Akkerman and the Towns of its District; Memorial Book
(Bilhorod-Dnistrovs'kyy, Ukraine)

Translation of
Akkerman ve-ayarot ha-mehoz; sefer edut ve-zikaron

(Akkerman and the towns of its district; memorial book)

Original Book edited by: Nisan Amitai Stambul

Published by Society of Emigrants from Akkerman and Vicinity

In Tel Aviv, 1983

Published by JewishGen

**An Affiliate of the Museum of Jewish Heritage—A Living Memorial to the Holocaust
New York**

Akkerman and the Towns of its District;
Memorial Book (Bilhorod-Dnistrovs'kyy, Ukraine)

Translation of *Akkerman ve-ayarot ha-mehoz; sefer edut ve-zikaron*
Akkerman and the towns of its district; memorial book

Copyright © 2020 by JewishGen, Inc.
All rights reserved.
First Printing: January 2021, Tevet 5781

Editor of Original Yizkor Book: Nisan Amitai Stambul
Translators: Ala Gamulka, Yocheved Klausner, Sara Mages
Layout and Name Indexing: Jonatan Wind
Cover Design: Rachel Levitan

This book may not be reproduced, in whole or in part, including illustrations in any form (beyond that copying permitted by Sections 107 and 108 of the U.S. Copyright Law and except by reviewers for public press), without written permission from the publisher.

Published by JewishGen, Inc.
An Affiliate of the Museum of Jewish Heritage
A Living Memorial to the Holocaust
36 Battery Place, New York, NY 10280

JewishGen, Inc. is not responsible for inaccuracies or omissions in the original work and makes no representations regarding the accuracy of this translation. Digital images of the original book's contents can be seen online at the New York Public Library website.

The mission of the JewishGen organization is to produce a translation of the original work, and we cannot verify the accuracy of statements or alter facts cited.

Printed in the United States of America by Lightning Source, Inc.

Library of Congress Control Number (LCCN): 2020952310

ISBN: 978-1-954176-02-7 (hard cover: 556 pages, alk. paper)

JewishGen and the Yizkor Books in Print Project

This book has been published by the **Yizkor Books in Print Project**, as part of the **Yizkor Book Project** of JewishGen, Inc.

JewishGen, Inc. is a non-profit organization founded in 1987 as a resource for Jewish genealogy. Its website [www.jewishgen.org] serves as an international clearinghouse and resource center to assist individuals who are researching the history of their Jewish families and the places where they lived. JewishGen provides databases, facilitates discussion groups, and coordinates projects relating to Jewish genealogy and the history of the Jewish people. In 2003, JewishGen became an affiliate of the **Museum of Jewish Heritage—A Living Memorial to the Holocaust** in New York.

The **JewishGen Yizkor Book Project** was organized to make more widely known the existence of Yizkor (Memorial) Books written by survivors and former residents of various Jewish communities throughout the world. Later, volunteers connected to the different destroyed communities began cooperating to have these books translated from the original language—usually Hebrew or Yiddish— into English, thus enabling a wider audience to have access to the valuable information contained within them. As each chapter of these books was translated, it was posted on the JewishGen website and made available to the general public.

The **Yizkor Books in Print Project** began in 2011 as an initiative to print and publish Yizkor Books that had been fully translated, so that hard copies would be available for purchase by the descendants of these communities and also by scholars, universities, synagogues, libraries, and museums.

These Yizkor books have been produced almost entirely through the volunteer effort of researchers from around the world, assisted by donations from private individuals. The books are printed and sold at near cost, so as to make them as affordable as possible. Our goal is to make this important genre of Jewish literature and history available in English in book form, so that people can have the personal histories of their ancestral towns on their bookshelves for themselves and for their children and grandchildren.

A list of all published translated Yizkor Books in the project with prices and ordering information can be found at:
http://www.jewishgen.org/Yizkor/ybip.html

Lance Ackerfeld, Yizkor Book Project Manager
Joel Alpert, Yizkor-Book-in-Print Project Coordinator
Susan Rosin, Yizkor-Book-in-Print Project Associate Coordinator

This book is presented by the
Yizkor-Books-In-Print Project
Project Coordinator: Joel Alpert

Part of the Yizkor Books Project of JewishGen. Inc.
Project Manager: Lance Ackerfeld

These books have been produced solely through efforts of volunteers
from around the world. The books are printed using the Print-on-Demand technology and sold at
near cost, to make them as affordable as possible.

Our goal is to make this intimate history of the destroyed Jewish shtetls
of Eastern Europe available in book form in English, so that people can
experience the near-personal histories of their ancestral town on their
bookshelves and those of their children and grandchildren.

All donations to the Yizkor Books Project, which translated the books,
are sincerely appreciated.

Please send donations to:

Yizkor Book Project
JewishGen, Inc.
36 Battery Place
New York, NY, 10280

JewishGen, Inc. is an affiliate of the
Museum of Jewish Heritage
A Living Memorial to the Holocaust

Notes to the Reader:

We apologize ahead of time for the poor quality of images in the book. Often these images had been scanned from the original Yizkor books which were of poor quality to begin with, being copies of old photographs. Each transfer results in loss of quality. We have done the best we could, given the original material and the resources and technology at hand. Even though images often appear of higher quality on computer screens, that does not transfer to high quality images in print. A reader can view the original scans on the web sites listed below.

Within the text the reader will note "{34}" standing ahead of a paragraph. This indicates that the material translated below was on page 34 of the original book. However, when a paragraph was split between two pages in the original book, the marker is placed in this book after the end of the paragraph for ease of reading.

Also please note that all references within the text of the book to page numbers, refer to the page numbers of the original Yizkor Book.

The original book can be seen online at the New York Public Library site:

https://digitalcollections.nypl.org/items/b3d683c0-2268-0133-32ec-58d385a7b928

or at the Yiddish Book Center web site:

https://www.yiddishbookcenter.org/collections/yizkor-books/yzk-nybc304238/amitai-nisan-akerman-va-ayarot-ha-mahoz-sefer-edut-ve-zikaron

In order to obtain a list of all Shoah victims from Akkerman, the reader should access the Yad Vashem web site listed below; one can also search for specific family names using family name option. These lists are continually updated by Yad Vashem, so it is worthwhile to periodically search these lists.

There is much valuable information available on this web site, including the Pages of Testimony, etc.
http://yvng.yadvashem.org

A list of this book and all books available in the Yizkor-Book-In-Print Project along with prices is available at:
http://www.jewishgen.org/Yizkor/ybip.html

Geopolitical Information:

Bilhorod-Dnistrovskyy, Ukraine 46°12' N 30°21' E and 293 miles S of Kyyiv

	Town	District	Province	Country
Before WWI (c. 1900):	Akkerman	Akkerman	Bessarabia	Russian Empire
Between the wars (c. 1930):	Cetatea Albă	Cetatea Albă	Basarabia	Romania
After WWII (c. 1950):	Belgorod - Dnestrovskiy			Soviet Union
Today (c. 2000):	Bilhorod - Dnistrovs'kyy			Ukraine

Alternate names for the town:
Bilhorod-Dnistrovs'kyy [Ukr], Akerman [Yid], Cetatea Albă [Rom], Belgorod Dnestrovskiy [Rus], Akkerman [Tur], Ir Lavan [Heb], Białogród nad Dniestrem [Pol], Alba Julia [Lat], Dnyeszterfehérvár [Hun], Walachisch Weißenburg [Ger]

Nearby Jewish Communities:

Shabo 5 miles SSE
Ovidiopol 6 miles NE
Mayaki 15 miles NNW
Mykolayivka-Novorosiyska 22 miles WSW
Odesa 26 miles NE
Olăneşti, Moldova 29 miles NW

Jewish Population: 5,625 (in 1897), 4,239 (in 1930)

Map of Ukraine with Akkerman (Bilhorod-Dnistrovskyy), Ukraine

Akkerman Memorial Book

Title Page of Original Yizkor Book

אקרמן ועיירות המחוז

ספר עדות וזכרון

מרכז המערכת: ניסן אמיתי (סטמבול)
חברי המערכת: ברוך קמין
שילדקראוט ישראל
בריליאנט שמואל
שכטר צבי
גורפיל שמואל

Translation of Previous Page

Akkerman and the Towns of its District

Memorial Book

Editor: Nissan Amitai (Stambul)
Editorial Board: Baruch Kamin
Y. Schildkrauth
Shmuel Brilliant
Tzvi Schechter
Shmuel Gurfil

TABLE OF CONTENTS

Akkerman City Plan		3
Prologue		4
The Jewish community in Akkerman from inception to destruction	Nissan Amitai (Stambul)	7
The pogrom in Akkerman in 1905	Mendel Kumorowski	83
Memories from the days of the pogrom	Yehoshua Harari (Berger) z"l	91

Parties and Movements

The beginning of "Tzeirei Zion" in Akkerman[1]	Tzvi Menuali	93
The association "Speak Hebrew!" - of the first youth organizations	Nisan Amitai (Stembul)	98
"Maccabi" Federation in Akkerman[2]	S. Segal and T. Manueli	102
"Gordonia" in Akkerman[3]	Sheftel Zukerman	113
The uniqueness of "Gordonia" in our city[3]	N. Amitai	117
"Gordonia" – the last chapter[3]	Chaim Zamir (Fima Chemerinsky)	127
"Hashomer Hatzair" branch in Akkerman[4]	Tzvi Giladi (Grisha Misionezhnik)	129
"Betar"[5] in Akkerman	Shmuel Gaber	135

Chapters of Memories, Lifestyle and Folklore

The Akkerman Steppe	Yakov Kushter	146
In the city I love	Y. Schildkrauth	146
Akkerman - the City of my Birth	Yosef Gur-Arye	153
Big Jabotinsky and "Little Jabotinsky" in our city	Yehoshua Harari–Breger z"l	158
My immigration to Israel in the month of Av 5681	Yehoshua Harari z"l	159
The first immigrants	Noah Zukerman	161
Chapters of memories from the days of my childhood	Binyamin Girshfeld	165
About the landscape and the climate	Yehoshua Harari	169
Akkerman - a corridor to the parlor	Yakov Zukerman	170
Artists and loyalists	S. Yisrael	173
From the bitter and the sweet	Y. Schildkrauth	176
The seven daughters of R' Mendel the carpenter	Y. Schildkrauth	179
Such a "Krishmelanu"	Nisan Amitai (Stambul)	181
Tit-bids from Akkerman (episodes and anecdotes)	Nisan Amitai (Stambul)	185
In bygone days	Chava Barnea (Dorpman)	189
A family tree (a tree and it's view)	Sheftel Zukerman	193
The Rabbi's house	Chaim Zukerman	197

A "note" – a memento	Yisrael Finkel	201
"I remember the days of old"	Efraim Abramowitch	204
Childhood and youth in Shabo and Akkerman	Baruch Kamin	206
Names and Nicknames [Y]	Z.M – Y.S.	211

Our High-School

A Symposium on "Tarbut" Gymnasium	A Shapira, S. Naamani, Y. Brudski	219
The Home, the High-School and the Movement	Baruch Na'amani	226
A "Foreign" Girl in Akkerman	Yehudit Karmi (Frenkel)	231

Artists and Cantors

About the Jewish Theater in our city	Yehudah Zigelvaks	234
The drama clubs	Frima Fejland	237
About Two Artists in our Town - Yosef Chaplin		240
About Two Artists in our Town (cont'd) - David Malchin		243
Cantors and Cantorial Music		244

The Holocaust

Not forgotten [Y] (poem)	S. Yisrolik	251
The destruction of Akkerman	Tzvi Manueli	255
Wartime Memories	Leyoba Asfis	258
The Prayer of the Saved [Y] (poem)	A. Plit	263
On my way home	Miriam Zamir	266
Between anxieties and hopes (Chapters of memories)	Rosa Weitzman (Gordon)	268
In the mission to save the Jews of Romania and Bessarabia	Baruch Kamin	272
The Flag	Shmuel Miniali	278
A Miracle did not Happen in Karnitchka	Berurya Har-Zion	281
A Story of a Name	Asher Shwartzman	283
The "flag-Day" ['tag-day']	Beruria Har-Zion	284
The Akkerman Jews during the War and after it	Kwitko Michael	285
Jewish survivors in the 1980s	Yakov Zigloks	289

Personalities and Characters of blessed memory

Avraham Ravutski z"l	297
Our ministers [Y]	301
Yakov Shmuel Halevi Truchtman z"l	302
Sergei Michaelowitz (Yisrael) Gutnik	304
My brother Yakov Berger z"l	306
Dov Shrira z"l	310
Professor Yitzchak Starec z"l	312
Moshe Hellman z"l	313

Pava Berkov z"l	Yehoshua Harari	314
Our brother Moshe Zukerman of blessed memory	Shmuel, Leib & Noah Zukerman	316
Leib Stambul z"l	Bruriah Ben-Zion	319
My uncle Yehoshua Harari (Berger) z"l	Yossi Shiloh, Ma'ale Shomron	320
Dov Harari z"l		322
Yehoshua Drory (Shura Volovich) z"l	N. Amitai	327
Zev (Wobcha) Kamin z"l	Tzvi Menuali	329
The lawyer Yosef Serper z"l		330
Doctor Shapira z"l	Alexander Shapira	331
Mendel Gellman z"l (Shohat)	Dr. Rachel Gellman–Neiger	332
Characters	Shmuel Geber	333

The Society of Emigrants from Akkerman and the Diaspora

The Society of Emigrants from Akkerman in New–York		337
The Society of Emigrants from Akkerman and the vicinity in Israel		340

Sons who fell in the Israeli Wars

Meir Zaltzhendler z"l	346
Avraham Neiman z"l	348
Avraham Feldman z"l	350
Yisrael (Srulik) Frank z"l	351
Avinoam Schechter z"l	352

The Towns in the district

Tarutino

Facts and numbers about the Jews of Tarutino	Eliyahu Feldman	354
Our Town Tarutino	Shmuel Brilliant	355
Notes From A Legacy	Dr. Yosef Laron z"l	369
From My Memories Of Tarutino	Shmuel Rosenberg	376
During The Days Of The Holocaust	Yehuda Bronfman	377
About Beitar[5] In Tarutino	Eliezer Shulman	381
Personalities And Charcters In Tarutino	Shmuel Brilliant	385
Public Servants and other Active Members of the Jewish Community		388
Eliezer Shulman, The Bible Researcher From Siberia		390

Artsyz

Artsyz	Shmuel (Milya) Gurfil	400
Artsyz my Town	Arie Kleitman	405

Tatarbunar

Tatarbunar		420
Tatarbunar and its Jews	Binyamin Gieker	421
The Tatarbunar Gordonia[3] Branch	Arie Shochat	423
Dr. Solomon Shalem	Binyamin Gieker	426
My home in Tatarbunar	Riva Zukerman – Silberman	428
The Gordonia[3] Congress		431
The Keepers of the Flame	Berurya Har–Zion	434
The Double Miracle	Berurya Har–Zion	436

Sarata

Sarata	Zvi Schaechter	438
Sarata	I. Ben–Hur (Altman)	444
About the "Bietar"[5] chapter in Sarata	Tzvi Schechter	448
About "Gordonia"[3] in Sarata	Elkana Altman	453
The Holocaust	Tzvi Schächter	455
Iziya's Story	Zvi Schächter	459

Byeramtcha

My Shtetl Byeramtcha	Moshe Shochet	465

Shabo

My Shtetl Shabo	Aharon Kaminker	475

Crochmaz

The Village Crochmaz	Yosef Koren	483

Former Residents of Akkerman and the Region in Israel	The Editorial Board	484
Akkerman émigrés in Israel		484
Tarutino émigrés in Israel		490
Artsyz émigrés in Israel		494
Tatarbunar émigrés in Israel		497
Sarata émigrés in Israel		498
Bairamcea émigrés in Israel		500
Shabo émigrés in Israel		501

Necrology 502

Name Index 508

Family Notes

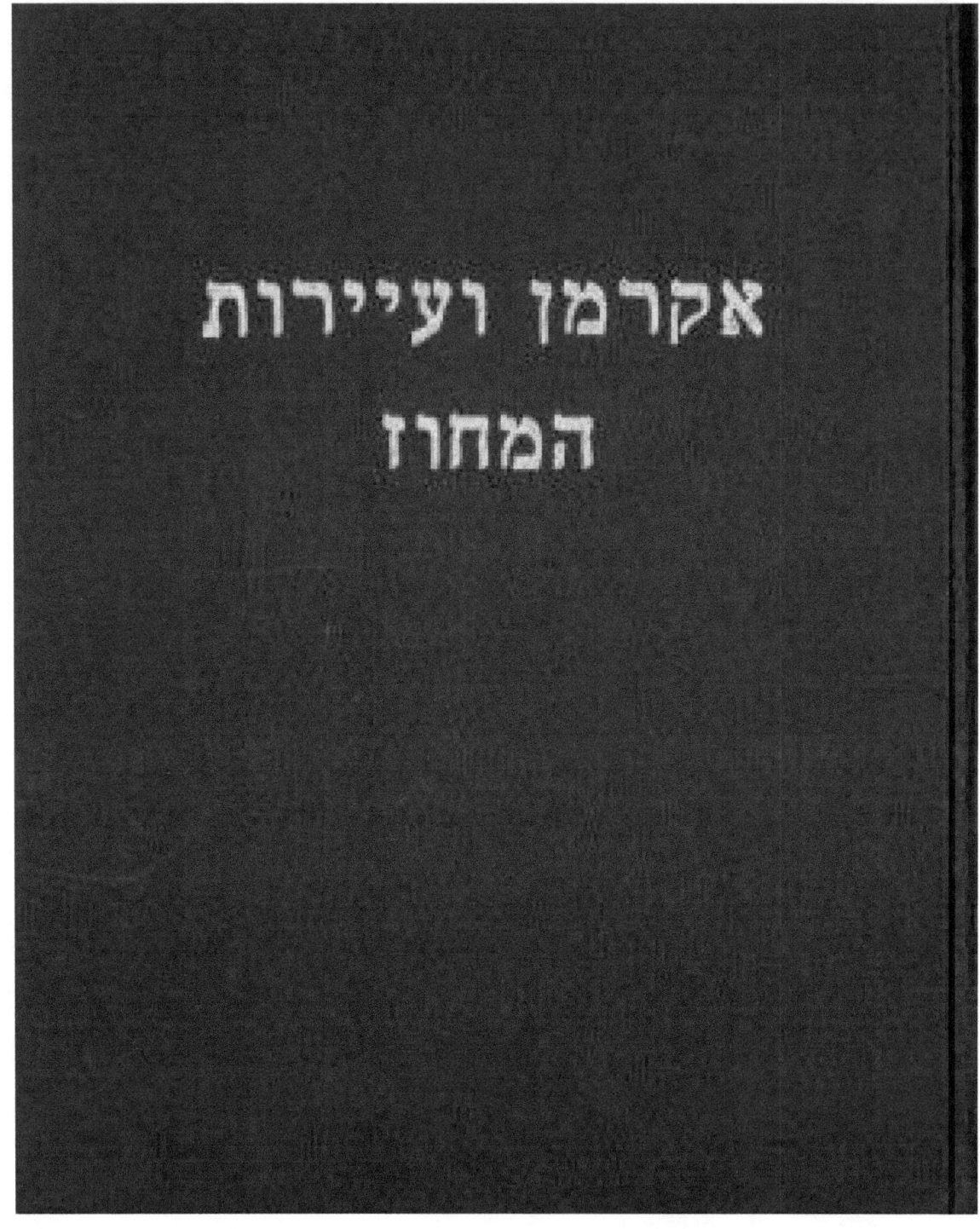

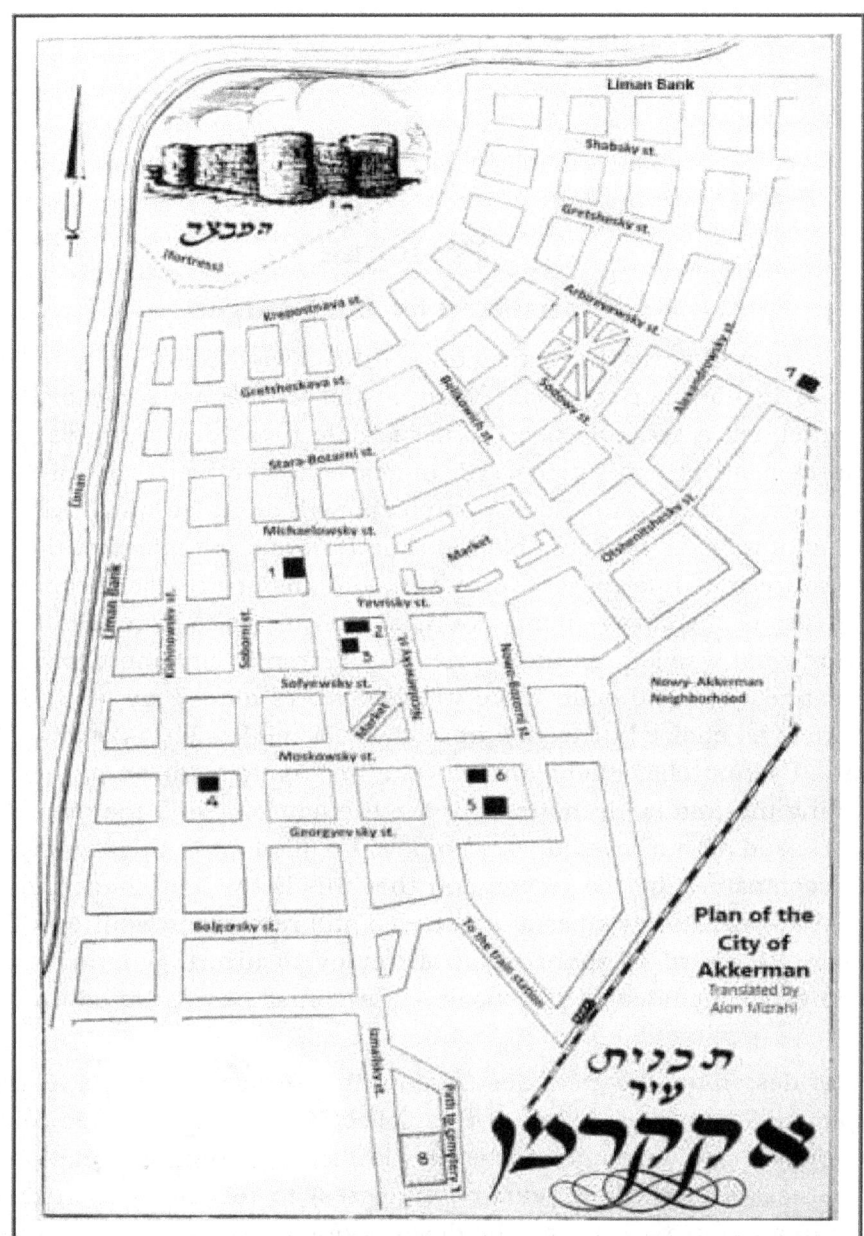

Akkerman City Plan

Map Key

1. "Ramselina" Synagogue
2. The courtyard of the three synagogues
3. The old Jewish hospital
4. Talmud Torah
5. The Hebrew gymnasium "Tarbut"
6. The Jewish Bank
7. The new Jewish hospital
8. The Jewish cemetery

[Page 8]
Blank page

[Page 9]

Prologue
Translated by Sara Mages

Many years have passed since the destruction of the Jewish community in Akkerman and the smaller communities in the district towns. Many of the former residents of these communities, who are now in Israel, felt a spiritual need to perpetuate these communities and raise, from the Vale of Tears, the memory of institutions and individuals who were so dear to us. For various reasons the publication of the Yizkor Book was postponed, and also now, with the publication of this book, we are not sure that we were able to properly shape the image of the lost communities. We did not have sources of information, archives, and historical documentary material at our disposal. With the loss of the Jews – many sources and memories were also lost, and we had no choice but to rely on what was left, on the survivors, one from a city and two from a family, letters from afar, old memories, etc. Although there were members among us, who thought that in the face of all this there is no choice but to give up and let them, Jewish Akkerman, Tarutino, Artsyz, Tatarbunar, Sarata, Byeramtcha, Shabo and all other towns, to go down to the depths of oblivion, but it is worth noting that many did not accept the thought of losing the memory of our parents, brothers and sisters, and all our loved ones who have instilled in us this legacy that in its light we walk. They were accompanied by the recognition that this is the last chance to save what can be saved, because year to year the number of those who still remember what was there and are able to attach word to word, shard to shard, as a testimony to future generations. If there are still some topics that are not included in this book – they must be attributed to the terms we were subjected to.

Also the chapter describing the great destruction, that each of us wants to know all its details, was not fully explored. The editorial staff of this collection did not see themselves as having the right to decide on details that were not sufficiently clarified regarding the final path of the martyrs. We let different witnesses (especially hearsay witnesses) to tell or write in their own words. It should be taken into account that not all the descriptions given in the book were written close to the time of occurrence, when things were still fresh in the memory. In many cases forgetfulness has done its thing, but, if after the publication of this collection additional sources will be discovered, or people who will be able to shed light on new matters, we will do our best to attach them as an appendix to the book.

Many years have passed since the curtain was raised and the sights of horror was revealed before us, but they did not make us forget and did not weaken, to a small degree, the great grief of the community and the individual, especially our heartache that most of the victims of the terrible Holocaust do not have a tombstone on their grave. Therefore, we dedicated a special section at the end of the book to commemorate their memory, and also the memory of the people of Akkerman and the towns of its district who fell in the Israeli wars or passed away in Israel. All words and details presented in this section – are the responsibility of the writers of the commemoration.

We see a need to thank everyone who helped us, a lot or a little, whether by writing a testimony, photos, etc., or by financial aid. May they all be blessed!

The editorial board of the book "Akkerman and the Towns of its District" December 1982
Tevet, 5743

[Page 10]

The Book's Editorial Board

Sitting right to left: **Shoshana Ramba (Hararit), Nissan Amitai (Stambul), Baruch Kamin (Kaminker), Yisrael Schildkrauth, Chava Barnea (Dorpman), Aharon Kaminker**
Standing right to left: **Shmuel Brilliant, Asher Brodsky, Tzvi Schechter, Binyamin Gieker, Shmuel Geber, Menachem Beider, Shmuel Gurfil**
The missing board members: **Binyamin Gershfeld, Bruria Har–Zion (Schwartzman), Yakov (Yani) Steinberg, Yosef Gur–Aryeh**

[Page 11]

The Jewish Community in Akkerman from Inception to Destruction
by Nissan Amitai (Stambul)
Translated by Sara Mages

Few sources were at our disposal for the purpose of writing this essay, and it is not our fault. It turns out, that few have fully explored the history of this city, which has undergone various incarnations, and regimes and many upheavals over the centuries of its existence. Our attempts to trace later sources, pamphlets and booklets published after the conquest of the city by the Soviets, also came to naught, for we have found that even with regard to the city's past, historians and Soviet record keepers have adopted their standards, which, as is well known, do not excel in excessive objectivity. So we had only one choice – to use material and quotes from various encyclopedias, as well as the documentation available to some researchers. Even when we discovered some contradictions between various sources – we did not try to straighten things out, and for the most part brought the different versions without taking it upon ourselves to be "the decisive third scripture among them." We had no pretense to write Akkerman's ancient history because we knew that the readers of this book are mainly interested in the knowledge about the life of the Jews in the city from the beginning of the formation of Jewish community in Akkerman to the bitter end, and this subject was especially on our minds when we began to dig into testimonies and archives, old newspapers and all the sources we came across. The writer of these lines isn't a historian or a researcher, and, therefore, the following shouldn't be seen more than an attempt to summarize things written, or said, on various occasions on this subject.

* * *

It is doubtful that there are many cities in the world whose name has been changed so many times by all sorts of rulers and regimes, who have been replaced in it frequently, as it happened with our city, Akkerman. The interesting thing is that in all the names the color white is somehow integrated in them. There is no doubt, that there was something about the unique style of Akkerman that emphasized the color white. Maybe because the brightness of the sun was different than in other cities, and maybe because the blue sky, which was reflected in the waters of the Leman River, was darker and casted a sharp white hue on the city? White is part of Akkerman's name in all languages and at all times.

Archaeological finds indicate that three thousand years before the Christian era there was already a population on the banks of the Leman who knew how to make iron weapons, they also raised animals and fished. We also know that in the first half of the first millennium BC, Scythians tribes settled on the eastern side of the Leman and Ostrogoths tribes on the southern side. In the 6th century BC, a settlement called Ophiusa was established on the banks of the Leman – which is Akkerman in the future. The Greek Herodotus, who also engaged in the study of the tribes that lived around the Leman, called Ophiusa by the name Tyras (by the way, the Greeks called the Leman the Dniester Tyras).

The author of the entry, Bilhorod–Dnistrovskyi, in the Israeli Encyclopedia (see volume 8 page 435), who relies on the studies of N. Iorga, V. Hyde, M.A. Halevi, A. Honigman and others, states that "Bilhorod–Dnistrovskyi is located in the place where the settlement of Tyras (Tyre?) was founded by Miletus' sons close to the year 650 BC." According to Ammianus Marcellinus (41.8.XXII), Tyras was formerly a commercial colony of the Phoenicians. As a Greek colony, Tyras was, for a short time, under the rule of Diadochus (heir[11]) Lysimachus, and in the 2nd and 3rd centuries BC was gained a great bloom.

[Page 12]

In the days of Claudius Caesar it was ruled by the Romans who exempted it from taxes and granted it tax rights. In the year 238 AD, German tribes took over the city. In the 6th century it was included in the territory of the Antes tribe who settled in the same area after the defeat of the Huns. Later, already before the 9th century, Slavic tribes sat there. The Khazars rule spread over Tyras, as on some other settlements who in the past were Miletus' colonies.

We are faithful to the testimony of Amianus Marcellius, because the excavations conducted at different times near the banks of the Leman and the Dniester revealed the foundations of houses, workshops, remains of water supply systems, sewage and coins, that there's enough in them to confirm his testimony.

We can assume that Tyras spread over a large area of about 200 dunam. The streets discovered stretched along the banks of the Leman to the "Acropolis," which formed the central part of the city, the place where the fortress stands today. The city's port in ancient times was in the place where the pier is now located, and to this place came boats and ships from distant places with cargo of various goods because Tyras was a free city and its trade relations were extensive.

The inhabitants of the city mainly engaged in farming, raising cattle and various crafts, and their ties with the settlements that stretched from the south and north of the Black Sea were very tight. They exported beef, honey, grains, fish, hides and wax, and imported expensive utensils, artifacts and decorations. Apparently, in the days of the Roman Empire Tyras was a commercial center for the environment, and the fact that it was granted privileges must have caused it to grow and prosper.

With the disintegration of the Roman Empire all kinds of tribes tried to take control of it. Its geographical location, proximity to the Leman River that was blessed with abounded of fish thanks to its sweet waters, the black fertile soil, the connection to the Black Sea, etc. – aroused the tribes' interest. As told above, in 238 AD Germanic–Gothic tribes took over the city but they were expelled by the Huns on their conquest campaigns in Europe. They also changed the name of the city and called it Touris. As they did everywhere, the Huns did here too – they exterminated and destroyed every sign of human culture that developed in and around the city.

After the fall of the Huns, and the disintegration of their rule in 451 AD, various tribes took over the city, but none of them lasted for long except for the Slavic tribes who stayed in the city for a longer time and also changed its name to Belgorod, meaning, White City.

(In parenthesis it is worth noting, that all the tribes that conquered the city changed its name, more of less, but, in all the names that they attached to the city the word white has been preserved, whether it is near the city or the fortress. The Byzantines called it Asprokastron – White Castle, the Tatars – Ak-Lova, the Genoses – Moncastro or Maurokastron, the Hungarians – Dnyeszterfehérvár, the Romanians – Cetatea Albă, the Turks – Akkerman and the Russians Belogrod and from 1812, with its conquest, they continued with the Turkish name, Akkerman, and most recently, from 1940, the Russians called it – Belgorod–Dnestrovskiy [White City on the

Dniester]. R' Yoel Sirkis Bach [BAyit CHadash], also mentions the "White City" in his book "Questions and Answers." The Russian chronicle, Nestor, (died in about 1100) also mentioned the city.)

There is no doubt, that the fact that the city frequently passed from hand to hand, from tribe to tribe, left its mark on its development, and it knew periods of ups and downs. It is known, that in the 14th century there was a settlement of Genova (Genua) merchants in the city who called it, Monoestro. They were joined later by others who originated from Ragusa. In the 15th century, the city was in the possession of the Moldavians, and because its place was at a crossroads between Lvov and Crimea, it had considerable commercial importance. In the days of the ruler, Alexandria cel Bun, the population of the city reached 20,000 inhabitants – Moldavians, Jews, Greek, Bulgarians, Armenians and Slovenians. This diverse composition of the population indicates that the city had an attractive power and its image was like "a window to the world."

The Turks also ruled the city for long periods. They settled in the city as early as 1420, but retreated after battles. In 1454, the Turks attacked the city from the Leman's side, but their attacks were warded off. In 1475, the Turks laid siege to the city and the fortress, which was in the hands of the Moldovans, and great losses were inflicted on both warring sides without the Turks being able to take control of the city. Only in 1484, Sultan Biazet II decided to conquer the city, at any cost, by seeing it as a key position for the takeover of Galicia and Poland. As it is told, there were constant battles for 15 days, and on August 16 of that year, the fortress fell to the Turks who massacred the defending inhabitants of the city and close to four thousand men and women were sold as slaves. The Turks destroyed the city and only about 200 remained of its previous inhabitants. The Turks called the city Akkerman (meaning, "The White Fortress").

Many battles have been fought between the Turks, the Moldovans and the Russians over the rule of the city, which passed from hand to hand, with each occupier trying to leave in it his impression and culture. In 1812, the city was conquered by the Russians who ruled it for over a hundred years, until 1918, and with that a new chapter began in the history of the city which quickly became a Russian city in everything. In 1918, the city came under Romanian rule, and after the Second World War it returned again to Russian rule who crowned it by the named, Bilhorod–Dnistrovsky.

[Page 13]

The Fortress

Akkerman is known in the world thanks to the fortress near the Leman River. Who, and when, started to build this fortress? – this matter is in dispute to this day. Of all the prevailing explanations on this subject, it is most reasonable to assume that the people of Genova (Genoa), who lived in the place for some time, initiated the construction of the fortress and even laid the first foundations. Its construction was completed in a later period, at the end of the 15th century during the Moldavian rule. An inscription, which was engraved in one of the fortress' towers, states that the fortress was built during the reign of the Moldovan, Stefan the "God fearing." The fortress was built according to the model and format of the Byzantine or European forts in the Middle Ages, covering an area of about 400 dunam, and together with the large square around it – close to 800 dunam. Twenty–six spires and towers stand out above the fortress. Its walls are impenetrable to bullets because their thickness reaches up to 5 meters. The length of the walls from the outside reaches up to 2 kilometers and their height to 11 meters. Positions and embrasures are fixed inside the walls. From the east, from the south and west, the fortress is surrounded by a canal whose depth reached up to 21 meters and width up to 10 meters. Even now, after the canal has been covered with soil, it reaches a depth of 14 meters in some places. The canal was dug 3 meters below the surface of the Leman and it has dams to stop the water. In times of war, the canal was filled with water to make it difficult for the enemy to access the fortress. A draw bridge hung over the canal at the entrance to the fort. There are three courtyards inside the fort and each has its own purpose. The largest courtyard was used for dwelling houses during a siege, the second courtyard for the garrison, while the third, the smallest one, for headquarters.

Bullets embedded in the fortress walls testify of the battles that took place at the site. For many years was an old rusty cannon inside the fortress square until the Romanians transferred it to the city's historical museum.

Many legends have been told about the tower and its turrets. Each generation has added its own personal touch to these legends and it is difficult to distinguish between imagination and reality in these legends, which added to the aura of mystery and romance to the fortress which is a kind of a hallmark and a sign of uniqueness of the city of Akkerman for many generations.

The entrance to the fortress in our time (after restoration)

[Page 14]
The Population and the Economic Life

The historian Anthony Babel states in his book, "La Besarabie," Paris 1926, that Tyras was the oldest city in Bessarabia, and this fact can be explained in the physical–geographical conditions of the place. It is no wonder that the Scythian tribes, who wandered with their flocks in the area, as well as the Phoenician sailors who came in their ships in a later period, chose Tyras as their place of residence. The fertile black soil, which yields large crops in rainy years, freshwater lakes with abundant of fish, pasture plains for herds of sheep and cattle, and horse breeding, a suitable and convenient place for mooring fishing boats and merchant ships – could they have found a more suitable place for their needs? Indeed, these conditions determined the economic development of the city. The residents in the area grew wheat and barley, rye and corn, various vegetables, fruit trees and vineyards on vast areas, and thanks to the fertility of the soil and the abundance of the seeds it produced, it was possible to raise various poultry and domestic animals during the winter. It is natural that the large crop, which accumulated in the threshing floor and in the winery, motivated the residents to cultivate trade relations with the settlements on the Black Sea coast and to export the crops of the fertile soil. The trade was conducted on the Leman River and the Black Sea and reached as far as the Crimean Peninsula, Greece, Rome, etc. The residents of the city, and the area, exported cattle, honey, grains, skins, wax, wine, etc. and so the foundation was laid for a flourishing and prosperous economy that emerged mainly in the 2nd and 3rd centuries BC (Klyuchnik, Bilhorod–Dnistrovskyi 1973). After the city was conquered by the Romans, who came to it after the conquest of the Dacia region, the new conquerors soon realized the special nature of the city and its importance to the development of the economy in the area, and this was probably the reason for the special privilege granted to the city by Claudius Caesar who freed the residents from taxes and defined it as a free city. Many boats and ships flocked to it through the Black Sea, or the Leman when it was not frozen, stocking up on the crops and grains they needed. We do not have reliable information about the economic situation in the city during the days of the invasions and rule of the nomadic tribes – a period that lasted nearly a thousand years – but there is evidence for the good economic conjuncture created in the area with the beginning of the settlement of the Genoese and the Ragusas. The Genoese applied their great experience, expanded trade relations in all directions, and greatly influenced this region to flourish and prosper as it had not before.

It shouldn't be forgotten that the large areas of Bessarabia were abandoned and without proper roads. A large number of nations who brought with them a medley of languages, sort of a "Tower of Babel" in biblical times, settled there. Also, the few existing roads were in danger and robberies and looting were very common. The industrious Genoese, who erected the forts in Akkerman, Bender, Soroca and Khotin in northern Bessarabia, knew, that first and foremost, they must secure the roads used by the convoys carrying the goods north, otherwise they wouldn't be able to market their goods, and they embarked on this mission and succeeded in it. Akkerman's location on a crossroads between Southern Poland and Crimea turned it into a very important strategic and economic position, and in this manner Akkerman and Kiliya became very important commercial centers. The experienced merchants of Genoa and Ragusa tightened the trade ties with Constantinople, Asia Minor and various ports along the shores of the Black Sea, especially – the port of Kaffa in Crimea. Traders from Poland arrived in Akkerman and bought wine, horses, grain, etc. and shipped them north. These ties did not cease even after the conquest of the area by the Moldovans, Akkerman, and the surrounding area, continued to fulfill the role of granary and supplied goods to the entire near and far environment. Romanian historians, among them N. Iorga, praise the fact that the Moldovan prince, Alexandru the Good, granted privileges to the merchants of Lvov who flocked on the roads of Wallachia to the coastal cities of the Black Sea, Akkerman among them. These special privileges were renewed from time to time by other Moldovan princes.

From this it can be concluded that even after Akkerman fell into the hands of the Turks, its fertility and special qualities did not cease and it continued to be an important economic center, although it went through a period of recession until the Turks established themselves in power. According to certain testimonies, there were about twenty thousand inhabitants in Akkerman before the Turkish occupation.

The great momentum in the development of the city, and economic sources, began with the Russian occupation in 1812. Their first steps prove that the Russians had a special interest in the development of this region. They made a kind of a "transfer" of the population and moved the Tatars and Moldovans, who did not like the Russians, into the depths of Russia. Many of them did not wait until they were transferred. The news of the Russians' repressive measures regarding the peasants, the obligation to enlist in the army, etc. caused them to flee to Wallachia and Moldova. The population of the place became very sparse and in order to re-settle the territories, especially the desolated "Budjak" region (Bender and Akkerman regions) in the south, which was emptied due to the expulsion of the many Tatars who made up the majority of its population, it was necessary to bring new colonists from remote areas.

[Page 15]

In 21.5.1816, four years after the Russian rule was established, Tsar Alexander I, instructed General Bakhmetyev, who was the Russian governor in Bessarabia, to take care of the colonization of the "Budjak" prairies, and see it as a very urgent role in the settlement of colonists in Bessarabia. The governor was also given permission to grant the colonists privileges and various benefits to attract them to settle in Bessarabia. Under this policy, German, Bulgarian, French from Lotharingia, Swiss, Bulgarians and Serbians settlers were brought in and granted the status of foreign settlers with special rights and benefits. Every family was given 60 dessiatin of land (about six hundred dunam) and relieved of their military service. In addition, the new settlers enjoyed a certain degree of administrative and cultural autonomy, including a long-term exemption from paying taxes, cheap credit for economic development and discounts. About twenty thousand peasants were also brought from the inner provinces of Russia, and they too enjoyed all the discounts granted to foreign settlers.

As a result of this Russian policy, important economic development began in the "Budjak" region, which also included Akkerman and Bender as one unit. The economic momentum in Akkerman was especially noticeable after it was separated from the Bender region in 1818 and turned into a district city.

The table given below proves the population growth in Bessarabia from 1816/17 to 1858, when a census was conducted in the cities ("Encyclopedia of the Diaspora" – A. Feldman):

City	Number of residents in the district cities		The growth %
	1816/1817	1858	
Khotyn	1500	13121	774.7
Soroca	2025	5410	167.2
Balti	3100	8077	160.5
Orhiyov	?	4305	?
Kishinev	5000	82683	1553.3
Bandar	1738	15188	773.8
Akkerman (1808)	1670	19963	1093.8

From this table we learn that only Kishinev [Chișinău] surpasses Akkerman in the rate of population growth. In 1818, Kishinev was declared the capital of Bessarabia and the authorities were interested in increasing the number of inhabitants in the city. Therefore, it turns out that during the first five decades of Russian rule the population of Akkerman increased by 18,266 inhabitants. In 1897, a census was conducted again and 28,258 residents were counted in Akkerman, meaning an increase of about 8,322 inhabitants over forty years, which proves a marked decline in the importance of the economy that gave signals in the movement of the population. It is worth noting, that the 1890 encyclopedic dictionary of Efron Brukhaus brings an estimate of 41,178 inhabitants in Akkerman for the year 1885, but this estimate does not seem reasonable for it is hard to imagine that in 12 years, until 1897, the population dwindled by 12,000 people.

In December 1930, the Romanian government conducted a census in the cities of Bessarabia and Aliba, and in that census Akkerman had a population of 34,485 inhabitants. It goes without saying, that for 33 years the city's population has grown by only 6,227 inhabitants. Presumably, some of them were residents who fled during the Russian Revolution and settled in the city.

In the above mentioned Brukhaus Dictionary, we find statistics on the sources of livelihood of the inhabitants of Akkerman and the immediate area in 1885. In that year there were in Akkerman: 304 vegetable gardens and 2,085 orchards and vineyards, 13 industrial plants and 551 commercial businesses. A district fair, called Nikolajevskaja Jarmorka, was held in Akkerman every year, from 6 to 28 December. The main products traded at this fair were: salt, fish, fat, wool and mostly wine. The municipality's revenue in this year (?) reached to the amount of 46,248 ruble, while the expenses to the amount of 47,218 ruble. The capital of credit institutions – 20,455 rubles (the customs house and three pharmacies are also included among these institutions).

With the Romanian occupation, Akkerman was cut off from Russia and its main port Odessa, and became a border city. The transfer of goods from Russia to Bessarabia was wiped out and, as a result, the economic situation worsened. The Romanians had no particular interest in developing the area. On the contrary, their aim was to attract a population to Romania and increase the Romanization of the area in which the influence of the Russians, culturally and economically, was very noticeable. All existing marketing was mainly directed towards the north. Indeed, Polish traders continue to come to Akkerman to buy wine and grain, but Akkerman in that period was no longer a commercial transit city through which goods moved north and south.

[Page 16]

Few are the details about the development of the city during the first half of the 19th century. From an article published in the newspaper, "Odesskij Vestnik," we learn that the residents in Akkerman and the district developed the wine industry and planted many vineyards. In 1842 there are already 800 vineyards in the city, meaning, that from the beginning of the Russian occupation until the date of the publication of the article – 1842 – the area of the vineyards grew by 150%.

If we can rely on Klyuchnik, in 1821 the wine industry crop was 40,000 buckets, whereas towards 1860 the crop amounted to about a million buckets. From the same source we learn that at the end of the 19th century there were 3 small sugar factories, 2 tobacco factories and 4 cotton factories in Akkerman. Brukhaus encyclopedia, like Klyuchnik encyclopedia, indicates that there were 72 flour mills in Akkerman, 5 jetties and 80 fishing points next to the Leman River and the shores of the Black Sea. Klyuchnik also mentions that with the declaration of Akkerman as a district city in 1818 it had 500 residential cottages, while in 1860 there were already 600 stone buildings out of the 2,953 residential buildings.

An economic downturn hit the city after the Russian authorities began developing the city of Odessa and its port, which quickly became the main port in the Black Sea for Ukraine and Russia. Also the development of the ports of Kiliya, Reni, Brăila and Galați on the Danube, caused a considerable decrease in Akkerman's status as a transit city for the import and export of goods. Although wine production and grain growth continued, but the aforementioned ports caused a considerable devaluation in the development of Akkerman port and, as a result, the days of the economic prosperity of the city and its port passed, and there was a long period of recession.

There was also a certain freeze in the industry during the period of the Russian rule and also in the days of the Romanian rule. With the exception of a few small industrial plants, which employed few workers in the industry of brick, roofing tile, canned fish, etc. The main marketing industry was fish marketing. Y. Schildkrauth lists in his book all types of fish that were marketed from Akkerman.

Carps and large heavyweight sanders, kefal [mullet], scomber [mackerel], fresh sardines swimming in lemon, big and wide flattened turbot with rivet bones, and "*buziot*" cracked and dried. The kefal was an important market in Akkerman because of its special taste. At a time when the kefal in the sea was still young and soft, and beginning to grow and develop, a fence was erected in a particular area in the sea. Fish food was used as bait for the tiny and skinny kefals, who floated and crept through the bars into the particular area. The kefal stayed there for a few weeks, fattened nicely, grew quickly and gained weight. They could not escape from the barred area back to the sea because the space between the bars in the water was quite narrow."

Apart from these, they also installed wide canals leading to the beach, and the tiny kefal fish were drawn into them as a refuge from predatory fish. These fenced areas were called "*yarikim*" and the fish – "yarichny kefal".

In its early stages the wine industry in Akkerman was quite primitive and the grapes were trampled by feet into large tubs. This, of course, was not the most hygienic way since the treading was done in cellars and also endangered the health of those engaged in it. Only later, presses were used to squeeze the wine and the work was done not in cellars but in the houses' courtyards.

Transportation

Akkerman did not excel in modern transportation. The main means of transportation in, and outside the city, were the carts and the "*bindiugot*" (long carts, open and narrow). The mean of transportation in the city itself was by "*drozkot*" (carriages harnessed to one horse), or "*peitonim*" (carriages harnessed to two horses). Before the First World War, a train operated from Akkerman north to Chisinau and after the Romanian occupation a line was also operated to Romania. At the same time, a railway line was laid from Akkerman to Odessa, but with the outbreak of the First World War the work on this line was stopped and not completed during the Romanian occupation. Y. Schildkrauth describes in his book a new way of, so to speak, modern transportation that was used before the First World War:

"One of Akkerman's wealthy Christian residents, named Pimilidia, decided to give the city a cheap, convenient and "modern," mean of transportation. To do so, he drove a "*konka*" (sort of a small "tram" pulled by horses). Narrow railroad tracks were laid on the city streets and crossed some of the streets – Izmailovsky, Sofievsky, Nikolaievsky, Mikhailovsky, Alexandrovsky, along the entire street on the Leman shore (Limania), and reached as far as the large flour mill of the Aswadorov brothers. In the big and long Izmailovsky Street, and in the city square in front of the fortress, was the main line of freight traffic. One harnessed horse easily pulled, as it was sliding on the polished tracks, dozens of iron wagons, closed and open, laden to the top with thousands of sacks of grain taken out of the granary. The horse brought them to the moorings and where their contents were emptied into the rigs and barges."

[Page 17]

This Pimilidia was a person with initiative and also gave Akkerman a more modern means of transportation when he replaced the horse with a large, old–fashioned locomotive, "which pulled in a crawl, with heavy exhalation and creaking, a long chain of railcars and platforms, loaded and full. It filled the streets with black, filthy and stuffy smoke, which was emitted from his old and used guts, and with its wild whistle disrupted the rest of the inhabitants and the normal traffic in this part of the city, and angered the population who cursed and sent all their bad dreams on the head of the "black demon." A few years later this mean of transport was eliminated and Pimilidia lost all his assets.

Convalescent Homes

An important branch of Akkerman's economy was the convalescent homes in its vicinity, like: Borysivka, Sargeivka, Tuzly, Budaki, Kordon, Bugaz and Shabo, each of them had its own virtues. So, for example, Budaki was famous for its "Dead Sea," meaning – the salt baths for those suffering from rheumatism in addition to the mud baths, and people suffering from rheumatism flocked to it from all over the country. Kordon, near Budaki, on the shores of the Black Sea, excelled in its dwellings, villas for rent that were, of course, intended for the wealthy. Shabo gained a lot of publicity thanks to a special variety of small light–pink grapes, which were sweet as honey, and many saw in them a kind of a remedy for lung and anemia diseases. Thousands of people from the north and Romania filled these convalescent homes to capacity in the summer season, which was an economic boom season for Akkerman. Indeed, it was a short season – just two months – but it was the "golden age" of Akkerman and the surrounding area. Farmers, merchants, and craftsmen of all kinds, eagerly waited for this season which covered the deficits of the entire year and everyone benefited from it. And so, Y. Schildkrauth describes the blessed season in his book: "When the recovery season began, the city took off its stiff clothing, "put its feet," simply and comfortably, inside the slippers, dressed in a "negligee" and behaved in the carefree way of the "cured." Akkerman's residents moved their wives and children to a health resort ("*kurort*" in a foreign language), and the husbands remained, abandoned and lonely, in the city to run their businesses and looked forward to Saturday and Sunday when they would come to stay with the family at the convalescent home."

The synagogue in the holiday village (Kordon– Budaki) at the convalescent home of M. Berg

Footnote:

So were called the army commanders who after the death of Alexander Macedon divided his kingdom among them.

[Page 18]
The History of the Jewish Community of Akkerman

When did the first Jews come to Akkerman? Who were the first and what motivated them to settle in this city? Unfortunately, to this day we do not have serious historical monographs on the first Jewish communities in Bessarabia and we also do not have reliable documentary material that we can base our attempts on answering the above questions. In any case, we have almost no documentary material on the beginnings of the Jewish settlement in Akkerman. The first testimonies on the presence of Jews in the city, and even these are very few, are from the 15th century AD and rely on foreign historical sources, or tourists who occasionally visited the place or any mentions in various books. Few documents have been preserved about the days of Turkish rule, although there is no doubt that by then there were already quite a few Jews in the city. Anyway, whoever wants to explore the reality of those days, and to unfold a picture of the life of the Jews then, their occupations and lifestyle, will lack the first infrastructure and will have to rely mainly on assumptions and guesses. Therefore, it is no wonder that we, too, groped in the dark as we tried to find an answer to the questions presented above.

The first mention of Jews in Akkerman, and it is also brought in the studies of A. Feldman, M. Davidzon and others, about the history of the Jews of Bessarabia, is related to the first century. One of the emissaries of Jesus Andrew, brother of Saint Peter, who was sent to bring the gospel of Christianity to the settlements on the shores of the Black Sea, tells that he arrived in the city of Tyras and found Greeks and Jews there. The very fact that this apostle mentions Jews proves to historians that he is not talking about a small number, but about many Jews. It is also possible, that the very presence of Jews in Tyras is the real reason for Andrew's journey to these places. Various Romanian historians also emphasize the fact of the presence of Jews in Tyras, Akkerman in the future, without bringing any further details.

Were there Jews in Akkerman during the days of the various tribal invasions of Bessarabia until the 11th century? We also don't have a reliable answer to this question. Presumably, the invasions of the barbarians and the many wars, that took place in the area, drove the residents away from the environs, among them also the Jews. We cling to the testimony of the Russian historian, Nestor (died about 1100), that the Khazars also ruled Tyras. On the other hand, there is no doubt that in the 13th and 14th centuries there were Jews in Akkerman, whether they came from Genoa together with the Italians who settled in Akkerman and have done a lot for the establishment of the trade and the economy in the city, or whether they arrived in other ways after the economic prosperity that began to show signs in the city and the surrounding area. There is also reason to believe that some of the Khazars' Jews, who are mentioned in Nestor's notes, remained in the place and maintained a traditional Jewish way of life.

The Metropolitan, Grigorij Camblack, author of the story of the life of the Christian martyr, Saint John's Day, who was murdered by the Tatars around the year 1300, mentioned in his story a Jewish settlement that was at that time in Akkerman, and even noted that the Jewish population in the city was concentrated in a special neighborhood. This Metropolitan of Moldova lived in the first half of the 16th century, and his story is probably based on folk tales and beliefs prevalent in Akkerman in the first half of the 15th century. According to the opinion of A. Feldman in the "Encyclopedia of the Diaspora," the Romanian historian, Nicolae Iorga, relied on the above story when he wrote that Akkerman was "full of Jews" in the first half of the 14th century, and they came there following the conquest of the city by the Tatars.

More reliable information about the Jewish community of Akkerman dates back to the 15th century, during the reign of the Moldovans who showed a tolerant attitude towards the Jews. During the reign of the Moldovan prince, Stephen the Great (in the second half of the 15th century), many Jews came to the cities of the Black Sea coast, among them Akkerman and Kiliya. In an article on the Jews of Bessarabia by M. Davidzon published in the periodical "*Gesharim*," it was said among others: "Mr. Khalifa wrote in his popular notebook about Bessarabia, which was published in 1914, that when he comes to the period of the principality of Stephen the Great, and when he speaks of the human material composition of the settlements in the coastal cities Akkerman and Kiliya, he counts, besides the Moldovans as locals, also the Greeks, Italians and Armenians, but his heart does not let him mention the existence of Jews there, even though everyone admits, and it has already been proven by historical document which cannot be denied, that when Stephen the Great sat on his throne of his principality there was already a strong and valuable Jewish community in Akkerman."

[Page 19]

The researcher, M. Davidzon, did not interpret on what basis he came to the conclusion that "a strong and valuable Jewish settlement existed in Akkerman in the days of Stephen the Great," and it is possible that this determination is far from historical accuracy. However, on the other hand, it is known that in the palace of Stephen the Great lived a Jewish adviser named Yitzhak ben Binyamin Shorr, who had a considerable influence on the state's affairs. It is also worth noting, that Yitzhak Beg, the Jewish physician of the King of Persia, also confirmed the presence of Jews in the area. This is another written proof that strengthens our determination that there was already a Jewish community in Akkerman in this period. We can assume that many Jews from Byzantium were pulled to this area, which had something to offer the Jews especially during the period of the expulsion of Spain, when they tried to find a hold outside the inquisition regime.

The first reliable information of a massive presence of Jews in Bessarabia tie to the eastern trade between Poland and the countries on the Black Sea coast, in which Jewish merchants from Poland took part in the late 14th and 15th centuries. Jewish merchants from Constantinople, which was already in Turkish hands, also passed through the cities of Bessarabia on their way to Poland, and presumably quite a few of them lingered in the place for a short or long time. According to documents discovered in the municipal archives of Lvov (Lemberg), it turns out that in the years 1467–1476 three Spanish Jews from Constantinople, who also had agents and aides, were active in the trade between Lvov and Constantinople. Although Akkerman's name was not mentioned in these documents, only Kiliya and Rani as places where Jews lived, it must be assumed that the Jews of Akkerman, a fortress and port city, also participated in this trade.

Since the 15th century, and mostly from the 16th century, there is already a lot of information about Jews in Bessarabia and Akkerman. The uniqueness of these reports is that they are of Jewish origin. In various sources we find information about merchants from Poland who passed in the cities of Bessarabia (Kiliya, Rani and Akkerman) for trade purposes. The rulers of Poland, Sigismund Augustus and Stephen Báthory granted concessions and special rights to merchants, or Jewish agents, who developed the trade between Poland and Turkey. Echoes of this movement of Jewish merchants from Polish cities to the cities of Bessarabia in the late 16th and early 17th centuries (1558–1616), were preserved in the books of questions and answers of the rabbis of that period: R' Yoel Sirkis (BAyit CHadash), R' Binyamin Aharon son of R' Avraham Selnik, R' Binyamin Meir son of R' Gedalia of Lublin (the Maharam of Lublin). From one of the answers of R'

Yoel Sirkis, written in 1591, we learn that in that year there was already a Jewish community in Akkerman with a rabbi and judges.

And so it says in this certificate:

"Before us, we the young people of the Holy Community of White, came to us... we wrote and signed our names here the White City, Monday 17 Sivan 5351 [9 June 1591]... I, Avraham son of R' Shlomo may he live a good long life... wrote here the Holy Community White... Binyamin son of HaRav R' Eliezer... witness Yakov son of HaRav R' Yosef Dayan, Yudah son of HaRav R' Yom Tov Dayan, Shlomo son of HaRav R' Yakov Dayan."

It should be noted, that during a certain period immigration from Poland and Germany to Eretz Yisrael was conducted through Akkerman. M. Davidzon writes in his article in "*Gesharim*":

"It can be assumed, that all the popularity and publicity in those days for Bessarabia in general and Akkerman in particular, maybe also came thanks to the Holy Land that the entire Diaspora aim for, and in all its efforts it sought the nearest and most convenient way to reach it, and already then there were many who found this path, Akkerman – Eretz Yisrael, to be the shortest and most convenient."

Another testimony, which confirms the convenience of this road for travelers to Eretz Yisrael, comes from the traveler, Riter Zebler, who in his records from 1479 advises Jews coming from the countries of Germany to Jerusalem to make their way on land: "First (they will travel) from Nuremberg to Poznan in Poland – 70 German miles. From Poznan to Lublin – also in Poland – 560 German miles, from Lublin to Lemberg – 530 German miles, from Lemberg through Wallachia (to Choczim – Khotyn) 530 German miles, from Khotyn to Weissenburg (Akkerman) on the sea, which is a city on the edge of Wallachia, 530 German miles. From Weissenburg, by sea, five or six days of travel to Samsun a city in Turkey, and from Samsun about six to seven days of travel to Shoket, etc."

Therefore, Akkerman was an important transit station on the immigration route of Jews to Eretz Yisrael. It is possible, that there were Jews in the city who were able to help the immigrants to Eretz Yisrael to continue on their way from Akkerman and beyond. There's also an assumption that there were also those among the immigrants who stayed in Akkerman for a while and even settled there after realizing that they could survive and make a living in this city.

Karaites

A chapter in itself is the matter of the Karaites in Akkerman. As is well known, many Karaites concentrated in the Crimean peninsula and from there spread across the environment. By the middle of the 16th century we already find the following Karaite sages in Akkerman: R' Yehudah ben Eliyahu Tishby, who completed and copied there in the years 5271-5278 [1510-1517] the book "*Yesod Mikra*" which was written by his grandfather, Avraham ben Yehudah; R' Keleb ben Eliyahu Tarno, who copied in Akkerman in the year 5291 [1530], the book "*Etz Chaim*" and in the year 5303 [1542] the book "*Gan HaEden*" both by R' Aharon ben Eliyahu Nicomedia, and also the well known Karaite sage, Caleb

[Page 20]

Afendopolo ben Eliyahu and his brother Shmuel Ha-Ramati (Encyclopedia of the Diaspora). The last, called R' Caleb Aba, who was a student of R' Eliyahu of Bashyazi, "lived at the end of his life in the White City (Weissenburg – Akkerman) and died there in the year 5270 (1509). In his book of poetic phrases and poems, "*Gan Hamelechn,*" one can also find two lamentations about the expulsion with God from foreign lands and the lands of Russia and Lithuania" ("*Gesharim*" – M. Davidzon).

A. Feldman mentions in his study, that in the second half of the 16th century the following Karaite sages stayed in Akkerman: Shmuel ben Shlomo Ramati, also called Ramati of Akkerman, and Eliezer ben Yosef Tzdik. There is reason to believe that the Karaite community continued to exist in Akkerman throughout the 17th century. In the Karaite cemetery in Chufut Kale there is a marker (tombstone?) "In memory of the honorable rabbi, the beloved Yitzchak, who is called Tzsli ben Eliya the elder who died in Ac–kerman on 8 Av 5424." Another helpful testimony is the Torah scroll that was found in the city with the inscription "Synagogue of the Karaite community of Akkerman," and on is written that it is from the 1500 (the Torah scroll was transported to Constantinople).

Many legends have been told about the tower and its turrets. Each generation has added its own personal touch to these legends and it is difficult to distinguish between imagination and reality in these legends, which added to the aura of mystery and romance to the fortress which is a kind of a hallmark and a sign of uniqueness of the city of Akkerman for many generations.

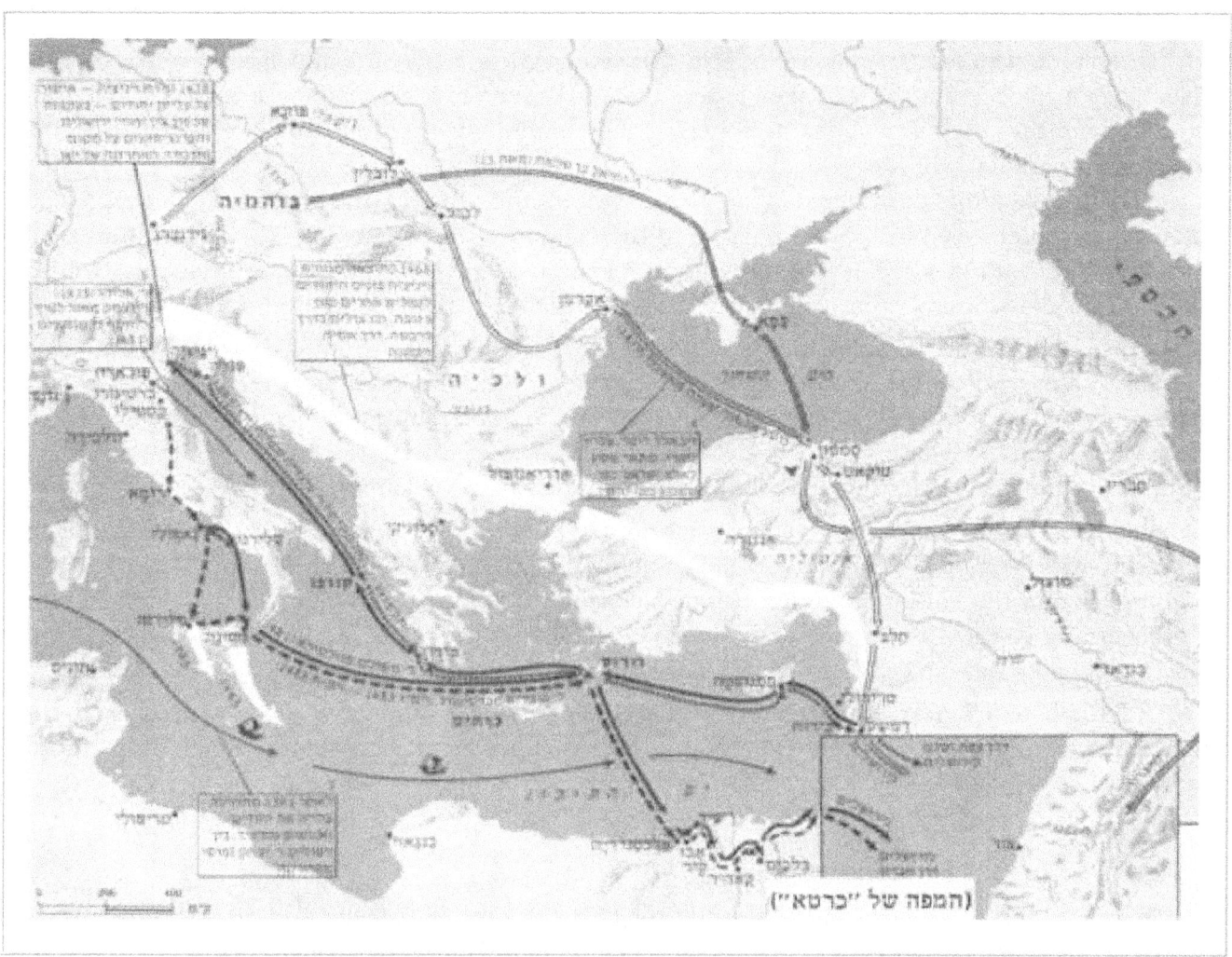

The route of immigration to Eretz Yisrael through Akkerman in the 14th century

[Page 21]

Y. Schildkrauth tells in his book:

"In the ancient and abandoned cemetery of Akkerman which, in the course of time, became a private vineyard and where later the new quarter, Novi Akkerman, was built, a long and narrow stone in the shape of a sloping roof was found during the excavations for the cornerstone of a new house. On both sides of the stone, to its lengthwise and widthwise, were deeply engraved letters arranged in even short rows. Apparently, the inscription on the stone was a song of praise for a deceased Jew from Akkerman, important and endearing. The eulogy is written in rhymes with words divided in places, in such a way that part of the word remains in one line and the other part is moved to the following line, a matter that made it easier for the writer to maintain the size of the row, or for the sake of getting the necessary rhyme, as was the custom of the rhyme writers and poets of that time.

Schildkrauth writes the following:

"This stone was laid for a long time in the synagogue's courtyard and many people came to investigate and decipher the damaged letters that had been erases over the years – for a long time, or many months, they were busy deciphering the contents of this tombstone. People from other cities of Bessarabia, who were also interested in this tombstone, came especially to Akkerman to assist the investigators of this tombstone (M. Davidzon and others). And these are the people from Akkerman who engaged in the deciphering of the content of the stone: the teacher M. Starec, the principal Yakov Berger, R' Haim Kaminker, R' Hirsh Brodetsky, R' Aharon Cohen, R' David Berkowitz, Yakov Rabinowitch, Leib Shohat, the writer of these lines and others."

I must add, that in a conversation I had with Mr. Tzvi Manueli, he emphasized that the person who made a crucial contribution to the decipherment of the inscription on the tombstone was the historian A. A. Harkavy, who came especially from St. Petersburg or Odessa, to decipher the inscription. Dr. A. A. Harkavy has dealt with the history of the Karaites and his many researches on historical subjects are still used today as study material in various universities.

According to the first letters at the beginning of each line, it turns out that the name of the deceased was Yehudah ben Tanach (?). It is not known to which community the deceased belonged to and the author of the tombstone's text, but it is most likely that the tombstone is from the beginning of the 16th century – the year 5287 (1527). Therefore, it turns out that even then Akkerman had a Jewish community with righteous and humble people.

The tombstone's text was copied on parchment in two copies and handed over to the community committee and Beit HaMidrash. The stone was placed in a special place in the cemetery.

[Page 22]

In the Days of Turkish Rule

The trade movement from Poland and Russia to Turkey, which passed through Akkerman, probably brought many Jewish settlers to Akkerman during the Turkish period. There is no reliable information about the economic situation of the Jews and their legal status at that time, but, presumably, they enjoyed the freedom of religious worship and were able to engage in their occupations. Various reports confirm that the Jews who lived in the Budjak plains, which was mostly inhabited by the Tatars, did not suffer persecution and even received legal protection from the authorities when needed. From this, it can be concluded that the Jews of Akkerman were not discriminated against and were allowed to engage in any craft. The Jews who lived in the fortified cities – and Akkerman is one of them – traded in brandy, tobacco, hides, grain and wines. From Poland they brought corals, cotton threads, coffee, perfumes, upholstery materials and fabrics as well as spirits.

Even in the 18th century, Akkerman was a transit for goods transported to cities on the shores of the Black Sea, but to a lesser extent than before. As mentioned, it was caused by the development of new means of transportation in Brăila, Galați, Ismail and others which slowed the pace of movement through Akkerman.

The Jews also engaged in various crafts. As in any Jewish community, there were butchers who are a necessity for every community, Jewish tailors who are also a necessity due to the prohibition of *shatnez* [linsey-woolsey], bartenders, Jewish tenants etc.

We do not have reliable information on the patterns of organization of the Jewish community during this period, but presumably there were some since Jewish public life was already created at that time in many Jewish communities. We do not know about the synagogues that existed then and their uniqueness. If any documents and testimonies have been preserved about the lives and the development of various Jewish settlements in Bessarabia, urban and rural, as well as about various synagogues and charities, then this is not the case with Akkerman. We are groping in the dark until the period of the Russian occupation of the area. The frequent wars between the Russians and the Turks in the late 18th century over the control of Bessarabia, had implications for the development of the Jewish community of Akkerman, which was one of the battlefields and depleted the local Jewish population. We have sources of information about the situation and lives of the Jews of Akkerman only after the defeat of the Turks and after Akkerman passed to Russian rule in 1812, as will be explained below.

General view of Akkerman

[Page 23]

The Jews of Akkerman Under Tsarist Rule in the 19th Century

After the Bucharest Agreement of 1812, the territories of Bessarabia passed from the Turks to the Russians. The frequent wars that have taken place in these territories depleted this region and its inhabitants. With the entry of the Russians masses of residents fled the cities and villages because they feared the Russians and the tsarist regime which was known for its harassment and the enslavement of the peasants to the nobles. The villagers especially feared the forced conscription of the population into the army, various taxes and economic decrees, and the harassment of the Russian administration. The first steps of the new regime were – the deportation of the Tatar residents, who were suspected as fans of the Turks, into Russia. The Budjak plains (Akkerman and Bender districts) were deserted, the population dwindled and the economic depression was well felt.

The Jews also fled from the region to places that seemed safer and more promising to them, and the population in the region was so sparse that the Russian authorities began to see it as a suitable place to for the exile of unwanted elements (the great Polish poet, Adam Mickiewicz, was also among the exiled to the Akkerman area and from there maybe the reference to the Akkerman's plains in one of his poems, as well as the Russian poet Pushkin).

With the passage of time, the authorities apparently came to the conclusion that this sparse region invites new occupiers and therefore decided to adopt a different policy. In instructions given by Tsar Alexander I in 1816 to the Commissioner of Bessarabia, Bohemteib, it has been said that he must take care of attracting new residents to Bessarabia, especially to the desolate Budjak region. As a result of this policy, masses of new settlers arrived in Bessarabia including French, Swiss, Germans, Bulgarians, Serbs and others, and people from other Russian provinces were also transferred there. The renewed momentum for the development of the region also brought masses of residents on their own initiative. With them were also many Jews who hoped to rebuild their lives in this part of the country, which seemed to them to have great potential for economic development. The authorities granted many concessions to the new settlers, distributed land to them, loans on favorable terms for the cultivation of the land and even release from the obligation of military service. At the same time, the Russian markets opened for products and produce from Bessarabia, and in the early 40s Bessarabia was already used as a large silo of the port of Odessa.

The Movement of the Jewish Population

It is not known exactly how many Jews were in Akkerman at the beginning of the 19th century. According to material found in one of the files stored in the archives of the governors of Wallachia and Moldova, there were only 90 Jews in Akkerman in 1808. Also, on the basis of the census conducted in 1817, it is not possible to arrive at a more accurate estimate of the number of Jews on that year, since Akkerman is included in this census within the boundaries of the Bender district without a separation for statistics between Bender and Akkerman. On the other hand, we know that Jews fled Poland to Bessarabia and the southern provinces because of the harassment.

The drought that befell Poland, and the economic depression, were also among the factors of immigration to southern Bessarabia. An expression of this is given in one of the stories of Mendele Mocher Sforim [Yankev Abramovich] – "The discovery of Wolyn," and so it is said in this story: "Out of trouble, my grandfather went to Wolyn during the days of the great famine, went down to Kishinev [Chișinău], the capital of Bessarabia – a land flowing with milk and honey, engaged in teaching together with other paupers like him and enjoyed all the good, ate mamaliga, for dessert ate fat-tail sheep, drank wine and lived there peacefully like all Jews, and knew no trouble."

Dr. A. Feldman explains in the volume on Bessarabia published by the "Encyclopedia of the Diaspora," that the new Jewish immigrants belonged to the economically and socially weaker classes of the population. They engaged in small trade or crafts and quite a few engaged in brokerage. Culturally they did not stand at the top of the ladder. Most of the immigrants to Bessarabia settled in the north of this region, or in the center, but most of them were absorbed in the south. The numbers speak for themselves. If in 1808 there were only 90 Jews in Akkerman, then in 1861 there were according to the count 1,797, and by 1864 the number of Jews had already reached 2,422. This increase in the Jewish population is especially noticeable if we compare it with other cities in Bessarabia.

[Page 24]

	According to 1816–17 census			According to 1864 census	
The district	The cities growth rate	The Jewish population	% in relation to all residents	The Jewish population	% in relation to all residents
Kishinev	2000	40.0	20385	24.7	919
Khotyn	1000	66.6	6342	48.3	534
Soroca	1020	38.7	4135	76.4	417
Balti	1975	39.7	3124	38.7	156
Orhiyov	?	?	3102	72.1	?
Bandar	110	6.4	4297	28.2	3771
Akkerman (1808)	90	5.4	2422	12.1	2591

As the economic and political pressure in the cities of the "Pale of Settlement" in Russia intensified – so grew the rate of immigration from there to Akkerman, so much so that in the 1897 census there were already 5,613 Jews who constituted 19.9% of the total residents in the city. On the other hand, there was already a certain slowdown in the growth of the Jewish population in the following years, and in the 1910 census 5,802 Jews were registered. It is reasonable to assume, that the development of new means of transportation caused a certain devaluation of the status of city of Akkerman as a transit city for trade, and from here also the small increase in the percentage of the Jewish population in the city.

In 1918, with the entrance of the Romanians to Bessarabia after the First World War, Akkerman was cut off from its living space, until now Russia, and the Jewish population decreased. In 1925, the Jewish population reached 5,000 people, while in the census conducted in 1930 there were only 4,239 Jews who made up 12.3% of the total population. In 1940, with the Russian occupation, the Jewish population grew and reached 8,000, which made up 16% of the total population, but there are completely different reasons for this increase and they will be discussed in the chapter on the Holocaust.

Employment and Economy

The sources of livelihood of the Jews of Akkerman were not different from those of the Jews of other cities in Bessarabia. It can be said, that they enjoyed certain reliefs and discounts that did not apply to other cities because of Akkerman's considerable distance from the international border of Russia.

In the of the authorities' directives published in 1818, it was determined among others that the Jews of Bessarabia constitute one of the nine ethnic groups of the population of Bessarabia, and they have to pay taxes and municipal tax like all citizens depending to their occupation: merchants in the city or farmers. They were allowed to trade freely in all areas of the region and also develop trade relations with other regions in Russia. Indeed, the directives also contained restrictions on Jews in regards to purchasing private land, but when it came to livelihoods, small trade and other trades, there was no restriction. Therefore, there is reason to assume that the Jews of Akkerman also enjoyed all the rights and discounts granted to the Jews of Bessarabia. They integrated into all branches of trade and crafts and even purchased plots of land for construction.

The agriculture in this area was in a state of rapid development, the vineyards areas have been expanded and wine production increased, thousands of dessiatin of grain and seeds were sown and many Jews entered the trade business, brokerage in agricultural produce, and even engaged in large-scale import and export. In the 60s of the previous century, the wine production in Bessarabia reached about three million buckets a year, while Akkerman's share was about a third. According to testimony of an authority figure (Zashtzuk), which is also brought in the research of Dr. A. Feldman, almost all the taverns in Bessarabia were owned by Jews and the sale of liquor was a Jewish monopoly. Zashtzuk mentions the "Jewish lessee, Karasik, who in 1873 leased the sale of beverages on state and private estates in the Akkerman district."

It is worth noting the large share of Akkerman Jews in the craft industries. They managed to get along with the Christian craftsmen and had almost complete control over certain trades: tailoring, furriers, shoemakers, tanners, etc.

In 1865, Count Stroganov informed the Minister of the Interior, on the basis of a report submitted to him by the governor of the region of Bessarabian region that all branches of labor, including those who require hard physical labor, are in the hands of the Jews.

The Jews of Akkerman purchased land not only in the city but also in the area to cultivate it. Under Russian law, the Jews were not allowed to purchase land and settle within a 50 verst [53.34 km] radius along the border, but they were able to purchase land near the Dniester. It is known that the owners of the Christian estates filed a petition with the emperor against the Jews who purchase land in places forbidden to them. The petition was sent by the Ministry of the Interior to Count Stroganov for investigation and opinion. Stroganov, who supported the demand of the landowners, asked for the opinion of the district management and the military governor, General Ilyinsky. The later suggested to forbid the purchase of lands by the Jews only in the districts of Khotyn, Soroca, Orhiyov, Yasi (Balti) and Kishinev, but to allow the Jews to purchase lands in the districts of Bandar and Akkerman.

[Page 25]

The local authorities in the towns occasionally implemented the law prohibiting the settlement of Jews in villages close to the border in the spirit of the above-mentioned regulation and expelled the Jews who settled there. It is known, that in 1890 fifteen Jewish families were expelled from Tatarbunar in the Akkerman district, and the reason was: they settled in the town after the set date, 27 October 1858 (the town was established in 1809). Even though Tatarbunar had the status of a town for the purpose of enforcing the anti-Jewish law, it was given the status of a village and the Jews, who were expelled from this village, move to cities where they were able to integrate into the economic life. In the second half of the 19th century the law was frequently enforced, but since Akkerman was a city the Jews within it did not suffer from this discrimination.

When industrial plants began to develop in southwestern Russia in the second half of the 19th century, and the first buds of a capitalist economy emerged, this process skipped Akkerman. Industrial plants were not opened in the city but, on the other hand, there was considerable momentum in the development of agriculture. The Jews bought the farmers fruit while on the trees and gave them payment on account. Even before the farmers began to sow there were Jews, who bought the grain in advance and by doing so the farmers' fields were enslaved to the urban Jews.

We find evaluations on the economic situation of Akkerman's Jews in various sources. The Maggid of Slutsk, Tzvi Hirsh Dainow, who visited Akkerman in 1869, wrote: "The Jews of this city most of them poor, destitute, needy and paupers – – – the status of the Bessarabian Jews is terrible and most of them are idler like their brothers, the Jews of Lita and Zamut." On the other hand, we find a completely different assessment with the author, Zalman Epstein, who described their situation in an article published in [the Hebrew newspaper] "*Ha–Tzefirah*" on the eve of the 1881 pogroms: "Their good physical condition (is similar) to that of the rest of the Russia's Jews – – – the trade, which is almost entirely in the hands of the Jews, will flourish here in a superior manner – – – thousands of steam carriages carry, year after year, the grain of the land to Odessa and from there abroad through the sea. Apart from this main trade, the trade in sheep wool, oxen and wine will also be very successful – – – the craftsmen will find their livelihood at ease and not in sorrow – – – there are many rich people here among the Jews." When he compares the situation of the Jews of Bessarabia to that of the Jews of Lita, the author says: "This country is truly like the Garden of Eden – – – also the poor people eat meat every day and drink wine, and for that their faces will produce life and emotional–strength."

Only 12 years differentiate between the first and second testimony – and the assessments are completely different. It is possible, that the second author used high and poetic language recommended by "*Bat Hashamayim*" [*Haskalah* movement] and it is possible that he saw it from his innermost thoughts. It is also possible that they both visited different places and hence the difference in vision.

Contrary to what has been said, we know from more qualified and less "poetic" sources that there was a considerable deterioration in the economic situation of the Bessarabian Jews, which began to show signs from 1880 onwards, and its traces were also clearly seen in the Jews of Akkerman. Due to the frequent deportations of Jews from the villages the cities were filled with many unemployed Jews. The 1880s and 1890s were known to be years of severe agrarian crisis in Russia. Grain prices in world markets deteriorated drastically and reduced the farmers' income. The crisis was felt in full force in Bessarabia whose economy was based mainly on agriculture. The emigration of Jews from the villages was well felt in Akkerman because there were no sources of livelihood for the new residents in the city. The stagnation in trade was well felt and many sources of livelihood were blocked as described in one source: "The shoppers stopped (buying), the merchants and the agents mourned and lowered their heads. Many are the artisans and laborers (craftsmen) who go idle."

At that time, many Jews in the city needed "*Kimcha DePascha*" in preparations for the holiday of Passover, and the growing impoverishment had implications in all areas of Jewish life in the city. The Jewish Colonization Association began to distribute support funds to the needy whose number increased. Many came to the conclusion that there's no choice but to take the wandering stick again and sail far and wide to seek subsistence and livelihood.

The Spiritual–Cultural Image of Akkerman Jewry

How did Akkerman Jews shape their spiritual–cultural lives during the tsarist regime? Is it possible to compare Akkerman's Jewry with that of Poland, Lita and Galicia in this respect? What were the reasons why the Bessarabian Jewry, Akkerman included, were not among the cultural and spiritual centers such as those in Europe at the time, and why they did not establish serious institutions for Torah study and raise generations of scholars, teachers, etc.?

It is not an easy task to answer these questions in a complete and comprehensive answer. We will turn to the sources and try to see what was written on this subject in those days. In 1832, an educated man named Tzvi ben Avraham Balaban of Brady, who was also called by the name Rabinowitch (and lived at that time in Kishinev), describes the situation in a letter to his friend: "Of all our brethren our allies, who live in European countries, the Jews living in the country of Russia stand on the lower step of the steps ascending in the ladder of wisdom ... but our brothers, residents of the district of Bessarabia, have not yet reached this step. Ignorant, stupid, and

[Page 26]

lacking resourcefulness, and anything that has an opinion, understanding and intelligence will be expelled from their homes... and the doctrine of man, even though it is always walking hand in hand with the innocent Torah, has been thrown behind their backs – – – the Torah, and good deeds, are considered nothing in their eyes, all the more so, wisdom and foreign languages. The interest and occupation of its residents, all day long, is to raise capital and save, to eat in revelry and drink the wine often kept in their caves at *mitzvah* meals" (published in "*ha–Boker Or*" [The Morning Light] 5660, 194–196).

If we remove the coverage of the rhetoric that characterized the style of that period, there is a very deadly verdict in these words on the Jews of Bessarabia, Akkerman included, and it is possible that several words were written for the glory of poetic phrases. But, for sure, there is a nucleus of truth in these words considering the Jewish human material that came to this region and scattered across the cities and towns of Bessarabia. They did not bring with them a rooted culture, generations of Jewish tradition, deep awareness for Jewish education and the like. They came from the weakest strata of the Jewish population, socially and economically, and they could not be expected to reach greatness and significant deeds.

The conditions in the towns of Bessarabia were not fit for cultural growth. We cannot forget that this region, villages and cities alike, was usually sparsely populated and, even more so, the Jewish population. What centers with a massive Jewish settlement can contribute and operate in the spiritual and cultural area cannot be done in settlements with low population. Patterns of Jewish tradition were not anchored within them due to the absence of a broad stratum of educated Jews who engaged in Judaism and the Torah. When the region of Bessarabia was occupied by the Russians, it lagged culturally and there were no serious educational institutions in it. This was especially noticeable in the small settlements. Wealthy Jews sent their children to study in the big cities such as Moscow, St. Petersburg, Odessa, Kiev, etc., but most of the Jews had to make do with what was, and what was culturally – was meager and poor.

The Jews enjoyed the political and economic constitution granted by the government to residents and new immigrants, and this helped to develop the patterns of life that were far removed from the traditional Jewish way of life, as it was, for example, in Poland.

The main aspiration of the Jews – to penetrate new branches of livelihood and trade and also to engage in agriculture (in the villages), motivated them to follow in the ways of the non–Jewish population, to imitate their customs and way of life. Many insisted that the Jews of Bessarabia did not observe the *mitzvoth* and the Shabbat. The northern region of Bessarabia had a more Jewish and traditional character than the central and southern part, but it also did not satisfy "*Shlomi-Emuni Yisrael*" [Union of the Faithful in Yisrael]. For example, R' David Eybeschutz, who was the rabbi of Soroca in northern Bessarabia in the first decade of the 19th century, complained about his congregation: "There are many defective things in them, among them those who speak aloud in the synagogue – and when the Sabbath comes they resent it by saying – that if they did not have the Sabbath they would earn money working in the Wine-House: – – – "Instead of engaging in the Torah on the Shabbat, they eat and drink and sleep and later go for a walk – – – and after half a day they light up a fire in the Wine House."

The very fact that Rabbi Eybeschutz repeatedly emphasizes the matter of the "Wine House," shows us the attractive power of the wine houses, which were probably numerous in this part of the country whose wine industry was its number one industry.

The influence of the Christian environment was great on the Jews. Unlike in Poland, there were many Jews in the cities of Bessarabia who walked bareheaded, sent their children to study in government schools and universities and not to "*hadarim*" and "yeshivot," did not adhere to kosher laws, etc. The intellectual circles, which arose in many cities, further alienated the Jewish youth from the religious-traditional life.

This general atmosphere also characterized the Jewish community in Akkerman. Akkerman's proximity to a cultural-economic center such as Odessa, as well as the close ties with the center of the Bessarabia-Kishinev region left their mark on the character of the Jewish community in our city.

It turns out that the process of Russification in Akkerman took on different dimensions than in other cities. It can be said, that this was an accelerated process, so much so, that many of those who dealt with the history of this region define Akkerman as the "other city," more "gentile," than other cities in Bessarabia, and there were also those who called it a "reckless" city from a Jewish point of view. The renowned preacher, Tzvi Hirsch Masliansky, one of the leaders of "*Hovevei Zion*" who gained a reputation for his sermons in Russian cities, also came to Akkerman in one of his journeys for a speech, or for a "sermon," and in his memoir he writes about his impressions from this visit:

"How different are Akkerman Jews from ordinary Bessarabian Jews! It is hard to believe they are from one district – – – their way of life, their customs, their clothes – are a copy from their neighbor, Odessa. Odessa spreads its wings over her little sister, Akkerman, imprinted on it the European seal and removed the cloud of the Bessarabian spirit – – – when you delve into the understanding, that Akkerman learned from Odessa only the "lawlessness," the rebelliousness of religion, the Jewish customs with their attributes, the sanctity of Shabbat and Jewish religious festival – – – the uneducated rule in Akkerman as in all the cities of Bessarabia."

[Page 27]

The Craftsmen Synagogue – on the east side

The girls' school of the teacher and principal Kaufman, 1902

[Page 28]

Even here we have before us a decisive verdict on the way of life of the Jews of Akkerman. If a personality like Tzvi Hirsch Masliansky, that we cannot associate him to a sect of extremist zealots, issues such a verdict and states that Akkerman learned only lawlessness from Odessa – are truthful words, and there is a place to assume that Akkerman was indeed different, and the change was not very visible to those who were accustomed to a different form of Jewish life in Jewish communities in Russia

The accelerated process of Russification in the southern regions of Bessarabia, "stabbed the eyes" of outsiders, who apparently could not come to terms with the complete control of the Russian language in Jewish homes, with a very small number of Yiddish readers compared to many Russian readers. From one statistic we learn, that the percentage of Russian readers in the district has reached 28 while in Akkerman to 43!!! – the highest in all the cities of the region.

It cannot be concluded on the basis of the above, that the Jews of Akkerman were detached from Jewish tradition and from the affinity to the sanctity of Judaism. On the contrary, there were also Hassidim in Akkerman who remained loyal to their rabbis and to various dynasties to which they belonged before they moved to Akkerman, but, in comparison, the number of "opponents" in Akkerman was greater. In any case, there is no doubt that there was never a center of Hasidim in Akkerman, the city marched in its furrow, apparently formulated a Jewish way of life that was in line with the needs, and the level, of the culture of the city's Jewish residents.

There is no doubt that also in the first half of the 19th century various rabbis sat on the rabbinical chair in Akkerman, but their impact is not noticeable and we are unable to tell about them. On the other hand, it is known that the rabbi of the city of Bandar, R' Arye Leib Wertheim, also had an impact on the Jewish community of Akkerman which was apparently under his spiritual patronage.

The first buds for the formation of a Jewish community appeared in Akkerman as early as the beginning of the 19th century. Three years after the city passed into Russian hands, in 1815, Beit HaMidrash had already been built and the very fact that the Jews saw the need, and were able to establish a spiritual center for themselves, indicates that they were already a serious part of the population at that time. From a notebook from 1807 found in the Beit HaMidrash, we learn that in 1865 there was a pogrom against the Jews of Akkerman (what was the nature of the pogrom? we do not know on the basis of these lists, but it must be assumed that there were no victims and the rioters were only satisfied with the looting of Jewish property).

"*Chevra Kadisha*" was also established in 1807. In 1828, the Old Synagogue was built (the future Great Synagogue) and 19 years later, in 1847, "*Chevra Kadisha*" also established the Old Kloyz.

The Craftsmen Synagogue was built in 1903, and until than the craftsmen prayed in a private room, dim and half-ruined, at the home of R' Chaim Prectman on Izmailovsky Street. According to what is told in Schildkrauth's book, on holidays and festivals the Jews also gathered for prayer in private homes, or in the apartments of various institutions, which became improvised places of worship during the holiday.

It is worth noting, that even if the Jewish community of Akkerman did not produce well-known scholars there were, within it, many scholars and God-fearing Jews who studied the Torah in private and in public, and kept a light *mitzvah* as a severe one. There were Shas and Mishnayot societies in Beit HaMidrash, and they marked the end of the study of a book in splendor and in a large audience alongside tables set for a meal, as the speakers season their words with Torah innovations and competed with expressions of proficiency and wit.

In his book, Schildkrauth lists the names of Jews in Akkerman who were great Torah scholars, such as: R' Moshe'le Zuckerman, R' Ben-Zion Chava-Libes (Schildkrauth), R' David Brend, R' Chaim Chava-Libes (Kaminker), R' Yosele' Levin, R' Hanoch Shapira, R' Aarale, R' Moshe Leker, R' Leibele the slaughterer (Hirschfeld) author of "*Penei Arye*," "*Amrei Baruch*," and others. It seems to me, that anyone who counts eight names in the city takes a little risk, for you never know if you are not missing someone worthy of being counted among the great scholars.

The Jewish education in the 19th century was concentrated only in "*hadarim*" and "Yeshivot" did not exist in Akkerman. Even though attempts have been made to establish Yeshivot they did not last long, either due to a lack of teachers or the lack of means to upkeep them. The first attempt was – to set up a "yeshiva" in Shagansky's home on Jewish Street not far from the Leman. This one lasted about two years. The second attempt to establish a yeshiva was held at the home of Shlomo Hacham on Mikhailovsky Street. It was kind of "modern" Yeshiva since hours were also devoted to secular studies such as: the history of Israel, grammar and arithmetic. However, also the "modernization" did not help and this Yeshiva did not last a year. In conclusion, if someone desired, or his parents desired, more serious Torah studies – he had no other choice but to turn to Yeshivot in Odessa or Kishinev.

[Page 29]

The gymnasium students in the school yard

The gymnasium students against the fortress' background

The gymnasium students against the fortress' background

[Page 30]

Schildkrauth writes about the study in the "*hadarim*": "There were different "*hadarim*" and Gemara teachers in the city. The well-known Gemara teachers in the city were: Rabbi Hirsh–Wolf, Rabbi Yossi, Moshe Yankel the long, Rabbi Moshe–Wolf, Rabbi Yizi, Yona the *melamed*, and others. There were also homeowners who imported "foreigners," meaning, outside of Akkerman, those lasted one or two "periods" and disappeared. An exception was Rabbi Nachum, whose students called him the "Angel of Death" because he severally beaten the student who did not memorize the lesson properly."

From various articles, published in the 1880s and 1890s in the general press, as well as in the Hebrew press, we learn that at that time there was a shortage of high school education in all Russian cities. Of course, the "*Haskalah*" [Jewish Enlightenment] "*Bat Hashamayim*" [Daughter of Heaven], also reached Akkerman, circles of *maskilim* had a subscription for Hebrew newspapers that came from St. Petersburg and Moscow, and the problems of the Russian Jewry were also at the center of the world of Akkerman's Jews. Indeed, the 1880s pogroms in Russia did not befall the Jews of Akkerman, but their influence was considerable and we will discuss this elsewhere in this essay.

Testimonies from "*Ha–Melitz*"

In issue No. 44 of the [Hebrew Newspaper] "*Ha–Melitz*" from 1889, an article was published on Akkerman. It was signed by "*Mishal HaDalponi*," which is probably the pseudonyms of one of the *maskilim* from Akkerman, and so it was said among others:

"...this city, where more than six thousand Jews will live in, will not excel in anything from other cities, and may even fall short of them regarding its spiritual life. We do not have here, as in other cities, different societies to glorify the Torah, to spread education among the Jews, to support the fallen and be gracious to the poor." The reporter did not write clearly, and did not explain to which societies he meant, and what's up with "to support the fallen and be gracious to the poor" in the spiritual life, as he defines. We only learn from this poetic article that its writer is distressed over the lack of association for the dissemination of education. In contrast, we read in Brockhaus–Efron dictionary from 1890, which is, undoubtedly, a more authoritative source than the reporter of "*Ha–Melitz*" in Akkerman that in 1885 there were 10 elementary schools in Akkerman and 596 boys and 18 girls studied in them. Among the educational institutions in the city there were also two pre–secondary schools with 4 classes, although this article did not mention the number of Jewish schools, or schools under Jewish management, but in "Iberskaya Encyclopedia" we found that Talmud Torah was founded Akkerman in 1882, there were also two schools for boys and two schools for girls, and a Shabbat evening school.

Presumably, the Jews encountered many difficulties in enrolling their children in government or municipal schools, but relative to their percentage in the general population, the number of Jewish students in these schools was higher than that of the other ethnic groups in Akkerman. The restrictions were particularly striking with regard to Jewish girls who, at one time, numbered fifty percent of all the girls in school, although it is not certain that there was a time when the Jewish population in Akkerman reached fifty percent of all residents...

In 1909, the municipality passed a resolution, under the pressure of anti–Semitic circles, to limit the number of Jewish students to only ten percent. The Jews had no other choice but to establish their own private schools so as not to deprive their children of education.

It is worth noting, that the Russian authorities did not approve the establishment of private educational institutions, fearing that they might be a source of social unrest that would foster opposition to the regime.

At the beginning, the private Jewish schools were far from Jewish education but, over time, there was a significant change in the trend of study, and this will be discussed later. In 1883, 41 students attended the private Jewish school owned by Gelfand. The second school was intended for girls and was under the direction of the teacher Bertha Davidovna–Kaufman.

The social–educational activity in the city, in the late 19th century, revolved around two big Jewish societies centered in St. Petersburg. The first was O.P.E – *Obshextvo dlia Rasprostranenia Prosveshenia mezhdu Jervejam v Rossii* (a company for the dissemination of education among Russian Jews), whose main activity, as its name implies, was in the field of education and assistance in the existence of Jewish schools or in Jewish administration. The name of the second society was, the society for the aid of poor Jews – *Obshextvo Posobija bednyn Jervejam*, and its duty was – financial support for poor Jews. Akkerman operated branches of these two companies and the Jewish intelligentsia in the city coordinated the social activities in both branches.

[Page 31]

The Jewish Community in Akkerman from Inception to Destruction (cont'd)

Welfare and Mutual Help

In addition the above societies there were also other philanthropic associations such as "*Malbish Arumim*", "*Maot Chitim*", "committee for the supply of firewood to the poor," and their names attest to their nature and role. Various public activists concentrated their public activities around other institutions such as: the Jewish hospital, Talmud Torah, and *Gemilut Hasadim*. The idea was – everyone, whose heart inspires him to act generosity, meaning – everyone chose for himself his field of activity and the association for which he wanted to act. The *gabbaim*, or "*kamitetshikim*," were chosen by their "close associates" and apparently did not adhere to democratic principles. We rely on the testimony of Y. Schildkrauth who writes in his book: "During those difficult times of the Tsarist rule, when there were no organized communities yet, the above-mentioned cultural-philanthropic societies occupied a prominent place in the Jewish life in Akkerman, and brought quite a bit of benefit to the Jewish population."

As noted above, the main philanthropic activity was concentrated in two associations that were centered in St. Petersburg. "The Society for the Distribution of Education" supported Mr. Gelfand boy's school, Kaufmann-Harmatz school, and also the Sabbath eve school, which was founded in 1895 and its purpose was to promote the education of young Jews who did not receive a formal education.

B. D. Kaufmann school, which was supported by "The Society for the Distribution of Education," stood out in its assimilation like all the schools supported by this society throughout Russia, and its principal was probably loyal to this line. However, it should be noted to his credit that it allowed the children of the poor to receive general education for free. The teaching staff of this school also included those with national-Zionist views, such as: Y. Boris Borisovich Kumarovsky, Simcha Wolman and others, who taught at a later period and tried to instill a Jewish national spirit in the school.

Y. Schildkrauth mentions the main activists in these two societies. Dr. Y. Shapira, Y. D. Brotzky, M. Krushkin, Hana Gvirtzman, Y. Einbinder, Natan Goldstein, B. D. Kaufman, and the renowned philanthropist Moshe Milstein.

Talmud Torah was established in 1882, and was first intended for the children of the poorest strata in the Jewish population. The circumstances were to his detriment because the management, and the teachers were not at an appropriate level for an educational institution, and the level of education was also quite low. The men of Beit HaMidrash were also the *gabbaim* and the activists of Talmud Torah, and according to the testimony of M. Kumarovsky they were of the opinion that "the level was sufficient for the children of the poor." It is not know if these words were said with irony, or the *gabbaim* of Talmud Torah really thought that poor children have to make do with a low level of education.

We learn a little about this institution from an article published in the [Hebrew Newspaper] "*Ha-Melitz*," No. 660 from 1895. So writes the author of the article, Yakov Zausmer, from Akkerman:

"On March 2, election took place at the city council house for *gabbaim* for the Talmud Torah building in our city. During the three years, in which the elderly *gabbaim* served, there was a great deal of neglect in the Talmud Torah building because no one supervised the needs of the building, both material and spiritual. And this time they expressed their desire to elected many of the new generation and in our city was a kind of war in peace between the old and the young, therefore this time the elections attracted the hearts of all the residents of the city and they talked about it."

The management, members of the younger generation, apparently introduced order in Talmud Torah and one of its achievements was – opening a course for the craft. The level of education has also risen. In 1908, Talmud Torah was released from the influence and control of the *gabbaim* of the Beit HaMidrash, and a new management was elected under the leadership of Y. Einbinder, Natan Goldstein, and M. Kumarovsky who instilled a new Zionist-nationalist spirit into the walls of Talmud Torah by inviting teachers like Meir Starec, Boris Borisovich Kumarovsky, and David Rebelski who was one of the activists of "*Poalei Zion*." M. Kumarovsky talks at length about the teaching methods of David Rebelski, and reveals that in this method was a consideration for the child's tendencies and skills. Attention was also directed to the situation of the children's parents, whose financial situation was quite poor, and so Mr. Kumarovsky describes the activities that began in this field:

"In the past the *gabbai* of "*Malbish Arumim*" appeared with a shoemaker, pointed with his finger at certain students and ordered the shoemaker to take the measurements for new shoes in the presence of the entire class of students. We have stopped this humiliating practice. Any help, with food or clothing, was given at the child's home, and in return we received good work that was done in the class by the children.

We arranged a medical service at the school by the Dr. Feigin who volunteered for this task. When the child needed medical help – and there were too many who needed it – the child was told that his treatment was not for his illness, but to make him "healthier." The management organized a parents committee for the school and parties at which the students performed. For many mothers from the city's back streets this was the only social gathering they were able to attend."

Here, we can see the beginning of the social and philanthropic activity in Akkerman, and perhaps this is not a beginning, but a continuation of the activity that preceded it.

[Page 32]

Later, between 1919-1912, the Jewish philanthropist, Yisrael Fokkelman from Akkerman, built a spacious two-story building for the needs of Talmud Torah. After several members of the administration left the city, and there were also changes in the teaching staff, there was a decrease in the level of education and members of the Yiddishism class in the city entered the administration. The assimilated Teacher, S. Chechelnitsky, was brought from Byeramtcha, and the management was composed of those who had never been elected to this position, such as R' Yisrael Kushnir, R' Yankel Kushnir, Shabtai Imias and others. After a while, the anti-Zionist "*Kultur-Lige*" ["Cultural League"] took over and another spirit entered the institution.

The Old Jewish Hospital

One of the oldest welfare institutions in Akkerman was the Jewish Hospital. It was founded in 1882 and was located in one of the houses of Dr. Alexander Kogen on Izmailovsky Street. This hospital, with its two rooms (one for men and one for women), did not excel in high level medical services but, nevertheless, brought great benefit especially to the poor population of the city. The hospital's limited medical staff was headed by Dr. Y. Shapira, who devoted a lot of time to treating patients without asking for payment. The practical director of the hospital was R' Meir Greenstein, who worked day and night to meet the needs of the hospital. R' Meir Greenstein was the omnipotent ruler of the institution and the sole determinant. M. Kumarovsky wrote about him that he was more of "a slave to the institution than a landlord." He was a tough man, but his devotion to the hospital was unquestioningly.

Other Institutions

Another public activist, who acted with devotion and loyalty, was Yitzchak (Issac) Grinstein, and his field of operation was the Society for Aid to Poor Jews, or as it called then in Russian, "*Obshcestvo pomoshchi.*" He was younger than R' Meir Grinstein, used to publish annual action plans and did not shy away from public criticism.

The affairs of the cemetery and burial were in the hands of *gabbaim* who appointed themselves and never stood for election by the public. These *gabbaim* terrorized the public and their fear especially fell on the rich. They probably knew how to "skin" those who needed their help, and when one of the wealthy fell into their hands they charged his family higher burial fees (perhaps to fill in what the deceased missed while he was alive...). Their rate of burial fees could not be appealed and there were rumors in the city that the cemetery affairs were not being conducted properly. However, there was no one to check the validity of these rumors, and even if they had found such – the *gabbaim* would not have made the inquiry easier for them.

In 1890, a philanthropic association named, "*Somech Noflim*" ["Supporter of the Fallen"], was organized, and in 1898 "*Kupat Gemilut Hasdim*" ["Interest-Free Loan Fund"] was established. It provided assistance not only to the Jewish residents of Akkerman but also to Jews from the immediate area. Each of these two associations had a group of *gabbaim* who volunteered their time for these institutions.

The new Jewish hospital (covered in snow)

[Page 33]
About the Immigration from Akkerman

As in all cities in Bessarabia, the immigration movement started to show its signs in Akkerman in the 80s and 90s of the previous century. It was caused by both economic and political reasons – the drought that befell Bessarabia, and also Ingatye's decrees on the expulsion of Jews from the villages that were at a distance of 50 versts from the border. These decrees were carried out cruelly, the Jews were expelled from their homes and their property was expropriated without prior warning. They were left homeless and without a livelihood. It is no wonder that for many Jews the decision has been made: to emigrate.

Also the 1880s pogroms in southern Russia constituted an important factor in the emigration of Jews from Akkerman, even though they did not directly affect the Jews of Bessarabia. The news about the pogroms, which were published in the press, undermined the Jews' sense of security and caused them anxiety because many thought that what happened today in other cities could happen to them the next day. The Jews sought refuge in various countries, but the main direction of immigration was: Argentina or Palestine (Eretz Yisrael). There was a real immigration in one direction – Argentina, while in the other direction – there were many plans but only a few fulfilled them.

The Immigration to Argentina

With the foundation of The Jewish Colonization Association [JCA], and the establishment of the special committee founded by Baron Hirsch for the selection of candidates for immigration and settlement on the land in Argentina, the immigration program to Argentina gained a lot of momentum. A rumor passed in all the cities of Russia and Bessarabia: there is livelihood in Argentina. The Baron came to the aid of the suffering Jews in Russia and many began to plan their departure from Russia. The representative of the Baron, Hirsch David Feinberg, went to cities in southern Russia and began organizing groups, each with fifty families, for settlements in Argentina. In Bessarabia alone six such groups were organized, one of them in Akkerman.

R' Yakov Shmuel Trahtman, a public activist, a writer and member of the Haskalah movement who published articles about Akkerman in the press, began to conduct the negotiations between the residents who were candidates for immigration and the representative of JCA, David Feinberg. M. Kumarovsky writes that R' Yakov Shmuel Trahtman has done a lot to publicize the city of Akkerman by corresponding with the management of the Hebrew press at the time and by his frequent articles in various journals. It is possible say, that he put Akkerman on the Jewish map. He was appointed legal representative of JCA in the district of Akkerman.

The immigration program to Argentina aroused great interest in all sections of the population: merchants, shopkeepers, mediators ("*mekler* – sort of a new class created after the expropriation of many Jews from the villages of Bessarabia), religious personal, etc. A delegation was sent to Argentina on behalf of the candidates for this immigration and it was headed by M. Berkowitz, a wise man with experience in agriculture. He examined the situation and conditions at the place designated for Jewish settlement and passed his findings to Baron Hirsch. His report was also published in his series of articles in "*Ha–Melitz*." In the report he states, that in order for the settlement to be successful it must be based on a broad footprint and provide a reasonable opportunity for the settlers to adapt (according to M. Kumarovsky, Berkowitz was interviewed by Baron Hirsch himself).

The first immigrants left Akkerman for Argentina in the years 1894–1895, and they established the village, "Primero de Maya," which was also known as "Moshavat Akkerman." M. Kumarovsky describes the beginning of the immigration from Akkerman to Argentina in these words:

"The writer of these columns remembers the separation of the immigrants from the residents of Akkerman. Dark skies with unfriendly clouds hung over their heads. Many Jews came to the synagogue for the last "*Shacarit*" prayer. The visit to the cemetery (to say goodbye to the deceased) passed in silence. After that, several carts, which drove the immigrants and their escorts, began to move. After a drive of a few kilometers the caravan stopped in a field to eat the last meal together. They drank a lot of wine, the thick–bearded men were hoarse and happy and the eyes of many shed tears of excitement."

After the immigrants arrived in Argentina, and settled on the land made available to them, letters from Argentina began to reach Akkerman. Most of them were full of satisfaction and personal fulfillment of the new settlers in the Argentine "Pampa." Yakov Shmuel Trahtman, the representative of JCA in Akkerman, published in journals excerpts of the letters he received from Yitzchak Hakham, Hochman, Weinstein, David the ritual slaughterer, Yakov Yakobzan, Zev Sheinberg and others. From them we learn that the immigrants were satisfied with everything they foundat the place of their settlement. So, for example, writes Yakov Yakobzan: "When I get out of my bed in the morning and my eyes wander over the square, I see that everything is mine: the house, the field, the animal, the tools, the chickens, and I lie in my bed in the evening and I know that my bread, water and needs are ready for me and my family, and on the next day I will not have to run through the streets and ask for food for my family – I sleep well and I bless God." In another letter it says according to Y. S. Trahtman: "We arrived safely and we found homes, bulls, horses etc. The settlement is full of charm, the soil is fertile, the air is fresh and healthy, it is close to the railway, a stream of water flows and passes through our boundaries and there are good living fish. In one word: we are happy! "

[Page 34]

No wonder that these "joyous news" of the "colonists" from Akkerman in Argentina spread quickly in the Jewish public and many were getting ready to follow in their footsteps. But it soon became clear to the settlers that happiness was far from them and in letters that arrived shortly afterwards completely different "songs" have been heard: lamentations and weeping for the bitter faith, about the attitude of Baron Hirsch's officials toward the settlers, the lack of working capital, lack experience, unbearable distress and suffering. It can be said to the credit of Y. S. Trahtman, that he also published a few of these letters for the public knowledge. And so we found in "Ha-Melitz" No. 232 from 5656, Tuesday *Parochet "Ki Thabo"*: "We received your letter, you order us to "to live quietly and peacefully and not to arouse an argument." As you know, we are all peaceful people – – – the officials stopped giving the farmers tools to work the land, the clerical house did not give us any help for sacred buildings such as a synagogue, a bathhouse with a mikveh, etc. "They have no business dealing with such things"– – – and what will we do if all the Jews of Russia are despicable and worthless in the eyes of these great masters, the Jews of France? As if we are not the sons of one father! Please do not forget us! We are your flock and you are our shepherd!"

The writer of this letter was a settler from Akkerman and Mr. Trahtman only reveals the initials of his name and surname: P.A.

In the letter signed by P.A. it is said among others: "To this day we have hoped that the difficult and bad terms of the contract will be replaced by others, but now we have realized our hope is in vain, everything is absurdity, and there is no escape – – – we are confused in a country not ours. We fell into the hands of hard masters – – – we were sold into slaves and we, our sons and our offspring to the end of all generations, will be, God forbid, enslaved for eternity."

There is no point in continuing with this letter since it is well known what happened to this settlement. The author, Alperson, describes the suffering of the colonists in his important book, "Thirty Years of Jewish Settlement in Argentina." The Jews of Akkerman were not the only ones to suffer. A long time has not passed and the settlers of "Primero de Maya" left the "Garden of Eden," scattered all over Argentina, every person turned his own way, to peddling, small trade, etc. In this way came the end of the new and productive dream of life that many of Akkerman's Jews had dreamed.

An old house in Akkerman

On the shore of the Leman River

The fortress kisses the Leman River

[Page 35]

The Beginning of the Immigration to Eretz Yisrael and "*Hibbat Zion*"

Y. Klausner tells in the "Encyclopedia of the Diaspora" about the beginning of the immigration to Eretz Yisrael from Akkerman:

"An association was established in Akkerman and fifty families registered in it. Among the registered members were many who were used to physical work. Most of the members had their own means. The association sent delegates to Constantinople, to Sir Laurence Oliphant. In 1880 he published his book, "*Eretz HaGilad*," in which he recommended the settlement of Jews in eastern Eretz Yisrael and actively supported the movement for the settlement of the country. In the spring of 1882, he visited Romania – Iasi and Bucharest – and from there traveled to Constantinople to seek a permit to settle Jews in Syria and Israel. Many Jews in Russia and Romania expected his help since they saw him as a wealthy and influential man."

In another place it is told about two emissaries, Y. Zusman and Eliyahu Steinberg, who left from Akkerman to Eretz Yisrael. They studied the conditions in the place, then met with Sir Laurence Oliphant and found out that his influence on the Turkish authorities was very limited, and he also has no means to assist the settlement of Jews in Syria and Eretz Yisrael. Therefore, they returned to Akkerman and reported their impressions and conclusions to the first members of "*Hovevei Zion*," who were getting ready to immigrate to Eretz. And so the plan to immigrate fifty Jews from Akkerman to Eretz Yisrael in the late 19th century was shelved.

From various articles published in the press, especially in "*Ha–Melitz*," we learn that a rather small circle of "*Hovevei Zion*" was active in Akkerman. The circle attracted followers for the idea of "*Hibbat Zion*" and also raised funds for the settlement of Eretz Yisrael. So, for example, was published in issue No. 176 of "*Ha–Melitz*" at the end of 5642: "Yehiel Treistman informs us from Akkerman that according to the annual account brought by "*Hovevei Zion*," a total of 466 ruble was collected in this city during the year, and in this account not a single name of a rich man, who contributed to the benefit of the workers in the Holy Land, is mentioned or counted"(quoted from Schildkrauth's book).

We find more detailed information in issue No. 766 of the same newspaper from 1894: Y.S. Trahtman, the reporter from Akkerman writes: "All for what reason? For what? That there was not a single person out of many in the entire city who challenged and dealt with this issue. The throats of famous preachers–talkers dried up in vain, our masters Massliansky, Korotkin and Yevazrav, who were here, preached, investigated, shouted and protested. Each of the listeners listened intently to their warm words which came from the heart and which, according to the commonsense, entered the heart. When they left the sanctuary for the daily life – each Jew turned to his business and trade." There is, of course, nothing in these words to compliment the Jews of Akkerman, but the bitter pill is sweetened by the final section of the same article: "Last year, the enlightened young man, Mr. Zelik Bayokansky, settled here. He is a *Hovev Zion* and a lobbyist, and he aroused the sleepers. He troubled himself, labored and toiled, gathered the people for a meeting and slowly slowly there was a movement in our city regarding the settlement."

We could not find a continuation to the activity of the "enlightened young man," Zelik Bayokansky, in "*Ha–Melitz*," but we know about the organization of "*Hovevei Zion*" in Akkerman that one of its activists was Leib Sharira.

In light of the ban during the reign of the Tsar to hold Zionist activities, the activities of "*Hovevei Zion*" concentrated in small circles and the meetings were held in private homes under the guise of family events, discussions on literary issues, etc. Apparently, these circles were composed mainly of members of the affluent class of Akkerman Jewry, but did not reach the wider middle class. Within "*Hovevei Zion*" was also an active group of young people who called themselves "*Bnei Zion*." Later, an "opposition" also appeared in the framework of the youth circle. These were young people did not find satisfaction in the limited action of the association and saw it as "stepping in place." They sought greatness, were interested in the liberation movements of other nations and in practical Zionism. Eventually they left the association and formed a new Zionist association called "*Ohavei Zion*." Among the activists within this association were Akivah Margolin and Binyamin Crossman. In the passage of time they immigrated to the United States and were active in the establishment of the Society of Emigrants from Akkerman in America.

The young circle grew and was later joined by: M. Kumarovsky, Meir Starec, Zise Gladstein, Ben–Zion Garin, Aharon Serper, Shmuel Gilbord, Yakov Icht, Rivkin and others. The Zionist leader, M. Sheinkin, who visited Akkerman several times, assisted in the development of this circle from an organizational and conceptual point of view. It is known about conceptual seminars organized by the circle and about lecturers specially invited to them, such as: Nowakowsky, Chemerinsky (who was known by his literary name R' Mordechai'le) and others. After a while, two groups of Zionist students were also established: "*Ezra*" and "*Kadima*," the Zionist activity branched out in their wake and received a new turning point. One of the activities in the "*Ezra*" group was Zina Helman.

There is no doubt, that at that time the Zionist activity in Akkerman was influenced by the activities in Odessa. Evidence of this were also the names of the various associations that emerged in the city and their names were similar to the names of the associations in the great and close by Odessa: "*Nes Ziona*," "*HaShachar*," "*HaTehiya*," etc.

[Page 37]

The groups' practical activity was reflected in the sale of the Jewish National Fund stamps, Zionist Shekel, signing for shares in the "Jewish Colonial Trust," standing by the bowls placed in the synagogues on holidays, collecting donations at weddings, bar mitzvahs and all sorts of other occasions. This activity improved the Zionists' prestige in Akkerman in the eyes of the main Zionist institutions, and all the Zionist conferences and conventions held in the major cities were attended by delegates from Akkerman. Akkerman delegations also attended Zionist conventions held away from Akkerman. So, for example, Meir Starec participated in the conference of Russian Zionists in preparation for the Second Zionist Congress held in Warsaw in 1898. He was also one of the ten delegates from Bessarabia who attended the Second Congress. A delegate from Akkerman attended the Russian Zionist Conference in Minsk in 5662. In the same year stamps were sold for the amount of 73 ruble.

In 1899–1900, Dr. S. Bandersky, a native of Kishinev who studied medicine in Odessa, worked in the region of Bessarabia and also in Wolyn, Russia, on behalf of the Zionist administration. When he completed his studies he moved to Zionist activity in Bessarabia and Akkerman was included in his field of activity. At a district conference held in Bandar on 4–5 July 1900, at the initiative of Bandersky, two delegates from Akkerman (Helfend and Prelis) also participated and in a report they gave in this conference they told about the activity for the teaching of the Hebrew language, courses on Jewish history and literature, and evening classes. This report made a good impression on the delegates and, among others, it was decided that every association should strive to establish a "theoretical association" such as the one established in Akkerman (as told in Y. Klausner article in the volume dedicated to Bessarabia in the "Encyclopedia of the Diaspora,").

Delegates from Akkerman attended the regional conference held in Kamianets–Podilskyi in 1901. At this conference those responsible for activities in the districts were elected and Sheinkin was appointed as the person in charge of the Akkerman district.

The Uganda Scheme divided the Zionists in Akkerman to those who said yes and those who said no. the representatives of five Zionists association ("*Bnei Zion*," "*Ohavay Zion*, "*Ezra*," and "*Poalei Zion*") gathered in Akkerman for a discussion on the Uganda Scheme, and after arguments that lasted more than eight hours a decision has been made against the authorized authority in Kharkiv (members of the Zionist General Council gathered at the home of Dr. Berenstein–Cohen and voted against the Uganda Scheme). The participants in the above discussion in Akkerman expressed their sorrow at the split in the Zionist movement, and claimed that the members of the Zionist General Council should have asked the Zionist associations for information on this important issue before making their decision.

In the summer of 1905, we find in Akkerman two factions of "*Poalei Zion*": the Jewish Territorial Organization with 60–70 members, and the Palestinians, or as they called themselves "*Zionei Zion*," with 40–50 members. The Palestinian faction of "*Poalei Zion*" established the "Palestinian workers' fund for laborers and clerks."

Meir Starec from Akkerman participated in the 1906 Zionist conference in Hälsingborg Finland.

The Zionist Activity

In 1910–1914, the Zionists in the city continued their regular activities, but it is known that in 1910 the government arrested six Zionists for the sale of Jewish National Fund's stamps which was prohibited by law. They were exiled to the Kherson region for two years. The names of the imprisoned: Gelman, Icht, Kanterovitch, Kumarovsky, Lis and Rivkin. The Zionist activity weakened, but in 1912 it resumed with a certain momentum and in camouflage. The seal of the "Society for the Promotion of Culture" in St. Petersburg served as a cover for any Zionist meeting.

Yehoshua Harari z"l told, that when his brother, Yakov Berger, returned from his academic studies in St. Petersburg, he joined the Zionist activities and even tried concentrate it with the intention of uniting the various factions and groups in order to strengthen the Zionist movement in the city. One of the factions was a group of workers who was under the influence of "*Poalei Zion*" and concentrated at the Craftsmen Synagogue. Among the activists of this group was also Leib Stambul who was influenced at the time by Borochov's lectures in Akkerman. In this group of "*Poalei Zion*" there were other activists whose names I don't remember.

After negotiations, this group joined the Zionist activity in the city. At the same time, Zionist propaganda also gained some momentum despite all the prohibitions and restrictions of the authorities, but at the outbreak of the World War it was also silenced.

[Page 36]

A group of "Agudat Ohavay Zion in Akkerman," 1904

First row on top, right to left: **unknown, Bronstein, Meir Starec, Reuven Shtulman, Zise Gladstein (picture of Dr. Leon Pinsker)**
Second row: **Yakov Haskin, unknown**
Third row: **Bernard Krausman, Mendel Kumarovsky, Ben-Zion Garin, Leibish Krasner**
Fourth row: **Aharon Serper, Shmuel Gilburd, Yitzchak Selinger, unknown, Meir Sviadush, Moshe Marinyansky**
Fifth row: **Akivah Margolin**
Sixth row: **Morris Gavshevits, Y. Kriper, unknown, Eli-Hersh Kriper, unknown**

[Page 38]
The 1905 Pogrom

The year 1904–1905 was, as is well known, a year of great calamity in Russia. Russia's defeat in the war with Japan undermined the foundations of the Tsarist regime and in its wake began a wild incitement against the Jews. It was conducted by the Russian People's Council ("*Soyuz Ruskov Naroda*"), which was called by the people the "Black Hundred" ("*Chornaya Sotnya*"). An atmosphere of pogroms hovered in the air and in the articles of M. Kumarovsky, which are published in this book, there an expression to this atmosphere and also a description of the events.

The pogrom arrived "late" in Akkerman by a few days and, as we know, the Kishinev pogrom preceded it. Akkerman's turn came after the region minister was forced to telegraph from St. Petersburg to end the pogrom in Kishinev. Akkerman's anti-Semite mayor, and the head of the church in the city, apparently envied the rioters of Kishinev and began to encourage the peasants to take revenge on the Jews. They interpreted the order of the region minister to stop the pogroms on the Jews as an only attack in Kishinev…

The self-defense, which was organized in the city in advance, concentrated about two hundred people: salesmen, laborers, high school students, and merchants. Its initiators were the Zionist circles in the city headed by Yeshayahu Brudsky, and the converted physician, M. B. Shar, whose heart was touched by the fate of his people.

The members of the liberal circles in the city, among them the Attorney General, the Justice of the Peace, the notary and several members of the city council – were unable to help: to withstand the growing stream of instigators and rioters. However, it should be noted, that there were some Christians who hid Jews in their homes and some of them even took to the streets and tried to calm the turbulent spirits.

Many Jews fled to nearby fields and gardens for fear of the rioters and quite a few were beaten by the farmers and their property was looted.

The pogrom amounted to seven dead, many were wounded, many shops went up in flames, 388 families were left destitute, and the general damage estimate – 960 thousand rubles. The murdered were: Michel Sternberg, Leib Fishman, Fania Steinberg, Leizer Wolman, Sioma Grinstein, Yisrael Buganov, Efrat and also an unknown Jew who was brought from the village of Kazatza. Six Torah scrolls desecrated by the rioters were also buried near the mass grave. These lines were engraved on a black marble tombstone:

> Stand here a human being and open the source of your eyes
> and if your heart is stone – it will melt into water at the sight of this mound
> beneath it found rest six Torah scrolls and eight martyrs.
> They died unlike any other person.
> They were murdered at the prime of their lives by cruel rioters
> who looted our property, sent fire to our homes,
> and in the synagogues they tore up Torah scrolls and desecrated them,
> they killed eight pure souls with severe torture
> on the bitter day, 7 Marcheshvan 5666.
> Here this mound is a witness, this tombstone is a witness, that the shame of
> our nation will not be forgotten until the malicious... [1] moves out of the country.

After the pogrom a special commission of inquiry, headed by Dr. Leo Motzkin, was set up in Berlin. The duties of the committee were: investigation of the events, collection of documents and evidence from the victims. For this purpose, special emissaries were also sent to visit all the cities where pogroms took place. The writer, Avraham Ludvipol, who stayed in the city for two weeks, gathered all the information on the victims, stolen property as well as photographs, documents, etc.

A group of Zionist teachers in Talmud Torah

[Page 39]

The new Talmud Torah building

A group of teachers and board members of Talmud Torah, 1908

Seating right to left: **Mendel Kumarovsky, Meir Starec, N. Zenkler, David Rabelski, Nathan Goldstein, Yisrael Einbinder. In the middle – the *shamash* Moshe**

[Page 40]

The Jewish Community of Akkerman

After the Russian Revolution of 1917, new winds began to blow in the country and many hopes also arose among all members of the national minorities who were looking for ways and forms to express their nationality. The depression that prevailed in all sections of the population after the war, the ruined economy, the mourning for the many victims, etc., slowly subsided and the Jews began to plan their lives according to the new regime and diffrent circumstances. With the secession of Bessarabia from Russia and its annexation to Romania in 1918, the economic distress increased and the two main philanthropic societies we talked about in the previous chapter, ceased their activities. Also the JCA Company, whose center was in St. Petersburg, stopped its aid operations. Akkerman was also cut off from Odessa, which served as an important economic and cultural center for the Jews of Bessarabia, and the city's Jews remained alone. Apparently, all these circumstances aroused the hidden forces in the Jews of this city and they began to understand the meaning of the ancient verse – "If I am not for myself, who will be for me?" They awoke from their stagnation and reliance on others and started to organize their public lives at all levels.

At the end of 1917, the Jewish community was established and its main forces came from the Zionists' ranks. Even the intelligentsia in the city, those "Russophiles" who saw the solution to the problems of the Jews with rapid Russification, who snuggled up on Russian culture and "Mother Russia" – sobered up from their dreams. In view of the Romanization imposed on the inhabitants by the new regime, and the means of repression taken by the new rulers, they had no choice but to approach the national Jewish camp and quite a few of them began to be active in the national institutions.

It is not to be understood from that that the path of the Zionists, who aspired the democratization of the Jewish community and to grant a prominent national identity to all institutions, received the support and sympathy of all. They had to struggle with three factors: the assimilated intelligentsia, the anti-Zionist camp (such as "*Kultur Lige*") and the religious public that concentrated around Beit HaMidrash. The struggle was not easy, but thanks to several dedicated leaders and the stubborn spirit of the Zionist camp, the Zionists managed to reach a dominant status in almost all the community institutions, direct them to constructive activity and prevent the takeover of the *gabbaim* and activists who acted on their own and did not receive the authority of the general public.

The first chairman of the community, who was elected in the free and democratic elections by the community council, was Dr. Yitzchak Shapira. After him served in this position according to turn: Hana Gvirtzman, Nathan Goldstein, and Moshe Milstein who was also known as the "benefactor" of the Jews of Akkerman. All of them served one or two terms and only the accomplished Zionist, Moshe Helman, served in this position for many years and initiated many activities for the benefit of the Jewish public in the city. He was liked by the Jews of Akkerman thanks to his good temper, boundless devotion to public affairs and the community institutions, and his personal honesty. All of this led to him to being repeatedly elected to the position of chairman of the community. His deputy was Yakov Berger, the gymnasium principal. For a certain time Yitzchak Feldstein served in the duty of deputy of head of the community.

Y. Schildkrauth writes in his book about the image of the community:

"The community in Akkerman was national-democratic, a matter that even Jewish Kishinev did not achieve. The representatives of the "*Yiddishe Kultur Lige*" in the city greatly helped in the struggle for a democratic community and its leaders were: the talented Y. Kogen, Yeshayahu Brudski, Akivah Kogen, H. Karolik and others. In contrast, we had to fight a lot with the "*Yiddishe Kultur Lige*" when we shaped the national image of the community."

It is worth noting, that other communities in Bessarabia shaped the procedure and practice in their communities according to the wording of the bylaws of the Jewish community of Akkerman. The community council was elected in a free and democratic election and each party, faction or group of members, was allowed to submit its own list and conduct an outreach campaign ahead of the elections. In the deployment of the community elections, information meetings were held on behalf of the factions and parties according to all the rules of democracy.

The first elected Jewish community was faced with difficult and embarrassing problems. It had to create something out of nothing while its coffers were empty. The Romanian government exchanged the currency of that times (the Russian ruble) for the Romanian leu, and even these exchanges caused many problems that this is not the place to detail them. The American Jewish

Joint Distribution Committee [JDC], which provided material assistance to Jewish communities that were dwindled after the war, came to their aid. A delegation on behalf of the JDC, led by Baruch Zuckerman, one of the leaders of "*Poalei Zion*" in America, visited many Jewish communities to clarify the most urgent needs. The Jews in the district of Akkerman received aid in the amount of 420,367 leu. It was a kind of a shot of encouragement that did not have the power to rebuild the ruins, but contributed a lot to the restoration of the Jewish life after the First World War.

[Page 41]

The committee for aid to the victims of hunger

Seating first row from the right: **S. Egul, Yosef Serper, Dr. Y. Feldstein, Moshe Milstein, Moshe Helman, Dr. A. Schwartzman, Y. Berger, M. Sharira**
Standing second row: **L. Risenzan, Dr. S. Zerling, Dara Goldman, Musi Gvirtzman, Y. Einbinder, Nathan Goldstein, Dr. M. Kruskin, Felik Berg**
Standing third row: **Nachman Smulbard, Yisrael Gurfil, Alexander Shapira, David Brand, M. Edlis, Mendel Gelman (slaughterer), Hana Karolik**

The Aid Committee for Ukrainian Refugees

Even before the first community council was able to stand on its own feet it was faced with a very serious problem – the necessity of providing aid to Ukrainian refugee, Jews who flocked to the border cities near the Dniester, Akkerman among them.

As we know, at the end of the First World War there was complete disorder and confusion in Russia which left its marks on all orders of life. Generals and various armed groups got organized and waged wars among themselves, and also with the Red Army which had not yet been properly organized. And this is how they acted on the ground: the soldiers of the "Reds," the companies of the "whites," and "Bat'ko Makhno" and Petliura gangs, consumed their anger, first and foremost, on the Jews who were subjected to plunder and looting. The Jews of Ukraine suffered and many fled for their lives, with a considerable number of refugees flowing in the direction of the Dniester and the settlements near its shores. Quite a few were blackmailed by all sorts of "smugglers," and there were also those who drowned in the waters of the frozen Leman after the thin layer of ice cracked, or shot by Russian or Romanian border guards.

When the first refugees arrived in Akkerman the Jewish public came to their aid. This was not the first time that the Jews of Akkerman have shown their willingness to come to the aid of their brothers. In "*Ha–Melitz*" No. 121 from the month of Sivan 5655, we read an article signed by "*Ish Yavne*" and in it is says among others: "I am glad to announce in the front page of "*Ha–Melitz*" that the fate of the burned Brest community also touched the hearts of our townspeople. During the holiday of Shavuot they read for shekalim, for the benefit of those who were burned, during the reading the Torah in Beit HaMidrash, the Great Synagogue and in the small House of Prayer. And the sum of the alms came to one hundred and sixty–seven rubles. On 22 May, they conducted a party in the amusement park in our city and the

[Page 42]

income was three hundred and seventy five rubles. Our townspeople are happy that they can help the unfortunate with a sum of more in five hundred rubles, and the leaders of our community have not yet finished" (quoted from Schildkrauth's book). Indeed, these sums, even at the rate of those days, were not large, but in light of the limited possibilities of the Jewish residents it can certainly be seen as a serious contribution.

Now, in the face of the wave of refugees from the Ukraine the community mobilized its best forces. The council elected a special refugee committee (as it was in other cities in Bessarabia) and it began collecting donations from the city's residents. In addition to the money received for this purpose from the JDC and former residents of Akkerman in the United States, this committee already had, more or less, sufficient means at its disposal to provide the many refugees with shelter, food and clothing. The committee also made sure to provide the refugees with documents that would protect them from the persecution of the anti–Semitic Romanian officials.

To the credit of the Jewish community, we must also write about the vigorous activity during the drought years that befell Bessarabia in 1925–26, 1928–29 and 1935–1936. The drought, and the economic crisis that plagued many countries in those years, led to the collapse of businesses and severe hardship within the Jewish population. Hundreds of Jewish families fell upon hard times and did not even have a piece of bread to eat. Those who were able to give in the past now received help from the community's hunger committee. The sociologist, Yakov Lestschinsky, describes the economic situation in Akkerman in the chapter on the economic life in Bessarabia in "Encyclopedia of the Diaspora":

"No less than 200 of the 1000 (Jewish) families in Akkerman are suffering because of the nagging hunger. The local committee handles the collection of donations from among the residents of the city in addition to the amounts it receives from the JDC. In November–December 1929, it spent nearly two thousand dollars on distribution of free bread, potatoes and firewood and even cash. If they had stopped the distribution of bread and potatoes – which was possible –

1000 Jewish people would have remained hungry for bread and expected to starve to death on the city streets."

In the newspaper *"Unzer Tsayt"* from 10.5.1929, there is also an article signed by the newspaper reporter in Akkerman, Y. Schildkrauth, about the help given by the Jewish community to needy Jews in Akkerman towards the holiday of Passover.

"The amount of help distributed (to the needy) reached in the month of Pesach to 650,000 leu. On this amount 300,000 leu were received from the central hunger committee, 100,000 leu from the Akkermanim committee in New-York, and 30,000 leu from the philanthropist, the opera singer Maxsim Karalik. The rest of the money (220,000 leu) was collated this month in the city itself. Of the above amount, grants were distributed to more than 15 small Jewish settlements in the Akkerman district in the total amount of 100,000 leu".... "In addition to that, thanks to the efforts of the director of the Moldova Bank branch, A. Sirotin, 1,000 kilograms of sugar were received and distributed among Jewish institutions that care for the poor population in Akkerman."

The community committee set up kitchens for poor children near "Tarbut" school and "Talmud Torah" and gave them free lunch. A special soup kitchen was also opened and free lunches were distributed to needy families. The management of these kitchens was in the hands of women who volunteered for this duty.

In another report from 11.12.1928, Y. Schildkrauth tells in *"Unzer Tsayt"*:

"Thanks to the intervention of S. Trahtman (member of the JCA company in Bessarabia), the local women's committee, which runs the free kitchen for the children of "Talmud Torah," received a subsidy from the JCA at the amount of 180,000 leu – 30,000 leu per month for six months."

The Participation of the Akkerman Community in General Activities in Bessarabia

The Jewish community of Akkerman actively participated in all kinds of activities with other communities in Bessarabia. Its representatives attended various national and regional conventions. On July 1930, an all- Romanian conference of the representatives of the Jewish communities was held in Bucharest. Its task was to organize the Jewish communities in Romania and also to protest against the attack of the Romanian authorities on the activities of the communities and the wave of anti-Semitism that befell the country. Akkerman was represented at this conference by the community chairman, M. Helman. A few days before this conference a delegation consisting of the chairman of the Kishinev community the lawyer Karl Steinberg, the chairman of the community of Akkerman M. Helman, and also the community of Artsyz, appeared before the authorities to demand a reinforcements to protect the Jews of Artsyz who suffered from the anti-Semitism of the Germans living in the town. According to the testimony of Y. Vinizky, the authorities responded to the representatives' request, reinforcements were sent and the Jews of Artsyz breathed a sigh of relief.

In 1935, the first all-Bessarabia conference was held in Kishinev with the participation of a delegation from Akkerman that included Moshe Helman, Yosef Serper, Yeshayahu Brudsky, Sirotin and Yaroslavsky. The discussion at this conference revolved around the famine that befell southern Bessarabia and the anti-Semitic threats against the residents of the area.

[Page 43]

At this conference it was decided to contact all the Jews in the region and require them to extend assistance to the casualties whose number was about 50,000. A special committee for the urgent needs was also elected and Moshe Helman and Yeshayahu Brudsky from Akkerman participated in it.

In the Second Bessarabian conference, which was called for 3.5.1936, HaRav Moshe Zukerman, Yakov Berger, Moshe Helman, Yosef Serper and L. Trachtenbroit represented the community of Akkerman. This conference discusses, among others, the amendments that must be included in the regulations of the Jewish communities in connection with their activities for Eretz Yisrael. At this conference sharp disagreements arose with representatives of the *"Kultur–Lige"* who, of course, objected to the proposed amendments. But thanks to the vigorous position of the Zionist representatives and Akkerman's representatives, the proposed amendments were accepted. Moshe Helman was re-elected to the General Committee.

We have given only a few examples of the community activity in the field of representation, but we can also learn from these few examples that the community of Akkerman was involved in all Jewish public activity in Bessarabia and Romania.

A chapter in itself is the Jewish activity in the general elections in the country, the municipal elections, etc. This activity had already begun in the run-up to the elections for the all-Russian constituent assembly scheduled for November 11-13, 1917. The Jews mobilized to support a list headed by Nahum Rafaleks (Nir), Avraham Ravutski (Akkerman native who lived at that time in Odessa. It would be told about him separately), and Shlomo Goldman.

The Jewish community also took an active part in the elections for the city council. This activity began in 1917 with the declaration of the Russian Revolutionary Government on the freedom of all nationalities to elect their representatives to municipal institutions. With the active support of the Zionist bloc, Jewish representatives were elected to the municipal council. However, these city councils were dissolved by the Romanians when they entered the region of Bessarabia in March 1918 and administrative bodies were appointed in their place.

In the years 1925-26, the Jewish communities, especially the Zionist bloc, revolted against the admission of Jewish representatives to the local municipalities. The Jewish vote was of considerable importance in these elections and it is no wonder that all the Christian parties also competed for this vote. After negotiations the Jews entered into an agreement with the Democratic Christian Party (National-Cernists). This list won the elections held in 1926, and many Jews entered the municipal councils in Bessarabia, including Akkerman.

It was not long before the Jews were disappointed with the Christian allies and the possibility of sincere cooperation with them. Therefore, independent Jewish lists had already appeared in the municipal elections on March 14, 1930. Municipal Jews had already entered the municipal councils in lists of Jews who defended Jewish interests without any dependence on Christian parties.

In the Romanian parliamentary elections, the Jews of Akkerman supported the independent Jewish list headed by Y. Lerner (Yaron) of Tarutino (his actions will be told separately in the Tarutino section in this book. The other candidates on this list were: Munis Wellman, Yitzchak Feldstein (Akkerman), Nachum Sirota, Nachman Stolberg (Akkerman), Moshe Shohat and Issac Shapira (Akkerman). The chairman of the community of Akkerman, Moshe Helman, appeared at the head of the least in the district of Izmail.

(Below is an election poster of the Jewish list for parliamentary elections in the Akkerman district)

Footnote:

The word government is missing for censorship reasons.

[Page 44]

On Aid and Welfare Institutions

Kupat Milve Vechisachon (the Jewish Bank)

The fund was established in Akkerman after the 1905 pogrom and was known by the name, "*Das Yiddishe Bankel*" (the Jewish Bank). It played an important role in the rehabilitation of the Ukrainian refugees who decided to settle in the city, as well as in the rehabilitation of merchants and craftsmen affected by the economic crises that often plagued the region.

As told in the previous chapter, the businesses of many Jews were destroyed during the pogrom. Their property was destroyed, their source of livelihood was lost and their world darkened. An important Relief Society in Germany – the "*Hilfsfareyn*"– came to the aid of these unfortunates and sent urgent financial aid to all the victims of the pogroms in Russia and Bessarabia, including Akkerman. The immigrants from Akkerman to the United States felt the need to come to the aid of the victims and also sent considerable sums of money. At the same time the idea of setting up *Kupat Milve Vechisachon* [Loan and Saving Fund] began to develop.

This was not an original invention of the Jews of Akkerman. In 1898, a cooperative fund was established in Vilna and its name reached the cities of Bessarabia. Three years later, the first cooperative fund in Bessarabia was founded in Kishinev.

The committee, which dealt with the distribution of aid that came from outside, was left with a considerable sum of money, and when the question arose how to use this money, it was decided to establish in Akkerman a fund similar to those established in Vilna, Kishinev and other locations. On 8 August 1906, the fund was established and was among the first eight funds established in Bessarabia on cooperative basis. By 1929, another 33 funds had been established and their number had risen to 41. The fund in Akkerman was affiliated with the "General Cooperation Alliance in Bessarabia," and thanks to a group of dedicated people to the fund (Hanna Gvirtzman, Yeshayahu Brudsky, the lawyer Serper, Michael Kruskin and others), it became one of most advanced and prosperous funds in Bessarabia. Every year a management was elected in secret and democratic elections. The annual meetings of the fund constituted a kind of an "exercise in democracy" for its participants. In meetings with a large number of participants, each member of the fund had the right to express his opinion, and since many exercised this right, sometimes the annual meetings lasted several nights. Among the candidates for the fund's management it was possible to find representatives from all strata of the Jewish population: merchants, people from the intelligentsia, artisans, Zionists, members of the "*Kultur–Lige*" and more, and the echoes of these meetings were heard in public many days after the date of the their gathering. It is worth noting the help that fund has provided to craftsmen for the purchase of tools, as well as to merchants for working capital in their business. One of the most important actions of the Cooperative Alliance in Bessarabia, after the First World War, apart from loans was the establishment of a mutual fund for deaths. These funds, according to their principles, were divided into three groups: "1) Payment to fund members according to the circumstances of deaths. The fund paid the heirs of the deceased a certain amount of this money – something that was customary in most funds. 2) Larger insurance payment for the death of elderly members and a fixed amount for the support of the deceased's family. 3) A fixed annual fee for all members and a fixed amount for the family of the deceased. The payment was – 200 leu for a year and the fixed support – 10,000 leu to the deceased family." (from Yitzchak Hitron's article on the Jewish cooperation in Bessarabia).

Yeshayahu Brudsky and Hanna Gvirtzman were known in Bessarabia as experts in the field of cooperation and more than once lectured at national conventions. In 1931, a regional fund conference was held in Akkerman and was attended by 26 delegates, representing 10 funds.

The activists in the Akkerman's fund were: Hanna Gvirtzman, Yeshayahu Brudsky, Puntish Sharira, Dr. Michael Kruskin, the lawyer Serper, Dr. Yeshayahu Kogen, Leib Stambul, Baruch Gacht, Hirsh Brudsky, Zise Goldstein, Nathan Goldstein, A. Brenson, N. Stolbrod, Yakov Yashpon, Yakov Rabinowitch, Y. Schildkrauth, L. Risnzon, Mati Adlis, Mendel Arbit, David Wisser, Mani Yaroslavsky. Perldansky, Hanna Zef, Dali Palikov, Gertz Abramowitch, and others.

The fund received a lot of help from the organization of former residents of Akkerman in the United States which occasionally transferred monetary allowance to the fund.

The Community's *Kupat Gemilut Hassdim*

After the First World War *Kupat Gemilut Hassdim*, which was initiated and managed by local activists, was liquidated. Indeed, the cooperative financial institution *Kupat Milve Vechisachon* existed, but it was a financial-banking institution subject to a procedure that required guarantees from all those in need of a loan and not everyone could afford it. There was a noticeable lack of a public institution that would give loans to the needy on more favorable terms. The community committee felt this shortage and in 1925 established *Kupat Gemilut Hassdim* with a based capital of 12,000 leu.

[Page 45]

We learn about the development of this institution from an article in the newspaper "*Unzer Tsayt*" ["Our Time"] from 1928 signed by Y.S. It tells that there was already 260,000 leu in *Kupat Gemilut Hassdim* and the fund distributes loans to the needy in the amount of 2,000 leu each. The significant increase in the fund's capital comes thanks to donations from former residents of Akkerman in the United States, as well as donations from local people.

During various periods of distress in Akkerman, many Jews who engaged in small-scale trade and handicrafts survived the economic holocaust thanks to the fund's loans. It is worth noting that most of the Jews who needed fund's grace repaid their loans as soon as possible.

The public committee for the construction of the new hospital and the Women's Committee Photographed next to the hospital during construction in 1929

Standing right to left: **B.L. Prelis, Y. S. Serper**
Seating right to left: **Mrs. Agol, Mrs. Einbinder, Dr. Kruskin, Mrs. Sirotin, Dr. Kogen, Dr. A. Schwartzman, Dr. S. Zerling, unidentified**
Standing: **Y.B. Brudski, Dr. Y. Feldstein, Nachman Stolbrod, Florence the construction supervisor, Leib Stambul**
Behind them standing (right to left): **Hanna Zef, the dentist Agol, the contractor Koskov, M. B. Adlis. Further up: M. G. Milstein, Y. Kvitko, A. Sirotin, M. Helman**
On the scaffolding – the builders

"Ort" school for girls for the sewing profession

[Pages 46-47]

The local "Keren haYesod" committee with the delegation from the center, 1924
Sitting, right to left: **Moshe Helman, Meir Starec, Yisrael Skoriski (delegation member), Yakov Berger, Dr. Spir (head of the delegation), Moshe Milstein, Shmaryaho Segel (delegation member), Dr. S. Zerling**
Standing, right to left: **Baruch Geret, S. Sternsaus, Wolf Gordon, Zise Gladstein, Alyakom Kaplansky, Yosef Aharonovich, Leib Stambul, Yosef Serper, Yosef Rivkin**

"Tipat Halav" of "OZE" society – dairy kitchen for children aged two to six, 1929–1928

[Page 48]

The public committee for the construction of the New Hospital

Seating first row right to left: **Dr. A. Schwartzman, Dr. Y. Feldstein, A. Sirotin, M. Milstein, M. Kruskin, Anna Sirotin, Bina Feldstein**
Standing second row: **Leib Stambul, Yisrael Kushnir, Moshe Helman, Shmuel Berger, Mendel Gelman (slaughterer), Baruch Gacht, Yosef Serper, Yosef Kvitko, Musi Gvirtzman, Dora Goldman**
Standing third row: **David Brand, Nachman Stolbrod, Avraham Krolik, Hersh Blinder, S. Prelis, M. Edlis, Hanna Krolik**

The Jewish Hospital under construction (back side)

[Page 49]

"Maot Chitim" – "Kamcha Depasha"

To the credit of the Jewish community of Akkerman must also be attributed the monopoly it had for baking *matzot* for Passover. The community did not allow any institution, or a private person, to bake *matzot* and took all legal measures against attempts made to bake private *matzot*. The profit belonged to the entire public, because every rich *matzot* buyer was required to pay "*Maot Chitim*" ["Wheat Money"] so that also the poor will be able to get *matzot* for Passover free of charge. It is worth emphasizing that they did not refuse, or evade, and even the assimilated and those far removed from religious tradition, observed this *mitzvah*. The group of porters, who brought the *matzot* from the bakery to the homes of rich customers, also brought the *matzot* to the homes of the poor so as not to embarrass those who did not pay. The community also provided the city poor with potatoes and wine for the four glasses. And so Schildkrauth writes in his book: "Rich and poor, without distinction, ate in Akkerman the same delicious *matzot* that were baked together. The poorest homeowner, who received the free distribution from "*Maot Chitim*" fund, received the same thin bright-white *matzot* – as the rich homeowner who donated his greatest contribution to "*Maot Chitim*." In this respect, Akkerman was among the few Jewish settlements in Bessarabia who observed the *mitzvah* of "*Kamcha Depash*" [flour for Passover] in this way.

"OZE"

This institution, which began its blessed activities even before the First World War, also contributed to the medical needs of the Jewish population. It was especially effective in the hospitalization of children and pregnant women. In "OZE" [*Obschestvo Zdravookhraneniia Evreev* – Organization for the health protection of Jews] it was possible to get free fish oil for poor children and medicines. The branch also served as "*Tipat Halav*" institution ["A Drop of Milk" – preventative medical services for mothers and infants].

"OZE" clinic was equipped with an X – ray machine, quartz lamps and diathermy, which were purchased thanks to a donation from M. Karalik. The active philanthropist, Dr. Shapira, stood at the head of "OZE" and the institution's activists were: Dr. Kogen, Dr. Zerling, Dr. S. Itzkovitz, and also Y. Brudsky, M. Kruskin, Yitzchak Feldstein, Alexander Shapira, Dr. E. Wilkomirski, Hanna Karalik, M. Yaroslavsky, Berta Fildman. The secretary was Y. Schildkrauth.

"OZE" not only provided medical assistance, but also conducted an information campaign regarding the preservation of the health of the Jewish population. In the newspaper "*Unzer Tsayt*" from 6 November 1927 it is told that the local "OZE" committee conducted "a week of health." On the first day of Sukkot, Dr. Kogen, Dr. Zerling, Y. Brudsky, Y. Serper and others, appeared at the synagogue and explained the duties of "OZE" and ways of maintaining a person's health. The doctors also talked to the students of "Tarbut" and Talmud Torah schools about the duties of "OZE" and information leaflets were distributed to the homes.

"ORT"

This institution was also established before the First World War but did not have its own school. At that time its role was limited to conducting craft classes and operating a small carpentry shop under the management of the carpenter, Chaim Britva. Later, a school was opened and its administration was composed of Berel Roitman, Leib Stambul, Nachman Stolbrod, Chaim Britva and others. They made considerable efforts to promote and improve this institution, but due to lack of financial means they were unable to establish additional departments. In the newspaper "*Unzer Tsayt*" from 27.3.29, in an article signed by "Anakermaner" we read:

"In the city of Akkerman that its total population reaches to 25,000 people, there are 10,000 Jews and about 300 families earn a living from craft. The rest make a living from trading grain, small trade, brokerage, etc. The trade collapsed due to the dire economic situation and many are the Jews who walk idle and reached the point of starvation. Because of the economic situation, many non–Jewish boys, and peasants, began to learn crafts and posed a serious danger to the continued existence of the craft industries on the Jewish street. Therefore, a large meeting was called with the participation of the representative of "ORT" center in Bessarabia and the agronomist, Haim Feigin, who addressed the gathering. The hall was full to capacity, not only with craftsmen but also with Jews from the various strata of the population. The speaker warned of the situation in the country and encouraged the Jews to send their sons to learn a trade. He also promised, on behalf of the center, financial support for the opening of new departments at the "ORT" vocational school.

However, the promised help they had hoped for did not arrive and the school did not progress satisfactorily.

[Page 50]

Free kitchen for children in the famine year 1929 with the women's committee

The first management of "Kupat Gemilut Hassdim" in Akkerman, 1907

Sitting right to left: **Yakov Sidikman, Dr. Y. Shapira, Ravutski, Ben-Zion Cohen, Y. Yishpon, M. Kruskin**

Standing: **Elisha Brenson, Shmuel Glefend, Hanna Gvirtzman, I. Vladimirovich Brudsky, Nathan Goldstein, Felik Preladenski, Y. Einbinder**

[Page 51]

The Jewish Hospital

The old Jewish hospital in Akkerman was established in 1882. The hospital building on Izmailovsky Street belonged to the philanthropist Dr. Korean. It was an old building with two-room, one for men and one for women, and the total number of beds was twenty. It was overcrowded and the sanitary conditions were poor. Despite the difficult conditions, this hospital played an important role, especially for poor Jews who needed it. The chief doctor, Dr. Y. Shapira, was the living spirit in the hospital. He devoted much time and effort to it and everything was done voluntarily. In 1924, Akivah Margolin, member of the Society of Emigrants from Akkerman in the United States, visited Akkerman. In view of the poor conditions of the hospital he encouraged the community council to purchase a plot of land and plan a new hospital, and undertook to raise the necessary financial means for the building from the former residents of Akkerman in the United States. The committee, which was elected for the construction of the new hospital, opened a fundraiser for this purpose among the city residents and the plot of land needed for the building was donated by Dr. Kogen. From 1925 to 1932, the Society of Emigrants from Akkerman in the United States transferred about 50,000 dollars for the needs of the building and the equipment for the hospital. In addition to this, there was also a significant contribution from Maxim Karalik, a native of Akkerman who lived in the United States. The construction of the hospital lasted seven years and on 7 October, 1934, the hospital was officially opened in an impressive ceremony in the presence of many of the city's residents and representatives of the authorities. The new hospital had 14 rooms and 60 beds, its annual budget reached 100,000 leu, and the medical staff included specialist physicians and experienced nurses. The level of the hospital was generally appreciated by the Jewish and the city's Christian residents who also needed its good services.

Farewell party for Akivah Margolin, member of the committee of former residents of Akkerman in New-York, 1924

Seating from the right: **the first two unknown, Hanna Gvirtzman, Mrs. Gvirtzman, unknown, Y. Berger, Shmuel Trackman, Mrs. and Akivah Margolin, Zev Krushkin, Yosef Rivkin, Nathan Goldstein, Shabtai Novak**

Standing from the right in two rows: **Zise Gladstein, R' Shmuel Berger, Mendel Arbit, Mrs. Moskowitz, Pinchas Milman, the cantor Moshe Cohen, Hersh Brudsky, R' David Braner, Felik Berg, R' Simcha Bronstein, Meir Obet, Hersh Blinder, R' Mendel Gilman (slaughterer) A.V. Brudsky, R' Haim Kaminker, Dr. Y. Kogen, Yakov Brand, Y. Yashpon, Mrs. Fidelman, Mrs. Zipa Berg, Mrs. Perlis, Berel Moskowitz, Yitzchak Arbit, Meir Starec, Shmuel Gelfand, the rest unknown.**

Home for the Aged

This institution, like other charities, has always been in financial distress, but served as an only address for the elderly who had no other address in old age. The person who got this institution out of the constant state of distress was, as stated in Schildkrauth's book – "A tireless stubborn old man, R' Simcha Bronstein, did not rest and worked hard until he obtained financial means and erected a new building for the Home for the aged. Mrs. Perlis, together with R' Simcha Bronstein, took care of the proper maintenance, sanitary, health and financial means of this important institution."

[Page 52]

The management of "Kupat Milve Vechisachon" with Baruch Gecht (board member), prior to his immigration to Israel in 1935

Seating right to left: **H. Brudsky, Y. Brudsky, Krushkin, B. Gecht, Y. Serper, Risnzon**
Standing: **M. Adlis, M. Arbit, D. Weisser, Grez Abramowitch, M. Yaroslavsky, Freldensky, H. Zef, D. Falikov, N. Stolbrod, S. Perlis**

[Page 53]

Public activists in the Jewish community of Akkerman and its various institutions and Zionist activists in the 1920s and 1930s until 1940

Chairmen of the community:

    Dr. Shapira Yitzchak – first chairman
    Hanna Gvirtzman – second chairman
    Goldstein Nathan – third chairman
    Milstein Moshe – fourth chairman
    Helman Moshe – fifth and last chairman

Vice chairmen served at different times:

    Berger Yakov
    The lawyer Serper Yakov
    Dr. Y. Kogen (*Kultur–Lige*)

Activists in the Community and its Institutions and Zionist Activists:

    Abramowitch Grez
    Einbinder
    Arbit Yitzchak
    Blinder Hersh
    Berg Felik
    Brudsky A.V.
    Brudsky Tzvi
    Bronstein Simcha
    Brend David
    Gecht Baruch
    Gladstein Zise
    Gelman Mendel, ritual slaughterer
    Helman Aba
    Zef Hanna (*Kultur–Lige*)
    Trahtman Avraham
    Yaroslavsky Muni
    Cohen Moshe
    Manueli Tzvi
    Stambul Leib
    Starec Meir
    Dr. Feldstein Yitzchak
    Perlis S.
    Dr. Zerling Shaul
    Kushnir Yisrael
    Krushkin
    Rabinowitch Yakov
    Risenson
    Schildkrauth Yisrael
    Sternsaus Shmuel
    Stolbrod Nachman
    Shapira Alexander

[Page 54]

The Zionist Movement in Akkerman, 1917 to 1941

The 1917 revolution, and the liberation of Russia from the Tsar's yoke, raised many hopes among the Jews of Bessarabia. There was a general feeling that they were on the verge of a new era, of freedom and the unloading of the yoke of bondage, a kind of a new "spring for the nations." The Jews of Akkerman, of course, were also among the harbingers of the end and the dreamers of the pink dreams.

Long before the great revolution, on 21 March 1917, the Revolutionary Provisional Government issued a proclamation announcing the abolition of all religious, national and political restrictions. It was natural that the national awakening among all nationalities of "Mother Russia" did not skip the Jewish national minority. The only movement that showed understanding for the current problems, and the dynamism required by the political changes in Russia – was the Zionist movement that under its flag gathered many who saw the solution to the Jewish problem in the renewal of Jewish independence in Eretz Yisrael.

In March 1917, the Odessa Zionist Committee to which the Zionists of Bessarabia were also subordinate, published a proclamation signed by Menachem Ussishkin, and so it was said among others: "Great events have taken place, bright chances for freedom and a life of happiness are opening up before all the people living on the land of vast Russia. Luck has finally begun to brighten the face of our suffering nation, and now it will stand up straight and cease to be a tortured stepchild." This proclamation did not fall on deaf ears also in Akkerman. Important homeowners in the city searched and found the way to the Zionist movement: Moshe Helman, Dr. Shaul Zerling, Miriam and Yitzchak Feldstein, the cantor Avraham Gotlib, Shmuel Sternsaus, the cantor Moshe Kogen, Dani Harol, P. Berkov, Rabinowitch, B. Hacham, K. Tabachnik, the brothers H. and Y. Karaninsky, Y. Schildkrauth, Z. Manueli and others. Zionist conferences were now held in public and openly, in cinemas and synagogues, and there was no need for camouflage although there were also those who feared the Gentiles' evil eye at the sight of this preparation in the Jewish public. Y. Schildkrauth tells that after the outbreak of the revolution, Akkerman prepared for a large demonstration accompanied by an orchestra, flags, and slogans calling for support for the revolutionary government. A group of Zionists planned to demonstrate with a Jewish national flag at the head of the procession, but there was another group who opposed it for fear that it might harm the Jews. And so Schildkrauth is telling: "They made a double-sided blue and white velvet flag, in the middle it was decorated with a large "Star of David" embroidered in gold, its rim was triangular, its thighs embroidered with gold and silver threads, and at its two sharp ends hung two gold tassels. The flag was hung on a long oak pole painted in brown lacquer and a silver "Star of David" was stuck in its head."

On the day intended for the demonstration the Zionists gathered in the synagogue courtyard to accompany the protesters from there. At the same time, a group of Zionists argued and flew into a rage over the question of the flag and could not reach a decision on whether to take responsibility for possible events. Then, what happened happened – at the height of the rage and quarrel, Ozer Feigin, the tall and wide, separated from the arguing group without the others noticing him. He grabbed Samet's blue and white flag, which was hung on a long oak pole, and before they had the time to give their opinion on this, he hurried forward as he was carrying the large heavy flag in front of him with his strong hands. The angry and furious group stood stunned... but they quickly shook off and began to chase after R' Ozer Feigin who ran with the flag... and so, while running, they joined the street demonstration together."

Later in this "spicy" description Schildkrauth is telling, the national Jewish flag was received with cheers by the Ukrainian group that also carried its national flag, and many Jews gathered around the national flag, which was carried high in Ozer Feigin hands, and no harm came to the Jewish demonstrators.

At the Seventh Zionist Conference held in St. Petersburg in June 1917, M. Starec and Y. Karaninsky participated as delegates from Akkerman (12 delegates from Bessarabia participated in this conference). When they returned from the conference they reported its action to Akkerman's Zionists.

In November 1917, after the Balfour Declaration, a wave of national-Zionist enthusiasm passed among the Jews of Akkerman. Eyewitnesses say that in the various assemblies, held in synagogues and public halls, they felt the great admiration of the masses of Jews who saw in this declaration the real end of exile. Rumors and legends spread in the city about ships standing ready in the port of Odessa to transport Jews to Eretz Yisrael. It was soon proved that these were nothing but false rumors and the stormy emotions cooled a little. The people, who were full of suffering and distress, tended to such rumors and hoped that redemption would come one day. This alone provided fertile ground for those who spread rumors of various kinds.

Indeed, ships did not wait at the port of Odessa, but, on the other hand, a group of young people who did not wait for miracles and did not rely on miracles, decided to pave their way to Eretz Yisrael. They were not members of a youth movement, and did not receive training in *HeHalutz*," but the love of the country and the vision of redemption burn in their hearts, and they did not shy away from difficulties and mishaps. They were: Yeshayahu Botoshansky, Aharon Brand, Yehusua Berger, P. Berkov, Avraham (Kafri) Dorfman, Avraham Molodowsky, Avraham Margalit, Serper, Noah Zukerman, Aharon Kaminker from Shabo and Yisrael Rabinowitch. This first group from Akkerman immigrated to Eretz Yisrael where there was no organizational body to absorb them. Without knowing what and who was waiting for them in Israel, they got up and emigrated.

[Page 55]

Sometime later, there was an attempt to organize a group of local young women for training for a working life in Eretz Yisrael. They leased a plot of land, grow vegetables and sold them at the local market. This attempt did not last long but a few young women immigrated later to Eretz Yisrael.

In the first all-Bessarabia conference, which was held on 4–8 May 1920, eight delegates participated from Akkerman: M. Starec, Yakov Berger, Dani Harol, P. Berkov, B. Hacham (later moved to Tarutino), Julius (Yehudah) Danovich, Yisrael Rabinowitch and Kuma Tabachnik. At this conference the discussions revolved around the questions of the ways of building the country, the forms of settlement and the ways of organizing the Zionist organization in Bessarabia. The debates were mainly between the General Zionists and *Tzeirei Zion*. According to what is told in David Vinitzky book, "*Bessarabia He-yehudit Be-ma'aroteha*" [The Jews in Bessarabia between the World Wars 1914–1940], Y. Danowitch and Avraham B. Hacham from Akkerman participated in this debate. They raised their concerns that the Jewish worker in Israel will be exploited by their wealthy employer, demanded that the country be built on the foundations of justice, criticized the private investment and obliged it to set aside a percentage of the profits for the benefit of the workers. In the early 1920s, Yuly Danowitch was a member of the *HeHalutz* center in Bessarabia.

With the annexation of Bessarabia to Romania in 1918, the Jewish public, especially the Zionist, was cut off from its center (Odessa) before establishing central institutions that would direct public and Zionist activity in the countryside. The above conference – the all–Bessarabia – gave its opinion on this, chose institutions, and organized the Zionist activities as well as the activities for the Zionist funds.

The Activity for the Funds

The collection of donations for *Keren Kayemet*, *Keren Hayesod*, *HeHalutz* and "Tarbut" funds was conducted with the approval of the Romanian authorities, and the Jews of Akkerman responded generously. The blue boxes of *Keren Kayemet* [Jewish National Fund] were at the homes of many Jews and the Zionist activists were busy emptying the boxes. Only after the Zionist youth movements were established this role was transferred to them. The fundraising for *Keren Hayesod* [The Foundation Fund] was carried out with the help of key activists, or emissaries from Israel who walked from house to house together with the local activists and raise funds. It is worth noting, that even in times of economic crisis and distress – and of course there was no shortage of them – Akkerman Zionists contributed willingly, each person to his ability. Some examples may validate our words. In 5698, which was a year of a difficult economic crisis, the sum of 13,924 Leu was collected in Akkerman for *Keren Kayemet*, while in 5699 the sum of 347,924 leu was collected for *Keren Kayemet* and the fundraiser campaign for "*Hagelila*" of *Keren Hayesod*. According to the size of the donations, Akkerman was in third place in Bessarabia, although according to the size of the Jewish population it was in ninth place. We also know that in *HeHalutz* week in 5687, 19,450 leu was collected in Akkerman and again it took third place in Bessarabia.

In the meeting of the first immigrants from Akkerman, which took place in Tel Aviv for the needs of this book, Noah Zukerman told about everything that preceded their immigration, and here is a summary of his words:

"I was not a member of any Zionist movement or youth movement. What motivated me to immigrate to Eretz Yisrael was the education I received at home and especially the great Zionist awakening that was felt in Akkerman after the Balfour Declaration. I still remember the big meeting held at the synagogue to mark the Balfour Declaration. The enthusiasm of the speakers reached its peak and swept the large audience as well. The speakers were Yisrael Rabinowitch, Meir Starec, Janowitz, and maybe someone else. I applied for a passport so that I could travel to Eretz Yisrael, but in the meantime I was drafted into the army and served for three months. At the end of August we were given a holiday to help the farms that needed working hands, and when I came home for a holiday I found the passport. I decided to leave as soon as possible. Yakov Berger gave me a recommendation for the Zionist organization in Bucharest where I obtained my visa to Constantinople. For travel expenses my father gave me 1,000 leu, my brother 1,500, my brother–in–law Yakov Rabinowitch an amount that I cannot remember. In any case, the money I had was enough for a stay of ten days in Constantinople with my friends Aharon Kaminker."

In the years 1927–1928, when the gates of Israel was closed, a group of 30–40 Jews members of the middle class who wanted to immigrate to Eretz Yisrael, was organized in Akkerman. In this group were small merchants, craftsmen, brokers etc. The majority were elderly families who could not reach Israel through the pioneering movement, and could not even obtain certificates by official means. This book tells about what happened to this group and we will not talk about it here, but it is worth emphasizing that the Zionists in Akkerman never reconciled with the decrees of immigration and sought every possible way to reach Israel, even through Cyprus, as this middle-class group has tried. Baruch Ghent headed this group.

[Page 56]

We do not have in our hands exact statistics on the number of Jews who immigrated from Akkerman to Eretz Yisrael, but there is a basis for the assumption that more than four hundred people immigrated by the outbreak of the World War.

The connections between the immigrants from Akkerman in Israel with the families who remained in Akkerman were very tight, but they were family ties that were expressed in private letters without any pretenses. Only once, to the best of our knowledge, these ties deviate from the usual course and received a kind of political mission. It was in July of 1935, when a proclamation was distributed in Akkerman towards the elections ahead of the Zionist Congress. It was addressed to "fathers and mothers, brothers and sisters, friends and members" and signed by former residents of Akkerman in Eretz Yisrael. The proclamation opens with an expression of gratitude to the Zionists in Akkerman who voted in the previous congressional elections for the Working Land of Israel list, and continues with the summaries of the achievements between congress and congress, with the conclusion being: "Vote for the List of the Working Land of Israel"

The following are the names of the signatories to this proclamation:

Shmuel Zukerman – Tel Aviv	Eliyahu Margalit – Kfar Gibton
Moshe Chaim Margalit – Rehovot	Binyamin Hirschfield – Kvozat Gordonia "Bezor- Netaim
Manos Freida – Kvozat Hasharon	Bruria Schwartzman – Karkur
Leah Berger – Rehovot	Nachum Liber – Tel Aviv
Ancel	Nissan Stambul – Kvozat Mesada – Hadera
Hinda Durpman – Tel Aviv	Yochevd Shapira – Jerusalem
Enya Malchin – Haifa	Aharon Dorfman– Tel Aviv
Yehezkel Manos – Kvozat Hasharon	Elisha Bedgi – Netanya
Nesia Zukerman – Kvozat Mesada – Hadera	Avraham Cornbleet – Ra'anana
Frima Zeider – Netanya	Miriam Gordon – Kvozat Mesada – Hadera
Leah Neiman – Kineret	Feibush Cohen – Hadera
Avraham Neiman – Kineret	Bast – Tel Aviv
Nachum Liber – Tel Aviv	Yochevd Shapira – Jerusalem
Kunicher	Shmunis – Hadera
Shlomo Gecht – Haifa	Aharon Kaminker – Tel Aviv
Sonia Margalit – Rehovot	Zipora Edlis – Tel Aviv
Zipora Margalit – Even Yehudah	Yochevd Shapira – Jerusalem
Rivka Cohen – Kvozat Mesada – Hadera	Ester Lapida – Haifa

David Malkin – Kibbutz Hashomer Hatzair – Ein Hai

Aharon Brend – Tel Aviv

Yisrael Manos – Mikveh Yisrael

Klara Licht – Kvozat Mesada – Hadera

Efraim Durpman – Tel Aviv

Rachel Goldberg – Kfar Saba

Yosef Glikman – Kvozat Mesada – Hadera

Shlomo Buloshin – Petach Tikva

Maliya Gordion – Ramat Gan

Avraham Dorfman – Tel Mond

Mendel Margalit – Rehovot

Sara Manos – Kvozat Hasharon

Reuven Manos – Kfar Haim

Yosef Chaplin – Kvozat Mesada – Hadera

Chana Dorfman – Tel Aviv

Yakov Yacobson – Kvozat "Bezor – Netaim

Leah Berkowitz – Tel Aviv

Shmuel Stetsky – Netanya

Nechama Kagalsky – Kvozat Mesada – Hadera

Aba Biranbaum – Kvozat "Avoka" – Pardes Hanna

Rivka Yitsá‚³ovits – Hadera

Frida Lederman – Kineret

Michael Shainer – Netanya

Chava Dorfman – Tel Aviv

Yehusua Bvolovitz – Hadera

Yehusua Berger – Pardes Hanna

Zarna Molodowsky – Tel Aviv

Baruch Cohen – Kvozat "Avoka" – Pardes Hanna

Avraham Molodowsky – Tel Aviv

Eliyahu Lev – Haifa

Sara Gelman – Afula

Niuma Kurin – Petach Tikva

Zvi Misonzik – Kibbutz Hashomer Hatzair – Magdiel

Yehusua Botoshansky

Zilia Gerber – Netanya

Avigdor Risenzon – Tel Aviv

Avraham Margalit– Binyamina

Mora Failand – Netanya

Enia Malchin – Haifa

Noah Zukerman – Tel Mond

Rivka Manos – Netanya

Yehezkel Manos – Kvozat Hasharon

Elisha Bedgi – Netanya

Yitzchak Toyerman – Petach Tikva

Frima Zeider – Netanya

Sonia Margalit – Rehovot

Miriam Gordon – Kvozat Mesada – Hadera

Feibush Cohen – Hadera

Botoshansky Shifra – Hadera

[Page 57]
The Library as a Factor in Zionist Education

There is no doubt that the public library was an important factor in the Zionist education systems provided to Jewish youth in Akkerman, and it is worth noting in detail the role it played. It was founded in 1917 by "Tarbut" society and two activists who dedicated the best of their time to it: Moshe Schildkrauth and Kumi Tabachnik, who collected books and donations for the library. The library was housed in two rooms on Moskovskaya Street and, in fact, was the first Jewish public library in the city. However, the two rooms were not only used to exchange books, but constituted a Zionist center. Almost all the Zionist activity in the city was concentrated within the walls of these rooms, the meetings of the funds committees, "*HeHalutz*," and also the committees of the parties that already existed at that time. Moreover, the first Hebrew kindergarten was also opened in the library rooms. Over time, rehearsals of "*Hazamir*" choir conducted by Cantor Moshe Kogen, rehearsals for parties and balls, and meetings of the circle "Speak Hebrew" were also held there.

After the death of Moshe Schildkrauth and Kumi Tabachnik, both died at a young age, the teacher Shmuel Sternsaus took on himself the management of the library. S. Geber wrote in this book about his dedication to this role. It is worth noting, that the readership in the library has grown considerably and "Tarbut" school provided the majority of readers since many students were helped in their studies by books from the library. Mr. Sternsaus took special care to enrich the section of reference books in the library, and with the development of the youth movements in the city saw a need to order many books that the counselors of the various youth movements can be assisted by them.

The library's two rooms bordered the rooms of "*Kupat Milve Vechisachon*" and belonged to it. In an article published in "*Unzer Tsayt*" we read an article under the title "A scandal related to the public library" and so it is said in it: "*Kupat Milve Vechisachon*" wanted to take part of the library space to expand its residence. On Saturday, a hole was opened in the wall shared by the library and the fund to annex part of the library area to the fund. The library management arrived on time and plugged the hole. At the meeting of the fund members a scandal broke out on this issue and it was decided not to touch or take over the area of the library (signed on the article – Y. Schildkrauth). The library remained unchanged until the entry of the Soviets to Akkerman in 1940.

"Tarbut" Society and "Tarbut" School

The crown glory of the Jews of Akkerman in general, and the Zionist movement in particular, was – "Tarbut" and the chain of its achievement: kindergarten, the Hebrew school and the gymnasium. Certainly, "Tarbut" would not have been founded without the help of a group of activists from all parties, but there is no doubt that Yakov Berger deserves all the praise. He knew how to cooperate with all the activists and with all the streams and marched "Tarbut" to the achievements it had reached.

Unlike other cities in Romania and Bessarabia, in which "battles" broke out between Yiddish and Hebrew fans for the place of one language or another in schools, there were no such struggles in Akkerman. When every national minority was given permission to develop its educational institutions, and to cultivate its language in these institutions, the assumption accepted by almost everyone in Akkerman was: Hebrew is the main language of instruction in Jewish schools.

The kindergarten of the Hebrew gymnasium, 1919

[Page 58]

Yiddish was the language of instruction only in "Talmud Torah," whereas in the first kindergarten of "Aunt Manya" and "Aunt Shoshana," and in the elementary school – Hebrew was the dominated language. The Romanians did not care. They were interested to push out the influence of the Russian language and the Russian culture, and they did not care with what language this would be done. Only a few years later, when the Romanians established themselves in Bessarabia, they began to narrow the steps of the Jewish educational institutions.

Many of former "Tarbut" students brought up in this book memories and experiences from their school days at "Tarbut" and praised their principal and the teaching staff, but it is worth emphasizing that the parents should also be praised. They sent their children to the Hebrew school despite the high tuition that the children of the affluent classes had to pay to enable the children of the poor to study in "Tarbut." Therefore, it was a commendable mutual aid.

It is interesting that schools, in which the language of instruction was Yiddish, disappeared in the course of time in Bessarabia, and even that under the pressure of the parents who preferred Hebrew over Yiddish. D. Vinitzky tells in his book "*Bessarabia he–yehudit be–ma'aroteha*" [The Jews in Bessarabia between the World Wars 1914–1940] that in the nationalized state gymnasium (No. 4) in Kishinev, whose language of instruction was Yiddish, a survey was held in May 1920 among the students' parents on behalf of the Board of Education. The parents were asked what language they would like as a language of instruction for their children. It turns out that out of 103 questioned, 92 answered that they prefer Hebrew and only two preferred Yiddish as the language of instruction. This survey indicates the mood on the Jewish street in Bessarabia, and Akkerman was no exception. The Hebrew language was generally seen as a wedge against assimilation' and, as already mentioned, the religious circles also preferred the Hebrew language as the language of instruction. No wonder many parents, who were far from Zionism or even hostile to it, became Zionists thanks to their children who attended the Hebrew school. There were, indeed, quite a few in Akkerman who sent their children to study in Romanian government schools but no ideological reasons motivated them to do so, just the benefit of it. Apart from the low tuition at the government schools, the education authorities have made it easier for the graduates to be admitted to Romanian universities, which was not the case for the graduates of other schools who had to pass supplementary government exams that were not at all easy.

Despite the reliefs, not many parents were tempted to the charm of the Romanian schools and have done their best so that their sons would be able to finish the Hebrew gymnasium.

Many praised the level of education in gymnasia "Tarbut" in Akkerman, but we also came across expressions of certain criticism. In an article in "*Unzer Tsayt*" from 7 December 1922, Yosef Ben–Daniel writes: "Tarbut" in Akkerman has a good kindergarten and a gymnasium, and thirty percent of the students study for free, but "Tarbut" committee conducts its work in a way that is too "family oriented" and during the four years of the committee's existence not a single general meeting has been convened."

The gymnasium principle, Y. Berger, with the teaching staff in 1928

Seating right to left: **S. Sternsaus, S. Helman–Sofer, Y. Berger, M.Y. Berman. Standing: B. Finchlet, S. Zukerman, Neami (secretary), the cantor M. Kogen, M. Starec, S. Zernivski**

[Page 59]

In the book mentioned above by Vinitzky the budget of "Tarbut" (including one kindergarten class, four elementary school classes and seven gymnasium classes) is published. In the year 1931–32, it reached the sum of 900,000 leu. The budget is calculated on a total of 200 students. The institution was facing deficits, and if not for the balls and fundraising campaigns that "Tarbut" activists held every year to cover the deficits, "Tarbut" institutions would not have been able to complete a single school year.

As mentioned, a few years later the Romanian authorities began to harass the Jewish educational institutions. And so we read in an article signed by *"A Feter"* (father) in *"Unzer Tsayt"* from 23.9.1929: "On Purim an administrative order arrived that requires the closure of the elementary school next to the gymnasium after nine years of existence. The director of the gymnasium, Y. Berger, immediately went to the appropriate institutions and managed to repeal the decree and open the school. The Jewish public opinion calmed down as they were confident that the order, on behalf of the central institutions, would also bind the local school superintendent. But it turned out that the supervisor did not take this into account, he managed to carry the matter for another week and canceled the studies of hundreds of children. Who knows how long the matter would have lasted if it had not been for the district superintendent, Bogdan, who was sent specifically by the education authorities to Akkerman to settle the matter and reopen the school."

Apparently that same government supervisor of education was a malignant thorn in regarding the school in Akkerman, since three months later (20.6.1929) another article was published in *"Unzer Tsayt"* and in it an expression of regret that the same supervisor, who was harassing the Hebrew gymnasium, has not yet been replaced and he does not respond to the teachers' requests regarding the end-of-year exams by the authorities. "We hoped – it was said in the article – that the same official would be fired but we were disappointed. After great efforts we were able to influence him to keep the teacher Tsheki away from the examining committee. The superintendent does not agree that the students of "Tarbut" school will take the final exams at the school itself, they are sent to be tested at the public school in Artsyz, and required to pay 800 leu for a test of one class and 1,600 leu for two classes." Even if the intent of these lines is not clear enough, it can be concluded from these two articles that the local Romanian Education Authority did not take kindly to the development of "Tarbut" institutions and harassed them with various excuses. It is difficult to assume that this harassment was not with the approval of the central education authorities, but it did not stop the development of "Tarbut" institutions. It must have increased the national consciousness of the Jews in general, and of the Zionist youth in particular, who realized that equal rights in Romania for Jews is a daydream.

*

Sources and Bibliography:

Encyclopaedia Hebraica. Encyclopaedia Judaica.
Encyclopaedia Brukhaus–Efron.
Iberskaya Encyclopedia.
Encyclopaedia of the Diaspora: articles by A. Feldman, Klausner and others.
M. Davidzon – A collection on Bessarabia – Eretz Yisrael.
Bessarabia a collection edited by Haim Shurer.
David Vinitzky – *Bessarabia he–yehudit be–ma'aroteha* – The Jews in Bessarabia between the World Wars 1914–1940 [https://www.jewishgen.org/Yizkor/Bessarabia01/Bessarabia01.html].

Articles by M. Kumarovsky on Akkerman.
Yisrael Schildkrauth – Akkerman the city I love.
Klutznick – Bilhorod–Dnistrovskyi published 1970–1973.
Pinkas haKehillot of Romania, A. Feldman.
Herget Encyclopaedia.
Conversations with Akkerman veterans – Y. Schildkrauth, Yehusua Harari and others.
Newspapers, "*Unzer Tsayt*" and others.

[Page 60]

The Pogrom in Akkerman in 1905
by Mendel Kumorowski
Translated by Sara Mages

Many factors prepared the ground and ripened the conditions for a pogrom in Akkerman and other cities in Czarist Russia. A prolonged agitation among the masses, the bloody march of 9 January 1905 to the Czar's palace under the leadership of the provocateur Gapon, the sailors' revolt in Kronstadt, and the extreme decisions of the "*zemstvo*" (institution of local government), etc. As is well known, the Czar surrendered to the pressure of the masses after the railway strike, and on 17 October announced that he would grant a constitution to the country.

As we know, at the same time the monarchists didn't sit idle and established the "League of the Russian people" which came to be known as the "Black Hundreds." Their main tactic was – to direct the masses' revolt not against the government, but against the scapegoat – the Jews. They were aided by the "Third Department" of the Ministry of the Interior, and by the press which preached and incited against the Jews. This reactionary organization opened tea houses which served as meeting places for the rabbles in each "Pale of Settlement." The incitement in these places against the Jews was obvious and well known. The Jews' property was confiscated and promises were given that the rioters against the Jews, and their property, would not be prosecuted. In addition, marches, accompanied by patriotic cries: "Beat the Jews – save Russia" were held in the streets.

The rioters' club in Akkerman was one of the best equipped and its driving force was Purishkevich, the extreme reactionary. Akkerman should have served an example for other cities in Bessarabia, and was chosen for this purpose in view of the fact that there was no serious liberal group in the city that would stand up to the wave of anti–Semitism and the lawlessness of the members of the "Black Hundreds" and their followers.

Mendel Kumorowski

The Jewish Self–Defense (*samoodbrana*)

We, the young Jews in Akkerman, were aware of the gravity of the situation. We felt what awaited us according to the behavior of the farmers. We also felt the change in the attitude of the intellectual circles toward the Jews, and began the organization of self–defense that would help us in time of trouble. We were not sure that our meager means would stand for us. I remember, that after my secret visits to our defense groups, I came to the conclusion that we fall far short of our enemies, both in terms of quantity and the equipment at our disposal, but, we didn't want to be like "sheep that is led to the slaughter," and preferred to defend ourselves. As the commander of the self–defense I announced that those, who were afraid, could leave the organization, and it should be noted that no one left. The morale of our members was high, which should be attributed to the Zionist recognition that prevailed in those days among the Jews. We learned a lesson from the pogrom in Kishinev and knew by heart Bialik's famous poem, "The City of Slaughter," which was written after this pogrom and was beautifully translated into Russian by Jabotinsky.

In January of that year, Dov–Ber Borochov and Hana Meisel visited our city. The latter encouraged us to act and to protect ourselves, and in our eyes she looked like the modern figure of Deborah the Prophetess. She was soft and gentle in her manners, but gave fiery speeches and her eyes flared when she

[Page 61]

spoke of the need of self–defense of Jews against the rioters. She had a hypnotic effect on us and aroused in us a spirit of heroism and courage. In her words she emphasized our moral advantage over the farmers and the mob that incited against the Jews. In one speech – she had a tremendous impact on us.

We began to organize and prepare, but we didn't imagine that the bloody clashes would take place at such a rapid pace. On Monday, 17 October 1905, the Czar's declaration of constitution was issued and aroused great joy, but, that evening, the rioters launched an attack in Odessa which lasted three days. We, in Akkerman, learned about the Czar's declaration the following day, on 18 October. I remember that the gymnasium students held a public meeting to mark the Czar's declaration and didn't encounter opposition from the local educational institutions. There was a festive atmosphere.

On Wednesday, 19 October, the postal service from Odessa was renewed and only then we learn of the bloody events there. We were aware of the imminent danger. After what happened in Odessa, the capital – what can we expect? An emergency meeting of the local council was held, but it ended without any real results. It seemed that no one was willing to deal with this issue. When Leon Asodorov spoke of the imminent danger of the "Black Hundreds," which was planning a pogrom against the Jews, a commotion broke out and the meeting was suspended.

On Thursday, 20 October, the rioters began to act openly. The markets were filled with farmers' wagons from the nearby villages. Kostia, Popov and Dinkowitz wandered among the farmers and in the "Black Hundreds" club, and incited against the Jews. That day I toured the city's streets. Many Jews stopped me and asked my opinion on the situation and what is in store for us. My answer was clear: we're about one step from a pogrom but the Jewish defense is ready and alert. I also said that anyone who can find a safe haven must do so.

That day, before dark, we began to stockpile weapons in my house. For security reasons the task of storing weapons was imposed on two boys aged twelve: Moshe Shteinberg and Gedalia Levit. The weapons at our disposal were – rifles, pistols, leather–whips, metal–whips, and bottles with explosives.

On Friday, 21 October, early in the morning, a group of self–defense members, 40 strong Jews, gathered in my house. Most were young and a few older. The headquarters announced that Matusis would be the commander of our sector. We placed a guard at the entrance to the house, set up a secret password, and began sorting and cleaning the weapons. The headquarters' announcements informed us of everything concerning the preparations of the rioters. Food was brought and we all ate something. Suddenly, the guard called me and asked me to come out. Moshe Levit, the father of Gedalia'ke who was one of our running messengers, stood outside and with tears in his eyes begged me to release his only son from his duty. His wife, he told me, was out of town and she would never forgive him if, God forbid, something would happen to their son. I explained to him that the service in the self–defense is voluntary, we do not force it on anyone and his son is free to leave. With the commander's permission, I took the boy out of the house and left him alone with his father so that he would be free in his decision. I heard that the father begged, wept and kissed his twelve year–old son, the son also cried, but he was firm in his decision to stay with the self–defense group and the father returned empty handed.

The young men, who gathered at my house, were in a good mood, as if we were not in danger of pogroms. Some were playing cards and some were drinking wine. The "Thief from Paris," as one of the young men was called, was lying on his back and inviting his friends to show their strength and try to move him. There were those who tried, but they weren't able to. Shimon Chudak played tunes on the instrument in his hand – a comb, while others accompanied him with a song. There were no signs of fear and cowardice. Outside, the farmers continued to ride in their wagons and many of them roared. They were excited by the speeches of incitement they heard in the churches. Icons were placed in the windows of several houses so that the rioter would know that their inhabitance were Christians. We have been told that Jewish homes were marked with chalk. We were ordered by the headquarters to be up all night. When the day got dark we saw bright light in the eastern sky, the city of Ovidiopol was on fire. The tension grew, but half an hour after midnight came the command to disperse.

A Feast Day of the Russian Church

Saturday, 22 October, was a feast day in the Christian Church in honor of the Virgin of Kazan, and on this day our Christian neighbors chose to demonstrate their Christian "love." Dawn came, the sun shone in the morning of that day, but we already felt that the sun didn't shine for us. All the synagogues were closed on that Sabbath. I don't know what happened in every Jewish home that morning, but I remember what I have done – I helped my wife and our baby boy to move to the home of Anna Nikolaevna, the principle of the girls' gymnasium. She was of an aristocratic family and was always friendly to my wife. She was a monarchist in her views, but she was too noble in her spirit and didn't join the people of the "Black Hundreds." I took my mother to Lavrentyev's home which was built like a fortress. She gave everything she had: her two sons were in the self-defense units and her daughter at the first aid station. When I parted from her she hung a metal tray on my chest, sort of armor. I didn't object because I knew that this "weapon" might easily turn into a frying pan... We were instructed by our headquarters to give the young men a good meal, but at the middle of the meal the "sobor" (church) bells began to ring. They were accompanied by roars of the crowd who left the church at the end of the prayers. The scouts, that we placed, informed us that a procession of Christians was moving towards the city center, but, in the meantime, there are no signs of violence.

[Page 62]

The Principal of the Russian Gymnasium

The sentry at the front door called me to come out. It turned out that the principal of the Russian Gymnasium stopped her carriage next to my house on her way from the church and she wants to talk to me. I was confused. Courtesy obliged me to invite her into my house, but for obvious reasons I could not do it and found some excuse. She gave me a penetrating look and said in a quiet tone: everything will be fine and, by the way, she suddenly asked me: are you at least well armed? Her cunning question confused me a little, but I answered her carefully, we, madam, are ready for anything. This is how her visit ended. Later, I learned that she joined the procession at city hall and delivered a passionate patriotic speech from the balcony. Meanwhile, our scouts continued to report that the procession had not yet dispersed and was moving toward the suburbs Popusoi and Turlaki. Dr. B.M. She'ar arrived to my house. He converted to Christianity many years ago and lived among the gentiles. Now, in time of trouble for the Jews, he returned to his people and offered his services as a commander of a riflemen unit. He looked at the weapons at our disposal and said – a splendid company. He spent some time with his fellow doctors and moved to another defense position.

The young man, N., turned to me and whispered quietly: "this march will return to the city." Poor fellow, he got caught in the idea that if he could get his sister's ring – he would be able to save the Jewish people. In the end he lost his mind.

The orders from our headquarters began to arrive one after the other and quickly: Get ready! Prepare the weapons! The password was – "Torah." We have to go to the synagogue's courtyard. Our commander, Matusis, divided us into small units and we were instructed to walk, on various routes, in the direction of the synagogue in order not to attract attention. I left with the last unit without locking the door to my house. We walked down Nikolaevsky Street and moved quickly. There were no people on the street. A frightened woman crossed the street and immediately disappeared. Like straw in a storm – I thought in my heart. Suddenly, I noticed a carriage advancing toward us. I was shocked when I saw my wife with the baby inside the carriage. They moved in the direction of our abandoned house. I quickly got them out of the carriage and together with them I went back to our defense group. My wife told me what had happened. When the principal of the gymnasium returned home from the church she said sweetly: tell me, my dear, are not you afraid to stay in this place? My wife fainted when she heard her question, and when she regained consciousness she immediately left the place which was meant to be a refuge for time of trouble.

Our column moves toward the corner of Nikolaevsky and Jevrejski streets. The only open door is that of Vilkomirsky's pharmacy where our first aid station is located. I leave my wife and the baby in this place and advance, together with my unit, in the direction of the synagogue.

All our defense units gathered in the synagogue's courtyard. We were a little confused when we heard that all our forces were reorganized. We didn't know the nature of the "reorganization." Kiselewski is trying to establish a fighting squadron, but without success. A command, in a loud voice, is heard from Yeshayahu Brodsky: "stand in three rows!" He also ordered one of the companies to stand under the pillars of the Great Synagogue, and two other companies to take positions in the courtyard. Brodsky stands in the center of the courtyard and Leon Esvodorov (not Jewish) and Dr. She'ar (the convert) stand beside him. Brodsky demands absolute silence and strict discipline. He updates us all with the information he receives from the scouts. Most of them are young Christians who mixed among the masses of farmers, and the most prominent among them was Beibik Brownstein, a courageous guy that a smile was always on his lips. After completing a mission he returned to us riding a horse he had released from a wagon while the owner of the wagon, the farmer, was looting... Among the volunteers in my unit was a Polish wine merchant from Warsaw who happened to be in Akkerman for his business. He asked for a pencil because it occurred to him that he had to write his will. One of the young men lit up a few matches and the wine merchant wrote his will to light of the burning match...

Now, the roar of the mob outside began to reach us. We hear clear shouts: "Vanka, come here!" "Vanka, hit". We also hear the sound of explosions. They smash windowpanes in the houses. Flames are visible west and south of our position. People are beginning to grumble in the defense units: when will we start the operation? But Brodsky demands and commands: "Quiet! For the time being there are only fires. There are no casualties. It is necessary to control the nerves. Rumor has it that one of the rioters was poisoned in Vilkomirski's pharmacy. But the truth is that the young woman, Fanya Steinberg, committed suicide in this pharmacy.

The Holocaust

Brodsky invites a few of us for a consultation and after that a third of our force was sent, under the supervision of Dr. She'ar, in the direction of Izmailovsky Street. When we started walking there our commander ordered us to shot once in their air. The psychological impact of this shot is enormous. Now we feel the soldiers who are ready to kill and be killed. In the corner of Sofievsky Street we were surrounded by a group of rioters and started to shoot at them. Two of them fell and the rest dispersed. We removed the burning material from the houses and shops which have not yet been torched. The market is burning before our eyes and we can barely stand the rising heat. Piles of goods are placed in the street corner. We saw the looters with piles of looting in their hands. They fled as we approached them. Here and there are also corpses. We divided into two groups. One turned down Izmailovsky Street to Georgievsky Street, while the group, to which I also belonged, turned left down Moskovsk Street, and again left in the direction of Nikolaevsky Street. In the corner of Sofievsky Street

[Page 63]

we ran into a crowd that looted Gutnick's shop. The leader of this gang was Kostia Popov. Later, we heard that his mother pleaded before him not to set fire to the bank since his father's store was also in this building which belonging to a Christian. His answer was: mother, this is not your business, do not interfere.

When the situation worsened, a third group of defense members, under the command of Liuba Shapira and Duba Lifshitz was ordered to take action. The information we receive is diminishing. There is a rumor that Kuznetsov, the chief of police, was shot by the rioters because he interfered with their actions. It seems that the army took command and the police joined the looters. One unit returns with the body of Michael Shternberg who was found dead.

Again, my group was ordered to go into action. There are sixty strong young men in the group and we started to move. Next to Druze's fish shop we saw a figure darting through the flames. It turns out that this is a Jew who went insane during the pogrom. We took him with us. We crossed market square from southwest to northeast. As we got closer the rioters began to run shouting: run away, their defense came! Again, we march down Nikolaevsky Street. In this quarter the situation is grave as in the market square. Houses are in flames and piles of goods are strewn in the street. As we passed next to Kogan's hat shop that half of it had already been burned, we heard the sound of a woman screaming from a building whose roof had been set on fire. We broke the locked door and found about twenty women with babies and children in the building. We moved them to Vilkomirski's pharmacy. Now we came into direct contact with the rioters. Neta Lifshitz's shop is wide open and we see the "intelligentsia," high school teachers and like them, among the looters. They dispersed after a few of our shots and only a few of them took shelter in various buildings in the area. A number of our men were ordered to locate them. Meanwhile, several members arrived with the prisoners, the villain Djokovic, agent of the "Black Hundreds." He almost managed to set fire to the pharmacy where our women and wounded had found shelter.

A few wanted to tie his arms and legs and throw him into the flames, but the order was – to cover his eyes and take him to the synagogue's courtyard. Our unit headed to Starobazarney Street, on our way back to our defense position. The thunder of army drums reached our ears. It must be that the regular army is behind us. We speed up our steps and cross to the other side of the street. When the first lines of our group reached the corner of Jevrejsk Street we heard three rounds of shots. Niunia Cohen, Moshe Klarfeld and Pinchas Sherira were seriously injured and Tzvi Weiser was slightly injured.

We, and also other units, returned to the synagogue. The question that stood before us: how the army would react? Will the soldiers attack us when we are in the synagogue's courtyard? Brodsky orders us to lie on the damp ground and keep quiet. In the darkness I try to locate Levonitz, who was sick with tuberculosis, and spread some garment under his body. This young Christian, the son of a Bairamcea's farmer, joined our defenders despite his poor health. Surely, strong moral motives have probably brought him into our ranks. In this respect, it seems to me that he is the greatest idealist of all of us, for there was no danger to him and his people.

I went to the hospital to check the effectiveness of the medical treatment. In the hallway I saw Shternberg's body. Inside – a vigorous and effective action. Dr. Izik Josipovich Shapira operated through the night without a break. I watch him as he was turning his face to the side and wipe the sweat off his forehead. His normally angry face seemed to have taken on another expression, a light of compassion and nobility was rising from his eyes.

The Respite

The soldiers didn't attack the synagogue. There's kind of a respite from the rioters. How long? Brodsky orders everyone to enter the synagogue, to warm up and rest. He turned to me, shoved a slice of bread in my hand, and announced that I had to attend the night watch. I reported to my position. The yard is empty and quiet. It is hard to get used to this quiet after the riots. My ears catch the sound of approaching footsteps. Someone is coming. I demand from the approaching figure to identify itself. He utters the password but, it is not "Torah" that comes out of his mouth, but "To–ro–ra," because of the cold or the excitement. It was one of our scouts – Markus, the son of a teacher and a Zionist. He was wounded in the Russo–Japanese War and recently returned home. Indeed, his homeland prepared a beautiful reception for him...

Dawn came. It is still quiet around. I ponder in my heart: who is watching over Levonitz, the sick volunteer, and who is guarding the murderer Djokovic? Both are gentiles, but, how great is the distance between them!

I listen to the conversation of two Russians returning from the banks of the Leman River. Interestingly, they talked about fishing and usual things, as if the days were ordinary days and nothing had happened. I struggle with the weariness that overtakes me. Brodsky approaches my position. I learned from him that the city is now under a military regime and therefore it was decided to disperse the volunteers. The dispersion begins immediately. Before the dispersion is completed, fathers and mothers come to the synagogue and anxiously looking for their sons. How good that I was able to assure them that nothing would happened to their loved ones!

It was also my turn to leave. I move, together with my brother, toward Learntube's house where my family is located. It turns out that shortly before I arrived to this house my mother and my wife sent someone to look for us. He went to my house and returned with a pair of rubber shoes and a skullcap which were interpreted as a sign of disaster. They breathed a sigh of relief when we appeared.

[Page 64]

Sunday, 23 October 1905

Leon Asodorov turned his specious house in Nikolaevsky Street to a place of refuge for the victims of the pogrom. He also tried to get the municipality's big hall for this purpose. We do not know yet how many families were hurt. Some are still hiding in the villages and others are hiding at the homes of non–Jews in the city. They had to pay protection fees in return for shelter in Christian homes, and the rate increased several times during the night. Hundreds of families, who lived in the city center, were hurt and property losses reached hundreds of thousands of rubles. Efraim Leib Fishman was brutally murdered. The homes of Moshe Peker from Popusoi, the brothers Schwien from Turlaki and Krichevsky's flour mill were burnt down. There is still no accurate and comprehensive report. The streets are flooded with curious gentiles. Simcha Itzkowitz leaves his house on Novobazarnia Street, tears his shirt and turns to the crowd of gentiles who gather there. "Here I am, shoot me, you miserable cowards!" They retreat and disperse in every direction.

Monday, 24 October 1905

Only today we managed to organize food supplies for the victims. The supply is run by women in the synagogue. Several pious Jews oppose it, but I manage to silence them. In the market I meet Ben–Zion Gorin and Moshe Reifman inspecting the ruins of their shops. I have no words to comfort and encourage them. Suddenly, the short bearded Shlomo Serper appears, his face is shining and he says" – these bloody events herald the coming of the Messiah. As stated: "*Akabta Demishha...*"

The assumption is that there will no longer be organized pogroms. However, we must be vigilant against individual attacks. It was decided that volunteers would guard the streets during the night.

Tuesday, 25 October 1905

Rumor has it that the local post office is flooded with telegrams from the United States, but most of the recipients are not in their apartments and therefore it is impossible to provide them with the telegrams intended for them. I hurried to the post office and among the pile of telegrams I found a telegram intended for me. I also helped other people to find their telegrams. The fact, that far from here, in the land of security and peace, there are people who are concerned for our safety, encouraged and comforted us during the difficult hours that pass on us.

During the day my wife's sister arrived in the city with her husband and also the rest of the members of the Gershon family. Their homes in the village of Divizia went up in flames and all their belongings were stolen. For three days and nights they hid among the crevices and the rocks along the shore of the Black Sea. On the third night the guards stopped two wagons that had arrived from Bairmacea. In one cart sat my aunt Haika as she was supporting her wounded husband, my uncle Gabriel Wallman. In the second cart sat Sara, daughter of the slaughterer Shimshon Kleinman, as she was also supporting her wounded husband, Yisrael Buganov. These two men fought with real heroism and now they are being taken to the hospital.

Wednesday, 26 October 1905

Dr. Trahtman told me that my uncle, Gabriel, has only a few hours to live and he is about to die. I stand at his bedside, see his agony and console myself that he is already unconscious. Suddenly he opens his eyes, he sees me and mutters: this is bitter! and again, loses consciousness. I spoke with Dr. Trahtman about my uncle's condition, but he left no room for doubt. There's no hope. This Dr. Trahtman is a brilliant intellectual. He is assimilated and a friend of Anna Nikolaevna, the principle of the gymnasium. Now he had suffered an unbearable disaster. How could he return to the parties at the home of the principal who was also caught in circles of the "Black Hundreds?" How could he stick to his theories and love the Russians?

Thursday, 27 October 1905

My uncle Gabriel passed away. He gave his life to protect his community. The local authority demands an autopsy. All my efforts to prevent it – failed. I took his body to one of the abandoned shops. I lit candles and gathered a group of people to recite Psalms according to custom. A handful of people accompanied him on his last journey and in the cemetery another nightmare awaited us. We had to wait for Dr. Kostirin and his assistant – both typical anti–Semites and from the leaders of the "Black Hundreds" gangs, to perform the autopsy. I felt as if my uncle Gabriel had died a second death. A grave was dug up for my uncle Gabriel next to the fresh graves of Efraim Leib Fishman, Michael Shternberg and Fanya Steinberg.

When I returned to the city in the evening the synagogues were already open and worshipers came and went. Afterwards, this location was designated as a memorial area for the martyrs. There were eight monuments. I wrote, were, because after the Second World War there was no trace of them.

(January 1955)

[Page 65]

Memories from the Days of the Pogrom
by Yehoshua Harari (Berger) z"l
Translated by Sara Mages

I was a six–year–old boy then and this pogrom is etched in my memory. Apparently, this is the first event I remember from my childhood.

It was Saturday before noon. The shutters (which were inside and not outside) were closed. Father moved the shutters a little, picked me up, and I saw a lot of people marching in a procession ("*procesja*") and waving flags in their hands. They were led by priests with large crosses. That's how it began. On Saturday night there was already a lot of confusion at home. My eldest brother, Yakov z"l, who was already fourteen years old then, went out often and brought news. Apparently, he was already in touch with the self–defense ("*samoodbrana*") which was located not far from our house, in the synagogue's courtyard. Suddenly, I heard the sound of "cymbals," it turned out that these were echoes of shattered windows. It was a few days after my mother gave birth to my sister Chana. Father decided not to take a risk and began to move us to the yard of our Greek neighbor, Manoles, who had a bakery in our neighborhood, at the beginning of Izmailovska Street. Behind the bakery was a large fenced yard and behind it were stables for horses. Women and babies gathered in a small room near the stables while the adults crowded in one of the stables next to the horses.

I remember that in the middle of the night my father took me out of the small room to relieve myself, and I saw that the sky was red from the flames that rose from the market. In the morning we all had to leave our temporary quarters at Manoles, and move to my grandmother's house in Michalowsky Street because it seemed to be safer there.

We moved to the house that behind it were grandmother's shops, close to the second market. I remember that also here we saw shops going up in flames in the second market, and the smoke rising from the burning wooden houses.

Seventy years have passed since then, and to this day I cannot free myself from the experience of the first pogrom I witnessed as a small child.

*"For these things I weep; my eye,
my eye runs down with water"*

(Lamentations 1:16)

[Page 69]

Parties and Movements

The Beginning of "*Tzeirei Zion*" in Akkerman
by Tzvi Menuali
Translated by Sara Mages

The Great Russian Revolution also caused a great public unrest in the Russian Jewry and a tidal wave in the Zionist movement that also didn't skip our city, Akkerman. At the same time the democratic Jewish community, the Zionist library, the Hebrew kindergarten under the management of Shoshana Zilbrleib (Puzis), were established. There was a different spirit in the Jewish street in Akkerman and Zionist activity began in all areas. Most of the activists were young, mostly students and a few high school students. Among them stood out: Fava Barkov who was a scholar and a brilliant speaker, Komy Tabachnik, David Kushnir, Yisrael Rabinowitch, Yuly Danovich, Bazia Hacham, Yosef Rivkin, Yosef Serper, Yakov Berger, Gelfand, the brothers Ajzik, Moshe and Yisrael Schildkraut, Kalman Kogen, Aharon Brand, Kulya Kogen and others. I was young then, almost a boy, but I followed every Zionist event and activity. It's possible to say - I was captivated to Zionism.

However, the situation has undergone a total change in a period of only one year. In March 1918, the Romanians took control of Bessarabia, instituted a reign of terror and repression, mostly in the border areas that Akkerman was also among them. This situation caused total paralysis in public and conceptual activity. Other than that, most of the young people left the city, a small group of *Halutzim* [pioneers] immigrated to Israel together the first immigrants of the Third Aliyah, while others - had scattered to all directions. With the group of *Halutzim* were: Fava Barkov , Yisrael Rabinowitch, Avraham Serfer Avraham Durfman, Shaike Berger, Yeshayahu Botoshansky, Zeidel Burotzin, Aharon Brend, Noah Zukerman, Aharon Kaminker, Freldansky, Margalit. Among the young women, who immigrated then, were: Yona Manos and Zukerman.

The news that arrived from Israel in the early years of the British rule was quite grim: unemployment, economic hardship, etc. A number of our first *Halutzim* left the country - a matter which, of course, caused a bitter disappointment.

In 1923, the year in which my story begins, there wasn't yet a slight sign of Zionist life in our city. The young generation tended to assimilation and was also charmed by the legends that circulated about the socialist paradise that was supposedly created across the Leman… In the summer of that year the Romanian authorities organized a mass transportation in a freight train to the seashore of Bugas. In one of my trips in this freight train

The members of the circle (Kružok) "HaTehiya"

Seating right to left: **Yehusua Harari (Berger), Klara Shutina, Yisrael Schildkraut, Moti Kushnir**
Standing right to left: **Misha Fraldnski, Avraham Rabinowitch**

[Page 70]

"Tzeirei Zion" committee in 1932

Seating right to left: **Lyoba Rozenbaum, Dora Goldman, Tzvi Menuali**,
Standing: **Yisrael Schildkraut, Aba Helman, Gertz Abramovich, Alexander Shapira**

I sat next the high-school student, Zeida Shapira, son of Heinich Shapira from the regular worshipers of Bait Hamidrash, and through a conversation during our journey I discovered that, like me, he's also a Zionist who dreams of Zion. After a few more conversations, following this conversation, we came to the conclusion that the time of action has arrived and decided to organize a Zionist circle. I drafted my best friends to this circle: Lyoba Schectman, Srulik Yelin and Shalom Vishnovitzki. Shapira drafted Misha Kroshkin, Aba Helman and Misha Frank. Therefore, apart from me, our circle ("*Kružok*") was made up of high-school students. For a certain period the circle operated in a limited fashion, meaning, strictly between ourselves, and we mostly dealt in the study of the theory of Zionism. All of our activity written and oral was conducted entirely in the Russian language.

Sometime later we decided to expend the circle and penetrate the wide circles of the government schools students because the Hebrew Gymnasium was still in its infancy. Due to the state of emergency in Bessarabia our activity was conducted clandestinely. Despite that it had a long echo and very soon the student circle "*HaNoar*" ["The Youth"] was organized and its driving force was my brother, Shimon Menuali z"l, and also Yehudah Brodsky.

The first public activity of our circle was... *Aliyah La'Torah* of students in Simchat Torah 1923 for the benefit of *Kern Hakayemet*. We enlisted the support of the students for this matter and the operation was crowned with great success. Many students streamed to the "women section" in the upper floor of *Beit Hamidrash*. Among them were those who were granted to do so for the first time in their life.

Another public activity of our circle was the Hanukah ball which was held at "*Tarbut.*" Many students participated with great enthusiasm in all the preparations for the ball. It was a typical ball for those days and served as kind of a demonstration "that our nation is still alive," the heart of the youth was with us and there was still a chance for the Zionist cause among the youth.

Our "*Kružok*" started to seek its way in Zionism. We contacted "*HaTehiya*" in Kishinev and asked for guidance. We sent Zeida Shapira to the youth committee in Kishinev in the hope that he would bring us a "program."

Zeida returned from Kishinev, but without the program...

I remember that we invited Yitzchak Schbartz z"l to give a lecture in one of the circle's meetings. He was a Hebrew teacher at "*Tarbut*" Gymnasia. His lecture left a great impression and we continued to hold meetings with him. Schbartz himself was a man of the Second Aliyah, but he returned to his hometown, Bielce, at the outbreak of the First World War. In his lectures he convinced us that the road to real Zionism is through the working Eretz-Yisrael. At the same time Jabotinsky became popular, the newspaper "*Rasviet*" appeared and the message of Revisionism also arrived to us. On *Tu B'eshvat* 1924, a well attended party was held at the apartment of Sioma Shimonovitz. Schbartz and also David Tcherniavsky, who was a math teacher at the Hebrew High-School, also attended. The establishment of "*Tzeirei Zion*" in Akkerman was officially announced in this party. Moshe Serfer was nominated as chairman, I as secretary and Zeida Shapira as treasurer...

With the first members of "*Tzeirei Zion*" were: Schectman,

[Page 71]

Yelin, Vishnevsky, Mati Preldenski, Aba Helman, Avraham Trahtman, Beti Levin, Aharon Dorfman, Shmuel Zukerman, Fenny Tulchinsky, Bruch Berger, Aliyahu Zilberlib, Estera Rabinowitch, Fenny Rabinowitch, Rosa Komorovsky, Mali Gordon, Manya Hohberg, Hirschfeld, Aharon Schinkovsk, Vaska Moskowitz. A year or two later, Yisrael Schildkraut, Ajzek Shapira and Dora Goldman joined the chapter and were among the most prominent activists. In a later period also joined: Gertz Abramovich, Aharon Roizman, Pinchas Pegorski, Lyoba Zunis, Malbina Feldman, Yitzchak Greenshpon, Fira Rivelnik, Dola Rosenbaum, Svaya Ribak, Natal Multiner, Vladia Scheinfeld, Malia Kaninker, Nioma Dudelzak, Tzvi Gerzenshtein, Sioma Segel, Melchin, Lyoba Rosenbaum, Ester Brodesky, Leyosia Zilberman, Filot and others that their names have been forgotten. With the transformation of the "*Kružok*" to a real party, Zionist Left, our public Zionist activity received a considerable momentum and our image rose in the public eyes and in our eyes. In Passover of 1924, "*Tzeirei Zion*" organized the fundraising campaign, "Pioneer Week," and we managed to collect the amount of 17.000 Leu which was, in the concept of those days, a huge sum. The centre of "*HeHalutz*" in Kishinev "burst with joy" when they heard the results of the fundraising in Akkerman. David Berfel, who was at that time the chairman of "*HeHalutz*" center, sent me a telegram of greeting and thanks.

The chapter of *"Tzeirei Zion"* in Akkerman existed and was active from 1924 to 1940. Of course, there were periods of high and low in the activities, but there was no break in the activities, I was active in all these years without a break. It should be emphasized that the appearance of *"Tzeirei Zion"* in our city was, in a way, a shot in the arm for the Zionist movement in Akkerman which was in a state of lethargy until we stood and in youthful vigor sprawled on the Jewish street and vigorously infiltrated the Zionist idea among the general public. Among those young people there were no geniuses who spoke flowery Russian like that of Pava Berkov who left Israel, but honest people who engaged in public needs with trust, spoke to the public in juicy Yiddish and not in Russian, which was spoken at that time in Akkerman, and carried with honor and pride the name *"Tzeirei Zion."*

Members of "Tzeirei Zion" in Akkerman

First row (sitting right to left) - **Roizman, Elick Zilberberg, Moskowitz, unidentified, Rabinowitch**
Second row (right to left) - Vilderman, Moshe Serfer, Ajzik Shapira, the teacher David Tcherniavsky, Tzvi Menuali, Porlodonski, Aba Helman
Third row (standing right to left) - **Beti Levin, Manya Gohberg, Yisrael Vishnivetzki, Baruch Berger, Baruch Serfer, Rosa Komorovsky**
Fourth row (standing) - **Y. Schildkraut, Dr. Shimonovich, Avraham Trahtman, Fini Tulchinsky, Avraham Dudlzek, Shmuel Zukerman**

[Page 72]

The Association "Speak Hebrew!"
- of the First Youth Organizations

by Nisan Amitai (Stembul)

Translated by Sara Mages

The political upheavals, and the many revolutions that followed, left their mark on the life and the existence of the Jewish youth in our city in the twenties of this century. Then, we didn't understand the political significance of all the great events (the World War, the Bolshevik Revolutions, the disengagement of Bessarabia from Russia and the beginning of the Romanian rule). However, we saw, with our own eyes, the convoys of refugees who crossed the frozen Dniester in the winter season in order to flee for their lives from the soviet regime and the famine that prevailed in Russia. We absorbed the atmosphere at home and the sensation of fear for the anticipated future. We saw the refugees who worked at paving the roads in the city and many Jews were among them, and had the feeling that the days are fatal days, but, as stated, it was just a feeling, the feeling of children, and nothing more.

We, the children, were alone and there was no one to help us with our wonder about the meaning of the events, anyone who would solve the problems that began to awaken in us. We knew that they were rightists and leftists, but we couldn't understand what is between those and those? and, what is cooking in the big world? Also the Zionist parties, which began to organize and form in the Jewish street, paid very little attention to the pondering youth. In this respect there was almost no difference between the parties. The General Zionist who dominated the public institutions in the city, "*Mizrahi*," the Revisionist and even "*Tzeirei Zion*" who, as their name, were young in years and experience - all of them were subjected to their own matters and problems. They were powerless to save and assist us, the youngest, the students of the lower classes of "*Tarbut*" Gymnasia.

We were 13-14 then. At the Hebrew gymnasium we studied Hebrew history and Hebrew literature, but we felt that we were required more than that, that we were able to do more than that since the days were "historical" days and required a lot. During breaks, and after school, we spoke among ourselves about the need to organize, to do something, to change something, etc. It is possible to say that all of us had the same feeling: it's time to do! I don't remember how the matter had started and what were the first steps toward organization, but, according to the best of my knowledge, Shura Volovitz (Yehusua Drori), Tzvi Shechter and Nisan Stembul were those who came to a decision to start to organize the youth, not on ideological basis, but on common linguistic structure - Hebrew. The natural tendency for youthful rebellion found an outlet for the energy that was stored within us and the feeling for the need for action. Since the spoken language at home, and also among the children, was Russian or Yiddish, the youthful rebellion, and maybe even the arising national consciousness, required that our main goal would be to speak in Hebrew, meaning, anyone joining our association will have to speak in Hebrew, and only in Hebrew, at home, in the street, at school, every day.

It is possible that another factor motivated us to establish an association based on speaking in Hebrew. The "*Kultur Lige*" [Culture League], which saw its goal to develop the Yiddish language and the Yiddish culture, was active in Akkerman (by the way, several members of "*Kultur Lige*" actually sent their children to the Hebrew gymnasium) and we rose as "antithesis" to the "*Lige*"…

Our first step was - to convene a meeting of the students of our class, to explain the objectives of our association that we initiate and "call them to the flag," meaning, the Hebrew flag. Just to spite, we decided to name our association "The Association Speak Hebrew!"

And so it was. At the beginning of the school year of 1927, the association was established with good luck and *Mazel Tov*. Many didn't join at first but over time, after we proved that our intentions were good, members from the gymnasium forth class and students of the second class also joined. We acted according to all the rules of democracy and elected a committee that, according to my best memory, included: Shura Volovitz z"l who served as chairman, I as secretary and Binyamin Gresfeld - treasurer, and also Tzvi Tzvi Shechter and Utza Kogen (Rachel Roll z"l). Sometime later, Sheptel Zukerman and other members joined the committee.

[Page 73]

The newspaper of "The Association Speak Hebrew!" in Akkerman

[Page 74]

We weren't satisfied with just talking in Hebrew and expanded the scope of our activities. The leaders of the parties, General Zionist and *"Tzeirei Zion,"* were invited to lecture before us on various topics, we held literary evenings, public and literature trials, and also started to empty the boxes of *Keren Hakayemet* and came as a group to lectures held by the Zionist parties in the city.

The crown glory of our activity - the internal newsletter designed for the members of the association. This campaign was a unique experience, and when I remember now with what awesome respect we handled this matter in those days - a smile passes on my lips… With the little money that we collected from the membership we bought a spirograph - kind of an oilcloth that you can duplicate a limited number of copies on it. We obtained the paper in an "original" way: since the grandfather of Yehusua Drori was a paper merchant and supplied sheets of paper to the stores, this grandfather hired us as "employees" and our only duty was - to count the sheets of paper that were sent to each store. In exchange for our work we received paper for the printing of our newsletter. We were novices at this task, we stained ourselves with the blue ink and stained every place that we worked in. Therefore, we arranged kind of a "rotation," every newspaper was printed in a different location and the housewives waited impatiently to get rid of us… We worked quite a lot for our newspaper. At times we had to copy the handwriting a number of times for duplication, but after such of an operation we had the feeling of satisfaction and personal fulfillment because, in this way, we gained support for our "idea" and strengthen "The Association Speak Hebrew!" For the sake of history it will be recorded that the first editor of our newsletter was Tzvi Shechter.

Later, with our maturity, we started to feel that our "platform" was too narrow. "The Association Speak Hebrew!" was no longer under our measure… we started to wonder about matters of supreme importance, searched for solutions for national issues, social issues etc. At the same time a group of students from the upper classes of the gymnasia organized and called themselves "Zionist Students." There was no difference between them and us and we agreed that the two associations should be united.

The riots of 5689 [1929] in Israel brought many additional problems, mostly the problem of the Arabs. The "Speak Hebrew" framework became more and more narrow and we came to the conclusion that speaking in Hebrew was very important but it doesn't solve the fundamental problem. Two years later the association disbanded, but it also served as a foundation for a youth Zionist movement as it would be told in one of the chapters.

Winter in the city park in Akkerman

[Page 75]

At the train station in Akkermann

"Maccabi" Federation in Akkerman
by S. Segal and T. Manueli
Translated by Sara Mages

"Maccabi" Federation in our city underwent various incarnations and stages. It began in the summer of 1917. In the summer of that year, Mr. Granovski arrived to our city from Odessa. He was active in the Zionist movement there and was among the founders of "Maccabi" in the city. Several members of "Maccabi" in Odessa came with him and organized a sports ball with a display of gymnastics at Stepidov's cinema. The gymnasts were dressed in blue and white and accompanied the sports exercises with national songs. They received a lot of applause from the audience and at that event it was announced that a "Maccabi" branch would be established in Akkerman. At that time there were no youth movements in the city, and for that reason many young people joined "Maccabi." However, the movement did not last long, the first enthusiasm quickly faded and the branch was liquidated a short time later.

The second incarnation of "Maccabi" looks strange and puzzling. In 1921, or at the beginning of 1922, a group of boys from the Government Gymnasium in Romania started to engage in gymnastics and various sports exercises. The name that they choose for themselves was - "Maccabi." We don't remember who the first members of this group were, but it is known that it was headed by a gentile named Kolia Bimbolov. What is even more puzzling - he gave the orders in Hebrew as he was marching through the city. Since this organization also had no public support - it also died.

The third incarnation of "Maccabi" began in the year 1925-1926. This time, the initiative to establish "Maccabi" came from our city's branch of "*Tzeirei Zion*" who aspired to bring the youth closer to Zionism and tried to achieve their goal through a sports federation. At the head of the organizing committee stood: Valya Milstein, T. Manueli and Y. Shildkraut. Also Simcha (Sioma) Segal was among the activists. Manueli and Shildkraut mostly acted in the field of culture. Due to the lack of suitable instructors the activity gradually weakened.

Now we arrive to the fourth stage. It was in 1928. At the initiative of "*Tzeirei Zion*" and "Maccabi," a literary trial was conducted on "Motke the Thief" of Shalom Asch. There was considerable income from this trial, and it was decided that it would be dedicated to the establishment of a fund for the strengthening of "Maccabi's" activity. At that time, Valya Milstein still served as chairman of the association.

In 1929, a convention of "*Tzeirei Zion*" in Bessarabia was held at the "*Halutz*" *Hakhshara* farm, "*Massada*," near Bălți [Beltsy], and Tzvi Maniali (Manoali) participated as a delegate from Akkerman. On his way back from the convention he stopped in Kishinev and had a consultation at the "Maccabi" center regarding to the renewal of the activities in Akkerman. The center recommended the sports instructor, Botoshansky, as an appropriate man from an organizational and sporting standpoint

A group of Maccabi gymnasts in training

[Page 76]

for the resumption of the activities of "Maccabi" in Akkerman. He was also promised a certain amount of money to cover his salary. A short time later the instructor arrived in Akkerman, started to reorganize the branch and, we can say, that he laid the foundation for an active and organized chapter of "Maccabi" in our city. For the first time a sports race was held in the city streets. It ended on Michaelovsky Street near the municipal park. That same year, a young man from the city of Bender (Tighina), who served as an instructor at the branch of "Maccabi" in his city, appeared before S. Segal and offered himself as a free instructor at the "Maccabi" branch in Akkerman. His proposal was accepted and a new committee was set up under the leadership of Dr. Shaul Zlering. Among the activists in the branch were: Valya Milstein, Manueli and Simcha Segal who served as secretary. In addition to them, several graduates of the Hebrew Gymnasia, such as Shaya Falikov, the brothers Yakov and Shmuel Rosenthal, and others, also joined. At the same time, there were various apparatus at the branch that enabled proper athletic activity. They also came to an agreement with the high school principal, Yakov Berger, that the school's gymnasium will be used for sports activity of the "Maccabi" branch in the evenings.

In 1931, Dr. Zlering immigrated to Israel and Tzvi Manueli was elected in his place. At the recommendation of the community leader, M. Helman z"l, the community donated a flag with "Maccabi's" logo. For the dedication of the flag a procession was held in the city streets to the sound of a band. It ended with a rally at the Great Synagogue. City leaders and community activists were invited to the rally, and the representatives of the government brought their blessing to the festive gathering.

Over time, with Tzvi Manueli's desire to free himself from the burden, we managed to bring new people closer to the activity of "Maccabi." Among them was Lazar Vladimirovich Groshman, who also agreed to serve as chairman for a certain period. When he moved to Bucharest, Dr. Akim Markowitz Wilkomirski was elected chairman of the association even though he wasn't a Zionist. He was, in fact, the last chairman of "Maccabi" until the Soviet occupation. Together with him were active: T. Manueli, S. Segal, Valya Milstein, David Waiser (owner of the notions store), and also Gretz Abramowitch - a member of "*Tzeirei Zion*" which continued to support "Maccabi" throughout its existence.

It is worth noting, that under the influence of the youth movements (*Gordonia, Hashomer Hatzair, Betar*), which began to develop great activity starting from 1929 and trained their members for immigration, Maccabi also experienced a certain agitation and its members demanded that "Maccabi" not only provide athletic activity, but also encourage its members for training and immigration. And indeed, in 1931, a national meeting of "Maccabi" was held in Romania and many members, mainly from Bessarabia, raised the demand to set up *Hakhshara* points [pioneering training commune] for the members of "Maccabi." A decision in this spirit was accepted at the conference, and "Maccabi" joined the "*Halutz*" movement. Members of the branch of "Maccabi" in Akkerman were among the first to leave for *Hakhshara* when they were established in Odobe?ti,,Ripiceni, Bucharest and Bāl?i. The first members who left for *Hakhshara*: Sincha Segal, Manya Licht, Sara Goldnberg, the brothers Levit, Fanya Abramowitch, Alyosha Barany, Mora Filand, Rachel Mutchnick, Batia Spinnern Sura Botoshansky and others. Our member, Yakov Rosenthal, traveled to Israel as a tourist to the Maccabiah Games, but he remained in the country. In this period, S. Segal was elected as a member of Maccabi center.

A group of "Maccabi" sports instructors

First row (seated right to left): **Yantzik Weinstein, Munia Trachtman, Alyosha Barany, Avraham Goldman, Shmuel Stetsky**

Second Row: **Buria Citron, Yisrael Ganpolsky, Isak Feidel (instructor from Kishinev), Mulia Rosenthal, Lifchitz**

Third row: **unidentified, Rotenberg, Lyuma Rotenberg, Izik Ganpolsky, Sioma Levit**

[Page 77]

In the years 1936-38, during the reign of the Jews-haters in Romania (Antonescu, Cuza, Goga), an order was given to close the *Hakhshara* branches in Romania and the *"Halutz"* center was forced to cease its activities. With the efforts of the leadership of "Maccabi," a license was granted for the establishment of one *Hakhshara* branch - "Masada Farm," in Bāl?i. the *Hakhshara* branch of *"Gordonia*'s" in Bāl?i, was also registered in this license under the name of "Maccabi."

At the outbreak of the war, the activities of "Maccabi" ceased throughout Romania, and all the emissaries to the youth movements were sent back to Israel, except for D. Guberman from *"Hashomer Hatzair"* movement who remained in Romania. The gates to Israel were locked, but many members of "Maccabi" managed to reach Israel in various ways, most, with the *Ha'pala* Movement (illegal immigration).

The branch of "Maccabi" in Akkerman at the flag raising celebration

Members of the committee sitting in the center (from the right): **Y. Greenshpon, M. Stretz, Leib Shohet, Dr. E. Wilkomirski, Lazar Grossmann, Pemi Baltaksa, Chaim Rosenthal. Greenstein, Shmuel Segal, Aba Hellman, Plock**

A group of "Maccabi" gymnasts

[Page 78]

Members of "Maccabi" with the sports instructors and the members of the Public Committee prior to the immigration of the chairman Dr. S. Zlering

Members of the committee (from the right): **Gretz Abramowitch, Y. Abramowitch, Y. Berger, Natan Goldstein, the chairman Dr. S. Zlering, Z. Miniely, Dr. E. Wilkomirski, unidentified, Falikov**

Members of Maccabi branch 1931-32

[Page 79]

A group of "Maccabi" gymnasts with the instructor Sioma Levit (on the right)

Maccabi parade with its flags on a Romanian holiday
The inscription on the poster - reexamination of the borders - means war

[Page 80]

"Maccabi's" chairman, Dr. E. Wilkomirski (the last chairman before the Soviet occupation)

"Maccabi" parade in Akkerman's streets

"Maccabi's" gymnasium with training equipment

[Page 81]

"*Gordonia*" in Akkerman
by Sheftel Zukerman
Translated by Sara Mages

From the distance of the years that have passed since then – more than forty years! – it is not easy to return to that period in our lives, when we were still young and beautiful and our perception of life, with its great and small events, was romantic and ideal. And yet, we were all imbued with a great ideal: emigration to Israel and self-fulfillment. It was preceded by *hakhshara* [pioneer training] in the "*Halutz*" and the expectation of the realization of the dream.

The youth movements arrived to Akkerman somewhat late. Akkerman's location at the south end of Bessarabia, kind of the "end of the world," caused that our movement started to spread first in the north. From Poland it moved to Bukovina, from there to northern and central Bessarabia, and only a few years later also arrived to us.

In the first twenty years of our century there were movements and Zionist groups of older people in Akkerman: "*Tzeirei Zion*," "General Zionists," "*Mizrahi*" and the Revisionist. There was, indeed, the Maccabi association, which was established before the Zionist youth movements and gathered many young people and children, but it was only active in the field of sports. Already in those years many young people immigrated from Akkerman to Israel. In 1920–21, an organized group of young people, age 20–21, immigrated to Israel with the *Third Aliya*. The immigration to Israel also flowed after them but it was mainly the immigration of individuals and not of an organized group like that of 1921.

With the establishment of the Hebrew gymnasium in Akkerman the best Jewish youth concentrated around it, even though not all of them were imbued with the same national and Zionist spirit which characterized the gymnasium students later. At the end of the 1920s, the gymnasium's youth was no longer satisfied with their studies alone and began to organize themselves in small cells, according to grade, at the Hebrew and Yiddish library (in the building of the Jewish Bank). They read books in Hebrew and Yiddish, read Zionist newspapers from abroad (*Ha'olam* from London, *He'atid* from Warsaw) and other local magazines and newspapers from Kishinev.

In those days a circle of students, limited at first, stood out and set the goal to speak in Hebrew, not only within the gymnasium's walls but also everywhere. "*Dabro Iverit*" [Speak Hebrew], was the name of this circle and it contained teenagers, age 14–15, that the national idea captured their hearts. From this circle came the first members of "*Gordonia*." In the year, 5689–1929, after the riots of the month of Av in Israel, and after the visit of the emissaries from Israel in Akkerman: Zev Meshi and Dov Shafrir-Giser – the branch grew and expanded and contained scores of members.

As stated, the branch started from the students of the Hebrew gymnasium "Tarbut." The driving force, in the organization of the "*Gordonia*" branch, was Shura Volovitz (Yehusua Drori z"l). He had an organizational skill and was stubborn by nature. He loved to read and loved to delve into the problems of the Jewish nation and the society. Yehusua did not neglect his studies and was also an outstanding student in his class. Active members, from his class and other classes, gathered around him. At first there were few but, later, whole classes from "Tarbut" school in the city joined "*Gordonia*." No more than two or three, outside the gymnasium students, joined "*Gordonia*." Over time, young people and children, from other circles, joined the branch of "*Gordonia*."

Already from its inception, the "*Gordonia*" branch in Akkerman captured a special place among the other branches of the movement in Bessarabia. It had its own uniqueness, a great cultural weight, knowledge of the Hebrew language, knowledge of history and the Bible, strong national recognition – all these contributed to the formulation of a special version of our movement in Bessarabia – Akkerman style.

Akkerman itself was a unique city in the landscape of the cities of Bessarabia: a district town, although not large in its population and without many Jews. It had a lively Jewish life and there was no shortage of Jewish institutions which were in every large or medium Jewish city. It was a pleasant, clean, orderly, and civilized city. It lay on the quiet Liman coast (the Dniester's lake that reached the Black Sea). It was greatly influenced by the nearby big city of Odessa, in its politeness and manners, as well as the Russian culture, the culture of the 20th century at its best.

[Page 82]

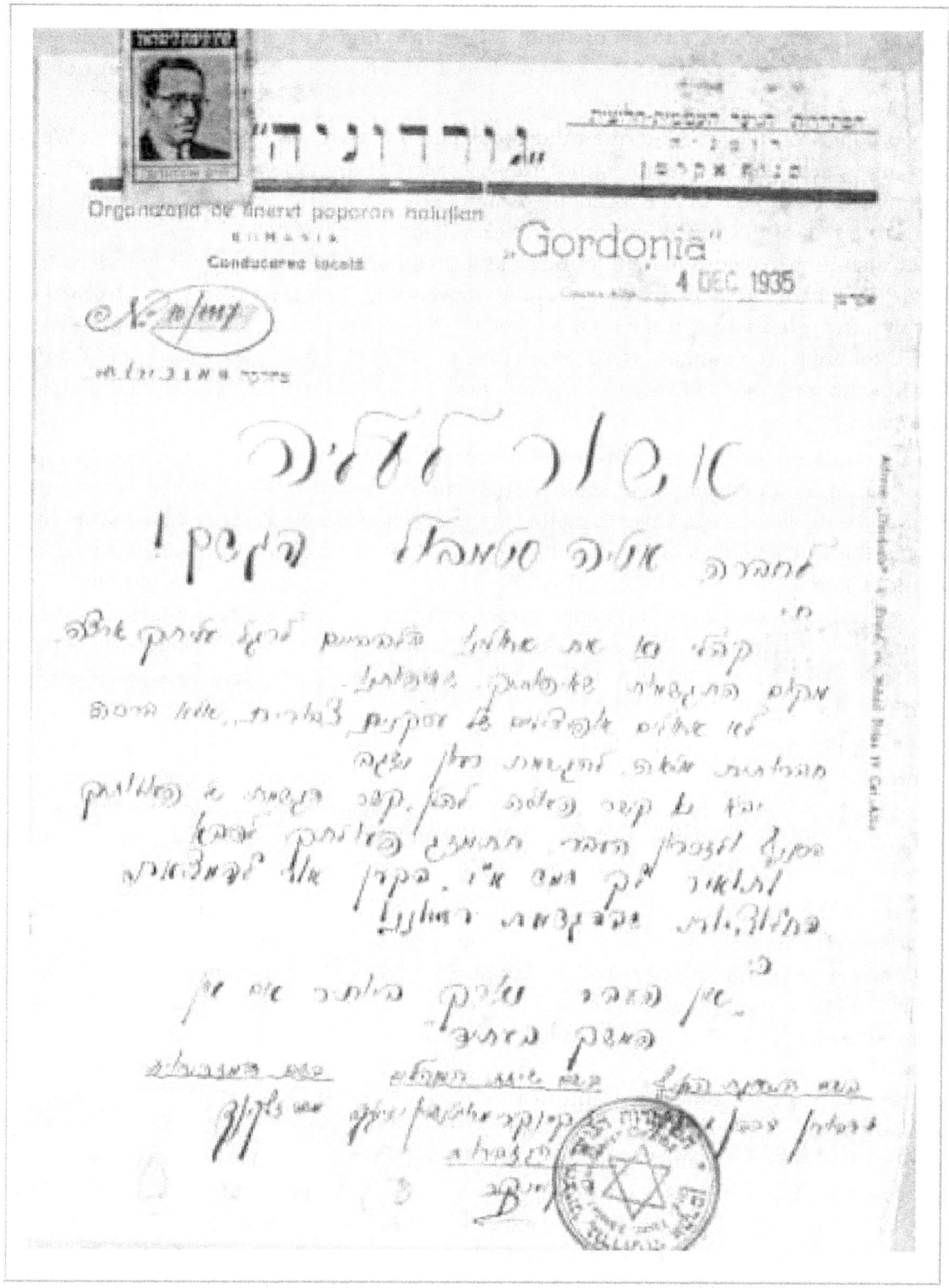

"Certificate of approval for immigration" that each member of "Gordonia" received from the branch before his/her immigration to Israel

[Page 83]

Akkerman was also influenced by the Jewish cultural life in the important Jewish center – Odessa. Only after the Romanian occupation, Akkerman, and with it all of Bessarabia was cut off from the Russian Jewry. However, the flow of Jewish refugees in the early years enriched Jewish Akkerman.

The "*Gordonia*" branch in Akkerman did not excel in the number of its members. We were not hundreds, as in some other branches, but those dozens of Jewish youth, students of the Hebrew gymnasium who gathered in the branch, designated it for the best. Good Jewish youth also gathered in the rest of the youth movements: "*Hashomer Hatzair*," "*Betar*" and "Maccabi." Over the years, they also immigrated to Israel, founded kibbutzim or were among their founders. There was a tradition of central activity in the national movement. Yehusua Volovitz (Drori) was called immediately after graduating from high school to the movement's center in Kishinev. Later, he moved to Bucharest, the capital city of Romania, to be in the main leadership of "*Gordonia*." He was active in the movement's center for a few years, until his immigration to Israel. Other followed his footsteps.

After the riots of 5689, when the gates to Israel were closed, many did not "jump" on the opportunity to immigrate because of the situation that prevailed in the country at the time. At the beginning of 1930, Baruch Zukerman (today Nemani, member of Kevutzt Masada in the Jordan Valley), was the first member of "*Gordonia*" in Akkerman to immigrate to Israel. I remember well the dozens of members who accompanied Baruch to the train station in Akkerman. There was great excitement and we, the young ones, envied him. Since then, each immigration of a member to Israel and each departure of a son of Akkerman to *hakhshara*, brought moments of excitement and enthusiasm to those, who gathered at the train station plaza, and sang from the songs of Israel and the movement.

There was no shortage of problems throughout the existence of the branch in Akkerman. There were financial difficulties in maintaining the club, and there were problems with the Romanian secret police in the city which, occasionally, harassed the members of the branch. We were assisted by a large number of friends of "*Gordonia*" in the local branch of "*Tzeirei Zion*." If they were not for us, we might not have survived.

Members of the Akkerman branch were active in all the movement's conferences, both regional and national. The center of the fifth region (Southern Bessarabia) was in Akkerman and Binyamin Gershfeld, and others in its wake, worked hard to establish new branches and operate them in the towns of our district and nearby districts. There were many conferences and regional meetings, in Akkerman and also in other towns (Tatarbunar, Romanovka), and all these brought us closer to wider circles of youth. Famous were the "*Zopiadot*," summer camps for the scouts, which were held on the shores of the Black Sea and nearby lakes. The members of Akkerman were aided by the members of Bucharest (the member, Rozman, will be remember for the best), who were knowledgeable in scouting and, together with the members of Akkerman, guided the regional summer colonies and contributed to their great success. In addition, the participation of the members of Akkerman in the executive colonies, although not in a large number (due to the distance of the place and the expenses involved in traveling to the remote Carpathian region), contributed greatly to the advancement of the active members of the branch. A great deal of effort was required to participate in the executive colony in the country far north.

The members of "*Gordonia*" in Akkerman didn't leave for *hakhshara* in droves – again, due to the distance of the locations of the *hakhshara* in Northern Bessarabia or in Moldova. On the other hand, their weight in immigration to Israel was not negligible. Surely, not all the graduates immigrated to Israel. There were those who continued their studies and immigrated to Israel later. There were those who weren't able to immigrate because of personal and family reasons and got stuck in their city. However, dozens of pioneers immigrated and to this day they live in kibbutzim, cooperative settlements and others.

It is only natural that there was a change in the management of the Akkerman's branch after the great immigration which began to flow into Israel in the mid 1930s. When the active members immigrated others joined the management of the branch. The branch did not always maintain its level and extensive activity as in the early years. There were ups and downs in the activity of the branch but, the "Akkerman uniqueness," was always kept.

With the graduates' emigration the connection between them and the remaining members of the branch was not severed. There was a connection of letters and every letter that came from the Israel, from one of the former active members, bridged those who were in Israel and the young members who had not yet gone to *hakhshara* or immigrated to Israel, built it and continued to live in kibbutzim.

Today, after 40–45 years, after the tremendous changes in the Jewish world, and after more than 30 years of the existence of the State of Israel, rise, from the depths of the past, the memory of the movement and the longings for that wonderful world of youth saturated with yearnings for redemption and hope for a new life. Life of Jewish youth, Zionist and pioneering, rooted in the history and culture of the Jewish people and builds its future in its old–new homeland. This memory, and the images and photos that have remained since, make us feel that we have not acted in vain, that we have not worked in vain. Over the years we harvested what we sowed then. "*Malu Asameinu Bar.*"[1]

Kibbutz Hulda

Translator's footnote:

" *Malu Asameinu Bar*" – "Fill our barns with grain"
Lyrics – Pinchas Lender
Music – David Zehavi
http://hebrewsongs.com/?song=maluasameinubar

[Page 84]

The Uniqueness of "*Gordonia*" in Our City

by N. Amitai

Translated by Sara Mages

Destiny's had was in the establishment of the branch of "*Gordonia*" in Akkerman because the members of "*Dabro Ivrit*," from which this movement was conceived and born in our city, were unaware of the existence of this movement, maybe because it was new in Bessarabia.

Late summer of 1929, at the month of August, our member, Rachel'a Gohebrg z"l, turned to me and asked me to go to her uncle's shop on Nicolaievskya Street, across from our home, because he wanted to talk to me. When I entered the shop, I found Mendel Davidson, brother of our teacher, Efraim Davidson, who was active in *Keren Hakayemet* in Kishinev. He gave me a short lecture about the pioneering movement, "*Gordonia,*" which supported the ideas and ideals of A.D. Gordon. He suggested that I join this movement and even gave me some circulars, from the main leadership in Kishinev, so that I could use them to attract followers to the movement.

I remember that on the same evening I went with the circulars to the home of Shura Volovitz (Yehusua Drori z"l). We read them carefully and, it can be said, that they aroused our curiosity. Truth to be told, that until then A. D. Gordon's name had not reached us and we knew nothing about his teachings. Therefore, we decided to learn about the man that the new movement was named after him. The next day we went to the local library and asked the librarian for A. D. Gordon's books. However, the librarian, our teacher S. Sterenhuss, informed us that the books were not available in the library, but he promised to order them as soon as possible. And indeed, a few days later the books arrived and that evening additional information material arrived from the main leadership.

We read the books with great interest. The man and his teachings appealed to us. The obligation to immigrate to Israel, integration into nature, joining the labor movement, social justice, collective life in Israel as a solution to inequality in human society, and a way to prevent the exportation of others. All these principles, which formed the foundation of A. D. Gordon's teachings, answered our hearts' wishes.

Therefore, we decided to bring the matter to the attention of other members of "*Dabro Ivrit*" association to which we belonged then. The association did not delve into ideological matters and was based mainly on one principle, speaking in Hebrew. When we raised the issue of joining "*Gordonia*" at the meeting of the association committee, and proposed to dismantle the existing framework and support the new movement, it aroused strong opposition from some members who saw it as an attempt to split the ranks of the youth. The argument on this issue continued for a short time and eventually the association broke up and its members joined three youth movements which were established around the same time – "*Gordonia,*" "*Hashomer Hatzair*" and "*Betar*" (the alliance of Yosef Trumpeldor).

In 1929, about a month or two after the start of the school year, the "*Gordonia*" branch was organized in Akkerman. Most of the students of "Tarbut" high school, who were previously active in "*Dabro Ivrit*" and "Young Zionists," joined the branch.

The following members were elected to the temporary leadership of the local branch "*Gordonia*": chairman – Shura Volovitz (Yehusua Drori z"l), secretary – Niosa Stambul (Nisan Amitai), treasurer – Binyamin Gershfeld, Utca Kogan (Rachel Roll z"l) and Chava Geber z"l. That same year, students from the lower classes joined the branch and soon we had three age groups: *Magshimim, Mitorarim* and *Tzofim.* All the members were divided into groups which were named after various settlements and regions in Israel. A group of older students formed the board of directors and instructors. The board of directors met twice a week, read the books of A.D. Gordon and clarified and rectified all the problems that have arisen. In order to expand our knowledge, the board of directors approached the teacher, M. Grossman, with a request that he would give us lessons in sociology and political economy outside the curriculum. He accepted our request and, for that purpose, we met twice a week in the afternoon at school. The lectures of the teacher Grossman broadened our horizons and led us to a serious study of various subjects.

[Page 845

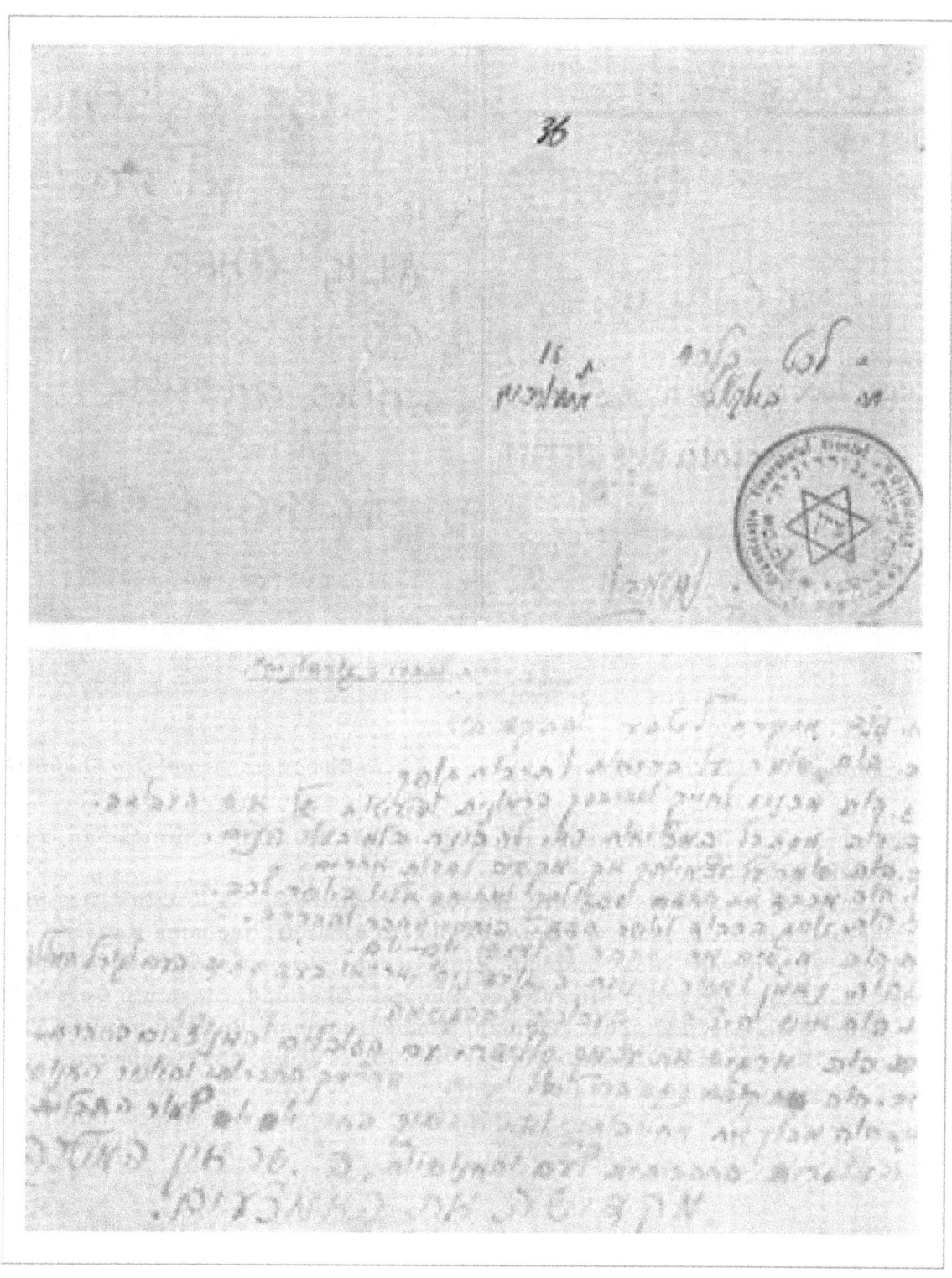

Membership card for "Gordonia" in Akkerman

[Page 86]

The "Gordonia" branch in Akkerman with the emissary from Eretz Yisrael Dov Shafrir (1930)

First row (seated right to left: **Nisia Shteinberg, unidentified, Yehudah Schwartzman, Yanchik Zukerman, Avraham Neiman**
Second row: **Aharon Dvorin, Shura Volovitz, Baruch Zukerman, Chana Kotziuk, Dov Shafrir, Chana Bravmann (from the Romanovka branch), Shaike Kushnir, Nechama Kahalski**
Third row: **Yasha Vishenivsky, Niosa Stambul, Klara Lechte, Frima Kotziuk, Nesia Zukerman, Chava Geber, Mania Schwartzman, Eliyahu Lev, Sheptel Zukerman, Binyamin Gershfeld**
Fourth row: **Sonia Berg, Glazman, Zula Feldman, Moshe Glickman, Buria Kaminker, Yakov Lev, Leah Berger, Rabinowitch, Chava Dorfman, Vitia Rozenbaum, Aba Bignbaum, unidentified, Avraham Kornblit**

A group of members of "Gordonia" (1931)
Seated (right to left): **Velvel Bignbaum, Mania Gordon, Lyuba Shmoish, Binyamin Gershfeld**
Standing: **Aharon Dvorin, Chana Manos, Aba Bignbaum**

[Page 87]

Emissaries from Israel

In 1930, the first emissary arrived to us from Eretz-Yisrael – the member Zez Meshi from Kvutzat HaSharon. His first visit in Akkerman was a real holiday for us. He was the first to bring us closer to the thought and teachings of the Labor Movement in Eretz-Yisrael. His conversations and lectures gathered all the graduates and also members from the younger age groups. The singing and dancing that emerged from our club brought an atmosphere of working Eretz-Yisrael. At the same time, the realization that we must fulfill our goal – immigration to Eretz-Yisrael – ripened in our ranks and our parents, who initially disapproved of their children's plans, also changed their opinion on this issue.

Our vigilant activity probably aroused the attention of the authorities because they turned to Y. Berger z"l, the principal of our school, and informed him that his students were organized in some kind of an organization that they weren't comfortable with. The principal of the gymnasium began to fear that something might happen to the educational institution because of us. One day, Shura Volovitz, and the writer of these lines were called to the principal and the conversation that took place between us was very difficult. Mr. Berger z"l demanded that we stop our activities in the youth movement because he feared that if we didn't stop, the authorities would harm the institution. We did not accept his opinion. We announced explicitly that we were operating under the license of the authorities and we will not liquidate the branch. Moreover, we expressed our opinion that the principal, who is a devoted Zionist, must help all the Zionist youth movements. He must explain to the authorities that our existence and our activities pose no danger to anyone, we do not oppose the existing regime and our only goal is immigration to Eretz-Yisrael. After the conversation we parted in a friendly manner and a handshake. It seemed to us that the principal agreed to the continuation of our activities, maybe because he had no choice.

The member, Shura (Yehusua Drori), was sent to the ideological seminar, which was held in the city of Balti with the participation of emissaries from Israel. And indeed, the seminar produced excellent results. Shura returned with many experiences and broader horizons and began to work diligently on expanding the branch and bringing in new members.

It should be noted that Shura (Yehusua Drori), was very much liked by all the members and had great influence on the students, in his class and also in other classes of the gymnasium. He absorbed the Russian culture from his eldest sister, read many works of Russian classics and studied the problems that arose in his reading, He had the ability to analyze and express himself, and in addition to all these, he was also blessed with organizational skills and his dedication to the movement knew no limit. Yehusua was always willing to listen to the words of others and accepted the opinions of others. He soon became well known in the movement, and in 1931, upon completion of his studies at the gymnasium, he was elected as member of the main leadership of "*Gordonia*."

The Focus of Inspiration

The chapter of "*Gordonia"s*" in Akkerman had its own uniqueness. One must remember, that the "*Gordonia*" movement in Bessarabia was established with some delay, after other youth movements preceded it and succeeded in capturing the best of the students. However, the branch of "*Gordonia*" in Akkerman managed to gather in its ranks most of the students of the Hebrew gymnasium.

A year, after Shura's election to the main leadership, he was sent as a delegate of the Akkerman branch to the national conference of "*Gordonia*" which was held at the *hakhshara* farm, "Masada." Until he was elected as a representative of "*HeHalutz*" center in Kishinev ("*HeHalutz*"center, together with the main leadership of "*Gordonia*," moved at that time to Bucharest), I served as chairman of the local branch. Later, the member, Sheptel Zukerman from the branch's young group was elected to the main leadership. Over time, other emissaries visited us from Israel: Michael Oved z"l from Kvutzat HaSharon, Dov Shafrir, Ben-Zion Gafni z"l from Kfar Vitkin, Aharon Kaminker who was on a private visit with his family, and others. As noted, we tried to bring the youth from the working class in our town to our branch. The task was not easy because it was difficult to overcome the gap that always existed between the youth who studied and the youth who did not. Much had to be done to overcome this gap. To those who joined, the branch was the only source of inspiration. Many among this youth remained in the Diaspora and perished in the Holocaust only because they didn't have the financial means to pay for the ship's ticket to Israel.

Graduates of "Gordonia" ("Magshimim") with Michael Oved – the emissary from Kvutzat HaSharon, Eretz Yisrael

First row, right to left: **Chana Dorfman., Rachel Goldberg. Michael Oved. Leah Neiman, Chava Dorfman**

Second Row: **Niosa Stambul, Klara Lechte, Riva Manos, Shura Volovitz, Mania Schwartzman, Leah Berger, Binyamin Gershfeld**

[Page 88]

It is necessary to note the close ties between "*Gordonia*" and "*Tzeirei Zion*" in Akkerman. It was mainly a cultural cooperation and we were often assisted by them. We also rewarded them and came to the many cultural activities that were conducted by "*Tzeirei Zion*." Thanks to our activities among the youth quite a few parents of the members of "*Gordonia*" were captivated by the Zionist idea.

The first district summer colony in the town of Tuzla was one of our most important activities in this period. The main leadership asked our branch to organize this colony. That is: a concentration of 60–70 teenagers for a period of two weeks, finding places to live, transport to Tuzla, food, cleanliness, health, and other things that we have not experienced so far. Three members took upon themselves the organization of the colony: Niosa Stambol, Binyamin Gershfeld, Buria Kaminker (Baruch Kamin). We rented a straw warehouse for a place of residence, recruited our kindergarten teacher, "aunt Mania" (Meniora Sharira), as a consultant and she traveled to the summer colony with her son.

A group of "Gordonia" graduates, 1931

First row, right to left: **Avraham Kornblit, Itzkowitz, Avraham Neiman, unidentified, Niosa Stambul, Golda Brand, Glassman, Binyamin Gershfeld**
Second Row, left to right: **Yosef Shankarovsky, Aba Bignbaum, Mania Gordon, Buria Kaminker**

Summer colony of "Gordonia" in Tuzla ("Mitorarim" group)

The supervisors and counselors that are sitting in the center: **Julius Meller (main leadership), Niosa Stambol, Mania Shrira, a doctor (Christian) responsible for health, Lyuba Shmoish (responsible for the kitchen), Binyamin Gershfeld**

[Page 89]

"HaSharon" group ("Mitorarim") of "Gordonia" with their director Niosa Stambul before his immigration in 1933

First row, right to left: **Mina Kauchansky, Fruma Lezer**
Second row: **Chaim Zonis, Rosa Gordon, Musia Chlapik, Etia Stambul, Niosa Stambul, Chava Kaninker, Webcik Kaninker, Izia Shankarovsky**
Third row (standing): **Shaike Shrira, Neuma Lev, Katya Abramowitch, Efraim Abramowitch, Yakov Zigelvaks**

    We contacted the local doctor who agreed to serve as a health consultant. In July 1933, about sixty members of "*Gordonia*" from the chapters: Akkerman, Tatarbunary, Romanevka and others, gathered in the place designated for the colony. On behalf of the main membership, the member Julius Meller from Chernovtsy, and the member Ben–Zion Gafni who was an emissary from Eretz Yisrael, conducted lectures and conversations. The colony was very successful and impressed all its participants.

    The branch in Akkerman was a regional center for branches in the area. At the initiative of the local members, or at the initiative of the main leadership, it also took care of branches, such as Romanovka and Bolgrad that did not belong to the Akkerman district. The active members of our branch often went to visit the small branches and held various informational activities there.

The First Immigrants

In 1931, the first members immigrated to Israel: Baruch Zukerman (Nemani, Kevutzt Masada), Frima Kotziuk–Marcus (Petah Tikva), Mania Schwartzman (Bruriah Har–Zion from Hadera), Chava Dorfman–Barnea (Tel–Aviv), and others. Other members followed them, left for *hakhshara* and later immigrated to Israel. Dozens of members of "*Gordonia*" from Akkerman are scattered in various settlements in Israel and they remember well the youthful kindness that the branch provided them.

There is no doubt that the branch has written glowing pages in the life of Akkerman's youth, who reached Zionist recognition without pressure from pogroms and persecutions, but only under the influence of systematic and continuous educational activity. The Zionist atmosphere at the gymnasium, the education for pioneering which was implemented in the framework of the branch, yielded remarkable results. It should be noted that even the youth outside the gymnasium was influenced by this atmosphere, and it is a pity that this influence did not bring everyone to the point of –emigration.

Whenever there was a rumor that members were leaving from the train station on their way to Eretz Yisrael – friends, parents and relatives flocked to the station to part with them. The excitement was great and all the way around the cries echoed, "we'll see each other soon!" Thanks to the immigration of the young people, members of the movement, many of their parents also immigrated, and so the conscience of the great Holocaust emerged and so they extricated from the claws of the great Holocaust.

[Page 90]

"*Gordonia*" – the Last Chapter
by Chaim Zamir (Fima Chemerinsky)
Translated by Sara Mages

Forty years have passed since we, my friends and I, parted from the city where we grew up, where we experienced childhood and adolescence experiences, and from which we have only memories, sad and joyful, and also longings. For us, born in the forties, Akkerman is not only streets, Kishinovskaya, Sobornya, Yevreyskaya, etc. Not even the Jewish businesses in Nikolaevskaya rise in our thoughts with the mention of the name Akkerman, but the first association, when we hear the name Akkerman, is - Gymnasia "Tarbut" which served as a spiritual and Zionist center for youth and adults alike. Yes, this building, the gymnasium building, had deepened our Jewish feelings, planted the love of the homeland in us, guided us in all our ways, formed the adult circles and all the youth movements centered around it. I cannot be objective. I know that there were important movements like "*Maccabi*," "*Hashomer Hatzair*," "*Betar*" and "*HaOved*," which gathered older members and was headed by Yisrael Schildkraut and Tzvi Miniali, but it is possible to say that the "*Gordonia*" movement "surpassed them all," in the number of its members, in its accomplishments, the number of immigrants and those preparing for immigration, and by everything that the movement contributed to Jewish life in Akkerman. Our adult counselors, Baruch Keminer and Yanchik Tzukerman, did not spare any efforts and were devoted, heart and soul, to the movement. They taught us, day and night, the pioneering Zionist doctrine and we can definitely say that they saw the fruit of their labor. After them came the turn of the younger counselors - the second generation in the movement's leadership - and they are: Vorobeichic Kaminker, Dudik Kogan, Efraim Abramowitch, Chava Kaminker, Kasya Roizman and others.

I remember, to this day, the conversations we had at the branch of "*Gordonia*" in Akkerman, as I also remember the sailings and the trips that we organized to the branches of "*Gordonia*" in the area - and we got as far as Shaba - for the sake of mutual acquaintance, the tightening of the movement's ties, etc.

After Kasya Roizman and Chava Kaminker immigrated to Israel and Efraim Abramowitch left to work for the movement's main leadership, we were left without guidance, but we did not stop to exist. Although, at that time, 1939-40, the persecution had already begun against everything related to Zionism and various movements ("*Maccabi*," "*Hashomer Hatzair*" and "*HaOved*") ceased their activities, we continued to operate on a very limited scale, without the same momentum and joy of life that were typical of our activities before, but we did not stop to exist, under no circumstances!

On winter evenings we gathered in one of the small rooms in the gymnasium, reminisced about days gone by, embroidered dreams of days to come, which will be better than the gloomy days of the present. During the summer evenings we sat on two benches outside, which were enough for all who came, and sang very sad songs that suited our mood in those days. I will only mention the names of those I remember from those days: Roska Gordon, Katya Abramowitch, Dvora'le Bilinowitch, Dudik Kogan, Vebtchik, Ayza Tzukerman, Aharonchick Trachtman and I, your servant.

On 28 June 1940, the city was captured by the Soviets. Our activities came to end and everyone went his own way.

Group of young members of "*Gordonia*" (scouts) in the late 1930s

[Page 91]

"Hashomer Hatzair" Branch in Akkerman
by Tzvi Giladi (Grisha Misionezhnik)

Translated by Sara Mages

The federation of *"Hashomer Hatzair"* in Akkerman was founded in 1928 and its founders were students of the Hebrew Gymnasium "Tarbut." It was a grassroots movement, which spoke to the heart of the working youth and managed to capture it to the Zionist idea. We gathered, around the branch, the Jewish youth who aspired to fully realize the Zionist idea. The Jewish residents in Akkerman lived under the harsh hand of the Romanians who lived right on the border. The separating Liman River winked to the youth… we were influenced quite a bit by the Russian youth. At the same time that *"Hashomer Hatzair"* was founded the rest of the youth movements were also founded: *"Gordonia," "Maccabi"* and *"Betar."* We acquired he inspiration and the values, on which we educated and were educated, from the Hebrew Gymnasium. In one respect, our activity was more difficult than that of other youth movements. We mainly absorbed the working youth while *"Gordonia"* mainly concentrated on the gymnasium students who spoke Hebrew fluently and it was easy to educate them. Our counselors knew that they had to work hard with these youth and only thanks to their loyalty, and boundless dedication, they overcome the difficulties.

Our branch was well organized and our members enjoyed their time there and also acquired knowledge and education. The members of the branch were also members of *"Maccabi"* and engaged in many sporting activities. Our performances, and parades in the city streets, delighted the hearts of the Jewish residents, especially on the holidays and festivals.

We were blessed with talented youth and did our best to encourage them. Our members were active in the "Yiddish Literary Theater Corner" under the guidance of Pesach Kleiman. We participated in many plays at the Municipal Theater and the proceeds from the shows allowed us to maintain our club. We considered it our duty to do everything possible to ensure our existence and published *"Hashomer Hatzair"* newspaper which helped to acquire members and fans for our branch. We became involved in the general Zionist activity in the city and the activities for the National Funds.

The world conference of *"Hashomer Hatzair,"* which was held is Vrútky (Czechoslovakia) in 1929, provoked unrest among our members when NEZAH (Pioneering Zionist Youth) left the movement. There were heated arguments following the split on the direction, and the ideology, of the movement, but we wisely and boldly tackled the problems and came out stronger because we knew how to direct our older and established members to help those who had ideological doubts.

We were helped by the emissaries who came from Israel. From among them I especially remember: Natan Bistritzky, Tzvi Zohar, Zev Bloch, Givony and Shadmi from Kibbutz Ma'abarot. The summer colonies that we arranged in the Carpathian Mountains, especially the summer colony in Kushna which ended with an executive day with the participation of Tzvi Zohar, left their strong impression and were a source of inspiration for the activities of our branch.

Counselors of "Hashomer Hatzair" branch in Akkerman

Standing right to left: **Grisha Misionezhnik (Tzvi Giladi), Shmuel Miniali, a counselor from the city of Bielce [Belz], Pusia Yarnowski, David Malkin**

[Page 92]

A meeting of "Hashomer Hatzair" in the Akkerman region

Graduates of "Hashomer Hatzair" in Akkerman

[Page 93]

In the course of time, youth from the studying youth circles joined the branch and the number of members considerably increased. There was a lot of cultural activity. Literary evenings and joint reading were held, as well as many entertainment and social activities. We also initiated the establishment of *"Gordonia"* branches in the immediate vicinity and helped to develop them. In 1932, the first group left for *Hakhshara* [training], and a year later our first members immigrated to Eretz Yisrael. The activity in the branch continued until 1940 with the Russian occupation.

We can now find the members of the branch in Akkerman in Kibbutz Kfar Masaryk, Kibbutz Ruhama, Kibbutz Shamir and other kibbutzim. They remained loyal to the movement that raised them and continued on their way.

Of the instructors who worked at the branch it is worth mentioning: Shmuel Miniali, Tzvi (Grisha) Misionezhnik, David Malkin, Pusia Yarnowski and Shifra Ternopol.

Group of graduates and administrators of "Hashomer Hatzair" in Akkerman

Right to left (seated): **Pusia Yarnowski. Ida Gordon, unidentified, Shifra, Manya Gordon, Yisrael Ganpolsky**
Second row (standing): **David Malkin, Shmuel Miniali, Grisha Misionezhnik, Batya, Liuba Shmoish, Chana Manos**

[Page 94]

Betar in Akkerman

by Shmuel Gaber

Translated by Sara Mages

In the summer of 1927, while visiting the community library under the management of Mr. Sternshis z"l, I came across a newspaper in which was an article about the activities of a youth group called "Brit Yosef Trumpeldor" in the city of Danzig. This article listed the principles and the foundations of this movement. At the end of this article it said that every young Jew is asked to submit, to a certain address, a handwritten essay describing the life of the Jewish community in his place of residence, and also indicate if there are young people in this community who want to build their future in Eretz Yisrael. We, a group of young people in Akkerman, students of "Tarbut," saw the need to respond to this article because the principles outlined in this article seemed to us. We sent our address and waited for an answer. This is how our first contact with the Betar movement began.

We met often, even before we officially belonged to this movement, organized trips, engaged in fishing, sailed in boats, etc. We borrowed the boats from the residents of the village of Tasir, who made their living in the summer from fishing and in the winter from collecting reeds for roofing. Our activity entered a higher phase after Yitzchak Starec, who studied in Italy and came to Akkerman for vacations, joined us Yitzchak's father was a loyal and devoted Zionist activist who showed great interest in distributing the Hebrew book. In Italy, Yitzchak was greatly influenced by Gribaldi's teachings and ideas, and it was reflected in all his conversations with us. From him, we first heard about the life of the Italian nation and its history, the gap between the various strata, about the Christian church that delayed the progress of the masses of Italian people, etc. Gribaldi, and his friends, were introduced to us by Yitzchak as leaders who led the masses of people in the struggle for freedom and liberation from bondage. He adorned these heroes with a charming aura of admiration and prestige, which may not have been so much in tune with reality, but was very much in tune with our tendencies and emotions, and our hidden longings. Yitzchak read us poems by Tchernichovsky, Frug and others, and also tried to convince us to choose different hobbies to avoid boredom and idleness. There is no doubt that he had a great influence on those who came into contact with him and, by the summer of 1928, there were already about 40 young people in our circle. The most prominent in this circle were: Aharon Braski, B. Arbit and Zvi Schechter. The last was a resident of Sarata, but was active in our circle during his studies at "Tarbut" in Akkerman.

One day, we received a letter from Danzig to which was attached a note from the Betar commission announcing the visit of the leader, Aryeh Dissentchik, to our city. The activity of the movement across the Diaspora was described on a separate page.

When we got the news we started to prepare for the anticipated visit. The main problem was - finding a suitable place for the meeting with the important guest since our one and a half room apartment was not suitable for this purpose. This problem was soon resolved. An empty warehouse at the soda factory owned by Y. Gershkowitz, which was far from the city center, was prepared for the meeting. After we renovated it, and equipped it with benches for sitting, it also served as our club.

One day, at the end of June 1928, we welcomed the distinguished guest at the train station. B. Rabinowitz and I represented the young branch of Betar, and the conversation between us was conducted in Hebrew. The visitor was interested to visit the city and meet with personalities, who were close to the Zionist idea but not yet organized in a party framework. The meeting of all the Betarim in the city was set for the early hours of the evening, and since also young people, who were not yet organized in our ranks asked to participate in this meeting, we decided that everyone can come. The meeting was very exciting. We asked the guest to lecture in Yiddish since only a few understood Hebrew, and he did. As he spoke, he also translated various words and concepts into Russian to facilitate their understanding. The hall, in which the meeting was held, was packed and many heard the lecturer's words standing. After the lecture there were also questions and comments from those present, most revolved around the issue of military education highlighted in Mr. Dissentchik's words. During the days of Mr. Dissentchik's stay, the branch leadership was established and an action plan was drawn up for the next six months. This was our first opportunity to become acquainted withthe aims and principles of the Betar movement, and the Betar organization was officially established in Akkerman. We were ordered to set up recruiting companies according to the instructions of the commission in Eretz Yisrael, to begin military training according to the possibilities in the place, and to prepare for immigration to Eretz Yisrael.

In October 1928, Akiva Brun (Kolya) visited us during his tour of Romania on behalf of the national "*HeHalutz*" movement, in order to explore the possibilities of recruiting Betarim for mixed *Hakhshara* companies. He also demanded that we prepare companies for *Hakhshara* towards immigration to Eretz Yisrael. We also heard from the visitor about a plan for a regional conference of Betar and the establishment of separate *Hakhshara* battalions in accordance with the decision of the institutions and the Betarim, who returned from "*HeHalutz*" general *Hakhshara* points and did not consider them asuitable framework for the training of the members of Betar.

I remember well the meeting with Kolya because I, and several other members (B. Rabinowitch, V. Hershkowitz and S. Frank), proposed that we join the Foreign Legion in order to study, in the framework of the legion, the theory of war under desert conditions so we would be able to implement the training, and the theory, in Eretz Yisrael. Kolya strongly rejected the idea and thoroughly explained the reasons for it, and we accepted his explanation.

Over time, the students of the Hebrew Gymnasium joined Betar and brought a new atmosphere to the framework of our branch. Along with that, we started to recruit Yiddish and Russian speaking members from other strata of the local population. Those, who excelled the most in the activity of recruiting new members, were: B. Arbit, B. Frenkel. A. Lapida, Shraga Cohen, Yosef Youngerleev, Z. Goldman and M. Girshfeld. With the increase of the number of members in the branch, a new headquarter, under the leadership of B. Arbit, was elected. His deputies were: the writer of these lines and Buria Rabinowitch. Yosef Youngerleev served as secretary and the sports instructor was Z. Goldman. Later, when A. Barski arrived in Akkerman, he was added as a cultural instructor. The members' activity was not only limited to activities within the framework of the branch, but for many other social and entertainment activities: joint visit to the cinema, walks in the public park, bathing in the sea and the Liman River, participation in the festivities etc.

Over time, a trio, which managed all the branch activities, was formed: B. Arbit, B. Rabinowitch and the writer of these lines. Each of this trio was in charge of a particular field of action. B. Arbit - the preparation of programs for educational activities with the emphasis on Zionist literature and joint reading from the books of Zionist leaders. B. Rabinowitch served as treasurer, raised money from various institutions and personalities, and also instituted the monthly tax every member had to pay. This tax didn't bring a lot of money, but it was also important educationally. I dealt with public relations, connections with institutions and personalities in the city, and also with other movements. It is worth noting that, despite the ideological contradictions between Betar and Poalei Zion we had a fair relationship and were helped, quite a bit, by Poalei Zion's large library for the sake of conceptual debates between us

[Page 95]

Group of Betar members in Akkerman

Of our active circles, it is necessary to note:

Camping circle, to which the affiliation was free at the choice of the members themselves. A training circle, that its main activist was my friend, Yakov Weinstein. The material for this circle was mainly drawn from the Scout's sources. A circle for fencing with sticks, which was a very popular sport in those days. A scout guide (Russian) agreed to teach us this sport since we saw it as self-defense training. Selected groups demonstrated fencing exercises in the festivities conducted by the branch. There was also a special circle for the preparation of public trials under the guidance of Busia Arbit. After his immigration to Israel the circle was guided by Aharon Braski z"l. Busia elected the presiding judge, the judges, the experts and the witnesses according to their education and skills. I remember that one of the issues that aroused a great deal of interest was restraint, in other words, the methods of reaction in Eretz Yisrael against riots and rioting Arabs. The first aid circle should also be mentioned. It was conducted in conjunction with sources outside the movement and, of course, was assisted by physicians' guidance. At Rabbi Youngerleev's recommendation, the circle received various tools and materials from the Jewish hospital, and great help was provided to us by Dr. Schwartzman.

[Page 96]

The residents of Akkerman were known throughout the area for their great affection for the beaches of the Liman and the sea. Therefore, it was natural that one of the most active circles during the summer was the circle for boating and swimming which was headed by Zenvel Goldman z"l. The circle rented fishing boats and trained the Betarim in water sports. The activities of this circle took place in the evenings, and sometimes until midnight.

The first contacts with the local Revisionist Party were established after the visit of Michael Yehenson z"l on Rosh Hashanah 1930. The most active liaison between these two organizations was M. Clapouch. These connections also helped us financially, and we rewarded the party with our activities towards the elections for the Zionist congresses and in other operations when our young people's help was needed.

From the days of my activity in Betar I remember, to this day, many operations and celebrations in all their details. I would never forget the celebration of "Vow Day," which took place on the birthday of the leader of Betar, Zev Jabotinsky. The Betar branch in Akkerman was also awarded the visit of Jabotinsky. It was in 1939, but, to my regret, I was not in Akkerman during this visit. When Jabotinsky arrived in Akkerman he told his escorts that he wanted to go to the Liman's shore and glance to the other side of the river in order to see, maybe for the last time (as he said), the coast of Tirsapol and Odessa. For a short while, the Betarim stood in formation, at absolute silence, with the leader of Betar at the Liman shore. Later Jabotinsky thanked his escorts to allow him this exciting visit.

After many members left for *Hakhshara* and immigrated to Eretz Yisrael, there was, of course, a change of personnel and a new shift entered into a blessed activity until the outbreak of the World War and the Russian occupation.

[Page 97]

Betar's Hakhshara group, among them members of the Akkerman branch

Betar formation next to the club

Group of Betar members

[Page 98]

S. Gaber, chairman of Betar branch in Akkerman

The commanders of Betar in Akkerman with the branch chairman S. Gaber

Group of Betar graduates in Akkerman

[Page 100]

Chapters of Memories, Lifestyle and Folklore

The Akkerman Steppe

I sailed to the ocean of a wide continent,
My cart was immersed in greenery, like a rowing boat;
Inside the steppe waves, in the sea of glorious flowers,
I pass the coral island of whispering thistle.

Twilight descends, not a road in sight,
I look up at the sky, searching for a guiding star,
There in the distance a burning cloud? a glowing morning star?
The Dniester sparkles there, Akkerman's chandelier.
(A. Mickiewiczs: "Crimean Sonnets"

In the City I Love
by Yisrael Schildkrauth
Translated by Sara Mages

In my eyes are reflected
the landscapes.
And paths I have trod
have straightened my stride –
tired and lovely steps.
(Leah Goldberg)

Akkerman, my hometown, the city where I went out into the world, where I grew up, where I took my first steps in public activity, in which I became acquainted with Zionism and started to dream of a Jewish homeland – – –

I loved wandering in the clean city streets after a pouring rain when all the sidewalks and roads, which were paved with black granite stones, were beautifully polished. The rows of trees on both side of the sidewalks dripped rainwater even after the rain stopped, and a few drops dripped from top the wet trees.

Luckily for Akkerman that it was built on sand that immediately absorbed rainwater without leaving muddy puddles. The rain washed the city streets and left it clean.

I loved the quiet summer nights when families sat in the courtyards enjoying the serenity of the night, listening to the croaking of the frogs in the swamps on the banks of the Leman, or the sound of the trumpet from the army barracks at the edge of the city.

I remember summer evenings when in our yard gathered Yeshayahu Gurin, Yakov Icht, my eldest brother Yakov, Yisrael and Mania Shrira – who later was the first Hebrew kindergarten teacher in our city and was known to all as "Aunt Mania." They watched the stars, measured celestial paths, and gave their opinions on the movements of each star as if they were astronomers by birth... As a young boy I joined this group and listen to their arguments. I heard names such as "Saturn," "Mars," the "Milky Way," etc. Thrilled and excited I stood next to these "astronomers" and marveled at their knowledge of the stellar moves and the paths of the sky. It is interesting that the moon itself did not receive much attention from this group, as if they did not find interest in it, except in the days of "new moon" at the beginning of each month.

[Page 101]

I loved waking with dawn in the summer to the clear voice of the Armenian "Karabat" and his continuous call, "He Bidile!" This "Karabat" wandered every morning in the city streets carrying in his hands his "Bidile" – a kind of a long and narrow Armenian pastry, and announced it aloud.

Osip Danilovich Rivkin

Short, a real dwarf, a forty-year-old single man was this Osip when I first met him. He was a man with a broad education, experienced in Russian culture and proficient in its literature, its prose and poetry, and, of course, his spoken language was Russian. He dealt with writing feuilletons in Russian for the local daily newspaper and his salary was very small. For this reason his clothes were also meager and shabby, and his shoes were worn out but with high heels probably to increase his short stature in the eyes of people. His colleagues in the editorial staff abused and ridiculed him mercilessly, but he restrained himself as long as he could continue to publish his daily feuilleton in the newspaper since he saw the essence and content of his life in his literary activity, and if he ever had the opportunity to hear words of appreciation about one of his feuilletons – there was no limit to his joy and that day was a happy day in his life.

One day, when he entered the office with his feuilleton he was greeted by Lyossi Constantiner, one of the editorial members, with the greeting: "Good morning Gospodin Kilometer!" Everyone stared at him in amazement and he explained: his weight – a kilogram, his height – a meter, and you have a kilometer... everyone broke out laughing but Osip Danilovich could not stand this insult. He left the editorial building, slammed the door angrily with a determined decision – not to return to this place again. However, his financial distress and especially his love of writing, which was like the elixir of life for him, overcame him and his decision. One morning he entered modestly the editorial building and sat at his desk as if nothing had happened. Since then he decided to take a different tactic: to laugh along with those who laugh at him and not to show that he was offended. It turns out that it was a good tactic because, over time, his friends got tired of mocking him and calling him by various derogatory names, and they let go of him.

Osip's father, R' Daniel Rivkin, a wise and educated Jew, of course treated his son and his shortcomings with compassion but unintentionally also gave him a certain nickname. One clear morning when Daniel stood with his associates, the "*Ogolnikim*," on a street corner and conversed with them on matters of utmost importance, he saw his son Osip skipping and running to editorial building. He told his interlocutors:

[Page 102]

look and see, my *ishon* [small man] is running there... from then on Osip was stuck with the nickname "Enosh'l" which was, in any case, more sympathetic than the nickname given to him by the editorial staff – "Kilometer."

Indeed, it was amusing and entertaining to see tiny Osip in his strange gait as he swung his right arm from side to side but, on the other hand, he was an interesting man who was versed in social issues. He knew by heart the poems of Pushkin, Moshe Krylov and others of the great of Russian literature and I really enjoyed sitting with him and talking to him on matters of literature and current affairs. All the abuse did not make him to lose his temper. He was full of joy of life and even content with what he had, even though what he had was bitter and tiny...

The "*Ogolnikim*"

The "*Ogolnikim*" were famous in Akkerman. They were sharp witted grain and wine merchants who stood at the corner of Nikolaevsky and Sofievsky streets (and for this reason they were called "*Ogolnikim*"). They negotiated with each other, talked about politics, gossiped and joked. From here, from the "Ogol," also came most of the nicknames that were stuck to the residents of our city, and from them it was possible to correctly define the nature, or the character, of the person bearing the nickname. Indeed, these were clever Jews and there was in them a kind of fusion of Motke Chabad and Hershele Ostropoler. With that, it is worth noting that they also helped to develop various public institutions, they were not stingy and they contributed quite a bit to the public life in Akkerman. I liked the "*Ogolnikim*" because they were always ready to help in a matter mitzvah and stand by the side of needy Jews in times of distress.

Hersh "The Exaggerator"

One of my favorite "*Ogolnikim*" was R' Hersh Sheyner, or as we called him, Hersh "The Exaggerator." He was tall and broad-shouldered, adorned with a tiny yellowish beard, his eyes were small and his nose – was a sizable nose, squashed a little, as if it was spread all over his face, in short – a nose that even our ancestors did not have... This Hersh was a wise Jew, had knowledge that came from actual experience, honest and pleasant to others. He was a constant source of jokes and catchwords, lies and exaggerations, and hence his nickname. There was usually some nucleus of truth in his stories, but to this nucleus R' Hersh added much more, from his imagination and exaggerations, to beautify the story and add a dash of grace and flavor to it. He told these stories in public as if they were adorned – with words of truth, quietly and calmly, and he enjoyed seeing the homeowners who listened attentively to his heartwarming stories.

He was not a native of Akkerman, from a distance he came to our city, but soon found his place among the city's dignitaries thanks to his intelligence, his extensive knowledge and joy of life. He liked to analyze, so to speak, the names of people and prove how incompatible they are with their true essence, and so he preached:

"The names and nicknames of people deprive their true essence. Take for example a Jew like Shabtai Kliger. Everyone knows how far he is from being smart, and he was given the name "Kliger" [wise]... And what would you say about a Jew like Hersh Vayser (white)? after all, the man is blacker than black... And a Jew like Avraham Nidriker (short) – what does he have to do with it when he, as we all know, is as long and slender like a *lulav*? And Alex Royter [red], the one from the petrol and Kerosene tanks on the Leman bank – is he a redhead? after all, his hair is as black as charcoal! And Hershel Blinder [blind] – what to him and this name, while he is gifted with sharp eyes and can see from a great distant... And why go so far? Take me myself. Please look at my face and see what kind of a "*Krasavets*" (handsome) I am – and I am actually called Hersh Sheyner [beautiful]!? So, and similarly, he preached *parashat* "names," but he also had other "*parshot*" which he generously adorned with exaggerations and catchwords that were later repeated by all.

Chairman of the community, the philanthropist Moshe Milstein

[Page 103]

The Uncles

Whenever I remember my uncles I see capotes [long black coats], beards, sidelocks and God-fearing men, and most importantly – good and merciful Jews who all served in holiness for his name.

Uncle Shalom Itseles (R' Shalom Brand), a tall bearded Jew, was "*Baal Korei*" [master of the reading] in Beit HaMidrash. He was widowed in his youth and remained a widower until the end of his life. He had six sons. On the Shabbat and holidays he read aloud the weekly Torah portion in Beit HaMidrash and was meticulous in biblical flavors. After his death his eldest son, David, inherited his place as "*Baal Korei.*"

Uncle Haim Chava-Leibes (R' Haim Kaminker), was an exalted scholar. His "right" in Beit HaMidrash was the blowing of the shofar on Rosh Hashanah and the *Ne'ila* prayer on Yom Kippur. He carefully observed the time of the *tekiah* [blowing] and on the conclusion of Yom Kippur he eagerly waited for the appearance of the first star. I remember that R' Shmaya Telenofer, who lost patience with the fast, hurried him every year: "Haim *blaz*! (blow!), but he did not answer him and only after the first star appeared he took his shofar, wrapped himself in his *tallit* and blew his *tekiah gedolah* after which all the worshipers declared "next year in Jerusalem."

Uncle David Chava–Leibes (R' David Dorfman), was "*Baal Musaf*" in Beit HaMidrash, he observed the mitzvoth and was heedful of a light precept as of a weighty one. In awe he approached the "pillar" [lectern] for the "*Musaf*" prayer and every word of the prayers came out of his mouth with clear pronunciation and pleasant melody. He died at a young age of a fatal illness and left my aunt Hinda, his wife, in widowhood with seven children. She took care of all the needs of her children, educated them in the spirit of Judaism and Zionism and some of them immigrated to Eretz Israel. She was also able to fulfill her wish, sometime later she immigrated to Israel and joined her family.

Uncle Moshe Itseles (R' Moshe ?aytsbli?), was first *gabbai* and "*Baal Korei*" in the kloyz and he accompanied his reading of the Torah with the sigh "*oy vey mameniu!*" Since his livelihood was plentiful as the owner a thriving fabric store, people did not understand why he sighed so much, and when he was asked about it, he replied: a Jew must sigh because the Jewish nation is in the Diaspora, and the addition "*mameniu*" for what reason? – because my honored mother was a great righteous woman. Therefore, my uncle earned the nickname "Moshe *mameniu*"...

Uncle Shmuel Chava–Leibes (R' Shmuel Gordion), was "*Baal Musaf*" in the kloyz on the Sabbath and holidays. He was kind, humble and gentle. When he wore the Sabbath capote and the black felt hat when he walked on Sabbath eve to the kloyz, it was possible to see the Shabbat Queen immersed on his slightly browned face which was adorned with a neatly combed black beard.

And above all, uncle Moshe Aharon Getzis – the "*matmid*" [diligent], a tall slender Jew with very long arms and legs. He was short–sighted and when he studied the Torah he wore a strange eyeglass frame without lenses, that one of the small holes was blocked with a round piece of tin, while the other small hole was completely open. What was the secret of these "glasses" – it was a mystery that no one knew its meaning...

[Page 104]

He was completely immersed in the study of the Torah and the fulfillment of the mitzvah "And you shall meditate on it day and night." Before dawn he made his way to Beit HaMidrash, summer and winter, sat down in his regular place by the big stove and studied incessantly. He was completely free from the worries of earning a living because his wife, Feiga, took care of it and she was a woman of valor. What bothered this uncle of mine was the fact that he could not keep the commandment of charity since the penny was never in his pocket. What did he do? He took an empty box of shoe polish, filled it with snuff, put it on his desk, and whoever is hungry – will come and smell, free of charge... this is also charity.

Dr. Shaul Zlering

Dr. Zlering arrived in our city at the invitation of the State District Hospital where he served as Chief Physician for the duration of his stay in Akkerman. From the beginning he was a foreigner in our city and no one knew his nature, until he turned to one of the city's Zionist activists and asked to purchase a Zionist shekel since that year was an election year for the Zionist Congress. Only then it became known that he was a Zionist and that he spoke Hebrew. During his studies in Switzerland he was chairman of the Zionist Students Association and was involved in public activities in the city. He was elected member of the community committee and served as chairman of the community culture committee. He was also active in "Maccabi," "HeHalutz," "OZE" and the Zionists funds, and lectured at the Hebrew gymnasium on subjects in the field of hygiene.

The management of Kupat Milve, 1924

As Secretary of the community culture committee I met with him frequently. I also visited him at his home since at that time he was also the chairman of the culture committee, and I had the opportunity to see how he educated his two daughters to love the Land of Israel. Everyone respected and appreciated him for his qualities and good temperament. Even the ultra-orthodox in the city treated him with respect even though they knew he was non-observant. Once, a quarrel broke out between him and R' David Brend, who was a distinguished scholar and opposed Zionism. In the heat of the debate Dr. Zlering said to David: in the end one of your children will also immigrate to Eretz Yisrael. R' David answered him: "is Dr. Shaul one of the prophets? After all, we know to whom the prophecy was given after the destruction of the temple"... "That's remains to be seen ..." answered Dr. Zlering.

[Page 105]

And indeed, a few years later R' David's son rebelled against his father, collected in secret the money needed for travel expenses, and one clear day escape from his home without saying goodbye to anyone and after many hardships he arrived in Eretz Yisrael. R' David did not reconcile with this son to the end of his life.

After a while the second "revolt" broke out in R' David's house. It was his youngest daughter, Dvora, who entered Gordonia and immigrated to Israel, but this time it was in her father's knowledge, though certainly not with his consent.

Dr. Zlering speaks at the meeting of former residents of Akkerman in Israel

In the 1930s, Dr. Zlering immigrated to Israel with his family. He integrated well into the Israeli society, continued to work in his profession and also engaged in public activity. The mayor, Meir Dizengoff, sent a letter to the Akkerman community in response to a request from the community committee regarding Dr. Zlering (see copy of this letter in this book). When I immigrated to Israel after the War of Independence, and I was still living in the immigrant house, Dr. Zlering immediately came to visit me to encourage me on my new path in Israel. This is how the connection between us was renewed, and when the organization of former residents of Akkerman was established he was the chairman and I was the secretary, and we worked together again in close and harmonious cooperation.

A malignant disease caused his death after surgery abroad and his bones were brought for burial in Israel. This good and pleasant man (was about 60 at the time of his death), was always ready to help a fellow man and justified his nickname given to him in Akkerman, "*A voyl mentshl.*"

The Jewish Bank

"*Das Yiddishe Bankel*" – this is how the Jewish bank was known by the "commoners." The bank's general meetings were attended by commoners and privileged people, and for many these meetings served as a platform to express their opinions. At these meetings it was possible to hear broken Yiddish spiced with faulty Russian, and vice versa. Therefore, it was natural that every annual general meeting became a kind of an entertaining show on a small scale. The "nail" of this "show" was usually the closing speech of the chairman of the bank's management, H. Gvirtzman the lame, who responded to the criticisms leveled at the management, which were sometimes very harsh.

This Gvirtzman was a former lawyer, who left his profession with the entry of the Romanians into Bessarabia because he did not want to identify with them. He was a clever and witty Jew and knew how to answer his accusers. He responded to the critics with sarcasm and a witty irony and without a shred of compassion. He took advantage of every slip of the tongue, and every mistake in the words of the debaters, and mocked them as the large audience accompanied his words with shouts and stormy applause. He had the upper hand, and a long time after the end of the "show," the general meeting, the Jews of Akkerman quoted his catchwords and jokes until the next general meeting of the bank.

"Tarbut" gymnasium

Last, but not least, our "Tarbut" gymnasium. It was a place of spiritual importance for the Jews of Akkerman and the surrounding area, for all the pioneering Zionist youth movements and everyone who spoke Hebrew. Although it was the center of our lives the gymnasium always suffered from a shortage of financial means, and it was necessary to organize balls whose proceeds were dedicated to the gymnasium. However, the value of these balls was not only in the financial gain, but also in their being a source of joy, entertainment and spiritual enjoyment for all the residents. A special team devoted themselves to the preparation of the artistic program of these balls and included among others: L. Berkowitch, Hersh Brudsky, Yitzchak Arbit and also me your servant. Each such program included sketches, humorous passages and satire that reflected the local experience, solo performances in music and singing, etc. These balls, as well as the buffets prepared by volunteer women, have become a tradition. The dancing continued until the third reserve – and the city of Akkerman rejoiced and was glad.

[Pages 106]

Akkerman – the City of My Birth
by Yosef Gur-Arye
Translated by Sara Mages

Zalman Shneur, the renowned writer and poet, opens the first chapter of his book "*Fendri HaGibor*" ["Fendri the Hero"] with these words: "Where are you Jews strong as oak trees? You, that in your eyes, the eyes of an innocent child, was hidden the force of life. You knew to give a hand and protect your brothers and sisters at all times of trouble. " Like him, I'll also open my memories of Akkerman: Where are you, the Jews of Akkerman, strong as oak trees, the innocent and righteous, laborers, farmers and simple folks, who only want to live in peace and tranquility, have bread to eat and clothes to wear. They were happy with their lot and content with little.

The Home of My Father of blessed memory

My father arrived to Akkerman in 1912 from the district of Ludmir in Wolyn (Poland-Russia) at the recommendation of his uncle, HaRav R' Yitzchak Wertheim, who served as a rabbi in the city of Bendery [Bender, Moldova] near Akkerman. In Akkerman, my father was accepted as a "Rabbi" (according to the family tree my father was a seventh generation to Baal Shem Tov) although it was customary in our extensive family that all the boys had to receive a permit to officiate as rabbis. In my father's family the title "Rabbi" was inherited from generation to generation, and for that reason all the sons were called - HR"HR (Half Half-Rabbi Rav). Anyway, my father served as a

Rav-Rabbi in Akkerman until 1935 because in this year he moved his place of residence to the capital city of Bucharest.

As it's customary, our house, a rabbi's house, was used as a public house. It was always buzzing like a beehive and people from all the circles of the Jewish population entered and left it, each person with his case and according to his needs. It should be noted, that in terms of religious life Akkerman was different from many cities in the Diaspora. It was customary to say: the most liberal city across Russia (in terms of Jewish religion) is Odessa, whereas the most liberal city in Bessarabia is Akkerman. The Jewish population in this city wasn't the largest and at the verge of the Second World War it didn't reach more than 8,000 persons. At first, my father had trouble acclimatizing among Jews who were free with their opinions because in the towns of Wolyn, from which he came, the Jewish population was ultra-orthodox. But, it's possible say that after a brief stay in Akkerman these Jews endeared him and he endeared them. Father appreciated the proper attributes of Akkerman's Jews: honesty, fine hospitality, decency, etc. I remember that when I was a child I used to hide behind my father's tall chair, which was made of bamboo, and listened attentively to matters of Jewish law that were brought before him. More than once these deliberations continued until well after midnight and my mother, may she rest in peace, found her child sleeping soundly behind the chair...

[Page 107]

Of course and as usua,l the discussions focused on matrimonial matters, between brothers and sisters, parents and their children, business partners, inheritances and wills, etc. The deliberations weren't always calm and sometimes the shouts between the "sides" frightened the children and the neighbors in the middle of the night. My father, who was endowed with an extraordinary patience, exhausted all the possibilities of compromise and didn't stop the deliberations before he had found the appropriate solution.

I remember an episode that characterizes the Jews of Bessarabia who, as we know, weren't known as great scholars like the Jews of Lita and Poland, but on the other hand were proficient in the laws of eating...From time to time my father was invited for litigation in one of the towns near Akkerman. The litigants were horse dealers. After my father issued a ruling to the satisfaction of both sides, one of the litigants declared in a loud voice that he was careful with the matters of the Sabbath to the highest level, and to prove it he opened and said: Rabbi, I once traveled from town to town. That day was Friday, so I whipped my horses with all my strength because I knew that the next day is the Sabbath and I had to reach the town by Saturday morning so, God forbid, I'll not violate the Sabbath...

Another story, which is also typical of the Jews of Akkerman, has reached my ears. My father told the story to his brother-in-law, HaRav Yosef Wertheim who was rabbi in Hurbieszow Poland, when he visited the city of Bendery before he immigrated to Israel. And so father told: it happened in 1913, the year in which he began serving as a rabbi in Akkerman. On Sabbath morning when father went to *Beit Hamidrash* he had to cross the fish market. And here he sees the chief *Gabai* of the Great Synagogue standing in the middle of the market. The *Gabai* greeted him with a broad Shabbat Shalom, but felt the need to add: "Have you heard such a thing? About two hundred carts of fish arrived to the market today and the price of fish literally skyrocketed - 30 Kopikot a kilo!"...

HaRav S. Ingerleib

Of course, there were also Jewish scholars in Akkerman, who were heedful of a light precept as of a weighty one, and we shouldn't learn from the individual about the entire community. I remember well the sharp-witted Jews who studied the daily *Gemara* page like: R' Chaim Keminker, R' Moshe Aharon, R' David Brener and more, but their number can be estimated in dozens and not in hundreds.

I remember the many gatherings that were held with great splendor on the Sabbath and on the holidays, but I especially remember the *mitzvah*-meals that were held on the last day of Passover to mark the miracle that happened to Baal Shem Tov who was saved from drowning in the Aegean Sea on his way to Eretz-Yisrael. According to the story the ship, in which Baal Shem Tov and his family traveled, capsized at the middle of the sea. They miraculously found an abandoned inn and in it they found dumplings kosher for Passover.

Since, as aforementioned, my father was related to the family of Baal Shem Tov (seventh generation), these meals were held with great enthusiasm and festivity, and many Jews (even though there weren't many Hassidim in Akkerman) gathered to celebrate. Father sat at the head of the table and the Hassidic melodies didn't stop until late into the night.

The Plan to Immigrate to Cyprus

An important event that is etched in my memory is - the plan, to immigrate to Israel via Cyprus that my father was one of its initiators. The matter occurred at the end of the 1920s. At that time the economic crisis was at its height and it was followed by distress and shortage. In addition, these were also years of drought that were well felt in Akkerman and its environment. The Jews have been hit hard by this crisis and walked gloomy and worried. At the same time my father z"l and other activists from the town like Baruch Gevet z"l, Steinberg from the town of "Shabo" and others, started to think seriously about immigration to Eretz-Yisrael and formed a special association for this purpose. However, the British Mandate Government had its own laws. Only a few immigration certificates were given to the wealthy, and only those who were able to prove that they were wealthy received them. I don't know who the main initiator of the plan was, but a number of important homeowners, who belonged to the association, decided that if they can't immigrate directly to Eretz-Yisrael - they'll be able to get closer to it. The plan was: to travel to Cyprus and stay there till the storm blows over, and from Cyprus to Eretz-Yisrael was just a matter of one jump. If my memory serves me, about five hundred Jews joined the aforementioned association. They paid membership fees to the association and decided to send two delegates to Cyprus in order to test the possibilities of existence there and, above all, to find the most efficient ways to travel from Cyprus to Eretz-Yisrael.

The delegates left, spent some time in Cyprus, returned to Akkerman and reported that it's pretty easy to settle in Cyprus and the immigrants are guaranteed good absorption conditions. However, it's not easy to move from Cyprus to Eretz-Yisrael and they shouldn't expect any benefits from the British Mandate Government. This report didn't encourage them and eventually the association was disbanded and the matter ended with great disappointment. However, the matter of this association shouldn't be forgotten because it proves how great the yearning for Zion was, and to what extent the Jews were willing to go in order to reach Eretz-Yisrael.

I immigrated to Israel in 1937 after a period of training that lasted for about three years. My father whispered to me when he accompanied me: you know, my beloved son that we strive with all of our might to immigrate to Israel. Therefore, be a good delegate and make sure that we would be able to follow you.

[Page 108]

With the outbreak of the Second World War all the roads and connections were disrupted. The "immigration request" that I sent to my parents didn't reach its destination and they were only able to immigrate to Israel in 1947. Father was awarded to see the establishment of the State of Israel, but he died of heart attack in 1952 at the age of 64.

It's interesting that shortly before his death he felt that his end was approaching and made all the efforts to publish his sermons and his lineage in two books: A)*"Binyan Shlomo"* - about the weekly Torah portions and the sermons and laws in the small tractates *"Berachot"* and "Shabbat." B) *"Sharsheret Hazahav"* ["The Golden Chain"] which included the sermons of the great Hassidic masters and the details of his genealogy and of his righteous ancestors.

Characters and Figures that are Etched in My Memory

Time has done its usual and erased a lot of things and people, but several characters from those days are etched in my heart and I'll try in the following lines to set, briefly, a memorial for them.

My friend, **Motale Shternish** z"l, was like a brother to me. We grew up and matured together, and my hand never left his hand. In 1928 I traveled to study in a Yeshiva in Kishinev and none of us was able to overcome the longing to the other, and indeed, a year later, Motale also arrived to Kishinev. He was a fine young man and a friend who knew to dispel any feeling of sadness or depression from each friend that he had met. When we walked together - and we were always together - people used to say: here is a pair of jokers. They mainly intended to Motale, but because I was always in his company this nickname also stuck to me. When I traveled to *Hakhshara* [pioneer training] - he also traveled, but he wasn't as lucky as I was and wasn't able to get the desired immigration certificate. According to information that reached me, Motale perished in 1942 in Odessa and I mourn him to this day because he was an intimate fried and I'll always remember him.

Shmuel Sternisht z"l was one of the teachers in Gymnasia "*Tarbut.*" He wasn't just a teacher, but a teacher in his heart and soul. In the manner of the people of Akkerman he was stuck with the nickname "Dubtzi" because he always told us the stories of Sholem Aliechm, especially the story "Motl, Peysi the Cantor's Son," who instead of learning to be a cantor became a nanny to Dubtzi the cantor's hunchback daughter. Big a small called the teacher Shternish "Dubtzi," but he didn't respond. A friendship developed became us because he was also the librarian. He allowed me to search the library and also let me borrow two or three books at a time. He gave me an appetite for reading and I'm grateful to him to this day.

R' Eliyahu Welbitesh z"l was my father's friend. He was a Talne Hassid and in his childhood he visited R' Dudel from Talne together with my father. He was a pleasant looking Jew, a successful merchant, and had a large family. Every morning he came to our house and inquired about the health of the family members. My father z"l honored him with the best *aliyot* [ascents] to the Torah, which were only given to the privileged, and it seems to me that this fact aroused the jealousy of the rest of the worshipers.

His grandson Yehusua (Drori z"l), who always accompanied his grandfather to the synagogue, befriended me. He later became one of the founders of "*Gordonia*" and one of the high officials of the Workers' Federation in Hadera [Israel].

R' Yosef Ben-Zion was a resident of Kamyanets-Podilsky in Podolia and no one knew how he ended up in our town. He was lonely without a relative or a savior, smallish and adorned with a very short goatee. All year long he taught the Torah to the Jewish children in one of the villages near Akkerman, and came to Akkerman for the holidays. Our family, who knew that he was lonely, adopted him and he ate with us each time he came to Akkerman. He had one weakness: he ate and talked very slowly. We used to say in our house - if R' Yosef Ben-Zion had finished his meal - it is a sure sign that dawn has arrived...

Sometimes, during the High Holiday he had the luck to be invited to serve a cantor in one of the towns. At Simchat Torah the clowns used to harass him and urged him to sing "*Adam Yesodo me-afar, ve-sofo le-afar*" ["Man comes from dust and ends in dust"] from the prayers of Yom

Kippur. He tried to trill his voice, but most of the times he wasn't able to. The kids tried to help him and threw handkerchiefs, towels and everything in sight at him, but he never lost his temper.

From my childhood I still remember other homeowners like R' Zeidl Auerbach who knew sickness all of his days. He was a scholar and an enthusiastic *Hassid*. He had a tremendous drinking power and was able to drink, all at once, the water that we kept in a copper jug. His friend was R' Moshe Wizblat who was very skinny, literally "skin and bones" as they used to say in our town. He was God-fearing and a *Hassid* and his nickname was "*Mamenyu*" [mother] because he used to wring his hands and emit a sigh that was accompanied by one word - "*Mamenyu*." He prepared himself for the next world and studied the Torah day and night. His wife had to take care of "this world", meaning that she had to earn a living, and for that purpose she had a textile shop. She was very proud at her educated husband and believed that thanks to him she'll also have a place in heaven.

[Page 109]

Big Jabotinsky and "Little Jabotinsky" in Our City
by Yehoshua Harari–Breger z"l
Translated by Sara Mages

I remember well the appearance of two great Zionist speakers in Akkerman, and they are: Ze'ev Jabotinsky, or as he was called then, Vladimir, and Yosef Shechtman who, due his rhetorical ability, was rewarded by the nickname "Little Jabotinsky." Ze'ev Jabotinsky was well known in Akkerman since he was a native, and a student, of the city of Odessa and his articles in "*Razsvet*" [Dawn], and other newspapers published in Odessa, gained a reputation in the Jewish world. Everyone talked enthusiastically about his rhetorical ability and quoted from his words, and he was especially admired in the youth circles. The topics of his lectures were on the state of the Jews and Judaism because, in those days, it was forbidden to call them in the explicit name: Zionism. If my memory does not mislead me, Jabotinsky had two, or three, appearances in Akkerman, but only one of them was engraved in my memory.

I was a teenager then, but I felt the great anticipation and excitement at home for Jabotinsky's visit. The Zionist activists in the city came to our home and spoke in a whisper with my brother, Yakov z"l, about the preparations for this visit. It was necessary, of course, to send an official Zionist representative to greet the distinguished guest by the ship, and the lot fell on Yosef Rivkin, who was known as "Anush" because of his low stature. Yosef Rivkin rented a carriage, and immediately after Jabotinsky got off the ship "Turgenev" traveled with him to the new "Petersburg" hotel. According to his story, Jabotinsky sat sullen and furious all the way, didn't open his mouth and didn't talk to the man who came to greet him. As they entered the hotel lobby, Rivkin, as is customary, quickly removed the coat from the distinguished guest. The guest did not say a word of thanks but said in Russian: "hang the coat and get out of here." Rivkin, who was very offended, hurried to talk with my brother. He expected, of course, that Jabotinsky would talk to him and he could later quote his words to Akkerman's Zionists, and he received such a welcome...

About seventy years have passed since then, and I still remember Rivkin in his insult. It may be that this fact influenced my attitude towards Jabotinsky's ways and actions, even though I heard from others about the courtesy and good manners of the great Zionist leader.

Jabotinsky's lecture was organized in Akkerman by a certain agent – and even that was a new thing in our city. The agent, of course, was interested in the full payment from every person who came to the lecture, and we, the youngsters, were not allowed to enter. Only after the efforts of our teacher, Stretz, we were given permission to enter and our designated place was in the orchestra pit, between the audience and the stage. The speech itself made a great impression on the audience and was, for a long time, the subject of conversation.

After a while, I had the privilege to be a witness to a brilliant Zionist performance of "Little Jabotinsky." It was in the period between the February revolution of 1917 and the October revolution of 1917. At that time, great preparations were felt throughout Russia towards the elections for the founding conference. The Zionists also organized "meetings" – propaganda meetings, and in one of them appeared Y. Shechtman, who earned a reputation mainly in southern Russia. One day, before the appearance of Y. Shechtman, there was a meeting in our city with the participation of one of the leaders of Poalei Zion Left, and if I am not mistaken, it was Zivion. This speaker remained in Akkerman and attended Shechtman's lecture. He sat quietly and when Shechtman spoke of the great truth that Zionism reveals to the Jewish people, Zivion jumped and interrupted him: "There is a proletarian truth, and there is a bourgeois truth." Shechtman immediately answered him with a verse from Pushkin's poetry and, of course, in Russian: "There is one truth that shines like the sun and bright as the day." The crowd cheered enthusiastically at the decisive answer, but Zivion burst out laughing at the answer. Shechtman answered him in the same language and again quoted a verse from Pushkin: "It is not funny at all when a despicable person contaminates an artistic creation of a painter like Raphael." And again, the audience applauded loudly to the sound of the verses of their beloved poet, Pushkin, whose poems were quoted by all at that time. Indeed, for a good reason they called Shechtman "Little Jabotinsky."

[Page 110]

My Immigration to Israel in the Month of Av 5681

by Yehoshua Harari z"l

Translated by Sara Mages

25 Kislev 5741, marks sixty years of my immigration to Israel together with six of my townsmen, and they are: Avraham Durfman (Kafri), Avraham Serfer, Avraham Margalit, Aharon Brand, Yeshayahu Botoshansky and Yisrael Rabinowitch.

All the formal arrangements for our immigration were as required. We traveled to Kishinev [Chişinău] and reported to Dr. Bernstein–Cohen, head of the Zionist organization in Bessarabia. He gave us a recommendation to Dr. Pineles, who was a delegate to the First Zionist Congress and lived in the city of Glatz. Dr. Pineles took care of our visa to Kushta-Constantinople [Istanbul], which, at that time, was an international sponsor city.

We left Akkerman in one group. All of our family members accompanied us to the train station and several mothers continued with us until we arrived to Glatz and received the visa to Kushta. We arrived there after a night in a stormy sea. Most passengers were seasick, but I was saved from it because of my frequent trips by sea, from Akkerman to Odessa, immunized me and I was able to walk among the sick passengers and provide help.

When we arrived to Kushta, I climbed with another member to the office of "*Vaad HaZirim*" (the Zionist management at that time), which was at the upper part of the city of Kushta. There, they wrote our names in the queue for an immigration visa to Eretz Yisrael. This office also took care of our housing during our stay in Kushta. Two hotels were at their disposal in city but they were occupied by *halutzim* who preceded us, so they took us to the town of Scutari [Üsküdar], on the Asian side of the Sea of Marmara, and after a stay of a few days we moved to "*Mesilla Hadasha*" [new path] colony.

The colony, "*Mesilla Hadasha*," was founded by the people of Bessarabia, among them two former residents of Akkerman: Alberg and Haimovich. The settlers in "*Mesilla Hadasha*" aspired to settle in Eretz Yisrael. When we arrived, we found there a school that its students spoke among themselves in fluent Hebrew, but many of the settlers started to move to the city and Turks worked in the farms.

One of the abandoned houses was made available to us and we waited, together with many *halutzim*, for a visa and a ship to take us to Eretz Israel. Among the *halutzim* in this place was also the writer, A.Z. Ben Yashar, who later served as secretary of the Tel Aviv municipality. He should be credited for the cultural activities that took place there.

A young Turkish man, who befriended me, managed the farm in our house. He taught me Turkish and I became kind of a translator, or the spokesman of our entire group...

From Kushta we left for Eretz Yisrael in the ship "Umbria." It was a large cargo ship and the five hundred passengers were housed inside a storeroom in unbearable density. The ship stopped in a lot of ports but we had no desire to go on tours and we were not even allowed disembark in the ports.

On December 5 1920, the eve of Chanukah 5681, we arrived in Haifa. The ship did not dock in the harbor and we were taken ashore by boats. We were welcomed by Dostrovsky, the representative of "*Vaad HaZirim*." He took us to an immigrants' house, equipped us with vouchers for meals in the workers' kitchen for a few days, and with – – – Quinine pills. Indeed, already on my first evening in Eretz Yisrael I learned to swallow these pills.

Pava Berkov waited for us at the gate. He arrived in Israel, together with our townsmen, Aharon Kaminker and Noah Zukerman, a few months before us. It is interesting that Pava Berkov, who was unemployed and even hungry, was not entitled to receive vouchers for the workers' kitchen. He warned us not to be tempted by the words of the instigators, who wandered among the *halutzim*, spread an evil report about Israel and mocked their immigration.

We were fortunate that the *Histadrut* conference, the founding conference, was held in Haifa when we arrived. It was natural that I wanted to visit this conference, and I even visited. However, it is truthful to say that I was not aware then of the great historical value that this conference might have over the years.

[Page 111]

Our townsman, A. Ravutski, who was a member of Poalei Zion Left, a minister in the government of the Ukrainian Republic after February 1917 and had to flee after the fall of this government – was also in Eretz Yisrael at that time. I was a guest at their home in Akkerman, and when I came to say goodbye to his mother prior to my immigration, she asked me to give her regards to her son in Israel. When I came to Israel I started to look for him. I have been told that I could probably find him at the *Histadrut* conference, and indeed, I located him there. His clothing caught my eye – it was probably a minister's attire, a matter that was out of the ordinary at a workers' conference. I have been told that he had purchased a ship, or several ships, and wanted to lay the foundation for a Jewish fleet, but the business had failed like many beginnings. After the riots of May 1921, he immigrated to the United States and for a while was the editor of Poalei Zion's journal.

When it became known to Aharon Kaminker and Noah Zukerman, who at that time already worked in Zikhron Ya'akov, about our immigration, they sent us a letter asking us to immediately come to Zikhron Ya'akov so we could work on paving the road from Zikhron to Shuni. Five, out of the seven members of our group, followed their advice and traveled to Zikhron, while Avraham Margalit and I remained in Haifa to take care of the transfer of the members' belongings. At the end of that week, on Friday morning, we managed to meet a farmer from Atlit who delivered all kinds of merchandise to shops in Zikhron. He agreed to load our belongings on his cart we and followed it by foot. At dark we arrived at the farmer's house in Atlit. We met the farmer's family, who lived in hardship conditions, and also constantly suffered from fever in the custom of those days. But, I remember that despite the distress he was proud to be a farmer and on Saturday morning, after we spent the night in his meager house, he took us on a tour of his little farm and proudly showed us the fruit trees that he planted among the rocks.

We left all the cargo in the farmer's cart (he brought it to Zikhron the next day) and Margalit and I started to walk in the direction of Zikhron Ya'akov. We passed the Arabic village of Fureidis and also lost our way a little. At dark we arrived in Zikhron Ya'akov in time for the Chanukah party that was held in the *moshava*.

The next day we wore work clothes, and according to the instructions of the "veteran" Akkerman people who emigrated a few months before us, we joined the builders' camp that dried the Kabara marshes, paved the Shuni road, etc.

[Page 112]

The First Immigrants
by Noah Zukerman
Translated by Sara Mages

I have been asked to recall my memories of Akkerman but, at my age – I already past the age of eighty – it is not an easy task since so many years have passed since I left my hometown. I'll try to bounce myself sixty and a few years back, and maybe I will draw something from the depth of the distant past.

I was born in 1898 to my parents Chana and Nachum Zukerman. My brothers Moshe and Leib and my sister Leah preceded me. All together we were ten children. I remember well, as if it was yesterday, my first day in the *heder* of the teacher Zeidel, when I was five years old, meaning, 78 years ago. My brother Leib accompanied me to the *heder* and, before we left, my mother z"l gave us two kopeks to buy lollipops to sweeten my first day at school. I studied two "periods" with Zeidel, and later moved to another *heder* where the Chumash with Rashi was taught. I remember one more detail from those days. On Friday, when my grandfather, Rabbi Zadok z"l, went to the bathhouse in honor of Shabbat, he passed by my *heder* and took me to accompany him to the bathhouse. When he entered the *heder*, all the children stood up in his honor, I earned half an hour and all the children were jealous at me for being released from the *heder* before them.

*A group of "first halutzim" from Akkerman at work drying
the Kabara marshes and paving the road to Zikhron Ya'akov, in 1921*

Seated from the right: **Noah Zukerman, Avraham Serfer, Aharon Brand**
Standing: **Avraham Margalit, Yehoshua Berger (Harari), Yisrael Rabinowitch, Aharon Kaminker, Avraham Durfman (Kafri), Yeshayahu Botoshansky**

I vaguely remember the days of the Russo–Japanese War of 1905. In order to erase the Russians' defeat in the war with the Japanese, the authorities tried to redirect the citizens' opinion to other matters and, as usual in such situations, the Jews were the victims. The slogan that was prevalent at the time was – "Hit the Jews and save Russia." In 1905, after the days of Sukkot, pogroms also broke out in Akkerman. Hooligans from nearby villages and the suburbs began to riot, looted, robbed and burned the Jews' shops and the terrible situation was unbearable. Many immigrated to countries across the sea, America, Argentina, etc. It was years before the Jews in Akkerman recovered, rebuilt the ruins, and life was back to normal.

We, the children, continued in the course of study, from Chumash and Rashi we moved to Gemara as usual at that time. My grandfather, Zadok z"l, passed away on the last day of Passover

1906. A large crowd came to accompany him at the funeral. Before the funeral my uncle Moshe z"l, who was the youngest son, was crowned the city rabbi in place of his father, Zadok z"l. Years later, my brothers, Moshe z"l and Leib, were sent to study at a Yeshiva in Kishinev [Chişinău], and in 1911 my brother Moshe returned from there with a rabbinical ordination. My father instructed him to teach me so he could save the teacher's salary. I studied with my brother until he was drafted into the army in 1913. He served in the army until July 1914, because he took advantage of a vacation given to him and fled abroad through the Austrian border. He reached Sadigora, the seat of the Rebbe that my father was one of his Hassidim. We exchanged letters, but in the aftermath of the war the connection broke off. It was renewed only after some time through the "Red Cross" because my brother was held captive by the enemy until the end of the war.

When my brother Leib returned, also with a rabbinical ordination from the yeshiva, I continued to study with him. In Sukkot 1914, my parents' youngest child was born, and he is Sheftel, member of Kibbutz Hulda.

I remember well the years of the war due to the great distress it that left its mark on everyone and also on me. There was rationing in essential foods and Akkerman, the city of wine, suffered the most because the export of wine to Poland stopped. Tragic news arrived from the various fronts, the Russians suffered many defeats and the civilians' mood, the Jews, included, was very bad. With the removal of the Tsar, in March 1917, a different wind blew around and hope arose for peace, a new era and the end of the bloodshed.

The Balfour Declaration in November aroused a new spirit in the Jewish population. The Zionist movement began to gain power. Yakov Berger was elected chairman of the Zionist organization. He organized public meetings on Zionists subjects, established the Hebrew gymnasium and aroused the Jewish youth to immigrate to Eretz–Yisrael.

In 1918, the Russian front loosened, the Austrians occupied part of Ukraine and reached Odessa, while the Romanians

[Page 113]

captured Bessarabia, and Akkerman was under a Romanian rule. Since the Romanians did everything they could to introduce the Romanian language to schools, many parents preferred to send their children to a Hebrew school, and by doing so, gymnasia "Tarbut" was given the opportunity to acquire many more students. Yakov Berger sat day a night and translated various text books from Russian to Hebrew. However, the older youth was not enthusiastic about the idea of studying at Romanian universities and preferred to travel to Western European countries to continue their studies. At the end of 1919, I also submitted a request for a passport to travel abroad, but, in the meantime, I was drafted to the Romanian army. In May 1920, I started to serve in the army but the Romanian did not enjoy my long service… On 31 July, I was given a month vacation, together with all the soldiers in my battalion, to help with the grain harvest. When I got home, I found the long–awaited passport and started to address my immigration issue. It was hard to get a visa, but I was helped by Yakov Berger who provided me with a letter of recommendation to the chairman of the Zionist organization in Bucharest. He directed me to the Swiss consulate and I received a visa to Kushta [Istanbul], and on the last day of my vacation from the army I embarked on a ship in Glatz that sailed to Kushta, and with that story of Akkerman ended for me. It is worth noting that I, Aharon Kaminker and P. Berkov, were the first *halutzim* from Akkerman. However, P. Berkov was not able to absorb in Israel, he left and his whereabouts are unknown.

I see a great privilege for myself for paving the road for the immigration of my family members, including my mother and my father z"l. They all took root in the homeland. I was also privilege to be among the founders of Kfar Hess in the northern Sharon plain, and my two sons also built their home in this village.

A group of first halutzim from 1920

Seated right to left: **Avraham Durfman (Kafri), Noah Zukerman, Yisrael Rabinowitch**
Standing: **Avraham Margalit, Yeshayahu Botoshansky, Yehoshua Berger (Harari), Aharon Brand, Aharon Kaminker**

[Page 114]

Chapters of Memories from the Days of My Childhood

by Binyamin Girshfeld

Translated by Sara Mages

From the days of my childhood I especially remember the image of my grandfather, R' Leibale' the ritual slaughterer (R' Yehudah Hirschfeld). He was a scholar and a God-fearing Jew, and for 46 years served as a *Mohel* and a ritual slaughterer in Akkerman. He wrote several books, which were printed in Jerusalem, on the laws of slaughtering ("*Pnei Aryeh*," "*Shaar Aryeh*," "*Amery Baruch*"). He was also a scribe and specialized in writing in tiny letters. His letters were written in flowery Hebrew and elegant handwriting. He used to straighten his white beard while reading the Holy Scriptures and left the hair that fell between the pages of the books. At times, we, the children, found his hair between the pages, and I remember that father used to say to us: "children, don't touch the hair, it's sacred!"

Grandfather passed away when I was six years old on one of the Sabbaths of the month of Kislev. I remember that father gathered all the children, informed them of grandfather's death, started to cry after he covered grandfather's face with a white sheet, got dressed in his everyday clothes and went to Beit HaMidrash.

My father also served the Jewish community of Akkerman as a ritual slaughterer until the outbreak of the Second World War. He was observant and zealous in all the religious values like the rest of the ritual slaughterers in the city: R' Mendel Gelman, R' Nachum Zukerman and Asher Malmud. On Sabbath eve and holidays, summer and winter, my father used to go to the "*mikveh*." He always returned with a guest to drink a cup of hot tea together and chat about this and that.

We had a Christian neighbor in our yard, who was a friend of the family, but he was a drunk. Whenever Grisha - this was his name - got drunk, he would come home singing and cursing out loud. He had a one-horse carriage, and it turned out that the horse memorized its way to the stable. When Grisha came down from the carriage, he used to open all the doors and gates, release all the geese, chickens and pigs, and announced in a loud voice: "All of you, go to hell!" He used to say to his son Favco, who was weeping bitterly: "You, you also get out of here, I'm not your father, I'm not the homeowner, I'm not a father and I'm not a husband, all of you, get out of here!" All the neighbors gathered to watch the show which was repeated often.

We lived not far from the [Dniester] Liman River, and in the scorching summer days we bathed in its pure and sweet water. Young and old flocked to the river bank, not only to bathe but also to nourish their eyes in the beautiful landscape, which was especially beautiful in the evening when the water merged with the blue sky and the bright stars sparkled around.

I spent many hours and days in our street, "Breiskya Ulica." Standing before my eyes is the building of the Romanian Secret Police that belonged to R' David Berkovic z"l. Across from it was a large courtyard with three synagogues: The Great Synagogue, Beit HaMidrash and the Kloiz. Akkerman's fourth synagogue was located in Izmail Street. This synagogue was called "*Ramsleina*" (craftsmen's synagogue), and excelled in its beauty inside and outside. On the Holy Ark, which covered the entire eastern wall, were different engravings and also the cantor's "pillar" was impressive. The *Gabba'im* sat on both sides of the "pillar," and the two exit doors were intended for the cantor and the singers who appeared on Sabbath eve and holidays. As we know, the

Germans held the remaining Jews of Akkerman in this synagogue until they led them to their last road.

Frequently, when I anchor in the region of my childhood and youth, I find myself in Akkerman's old Beit Midrash where I spent quite a lot of my time. The renowned Jewish writers dedicated a prominent place in their work to Beit HaMidrash and I, of course, will not add anything new in my description. From the dawn of my childhood I absorbed everything that took place within the walls of this Beit-Midrash. The special Jewish experience came to expression inside it, and I remember all the worshipers, the important homeowners and the least important homeowners, according to the order of their seating, as I remember all kinds of events in this Beit-Midrash that stand alive before my eyes.

[Page 115]

The extensive Girshfeld family

The entrance gate to Beit HaMidrash

[Page 116]

From among the various personalities, that I remember now, I'll appoint: R' Yosel Ben-Zion, son of Efraim Tzvi, who liked to drink and ran a lot to do his "little business." In the bathroom he used to run into a pile of stones and woe to the one who was captured in his hands; R' Moshe was able to sing, and when the Gentiles gave him a small coin, he sang the "*Tochecha*" [rebuke] and showered them with curses in the Holy Language that they couldn't understand; R' Leizer the blind, who had a bass voice, was mostly begging for alms in funerals; Babe *de lange* [the tall], who was in charge of the women's "*Mikveh*," also served as the prompter in the women's gallery of the Great Synagogue and read from her "*Tze'nah u-Re'nah*" in a loud voice; R' Idel always talked to himself and cracked seeds constantly. Every once in a while he was seized with madness and it was necessary to tie him with ropes; Yasha the newspapers seller, who was semi-paralyzed, used to come to parties that he wasn't invited to dressed in a black suit, a shirt with a white collar and a bow tie, and his face shone from joy and happiness; Pessi was the cantor's helper at the synagogue. He recited "*El malei rachamim*" for a fee, and lengthened and shortened the prayer according to the price that he was getting... and there were more and more characters like them.

Now I see before my eyes the elderly, R' Motel Feigin, as he's sitting and praying at the eastern-wall. He was one of the richest men in the city, a handsome Jew that his beard was white from afar and his opinion was accepted by others. And there were other respected homeowners who were Torah scholars and proficient in *Shas* [six sections of the *Mishnah*] like: David Brand, the brothers Granick, Aharon Cohen, Chanich Shapira, Haim Kminker, Shmuel Berger, Yakov Grishfeld and others.

And if you have a public event that isn't related by any means to Beit HaMidrash - a wedding, Brit Milah, Bar-Mitzvah, "*Yahrzeit*" and, of course, also funerals. Now, echoes in my ears Shmuel Gordon's "*El malei rachamim*" before the departure of a funeral. I also see the beggars standing at the roadside and hear the voice of Leizer the blind calling: "Give elms to the poor!" The class differences were especially prominent at the funerals. Besides the coffin-bearers, who volunteered to do so, only a small number of Jews were dragged to the funeral of the poor and the beggars knew in advance that they will not fill their bowls with donations. It wasn't the same when an important person passed away. He was rewarded that the masses will accompany him, by foot or by car, and the beggars also won a "fat share" and their bowls were filled with coins.

And now I hear the wailing of a woman who bursts in the direction of the Holy Ark. In those days it was probably the last resort in times of danger. "Jews, Help!" - she would shout in bitter tears - help - my son is struggling with something worse than death." And merciful Jews, sons of merciful fathers, immediately rushed to help, recited Psalms or just fulfilled their obligation by saying "*Brukh hu Ubarukh Shemo*" ["blessed is He and blessed is His Name"] and "Amen."

And here I hear the fiery speeches of the emissaries from "*Keren Hayesod*" ["United Israel Appeal"] or "*Keren HaKayemet*" [JNF], about the redemption of the Land of Israel during the break between "*Shacharit*" and "*Mussaf*" prayers in Beit HaMidrash. The orthodox Jews took advantage of this opportunity to warn that the Sabbath isn't kept in Eretz-Yisrael, and the emissary's words were swallowed by the interjections.

There was a flurry of emotions in Beit HaMidrash when a controversy broke out between the old rabbi and the young rabbi. The first - well versed in *Poskim* and the Talmud, while the other - a rousing preacher and a pleasant cantor. Things came to such an extent, that when three Jews died in one day, many claimed, that the fire of the great controversy has caused this disaster.

The members of Beit HaMidrash kept the flame burning and belonged to "Agudat Yisrael" or "Mizrachi." Beit HaMidrash not only served as a place of worship, but also for all the needs that Judaism was associated with. Here, groups studied "*Mishnayot*," "*Ein Ya'akov*" and "*Tehillim Zager*" [recited Psalms]. The parties for the Torah scholars, who finished the reading of the book, took place here. These parties ended with the rabbi's sermon and the eating of *knaidlach*, and sometimes, especially on Lag BaOmer, also the smell of goose fat rose from Beit HaMidrash... The melodies before the "Mincha" prayer also emerged from there on the Sabbath, and I especially remember the sorrowful melodies, which were sung during "*Shalosh Seudot*" [the third meal eaten on the Sabbath], when the Jews parted from the Sabbath Queen.

Of course, the *Shamash*, Yisrael-Moshe, conducted with honesty and dedication the great preparations for the holidays and festivals, while the honorable Rabbi Roler gave sermons on the Sabbath and holidays. As usual, he always ended them with the blessing - "*Veba lezion goel venomar* Amen.*"

I close my eyes and see Beit HaMidrash on Tisha B'Av, its benches overturned, *"beralach"* [snails] are thrown from different directions, and the sad melody of *"Eikhah"* [The Book of Lamentations] is piercing Beit HaMidrash.

Especially etched in my memory is the special status of the "bowls" on Yom Kippur before *"Kol Nidre"* prayer. Young and old sat, each in front of the bowl that he was in charge of, and his eyes examined every donor and every donation. Is that the voice of the cantor Avraham Rybak that is rising in my ears? "For all of these, God of forgiveness, forgive us, pardon us, grant us atonement."

[Page 117]

I also hear the silent weeping of R' Motel Zarchi, a God-fearing Jew with a thin beard who always had a gloomy expression in his tortured face. When I was a child I loved to look at his face because, for some reason, it seemed to me that light was strewn on it, as it's written "Light is sown for the righteous." When the worshipers reached *"Shema Yisrael,"* R' Motel prolonged the last word of this verse and the cantor wasn't able to continue until R' Motel had finished his trill.... Interestingly, the worshipers in Beit HaMidrash weren't satisfied with their own cantor and were eager to hear *"Lishmoa El Harina Vel Hatfilla"* ["Let us listen to the song of our prayers"] from good cantors like Moshe Cohen, Nisan Kentor and Tzvi Krankurs who prayed in the Great Synagogue. The Jews of Akkerman had a special affinity to Cantorial music, and even the secular and assimilated Jews, who didn't want to give up a "piece" of Cantorial music, flocked to the Great Synagogue. Nonetheless, a Jewish heart...

About the Landscape and the Climate
by Yehoshua Harari
Translated by Sara Mages

From the summit of my 80 years on earth, after 60 years of life in Israel in which I dried swamps, paved roads and built many houses, including my home, I'm still tied by bonds of love to my hometown, Akkerman, where I spent the first twenty years of my life.

Indeed, the landscape of my birthplace left its mark deep in my soul. The city lay on a hill surrounded on one side by the water of the [Dniester] Liman River, and on the other side by vineyards, orchards and fields. The long shore of the Liman River was used for growing vegetables, reeds, fish farming and storage of timber, and the Liman's port connected us with the city of Odessa - the Jewish metropolis. The river froze in the winter and the snow accumulated to a great height. The ice was stored in cold-cellars and lasted for the entire summer.

In the summer, the swimming beaches stretched from two directions on long bridges which were supported by poles. There was a beach for men, and quite far from it, a beach for women. The timber from the warehouses floated by the beaches and helped the children to learn to swim. Those, who weren't lazy, were able to take a hot shower because one of Asbsorov's three flour mills was located on the beach. Later, also the electric power plant was located there. The plant used the Liman's water to cool its machines, poured the hot water back into the river, and here you had a hot shower. However, in the winter it was necessary to go to the *"Bania"* - a public bathhouse with steam.

The frosty winter landscape with temperatures that reached between 25 to 30 degrees below zero, and the large piles of snow that accumulated in the streets, is well remembered by everyone who lived in Akkerman. It should be noted, that the city residents knew how take advantage of the summer season for the winter season by collecting firewood, pickling vegetables (even watermelons) in big barrels, and accumulating a stock of "*powidło*" [fruit stew] from the fruit of the season. I remember that Yosef Beretz, a resident of Kibbutz Degania who visited Bessarabia, sent an article to the weekly "*Hapoel Hatzair*" ["The Young Worker"] and its title was - "Cooking *Powidło*," because every place he visited he came across this phenomenon.

The temperature difference between summer and winter was very large. Thanks to the high temperature in the summer all the vegetables and fruit that we know in Israel, apart from subtropical fruit and citrus trees, grew in our place. Huge quantities of fruit and vegetables streamed to the city, and the watermelons piled high. Dozens of carts with apples and plums arrived to the market, and as a child I was impressed with this abundance.

Many wrote and sang about the blessed land of Bessarabia and the abundance that fell in its share, especially in the south. When we lived in Izmailosky Street I always saw the convoys of railcars on the tracks and the "*bendigot*" [stevedores], who lined up in the direction of the Liman and filled the "barges" (the tankers of those days) with wheat, grain, barley and corn that were sent abroad. I remember this sight to this day.

A chapter in itself is the wine industry. During the harvest time the whole city was marked by this. Merchants, who even came from Warsaw, and all kinds of "religious ministrants" ran around the streets of our city to make sure that the wine barrels, which were exported abroad, were strictly kosher.

We can't separate the Turkish fortress ("Krepost") from the landscape of Akkerman. It was shrouded in mystery and various legends were told about its towers and dungeons. Also the two town squares, one in the city center and the second in the other end, constituted, of course, an integral part of this landscape.

[Page 118]

Akkerman - a Corridor to the Parlor
(a Chapter of Memories)

by Yakov (Jancik) Zukerman

Translated by Sara Mages

When I try to remember Akkerman, my childhood, personalities, landscapes, events and experiences from the past, I'm amazed how little I remember from there. I only remember a little bit about public affairs and personalities who were active in the Jewish community. It seems to me that it's possible to explain this phenomenon by saying - that, in fact, we didn't live there when we lived there, because our existence focused on the Land of Israel. We sat on the banks of the Liman River and sang songs about Lake Kinneret. We walked in the square by the fortress and our heart was in Kibbutz Degania or Masada. Even when we were there, we knew very little about the public life that occurred in the community or in the synagogue, and the "politics," which was conducted in the conversations of the idlers of "*Agudat Yisrael*," didn't interest us at all.

I started my formal education in Manya's kindergarten. She was an educated woman, saturated in Russian culture and talented. It was necessary to have some degree of boldness to manage, as much as possible, this kindergarten purely in Hebrew. The song, which is known to every child who attended kindergarten, is echoing in my ears: "On a window, on a window, stood a beautiful bird." The kindergarten teacher Manya explained to us the meaning of the Russian words, and then started to work hard on introducing the melody. I progressed from kindergarten until I graduated high school. I'm sure, that many have already raised their memories in this book about the good teachers that we had in high-school, and first and foremost, about the image of the principle Berger. For sure, they didn't spare praises at his expense, but let me mention a particular disadvantage. As a teacher, Dr. Berger, who was highly knowledgeable, didn't know how to teach it to others. We can say about him that he was like a samovar full with water, but his tap was faulty. He knew eight languages, including Arabic. I think that he learned this language by himself, since it's clear that there weren't any Arabic language schools in Akkerman or in Odessa. Maybe he studied Arabic in Leningrad, because for some time he was the secretary of "*Tzeirei Zion*" in Leningrad. At any rate, he was a renaissance man to the full meaning of the word, and his mark was evident in the institution that he managed and nurtured. We had another interesting teacher - Feinbelt. He had a good pedagogical method and was a superb teacher.

When I was ten I joined "*Gordonia*." I arrived there directly from the "Hebrew Speaking Association." At the chapter, and at school, we only spoke Hebrew between us. I only started to study Yiddish at the age of 15, and it's no wonder that people said that I spoke Yiddish like a real Gentile... In fact, I didn't need any Yiddish because we spoke Russian at home. My mother was a teacher in a Russian elementary school, an amateur singer, a collector of Ukrainian and Russian songs, and we had close ties with Russian families. And if I didn't need to know the language for my teaching job with an "*Achvah*" group, whose members came from the middle class and only spoke in Yiddish - I would have remained, to this day, a "total Gentile" in terms of my knowledge of the Yiddish language... However, for us, the "*Gordonia*" members, the Hebrew language was like a mother tongue. We spoke, of course, in Ashkenazi accent, and only in 1930. when the first emissaries came from Israel we started to speak in a Sephardic accent. The teacher Epstein, who came from Israel, was the first to speak in this accent in Akkerman. He was like a second Eliezer Ben-Yehudah. He only spoke only in Hebrew with Jews and Gentiles. At first, everyone made fun of him but, slowly slowly, he accustomed everyone to turn to him only in Hebrew. He didn't deviate from his way or speak in any other language. It's worth mentioning that the son of the teacher and librarian Sternshis only spoke in Hebrew although his mother wasn't a Zionist.

From among the leaders of the Jewish community I especially remember Stretz who prepared me for my Bar-Mitzvah. He was a unique figure, a man of values who remained loyal to the principle of self-employment. He chopped wood with his own hands and didn't use a water-drawer. He put a yoke on his shoulders and brought the water to his house. This matter seems very strange in light of the way of life in the city in those days. He only had one son, and when his son entered the ranks of the Revisionists he stopped talking to him... I remember, that when he taught me the *Haftorah* for *Parashat* "*Chayei Sara*" which dealt with Abishag the Shunammite, I started to shower him with embarrassing questions

[Page 119]

about the behavior of King David toward the young girl Abishag. Stretz complained to my mother that I was teasing him with my questions and throwing him out of balance....

Another interesting character was the principal of "Talmud-Torah" School, who was also a teacher. His name, Tchichelnitzky was a bit strange and caused many jokes among my group of friends. He used to whip his students with a special kind of whip ("*kanchik*"), and in this respect he was "unique" in Akkerman. Incidentally, "Talmud-Torah" was under the influence of the *Yiddishistim* [advocates of the Yiddish language].

The members of "*Agudat Yisrael*" congregated in Beit HaMidrash. I had a "*shtot*" [a permanent seat] in this Beit Midrash despite the fact that I wasn't a God-fearing Jew. I actually won a "*shtot*" in the eastern wall after my father got into an argument with "Beit HaMidrash" and kept away from this place. Since then, I came to Beit HaMidrash by myself, sat in "my *shtoat*," and found myself in the company of important homeowners, masters, and influential persons in the terms of Akkerman of those days... Apparently, they treated me with some kind of respect because my great-grandfather, and also my grandfather, served as rabbis. Also, my second grandfather (on my mother's side) wasn't a worthless person, and he is - "*Yankel der heizeariker*" - the cantor who was famous not only in Akkerman (by the way, I was named after him). I wasn't awarded to know him, but I know that he was one of the great cantors and that he also composed several payers. He is well praised in "Encyclopedia of Bessarabia," in the chapter about Bessarabia's cantors. He was given the nickname "*heizeariker*" [hoarse] because of this incident.

During the days of the 1905 pogrom he hid for several days in a cellar from fear of the rioters, and when he came out his voice became hoarse. It was told about a competition between him and the famous cantor "Nissan der Belzer," and my grandfather (actually - his voice) had the upper hand. He left Akkerman after the aforementioned pogrom, traveled to Czechoslovakia and England and many flocked to hear his prayers. I own a booklet of prayers that were composed by this grandfather. My uncle, one of the sons of "*Yankel der heizeariker*," was also a cantor and a slaughterer. He studied at the conservatory and was the one who managed to decipher his father's writings. Later, he left the *chazzanut*, studied medicine and became a surgeon. Apparently, the musical talent, which characterizes several members of our family, is hereditary and originated from my grandfather and maybe also from my grandfather's grandfather. Anyway, mother received a good measure of musical education from grandfather Yankel. She knew many songs and recorded every song with a folkloristic character in her notebook. To this day, my mother's melodies are echoing in my ears, and on the wings of these melodies I'm also carried to those days.

If I mentioned Beit HaMidrash, it should also be noted that the people of Beit HaMidrash conducted all the affairs of the city. The "tax," which was entrusted in their hands, was the main source of income of the Jewish community, and those who hold the pay - also hold the opinions... I remember that David Brand, one of the people of Beit HaMidrash, was almost the only ruler and ruled everything that was related to public affairs. Frequently there were disagreements between the people of Beit HaMidrash and the Zionists, and I remember, that in not one case, the Zionists were the losers. It's difficult for me to remember the nature of the battles that took place in those days, for as I said at the beginning of this article, I wasn't involved in them and they didn't concern me at all. When I was in Akkerman I saw myself as Mordecai Tzvi Manne, the poet from the Haskalah period who is "standing still on top of a hill," his soul is yearning to Zion and he's asking: "Where are you, where are you the Holy Land, my soul yearns to you." For us, Akkerman was only the corridor to the parlor. Our hearts, opinions and feelings were given to Eretz Yisrael, to the parlor, and everything that happened in the corridor was unimportant and insignificant.

[Page 120]

Artists and Loyalists
by S. Yisrael
Translated by Sara Mages

Like in most cities in Bessarabia the majority of the Jewish population in Akkerman was merchants and professionals. However, also the craftsmen constituted a significant portion of the population, and there isn't a profession that the Jews didn't engage in. In our city, there were a number of crafts that the Jews and Christians dealt with together like: carpentry, shoemaking, glazing, painting, electricity, baking, tailoring, bathhouse attendant, etc. and there was also one Jewish blacksmith - Avraham Grynszpan. On the other hand, there were also professions that were only in the hands of the Jews: tailors, watchmakers, milliners for men and women, photographers, goldsmiths, dental-technicians, furriers, dressmakers, bookbinders and tinsmiths. It should be noted, that most of the craftsmen in our city were involved in the public life and served as community leaders.

There's no doubt that it's fitting to place the tailor Leib Stambul, who was a loyal and dedicated public activist, at the head of the privileged and honored craftsmen. He was elected as a member of the community council, was a member of the board of "*Tarbut*," "ORT, ""*Maccabi*," the New Jewish Hospital, and more. It can be said, that most of the important public institutions in Akkerman enjoyed the public activity of Leib Stambul. A chapter on its own is his Zionist activity. He was one of the first members of "*Hovevei Zion*" in the city. Later, he was active in the "General Zionists Party," the committee of "*Keren Hayesod*" [United Israel Appeal], "*Keren HaKayemet LeYisrael*" [JNF] and even in the "*Halutz*" committee.

It goes without saying, that he educated his son and daughter to Zionism and Zionist fulfillment. His son Nisan, who was one of the activists in "*Gordonia*," immigrated to Israel after his graduation from the Hebrew High-School. In 1936 Leib Stambul followed his son and immigrated to Israel together with his family.

Upon his arrival to Israel he didn't stop his public activity. In 1950 he was one of the founders of the "Society of Emigrants from Akkerman" and the society's "Loan Fund." He maintained close ties with the former residents of our city. Everyone knew that Leib Stambul was the best address at time of need. He was rewarded to live to a ripe old age and enjoyed his children and grandchildren. He passed away in 1968.

The tailor, Yakov Yashpan, was among the founders of the craftsmen's synagogue and also served as the *Gabbai* [beadle] of this synagogue together with the lawyer Bendik Axelord. He was tall and handsome, well dressed, good natured and honest, and was valued by the residents of our city.

Fondly remembered is the tailor Wasiniwesky who was highly accepted by his clients, Jews and non-Jews, who were among the crhme de la crhme of the city. He gave his children a Jewish education, and his only son was among the activists of "*Tzeirei Zion*" in our city.

The watchmaker R' Ben-Zion Kogen, who was known by his nickname "Ben-Zion *der zeigermacher*" [the watchmaker] or "Ben-Zion *der weiser*" [the white], was a Jew with a gracious facial expression and a long beard. He was a God-fearing Jew who didn't skip a prayer. He was one of the respected craftsmen, did his work faithfully and honestly and acquired a lot of friends.

Another watchmaker, who was also a public activist, was Berel Roitman. He represented the craftsmen in a number of public institutions and was among the activists of "*HaOved HaTzioni*" ["The Zionist Worker"].

A special character was Yeshayahu Greenstein the silversmith. He merged *chazzanut* [Jewish liturgical music] and silversmith. He also hummed various *pirkei chazzanut* [Cantorial pieces] and trilled his hoarse voice when he sat at his workbench. Chazzanut was a hobby for him, and when a synagogue in the city wasn't able to obtain a cantor for the holidays, R' Yeshayahu was always willing to lead the prayers. He also organized a small choir that accompanied him - and also that on his own expense.

From among the carpenters in the city it's worth noting Haim Britva and Teshmerinski. The first was a Zionist activist, a member of "*HaOved HaTzioni*," and also taught woodworking at "ORT" school. He was also among the activists of the Zionist funds. The second was highly respected for his honesty and good manners. He was rewarded to immigrate to Israel with his family.

If we move to the printing profession we should mention two noteworthy Jews, and they are: Pinchas Aksler who was an active member of the "General Zionists Party," and helped all the Zionist parties in preparing their printouts, and Gedalyahu Goldfarb who was a "burnt" *Yiddishist* [advocate of the Yiddish language], a member of the "*Kultur Lige*" ["Culture League"] and a supporter of the Yiddish School. Despite being one of the opponents of Zionism, he couldn't convince his daughter to follow this road. She immigrated to Israel and built her family here.

[Page 121]

Another *Yiddishist*, Fruma Feinland, who was also an activist in "*Kultur Lige*," was rewarded with a similar fate. Her daughter also immigrated to Israel and established a family here. Fruma, who sewed hats for women, was among the founders of the "Yiddish Drama Club." She was the "star" of this club and played many roles in the plays that were produced by the club and even gained success. This hobby was often at her own expense because the burden of income was imposed on her after her husband died at a young age. Her many friends, who respected and admired her, were loyal to her and only ordered their hats from her. She went through many difficult years during the World War, but she managed to reach Israel and was rewarded to live to a ripe old age in the company of her daughter and her family.

There was also an interesting character among the locksmiths, and he's - Pinchas Milman. He was among those who came to the synagogue early in the morning. Before the onset of the prayers many Jews, who enjoyed listening to his tales about people and events that he encountered in his occupation, gathered around him. Not to mention the many stories that he had told about America, the golden land, and about all the great things and wonders that he saw there when he visited his eldest son who lived there.

We'll also mention the tinsmith Eli Ber Kizlman, A kind-hearted Jew, short and skinny, what was called in Yiddish "*a dravene Yeddel*" [a small Jew]. He was among the builders and the *Gabbaim* of the new "*Kloiz*" and donated a Torah Scroll. For the festive grand opening he was carried from his house to the "*Kloiz*" accompanied by kleizmer band. His only son served as a cantor in the craftsmen's synagogue and later in London.

Apart from them, there were many other craftsmen from the working class who lived from the labor of their hands. Some of them engaged in public activities, each person in his own field. They were honest and "modest in their thoughts and deeds" in the words of the poet [Bialik] in his poem "I'd rather be with you."

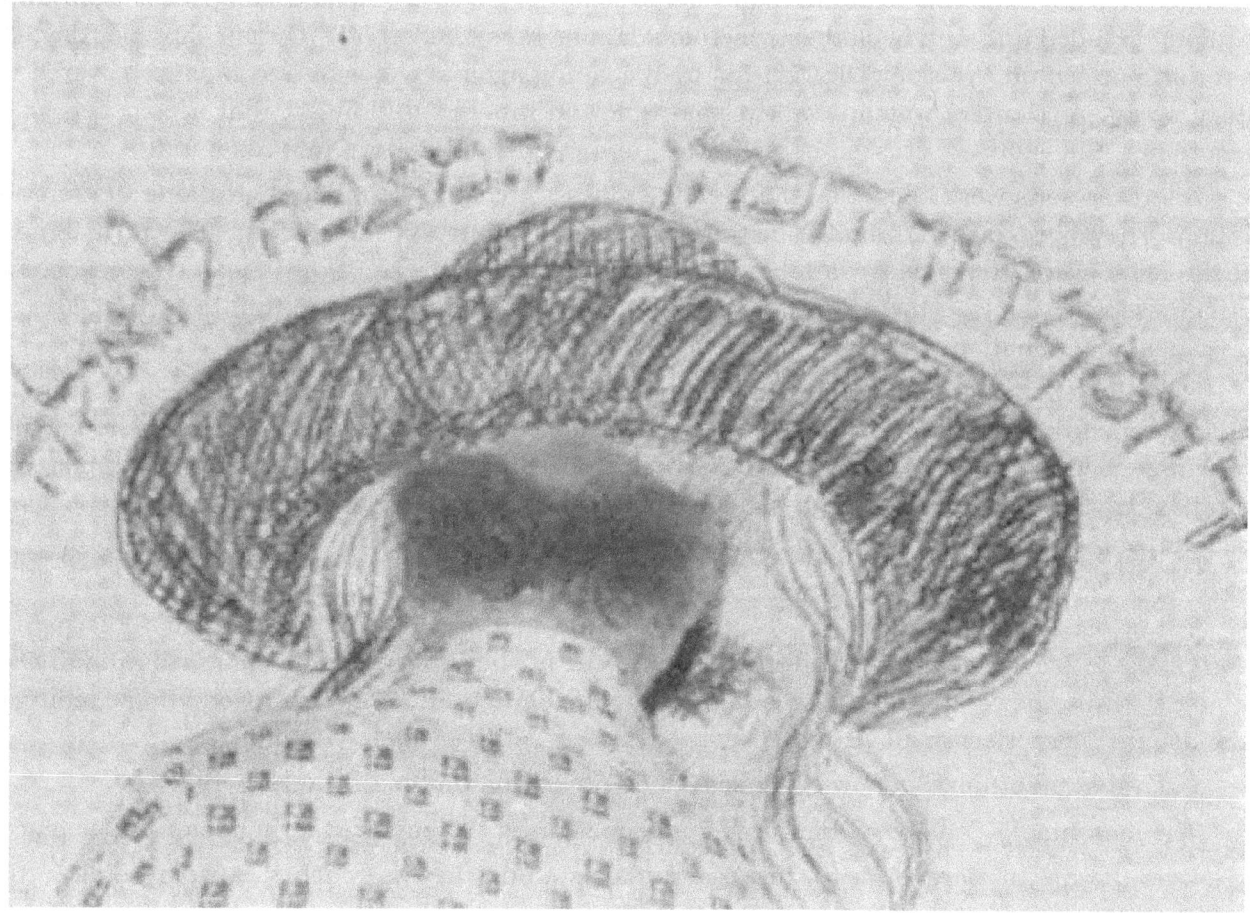

[Pages 122]

From the Bitter and the Sweet
(crumbs from the way of life)
by Y. Schildkrauth
Translated by Sara Mages

A. Measure for Measure

One day two important homeowners met in one of Akkerman's streets. One was Chone Gewirtzman the lame who was also a lawyer and an active leader in the cooperative. The second was one-eyed Hersh Brodetsky, an intelligent cultured man who was active in public affairs. Hersh Brodetsky, who had one eye, asked Chone who limped on one leg: well, R' Chone, how it goes? Chone the witty answered immediately: as your eyes can see…

B. Only a Doctor

Ozer Schwinn was very rich but also a great miser. He, together with his three sons, traded in grain, wine, wool etc. and accumulated a large fortune. However, it didn't stop Ozer from always walking in faded and untidy clothes which looked like rags on his body. On one summer day, Ozer sat and napped on the sidewalk with his body leaning against the wall and his face covered with dirty sweat. A "Gentile" woman walked past him and innocently thought that a poor beggar was before her. She stopped, crossed herself twice, and pushed a handout into his hand…

His three sons were known by the name "Z'lobes," and they were like their name - clumsy and rough. They lived in a farmhouse in the agricultural suburb of "Wershina." The furnishings in their house were very modest: a long wooden table, a few beds and long wooden benches. Their stinginess was visible in their house. Everyone knew that there was no reason to turn to Ozer with a request of a donation. It was a wasted effort. Ozer would never give.

One day, the "spirit of insanity: entered one of Ozer's daughters. Her soul craved to study and all of Ozer's arguments that he doesn't need a "*melumed'te*" [educated woman] in his house and it will also cost him a great fortune - didn't help. The daughter insisted and even completed her studies at the government's high-school. When she reached marriageable age they began to search for a husband for her and since the pretty maiden was also educated, her father, Ozer Schwinn, declared that he will not take less than a doctor as a groom for that daughter.

Yosale' Segel the matchmaker search and found in the village of Shabo near Akkerman the son of David Meyrson who studied in the third year at the university. He came running to Ozer's house with the news: I have! I have a doctor for your daughter! He's from a good home, educated, handsome and perfect in all virtues.

Ozer answered him: So, how expensive? Meaning - what is the desired dowry?

The matchmaker answered him: half a million. This is the payment for a doctor in our place.

Ozer began to bargain with the matchmaker until they've reached a compromise: three hundred thousand.

When they were on the verge of writing the "Tannaim," Ozer remembered to ask: what kind of a doctor is this young man? Yosale' the matchmaker answered him: the groom is studying veterinary medicine and this is a labor that honors its owner.

Ozer became angry and shouted: "what? For three hundred thousand you offer a "horse doctor" for my daughter? You are a thief! You are a leech! Get out of my house and don't show your face again in this place!"

Yosale' took off immediately, the match was canceled and the matter became the topic of conversation in our city.

C. A New Face

Kalman Kogen was one of the Yeshiva students in Beit HaMidrash. He came from a good home, earned a good living, but he had one flaw: he didn't have a beautiful face. To cover his ugliness he always dressed in fancy clothes. In one of the weekdays he came to Beit HaMidrash dressed in a new suit, a new hat and a fancy tie. He made an impression on his friends but Pisi Lewin, who was both witty and cheeky, was also there. When he saw Kalman's fancy outfit he said to him in these words: "look Kalman, if you can spend so much money on new clothes why don't you also buy yourself a new beautiful face?"

D. The Fate of a Jewish Master

Moshe Milstein was one of the wealthiest men in our city. He had mansions with large gardens around them, vineyards in the vicinity of Akkerman and in nearby Shabo, grain business etc. In addition to all of that he was the chief executive of the shipping company that

[Page 123]

sailed its ships in the waters of the Black Sea and the Dniester River, and during the Romanian rule he also served as a bank manager. Therefore, it was no wonder that his name was carried on all lips and the most popular blessing in Akkerman was: if only you can reach the rank of Moshe Milstein!... He donated a lot of money to public needs and the highlight of his contributions was the building that he established for the Jewish school in one of his gardens. When "*Tarbut*" association was established in 1918, he dedicated the building to the Jewish High-School and the Jewish council's offices were also located there.

One evening, in 1929, Moshe Milstein invited Moshe Herman the chairman of the community council, and the lawyer Yosef Serfer who was a member of the community presidency. He locked himself in one of the rooms with them and revealed a secret: his businesses are in trouble, the situation is unbearable and he's unable to pay his debts. In order to pay his debts and save his good name he decided to mortgage all his buildings and vineyards. Since the building that housed the high-school and the community offices is also registered in his name, there is a danger that they'll also put a lien against it. Therefore, he asks them to hurry and do all the official arrangements in order to transfer this building under the Jewish community's name so it won't fall in the hands of strangers.

At the same time he asked them not to reveal his secret in public because of the "evil eye" and other dangers related to it. Hurry, as much as possible, to take out the building from my hands so you won't miss the dateline.

The community leaders pledged to quickly take all the necessary steps and keep the secret.

E. The Repentant

There were several converts in Akkerman: the son of the lawyer Toporov, the lawyer Zwillinger who often served in the role of an attorney, not for the sake of receiving a payment, in trials concerning the dignity of a Jew and Jewish public interests, Dr. Hacham, son of Shlomo Hacham, who returned to the bosom of Judaism after the Revolution of 1917, Dr. Scher, who was one of the organizers of the self-defense unit ("*Samoobrona*") in our city and commanded a division during the pogrom of 1905 in Akkerman, and others.

We should talk here about the last one. Toward his old age Dr. Scher left his Christian wife, children and grandchildren, and a repentance ceremony was held on one of the Sabbaths in the craftsmen's synagogue. Dr. Scher was called to the Torah, and from the synagogue's *Bima* he expressed his regrets as he was barely holding his tears. He asked the congregation and all the Jewish community to forgive him for the disgrace that he had caused to the Jews when he converted from Judaism to Christianity. After Dr. Scher's words of confession the synagogue's *Gabai*, the lawyer Bendik Akslrod, congratulated him on the occasion of his return to Judaism and wished him a long life. In his words he mentioned his activities for Jewish interests and his stand against the rioters in 1905. At the conclusion of his words he said: we've all heard your request for forgiveness and we owe you an answer, and the answer is: "I forgive you as you ask!" and the congregation replied: "We forgave."

Those, who were present at the craftsmen's synagogue, testify that it was an impressive and shocking event.

I, the writer of these lines, also attended this dramatic event in the synagogue.

[Page 124]

The Seven Daughters of R' Mendel the Carpenter
(From the Jewish way of life in our city)
by Y. Schildkrauth
Translated by Sara Mages

When R' Mendel was widowed, may the same thing not happen to us, when he was still in his early fiftieth he had, neither more nor less, seven daughters in his house. They were, to say the least, not beautiful, and neither of them was a candidate for the title of Bessarabia's beauty queen. Besides that, R' Mendel was very poor and was unable to give a dowry, and in those days everyone knew that if there is no dowry - there are no grooms.

So, the girls sat at their father's house and no one paid attention to them apart from the city's clowns who gave them the nickname "*Benot Zelophehad*[1]." This nickname was accepted by all because no one was able to explain why Mendel's daughters were given this nickname. The only explanation that I've heard is - that it was given to them because they were orphans and remained virgins for many years.

We can't say that young men never stepped on Mendel's doorstep. On the contrary, they stepped. Store clerks, craftsmen, craftsmen's assistants etc. spent every Sabbath eve in the company of these girls. They cracked seeds, chatted about this and that and even danced to the late hours of the night, but, it never came to "realization," meaning, marriage. Mendel's heart ached when he saw his daughters getting older from year to year. Sometimes he uttered a sad monologue, which was mostly seditious words against the young men who take advantage of his daughters for recreation, love games, etc., in the ears of those who were willing to listen.

One day, a rumor passed in the city: one of Mendel's daughters is getting married, and not just to a young man, but to Zalman Tchernilov, Zalman of the hats, meaning that he produces hats and also sells them in his shop in Akkerman's main street. It was a good match by all accounts, and the matter became the topic of discussion by all. Before people had the time to properly spin the story of this marriage, a new rumor circulated: R' Mendel's second daughter is getting married to Golobow the furrier. Apparently, Mendel's distress was observed from the Heavens and the matchmaker of all living took pity on "*Benot Zelophehad*." Before long it was the turn of two additional daughters: one married to the owner of the kiosk, Zalman is his name, and the other to a salesman in Liza Steinberg's grocery store. In short, a wedding followed a wedding and the traffic in R' Mendel's house increased from day to day, just like in a train station…And why should we extend in a place that we have to shorten? Less than two years have passed and Mendel's house was emptied from all the daughters. Chaim Frechter, the owner of the tavern, was the one who took the youngest daughter, and Mendel remained alone.

All the efforts of the city's clowns, the "*Ogolnykim*[2] " and the gossipmongers to explain this puzzling spectacle came to naught. It was impossible to settle the matter logically, and the sages of the generation concluded and said: it must be the finger of God that wrought this miracle. Who could have imagined that Mendel's daughters will be grabbed like fresh buns when everyone knew that they were not so fresh and they had not dowry. What is there to say? When the Divine Providence intervenes in worldly matters it generates great things.

The birds have left their nest and R' Mendel remained alone at home. Theoretically, he should have been happy that he was released from the sorrow of raising daughters and from his financial worries, but he was far from happy, he was sad and he was bored. He had an eerie heaviness in his heart because it was difficult for him to get used to the new situation and to the pace of the weddings.

It was not only difficult for him. It was also difficult for the city's clowns to accept the changes. For many years "*Benot Zelophehad*" were the subject of their jokes and now they were left without a subject. After a consultation they decided that the matter needs to be examined. It's impossible - they claimed - that there isn't another daughter in R' Mendel's house. From then on, they started to visit R' Mendel's apartment every night. They knocked on the door and asked: R' Mendel, do you have another daughter? Every day, or rather, every night, before R' Mendel had the time to close his eyes and before he wove the threads of his first dream, they woke him from his sleep with the same question: Do you have another daughter?

[Page 125]

R' Mendel was beside himself. He complained before the city's homeowners, asked for mercy and claimed - I suffered badly before my daughters got married so why do I have to go through the same agony after they got married? What do they want from me? Is there a shortage of modest girls in the city? Is it not enough that I placed seven daughters? They should go and knock on the doors of those who didn't bring even one daughter to our world.

It turns out that the city's clowns also have a Jewish heart, and when they realized that their prank agitated R' Mendel's soul, they decided to let him go him and find another victim for their practical jokes, and R' Mendel found his peace.

Translator's Footnotes:

Benot Zelophehad - "Daughters of Zelophehad."

The *"Ogolnykim"* were grain merchants who stood and gossiped at the corner of Nikolowski and Sobieski streets.

[Page 126]

Such a "Krishmelanu"
by Nisan Amitai (Stambul)
Translated by Sara Mages

There was a Jewish man in Akkerman and his name was *"Leizer der Blinder,"* and so he was called, may it not befall on us, because this Leizer was blind. However, despite his blindness he knew all the Jews in the city, knew where they lived and what they did, and even knew how to get to them. He knew everyone - and everyone knew him. And why is that? Because this Leizer had a special role, he had the "possession" on all the *"Krishmelanus"* in Akkerman. If you don't know the nature of these *"Krishmelanus,"* I will explain it to you. *"Krishmelanus"* is a large number of *"Krishmelanu,"* and its interpretation probably came from the word *"Kriyat Shema."* And if you want to know how *"Kriyat Shema"* turned into *"Krishmelanu"*- the people of Akkerman have the solution. They were experts in the disruption of *Leshon Hakodesh*, names of prayers etc.

Well, Leizer's "possession" was to conduct the prayer of *"Kriyat Shema"* in the Jewish Maternity Hospital one day before a newborn was brought in the Covenant of Avraham Avinu. He didn't lead the *"Kriyat Shema"* on his own, he added to himself a group of boys who also received a payment for the *"Krishmelanu."* The mothers gave the boys cookies and candy, whereas Leizer was paid in cash for his trouble. It can be assumed that the business was worthwhile for him, and the proof is - he never relinquished this livelihood and the "possession" on it.

There was another man in Akkerman and his name was Chaim Klorfeld, but the *"Ogolnykim"* of Akkerman nicknamed him Chaim *"der langer,"* and if they called him that way - so would we. Chaim *"der langer"* wasn't only *"langer"* (long), but also a wise Jew who loved to joke.

One day, and that day was a summer day, our Chaim walked in a city street a little bored and probably pondering in his heart: on whom can I play a practical joke on this summer day and relieve some of the summer's boredom? As he was thinking so and so - Leizer *"der blinder"* came toward him. An idea flashed immediately in Chaim Klorfeld's head. R' Leizer - he said to him - you probably know that a certain Jew from Bucharest lives in my yard. A son was born to him, his eldest son and, God willing, the *"bris"* will take place the day after tomorrow. Don't forget to conduct a proper *"Krishmelanu"* in his house, and you may rest assured that this Jew will pay what you deserve, because he's not one of the wimps, some say that he is a very rich man. Don't forget, for God's sake, tomorrow afternoon!

Leizer's face lit up when he heard the news. He knew well where the yard of Chaim *"der langer"* was, and in the afternoon of the next day he gathered a large group of boys, as appropriate for a Jew from Bucharest that the gossipers say that he's a very rich man. He burst with shouts of joy, together with the children, to the house of the Jew from Bucharest in the yard of Chaim "*der langer,*" and without asking questions started to pray "*Kriyat Shema*" with great enthusiasm and in the most festive style.

As they conducted the ritual of "*Krishmelanu*" the shout of - Woe is me! - sounded from the next room. It was accompanied by the cries help! help!, and the voice, the voice of the mother who became hysterical after hearing the prayers of R' Leizer and his group of helpers.

The Jewish women, who heard the cries in the yard, quickly entered the apartment of the "Jew" from Bucharest and saw R' Leizer and his group of children at the peak of their ecstasy, trilling their voices and swaying their bodies the way you shake a *lulav* on Sukkot. What are you doing here? - the women shouted, get out of here, fast!

Why do we have to leave? - says "*Leizer der Blinder*" - we came to conduct a proper "*Krishmelanu*" for the newborn and his mother and wish them *Mazel Tov*. I don't understand why the woman is shouting as if she was slaughtered by a sharp slaughterer's knife. The most important thing is - I want them to pay me and give some candy to the children.

So? - the women said - you're waiting for your payment? We advise you to run away from here with the boys

[Page 127]

as long as you're still alive, otherwise, you will get such a beating that your ancestors and your forefathers never knew. This Gentile, the tax collector from Bucharest, will beat you hip and thigh if he would come here and see what you have done to his wife. He will dismantle your bones, one by one, and grind them very thin!

What, a Gentile? - said one-eyed Leizer - after all, Chaim "*der langer*" clearly told me that a Jew lives here, a distinguished Jew from Bucharest, a very rich man!

The righteous Jewish women didn't respond to his puzzling questions because first of all they had to calm the Christian woman, explain the tragic mistake and beg her not to tell the whole matter to her husband. R' Leizer stopped the "*Krishmelanu*" prayers in the middle because he understood that this time he fell victim in the hands of Chaim the long. He no longer waited for his payment because he was afraid that he would be forced to read "*Kriat Shema*" before death, and this time, specifically for his own body. Leizer "*der blinder*" left with pain and shame together with his "holy sheep."

In Akkerman City Garden

Corners in Akkerman's City Garden.

The Liman River

In Akkerman's City Garden

[Pages 128]

Tit-bids from Akkerman
(episodes and anecdotes)
by Nisan Amitai
Translated by Sara Mages

When Shmuel Trachtman, the renowned author and scholar retired, he settled in Akkerman and established a sophisticated and modern bathhouse. His house was almost the first house that those, who came to Akkerman by sea, encountered. Those who came in a different way - were drawn first to the impressive shop in the corner of Ismailsky and Moskowakaya streets that its owner, Y.P, was famous for his ignorance and rudeness.

Mr. Trachtman used to say that those, who came to Akkerman for the first time, might come to wrong conclusions. Those arriving by sea - will definitely say: if the manager of the bathhouse is a very educated man, the richest man in town is probably a lot more educated than him. On the other hand, those who come to the city by land will definitely say: if the richest man in the city is such an ignorant, the fellow who runs the bathhouse is probably worthless!...

* * *

A Jewish shopkeeper was convicted in Akkerman because he opened his shop ten minutes before the time allowed by the order of "Tablani days, " the days in which special prayers were held for the life of the royal family. The man asked for the services of the lawyer Zwilling. When the case was discussed in court in the presence of three judges, Zwilling asked permission to verify the time by comparing his watch to the judges' watches. It turned out that each watch showed a different time. "Your honorable judges", Zwilling said, "if your watches are so far from being accurate how could you blame a poor shopkeeper whose watch is undoubtedly not as perfect as your watches? " the trial was cancelled.

* * *

After the revolution of 1905 there was a significant tendency for baptism among young Jewish men and women who sought a university education. A liberal priest, who was a novice at the Armenian-Gregorian Church in Akkerman, was a very convenient man. Candidates for conversion arrived from Odessa in the "Turgeneiv" ship, quickly got rid of the matter, and returned on the same day and in the same ship to Odessa as proper Christians. A matter of no importance. Jabotinsky denounced these knights and called them "converts, members of the Armenian-Gregorian faith. "

* * *

Grain export was the main industry in Akkerman. At the beginning, several merchants did rather well, but over time they fell victim to market fluctuations and became destitute. Each one of them. When a merchant sent a shipment to Odessa, he wrote the purchase price in his notepad in Yiddish or in Hebrew. Later, he also wrote the proceeds from the sale. If there was a loss, the registration in the notepad showed: remained in Odessa (in Hebrew).

* * *

Zusman was a God-fearing Jew and never missed a prayer. When the trading season was at its peak, he used to get up very early when it was still dark outside. By law, it too early for the *Shacharit* prayer, and it was impossible to pray later in the market place. Zusman solved this problem successfully. He wrapped himself in his *Tallit* and *Tefillin* before he went to sleep, and by doing so he fulfilled his duty before nightfall.

* * *

Once, there was a great commotion in the city. It was when scientists notice that a comet was moving and getting dangerously close to Earth. The collision of the comet with Earth was considered possible and people were very excited. The matter was discussed at length in the synagogue between *Mincha* and *Maariv*. Those, who explained the news, held the audience spellbound. Only one wagon owner remained skeptical. Imagine - he said to another wagon owner - that the two of us meet on a narrow road in a very dark night. Do you think that we will pass unscathed? All the more so, God is the one who leads his world in the wide open space.

* * *

[Page 129]

K.B. bought a pair of new horses and was about to go on a journey around the city's streets to show them off. However, to his great embarrassment the horses refused to move. A crowd of spectators gathered quickly and a few of them gave him various tips. K.B., who was very angry, answered them: please present your ideas in writing and don't forget to paste a stamp.

* * *

Akkerman was abuzz the day Plehve, the Russian Interior Minister, was murdered. It was possible to hear discussions about the startling news in every corner. Women even forgot their shopping at the butcher shop and wanted to learn additional details about the event from each other. One woman said with sympathy: this is a hard way to make a living - a difficult livelihood.

* * *

After Plehve's murder the following legend was widespread in Akkerman.

The late Dr. Herzl decided to call Plehve to the Heavenly Court because of his persecution of the Jews. He sent Moshe (Moishe), the *Gabbai* of the Kishinev synagogue who died a martyr, to call Plehve, but Plehve refused - again and again - to come. At the end, Dr. Herzl told Moishe: go now for the last time. If you can't bring him in one piece, bring him in pieces, but this time he must come.

* * *

During the Russo-Japan War, the public followed each newspaper edition with anxiety. One young man, rich but uneducated, subscribed - according to the spirit of the times - to the Saturday edition of *"Odeskia Novosti"* which contained a photographic section with many pictures of warships. In his clumsy way the young man spread the paper upside down and immediately called his family: please look - another ship capsized.

* * *

Chaim-Yankel Kitzis and Shalom Levinton were two prominent exporters in the community. Each one of them paid his financial obligations differently. As exporters of grain they used to buy from the local merchants. When a merchant gave his goods, he came to receive his payment. Kitzis received him with friendship, conducted a long conversation with him, and eventually influenced him to come and get what's due to him the following week. A week later, the same episode was repeated. Finally, at the end of the third week, the merchant received his payment in the form of a check to Trabuti and associates, Odessa, for payment in twenty one days. Shalom Levinton wasn't so. Without exception, each merchant, who came to get his payment, received an envelope that contained an invoice and all the money that was due to him without unnecessary talk.

It seemed that Levinton belittled the merchant's dignity in favor of the latter. People used to say that Kitzis loves the Jews and Levinton didn't like them.

In Akkerman's city garden

In Akkerman's train station

Akkerman's city garden in the winter

[Page 130]

In Bygone Days
by Chava Barnea (Dorpman)
Translated by Sara Mages

A. The Band

As we know, "*Tarbut* Gymnasium" was the crown glory of our city and this was largely thanks to Yakov Berger - the talented man who headed it. Certainly, quite a lot will be written in this book about the many achievements of this man, but I intend to devote my words to the Gymnasium's brass band which was conducted by Yosef Pelikof. Several members of the band are currently living in Israel, and we often reminisce about the many performances of the band which had a reputation in the city.

I especially remember the band's performance in the marches that were held in the Romanian national holiday. The students of the Hebrew Gymnasium marched dressed in uniform, together with the students of the Gymnasiums and state schools, along Mikhailovsky Street accompanied by the sound of our band. The principal, Mr. Berger, invested considerable efforts before each march because he knew that the Gymnasium's performance might determine the Jews' honor in the Gentiles' eyes. We, the students and also the musicians, were infused with the spirit of mission because we knew that many Jews and non-Jews will stand on both sides of the street and closely watch our performance which will be the topic of conversation by all.

However, the Gymnasium's band wasn't only tested during these official marches. I now remember the traditional trips on *Lag BaOmer* in which all the youth movements in the city participated, every man by his own camp and every man by his own standard, to the rhythm of the band's marching songs...

At this opportunity we should remember the man who contributed to the development of the musical activities in our city: Moshe Cohen, who organized the municipal choir *"HaZamir"* that appeared in various dances with great success. He himself had a fine and pleasant voice. However, the choir only existed for a short time. He taught us solfège and endowed us with the first sounds of the Hebrew songs that were popular in those days. The choir, which was under his direction, participated in the various parties that were held in Gymnasium to the enjoyment of the many guests..

Members of the Gymnasium's band with its conductor Yosef Pelikof on his wedding day

[Page 131]

"Tarbut" Gymnasium's band

First row sitting from right to left: **Yoske Koren, Bitelman**
Second row: **Pelikof Moshe, Rosental Yakov, Britawa Siyoma, the principal Y. Berger, the band's conductor Yosef Pelikof, Yasha Wienstein, Wisniewski Yasha**
Third row: **Yoske Zeplin, Frumer Musya, Kaplinsky, Zukerman Sheptel, Goldman Zemba, Frank, Lushek Filya, Abramowitch Musya**
Fourth row: **Gewet Siyoma, Girshfeld Binyamin, Lev Yasha, Toyrman Yitzchak, Rabinowitch, Kogan Izaya**

[Page 132]

B. Purim Eves in My Family

My extensive family in Akkerman excelled in a way of life that was based on Jewish tradition and customs which charmed of the youngsters in the family. It was especially expressed on Jewish holidays. It was customary that each branch of the family had a "possession" on a certain holiday, meaning: it hosted the whole family in "its" holiday. The holiday of Purim belonged to aunt Beila from the Shteydakot family, and I remember that I, and my entire family, waited impatiently for the traditional visit to the home of aunt Beila. The traditional pleasant atmosphere in this house probably caused it.

The preparations for the holiday began two weeks earlier, and the swallow that heralded the arrival of the holiday was aunt Beila who used to come to our home to ask my mother z"l all kinds of questions about this and that, until she reached the point. And what was the point? - to remind us that the holiday of Purim "belonged to her" and, God forbid, all of us, young and old, shouldn't forget to come to dinner.

My mother, who knew from the outset the reason for this visit because it was repeated year after year, responded with a cheery face: "My dear Beila, how can I forget? After all, it's well known that Purim is your holiday. We'll come, all of us will come!"

And indeed, Purim feast at my aunt's house was a real experience. The parlor was properly polished, the big chandelier above the table shed a lot light, the traditional delicacies for Purim were delicious, and the big table was tastefully set. My pretty aunt and her tall and beautiful daughter Chana knew how to add to the festive atmosphere the way they welcomed their guests. The good atmosphere aroused everyone to participate in a sing-along until the arrival of the promised "dessert," which has become a tradition in every Purim feast. The cantor, meaning Yisrael, sang along with everyone and didn't make an impression that he was the star that everyone waited for his performance... However, when his turn came, he proved that he was indeed the "star." He was an expert in reading the works of Shalom Aleichem, and every year he also added something from his works to the delight of all the participants in the meal.

And so, we sat in an atmosphere of holiday and happiness to the wee hours of the night and enjoyed the splendor and taste of Purim in my aunt's house.

"Budky" beach 1926

[Page 133]

A Family Tree
(a tree and it's view)
by Sheftel Zukerman
Translated by Sara Mages

On the seventieth birthday of our brother, Zadok Zukerman, who lives today in Herzlia, all the members of the extensive family and their descendants gathered at the home of his oldest daughter and son-in-law, Malka and Zev Golani, in Herzlia. Not all the family members came. But, nevertheless, about seventy "Zukermanim" gathered.

In honor of this family event, a page with a diagram of a "tree and branches, "the "Zukermanim's stocktaking" to the month of Tishrei 5739, was prepared and distributed to all the participants. This page, which was snatched by everyone as a keepsake, was not only given to the sons and their descendants, but also to other relatives (cousins etc.). We are grateful to Malka and Zev Golani who prepared this handsome family page.

Who are our parents, the head of the lineage?

The father of the family, Nachum Zukerman, was born in 5630 (1870) in the town of Azarnitz, Ukraine. His father, HaRav Zadok Zukerman, was the rabbi of the city of Akkerman for many years. The family probably moved to Akkerman from the Ukraine around the 1860s. Our grandfather, HaRav Zadok Zukerman, was a descendent of a Ukrainian rabbinical family, and one of his ancestors was a famous rabbi, the *Bach* [Yoel Sirkis], who, as it was customary in those days, was named after one of his books.

I remember the tombstone of grandfather, Zadok z"l, in the first row at the entrance to the Jewish cemetery of Akkerman. It was in the form of an "*ohel*," and was located in one of the most distinguished places as befits the man who was the rabbi of the city for many years. When our father, Nachum, died in 5685 (1925), he was buried in the second row near his father's grave. Every year, in the month of Elul, I visited the cemetery with my mother to pray at the graves of my ancestors, as was customary in Jewish communities.

My father z"l studied at the Yeshiva and was certified to be a ritual slaughterer. He was one of the four ritual slaughterers of Akkerman. He died after a long illness on 12 Elul 5685 (1925). Until his death he was a Torah scholar and an ardent Hassid of the Rabbi from Sadigura. His image appears before my eyes (he died when I was 11) – as a tall Jew with a beard and he's dressed in a black *kapote* [long coat]. A "*yarmulke*" was always on his head when he studied the *Gemara* or other sacred books. On the Sabbath and holidays he dressed in his holiday clothes and walked slowly to the Hassidim's "*Beit HaMidrash*" which was located in the synagogues' courtyard. On the Sabbath he usually returned with a "guest for the Sabbath."

Father didn't stand out in public activities probably because he was always busy with matters of livelihood. Even though he had to support the eleven children who were born to him over the years, he was very devoted to his Rabbi from Sadigura. Once a year he visited his "rabbi" and spent 2-3 weeks in his "court"...

Mother z"l, Chana Zukerman from the Horovitz family, was born in Akkerman in 5634 (1874), and the origin of her family – Southern Bessarabia. Her father, HaRav Eliyahu-Chaim Horovitz, was the rabbi of the city of Kilya which was located on the bank of one of the tributaries of the

Danube River. I remember well my elderly grandfather, Eli- Chaim, when he came to visit us and when I visited him when I happened to be at the branch of "*Gordonia*" in Kilya. The family tree of grandfather Eliyahu-Chaim Horovitz refers to the sons of the "Horovitzim", the descendants of R' Isaiah HaLevi Horovitz who is better known as the "Shelah ha-Kadosh" after the title of his well-known book "*Shenei Lu?ot HaBerit.*" Therefore, on our mother's side, we are offspring of "*Shelah ha-Kadosh*" and all of us are proud of this relationship.

I will always remember our mother Chana as the mother of the big family. She was awarded to raise 10-11 children, big and small. The house was always full, but not too full because of the age difference (there's a difference of 22 years between me, the youngest, and my older brother).

My parents' home, despite the religious atmosphere, the observance of the commandments, and the daily prayer in the synagogue, was also a Jewish-national and Zionist home. I envision the books in Hebrew and Yiddish - which were on special shelves, next to the beds or on top of the wardrobes. The general book case only contained the *Gemara, Mishnaiot* and other sacred books.

[Page 134]

For many years we lived near the Jewish library (Hebrew and Yiddish). In the afternoon, Shterenshis, the librarian and teacher, passed next to our apartment on his way to open the library. Therefore, we were able to plan our visit to the library to exchange books. The following newspapers came to our house regularly - "*Unsere Zeit*" from Kishinev, "*Ard un Arbayt*" of "*Tzeirei Zion,*" "*HaOlam*" the weekly journal of the "World Zionist Organization" which came every week from Great Russell Street, London. We were very proud of this newspaper which came straight from London... Books, which were published by "Stiebel" and "*Tarbut,*" were also found at our home. The kids read children's books and also studied from the collection of "*Olam Katan*" [small world] which was published at the beginning of the century. We spoke Yiddish at home even though everyone was fluent in Russian and Romanian. We also spoke Hebrew because the young children (four of us) studied at the Hebrew Gymnasium.

The children's education was varied: the first - the three sons - studied in Yeshivot and received rabbinical ordination. Only one of them went the way of his ancestors and became a ritual slaughterer (our brother Leib Zukerman). The sister, Leah, studied at the government school for girls (in the Russian) in Akkerman and also studied external studies. The fourth son, Noah Zukerman, who also studied in a Yeshiva, was the first son to immigration to Israel. He defected from the Romanian Army and traveled to the port city of Constanța on the Black Sea coast. There, he "slipped" to a boat that brought him to the shores of Israel in the fall of 1920. Two sons, Zev and Shmuel, studied at the Russian trade schools in the city even though they studied the Torah and a little Hebrew before that.

A new period in the education of the children in the Zukerman family began with the seventh son, Zadok, and I mean the Hebrew education at the primary and secondary (gymnasium) school of "*Tarbut*" association in our city.

At the end of the First World War Bessarabia was returned to Romania. At that time, Hebrew schools of "*Tarbut*" society were established in the regions west of Tsarist Russia, from the Baltic Sea to the Black Sea in the south (Lithuania-Latvia, Eastern -Polandand Bessarabia). The new authorities, in their wish to push out the Russian language and culture that dominated the streets and spoken by Jewish families for centuries, encouraged the establishment of a network of these schools. Most were private schools who didn't receive rights from the government. The graduates of these schools had to take additional exams so they could continue their higher education at the university.

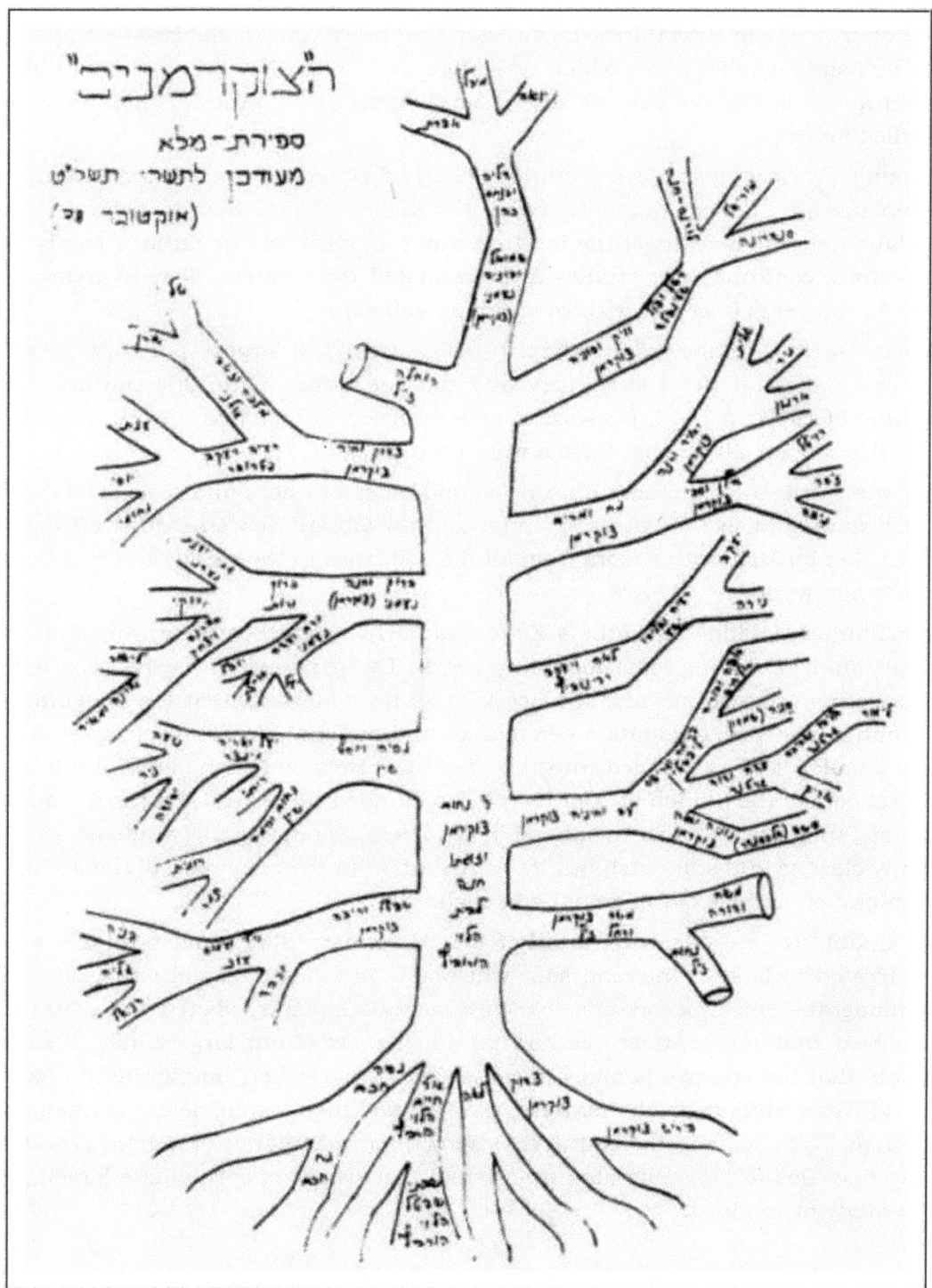

The Zukerman family: a tree and its view

[Page 135]

Zionist and Hebrew activists took advantage of this situation and established a primary school in almost every district city in Bessarabia. Later, they also established a Hebrew Gymnasium. The study at the gymnasium was for a fee, which was often quite high. Not everyone was able to pay tuition, and after a year or two the parents sent their children back to the Romanian Gymnasium where they studied for free.

The Zukerman's four young children studied at "*Tarbut*" school. The first, Zadok, studied only for 2–3 years because after father's death he traveled to Kishinev to study in a Yeshiva. He studied to be a ritual slaughterer so he can get the job that was the "right" of our father's family. We, the three young children, continued our studies and graduated the Hebrew "*Tarbut*" Gymnasium in Akkerman after 12 full years (together with the primary school).

Akkerman was greatly influenced by the city of Odessa, the largest port city in southern Russia, but it was mostly at the 19th century and the beginning of the 20th century, until the October Revolution of 1917. In 1918, Bessarabia was returned to Romania, the border was closed and sealed, and the contact with Soviet Russia was severed.

I remember the stories that my parents, uncles and older brothers and sisters told me about "Odessa, the Jewish metropolis," about its splendor and the vibrant Jewish Zionist life in it. About the harbor which was bustling with sailors from all the countries in the world, and to differentiate, about the city's "underworld"...

Our brother Shmuel, in addition to the 4 Zukermans who studied at the gymnasium, was the school's secretary and its driving force for many years. The gymnasium wasn't only a place of study for the Zukerman's sons, but also a place for cultural entertainment for the entire family. The famous Chanukah parties, graduation ceremonies and national Zionist meetings took place in the gymnasium's hall. All of us blended into the life of the Hebrew Gymnasium and were active within it. The first core of the branch of "*Gordonia*" was founded there, and the three "young" sons of the Zukerman family were active members in it. There weren't many students in "*Tarbut*" Gymnasium (only close to 200 students), but its contribution to the education of the Jewish youth to Zionism, immigration and life of fulfillment was high.

Without a doubt we are the **only family** from Akkerman that almost all its sons and daughters immigrated to Israel. Only one son, who's also has ties to Israel and visited it three times, didn't immigrate. His descendants, who are veteran Zionists, visited the country many times. We often hear from our townspeople how proud they are of our large family. It's true that we were fortunate that the last two families, together with our mother, immigrated to Israel after the Second World War and its tribulations. Here, they merged their strong desire to immigrate and their desire to build their home in the country. Dozens of grandchildren and great grandchildren live in Israel. No one, God forbid, emigrated from Israel. This is the epopee of one Israeli family, if only there were many more like it.

The extensive Zukerman family

[Page 136]

The Rabbi's House
by Chaim Zukerman
Translated by Sara Mages

More than forty years have passed since we left Akkerman to the "mercy of the Gentiles" as it changes the names of its squares and streets, perpetuates its history and the names of its various conquerors, but it never left our memory. Our Akkerman had infinite power when it clung to the shore of the Leman River that its silent waves cleaned the walls of its legendary ancient fort.

Beautiful and proud Jews lived in Akkerman, Jews who settled there by chance when they sought a source of income and sustenance. They struck roots in the city and added a lot to its beauty and charm. I close my eyes for a moment and envision various scenes from my childhood and youth. Here is the market with its many shops and Jewish merchants waiting in their doorways for a buyer; here are the vendors lurking nervously, they're also looking for buyers for their wares; a woman is offering a chicken for sale – the revenue from this chicken – her only income; and here's the corner of the taverns and the strong smell of vodka reaches my nostrils.

And here's the corner of the haberdashery stores, the bakeries and grocery stores and in their center – a square. It stands empty all the days of the week and only fills with farmers and agricultural produce on market days. Here's a farmer sitting in the corner and eating *challah* with herring and a bottle of vodka next to him; and I see more and more pictures in my closed eyes.

Akkerman was a Jewish city. All its synagogues were concentrated in one yard and each synagogue was unique and a world unto itself. And to differentiate – the church that the ringing of its bells brought a reminder to the Jews, a threatening reminder from ancient time to our days.

We, the members of the rabbi's family, lived in the shadow of this church. I remember the road that led to the church on Sunday and Easter, and the galloping horses that frightened the hearts of the Jews. Our house was in a large courtyard with a lot of neighbors and a well stood in its center. Behind the courtyard sprawled an orchard and a vineyard, a barn with a lot of cows and warehouses with a stock of barrels that were used to store wine.

I see father hunched over the *Gemara* studying a *Sugia* [Talmudic discourse on a topic]. By the sound of his voice I was able to tell if and when he managed to overcome the severity of the *Sugia* and start learning a new one. He had time for Torah study and for ruling on religious laws and *kashrut*, meetings with the city leaders and walking to the synagogue with a close friend. This walk was seasoned with words of Torah and wisdom

During the holidays his "sermons" at the Great Synagogue were saturated with wisdom and wit. They weren't just seasoned with quotations from the Bible, but also with words of secular philosophy of ancient and modern philosophers that weren't strangers to him. He repeated, again and again, that Jewish thought and the Torah influenced their contemplation. He fascinated the worshipers with his words and the synagogue was full to capacity each time he gave a "sermon" on current affairs.

Our course of life and daily existence were rooted in the Torah and tradition, and every holiday cast a special atmosphere on the house. On Passover eve the city's Jews came to the rabbi's house to sell the *chametz* to a Gentile from Turlaki. The last day of Passover, which is the day of the death of my grandfather HaRav Zadok, is engraved in my memory. After his death the rabbinate was transferred to my father who was "ordained" by the genius rabbi "*Der Alter* from Constantine." Later, he was also "ordained" by the genius rabbi, R' Soloveitchik, from Brisk. On that day all the relatives and family members gathered at our home and the preparation for that day was great and exciting.

I also remember well the days of *Gittin*. Gloom settled on the house on the days of *Gittin* because home and family ceased to exist. In one corner in father's room, which was filled with scared books, lay the "*halitzah*" shoe that, as we all know, freed the widows from their "*aginut*." We, the children, were taken out of the house so that we will not see the procedure of the *Gittin*. By the way, in the divorce certificate the addition, which is called "Weissenberg," was written next to the name of our city because of the power of an ancient custom.

[Page 137]

Besides the yard, the orchard and the wide spaces around us, we, the children, had another hidden treasure that cannot be described in words, and the treasure is – our mother. She was the center of the house and the supreme authority. Those who came to the rabbi's door knew that she was in charge of the rabbi's public relations. She engaged, from early morning until late at night, in matters of the house, the education of the children, etc. Sometimes, I pestered her with my various questions including the eternal question that only a child like me allowed himself to ask: Is there a God or not... Mother showed great patience to my embarrassing questions and didn't let me go until my claims were closed. I'm sure that she didn't tell father what bothered me because he didn't have great patience to my heretical questions because, after all, he was a Jewish rabbi.

There were brothers and sisters at home and each had his own living space. The atmosphere in this house merged with the atmosphere of the city's Jewish community. The war brought an end to our home and its unique atmosphere.

HaRav R' Zadok Zukerman and His Sons

The book "*Ohalei Shem*," which contains details about rabbis in Jewish communities, includes these details about R' Zadok Zukerman and his two sons: Efraim and Moshe.

On R' Zadok it is told, that he served in the rabbinate in the towns: Harishkivkek, Azarnitz and Akkerman for fifty years and he is the grandson of HaGaon, our rabbi R' Heschel zt"l, offspring of HaGaon [David ha–Levi Segal], author of "*Turei Zahav*" ["Rows of Gold"] zt"l, and grandson of the illustrious Rabbi, R' Eliezer of Tavashville, one of the disciples of Baal Shem Tov zt"l and grandson of HaGaon, R' Moshe zt"l, president of the court of the community of Vinnytsia at the time of Baal Shem Tov zt"l.

On his son HaRav R' Efraim it is told that he was ordained for teaching by the rabbis of Mohyliv–Podilskyi, and in the year 5642 was accepted to teach in the city of Azaritz in the Podolia Voivodeship and in the year 5644 in the city of Mezhirov. His Torah innovations were printed in the responsa of Rabbi Malkiel Tzvi HaLevi, president of the court of the community of Łomża.

On Rabbi Moshe, son of Rabbi Zadok Zukerman, it is told, that he was born in 5640 and appointed rabbi in 5666. He was ordained for teaching by HaGaon R' Chaim (HaLevi) Soloveitchik, may he live a good long life, of Brisk, and HaGaon R' Shmuel Avraham president of the court of the community of Alt Konstantin [Starokostiantyniv]. In the *Ketuvim* there are also questions and answers that he negotiated in *Halakhic* discourse with the outstanding rabbis of the generation, and in the book "*Divrei Malkiel*" of HaGaon of Łomża an answer was printed to the question of Rabbi Moshe Zukerman.

HaRav Moshe Zukerman, the Rabbi of Akkerman

[Page 138]

A Letter of Recommendation

(copy of a letter written by our grandfather z"l – R' Zadok Zukerman the Rabbi of Akkerman, written in 5666, the month of Heshvan, November 1905, close to his death).

With God's help, Thursday Parashat Chayei Sarah
5666, Akkerman

When the bearer of this letter, R' Dov may his light shine Gottlieb, leaves our city and sets out to a place, where he is not known, to apply for a position in one of the congregations that God has summoned before him, we come to testify of him and tell about his honesty and good qualities. He has been a cantor in our community for seven years and we hold respect to him because he is a great and famous musician, who sings nice things that he himself wrote with a choir of singers and his voice is also pleasant. And therefore he acquired for himself a lot of love and affection in the hearts of all who heard him and, in addition to that, he is a beloved and valuable man. He is involved with people and he is also honest with God and his religion. At such time he is not a common phenomenon, there is no cantor who sings like him, he will not leave the teachings of God and he respects it in all its details. We also knew very well his late father, R' Yakov z"l, who was a beloved respected scholar and God–fearing. And this time the cantor, R' Dov may his light shine Gottlieb, was forced to leave our city because of the pogroms that befell us in the past three weeks, the bandit rioters surrounded our city and robbed all the people of our city, and after they had done as they pleased, they plundered and looted all the trading houses and, before they were satisfied, they set fire to the shops and houses of the Jews and burnt the whole city. Most of the people of our city remained naked and destitute, every person's heart was horrified to the sight of a man who was once affluent and wealthy and now became a destitute who extends his hand to receive bread from the charity fund, and there were also many dead in our city that the rioters attacked murdered, and the people who remained fled from them, from among the lions teeth and the jaws of the heretics and there was only one step between them and death. Therefore, it is easy to understand the magnitude of the distress that prevails in our city and why he should leave our city. And if not for the riots, robbery and disaster in our city, he would have remained the cantor of our city for many years to come. Therefore, the sacred debt is imposed on each and every person to receive him (…) and, thanks to this God will strengthen his people, protect them from all trouble and distress, and save them from the beasts of prey.

The petitioner – Zadok the Rabbi of Akkerman
(seal: Zukerman the Rabbi of Akkerman)

[Page 139]

A "note" – a Memento
by Yisrael Finkel
Translated by Sara Mages

The immigrants from Akkerman to Eretz Yisrael received emotional farewell from their friends and family members who remained in Akkerman. The joy of the immigrants, and the sadness of those who remained, mingled together. Tears of joy and sorrow mixed together. To this day I remember the sight at the train station in Akkerman on the day of my immigration as a member of "Gordonia." Almost all the members of the movement came to accompany me and my friends, and a few moments before the train moved one on the members tucked a small note in my hand and it is kept with me to this day. When I had the time to look at the note after boarding the ship, it became clear to me that it was not just a note, but a poem written by my friend, Musia Rotenstein, and in it he expressed his strong emotions towards my migration. I keep this note as an amulet and it is worth bringing it to the knowledge of our townspeople as it was written.

I haven't heard anything about the author of this passionate poem since my immigration, and I have no idea what happened to him, but the emotions of the heart and the outpouring of his feeling in this poem are not only his, but of all the young people of Akkerman in those days (according to rumor the writer of the poem perished in the Holocaust).

This poem will be an everlasting memento for you!

To the Immigrant

by M. Rotenstein

You, the immigrant to the homeland
To establish a home there for the suffering Jew,
Please carry the blessing of my trembling soul
Deliver the sorrow of my withered heart!

He cries in the daytime, and also howls at night
On the condition of his people living in exile:
Because joy moved away and happiness passed
He can no longer tolerate poverty...

Please deliver to the flourishing Land of Israel,
That we shed many tears for her,
Tell to every home, to the forest, to the grass,
That out of abundance of longings we walked away them!

Bring a blessing from me to Lake Kinneret,
To the mountains of Lebanon, to the valley, to the ravine,
Tell that my soul is thirsty for them
Say that I will be hungry for them the rest of my life!

Notify my people who are there in Israel
That I worried about them many times.
That I asked a lot, read, wrote
And even now I devote my life to them.

Kiss the land of our patriarchs for me.
Sing the anthem for you!
"Let your hands be strong – the immigrants to our country.
all of you, build the homeland."

Akkerman 26.3.1936

לְעֶבְרְךָ עָת יִהְיֶה לְךָ פְּירִידָה

אֵשׁ הַגְּאֻלָּה!
(שיר א. שלונסקי)

אַשְׁרֵי הָעָם אֲשֶׁר אֵשׁ הַגְּאֻלָּה
בִּדְבַקִים עַל אָדְמוֹ לְבַדֵּי הַסְלָע,
תֹּאכַל-לוֹ בִּרְמַת עוֹלָמִי הָרָצוּא
בִּמְאוֹד אֵשׁ לִבּוֹ הָרוֹעֵד!

בֹּעֲרָה הִיא שׁוּמָה, וְחֻמָּהּ לֹא פַחֲנָה
אֵשׁ אֲדַּק קֵץ וְאֵין חֲמִים בִּלְעָדָיו:
כִּי הַדְּרָכָה לֵעֵינָיו וְלֹב הַשָּׁוֹן
לֹא נָטָה אֶל רֶשֶׁף עַד הַסֵּתֶר...

תְּמוֹרָתוֹ לְפִגְרוֹ וְעַל רֹאשׁוֹ הַלֶּהָבָה,
כִּי לֹא בְּשָׂרוֹ אֲשֶׁר לָטְלוֹ;
סְפִי לוֹ כִּי בְּעֵר לוֹשֵׁן, בֹּעֵר לוֹ
כִּי דְּרוֹר לְאֻמִּים וְקִיָּמָם יִפְעַל.

אֵשׁ הַגְּאֻלָּה נָשָׂא אֵת יָם הָעֹרֶף
אֵת הָרֵי הַצִּפּוֹן אֵשׁ הַצָּפוֹן אֶת הָשׁוֹן,
סֻפַּר פְּלָסֶת לְשׂוֹנוֹ דַּעַת
תִּאמֵר פָּלַסְתֵּ הֵבִיא עַל וְי!

הָעֹלָם לָעוֹם יַעֲשׂוּ הַלְּעֻמִּים אֵם מֶלֶך
שָׁלַט בִּלְעֻמִּים זָה לְזָה לִצְמָחַל!

[Page 140]

"I Remember the Days of Old"
(From a letter from Siberia)
by Efraim Abramowitch, Siberia, the Soviet Union
Translated by Sara Mages

It's our *mitzvah* to tell, and not just a mitzvah, but an obligation to tell about the founders of our Hebrew School in Akkerman. The young generation must not think that everything came to us ready, as a gift of God above. It's the fruit of hard work of many people who devoted their life to one goal: educating the young generation. Indeed, in Israel, no one wonders when kindergarten children appear in a play or in a radio program in Hebrew. It's natural and obvious. However, imagine in your souls: a city in Southern Bessarabia, far from the center, the dominated languages in the area are Russian and Romanian, and within this environment the kindergarten children of our school appear on the stage in fluent Hebrew.

I now remember events from fifty years ago, and I was then a boy of five. Our kindergarten class prepared the play "Yitzchak and Rivka" in Hebrew, and although more than fifty years have passed since then – I remember to this day the words and melodies of this play. I see before me the hall full of people, the parents who draw satisfaction from their children, and our teacher – "aunt Manya" (so we affectionately called Manya Sharira who died a few years ago in Kishinev at the age of 93). She used to peek behind the curtain and followed the play, on which she invested a lot of work, with great excitement and anxiety.

Why did I start my memories from kindergarten? because it was the first link to the school that was established by "*Tarbut*" association in Akkerman. The initiator and founder was Yakov, son of Shmuel Berger z"l. He worked together with a dedicated group of teachers who tried to create something out of nothing. However, the birthright mainly belongs to – Berger. He knew how to instruct and guide in the right direction, was very knowledgeable in all areas of Judaism, knew foreign languages, and of course, all these helped him in carrying out his job. He was the organizer and coordinator of the "educational process" – meaning, the daily education program.

I remember how I looked at him with admiration. He knew everything. Here he appears in our class and gives us a Bible lesson, and a short time later he returns to us and teaches us the doctrine of laws. The treasure of his knowledge aroused a lot of wonder. To this day I remember his lessons and lectures about Shalom Aleichem and other writers of his time. Also his public activity was very extensive. The goal, which he placed before him, was that the school, under his management, would also be an educational institution that will help the students to foster their own personality.

We will not deprive the rights and contributions of other teachers. Is it possible to forget the lessons of our literature teacher Meir Grozman? Or the math lessons of our teacher Yeshayahu Neiman? I'm jumping from one to the other because the chronological order isn't the determining factor. I just wanted to highlight the impression that the school had left on me, and for sure, also on each of the students. We grew, matured, and the chain of life continues. We became parents and grandparents, but the school's place in our life remains firm and abiding, as a lighthouse from the days of our youth.

The last years, 1937-1940, were very sad years. In 1938, the **Goga-Koza** government rose to power and the school was closed. It was a difficult blow to the Jewish population. Among the decrees of that time was a decree which required each Jew to prove that he was born in the place. It was a condition for citizenship. In those years I've seen Berger in his work at the Jewish community as *Rav MeTa'am* [the rabbi on behalf of the government]. He had to search hundreds of documents. Dozens of people visited him every day because many were afraid to lose their citizenship and rights. He worked hard, above his powers, and tried to help those who turned to him. I see him with a satchel full of documents. He rummaged through them after he returned home from a day of hard work.

The Goga-Koza government fell and its evil decrees were abolished. Many appreciated the great help that they've received from Berger during the difficult period.

[Page 141]

I envision Berger's work room and the large bookcases along the walls. He was always absorbed in his work and I've never seen him idle. In July 1940, when we separated, he left me several books as a gift, among them were the history books of Dubnov. He was 48 years old when he was expelled from Akkerman. In an instant, all that has been achieved over many years was destroyed.

Until the beginning of the war he worked as an accountant in a place that was a distance of 40 kilometers from our city. Somewhere it's said that whoever planted a tree or left behind a student – his life had not been wasted. Berger's memory will never be forgotten because he didn't leave one student, but hundreds of students who will always remember him. Although his burial place is unknown, his tombstone is stable because each one of his students who survived carries his memory with him.

When I happened to be in Akkerman together with David we went to visit the school building. Now this building is used as a hospital. Indeed, this is also a vital and important institution, but I said to my son at the time: look, this was the nest of our education, the spring from which we drew our youth, and now – it's destroyed and gone.

*Efraim Abramowitch on his visit to Akkerman in 1981
Against the fortress' background*

[Page 142]

Childhood and Youth in Shabo and Akkerman
by Baruch Kamin
Translated by Sara Mages

The Story of My Life – the Days of My Youth

From my youth I remember the thunder of the cannons of the Red Army who retreated to the eastern side of the Dniester River, and the thunder of the cannons of the Romanian Army which entered the town of Shabo, a distance of 5 kilometers from Akkerman. In the cellar of the house of my grandfather, who was a rabbi and a slaughterer, I saw my frightened family and…I was afraid with them. It was dark in the cellar and only faint rays of light penetrated into it. At night, a lantern threw dim light and black shadows which increased the feeling of fear in me. Our days and nights were difficult and scary. After a few days we left the cellar and returned to our homes, to the yards and the streets that were full of sand. Silence prevailed in the area… the sun rose again for us and there was light. Romanian soldiers rode their horses through the streets and threw candy and sugar – commodities that we didn't have during the days the war.

We, the children, ran through the streets and collected the candy and sugar cubes. We were very happy to see the beautiful horses of the Romanian cavalry. My father, mother and I returned to our apartment which was at the upper part of town. Next to the apartment was a large sandy square and in its center stood a deep well. A large wooden bucket was tied to a long pole and large stones were attached to one of its ends. The bucket was lowered into the well and cold fresh water, which revived the soul of a man and beast, was drawn from it. Next to the well was kind of a wooden sink which was used to water the animals. The children always found interest around the cold water well, especially in the horses and cows that stood next to it. In the building where we lived (a new building with many apartments), one of the apartments was confiscated for a Romanian captain, a commander of a company of soldiers. Twice a day he conducted a roll call in the sandy square as he was riding his beautiful horse. All the neighborhood children watched the spectacular parade and all of us wanted to be a captain riding on a beautiful horse, dressed in magnificent uniform and adorned with gold and silver medals. At night, we dreamt about soldiers, horses, guns and waged wars...

Shabo was an interesting town in terms of its beautiful nature and diverse population which included several thousand Russian and Ukrainian residents, and also about sixty Jewish families. The environment was rich in vineyards which stretched for tens of kilometers. The soil was fertile and produced wheat, corn, fruit-trees, watermelons, melons and vegetables. Along the way, from Akkerman to Shabo, there were vineyards with a special variety of medicinal grapes. Near Shabo was a Russian-Ukrainian-Jewish town, the "Colony," which was name after the Swiss colonists who spoke German and French and were Lutherans, Catholics and Calvinism. Each religious sect had its own church. The Lutherans, who were the majority, had the largest church in the middle of the colony. The Calvinism had a small and modest church at the entrance to town. The colony was beautiful, well planned, its streets were wide and straight and beautiful trees lined both sides of the street. The beautiful buildings were built in a western Swiss style with big yards and wide warehouses... The yard of the big Provoslavit Church separated the town of Shabo from the colony. All the residents of the colony had a yard with chickens, horses, cows, dogs and cats, all by example and pattern of Western-Europe. The entire colony was immersed in greenery. The Swiss brought with them many varieties of fine grapes which acclimatized well in Shabo's sandy soil. Fish was also in abundance. Different species of fish were raised in artificial ponds at the mouth of the Leman River. They were used as food for the many vacationers who flocked here during the summer season. The smell of wine and fish rose from each yard. Traders came in droves from all over the country and even from abroad (especially from Poland and Czechoslovakia), and conducted large export businesses in fish and wine. Among them – many Jews who were interested in kosher wine. My grandfather, who was a rabbi and slaughterer, was also among the kosher wine producers because the income from the rabbinate and slaughtering was insufficient to support his large family of seven children. A large warehouse, which was used for storing hundreds of liters of kosher wine, stood in the yard. The wine was produced by Jewish workers and under my grandfather's supervision. Most of Shabo's Jewish residents engaged in trade and wine production, and only a few engaged in craft.

[Page 143]

I remember two shoemakers. One of them, Yitzchak Veler, was short, plump and highly active in public and cultural life. He was a talented actor in the Yiddish theater that was established in the place. Over time, the town of Shabo and the colony got closer to each other. The educated young people married each other, and the adults traded and worked together. On winter evenings, young people from the town and the colony climbed on top of the hill to watch the magnificent scenery of the Leman River and its frozen waters which glistened in the moonlight, or to skate on the frozen lake. On Sunday and holidays they played "cricket" in the town and in the colony. This game was brought from Switzerland and became the primary game of the place.

On the shores of the Leman, a distance of a few dozen meters from grandfather's house, were ornamental trees, tall reeds and natural recreation and bathing places. During the spring and summer we were able to sail and swim in the Leman, while in the winter the Leman was covered with a thick layer of ice and snow and strong cold winds blew from the river. This area was used as a place of crossing for the Communists who fled to the Soviet side and quite often shots pierced the air. More than once the bodies of the victims were left lying on the ice till dawn. Thereby, the river was a source of calamity for nature and man.

When the war ended, and I was then a boy of four, our family moved to live in the county city of Akkerman, while my grandfather's family continued to live in Shabo. My grandfather had seven sons and daughters and my father was the eldest. My grandmother was a beautiful woman, a diligent worker, and her children and grandchildren enjoyed her excellent food. She was a devout and observant and at the same time also progressive. She accepted the changes of times and advanced in everything that was related to the children's education. Grandfather was a scholar, the son of Rabbi Velvel from Zhabokrich (Podolia), and grandson of HaRav Pertz who came to Bessarabia to serve as a slaughterer and established a home and a family there. He got up at dawn to study the Torah and the melody of his *Gemara* blended in perfect harmony with the chirping of the birds. I liked to lie in bed in the morning and listen to the melodies and the chirping, and with them, the strong smell of the morning and the blossoming acacia trees. After the prayer and the meal, grandfather slaughtered chickens that the local people brought to him, and around 10 o'clock he devoted himself to the production of kosher wine. At four o'clock he went to the slaughterhouse and when he returned home he brought "pieces" from each animal that he had slaughtered [legs, liver, intestines, heart, tongue, lungs etc.) which, according to custom, belonged to the slaughterer. Grandmother sold some to the neighbors and used the rest to prepare tasty meat dishes for the entire family. The menu on Sabbath was varied: "*holodez*" [jellied meat], "*pizya*" [chicken wings in lemon sauce], liver, knishes, intestines, etc.

During the inflation, after the war, my father bought a large building with seven apartments on 35 Kischinovsky Street in Akkerman. It was across from the Russian bathhouse of the Gentile Bishlaga, who was rarely sober.

One of the fortress' towers

Behind the bathhouse, across the street, lay the Leman River, a tributary of the Dniester River. Most of the apartments of our building faced the street and a wide circular yard surrounded them. There were large warehouses in the yard and the fishermen used them to store fish. The tenants also used the cellar, especially on hot summer days. One of the warehouses was leased to the soap factory. North of the Russian bathhouse, across the street, on the shore of the Leman, was an artesian well with a hand pump that supplied water to the residents. During the winter, when snow storms raged on the shores of the Leman, it was difficult to draw water from this well. South of the bathhouse, across the street, was a large empty plot and pigs ate the tall weeds that grew there. The neighborhood children rode on **the** pigs and organized racing competitions. The pigs immediately felt the uninvited guests who were riding on their back and started to gallop and jump. Whoever sat the longest on the pig's back – was the winner of the race. The Jewish children were always carful that their parents wouldn't notice them because riding on a pig was also considered an offense.

The fishing village of Turlaki was three kilometers from our building. The reeds that grew there were used to cover the roofs and also to heat the ovens on cold winter days. The Leman was a good source of income and hundreds of fishermen left day and night to fish in its waters. At the same time, the Leman was a place for bathing and recreation. Thousands of people spent time, ate, swam and rested on its long beach. Sailing a sailboat or a rowboat was an impressing sport, and it was a pleasure to see the many white sails on the horizon. We always had to remember not to cross the four–kilometer area of water

[Page 144]

which belonged to the Romanians, and not to enter the Soviets' territorial water. In the winter, the Leman was also used as a place for ice skating. To sum up: the Leman was a natural treasure, an asset to all the residents of Akkerman and the surrounding area.

During spring and summer the sound of singing came from the river day and night. The area was well-guarded by border guards because it was a border region. At night, the lights of Turlaki, Iaki at the mouth of the Dniester, and Ovidiopol on the Soviet side of the Leman winked at us from a distance. The southern end of our street, Kischinovsky, reached the foot of the ancient fortress that the city was named after – the white fortress – although the fortress ceased to be white and blackened over time from all the wars that were raged around it and on it. The water of the Dniester River surrounded it on three sides and the water channels, which were blocked over the years, tied it to the shore. The area of the fortress was huge, there were residential areas, military batteries and mysterious underground caves. Various legends circulated about the fortress and excited the imagination of young and old, and especially the women who believe... These legends passed from generation to generation and became an inexhaustible source of stories that were told by veteran fishermen and sailors.

In this area, at the bosom of nature, I grew and absorbed the love of landscape, nature, water, vegetation, fisheries, history and romance. It was an inspiration for my small and large acts for others. In my thoughts I often return to Kischinovsky Street in Akkerman, my place of residence in the distant past, and I draw from its special atmosphere.

Gordonia's summer colony in Bodki – 1934

[Page 145]

Names and Nicknames
by Z.M – Y.S.
Translated by Libby Raichman

Z. M. and Y. S. got together and raised from the abyss of oblivion a long list of names and nicknames of the Jews of Akkerman. Even after they checked the list and took out insulting nicknames – we can see there is still a long list left. Since most of the nicknames are based on the Yiddish language, we also give the introductory to this list in this language, because the taste and the charm of the nicknames will be impaired if we try to translate them into Hebrew.

* * *

Tz. M. and Y. Sh got together and saved a long list of names and nicknames of the Jews of Akkerman, from oblivion. Even after they refined the list and removed offensive names – as we see, a long list remained.

In almost all the towns and villages in Bessarabia there were Jews with nicknames and assumed names that the town or the village attached to them, but nowhere, were there as many nicknames as there were in the Jewish town of Akkerman. Without exaggeration: there were hundreds. As it says in the verse: "there was no house without … a nickname". The reason for this, one might assume, was that in our town of Akkerman, there were great champions in this area, who were qualified to detect the faults, or the weaknesses of every Jew, and on this basis attached a nickname to each one. These "champions" came from among the wholesalers and the young men in the prayer houses, who saw to it that no Jew in Akkerman, God forbid, would remain without a nickname… .

For the compilers of the nicknames, it was not so easy to evoke all these nicknames, that reflect to a certain extent, the specific folklore of the Jews of Akkerman. Aside from this, one needs to take into consideration that certain nicknames cannot be printed for aesthetic reasons, that the "champions" of the nicknames did not consider, but we must consider them… .

A א

Avraham Anatre: Avraham Goldenshtein, lived in Izmialsky Street.

Aharon Hak [an axe]: His face had the shape of an axe.

Utshette [Itshe]: Meir Kagan. His father Reb Fyve called him Itshe–Meir and with time he was called Utshette.

Enoshl: This means a small person, the diminutive Danielovitz Rivkin.

Avraham Gezetshik [a newspaper]: Avraham Edliss was the "distributor" of all the newspapers that used to arrive from Odessa before the First World War.

Isaac Bublitshnik [bagel maker]: Isaac Perlin. He was the main baker of bagels in the town and for the entire vicinity.

Asher Karpovitz [a carp]: Asher Bronshtein who was caught, not to be repeated, when he tried to carry off a fresh, wriggling, large carp and binge on it himself.

Ugolnikkes [ugol is coal]:They were grain and wine merchants. Their exchange was at the "Ugol", sometimes at Motl Fagin's tavern and later at Eli Krasniansky's store. They were big jokers.

Alter of the Kosse:originally from Kosse, a suburb of Akkerman – The Kosse.

Avraham Shabolatter: Avraham Zektzer, originally from Shabolat (Sergyevky).

Alter Chazan [cantor]:Alter Melnik.

Aharon Kuzniyetz [a forge]: Aharon Grinshpun – a blacksmith.

[Page 146]

Avraham Moshe Fyvelles [son of Fyvel]: Avraham Riebak.

Avraham Yuchentzes: Avraham Prechter.

Aharon Fyvelles [son of Fyvel]: Aharon Kogan.

B ב

Berel Bik [an ox]: Berel Rabinovitz. The entire summer he kept an ice–room, packed with ice to sell .

Bronzeboi [froth]: David Berman. He would spray every face when he spoke.

Boruch Voyenne [soldier] : Gamshiyevitsh, dealt in rags, a thief, a drunk.

Binyamin Semmen: originally from a village called Semmen.

Berel Slon [elephant]: Berel Bezprozvanne. His face with his long nose resembled an elephant's trunk.

Benny Hikkevotte [stutterer]: Benny Rubtzinsky, was a stutterer.

"Barulke"]: Motti Parladansky.

Ber Akkerzsher: Ber Kolyesky, originally from a German colony called Akkerzshe, between Avidupol and Odessa.

Benny the Roiter [ruddy]: Ben Tzion Vassilevsky.

"Bureshke": Hersh Elberg. Why "Bureshke"? – not clear.

"Bobtzi": The Bass family. She was the Madame of a brothel on Starobazarny Street.

Brynne the Modistke [Milliner]: a famous milliner in the town.

Benderer: Parkansky, originally from Bender.

"Bufty" [an actor, a buffoon]: Yisroel Sverdlik

"Benny Getz": he came from a many branched Chassidic family. His great–grandfather was Aharon–Getzy

Bobbe Gelly [yellow/ginger]: Famous for her cows. She provided kosher milk for the religious folk.

Boruch Hurtzele: Boruch Gelman.

Ben Tzion Chave Liebe's [son of Chave Liebe]: Ben Tzion Shildkroit.

G ג

"Genzele" [a little goose]: Yisroel Lazar, who looked like a goose.

"Garlotshov" [neck]: Fishman, a staroveshnik [an old mind]. He and his sons were all thieves and drunks.

Gittel the Gannefte [the thief]: Gittel Tzibulevsky, simply had a "weakness" for stealing.

D ד

Dovid Kapelush [man's hat, a fedora]: Dovid Ginzburg. He would "dress up" during the week, summer and winter and wore a hard, black hat (kotyelyok).

The Bikl [the ox]: Yisroel Spivak.

Dovid Hon [rooster]: Dovid Braverman. He would run around the marketplace, shrieking and crowing like a rooster while selling bruised and rotten fruit of various kinds.

The Reiche Kabtzinte [the rich pauper]: Mrs. Nudelman was very poor but had the presence of a rich woman.

Der Trespolyer: Motl Ratner, a handsome Jew, proprietor of houses, originally from Tiraspol.

Der Lekachbekker [the honey/sponge cake baker]: he and his children were famous as specialists in baking these cakes.

Dovid Chave–Liebe's [son of Chave–Liebe]: Dovid Dorfman.

[Page 147]

Dovid Kotter [a male cat]: Dovid Zonnis, served the gentile nobleman Navrotzki. He had bad luck from a black tom cat.

H ה

Haman Vodovoz [transporter of water]: a sham, a water–carrier, who would not give a drink of water even in the greatest heat. He was therefore crowned with the name "Haman".

Hersh Moldovon: Hersh Kardonsky, originally from the village of Moldavonesh, in the vicinity of Akkerman.

Horbetsh [hunchback]: Alter Sapoznikov, the boot polisher who had a hunchback.

Hersh Guzmanzogger [exaggerator]: Hersh Shainer.

Hershl Shaibes: Hersh Blinder.

V ו

Voyenshiche [tailor]: Sorre Gamshiyevitsh. Her husband, a tailor, patched clothing. She hung up a sign "Tailor to the Army" and was therefore called Voyenshiche.

"Vodyanke": Dovidke Feldman. Why he was called "Vodyanke", is unknown.

"Vatuti" ["vatte" is padding]: Shlaymele Missonzshnik, a tailor.

"Varenik" [a dumpling]: Izenber, a shopkeeper, had a face like a dumpling.

Z ז

Zeleny [green]: Segal, the printer. Why "Zeleny", is unknown.

Zundel Pakkenarreger [itinerant bookseller]: Zundel the bookseller used to carry a large woven basket with all kinds of books and story books. Originally from Lithuania. Familyunknown.

Zynvil Vattenmacher [cottonwool and padding maker]: Zynvil Zaslavsky. He had a machine to produce padding.

"Zigotte": Yankel Ziggelvaks. He was a big clown at school. His friends compared him with great envy – to the comedian, the artist, Zigotte.

Zeidl Puziniok [big belly]: Zeidl Averbuch, the treasurer in the synagogue, coarse and fat like a big belly.

"Gendarme" [policeman]: Shmuel Berger. He was a tall, strong, respected Jew. He walked tall like policeman.

Zeilik Mukumel [flour grinder]: Zeilik Milman, a story, a tale. His father had a mill at the "Vershinne".

Zeilik met a farmer, an acquaintance who asked: How is your father? Zeilik answered: "mukumelle" meaning – he is grinding flour. Since then, the nickname "Mukumel".

Zeilig Eli–Chaims [son of Eli–Chaim]: Zeilig Gurevitsh.

CH ח

Chaim the Langer [Chaim the long one]: Chaim Klurfeld.

Chayenke Shtink: Chayenke Magalnik was, not to be told to anyone, a very smelly person.

Chaim Balebottish [right, respectable]: A tailor, a big bungler who would make excuses for the defects in his tailoring with the motto: it should be right.

"Charitke" [mistress]: Avraham Krasniansky. Why "Charitke"? – because of a matter with a gentile girl.

Chaim the Meshugenne [Chaim the madman]: a good-natured madman, whom they would tease and with whom they would clown around and then provide him with all his needs.

"Chunchuzn": This is what all the Chassidim in the town were called. How they came to have the name of a wild tribe of the Asiatic steppes, is unknown.

Chaim Chava–Liebes: Chaim Kaminker, son of Chava–Liebe.

[Page 148]

T ט

"Titulesku": This is what Pinny Tultshinsky was called.

"Tshempulyetti": Yisroel Rabinovitz.

"Tshornomazi" [blackbeard]: Abramovitsh. His face had a black overgrown beard.

"Tuste": Alterman. A somewhat dazed character and a drunk.

"Tentzer" [dancer]: Nachman Reznik, would hop, and dance a little when he walked.

"Tshubuch": Fiddelman, a sheet metal worker. Why he was called "Tshubuch", is unknown.

Y י

Yisroel the Toiber [the deaf one]: Yisroel Tultshinsky.

Yossele Nidde: Yossele Segal – a bit of a broker, a bit of a matchmaker, a small petite Jew with a yellow lined face, like Nidde.

Yankel the Heizerikke [the hoarse one]: Cantor Yankel Gottloib, a well-known leader in prayer. He prayed all his years in the synagogue with much warmth and pleasantness, with a hoarse voice.

Yehoshua Kaloshnik [galoshes]: Yehoshua Bailis, the greatest specialist in the town for repairing galoshes.

Yisroel Bolgar [from Bulgaria]: Yisroel Brodtzky, originally from Bulgarian village in the vicinity of Akkerman.

Yankel the Viser [the white one]: Yankel Kogan the watchmaker who had an unusually clear white face.

Yankel Krassiltshik [dyer]: Yankel Zilberberg. He was once a painter but recently he dealt with fish.

Yashke Starozumne [old way of thinking]: Yashke Gelman because he was cunning.

Yashke Gazettshik [newspaper seller]: Yashke Vineberg, semi crippled. He would drag himself around all day in the town, with great difficulty, selling newspapers.

Yossel Leibeles: Yossel Levin, son of Leibl.

Yeshia Nachmans: Yeshia Rabinovitsh, son of Nachman.

L ל

Lechtzieren: Tinkelman, used to produce lecht.

Leib Daitsh [German]: Leib Kelzon, originally from Austria – Hungary.

Luzer Sposov [a trick]: Luzer Vladimirsky. Everything that he made, he said, was made with a trick.

Leizer the Blinder: He was blind and very popular in the town. He was involved in the community. No one knew who his family were.

Leib Goy [ignorant of Jewish traditions]: Leib Perlis, a somewhat rich Jew, but he was a wild, coarse man, an ignorant person.

Leizer Nusatte [large nose]: Leizer Grinshpun. He had a big nose and therefore had the name Nusatte.

Leah the Shvartze [the dark one]: she was dark like a gypsy.

Leib Sussy: His family were unknown, only that his name was Leib and that he sold soda-water.

"Liyustra" [chandelier]: Elyusha Bendersky.

M מ

Morskye Grabittel [sea port]: Brodtzky had a buffet on a steam boat at the port, and would fleece one's skin with his prices.

Moshe Havdolah: Moshe Kogan. He was long and narrow like a Havdallah candle.

[Page 149]

Motl Chalomot [dreams]: Motl Weiss. Why dreams? Unknown.

Mendel Shpan [stride]: Mendel Milman, a locksmith. He had long feet and a broad stride.

Moshe Bass: Moshe Vineshtein, a metal worker who was the bass voice in the synagogue choir.

Moshele Veggele–Shtuper [wagon–pusher]. No one knew who his family was. He was only a small Jew with a sparse beard who would drag a huge wagon on 2 wheels and served all the established members of the community.

Motti Pegger [a corpse]: Motti Goldenshtein, unemotional, therefore like a corpse.

Motl Litvak [Lithuanian]: Motl Zarchy, originally from Lithuania.

Mal'ach HaMavet [the angel of death]: a strange Jew, a teacher of Gemarah, a sick man, an asthmatic. While ill he would beat and pinch the students until they bled. He beat one student to death and then he himself fell and died.

Mottele Beider [bath attendant]: Motl Weisberg, a heavy drinker, was the bath attendant in the town's bathhouse.

Moshe Mamenyu [mommy]: Reb Moshe Vytzblit. He would always groan: Oh, woe, Mamenyu.

Marke Varrenik [dumplng]: Markus Kutshiuk. Why "Varrenik"?

Motl the Shvartzer [the dark one]: Motl Shechtman, a shoveller. He was very dark.

"Malyutke" [baby]: Magalnik, a boot polisher. Why "Malyutke"?

Motl Eigenheim [own home]: A fine man, a home–owner, Motl Berkovitz, originally from the German colony in the vicinity of Akkerman.

"Megege" [idler, dawdler]: Grinshpun. Why "Megege"?

Max Linder [soothe]: Issachar Gamshievitsh. Why "Max Linder"?

"Mazzieppo" [a hero] Reuven Gelman. Why "Mazeppo"?

M'shumedet [destroyed]: Nemtshenka, committed suicide as a young girl.

Moshe Pippik: The pharmacist, Moshe Pippergal.

Mendel Munishes: Mendel Malkin.

Moshe Itzelles: Moshe Vytzblit, son of Itze.

Meir Shikkeles: son of Shikke – a name derived from Yehoshua.

Moshe Aharon–Getzis: Moshe Shinkarovsky, son of Aharon Getzy.

N נ

"Nydenne" [found]: Itzkovitsh. He was employed to remove the garbage from the town, and he dealt in goats. Once he lost a horse, a mare, so he ran around looking for it and finally found it. Whomever he met, he told the news: Nydenne kobille! [I found my mare].

Nachman Kelbel [small calf]: Nachman Perliss.

Nachum Zsheliyenzshik [mender of pants]: Nachum Gershkovitsh. Dealt with old pants.

Noach the Izenner [the metal one]: Noach Zaltzman. Had a metal store at the marketplace.

Nuske the Toiber [the deaf one]: Natan Moisyevitsh Goldshtein.

S ס

Sonky Zolotye Rutshka [golden pen]: Sonki Gershkovitsh. She was simply, a thief.

"Skazshenne" [crazy]: Finkelshtein, was a skazshenne, a crazy person.

Smiyetsa [smile]: Avraham Weisberg always had a silly smile.

Skory Pomoshtsh: Feige Ladizshensky would carry 2 full baskets with fresh bread for sale call out: "spasytiye, spasytiye, svizshi chliev"– "save, save, fresh bread".

[Page 150]

Sanni the Roiter [the ruddy one]: He used a wheelbarrow to distribute his merchandise. He had a ruddy face. No one knew his name.

Suslik: Gritshevsky traded with felechlech of suslikkes.

Smakartinnef [junk]: Dr. Markotin.

AYIN ע

Eli–Ber Blecher [metal worker]: Eli–Ber Kizzelman, a metal worker and trustee of the synagogue.

Azriel Leibeshis: Azriel Helman, son of Leibesh.

P/F פ

Peremishl: Avraham Shpiegelman. Why "Peremishl"? unknown.

Feige the Sarvern [maître d'/waitress]: she would bake layered cakes with fruit, for the weddings of wealthy Jews.

Poltora Zshida [a 1½ Jew]: Reb Sholem Finegersh, a merchant. He was exceptionally large, tall and broad and wore size 55 shoes.

Fyvl Turlakker: originally from the village Turlak, close to the town.

Pinny Kabak [pumpkin]: Advocate Pinny Shteinberg. He was fat, coarse, with a big stomach. He took on the appearance of a pumpkin.

Polkovnik [colonel]: Feldman, a metal worker. He was a soldier in the Nikolayev army. He took long firm strides like a member of a regiment.

Purishkevitsh: Zbarsky the pharmacist. Why "Purishkevitsh"? He was a very bad Jew and did not respond to any hardship in the town.

Fonfish [nasal]: Avraham Goldman, he spoke nasally.

Parah Adumah [red cow]: Mrs. Tabatshnik. She had red hair and was 'a big cow' – very stupid.

TZ צ

"Tzelke" [virgin]: Yisroel Kushnir. He received the "beautiful" pleasant name Yakobu because he did not have children for many years.

Tsegynirte [gypsy]: Chaike Segal.

K ק

Kuter [male cat]: Velvl Zonnis, a shopkeeper who had dark angry eyes and resembled a black cat.

Kishkelech [intestines]: Azriel Helman. His father was a ritual slaughterer and he liked fat, slaughtered intestines.

"Kolokoltshik" [a small bell]: Radzivitzke, a metal worker. Why? Unknown.

Krivorutshke [deformed]: Leib Schvartzman, had a crooked hand.

"Kurotshke" [hens]: Puli Feld. He would walk around nodding his head, like a hen.

Kvatshke [brooding hen]: Zelik Milman's wife. When she spoke, she cackled like a brooding hen.

"Kitayetz" [Chinese]: Puntshik Buchner had a yellow face like a Chinaman.

Kressy the Chazante [wife of the cantor]: The widow of the well-known cantor, Yankel the hoarse one.

R ר

Rayze the Horbotte [hunchback]: Rayzi Glazman was a hunchback.

Rieve the Goldshmideche [Goldsmith, fem.]: Rieve Izbelinsky, because her husband was a goldsmith.

Rayzi the Milchikke [milk]: Rayzi Elishkevitsh. A very pious woman who kept cows to provide religious Jews with kosher milk.

Ribono-shel-olam [God of the universe]: Yisroel Chacham and his son Pinni. Why?

[Page 151]

SH ש

Shlomo Shtukes [ruses]: Shlomo Zilberman, a wine merchant. He used to say that everything isdone with ruses.

"Shotambula": Hersh Cheikis. Why? Unknown.

Shimon "Butz" [fat slob]: Shimon Rabinovitsh because he was a fat slob.

Shalom Slabay: Shalom Riebak, a tall, strong man. Out of curiosity he was called "Slabay".

Shmuel Neizl [nose]: Shmuel Milman, because he spoke nasally.

Shuel Karnaliyevikker: Shuel Itzkovitsh, originally from the village Karnaliyevki, in the vicinity of Akkerman.

Shuel Kozak: Shuel Mutshnik: originally from a village in the vicinity of Akkerman – Kazatshe.

Shalom of the Bolnitze [hospital]: For many years, he was head of the hospital.

Sharik [means of contraception]: Dovid Moshe Yaroslavsky. His mother used "Sharikkes", to prevent her becoming pregnant but the little boy Dovid Moshe, broke through the Sharikkes so he was called Dovid Moshe "Sharik".

Shlomo the Toiber [deaf]: Shlomo Rottenshtein, a hat-maker.

Shmuel Yisroel Avromtzes: Shmuel Berger, son of Avrom.

[Page 155]

Our High-School

A Symposium on "Tarbut" Gymnasium
by Alexander Shapira
Translated by Sara Mages

I served as a teacher in the gymnasium for four years, in the years 1921-1923 and in the years 1931-1932, and I can say for sure: these were the most beautiful years of my life. The atmosphere in the institution, the collaboration between the teachers, especially the spirit of the principal, Berger, which prevailed in the gymnasium, created a good spirit and a good atmosphere.

As we know, the gymnasium grew out of the kindergarten under the management of aunt Manya, but by the time I started teaching, there were already three grades in the institution. I started teaching even though I was not a qualified teacher but a graduate of the government gymnasium. Mr. Berger offered me to teach geography and history in Hebrew, maybe because he knew that I had some teaching experience because I gave private lessons to students in these subjects, or because it was difficult in those days to get Jewish teachers to teach in Hebrew, and he did not want to give the Christians a foot hold in the gymnasium. His offer surprised me to some extent because I graduated from the government gymnasium in 1921, and although the proposal itself appealed to me, I still had concerns about my success in the proposed role. Therefore, I consulted the principal of the government gymnasium and he greatly encouraged me to accept the position offered to me. I remember his words very well: "the Hebrew Gymnasium students will excel in their studies, and I know you can be trusted."

With awe and reverence I entered as a teacher to the classrooms that did not contain many students. In the second grade, for example, there were only seven students aged 13-14 and this, of course, allowed close contact with each of them. Outside the classroom everyone called me by my first name, but in the framework of the class I was addressed in the official version: "Mr. Teacher."

Among the teachers, who were at that time in the gymnasium, I especially remember a Hebrew teacher from Eretz Yisrael and his name was Epstein. He arrived in Akkerman after he fell ill with a certain disease in Eretz Yisrael and the doctors ordered him to change his place of residence.

As stated above, during the first two years that I taught in the gymnasium I got to know the principal, Berger, and I was very impressed with his personality. He had a sense of leadership and was very knowledgeable in various fields. I have no doubt that he was destined for greatness and Akkerman's framework was too narrow for him. Obviously, the great development of the gymnasium was largely due to the efforts that Berger invested in it.

When I returned to Akkerman in 1931, after I was released from the army and after a period of training in Belgium, I found almost the same communal workers that were there ten years ago. They were headed by Hershel Brudski, Yitzchak Arbeit (he has two sons in Haifa) and others. In this period I taught Romanian in the gymnasium and in one elementary school classroom.

There were also no noticeable changes in the teaching staff during the years of my absent from Akkerman and the good atmosphere was preserved. The number of students increased by a considerable proportion, and most of them were not necessarily wealthy. It was customary to accept every student who applied regardless to the parents' financial ability which is, perhaps, the uniqueness of the gymnasium in Akkerman.

Almost all the students in the institution belonged to a youth movement. The curriculum at the institution was similar to that of the high school curriculum in Romania and conducted according to the government program. However, a definite national spirit prevailed in the institution and it can be said that every teacher in the gymnasium was a Zionist. Supervisors from the State Department of Education frequently visited the institution, and the gymnasium's principal knew how to get along with them. To this day, I keep in touch with my former students and our shared memories of those days are refreshing and encouraging.

[Page 156]

The Hebrew Gymnasium "Tarbut"
Tecsesti–Alba, Romania
Diploma

[Page 157]

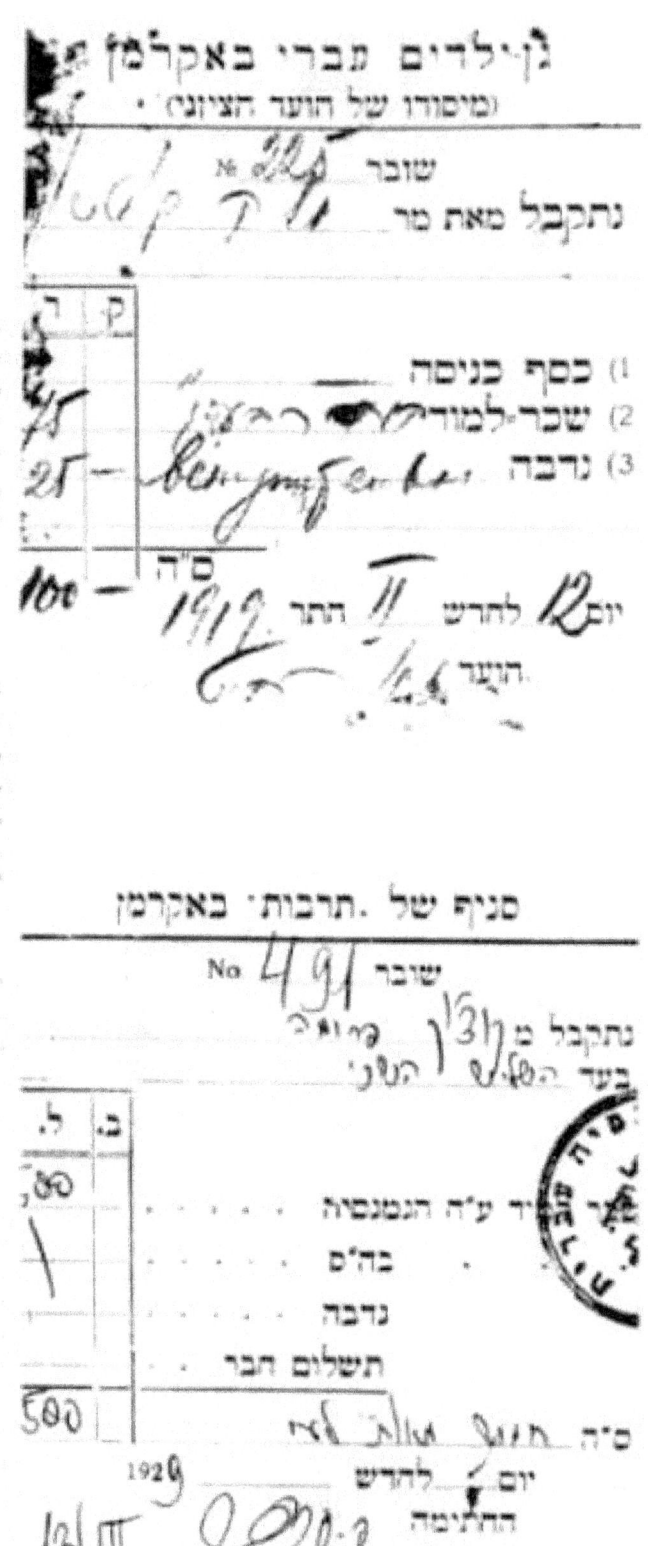

The teachers of "Tarbut" School during the years of the gymnasium's existence:

Kindergarten Teachers

Stretch Sara (aunt Sara)
Puzis Shoshana (aunt Shoshana)
Kaminker Risia
Shrira Mania (aunt Manya)
Rabinovitch Hadassah (music)
Zuckerman Batya –Friedman

The Principal – Yakov Berger

Teachers

Epstein – Hebrew
Epstein Sara – (kindergarten teacher – teacher)
Berman M. – French
Gleichman
Grozman Meir – Hebrew, history, psychology
Glinberg
Davidson Efraim – Hebrew, Bible
Helman Sonia – Latin
Charol
Cohen (Kogen) Moshe – singing and music
Malamud Etya
Novak – Hebrew, Bible
Nutov Moshe – biology, natural sciences
Yehusua Neiman – mathematics, physicsv Stretch Meir – Bible
Serfer Boia
Feinblatt – Hebrew
Fisher Leah
Plutizer Faniav Zukerman Zina
Tcherniavsky Moshe – mathematics, physics
Dr. Zerling Shaul – hygiene
Rabinovitz Chavav Schwartz – Hebrew
Stern – Hebrew
Sternsaus – Hebrew, history
Shapira Alexander

Secretary: Zukerman Shmuel
Supervisor – Goldman Dora

[Page 158]

Shmuel Naamani

I started working in the gymnasium in October 1922, and from 1924 to 1933 (except for the period of my military service) I served as secretary and treasurer. How did the gymnasium manage to balance its budget? We did not receive a large allowance from the municipality, from the community's *"Korovka"* money [tax on consumer goods and commercial transactions] and "Tarbut" center in Kishinev [Chişinău]. However, all of these, in addition to tuition, were not enough to ensure the payment of the teachers' salaries. Therefore, special activities, balls and the like had to be organized to fill what was missing in the budget. Sometimes, as treasurer, I had to play a very unpleasant role and sent home students whose parents did not meet their financial obligation. We usually tried to avoid these steps and only punished those who could pay – and did not pay.

I collaborated the whole way with Mr. Berger. At times, I was really amazed by his maneuverability of the Ministry of Education's inspectors. Not all the teachers had the qualifications required of a high school teacher, and if a certain teacher aroused the suspicion of the inspector, who began to question him, Berger always managed to distract the inspector with another matter and in this way rescued the particular teacher from the government inspector. The gymnasium was not just a teaching institution, but the spiritual center of 1,200 Jewish families who centered in Akkerman. All of the school's halls and equipment, including the gymnasium and its equipment, were available to the public and the activities in the school were conducted day and evening. Every Zionist emissary, who visited the gymnasium, praised the many achievements of the dedicated teaching staff, especially the principal who worked diligently on the development of the institution.

Asher Brudski

I was eight-and-a-half years old in 1919 when I took the exams to be admitted to the gymnasium. Twenty five children, whose parents wanted them to attend a Hebrew school and not be forced to desecrate the Sabbath as the students of the government school, took the exams with me. It is therefore not surprising that among the first students were the children of religious families, butchers, rabbis (Zuckerman) and others. More than sixty years have passed since I took these exams, but I remember this ritual well. My examiner was Berger who sorted out the students according to their knowledge of the Hebrew language. He asked me the meaning of the word *tachana*, and I replied "a mill." Berger said: nice, but there is another kind of *tachana* and I did not know he meant the train station. In arithmetic I was asked how much is it 8 times 3, and I was able to answer correctly. On the basis of these questions he classified me to first grade. Those, who knew less than me, were sent to the preparatory program.

As we know, Milstein made his building, which was initially used as a Russian school, available to the gymnasium. A large courtyard surrounded the building and, apart from the classrooms, there was a large hall which was also used for various conferences. Once, I opened an old cupboard, which stood in the gymnasium's building, and discovered a treasure trove of books in Russian. Almost all the books were of Russian classical writers: Pushkin, Tolstoy, Turgenev, Dostoyevsky, etc. I remember that I showed these books to my best friend, Sheraga Cohen z"l, who was an avid reader, and he jumped at this finding as if he had found a great booty.

The Russian language was taught in the gymnasium also after the Romanians entered Akkerman, but, slowly-slowly, the process of Romanization intensified and all sorts of unfortunate people, who were sent to us by the Ministry of Education, had to oversee this process.

In class we spoke in Yiddish that many Russian words were incorporated in it. And so we used to say, for example: "*gib mir di spichki* (give me the matches) or "*tetrad*" (notebook). In my class there were only two children who did not know Yiddish. The "*Yiddishstim*" did not have their own school and they barricaded themselves in the "League" library that most of its books were, of course, in Yiddish.

Of the teachers in the gymnasium it is worth noting some special characters. One of them was my first Hebrew teacher – Stern. He was an elderly Jew with a beard, spoke Hebrew in Ashkenazi accent and understood all the paths of the language and its development. However, most of his strength was in singing. He taught us Israeli songs that were the hits of those days (*Hayarden Mitlakhesh, Zion Tamati*, and more). In these songs we poured our feelings with him. By the way, Stern's daughter was the wife of the well-known writer Aharon Ever-Hadani (Feldman).

A special character was also the teacher Epstein. His wife was a kindergarten teacher and he arrived to us from Eretz Yisrael. Like Eliezer Ben-Yehudah he decided to speak only in Hebrew, whether they will understand him or not. He did not deviate, not even a tad, from this sacred principle and spoke only in Hebrew with the gentiles in the market and with the shoe shiner. It turned out that they understood him. His nickname was "The teacher Shalom," because he greeted everyone he met with Shalom in Hebrew.

I remember well two more teachers–educators, and they are the teacher Schwartz (Hebrew) and Tcherniavsky (mathematics). Schwartz helped a lot to Tzeirei Zion with his activities. These two teachers taught us for several years and probably did their work with faith. The fact is that when I immigrated to Israel, many were amazed by my eloquent Hebrew speech, my knowledge of the names of the communities in the country and the correct pronunciation. It is also the right of the teacher "Shalom" who made efforts to teach us to distinguishing between *Aleph* and *Ayin*, *Het* and *Kaf* and the like.

[Page 159]

The teacher Sternsaus, whose nickname was "3 *Mal Ka*" (the acronym: Commissar *Kern Kayemet*) is worthy of special recognition for his great dedication to the public library. He made sure that every Hebrew book was found at the library and all his activities in this field were voluntary.

And last but not least, the teacher Feinblatt, who was probably our best teacher. I especially remember his lessons on Yiddish literature.

In 1928 I graduated the gymnasium with the first class. In total we were eight students who graduated because many dropped out over time for various reasons. In any case, among the first graduates were only two that were not included among the first twenty-five students who were admitted to the gymnasium as is told above.

My father was very active for "Tarbut." He was a General Zionist but not the kind known to us today. He was a Zionist from Weizmann's "*heder*" and towards the election campaign he came out with all the ammunition and worked day and night for his party.

There were two committees next to the gymnasium: a parent committee and "Tarbut" committee. My father was the secretary of both committees and his dedication to the gymnasium knew no bounds. I remember that he went out to the market, grabbed gentiles who led wagons loaded with bulrush, which was used for heating, and sent them to the gymnasium so that, God forbid, the children would not suffer from the cold. Since he was often an arbitrator in conflicts between a Jew and a Jew, he put two conditions before them before hearing their claims. One – that they would accept his decision, whatever it is. Second condition – instead of an arbitration fee they would give a gift to the gymnasium.

How the gymnasium balanced its budget – is a wonderful thing. It was impossible to exist from the tuition and, in addition, there were quite a few students from poor families who did not pay at all. There's no doubt that the allowance they received from the authority was minimal, and if it wasn't for the various activities, especially the balls whose revenues were dedicated to the gymnasium, the existence of the institution was in danger.

The balls also had a social value apart from their economic value. They employed a lot of people who volunteered, each in his field and ability to help. The preparation for the balls was evident throughout the city. In the Purim balls, "*HaMasmer*" [the nail], a parody of Megillat Esther was read in the traditional tune and whipped, without mercy, people and institutions of Jewish Akkerman. If I am not mistaken, it was written by three people and they are: Schildcroit, Lyuba Berkowich and Hersh Brudski. One verse is etched in my memory: "whoever can do the job has a blessing from it." The intention was for those who sat next to the "*Korovka*" plate, meaning, communal workers who did not enjoy themselves while performing their duties.

The snack bar in these balls, which was laden with wine, liqueur and cakes prepared by volunteer housewives, was also a serious source of income. "Tarbut" committee waited impatiently for the income from these balls to pay off debts, pay the teachers' salaries, etc. Apart from these balls, there were also parties only for the students, such as the Tu B'Shvat party when all the students received small packages containing carobs and figs – fruits from Eretz Yisrael. The principal, Y. Berger, gave a festive speech and every year he told us that the goats eat carobs in Eretz Yisrael, and when we eat these fruits from Eretz Yisrael we can feel the taste of the homeland. I also remember the great assembly, which was held at the Craftsmen Synagogue in 1925, to mark the opening of the university in Jerusalem. My father gave a speech in Hebrew and the grocer, Pesach Levin, who was also given the honor to speak at this assembly, announced in Yiddish: "there (in Jerusalem) the bride is open, and here sits the groom." After the assembly a festive parade was held on the city streets.

Every year, on May 10 – Romania Independence Day, the gymnasium students participated in a parade on the city streets along with the students of the government gymnasium, military units and more. The gymnasium's orchestra accompanied the marchers with its music and masses of Jews, who crowded in the streets where the parade passed, enjoy the sight of the students of "Tarbut" who marched in formation.

[Page 160]

The Home, the High-School and the Movement
by Baruch Na'amani, Kvutzat Massada
Translated by Yocheved Klausner

During one of our family events, our granddaughter asked: How come that the members of our family did not make Aliya together, but separately, and it took several years until all (except one) were gathered in our land: seven brothers, two sisters and Mother, who arrived illegally at the end of WWII?

This is what I answered, in short:

Our home in Akkerman was a religious home. My father z"l was a ritual slaughterer [SHU"V], the son of the town rabbi, who had come to Akkerman from the Ukraine at the end of the 19-th century. Most of his brothers – my uncles – officiated as rabbis in Akkerman or various other Ukrainian cities. My mother z"l, was also of a family of rabbis for many generations: the Horowitz family, whose ancestor was "The Holy SHEL"A [Yeshayahu Halevi Horowitz].

Our home was "soaked" in the love of Eretz Israel. My grandfather, my mother's father z'l was born in Eretz Israel and his family "went into exile" according to the order of the rabbis and doctors at the time. Since we were a family blessed with many children, we were divided into three generations: a. the adults studied in the Yeshiva in Kishinev; b. the middle generation studied in the secular high-school; c. the young generation studied in the Hebrew high-school. All had in common the religious-traditional home, where a Zionist atmosphere reigned.

I shall tell here only about those who studied at the Hebrew high-school.

For us the school was a *Mikdash-me'at* [a Temple] which embodied the love for Eretz Israel and the study of the Hebrew history and literature. The wide hall was decorated with the portraits of the writers and poets that we admired and loved: Ahad Ha'am, Bialik, Mendele, Tchernichovski, Shalom Aleichem and others. We kept the Jewish holidays. On *Tu Bishvat* [15-th in the month of Shevat] we sat in the big hall, outside was cold and the ground was covered by the white snow, and we were singing "In Eretz Israel the sun is shining and the vines are blooming." With our spirit we saw not the cold in the hall and outside, but the sun and the warmth in Eretz Israel.

Bialik's poem *Basade* [In the Field] made a great impression. We read and reread the words: "Like a poor man I stand before the splendor of the growing grains," "It was not my own drops of sweat that wetted the black earth;" "You are dear to me, my fields, since you remind me of my far brethren" etc. If we add to all that the influence of the Zionist youth movements in our town, we shall understand how deeply ingrained in our souls was the idea of fulfillment and Aliya.

In our young eyes, Akkerman was the end of the world. The train arrived from one direction only, and went back the same way. There was no continuation of the railway, except for some 20 kilometers in the direction of the sea. We felt cut off from the rest of Bessarabia and only weak echoes of what happened in other towns and villages, in the center of the country, reached us. The rumor about Zionist youth movements reached us through emissaries from the Holy Land and activists of the JNF, who came to our town rarely. In time, various youth movements were established as well, but they were not connected with the movements in the rest of the country or in other countries. Only during the summer of 1929 a branch of "Gordonia" was opened in Akkerman. One of the emissaries who visited in town convinced the young people to join. I was out of town that summer – I was in the resort town Budaki – and when I returned I found the Branch wonderfully organized, the heads being Shula Wolowitz z"l and Nissan Stambul (Amitay), may he live a long life. I joined immediately and was appointed secretary of the Branch shortly. The branch numbered several hundred members, in three sectors: the scouts, the awakening ones and the realizers. From the hours of the afternoon until late in the evening our Club was full of people, children and youth, who were guided by and listened to the adult "guides". Hebrew speech and songs were heard to a distance.

In the spring of 1930 I asked to be sent for training in the "*Hechalutz*", as was customary. But the delegates who in the winter of 1929 visited us tried to convince me to continue my work at the Branch, since I had a "Pioneer-Zionist" conscience and I had a good knowledge of Hebrew, and training at "*Hechalutz*" would not add much.

[Page 161]

I answered affirmatively and I remained, continuing being a guide at the Branch, and I was promised that my Aliya would not be delayed much and I will receive the much awaited "certificate" without my training in the "*Hechalutz*."

Indeed, by the end of May 1930 I made Aliya. On 29 May I arrived by ship to Jaffa. As every new immigrant, I was very excited; I jumped in the little boat which took us to the shore. While doing that, I forgot in the ship a coat and a small suitcase, and the ship continued its journey to Alexandria in Egypt. After the famous "quarantine" we were taken to the "immigrants' house" on Aliya Street in Tel Aviv. While staying there, I had to make a decision about my next step in the country. Thoughts about continuing my studies were in my head (I was a graduate of the Hebrew School), or joining a *kibbutz*. I visited my two brothers in Zichron Yakov (my brother Noah had made Aliya in 1920 and my eldest brother z'l in 1926). I went to Jerusalem to check out the Hebrew University on Mount Scopus and to get information about the faculties that had just opened. After discussing the matter with students and with the secretary of the university and after hearing a lecture by David Yelin on the Hebrew poetry in Middle-Ages Spain, I decided that my life in this country would be only through full self-realization, which meant life on a kibbutz. By chance I was informed that at the Rechovot branch of the Gordonia movement the meeting of the General Council of Gordonia was taking place. I decided to go there, to meet personally the group and the leaders of the movement, and I was not disappointed. The meeting of the Council opened on Friday night and the participants were, as far as I remember: Chaim Arlozorov, Binyamin West, Gershon Chanoch, Yakov Zandberg (head of the Committee of Culture of the *Histadrut*), and of course Pinchas Levanon (Lubianiker) and others. The discussions were on a very high level and made a deep impression on me, a young man and a new immigrant. During Shabat I got to know the few members of the group and in particular a member of the Romanian *Gordonia* group, Dov Misha'eli (Mushinski z"l. He told me about the Hadera group, where I intended to join.

Indeed, at the end of the meeting, I finished all the formalities in the "immigrants' house" and toward evening we arrived by train in Hadera (I and Dov z"l) on the "Bussel Hill", where The Gordonia A group (later relocated to Hulda) and the Gordonia D group (later to form Kibbutz Massada) were located. The two groups lived in one camp, and only the dining hall was divided by a wooden wall, three quarters of the area belonged to group A and one quarter was ours. One part of or camp was empty. To my question "where are the people" I received an unclear answer – something like "they will soon return"....

I checked out the camp, the barracks where I was to live, I met the members of the Gordonia A group but I didn't meet the members of my own group. Only at dinnertime I discovered the "great secret": our group numbered only 5 members and at dinner we were only 4, since one was at Gan-Shmuel, where she participated in a course. One month after I arrived, the first baby was born: he was the first baby of the world Gordonia movement and was named Aharon David, after A.D. Gordon. I should mention that on the day I arrived in this country the British government issued the law against Aliya.

But little by little, during the next few months the Aliya gates opened and the number of our members began to grow; by the end of 1930 we were already 12 members.

On the development of the group, its longing to establish a kibbutz and the founding of our kibbutz in the Jordan valley we can read in the book *Kevutzat Massada*, published in 1962, 25 years from its foundation, edited by me.

Leib Stambul lighting memorial candles at a conference in Israel at the 40

[Pages 162-163]

Students of the Hebrew High-School in 1920

First row from right: **Atiya Berg, Katia Gilbord, Vitia Rosenbaum, Shura Bronstein, Musia Frumin, Sviba Berkowitz, Soya Gelman, Utza Kogan, Sara Stulbrod, Baba Axelrod, Soya Brand, Nyusia Stambul, Bitelman, not identified**

Second row from right to left: **Binyamin Girshfeld, Musia Abramowitz, Boria Kaminker, Abramowitz, Yosef Tzeplin, Shura Wolwitz, Zamba Goldman, Riva Ingerleib, Gaber Chava, Kogan, three not identified, Nechama Kahalski, not identified, Yashke Weinstein, Malina Teuerman, not identified**

Between the 2 rows, sitting: **at right the kindergarten teacher Sarah Startz and at left the kindergarten teacher Shoshana Silberfarb**

Third row from right to left: **cleaning woman, David Malkin, Moshe Ingerleib, the teacher Sternshis, the teacher P. Stern Malmud, the principal of the school I. Berger, Asher Brodeski, Tzadok Tzukerman, the teacher of the Romanian language, Sokoloski, M.I. Berman (teacher of French), not identified, Manus Reuven, Eliezer Ingerleib, Baruch Gershfeld, Israel Manus, not identified, Finsburg, Reginowitz, not identified**

Fourth row from right to left: **the first two not identified, Ester Brodeski, not identified, Sioma Laker, Riva Roizman, Giora Gurewitz, Atiya Margalit, Milia Sherira, Chana Levin, A. Lis, Riva Kogan, Leah Berger, Shura Kesselman, Palikov, Bentchik Palikov, not identified, Eisman, Meir (Mira) Botoshanski, Korin**

Fifth row from right to left: **Goldman, not identified, Bunia Eisman, two not identified, Liuba Shmoish, Frima Kotchuk, not identified, Giora Roitman, Atiya Berg,, Chava Dorfman, Yente Weissberg, Yitzhak Teuerman, Elik Berg, Marusia Rabinowitz, Chana Dorfman, Byoma Brand, Leah Berkowitz**

Sixth row from right to left: **Chaim Brand, Bonia Eisman, not identified, Tzukerman (?), Mulia Rosental, Z. Kogan, not identified**

Seventh row: **Brodeskki, Grisha Rabinowitz, B. Chefetz, Idke Brand, Sheike Kushnir, Bosia Arbit, Milman, Zeplin, Shlomo Gecht, Zukerman, Izia Goldman, S. Minieli, not identified, Shmuel (the attendant of the school), Sinilnikov, Gordon, Sioma Britava**

[Page 164]

A "Foreign" Girl in Akkerman
by Yehudit Karmi (Frenkel)
Translated by Yocheved Klausner

I was not born in Akkerman and I don't know whether I have the right to participate in this book, but I am connected by many strings to this town, where I spent some of the most beautiful years of my life, and maybe this can serve as my privilege...

I was born in the town Lyova on the River Prut, very far from Akkerman. But when I finished the local elementary school my family decided that the best and most suitable place to continue my studies would be the Hebrew High-School in Akkerman, which was famous as a national educational institution. No doubt that the fact that two of my uncles (the families Shapira and Frank) lived in Akkerman helped much to make that decision, but there is also no doubt that the good name of the "Tarbut" school played a decisive role.

In the fall of 1929 I packed my things and left little Lyova on my way to the "big city" Akkerman, which was indeed a big city compared to my town of birth. I shall not try to describe all my experiences connected with this drastic change and not my difficulties and pain of adjustment, since they are described in many books and are characteristic to any young girl who leaves the house of her parents and goes to live in a big city. My fate was not bad, since very soon I realized that my choice was good and the Tarbut high-school is kept in my memory to this day, as the institution that helped much in my education.

I remember my first day in school: young boys and girls, during recess running noisily around in the long corridor, full of young happiness and a great feeling of friendship. I was standing alone in a corner and did not take part. I did not know any of the students and everything looked strange to me and I had the feeling that I shall never adapt to what I saw around me. All of a sudden, I saw a familiar face, and a person approached me. I thought I was dreaming: it was my first teacher at the elementary school in Lyova, the teacher who taught me the Hebrew Alphabet and helped me learn to read. He was my first teacher,

The principal of the High School Yakov Berger and a group of teachers, 1928

[Page 167]

whom I loved and cherished, the teacher Gruzman, who had moved to Akkerman and was a teacher there. I shall never forget the meeting with him. This was my salvation in those difficult days, when I was so alone. My renewed connection with this teacher was not interrupted, until I finished high–school. He helped me find my in the new environs, Akkerman and the new school.

At that time, the high–school was the spiritual center of the Jews in general and the Jewish youth in particular. All roads led there and it was active during school hours and after them. Performances, sportive events, outings, sailing on the Liman and other activities of the movement – all were focused in the school, which was the **home** for all students, and more so for a lonely girl like me who had come from a foreign land. I was charmed by the atmosphere in school, by the good spirit of Yakov Berger that was felt everywhere and by the enthusiasm of the teachers. Our class was in particular united in spirit, most of the students were members of the Gordonia movement and worked hard on the preparations for Aliya. I do not have exact numbers, but I shall not exaggerate if I say that most of the students of my class did make Aliya and it is still possible to locate them in the kibbutzim Massada and Nir–Am, carrying on proudly the legacy of our former school.

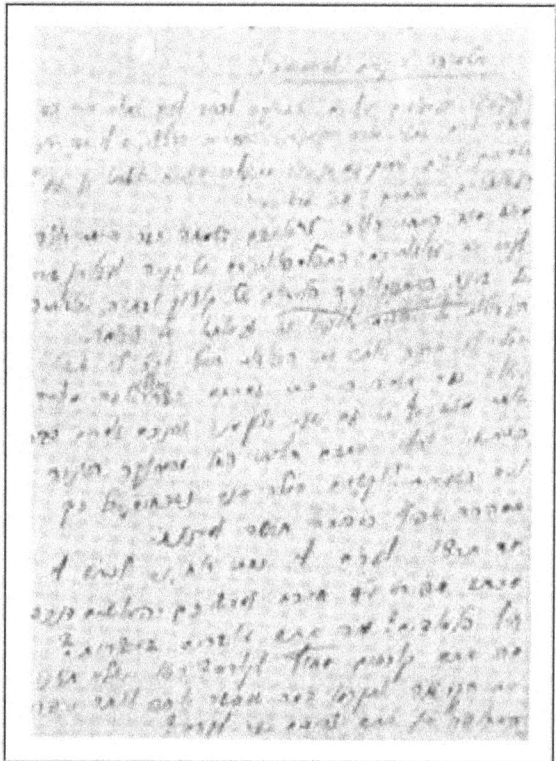

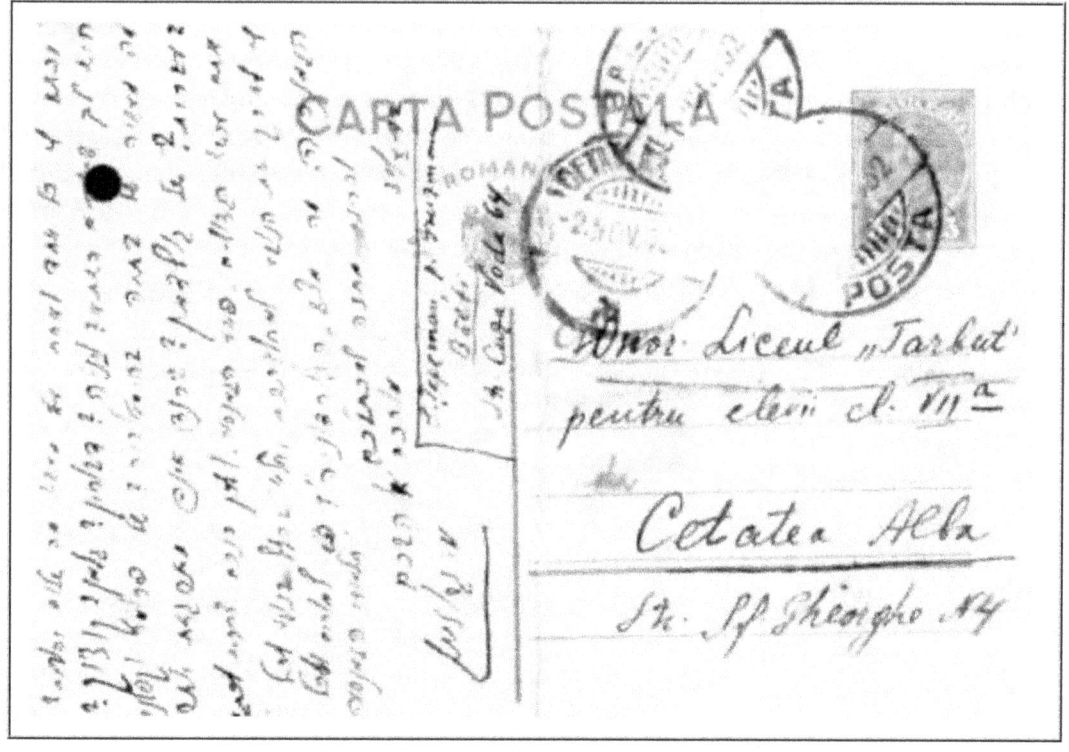

A postcard from the teacher Gruzman to his students

[Page 175]

Artists and Cantors

About the Jewish Theater in Our City
by Yehudah Ziglevaks
Translated by Sara Mages

The moments, in which I clung to the theater for the rest of my life, are well guarded in my memories from the days of my youth. It happened when I participated in the presentation of the play "*Di kishufmakhern,*" (The Witch) by Goldfaden, which was performed by a troupe of amateur actors on the Jewish stage in Akkerman. Then, I fell in love, with every fiber of my soul, with the Jewish folk theater. The participants in this play constituted a small group of cultural people in our city at the beginning of this century whose challenge and mission was to bring the theater to the Jews of Akkerman. The most prominent among them were: Pesach Kleiman, Gedalia Goldfled, Yeshayahu Greenstein, the artist Puterman, Brofman, Brudsky, Ms. Puchslman, Ms. Feiland and others.

In their artistic activity they were mostly influenced by the theater of Avraham Goldfaden in Iasi [Romania], and the visit of theater troupes from Odessa and Vilna who became well known for their artistic level.

In the 1920s, due to various reasons, and mostly because of the frequent changes of government, this group ceased its activity and dispersed. In those days I hadn't thought, even in my wildest dreams that I - a simple and modest boy from the lowest layer of society, would be lucky to open a new chapter in the Jewish theater in our city, but so it happened.

From early childhood I clung to the Jewish folk song. I was fascinated by the joy and sorrow of this song that our ancestors, and forefathers, immersed their yearning and longing in it. I organized actors for the days of Purim (*Purim-shpiler*), teams for entertainment at weddings and other celebrations. I had no real pretension for theatrical acting and I also didn't attribute any importance to my occupation or my hobby.

In the years 1926-1927, I made the first steps for the establishment of a theatre together with my friends Solomon Guzman (now - a resident of Haifa.) and Grisha Misionezhink (today - Tzvi Gilady, a member of Kibbutz Kfar Masaryk). The name of the troupe that we established was "*Das Dramatische Vinkel*" (the artistic corner). Our first experience in this framework was the presentation of the historical play, "The Viceroy" by Feyman, from the period the inquisition in Spain. It took considerable effort and, I wouldn't exaggerate if I say that each one of us, the initiators and the players, invested his best efforts and talents in this play. Materially, our situation was dire. Public officials and the public institutions didn't take us seriously and haven't extended any assistance. We encountered many difficulties to find a suitable hall to hold the rehearsals and we didn't have the appropriate customs, stage sets, makeup, in one word: we lacked all the items that without them a theatrical troupe cannot exist. Our requests for help - weren't answered. I remembered that when we turned to Mr. Tchichelnitzky, the principle of the government primary school "Talmud Torah," with a request to allow us to hold rehearsals in the evenings in one of the school's room - we encountered an absolute refusal. Therefore, our first rehearsals took place in the school yard, outdoors…

Some time later we found kind of a shelter at the private home of our friend, Lyoba Wilderman, in Izmaylovskoye Street. The premiere was held at the municipal theatre "Regina Maria," which was owned by Schneider and Sklyarov, and it was huge success. The next day the local press noted the professional level of our troupe and emphasized the impressive victory of the new Jewish dramatic troupe in Akkerman. It is noteworthy that most of the participants in the play were young men and women, sons and daughters of the simple people. I will mention those that I remember from those days: Yisrael Gonopolsky, Yakov Kushnir, Yitzchak Gordon, Ajzik Eisenberg, Zev (Volodya) Zeplin, Polik Grohovcky, Peretz Kleinberg, Ms. Lyoba Wilderman, Reya Goldenstein, Pusya Voronovskaya, the couple Schuman, Moni Tishler and others.

Especially noteworthy is the violinist Sklyarov, Reuven Kaplinsky, Filya Lushak and the pianists Fima Goldman and Ms. Tabachnik. Shakhnazarov arranged and conducted the music and the make-up artist was Belkin (the last two were actors from the local Ukrainian theatre who extended their help). I should also mention the help of the official, Kalman Frechter, who obtained the permit from the police. The promoter, Julius Talmazan, also helped us to some extent.

[Page 176]

Over time we managed to bring to the Jewish stage a long line of plays, concerts, balls and evening entertainment which were accompanied by raffles and dances that lasted till dawn. The public got used to us, was attracted to our plays and gradually we won the appreciation of young and old who streamed to our performances at the halls of cooperative "Frima," the halls of the high-school, "Talmud Torah" and others.

When we became successful we left for performances in the provincial towns, presented plays in Shabo, Tatarbunary, Artsyz, Siert and other locations and received a warm welcome. We handed over our revenue to charitable funds and various public institutes. The play, which won a special success, was "*Di tsvey Kuni-lemels*" [The Fanatic, or The two *Kuni-Lemls*] by Goldfaden, "*Der Katarznik,*" the comedy "The bride of three grooms," and also plays of I. L. Peretz, Shalom Aleichem and Yakov Sternberg. I was the comedian of the troupe, and if I'm allowed to say about myself, I succeeded mainly in character roles and comic songs which became hits because they were being heard later in every Jewish family.

Generally, many troupes and famous actors, such as M. Fishzun, P. Bartov, the brothers Fridman, the Kochanski family, Dina Kenig, Sidi Tal, Adolf Tepner, Yitzchak Chavis and others, came to our city Akkerman. Of course we received advice and guidance from the famous actors for our artistic activities. At the end, I was forced to travel to Bucharest to receive the title of professional actor because it was an explicit demand of the authoritative authority of our city. And indeed, I successfully completed a special course, was successful in the exams and received a certificate confirming that I was a professional actor. My friend, Solomon Guzman, also received such a certificate and devoted many years to the Jewish theater in Bessarabia.

In 1947, I was invited to participate in the theatre, "Sevilla Pastor," and wandered with this theatre in the cities of Czechia, Austria and Belgium. In the course of time new faces appeared on the stage in Akkerman and I had the satisfaction that I was among those who paved the way and saw those who continue the road that I've started. Of those, who continued on our way, I will mention: Shulka Hacham, Yakov Nodelman, Yisrael Segel, Yafim and his sister Janet Ludizenski, Klara Sverdlik, Roza Zeider, Anya Maglnik, Zina Polonskaya and others.

In 1940, with the conquest of Akkerman by the Red Army and the establishment of the Soviet administration, also came the end to the artistic activity in the city and the Jewish amateur troupe dispersed.

The amateur theatre in Akkerman, 1928
From the play "The Viceroy." In the photo Shlomo Guzman as Sebastian and Misionzink as Alonzo

[Page 177]

The Drama Clubs
by Frima Fejland
Translated by Sara Mages

It wouldn't be an exaggeration if we say that despite the fact that it was an amateur theater, it was theater of quality that its actors acted as if they were professional. It was founded under the influence of the troupes and the Russian theaters from Odessa who often visited our city and a large crowd of Jews, lovers of the theatre, flocked to them. Odessa had a great influence on Akkerman and radiated on it from its spirit and culture.

At the late nineties of the past century, a Russian club, which called itself *"Literaturnyi-Artisticheski Kjudozheveny Teater,"* meaning, a theatre for literary-artistic acting, was organized in Akkerman. Over the years it changed its name to "The Russian literary drama club." In fact, it was kind of a school for the study of acting and artistic reading. In 1900, I was among the students of this club together with other young Jews who showed tendency for acting.

This club was associated with a similar institution in Odessa, "The school of theater," that its teachers and counselors also served, at the same time, as teachers and consolers in the Akkerman course. From time to time the club presented various plays before a limited audience and in order to advance its students it brought famous actors from Odessa who appeared in the plays together with the students of our course. In doing so, the leaders of the club assumed that they would be able to provide fluency and stability in acting to their students. I remember that among those, who appeared with the students, were famous Russian actors like Maious Pettifer and his wife, Svoboda, Ronitch (one of the founders of the Russian cinema) and others.

In 1910, several Jewish students of the Russian course got together and decided to try to establish a Jewish troupe. Three reasons prompted them to do so: A. their desire to improve the image of Jewish Akkerman. B. they assumed that the Jewish intelligentsia would support a troupe that present Jewish plays and it will also serve as a barrier against excessive Russifinaction. C. their desire to release the artistic powers that were imprisoned in several Jewish actors, and by doing so to cause additional artistic awakening and bring a release of cultural-artistic potential among the Jewish youth.

The driving forces of this club were: Felick Doyben and Pieterman. The first had a good voice and a pleasant appearance and received a lot of applause when he performed before the audience. Many young people, who eventually became activists in the Jewish public life, gathered in the club. Among them Shabtai Novak who was later the director of the Jewish Bank, the pharmacist Geisman, the lawyer Grisha Echselrod, Berta Fidelman, the writer of this lines whose nickname as an actress was Amirf (the opposite of Frima), Pesach Klaiman, Roselia Warszawskaya, Grisha Adlizki (the owner of the flourmill), the brothers Aharon and Ozer Krasik, Chaya Brofman and her brother David, Max Krolick (activist in the Jewish community), the cantor David Feldman and his sister Fania and others. A choir also operated next to the club and Lisa Helman and Chaya Brofman were among its soloists. Belkin, the troupe's make-up artist, was also the make-up artist of the Russian troupe. The shows were held at the Schneider-Skliarov cinema. The last was an avid music lover and also conducted the choir. Since our plays were held every Saturday evening we were nicknamed *"Sobrertnikim"* - Sabbath observers.

I remember that the first play that we presented was "Scattered and widespread" by Hirschbein. After it, we presented "Shulamit" by Goldfaben, "Money and Disgrace," "Chasia the orphan," "The slaughtering," "To be a man" and others. We deliberately chose plays with Jewish topics and way of life because we wanted to bring the Jewish audience closer to our troupe and also prove that "the situation is not yet desperate" and we do not have to be ashamed of Jewish writers and dramatists in comparison to those of the Russians. Only after we realized that we achieved this goal - we started to present plays of writers of other nations such as "The Wild Duck" and "Nora" by Ibsen, "Thoughts" by Andreyev, Potash and Perelmuter etc.

[Page 178]

After each of our performance a review was published in the local newspaper, "*Akkermanskaya Gazetta*," and we, the actors, waited anxiously for this review because we didn't get other newspapers. The rehearsals took place in my apartment and also at the Piterman's house. It is worth mentioning that we treated our role with reverence, we appeared on time to each rehearsal and memorized the text very well. In one word, we have done everything on our side to gain success and delight the viewers. And indeed, the audience responded to us, the stands were full and there were also Russian theater-lovers who came to our shows despite the fact that they didn't understand Yiddish. No one wanted to pay for our expenses and our only income was from the selling of tickets. This matter proved that there were many in the Jewish community who streamed to our shows. It is possible to say, without fear of exaggeration, that each new show that we brought to the stage became an experience for the audience and, of course, also for the actors.

The Jewish theater existed for about sixteen years with the above mentioned group of actors. Various reasons caused its dissolution. Doiben Felik, one of the main activists, immigrated to the United States, others also immigrated, financial worries made it necessary to devote more time to various businesses and occupations, and so the curtain fell.

Fell but not completely. Apparently our toil wasn't in vain. The seed that we planted - was well absorbed and many years later a Jewish artistic troupe, which lasted until the entrance to the Soviets to the city in 1940, was established again in Akkerman

(Written by Nisan Amitai - Stembul)

A notice for the Symphony Orchestra concert

[Page 179]

About Two Artists in our Town - Yosef Chaplin
Translated by Yocheved Klausner

Yosef Chaplin

He was born in 1914 in Odessa and in 1919 his family moved to Akkerman. He studied at the Tarbut Hebrew High-School, joined the Gordonia Movement and is a member of *Kvutzat Massada* in the Jordan Valley to this day.

In his youth he began painting and studied at the Beaujar Painting Academy in Paris. In 1943 he was accepted as member of the Association of Artists and Sculptors in Israel and served as teacher of painting at the "Valley of Jordan School" and the school on Kibbutz Ashdot Ya'akov, at the Chagall House in Haifa, at Yad Labanim in Petach Tikva and at The House of Culture in Kfar Saba. He also participated in Group Exhibitions in London, Paris, Switzerland and South America.

In 1956 an exhibition of his work was held in Paris on Faubourg Street, Saint Honoré. The reviews were excellent. Some of the reviewers mentioned, that the oil paintings reminded them of the great works of Mokadi (the great Israeli artist) by the brown-reddish color as well as by the pale, sad faces. He painted with sensitive and gentle lines. One of the reviews of his exhibition at The Chagall House said, among others: "This is one of the most beautiful exhibitions that we have seen this season. Yosef Chaplin, a member of *Kvutzat Massada* and graduate of the Paris

Academy of Fine Arts not only paints, but composes music of lines and color; his paintings sing, are poetic and sensitive to beauty and movement". - - -

[Page 180]

Chaplin did not join any special line, some define him as an impressionist and some say that he has remained "stuck" between the various modern currents.

In other reviews we read about the subjects of his creations, that stem from the environment in which he lived, Kibbutz Massada. The local atmosphere is strongly expressed in his paintings, in particular mothers and children on the kibbutz. - - - He distanced himself from plain ornaments and from any technical tricks. His painting is cultural, balanced and perfected on the canvas to the last centimeter. He takes his work seriously and regards it as a constant part of his life within the working society, - - - an artist who knows his way and sincerely devotes himself to his art every free minute.

In an interview published in the *Al Hamishmar* newspaper Yosef's words are quoted: "To the things that I am painting I try to add movement, but most of all sound, music. It is said about me that I am a lyrical artist, a painter of atmosphere - - - I don't paint according to a fixed plan. When I have an idea I try to express it on the canvas. When I feel that I have taken a wrong turn I leave the canvas and restart on a new one. When I feel that the painting is finished, I leave it. Sometimes I feel that I want to return to a painting that I had already finished, but I try to avoid that". The title of this review, published on 8.8.78, is revealing: "The colorful songs of Yosef Chaplin".

[Page 181]

David Malkkin

He was born in Akkerman to a respected man, R'Mendel Malkin. He went to the Hebrew High School "Tarbut" and was one of the founders of the branch of *Hashomer Hatza'ir* in Akkerman and one of its first instructors. His painting and sculpting talents were already apparent in his youth. He devoted much time to it and decided that he wanted to study.

In 1934 he made Aliya and joined the group of the *Ein Chay* kibbutz in Magdiel. The condition of the kibbutz at that time, in particular his own strong desire to study and develop his talents forced him to leave the kibbutz. He relocated to Jerusalem and began to realize his aspiration. His first teachers were the artist Barnar and the sculptor Norman.

During WWII he joined the "Jewish Brigade" and at the end of the war he began to study at the Academy of Milano, Italy, then at the Academy of Firenze and Rome, graduating cum laude, and had exhibitions as an Israeli artist. Next he relocated to Paris and remained there. He exhibited also in Jerusalem, Haifa and Tel Aviv.

According to the reviewers, Malkin's main strength was in portraits. He knew how to catch the main lines of a person's face and present them in a most impressive form. His heads looked alive, and sometimes funny. An insolent face of a woman, a good heart of an elderly man, the honesty of a postman, the sweetness of a small boy – all these and others like them are looking at us from the paintings of this artist.

[Page 182]

Cantors and Cantorial Music
Translated by Yocheved Klausner

The cantor Gottlieb and his choir

The Akkerman Jews had a special connection with cantors. In this respect there was no difference between religious and non- religious, fanatic and heretic. When the cantor was famous and he was known to have a pleasant voice and a special style, everybody came to listen to the "prayer and singing." Perhaps the proximity to Odessa awakened the strong feelings for cantorial music in the Akkerman Jews, since Odessa was famous for its great cantors, Razomani, Pinchas Minkovski, David Roitman and others, who filled the synagogues in any place they visited. The cantors were aware of the fact that in Akkerman there was a great number of "mavens" in cantorial music and they never skipped Akkerman during their travels. We shall describe here several of the Akkerman cantors; most of them passed away but some are still with us, and some are still leading the prayers.

Yakov Gottlieb

Known by his nickname "Yankel the hoarse" or "Yankel with the husky voice" – he certainly deserves to be the first on the list. He was born in 1852 Trostyanitz near Odessa, was blessed with a pleasant alto voice and was a member of the cantor Betzalel Odesser's choir. For some time he was cantor in Odessa and was very appreciated. After he married the daughter of a rich man in Akkerman he moved to Akkerman and was cantor in the *Bet Midrash*. The musical critic Ycht wrote about him: "He was a great artist" – and the Akkerman Jews liked that. The great cantor Yerucham the Short One invited him once to the Sabbath prayer in his Berdichev synagogue. After the prayer he said: He should not be called Yankel the hoarse, but Yankel the slaughterer, because with his prayer he slaughters all the other cantors... His voice had become husky when, during a pogrom he hid in a damp cellar and caught a severe cold. But he did not lose his charm and grace. His special *Nosach* [prayer version] and pleasant music attracted crowds of Jews to the *Bet Midrash*. He was the teacher of many cantors who later became famous, among them: Mordechai Patashnik, who had been a member of his choir, Pesach Crasnov, who was later cantor in Montreal, New York and Brooklyn, and others.

[Page 183]

Cantor Moshe Kogan with his choir

First row from right to left: **Yochanan Shoshok (the conductor), Unknown, Mote'le Gershfeld, Avraham Neiman, Yehuda Siegelwachs, the cantor Moshe Kogan, Sioma Itzkowitz, Sheftel Zuckerman, Siegelwachs**
Second row: **Magazinik, Kutchuk, Peretz Kleinbord, Yakobsohn, Zunis, Gordon, Unknown, Unknown, Pesach Kleinman**

He died young, in 1900, while reciting the prayer *Av Harachamim*.

His three sons followed in their father's path, were blessed with pleasant voices and continued the line of the Gottlieb cantors: Aharon Dov was cantor in the *Bet Midrash* in Akkerman after his father's death, and served six years. After the 1905 pogroms he moved to Sadigura and then to Baungwar, and finally to Newcastle in England. As a child he sang in his father's choir with his sweet soprano voice and learned from him a great deal. He composed the music for many prayers of Sabbath and the "Three Festivals" [*Pesach*, *Shavuot* and *Sukkot*].

Aharon Dov's son, Yankel's grandson, who sang in his father's choir in Baungwar and Newcastle, continued the tradition and is now cantor in England.

David Gottlieb, Yankel's second son, also had a pleasant voice, learned the prayers from his father and inherited his qualities. At first he was cantor in the *Bet Midrash* and later in several towns in Russia. He perished in the Holocaust.

Avraham Gottlieb, the third son, also learned from his father, was a member of his father's choir, was cantor in the *Bet Midrash* and later in London.

Mordechai Leib Yakobsohn

At the time Yankel the hoarse was cantor in the *Bet Midrash*, Mordechai Leib Yakobsohn was cantor in the Great Synagogue. He had a strong voice, but he did not attract the crowds as did Yankel, because of his somewhat cold and impersonal performance. In an article by M. Greenstein published in *Hamelitz* 246 in 1894 it was related that Jews gathered in the Great Synagogue to pray for the recovery of the ill Emperor. The representatives of the Municipality and the Authorities were present as well. The cantor was M. L. Yakobsohn, who was praised in that he "sanctified the name of the Jewish People in front of the officials, who listened to his prayer and singing, and were astonished by his strong and beautiful voice, and asked him to appear with his choir in the theater, in a charity performance for the hospital."

[Page 184]

Moshe Kogan

He was cantor in the Great Synagogue and music teacher in the "Tarbut" Hebrew School. He was an active Zionist, was involved in community matters and founded the Zionist choir *Hazamir* [The Nightingale]. He had a beautiful and pleasant tenor voice. During Holidays and during the "Days of Awe" [*Rosh Hashana* and *Yom Kippur*] He was accompanied by a choir. Since he smoked much, his voice became husky and he had to stop, to the regret of the members of the Great Synagogue.

Nissan Truker

He took Moshe Kogan's place in the Great Synagogue. He was born in Kishinev to his father R'Chaim, himself cantor and *shochet* [ritual slaughterer and examiner]. As a child he helped his father in his prayers in the Synagogue in Călăra°i, as one of the "singers." Yona Danziger, a famous cantor in Kishinev, taught him the fundamentals of the profession as well as solfège. At the age of 21 he was already cantor in Foc°ani and later in Bucharest and Gala?i. He was invited to the Great Synagogue in Akkerman and won the sympathy of the synagogue-goers by his pleasant voice and beautiful praying. He was active in public life and was member of the "Tarbut" committee. In 1949 he made Aliya to Israel and prayed in the Great Synagogue in Tel Aviv and other places.

Mendel Malkin

He was born in Akkerman in 1906 and received a religious education at home, by his father Rabbi Israel Malkin. He was a student at the Kishinev Music School and studied voice development with Professor Angelo Disconti. In 1924 he began working as cantor in the *Ahdut-Kodesh* synagogue in Buhu°i (Romania) and continued there until 1940. Then he relocated to Bessarabia.

Israel Swet

He was a pupil of the well-known cantor Razomani. He began his career as cantor in the Craftsmen's Synagogue in Akkerman and later worked in the Great Synagogue. He had a strong tenor voice and his prayers had a special sweetness – and he became famous in the synagogue-world. I. Schildkraut noted that when Israel left Akkerman it was difficult to find a cantor to replace him.

Zvi Kernkurs

He was born in Kishinev, the son of R'Moishe the leader of the ritual slaughterers. He was a member of the choir of the famous cantors Avrahm Kalechnik and Yehuda-Leib Kilimenik. His *Nosach* [version of prayer] was traditional, as he had learned from his teacher Zusia Serebreinik. Starting in 1924 he worked as an independent cantor. During several years he served as cantor in the Craftsmen's Synagogue and later in the *Zivchei-Tzedek* synagogues in Gala?i and Bucharest. He made Aliya and prayed in the *Ohel-Shem* and *Bilu* Synagogues in Tel Aviv.

Ben-Tzion Keiselman

He was born in Akkerman, the son of Eli-Ber Keiselman, a pious craftsman who was also *Gabbay* in the Kloiz and was nicknamed "Eli the tinsmith." His own nickname was "Bashke the Cantor." He served as cantor on a yearly basis in the Craftsmen's Synagogue in Akkerman and later he moved to England and was cantor there as well.

David Feldman

He was the son of a wealthy *baal-bait* [respected man, lit. "House-owner"] and served as cantor in the Great Synagogue. He had a beautiful tenor voice. From Akkerman he moved to Bandar and from there to Czernowitz. Made Aliya in 1944, settled in Tel Aviv and was cantor in several synagogues, among them the Great Synagogue in Tel Aviv.

Moshe Levitzki

He was born in a small town in the Minsk District. At the age of 18 he arrived in Odessa and participated in the choirs of the famous cantors Pinchas Minkovski and Efraim-Zalman Razomani. His first position as cantor was in Akkerman, and after he became famous he moved to Kiev. He was born in 1881.

Chaim Barkan

After the *Gabbay*s of the Great Synagogue fired the cantor M. L. Yakobsohn they hired Chaim Barkan to take his place. Barkan had great success and won the hearts of the public. He was cantor there for a period of many years.

[Page 185]

Meir (Mario) Botoshanski

Meir (Mario) Botoshanski

He was born in 1913 to a wealthy family in Akkerman, his father was Sioma Botoshanski. As a boy of 8 years he won the admiration of all his listeners when he sang solo as a member of the synagogue choir. His first teacher was the cantor Moshe Cohen, who taught him the fundamentals. When he was thirteen he attracted everyone's attention when he sang at his own Bar-Mitzva party. He went to the "Tarbut" School in Akkerman. In view of his marked musical talent his parents sent him to Kishinev, where he studied music with Professor Zacharov and at the same time studied at the *Magen David* Yeshiva, under the supervision of the well-known Rav Tzirlson. He continued his musical education in Milano, Italy and later in Rome. In Rome he attracted the attention of the Rabbi of Rome, Prof. Angelo Sacerdati, who invited him to take the position of cantor in the largest Sephardic synagogue in Rome – a very rare occurrence for a cantor of Askenazic descent...

Cantor M. Botoshanski had high aspirations in the area of prayer music and singing in general, and went to the United States to further his musical education. He studied music and voice development with the greatest experts in the field and appeared with the greatest cantors in the USA. Very soon he acquired fame as a unique commentator of Jewish and Israeli music and was often invited to give concerts and appearances on the radio. During 20 years he substituted for the well-known singer and cantor Richard Toker in the *Adat Israel* synagogue in the Bronx and later was invited to be cantor in the *Sha'arei Torah* synagogue in Brooklyn. Presently he is cantor in Florida, USA.

Among the Akkerman born who were members of the synagogue choir and became later famous cantors abroad we should mention also the cantors Talmezan, Shoshtchuk and Dorshkind. In addition to all those that we have mentioned above, many of the best cantors performed in Akkerman as visiting cantors, among them: Rozumani, David Roitman, Moshe Steinberg and others.

[Page 190]

The Holocaust

ש. ישרוליק

נישט פארגעסן !

נישט פֿארגעסן קיין טאָג, קיין שָׁעָה אַפילו
וועגן אַ שײן בליִענדע אידישע קהילה
ווי אידן האבן געזעלשאַפטליך גערִיכטעט
געבויעט אָנגעשטאַלטן לתפארת ולתהילה,
ווען רוצחישע הענט זיי אלע פֿארניכטעט.

. . .

עס פליסט דער דניעסטער טײַך זײן לאנגן וועג
חדשים, וואָכן, פיל לאנגע טעג,
שלענגלט שמאָלע, שטילע וואסערן
גלײַך צום שווארצן ים זײ פלאסערן.

צווישן דניעסטער טײך און ים דעם שווארצן
מישט ארײן זיך אַ "פֿארמיטלער", מיטן גאנצן האַרצן
צעשפּרײט זיך פליסיק-גײענדיק דער "לימאַן",
אויף זײנע ברעגן זיצט די שטאָט אַקערמאַן

גאסן לאנגע, גאסן גלײַכע, שורה נאָך אַ שורה,
אויסגעצויגענע סטרוגעס, גלײַך ווי אַ ווִירעַ.
אַ פעסטונג נעמט די שטאָט אַרום,
אַ הויף אַ גרויסער, ווענט דיקע, אלט און קרום.
אַ באַשנײע, שמאָל און הויך, אין הויף אינמיטן,
פֿאר אַ "גוט אויג" די שטאָט פֿארהיטן.

זומער דאַרט אין שטאָט בויעמ בלײעַן,
פייגעלעך זינגעמ, שפרינגען, פליען,
בויען נעסטן, "פֿירן ליבע" און רוהען.
קומט אַ רעגן, וואשט די גאסן רײן.
באלד שפאַצירן מײדלאַך מלא-חן.
רעגן-טראָפן פאלן פון די בוימעלעך,
שפילן-טאַנצן אברעמעלאך-פרומעלעך.

[Page 191]

די שוהל, די שנײַדערשע, הויבט אַ דאַך צו הימלען.
אויפן דאַך באַזעצט אַ פּאָרל טשערנאָהאָזן.
אַ נעסט דאָרט בויען, האָרעווען, טומלען,
ברײַנגען פּרודיקלעך, שינדלען און גראָזן.
שוין ליגן אייעלעך אין נעסט פון די שינדעלעך
און פון זיי אַרויסגעפיקט צוויי קליינע "קינדערלעך".

די נעסט אַ גרויסע, קײַלעכיק ווי אַ שיסל,
שטײַט אַ טשערנאָהאָז אויף אײן פיסל,
האַלט אין צווייטן אין לאַפּקעלע
אַ גרין, צאַפלדיק, קליין שזאַבקעלע -
"פּרישטיק" פאר די קליינע וואָס אין נעסט געזעסן,
ציען העלדזעלאַך, אָפענע פיסקעלאַך, עסן-פּרעסן.

דער זומער באלד פאַרבײַ - נישט פאַרגעסן.
טשערנאָהאָז פאָראורטפֿט זיין לאַנגן האַלדז אַרוגנטער
קנאַקט מיטן שנאָבל, זאָגט אָן: עס קומט דער ווינטער!

* * *

אַ שטאָט מיט פעלקער פיל, גרעסערע און קלענער
אוקראַיִנער, מאָלדאַוװענער, קריסטן און אַרמענער.
פיל שפּראַכן, פיל מִנְהָגִים - פאַרשיידן,
און צווישן אַלע - אַ קהילה מיט ייִדן:
פּרומאַקעס, חֲסִידִים, גרויסע לַמדנים.
פיר שוֹחֲטִים, מלַמדים, צוויי רבָּנים.
אַ בינטל "אויסגעלאָסענע", סאָציאַליסטן,
און פיל טרײַע, טיכטיקע ציוניסטן.

אַ "תרבות" גימנאַזיע, אַ קינדער-גאָרטן,
אויף העברעאיש אַלץ געלערנט דאָרט.
זעהט נאַר ס'אַ גוטע יוגנט אַרויס פון איר:
"גורדוניה", ביתּ"ר, "השומר הצעיר".

נישט פאַרגעסן "צעירי ציון", "העובד", רעװױזיאָניסטן
ווי אויך די ויצ"א און "אלגעמיינע ציונסטן".
דערצו נאָך: "קולטור ליגע" און אַ הײַפּטל בונדיסטן
נישקשה פון אַ געזינדל, פיינע "סחורה".
צוזאמען מיט דער ייִדישיסטישע "תלמוד תורה".
בקיצור - די גאַנצע קלאַפּער געצײַג, מכָּל המינים,
גאָרנישט געפעלט - לויט אַלע דינים.

[Page 192]

אַקערמאַן - אַ שטאָט, אַ קרייז רעזידענץ,
מיט אַ היבש ביסל יידישע אינטעליגענץ.
פיל געזעלשאַפטלעכע יידישע אַנשטאַלטן,
די קהילה געזאָרגט זיי אַלע אויסהאַלטן.
"אָזע", "מכבי", אַ שולע פון "אָרט",
דוכט זיך, גאָרנישט געפעלט האָט דאָרט.

אַ פרשה פאַר זיך געוואָרן די שולן.
נישט נאָר צום דאַוונען, אויך צום קהלן.
די "שניידערשע שול", אין אַ הויף אַליין,
ביי געבויעט הויך און שיין
אויסגעשטעלט אין אַ הויף, אין אַ ריי,
געשטאַנען אַנדערע שולן - דריי.
די גרויסע שול, אין הויף אינמיטן,
הויך, ברייט, מיוחס׳דיק ווי אַ מחותן.
אַ שוהל, אַ "קאַלטע", צום דאַוונען בלויז,
צו איר האָט זיך געטוליעט די קלויז.
אָפּגערוקט אין אַ זייט, מיט פּאַרכט און מורא -
דאָס "בית מדרש" - צום דאַוונען און לערנען תורה.

. . .

יידן סוחרים, מעקלערס, קלייטניקעס,
שניידער, שוסטערס, און אויך טאַנדעטניקעס.
נישט צו פאַרגינדיקן, פיל בעלי-מלאכות,
שווער געאַרבעט צו פאַרזאָרגן די משפחות.

אַ נאָמען געהאַט די אַקערמאַנער יידן,
מיט אָפענע הענט, גרייט העלפן און געבן,
ווי עס שטייט אין די הייליקע ספרים געשריבן:
"הפותח יד - נותנים לו", ווען אַ האַנט אויסגעשטרעקט -
ווערט זי גלייך מיט וואַרעמקייט פאַרדעקט.

יא, אַ נאָמען געהאַט די אַקערמאַנער יידן - - -
מבינים אויף קונסט, אויף חזנים,
זייער יידישקייט - געהאַט אַ פּנים.
מאַסענווייז געשטראָמט הערן אַ מגיד,
אַ גוטן רעדנער הערן, אפילו דער נגיד.

. . .

[Page 193]

וואו זענען זיי איצט? אלע מיטן אומגליק אוועק
דערמאנסט זיך, כאפט דיר א גרויל, א שרעק.
נאַצישע רוּמעַנער, פֿאַרבלוטיקטע העַנט,
געקוילעט ייִדן, געשאָסן, פֿאַרברענט.
אויך די וואָס זענען קיין אַדעס אַנטלאָפֿן,
האָט די נאַצישע האַנט דאָרט געטראָפֿן.
די אַלע וואָס זענען אין אַקערמאַן פֿאַרבליבן –
אַלע פֿון די הײַזער ארויסגעטריבן.
אין "רעמעסלינע" שול, איך זעה זיי ציטערן,
אין דעם טאָג דעם פינסטערן, דעם ביטערן,
אײַדער מען האָט זיי געטריבן אין די גאַסן,
אויפֿן וועג אין "קערניטשקע" – דאָרט אויסגעשאָסן.

איך זעה קינדער זיי טאטע-מאמעס האַלטן,
איך זעה טייערע קרובים חברים, געשטאַלטן.
איך זעה זיי אלע מיט מיינע גייסטיקע אויגן,
איך זעה ווי די תליה ווערט איבער זיי געצויגן.

איך הער זייער לעצטע תפילה, זייער אך און ווי,
און פֿון טיפן הארצן רייסט זיך מיין געשריי:
רבונו של עולם, וואו ביסטו געווען?
ווי האָסטו דאָס אלעס געקענט צוזעהן?

שוואַרצע ראָבן, שנאָבלען רויטע,
שוועבן – פליען איבער קערפער טויטע.
שוואַרצע ראָבן קראָקען: קראָאה, קראָאה:
"די ייִדן זענען שוין נישטאָ"...

גאָרנישט געבליבן פון א גאַנצער עדה,
אלע, אלע, געפֿירט צו דער עקדה.
דאָס הארץ ווייטאָקט, דאָס בלוט טהוט זידן,
נישטא שוין מער די אַקערמאַנער ייִדן.

אומגעקומען, פֿאַרניכטעט, א גאנצע קהילה,
נישטא קיין ווערטער זיי באוויינען אפילו.
שוועסטער, ברידער צוזאמען און באזינדער
טאטעס און מאמעס מיט קינדער
אויך פון די אַרומיקע שטעטלאַך צוזאמען
זענען אלע אוועק מיט די פלאמען

און די גאָט, דיין משפט איז גערעכטיק
גאָט איז הייליק, גאָט איז מעכטיק
זאָגט א "קדיש", פיל מיט צער
קיינעם האט ניט פֿאַרמיטן דאָס געפֿאר:
אַקערמאַן, ביִראַמטשע און טאַטאַרבונאַר,
טאַרוטינאַ, אַרציז, סאַבאַטע און שאַבא
יתגדל ויתקדש שמיה רבא... – – –

[Page 194]

The Destruction of Akkerman
(From statements at the gathering of former residents of Akkerman in Tel-Aviv, November 1950)

by Tzvi Manueli

Translated by Sara Mages

We gathered today to honor the memory of our loved ones, the Jews of Akkerman, who perished in the great Holocaust of the Jewish people. We, the remnants of the destroyed Jewish community, came to lament the martyrs - parents, brothers, sisters, relatives, friends and acquaintances who weren't even awarded with a tombstone on their grave. There are no words in our mouth to recount and describe the great tragedy, but, I see it my duty to describe the great disaster because, at the present, I'm the only person in Israel who visited Akkerman after the war and saw the great devastation with his own eyes. I cannot find peace in my soul. I have to include you in the sights of horror, tell you what I've been told, and share the feelings, sights and impressions with you. Yes, I saw with my own eyes the few survivors who remained in Akkerman. I spoke, not only with the few Jews who remained in the city, but also with Christians, acquaintances and former neighbors. I tried to rescue the information about the bitter end, but, to my great sorrow, I couldn't write all the testimonies and all the things that I've heard because I've been warned that written words can cause trouble under the conditions of post-war Soviet regime. In retrospect, I regret that because I forgot many details. One episode is engraved well in my memory: it was on Yom Kippur 1943. I was staying with the brothers, Shaike and Beske Yeroslavski, who lived at that time as refugees in Vakabaz Kolkhoz, somewhere in a remote location in Uzbekistan.

In conversation, I've been told that Shaike corresponds with survivors from Akkerman who live all over Russia, and also manages the strangest "account book." In this book, which I've seen with my own eyes, were pages of income and expense. Shaike registered each survivor from Akkerman in the income page, and each person who had perished in the expense page. Kind of a "bookkeeping"… Unfortunately, the "expense" was much greater than the "income"…

In my meetings with various friends (Leibele Shochat, Finya Tulchinsky, Mendel Gelman, David Berkovic and others), we tried to reach an estimate on the number of victims from our town, and the estimate was very bleak. Many families returned to Akkerman from Romania after the annexation of Bessarabia to the Soviet Union, and it's likely, that in 1941 there were about five thousand Jews in Akkerman. When I visited Akkerman at the end of 1945, there were only 250 Jews in the city (children included). According to a conservative estimate, about two hundred and fifty people remained stuck in various locations across the Soviet Union. That is to say, that four thousand five hundred Jews perished in different ways - hunger, epidemics, during the evacuation, in the bombing and at the hands of the Nazis and their helpers. The liquidation was carried out in stages and the spiritual-cultural extermination began before the physical liquidation. All the Jewish institutions and organizations, including the educational institutions, charitable organizations and everything that was established and cared for by the Jews for dozens of years, was eliminated and dismantled immediately after the annexation of Bessarabia to the Soviet Union. Only the houses of prayer and the cemeteries remained. It was kind of a cold blood pogrom which left its impression in every Jewish home and in each Jewish heart. A wave of arrests began immediately after the "honeymoon." Suddenly, the activists, Zionists, and all who played a role in the Jewish public life, disappeared from the city. On the night of 13 June 1941, in the middle of the night, they "raised" hundreds of people and deported them to the plains of Siberia, Ural and Baikal. Among the exiles were: Moshe Hellman who served for many years as the head of the community, Yisrael Eibinderr, the Yeroslavski brothers, Kuty Vilderman, Shalom Teplizki, David Berman, Shmuel Gelbord, Yosef Kvitko, Hanina Krasninski and others. Only a handful of exiles held on and none of them returned to his hometown.

In June 1941, when the war broke out between Germany and the Soviet Union, the Jewish youth was recruited to the Red Army and labor battalions. It should be noted, that many of these recruits remained alive. However, dozens of them have fallen in the battlefields.

When the Red Army began to retreat from Bessarabia, many of Akkerman's Jews started to stream to nearby Odessa because it was impossible to travel in the other direction. Only about five hundred Jews remained in Akkerman. Most of them were members of "Beit HaMidrash" who developed a theory that when the Romanians will return to Akkerman they wouldn't hurt religious people who opposed the Bolsheviks.

Among those, who preached not to move from the place, were: David Brend, Henoch Shapira, Chaim Kaminker, Pisia Levin, Hersh Ternopolski, Hershel Blinder, Moshe Leker, Gernik and others. Apart from them, there were also many among those who were deported to the villages and their property was confiscated by the Soviets,

[Page 195]

These deportees, who received a passport with Article 39, also decided not to leave Akkerman. They hoped that they wouldn't be harmed because they were the victims of the Soviet regime. All of them made a tragic mistake in their calculation. Of all the Jews of Akkerman only two converts remained alive: Kalkin and Leuba Shmoish who converted to Christianity and married a Romanian. From them, and from local Christians, I was able to get details that shed light on what had happened in Akkerman after the withdrawal of the Soviets. It turns out that farmers from Papushoi and Turlaki began to stream to the city before the last soldiers of the Red Army retreated. They broke into the Jews' apartments and stole everything on sight. Robbers, from the local mob, murdered Idel Brand (son of Shalom) and Chaim Klorefeld. At the end of August and September 1941, the Romanian campaign of revenge against the Jews has reached its peak and the number of victims among the Jews is estimated at 800.

The Jews, who remained in the city, were concentrated at the Craftsmen's Synagogue and held there for three days without any food or water. Then, they were taken to the road leading to Shabo where they were murdered with machine guns. On Yom Kippur of 1945, at the time of my stay in Akkerman, David Berkowitch turned to the worshipers with a call to bring the bones of the martyrs to Jewish grave. I don't know if something has been done in this matter.

Captain Okishur, who was the city's commandant, initiated and organized the massacre. He was the chief executioner of Akkerman's Jews. His assistants were: Commissar Teodorescu, Penca Stompotolo, and several local Christians who specialized in the discovery of Jews who managed to find a place to hide.

Also those who, so to speak, managed to reach Odessa, didn't escape the bitter fate. The progress of the German Army was very fast, and at the end of August it already stood at the gates of Odessa. Many, including a large number of our townspeople, were killed in the bombing on the city and many were killed during the evacuation from Odessa.

The evacuation of the refugees from the besieged city was very slow. It was difficult to obtain an exit permit, and after the permit was obtained - it was difficult to find a place in the ships that were intended to evacuate the civilian population. The refugees constituted a heavy burden on the besieged city and the authorities didn't treat them kindly... No wonder, that there was kind of a fatalistic mood among the refugees: "come what may" - many said - "we will remain here!" Against this background, one can understand the reasons why most of Akkerman's refugees remained in Odessa (their number is estimated at more than 3000). Only 800-1000 managed to leave the city and wander for many weeks in long trains, in arduous and tedious journeys of thousands of kilometers, until they arrived to remote settlements in Kyrgyzstan, Uzbekistan, Shakerya, etc.

The evacuation roads were also deadly, the trains were bombed and many were killed on the way. Two refugee ships, which also included Jews from Akkerman, were sunk in the Black Sea by bombers. Due to the terrible conditions in the various *kolkhozy*, the "lucky ones" weren't able to hold on. I have a long list of our townspeople who met their death in these places of refuge.

What happened to the Jews of Akkerman who remained in Odessa? On 12 October 1941, Odessa was captured by the German-Romanian Army and the terrible campaign against the Jewish population immediately began. On November 1941, there was a big explosion at the headquarters of the occupying army in Odessa. On November 17, in retaliation for this act, which was carried out by Soviet partisans, thousands of young Jews were hung on electric and telephone poles. Among them were also young people from Akkerman: Edika Brand, Idel Roizman, Averbuch (the watchmaker), Sopha Weisman from Tatarbunary, Sudkowitc, Sioma Erlich, Sonia Rubinstain, Dr. Ritenberg, Shmukler and others. One day, the occupation authorities issued a statement that all the Bessarabians, who wish to return to their hometown, should appear at special stations with their belongings, and from there they would be transported to Bessarabia. Thousands of Jews, among them many from Akkerman, crowded in long lines. All the "repatriates" were concentrated in Dalnik near Odessa. They were locked in huge ammunition warehouses and set on fire. I've read the Committee of Inquiry report on the massacre in Odessa. This committee determined that the warehouses burnt for three days and about 2500 Soviet citizens were burnt alive in them. This report doesn't say who these citizens were, but it's known that most of them were Bessarabian Jews. In the winter of 1942, dozens of Jews, including Jews from Akkerman, were sent to the camps in Transnistria. A tiny percentage of the deportees survived.

It should be noted, that several public figures from our city, especially Yosef Serper and Shaike Feldman, tried to organize any kind of help under the most horrible conditions. Many, of those I spoke to, commended the vigorous activity of Shaike Feldman for the benefit of the refugees from Akkerman who were in Odessa. Eventually, he and his wife died of typhus. His daughter Rosa, who lived in Bucharest, managed to obtain a special permit to take her parents out of Odessa, but she was too late. Only fifty Jews survived out of the 3000-3200 Jews who fled from Akkerman to Odessa. Most were in Transnistria, some came to Israel and they are here with us.

In this manner an entire Jewish community was annihilated.

[Page 196]

Wartime Memories

by Leyoba Asfis

Translated by Sara Mages

The light of the sun of the month of June flooded the city. The linden bloomed, the acacia blossomed, the city sparkled in its cleanliness and the bustle of people's voices mingled with the noise of cars and carriages. That Sunday, nothing heralded the impending disaster.

Indeed, the disaster came abruptly. It burst from all directions like a mighty sandstorm, through wide open windows and doors, top to bottom. At night, the Germans bombed Brest and Kiev, and in the morning, of the same day, everyone already knew that the war broke out. The brilliance of the sun faded in an instant, people's faces wore gloom, grief burst to their eyes and to their life.

To my life, and I was then an eight year old girl, sorrow burst three days later, on 25 June 1941, when my father, Viktor, and his three brothers, Avraham Michael and Lyoska, were recruited to the war. The four of them were brave, fearless, and all the notorious thugs were afraid of them and their receiving end. At that time the recruitment hasn't yet started in Bessarabia, but the four brothers, who've "lost" their documents, registered at the Military Registration Committee as natives of Russia and for that reason they were sent to the front. They defended Odessa and Kerch, Sevastopol and Stalingrad, and pushed the Nazis westward.

The evacuation began in Akkerman. The Jews turned to those who advised them to flee from the city with an argument: Where do we escape? Where is the safest place of refuge? Can we leave the few possessions that we've accumulated after many years of toil? And what would the Germans do to us? Who knew what is known? As opposed to them, there were those who packed their belongings in large bundles, as they were weeping and wailing, crossed to Ovidiopol by ferry, and from there - to Odessa.

My parents, who were also among those leaving, hated the Romanians and didn't wait for the Germans. For three weeks we wandered in wagons. The Germans bombed us more than once and heavy rain fell down on us. We traveled together with people from Akkerman, the elderly, women and children. After an arduous journey and many tribulations we arrived to Rostov, and there, we were scattered to different villages. The Don Cossacks, who aren't considered to be very good people, received the Jews with kindness, they fed us and hosted us in their homes. At the same time, our Akkerman was already in the hands of the Germans. Odessa was in flames but still defended itself. My father fought there and was even wounded in his leg. There were eight men from Akkerman in his battalion: Issac Lublinsky, Sonya Yelin, Avrasha Katz and others whose names I don't remember. Six men were killed by grenade thrown to the place where my father was.

Odessa fell. The Germans bombed Ukraine while we were in Stalingrad. The first reports of the Germans' massacre of the Jews of Odessa began to arrive. Among those killed were my mother's nieces and nephews, the Talmazan family, the Kosoy family, and my father's relatives.

We lived in a Jewish *kolkhoz* in the vicinity of Stalingrad. All the duties, starting from the chairman of the *kolkhoz* and ending with the cleaning personnel and the stables, were in the hands of the Jews. Each and every one was subjected to his sorrow and grief but the small village, in which only a Jews lived, served as half consolation. Jewish women, who were used to life in the city, worked hard from dawn to late at night: they harnessed horses and oxen, plowed the fields, drove combines and tractors, and took care of the children and all the housework. At night, they cried as they remembered their husbands and their sons who weren't with them. Indeed, they were real heroes who didn't get a citation, but, of course, they deserved it.

It may seem strange, but the fact is, that pain and sorrow is also expressed in singing. On summer nights, after a hard day's work, when Stalingrad served as an arena for bloody battles, and also on cold winter nights - the women gathered in one of the homes and poured their bitter heart in Russian and Ukrainian songs. However, the sad songs in Yiddish especially fascinated me. It was a soft singing, in very low tones, so as, God forbid, not to wake the sleeping children.

[Page 197]

Anxieties and Hopes Serve Interchangeably

1942. The High Holidays and the Jewish holidays arrived. I remember well the first day of Rosh Hashanah. There were no bombings on that day. The small houses dipped in the morning dew and the sun painted the trees in a shade of golden-emerald. That morning all the residents of the village walked to the house where the Rabbi of Kharkov and his wife, the Rebbetzin, lived. They went to the prayer dressed in holiday attire and the rabbi's house, which contained *mahzorim* and *tallitot* for the worshipers, turned into a synagogue. Everyone prayed for the welfare of their loved ones and their relatives, and for the end of the war. The same thing was repeated on Yom Kippur. Before Yom Kippur, a delegation from the district administration arrived with a demand that everyone, without exception, must go to work on the sacred day. However, all the Jews in the village refused to desecrate the sanctity of the holiday and went to pray. The arrests began the next day. The chairman of the *kolkhoz* was sent to the front, the activists were deported and the foremen were punished.

Odessa was liberated in 1944. We, the children, ran every morning to the district administration building to hear the official announcements on the progress of the army, and accordingly moved the pins on the map of the Soviet Union. People waited with tension and anxiety for the postman. Who can guess what he might bring in his satchel? Just not that - many thought - just not the official statement with the bitter news - "Fell as a hero defending the homeland"... Small joys accompanied the great anxiety with the liberation of well-known cities: Kharkov, Kiev, Vinnytsia, Poltava, etc. People's faces lit up each time we received a word about the liberation of a city, and it seemed, that mountains of grief disappeared from over their heads for a brief moment.

On 23 August came the news that rocked our hearts: Akkerman was liberated! We started to make arrangements to return home and also started to search for our relatives. The search was drastic because, as we were looking for them - they were looking for us. We knew that when we return to Akkerman we would only find the ruins of our homes.

The Great Change

On 25 June 1945, we finally approached the shores of the Lemen River. We sailed in a ferry between empty wine barrels,, barrels of herring and wagons loaded with straw. We felt the unique smell of the water of the Lemen River, and saw, with our own eyes, the famous fortress. However, the city greeted us with "thundering" silence and the wilderness of the destroyed houses. We felt as we were treading on a "cemetery." Mounds and ruins and ashes of fires. It's impossible to describe what took place in our hearts when we saw the images before us.

We were lucky. My father and all my uncles returned from the war, but there were many families who lost their loved ones. Hundreds of families were shot in the suburbs of Akkerman, and hundreds of Jews from Akkerman, who sought refuge in Odessa, perished there. We were happy with every Jew who survived and returned, and cried bitterly when we remembered the many who did not return.

Life continued to flow its course despite everything. People worked, ate, when there was something to eat, cleared the rubble, rebuilt the city and renewed its face. A new generation grew. We, the children of the 50s, were far from Judaism. No one told us about the Maccabim and Bar Kokhba, the name Herzl didn't say anything to us, and the same was for names like Jabotinsky, Ben-Gurion, Weitzman and others. We had no interest in Zionism and Judaism because we weren't educated in that direction. We weren't even excited by the name Israel. And yet - we were Jews. We searched for Jewish friends, sang songs in Yiddish, even though we didn't speak in this language, we ran to concerts of the actress Sidital and performances of actors from the Jewish theater in Moscow. We were excited by the singers Ana Guzik and Nechama Lifshitz, and enjoyed the records of Emil Gurevich and Appelbaum even though only a few understood their Yiddish. So were things.

Years have passed. The Six Day War in Israel removed the cataract from our eyes, pulled the curtain, and the world behind the Iron Curtain was unfolded before our eyes. We started to think about ourselves, about our essence and our Judaism. At that time we also started to correspond with our relatives who left the Soviet Union and immigrated to Israel in 1957. We started to take interest in everything that was said and written about Israel in the newspapers, and also tried to read between the lines. We discovered ourselves. We discovered that the Jews have their own country, a homeland with all that involved in it and arising from that. We told that it to our ten year old son. At first, he didn't show much interest in our stories. He had his own world. The Soviet regime left its mark on the course of his life and his thoughts. He was a young Russian in everything. The turning point came six years later, when he was sixteen, after the death of his beloved grandfather and the Yom Kippur war in Israel. This turning point was helped by his clash with a police officer who threw in face "Here isn't Golda Meir's government." He became interested in the State of Israel and read the letters of our relatives who lived Israel. We understood that his eyes opened, that the seed of Judaism was sown in the furrows of his heart.

Farewell Forever

1975. The sun of the month of June is warming our old city, and the linden and acacia are blooming again. There's peace and quiet around. The four of us are walking around the city: I, my husband my son and daughter. We're passing the same roads that we've passed in our childhood and nourish our eyes in everything around us.

[Page 198]

The city's park is clean and well maintained. The birds greet us with their lovely singing and the goldfish swim around the pool and shake their heads and tails. The fountain's water jets spray fresh water on us, an orchestra is playing a new-old waltz on a small stage, and for some reason I feel that they play the song in our honor:

> Many years have passed
> and our weeks ran away.
> I'm no longer young

> and you're not a little girl
> in a white dress.
> White sneaks to my temples
> and also your hair is graying slowly---

So it was. Indeed, our hair hasn't yet turn white, but we didn't stay as we were in the distant past

When we left the city's park we passed by the school on Mikhailovskaya Street, which is now called Lenin Street. I once started to study there and now my husband works there. The friendship between my husband and I was tied at that school. Our love was born here and now our children go to this school. We pass by the institute (previously a school for boys) and remember our student's days. Our ears attuned to the quiet waters of the Lemen River and our eyes are raised in the direction of the ancient fortress. It seems that the sailboats separate from us like pure seagulls. We walk in familiar streets and we have no power to part from them and the many buildings who tell of our childhood. We arrive to the cemetery - the last stop of every person on earth. Above the stones we see the pictures of our relatives. We part from them forever. We feel as if they accompany us with a blessing for our new path. Yes, we are traveling to Israel. They, our loved ones, weren't awarded to do that, but, they accompany us with a silent blessing.

On 27 July 1975, we left Akkerman, our birthplace, forever, but wherever we would be, they'll also be with us. We'll carry their memory everywhere. To this day the name Akkerman is ringing in our ears, echoes, like the first cry of a newborn baby, like the first word, "mother," of a little child, like the first kiss, like the first waltz. Echoes, and reminiscent of what has been forgotten.

Translated from Russian: N. Amitai

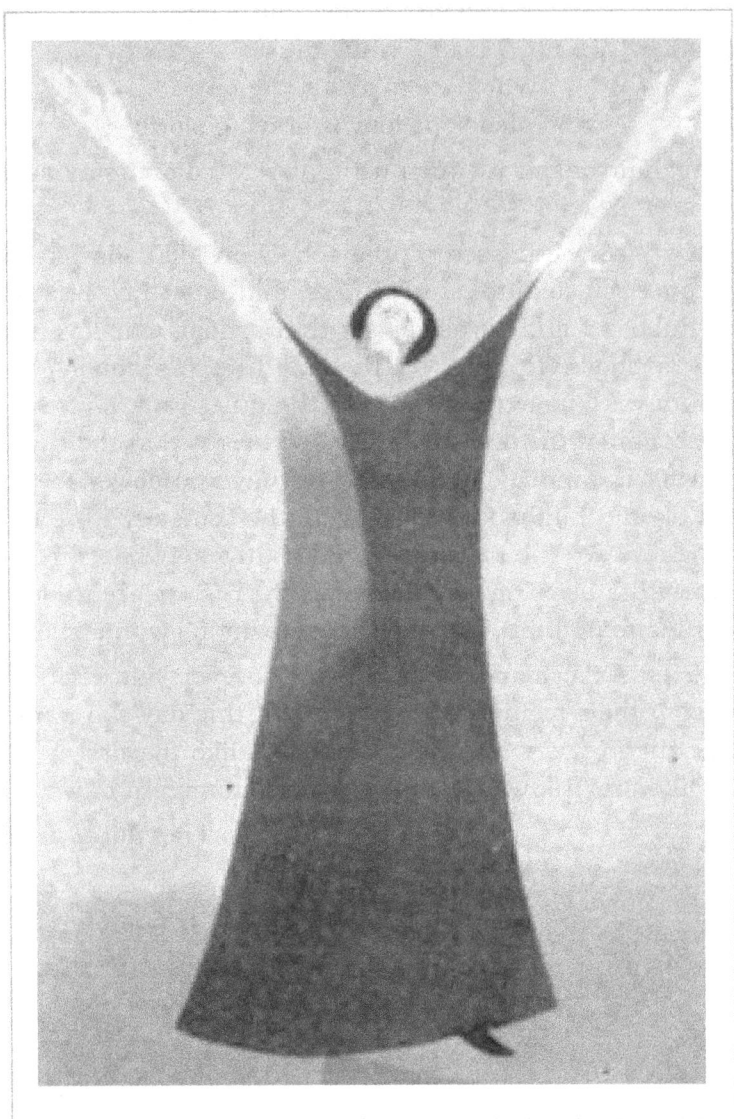

I will lift up my eyes to the mountains;
From where shall my help come?
{Psalms 121:1)
(Drawing of the artist Ben)

[Page 199]

א פליט

די תפילה פון א געראטעוועטן

יא, מיינע טייערע, איך האב זיך געראטעוועט,
איך בין געבליבן לעבן - אויב דאס הייסט לעבן.
יא, איך עם פרישטיק אן מיטאג, איך גיי אפילו אמאל דאוונען,
אבער גלויבט מיר, טייערע מיינע, עס דאוונט זיך נישט?
ווי קאן איך דען דאוונען? איך ווייס דאך דעם פירוש המלים
פון "יתגדל ויתקדש שמיה רבא"...
קאן איך דען א לויב געזאנג צוטראגן צו דעם אלמעכטיקן
וואס האט אלץ געזעהן און געהערט - און געשוויגן?

*

יא, מיינע טייערע, איך האב זיך געראטעוועט, איך לעב,
אבער טאג איין טאג-אויס באגיס איך מיט מיינע טרערן
דעם וועג פון אקערמאן קיין קערניטשקע, אייער לעצטן וועג,
וועלכן איך האב נישט מיטגעמאכט מיט אייך צוזאמען,
אבער איך זעה אים בעשיינפערליך, איך פיל אים
מיט מיינע אלע רמ"ח און שס"ה, מיט מיין גאנצן וועזן.

*

פרייטיק צו נאכט, ווען איך זעה די שבת ליכט אין די פענצטער -
זעה איך די תפילה׳דיקע הענט פון מיין מאמע
בענטשנדיק ליכט און לאזנדיק א טרער;
און אין א פשוטן מיטוואך, גייענדיק אין גאס -
גייען מיט מיר הונדערטער אקערמאנער יידן.
איך שמועס מיט זיי, איך קאן דאך יעדן באם נאמען אן צונאמען.
פיינע יידן, שיינע יידן, הארציקע יידן.
איך וויל זיך פון זיי דערוויסן דעם גרויסאמן סוד:
פארוואס? פארוואס? וואס האבן זיי געפילט אין די לעצטע מינוטן?
ווי זענען זיי געגאנגען פון רעמעסליענע שול קיין קערניטשקע?
וואס האבן זיי געזאגט צו זיך אליין, צו זייערע קינדער?
איידער זיי האבן דעם לעצטן אטעם געאטעמט?
אבער זיי שווייגן, א ווארט לאזן זיי נישט פאלן.
פונקט ווי זיי וואלטן געוואלט איך זאל אליין טרעפן,
איך, דער לעבן געבליבענער...

*

אלע טאג שטיי איך אויף און דאוון "מודה אני",
אבער מיין "מודה אני" איז גאר אן אנדערער,
נישט דער וואס מען האט מיר אין "חדר" געלערנט.
איך דאוון צו אייך יעדן באגינען,

[Page 200]

יא, איך האב זיך גערארטעוועט, איך לעב!
אבער ביז היינט קאן איך ניט פארשטיין דעם סוד:
פארוואס איך יא, און איר נישט?
בין איך דען בעסער פון אייך? האב איך א גרעסערע זכות?
מיר וועט קיינער איבערצייגן אז דער גורל האט אזוי געוואלט.
ווער איז דער גורל? וווּ איז דער גורל?
האט ער געוויגן אייערע מעשים טובים און פארגלייכט מיט מיינע?
פארוואס קומט מיר לעבן און אייך טויט?
דערפאר איז מיין פרימארגנדיקער "מודה אני" אזוי אנדערש.
דערפאר שטיק איך זיך אין מיין צער און טרויער,
און מיינע אלע פראגע צייכנס שוועבן אין דער לופטן,
קיינער וועט זיי נישט פארענטפערן.

*

"ויבוא הפליט – ויגד לאברהם", אזוי שטייט אין דער תורה געשריבן,
אבער וואס האב איך געהאט צו זאגן מיינע ברידער דא אין לאנד?
איך האב זיי דערציילט אז איר האט זיכער אויסגעהויכט די נשמה,
אין קערניטשקע אדער אין אדעס, ווי איר האט זיך געוואלט ראטעווען,
מיט "שמע ישראל" און ארץ-ישראל אויף די ליפן;
איך האב זיי געזאגט אז איר האט זיכער געקלערט וועגן זיי –
און נאך אזעלבע בשורות האב איך, דער פליט, געבראכט מיינע ברידער דא
זיי האבן געהערט – און געשוויגן, שטארק און הויך געשוויגן,
אזוי שטארק אז איך האב געוואלט זיי א טרייסל טאן און זאגן:
"הערט אויף שווייגן, שרייט בעסער"!
יעדער איינער מיט זיין טרויער, מיט זיינע קדושים,
יעדער איינער איינגעטוליעט אין צער און פיין,
קדיש-יתום.

נאר איין מאל אין יאר זאגן מיר "קדיש" בציבור,
איין מאל אין יאר – זענען מיר זיך מתייחד מיט אלע קדושים צוזאמען.
דער חזן זאגט קדיש און "אל מלא רחמים" פאר דער גאנצער עדה.
און איך קלער בשעת דער תפילה: וואו זענען די רחמים
פון דעם "אל מלא רחמים"?
איך קלער וועגן דעם "מארש" פון הונדערטער יידן
בארוועס און נאקעט אין די אקערמאנער גאסן אויפן וועג צום אומקום.
וואו ביסטו דאן געווען "אל מלא רחמים"?
איך טרייסל אפ פון זיך די כפירה'דיקע מחשבות.

[Page 201]

ווער ווייסט ווי ווייט זיי קענען דערפירן?
זיי מיר מוחל, אלמעכטיקער, אבער די מחשבות לויפן מיר נאך,
און צוזאמען מיט זיי פנים׳ער, געשטאלטן, קינדער, קינדער, קינדער –
די אזכרה ציט זיך, דער חזן דאוונט, א רעדנער רעדט,
אבער איך הער נאר אייער שטימע, אייער יאמער און געוויין –
איך גיב נישט דעם "קדיש" מיין "אמן".
איך שטיי מיט איך אין קערניטשקע
און אין מיינע אויערן קלינגט אן אויפהער אייער תפילה.

The 1903 pogrom in Kishinev

[Page 202]

On My Way Home
by Miriam Zamir
Translated by Sara Mages

On July 1941, the war between Germany and Russia broke out and the Jews of Akkerman were forced to leave their homes. Our Christian neighbors mocked us: "You're running away together with the Communists, but we have no reason to flee, we're in our home."

At the same time my brother returned from the prison in Odessa. He lost a lot of weight and aged beyond recognitions. The only way to escape was - through Odessa, but my brother insisted and claimed: "Death is better than to return to Odessa." Since he lived for some time in the German colonies in Bessarabia, it never occurred to him that they could be so cruel. However, after he realized that everyone was fleeing, he had no other choice and joined us together with his family. When we got to Odessa he didn't want to move from there, and ultimately, his fate was the fate of 135 thousand Jews of Odessa - annihilation.

My family decided to continue our flight. We looked for a way to get on a ship and sail from Odessa. On 10 September, a ship sailed with 3500 passengers, most of them were wounded in the war, but on the following morning it was bombed by the Germans and sank. On 18 September, we managed to get on a ship and sailed under the cover of a smoke screen but, sometime later, a squadron of German planes spotted us and started to bomb us. When the anti-aircraft guns didn't let them to sink us, they aimed their fire against Odessa and saw the city go up in flames from the ship's deck.

Our ship, whose name was "Krim," turned in the direction of the Crimean Peninsula, not for from Novorossiysk. In the morning of the third day of our sailing, the ship was hit by a naval mine. Fortunately, the damage was on the side of the food storeroom and not in the ship's bow. About one hundred people, who were standing on the deck, were thrown into the sea from the intensity of the blast. Sailors lowered lifeboats and started to save women and children. It's difficult to describe the nightmare that we had gone through. The boats, which dried in the sun, filled with water and began to sink. The captain called for help by radio. Motor boats sailed towards us from the Crimean Peninsula and their sailors somehow managed to plug the gap that opened on the ship. When the boats arrived, people started to jump into them and the cries of children and mothers were heart-rending. Due to overcrowding on one side of the ship, the ship tilted on its side and miraculously didn't roll over. Sometime later, a towboat arrived and towed us to the shores of Novorossiysk. Thousands of people gathered on the beach to see the survivors. We were taken off the ship exhausted, shaken and soaked to the marrow of our bones.

The residents of Novorossiysk, most of them Russians, tried to help the refugees. They served us food, a hot drink, etc. I became friendly with a woman, and when I told her that I know how to sew and want to earn a living from this craft, she took me to her home. I mended old clothes, sewed new ones, and in exchange for my work I received cooked food that I brought to my family.

One day, it became known to me that a train, with wounded from the front, is getting closer to the city. I, my husband, my son and my elderly mother (our daughter died on the way to Odessa), climbed on one of the cars without permission. The train, which stopped frequently, was bombed by planes and young and old jumped out of the car in panic to save their lives. From time to time, this train suddenly began to move and left many people in the middle of the field. There is no way to describe the terrible tragedies that took place. I remember that one of the mothers took three of her children off the train, and when she went to get the fourth - the train suddenly moved and separated the mother from her three children. Shouts and cries accompanied us until we arrived to Stalingrad. We didn't get an enthusiastic reception when we arrived to Stalingrad. Many lived in the streets, the hospitals and the public buildings were filled to capacity. The city was in a state of chaos. Thefts and robberies were daily occurrence. Government officials came quickly from Kamyshin and from the *kolkhozy* in the vicinity and started to recruit professionals. We were also

[Page 203]

recruited. We were told that they would take us to a village in Upper Volga and give us the homes of the Germans who were exiled to Siberia. We saw ourselves lucky and hoped for the best. In the morning, after an overnight stay in the village of Gamlenky, they took us to various *kolkhozy* in the surrounding area.

The "houses" that were given to us were nothing but clay huts. The windowpanes were removed from the windows and the doors were pulled off their hinges after the previous occupants left. The floor was also made of clay. We were told: you may choose any apartment you want. Before we managed to get organized we saw a notice in this wording: "Those who do not go to work - will not get bread!" The bread that was given to us was inferior and many became ill with gastric diseases. Sugar, salt, onion etc. - were nowhere to be found. Red beets served as sugar, and also the babies didn't get sugar. We held on for the entire winter despite the unbearable conditions When the Germans got closer to Stalingrad, entire *kolkhozy* and villages were evacuated and their residents started to arrive to Gamlenki and to the neighboring villages.

The *kolkhoz*'s officials liked the huts that we worked so hard to renovate, and after we were evicted from them, we moved to a grain warehouse which served as a place of residence for four families.

In late autumn of 1942, my 52 year old husband and my 19 year old son were drafted to military service and I was left alone with my elderly mother. In the winter of 1943, we received an evacuation order. One night, we were loaded onto a truck and taken to the train station in Gamlenky. At the same time, a silo full with grain went up in flames and the smoke, which rose from there, chocked us. We couldn't even eat.

Several days later, a freight train, which was loaded with tanks and spare parts for damaged planes, arrived from the front. Some of its cars were used to transport coal. We climbed on it and traveled without knowing where. Several cars were disconnected at different stations and people got stuck in places like: Uzbekistan, Kazakhstan, etc. Our fate was to be thrown in Uzbekistan, a godforsaken region where backwardness and poverty were really desperate. We were thrown together with forty people and were told to wait for a ship that would carry us forward. I ran to the nearest village to get some food and during my absence my elderly mother took off her shoes and fell asleep. During her na,p her shoes and her suitcase, in which she kept the shroud that she prepared for a time of need, were stolen.

Finally a ship arrived and took us to the city of Przheval'sk in Kyrgyzstan. From there, we were transported to all kinds of remote places. I, my mother, and an elderly couple from Odessa (Ziglis), arrived to a place, which wasn't a village or a city, and its name is Tyon. The local residents were prisoners who were sentenced to 20-30 years imprisonment because they were - bourgeoisie. We were given shelter with a family of four children who lived in one room. The father of the family was in the battlefront.

I noticed that there was a manual sewing machine in the apartment and offered to sew all kinds of clothes so we'll sell and buy food with the money. When the landlady heard this proposal she responded: "God Forbid! I cannot allow a Jewish woman to make a living from my sewing machine. After all, it's the Jews' fault that we were brought to this remote location."

It's difficult to describe the suffering and our hard work. Our job was - transporting wheat from place to place. We barely held on. I started to make attempts to locate my family members who were scattered in different locations.

Translated from Russian: Nisan Amitai

[Page 204]

Between Anxieties and Hopes
(Chapters of memories)
by Rosa Weitzman (Gordon) – (Kibbutz Hanita)
Translated by Sara Mages

1939 was intended to be the year of my immigration to Israel. I finished *Hakhshara* at "Masada" near Bălți and returned, out of a sense of security, to my home in Akkerman to start preparing for the expected immigration, but it was not as I imagined. All matters - not just mine - received another turn in that historic year that sealed the fate of millions. As soon as I arrived to Akkerman I felt an alarming unrest. Everyone was expecting different developments and the rumor said that the Russians are about to conquer all of Bessarabia. Musia Shapiro, one of the of the communist youth leaders, who later became an omnipotent ruler in our city, remembered our old friendship and came to warn me that I must leave Akkerman as soon as possible because after the regime change I will have a lot of difficulties and wouldn't be able to emigrate. I was confused and frustrated. The members, with whom I went through *Hakhshara,* were immigrating to Israel with *Aliyah Bet*, and I was still waiting for the announcement of my legal immigration date. I finally got the message I was expecting from Gordonia's main leadership in Bucharest that I should come to the capital immediately regarding my upcoming immigration. I parted from my family and traveled to Bucharest. I have been told that there was a chance that I would immigrate soon and I should be ready to leave for the road. There was no limit to my happiness. I sent a telegram to my mother and my sisters and told them the news.

At the very last moment there was a change. I was asked to give up my turn for the benefit of a sick young woman from the "Buslia" federation who had to immigrate immediately with her husband. I was told that it was only a few weeks delay, and I agreed to give up my turn. I returned to Akkerman to be with my family in the few weeks left until my immigration.

I felt the tension in the city. We did not know what lies ahead. Musia, my friend, told me that it would have been better if I had waited in Bucharest for the date of my emigration because a serious turn in the conditions and circumstances may come any day. However, he saw the need to add while patting my shoulder: "don't be scared, we won't touch you." A message arrived again from Bucharest: we haven't forgotten you, you have to wait patiently."

Where do you take patience when the war in Europe is spreading in full force and everyone predicts that there will be drastic changes in our regime?

In June 1940, Soviet troops invaded Bessarabia and, as a result, all the *Halutzim* who were unable to immigrate were in great distress. We meet every day, talk and consult. David Cohen z"l, Musia Rotenshtern z"l, Efraim Abramowitch May he live, myself and another member are trying to find a way to save ourselves. Something is emerging on the horizon. Hope and despair mix together. Everything is vague. Bucharest announced that someone had been sent to bring me there, but unfortunately he was caught by the Russians and exiled to the depths of Russia. I remained stuck.

Meanwhile, the new regime began to show its true colors. The "capitalists" were exiled and all their businesses were confiscated. The activity of all youth movements ceased, as did all social-party activities. Everyone feared for his life. The communists in the city rose to prominence. They were headed by Musia, who traveled in the city streets in an open car and sealed the fate of each person. I started looking for any kind of work because I had to prove that I was a productive element. I started to work as a cashier in a restaurant that was confiscated from its owner. My Zionist past did not make me feel safe even though Musia came to our house and tried to reassure me that nothing bad would happen to me (in the end he also went through a period of suffering. Apparently he was disappointed with the regime, which did not find him reliable, and was also exiled). We knew we were being followed, all the more so after Efraim Abramowich was arrested together with his family. This imprisonment shocked me. I pondered in my heart if, sooner or later, I would also go through a period of trouble and suffering.

Meanwhile, the war broke out between Germany and Russia. In the city - disarray in all areas. Many are leaving the city and only a few delude themselves that the war would end quickly. The city is slowly emptying from its inhabitants. Many flock to Odessa in the hope of finding refuge there. You can't leave Akkerman

[Page 205]

without permission, but my mother, my sister Sonia and I, do not receive such a permit. The reason is probably in our Zionism. We want to leave, at any cost, and only on the last day, at the last hour, we were also given permission to leave Akkerman.

Our first stop on the way to Odessa was Ovidiopol. In this city we received a very "warm" welcome - a heavy bombardment with many victims. Miraculously, Dodik Cohen z"l appeared as a messenger from the High Providence and with his help we arrived at the train station. When we arrived, after many hardships to Odessa, we became refugees with all the implications of this concept. Those who had relatives - went to them, and those who did not - sought refuge wherever they went and expected the mercy of others. I remember that hundreds of Akkerman's residents gathered every day in a public park in Odessa to hear the news, to receive coupons for bread and share stories of sadness and grief.

It was clear that within a few days Odessa would be captured by the Germans. Time has worked to our detriment. Many of Akkerman's residents left Odessa and advanced, in all sorts of ways, toward the depths of Russian. Every day I met with Musia Rotenshtern, Yakov Ziglwaxs, Gitia Brend and Mischa Zalkind, but in these meetings we couldn't alleviate our distress (Mischa was recruited, participated in battles in Odessa and was killed). As the shelling intensified, and after we began to see German cannons when we stood on a high floor of a building, we came to the realization: there is no point in staying in Odessa, we must flee.

To my happiness, a rumor spread that there's one way to escape, but it's very dangerous, through a mined sea. We decided to gamble on this option even though we had been warned that the risk was very high. We had nothing to lose. My mother and sister said it was crazy to go out in such a dangerous way, but there was no other choice. We were able to get a truck and arrived with our belongings to the port of Odessa, but we entered the ship without our belongings which were thrown into the sea.

On our journey we had to pass through a heavily mined area. For two days and nights I did not know where my mother and sister were. But, in the end, we all got to Novorossiysk. There, too, we were greeted with a heavy bombardment. We continued our journey and reached Stalingrad. Many of the passengers stopped there, but we continued to travel to get as far as possible from the front. On 13.10.1941 we arrived in Karaganda Kazakhstan and stayed in Siberia until 1945. I was cut off from all my acquaintances and friends and only had some contact with Ephraim Abramowich who sat in prison. I served as a teacher and secretary in a Russian school, and was eagerly waiting for the day that I could renew the relationship with my friends and Eretz Yisrael.

At the end of the war we left for Kishinev, because my sister married a native of this city who served in an important role in this city and was called by the Russians to return there. I worked in bookkeeping, but all my thoughts were focused on one single issue: to get in touch with my friends from the movement and find a way to get to Eretz Yisrael.

Among those, who came to see us when we returned to Kishinev, was also Munia Feldman. He was the first to bring the news: a certain young man came from Bucharest and he's trying to get in touch with former members of the movement and resume the activities, but underground. All efforts were directed at the attempt to illegally cross to Romania. I will confess, and not be embarrassed, that I have treated this message with such suspicion that I asked him to stop talking to me about it. I have never been a great hero, and all the hardships I had gone through during the war added fear to my natural fears. So I continued to work and tried to get used to the new circumstances, but I did not give up and a glimmer of hope kept shining on me.

I continued to treat with great suspicion every piece of news about connections with the "outside, " and yet I did not stop hoping for a change. One day - and it was on May 1, 1946 - in the midst of May Day celebration, Rabinowitch from Chiţnău approached me and whispered to me: get out of the lines. There's a young man here who wants to see you. You must come to meet him at the home of the Portnoy family from Uriv [Orhei].

And again, hope mixed with fear. I ran home impatiently to consult my family, whether to go to a meeting with this man who came on a certain mission, not knowing the nature of it. Maybe it's just a trap?

We made a positive decision despite the risk involved, and I set out to meet the anonymous emissary. The conversation was short. After making sure that I was Rosa Gordon, he introduced himself as Zelig Weitzman and told me that he was working on establishing a contact between former members of the movement and the illegal crossing of the Russian border in order to immigrate to Eretz Yisrael. He asked if I was willing to join while emphasizing the risk involved and the need to keep it a secret. I was shocked and frustrated. I was not ready to give him an answer right away and asked for time to consult with those closest to me.

When I told my family about it, my mother ruled immediately: destiny has summoned you this young man and you have to trust him. I was in a serious dilemma because it was just for me and older people were not taken into account. I was very attached to my mother, to my sister Sonia and her husband. I couldn't imagine life without them. On the other hand, I knew that this might be the last chance. The emissary, Zelig Weitzman, who later became my husband, helped me make the decision. Slowly, members I knew from the Gordonia *Hakhshara* period, as well as members from other locations, started to come to our house and in this manner the home of my brother-in-law and my sister became the center of the underground activity. Zelig had forged papers and in Kishinev he was "a guest who stayed overnight. " During the day he had meetings with members and at night he slept on a bench in a public park in the city center. My brother-in-law, Avraham Gunmacher, a very noble and faithful man to the family, couldn't come to terms with his condition and invited Zelig to live in his apartment despite the danger.

[Page 206]

One day, I was summoned with four members to come immediately to Chernivtsi in order to cross the border. I got up and traveled without thinking much, but, unfortunately, something happened at the last minute, as it happened to me often, and the border smuggling was postponed. I returned to Kishinev and felt the change in the attitude towards me in my workplace. They began to suspect me and probably my sudden trip, without permission, cast suspicion on me. I also heard a rumor that they were going to put me on a members' trial and my only hope was that I would be able to escape before that.

On the eve of Rosh Hashanah 1946, I received a message from Zelig that I should come immediately to Chernivtsi. When I got there, Zelig met me at the train station and informed me that he had to join our group because they started to follow him and we were leaving at night. His frequent trips from Kishinev to Chernivtsi raised suspicion, his papers were forged and he had the feeling that the zero hour has come for him. We met in Dvora Blinovitch's room and received the last instructions from Zelig. In our group were: Aharon Bratini, Shimon Rabinowitch, Zelig and I. Of course, the papers in our hands were also forged and we had to declare, in case we got caught, that we were some kind of medical committee assigned to a particular mission... We walked a long road full of obstacles and I occasionally choked with fear. The sounds of the border patrol, and the barking of the tracking dogs, echoed in our ears. We knew very well what we can expect if we were caught. We reached an electrified fence that Zelig passed the members through one of its opening, and we also passed through this opening.

We breathed a sigh of relief as we crossed the Romanian border and reached the town of Siret south of Bukovina. From there, after a short stay, we left for Bucharest and met Meir Zait and Baruch Kamin who worked for the movement. I won't even try to describe the excited meeting. They looked at us as if we have come from another planet. Everything seemed to be in a different light. We began to believe that we would achieve what we dreamed of for many years.

In consultation with Zelig and the "*Bricha*" operatives, it was decided, despite all the dangers, that Zelig must once again travel to Russia to collect more members for the same mission. Zelig, of course, accepted the "movement's judgment " and set off and I, already his fiancée, had to wait for him in one of the *Hakhshara* points. Sometime, afterCed Zelig left for Russia, alarming news began to arrive. A number of members had been arrested and Zelig's life was in danger. And again, I agonized with anxious anticipation. Am I doomed to go through torment again?

One day, Zelig miraculously appeared. Our wedding was held in Bucharest and was attended by many of our members who came from Russia. In the meantime, we began to feel that we were being followed, and we had to leave Romania before it was too late. Together with Baruch Kamin and his wife, we fled to Hungary, but even there we couldn't sit peacefully because we were being followed. We fled to Italy where we finally breathed a sigh of relief. In Italy we met Issachar (Iscah) Haimovich who served as an emissary from Israel. I was very excited because I owed him thanks for the material and mental help he had given us during the war. He made sure, every month, that I would receive a food packet that kept us from starving in the harsh and bitter days.

In Italy we were with a group of about forty members who escaped from Russia, and we continued to live together as a big united family. Zelig and I were able to immigrate to Israel with *Aliya Daled*, whose living spirit was Shulamit Arlozorov, and arrived at the place we longed for - Hanita. There was no limit to our happiness, but there were also shadows that clouded this happiness: news came about members who were caught on their way from Russia and received five to seven years in prison. Among them was also my brother-in-law, Avraham Gunmacher, who literally sacrificed himself for the common cause. People, who were with him, told me that he was very happy when he learned that I arrived safely to Israel. He did not achieve that, he died in the Diaspora. After a lot of hardships, my sister, his wife, managed to get to Israel. My mother also lived with us in Hanita for a few years and those were the most beautiful years of her life, but that's another story.

Now, that I am already a grandmother to grandchildren, I often tell them the sad stories of those days, but they are an important chapter in the history of my personal Zionism, and also of others.

[Page 207]

In the Mission to Save the Jews of Romania and Bessarabia

by Baruch Kamin

Translated by Sara Mages

It is no coincidence, that among the dozens of emissaries from Israel, who were selected for the mission to rescue Jews from the Diaspora during the Second World War, were many from Bessarabia. There were several reasons for this: the special status of the Zionist movement in Bessarabia, which was formerly part of Russia, and later, between the two world wars, part of Romania. The proficiency of the former residents of Bessarabia in both languages - Russian and Romanian, and maybe we should mention the decisive reason: their passion for the war against the Nazis and providing help to their relatives and loved ones who remained in the Diaspora. Many former residents of Bessarabia enlisted in various auxiliary units in the British Army, and later, with the establishment of Jewish combat units ("Buffs"), many of them enlisted in these units assuming, that in this way, they would be able to fulfill the above two goals that stood before their eyes. However, as is well known, the Allies refrained from transferring Jewish combat units to the front on various excuses, justified and unjustified, and in the meantime the mass-murderers carried out the work of extermination, and also the Jews of Romania and Bessarabia received their punishment. Many of them were concentrated in camps in Transnistria and their end was also near. After vigorous activity on the part of the authorized institutions in Israel, it was approved to parachute emissaries to Romania, and other European countries, in order to save all that can still be saved and organize the escape of Jews from Europe to Eretz Yisrael.

Among the dozens of emissaries, who were selected for parachuting in Romania, were also two from Akkerman and the surrounding area: Dov Harari (native of Byeramtcha who was educated in Akkerman) and the writer of these lines, a native of Akkerman. Fate summoned us together again and this time as a parachuting pair, because paratroopers usually parachuted in pairs. I was in

Egypt with Dov and we trained together. In the morning of 1 August 1944, we parachuted together to Romania.

When we arrived in Bucharest each of us turned to his field of activity. Dov - for the establishment of his movement "*Habonim Dror*" and the centralization of the written expenses of "*HaHalutz*," and I - to the establishment of "*Gordonia*" which was my movement before my immigration. I saw my main role in bringing Jews to Israel, and after a while I began to organize the "*Bricha*" [escape] from Russia to Romania and from Romania, through Hungary and Yugoslavia, to Eretz Yisrael.

In August 1944, the war was still in full swing, the Soviet army camped on the Romanian border and the Germans still ruled the territory. At that time, many Jews from Bessarabia, among them many from Akkerman, managed to infiltrate from Transnistria to Romania and were found in the country's major cities, especially in Bucharest. Their financial situation was very bad and we began to distribute allowances to the needy from a special fund set up for this purpose. Bucharest was an open city, those who managed to get to this city found refuge there and therefore we encouraged this infiltration as much as possible.

On the second day of my second arrival in Bucharest from Israel, November 1945, Shaike Trachtenberg introduced me to a Jewish officer in the Soviet army named Weizmann. This officer took off his uniform, wore civilian clothes, and all his ambition was - to immigrate to Eretz Yisrael. Shaike (now his surname is - Dan), and also me, have done our best to persuade this officer to return to his first "being," that is, to put on his officer's uniform, cross the border into Russia and serve there as an emissary for the "*Bricha*." He would locate the Jews in Kishinev and Chernivtsi, help to smuggle them to Bucharest, and from there the road to Eretz Yisrael was already short.

Weizmann accepted our offer, agreed to leave his wife in Bucharest and took on the mission. When he introduced me to his wife, it turned out that she was none other than Rosa (we called her Rosczka) Gordon from Akkerman - my hometown. It's hard to describe our excitement when we met. From her I received the first greeting from my family and townspeople, as well as from the members of the "*Gordonia*" movement. Rosa told - and we both cried non-stop.

For a whole night she told me about destruction and killings, about the wanderings of Akkerman's Jews as far as Siberia and Tashkent and all the atrocities and torments that befell them, about the members of "*Tzeirei Zion*" whose only aspiration was to find a way to immigrate, etc., etc.

[Page 208]

I would never forget the "greetings" I received from my city' and my townspeople' after a long separation from them. Even after I parted from Rosa I couldn't stop thinking about all the sad information I received from her. From now on my activity at the "*Bricha*" center increased. I believed that I would be able to provide the only way out to the Jews of my birth-place - Akkerman.

With the liberation of Southeast Europe, the roads to the Mediterranean ports were opened. The chances of escape increased and many former residents of Akkerman began to move in the wake of the Soviet army and concentrated in Bucharest.

The Feldstein family was the first Jewish family from Akkerman I met. I then met with Kvitko, Itsikson and others and, at a later stage, with Schildkrauth, Kroyt, Menuali, Zukerman and others. Romania was the center of escape through the ports of the Black Sea and the Adriatic, Turkey and Syria. The traffic was heavy. The Black Sea was still full of mines, but this did not deter those for whom immigration to Israel was the only way out after the horrors of the war. Also the hostile attitude of the Mandatory Government and the rickety ships, in which the immigrants made their way to Israel, did not frighten those who had faced fear for a long time. We, the *"Bricha"* activists, were mainly faced with the problem of how to concentrate in Bucharest masses of Jews from Transnistria, among them many from Bessarabia and Akkerman, and extend first aid to them until their time comes to travel to Israel. The Soviet occupation authorities aided the activity because they were interested to free themselves from the burden of the displaced Jews and, on the other hand, also wanted to cause trouble for the British Empire. The goal I set for myself was to pave the way for the immigration of Jews from Bessarabia, Bukovina and Northern Transnistria, by all means. I was looking for a suitable person to move to Chernivtsi, which was now under Russian rule, and in which masses of Jews were concentrated. From Chernivtsi it was possible to contact Bessarabia, which was our main destination. This man had to bring to these Jews the message that a chance for immigration had opened up, and to organize and guide them without the Russians' knowledge. We soon had the opportunity to meet such a man, and he's - Leizer, today Professor Tur-Kokhba, Dean of the Faculty of Life Sciences at the Tel Aviv University, who was a native of Northern Bessarabia. On 20 December 1944, Leizer is telling, Sheiko, who was the representative of the *"Bricha"* in the Bukovina border, transferred him to Siret and from there he traveled by cart to one of the villages in the area. After hiding during the day at the home of a farmer, he managed to reach Chernivtsi with the help of border smugglers and met with Beresh (now in Ein Harod). Beresh painted posters for cinemas, but his main occupation was preparing forged papres for the Jews who concentrated in Chernivtsi. Meanwhile, Zelig (today member of Kibbutz Hanita), also arrived in Chernivtsi and he, too, joined the mission of smuggling Jews to Bucharest. Rumors of the possibility of immigration from Bucharest spread rapidly throughout the youth and Zionist circles in Russia, and reached as far as Central Asia where there was a great concentration of Bessarabian Jews. These Jews were extremely happy when they learned about the two paratroopers (Dov and I) from Akkerman, which were known to many of them from the days before the war. Needless to say that, we too, waited impatiently for the meeting with the people of Akkerman, and it can be said that "more than the calf wishes to suck - does the cow yearn to suckle" meaning, our passion and willingness to bring them to Israel was no less than their desire to immigrate.

From December 1944 to March 1946, hundreds of Jews from Chernivtsi and Bessarabia arrived in Bucharest. Two centers were activated on the Soviet border to help the escapees: Siret and Rădăuți. The refugees, who arrived in these places, were equipped with appropriate papers, clothing and money for initial expenses. The activities of Zelig Weizmann greatly helped to increase the smuggling rate. It was necessary to overcome a lot of mishaps, the roads were dangerous, and if it is said "with cunning you shall wage war," it can be said that with cunning we also made *"Bricha,"* and this is not the place to list them all. Our activity lasted until 6 March 1946, when the repatriation of Jews from Northern Bukovina to Southern Bukovina in Romania began.

Yisrael Schildkrauth, of the leaders of *"Tzeirei Zion"* in Akkerman, is telling: in 1945, when the war ended, I traveled with my wife to Kishinev. When I arrived to my previous apartment I found out that it was occupied by a Jewish family from Russia. I've been told that this Jew from Russia knew about my Zionist past, and if I started harassing him with a lawsuit to evict him from my apartment, he might report it to the authorities and then I would live not in my previous apartment but in a Soviet prison... I was helpless until a rumor reached me that "Jews travel to Chernivtsi and from there they travel on." I got up and traveled to Chernivtsi. I went to

Chernivtsi's market to meet Jewish acquaintances and learned that the border to Romania was already closed. I did not have a choice but to rent a room and live in Chernivtsi until the rage passes. Two months later they started again to register Jews who wanted to cross to Romania and a committee was set up for this purpose. An officer of the Red Army also participated in the committee, and a Jew, who knew Russian and Romanian, sat down and registered the candidates. After a while this Jew passed away and a Jew from Akkerman, named Magzinik, took his place. There was a rumor that this Jew was taking 5,000 ruble for arranging a travel document. I came to Magzinik's house several times, but each time his wife told me that he was not at home. I was close to despair, but one day I met this Magzinik on a city street and he told me: " Schildkrauth, why

[Page 209]

don't you sign up for the trip to Romania?" I told him; where would I get 10,000 ruble for two people? He answered me: go and register because ten thousand people already registered and one day the registration will close. Don't be afraid, go to "Zaks" (Russian institution for civil registration), register without paying and don't worry about the payment. I did as he advised, I signed up without paying and after a while I learned that other people from Akkerman signed up without paying, including Zieglwax, Menuali and others. Two months later, I met this Magzinik again and he said to me: prepare firewood for the winter. Chernivtsi belongs to Ukraine, we sent the papers to Kiev and there is reason to believe that instead of Romania they would send us to Siberia... It is easy to describe our anxieties until a rumor spread that in the morning a special window was opened at the NKVD to distribute numbers to those who wanted to travel to Romania. I went to Magzinik and he told me that he has the number 8,000 while I will have the number 10,000...

I crossed the border one kilometer from the town of Siret in Romania. There were many carts there and also a man from the "Joint" who transferred the refugees to the synagogue's courtyard. All night we lay on our packages and in the morning I went to look for a "contact." Acquaintances told me to go to a certain room, and when I got to that room, I was terrified and frightened because there were slogans of Stalin, Lenin, Marx, etc. on the walls. I ran away in a panic. That day, I met a guy named Shaike who invited me to come to him, to the same room from which I ran away, and he offered me a sum of money saying that the money was sent to me by Baruch. I was afraid to take the money and asked him to tell me who Baruch was, and then he revealed to me that the man was none other than Baruch Kaminker. I breathed a sigh of relief, took the money I really needed, and together with Menuali rented a room for one night. I then traveled to Galați ;while Menuali traveled to his wife's sister in Ploiești. After Passover I traveled to Bucharest. I met with Baruch who provided me with financial help that allowed me to bring my wife and get organized until our immigration to Israel. By Baruch's recommendation to the "*Ihud*" party I started to work as an instructor in cities and towns in Romania.

Tzvi Menuali, who was chairman of "Tzeirei Zion" in Akkerman, is also telling a similar story. He, and his brother Shmuel, also arrived in Chernivtsi based on the rumor that from there it was possible to travel further in the desired direction... They crossed the border to Romania and when they arrived in Siret they received a telegram from Baruch Kamin that the members of the "*Bricha*" would take care of them and transfer them to Bucharest. In Bucharest they also received financial aid from the Israeli aid fund, and in June 1947 traveled through Hungary, Austria and Italy and arrived in Eretz Yisrael.

I could also bring here the story of Zadok Zuckerman, son of Akkerman's slaughterer, and other stories that can testify that the same "mysterious" Baruch did not forget his Jews, the Jews of Bessarabia in general and the Jews of Akkerman in particular. If I may testify for myself, I will only say this: I did my best to help Jews to reach safety. It's hard to describe my excitement with each meeting with a Jew from Akkerman. The best reward I've received was a poem dedicated to me by the well-known poet, Bartini, who was also among those helped by me.

On my return to Israel, at the end of my mission in Romania, I was elected to the Second Knesset as a representative of the Romanian immigration. I'm allowed to admit, without boasting, that my heart overflowed when I stood on the Knesset podium to deliver the oath of allegiance. In my imagination I saw my father and mother, all my family and the Jews of Akkerman who were executed. I also saw myself as their representative. I pondered in my heart: I must justify this trust given to me by continuing the struggle for the immigration of Romanian Jewry. This was in 1954, when the communist regime in Romania plotted against immigration and Zionist activity. Zionist and immigration activists in Romania were arrested and imprisoned and many of them were prosecuted for espionage and treason. As a new and young member of the Knesset, I had to, of course, learn the ways of parliamentary activity, and so I've done, but the issue of immigration from Romania was my top priority. Together with the member of the Knesset, Idov Cohen, also from Romania, I began to initiate, in cooperation with the institutions of the Jewish Agency for Israel and the Ministry of Foreign Affairs of the Government of Israel, protest rallies in Israel and abroad against the suffocation of immigration from Romania. These rallies received many responses and I especially remember the words of Emanuel Celler, member of the U.S. House of Representatives in Washington, following our wave of protests. In addition to the protests, we also announced a hunger strike of communal workers, immigrants from Romania, as a sign of solidarity with the Prisoners of Zion who are rotting in prison in Romania. The fast began on 24 May 1954 at the Great Synagogue of Tel Aviv. Among the participants in the fast were, of course, the two members of the Knesset who represented the Romanian Jewry: Idov Cohen and I. According to our proposal, the Knesset presidency gave urgency to the proposal we submitted regarding the Prisoners of Zion in Romania. In the speech I delivered in the Knesset on 25.5.54, to substantiate our proposal, I described the situation of the Romanian Jewry during the Nazi occupation and everything that has happened to this Jewry since then to this day. I noted that the wave of arrests and trials came as a result of the wild incitement of the Romanian *Yevsektsiya* [Jewish section of the Soviet Communist Party]. From the Knesset podium, I sent a warm greeting on behalf of all the participants in the fast, and on behalf of all the Romanian Jews in Israel, to the Prisoners of Zion who are rotting in Romanian prison.

All the Israeli newspapers reacted to our activities, especially to the forty-five communal workers who emigrated from Romania. Many telegrams of encouragement and solidarity with our fast and protest arrived to the Great Synagogue, as well as large delegations of

[Page 210]

rabbis, communal workers, workers' representatives and many different public organizations. The Society of Emigrants from Bessarabia invited all its members and activists to the place where we fasted to express its appreciation and solidarity. We were also visited by the Prime Minister Moshe Sharett z"l, the Speaker of the Knesset Yosef Sprinzak z"l, and the chairman of the board of directors of the Jewish Agency for Israel, Berel Loker z"l. We spent the days of fasting reading, studying the Talmud, talking, etc., each person according to his inclination. Dr. V. Abelis, director of *Kupat Holim* in Jerusalem, was the medical supervisor of the participants in the fast. After five days of fasting, the hunger strike was stopped at the request of President Yitzhak Ben-Zvi, which was brought to us by his wife and his Military Secretary. Over twenty thousand people visited us during the five days of fasting, and many newspapers abroad wrote about our protest. That was our goal - to arouse public opinion in the world - and that goal was achieved.

Since then, things have changed. Today's Romania is the only country in the Eastern Bloc that has diplomatic ties with Israel. Is it possible that our vigorous response, from many years ago, also has some part in the current situation?

The hunger strike at the Great Synagogue of Tel Aviv for the Prisoners of Zion in Romania, 1954. Moshe Sharett visits the participants in the fast. Baruch Kamin is standing next to him.

[Page 211]

The Flag
by Shmuel Miniali (Netania)
Translated by Yocheved Klausner

Who, among the Akkerman Jews, does not remember the blue-white flag that was carried high during every important public event and in the front of all the national parades and Zionist demonstrations? This flag touched all Jewish hearts in Akkerman and filled them with pride.

As the rumor said, this flag was made illegally at the time of Herzl and the first Zionist Congresses by the few Zionists who lived in our town. It was made of expensive silk, the Star of David was of golden color and it carried the inscription "Carry to Zion the Flag, the Flag of the Camp of Yehuda." This flag symbolized for us the national revival and the hope for a Jewish State.

A respected resident of the town, perished in the Holocaust

During many years was the flag kept in the "craftsmen's synagogue" and it was impossible to describe the feeling of happiness felt by those who happened to carry the flag, which was quite heavy, while leading a procession. The strongest youngsters were chosen for this task. As a student in the high-school, I often had the opportunity to argue with the attendants of the synagogue (Yashpun, Shayke Shlein and Chaim Leib Speevak), asking to borrow the flag for a parade. Sometimes it was not easy to make a decision.

Several times I had the privilege to be the carrier of this flag at the head of a parade and salute the authorities who were standing on the official platform on Michaelovska Street near the public park. At the head of those parades, always walked the High-School orchestra, directed by the Brothers Palikov.

In 1940, as the Soviets occupied the town, the flag disappeared and nobody was interested to know its fate. I had the good luck to see it for the last time, one or two days before the war broke out – the last days of the Soviet rule in Akkerman. This is the story:

At that time I was living in the Kwitko House, not far from the Craftsmen's Synagogue. One day, I passed near the synagogue and noticed that the door to the basement near the gate was open. I thought that I should look in, to see what was hidden in the cellar, which was familiar to me since my childhood, when I was part of the choir that accompanied the cantor of the synagogue Moshe Kogan z"l and we would change our clothes there before our appearance. My eyes noticed immediately, that our dear flag had been thrown on a pile of waste, old and dirty. My hart ached seeing the humiliated flag, whose fate was similar to the fate of the Akkerman Jews.

Scared and full of fear I left the place, hoping that the flag would be crowned again sometime.

[Page 212]

[Page 213]

A Miracle Did Not Happen in Karnitchka
by Berurya Har-Zion
Translated by Yocheved Klausner

Many holidays and other events were celebrated in our school in Akkerman, but etched in my mind is the memory of the holiday of Lag Ba'omer. It is not one of the major Jewish holidays, but I remember from those far years all its details, as if it were today. Maybe the reason is the memory of our parade through the streets of the town, which touched our hearts and filled it with Jewish pride. Indeed we had parades in honor of the Romanian national holidays as well, and our school excelled in organizing them, but we never received the highest grade among the other schools.

Not so on Lag Ba'omer. This holiday was all ours, created for us, part of our history and our heritage. The preparations would begin long before the holiday, and on the morning of Lag Ba'omer the principal of the school would walk between the rows of students, check if the shoes were shining, if the buttons of the shirts were in place, if the shoelaces were tied well, etc. – exactly as before a general Romanian holiday. I confess, that all these procedures annoyed me and I would think: what can be the connection between this Jewish holiday, which symbolizes the heroism of the Jews, the Bar-Kochba revolt, Rabbi Shimon Bar-Yochai, and the strange procedures of the holidays of the Gentiles? But I would forgive the principal, after I heard his speech, which I remember well, since he repeated it every year and no wonder that we remembered it...

In the neighborhood of our town there were many places with beautiful fields, full of fruits and vegetables, but everybody knew that on Lag Ba'omer our aim was only one place – Krinitchka. Indeed, this was a place which was, apparently, created for Lag Ba'omer. There were many legends about the nearby spring, the tall cross, the many events that had happened there etc. One legend I remember well:

Many years ago, a group of fishermen lived there, whose sustenance depended on fishing alone. One day, the well that served the inhabitants of the town dried up. People died of thirst, babies perished, epidemics broke out. As the situation got worse, almost all residents decided to leave the place. Only very few remained, and all winter they drank snow water. When spring came and the snow began to melt, someone noticed some water under the snow. They followed the little stream and found a spring with sweet and clean water. At the place they erected a small building with a big cross on the roof, as thanks to God Who sent them water. This legend accompanied me through my entire childhood.

I think that they could not have chosen a better place for our outings. The usual fine weather in the month of May, clear skies, green trees all around, intoxicating bloom, chirping birds, blue water of the Liman – all this fused with the surrounding landscape. No wonder that the Lag Ba'omer songs echoed during our parade with enthusiasm and youthful beauty: many weeks before the holiday we anticipated the experience and longed for it.

In the afternoon, after the lower-grades pupils returned home, the upper grades would gather with their teachers under a large tree and have a long discussion. The teacher Tcherniavskki would mix his tales and songs with Russian words, and I remember in particular the Hebrew song *Al tira avdi Ya'aov* [do not be afraid, my slave Yakov], inlaid, like a gem, with stories.

Sport events, bicycle races, various games – were the special agenda of the day. The echoes of our songs were heard all around, and even the Christians knew what this holiday meant for the Jews. Only late afternoon, when the sun began to set and a violet-greenish light would spread at the edge of the sky – we began preparations to go back to town.

[Page 214]

After more than thirty years, in 1966, I visited Kishinew and met my kindergarten teacher Mania Sherira, and we reminisced about the Lag Ba'omer festivities. We sat in a room with the shutters closed and remembered those old days. How sad it was to hear, that Krinitchka, where Jewish children would gather with songs on their lips to remember Bar-Kochba and the heroism of the Jews – was the last station of thousands of Jews from Akkerman, who perished there with the words *Shema Israel*, and not *Al tira avdi Ya'aov* on their lips. I said to Mania: Why did the powers of nature not react? Why did the lake not erupt into the air? Why did the trees not tremble at the moment of destruction, the same trees in whose shade we sat on Lag Ba'omer? How could all these be silent witnesses to those indescribable things?

Indeed, the miracle that happened so many generations ago has not repeated itself. The soil, which in those far days of Lag Ba'omer festivities drank the songs of our youth and the burning of our hearts – now drank the blood of our beloved. The place, which had symbolized youth and hope for the children of Israel, now symbolizes for all of us the bitter end of the Jews of Akkerman and surroundings.

By mistake, the wrong picture was printed on page 214. Below is the correct picture:

Memorial service for the Shoah victims at the Akkerman Meeting

[Page 215]

A Story of a Name
by Asher Shwartzman
Translated by Yocheved Klausner

I wouldn't tell a personal story if I hadn't thought that it would be of interest not only to me. In any case, I learned a great deal from this tale – the story of my first name.

Asher was the name given to me at my Brit Milah [circumcision]. But in fact, I never used this legal name of mine. There were many reasons for that: I was ashamed; I was afraid of the reaction of my friends on the street and at the playground, and my teachers, who might mock this strange name; I was afraid of the reaction of the various officials when I had to fill forms in some office. When I reached the age of 14-15, the shame with my "strange" name turned into real pain. It became an obsession. I began comparing my name to Russian, Ukrainian and other names. I longed to understand the problem – why was my name worse than other names? Why should I be ashamed with the name that was given me at my birth? The result that I came up with was that a Jewish name could not be equal to other people's names. Jewish names were names of a nation of merchants (although my father was a laborer and my grandfather was a cobbler), a nation of weak people (my father was a proud soldier in the Red Army and fought the Germans and fell in battle with his weapons in his hands), a nation who remained in Tashkent the length of the war... My inferiority complex in face of other nations grew deeper.

This was not easy for me, maybe because of my character. After some time, I discovered that many Jews changed their names and took Russian names, but my own character was strengthened by the reality, the surrounding conditions and the neighbors and I abandoned the idea of changing my name. My name remained proudly written on my identity card, my matriculation diploma, my army card, my university diploma and my marriage document. However, I gave in at the end, following two things that forced me to change my "unhappy" name. The first happened after I graduated from the university and I began working as a teacher at a teachers college. It was not easy to be a teacher when your name is Osher Osipowitch... The second case – after my first daughter was born, I thought to myself: What is the fault of my children? Was it not enough that I was suffering? I decided to change my name and I chose the name Leonid. This name was printed in my identity card, so my children could use it, and the old name Osher remained on all other documents.

When I made Aliya, my new name – Leonid – was on my "immigrant card" and my new identity card. I decided to adopt back my original name Osher but a new problem arose: many people, who knew me as Leonid, were wondering about the Hebrew name and I had to give lengthy explanations. For me it was not a minor change, but a return to my origin. I belong to my name and my name belongs to me and with it I feel that I am myself.

[Page 216]

The "Flag-Day" ['tag-day']
by Beruria Har-Zion
Translated by Yocheved Klausner

I remember, when I was a pupil in the lower grades of school, my desire was to be one of the carriers of the "blue-white box" on the "tag day" (when we collected money for the JNF and every donor received a little blue-white tag to pin it on his/her shirt). At the time I did not know what the real meaning of the "blue box" was, but my relation to it has not diminished. Knowing that it was very dear and very important was enough for me.

We went out in pairs, one of us carrying a large cardboard in the shape of a star-of-David with the tags arranged on it like flowers and the other carrying the box. It was Sunday and the street was full of people. We were assigned the stretch between Michalovski Street and the town park, where there were many Jewish shops. Our instructions were to approach every person and enter every shop, Jewish and non-Jewish. When we came near one of the stores, my partner told me that I will have to go in myself, not telling me the reason. I entered the store of Mrs. Constantiner and the owner received me with shouts: Again you came to beg?? I asked many times not to come to my store. Go to your Palestine, you insolent and dirty youngsters, the Arabs will slaughter you there. Don't come here anymore!

I was stunned. I was not ready for such a "welcome." I didn't understand why she said "dirty." I tried to say something, but this increased her fury and shouts, and I ran away, ashamed.

My next "tag-day" was *Tu Bishvat*. This time I knew more about the Box and its purpose. Again I was assigned the same street as on *Lag Ba'omer*. When I reached the Constantiner store, my heart began to beat strongly. I peeked into the store and saw two people: a young officer and a lady. I decided to go in, and offer the young couple the tag. The owner started to yell again, but I was ready and managed to say: "Sorry, we did not come to you, but to the people in your store. I approached the pair and offered them a tag, explaining the purpose of JNF, as we had been instructed. The officer responded politely and gave a nice contribution. The owner of the store was furious again, but I felt that I won and thanked them, as I was taught to do. But I also felt the need to take revenge on the lady owner; when I was at the door I said to her: We shall always visit your store, but you should know that we are not coming to you, but to your customers, whom we already know…

[Page 217]

The Akkerman Jews During the War and After It
by Kwitko Michael
Translated by Yocheved Klausner

Very often I find myself thinking about the bitter fate of the Akkerman Jews. A while ago I heard from my friend S. Rosenthal that no more than 12-15 families are living in Akkerman nowadays. The town itself has grown and developed, but its 5000 Jews have perished. Why did the Akkerman Jews "drink the poison cup" in its entirety? Why was their fate so cruel? Why did they not flee and escape before the end came?

I think that there were several reasons, which depended on the Jews themselves. I would like to mention some of them. In 1918, when Bessarabia left Russia and became united with Romania, the Akkerman Jews lost the center town that they loved, Odessa, which had remained in the hand of the Russians; but little-by-little they got used to live without Odessa and accepted the fact that Akkerman was under Romanian rule. Moreover, they learned to make maximum use of this fact. The Romanian anti-Semitism, which was felt very well in other towns, was almost not felt in Akkerman, and during 29 years, until 1938, the Jews could lead quietly a regular life. I think that this quiet life was, partly, the reason that did not hurry to leave the town when the days of the Holocaust came. There are testimonies that the Jews who gathered around the Bet Midrash listened to the attendants and leaders and decided not to leave the place. This influenced others as well and they didn't move out.

A second reason, and maybe this was the most important one, which convinced the Akkerman Jews not to move out from Akkerman, was the great disappointment from the Communist regime. Many have felt this disappointment, even among those who had been members of the Communist Underground. Very few maintained the hope that the communist regime would save the Jews from the danger of Nazism and bring them peace. The Jews did not trust the Soviet rule at all; some of the moves of the Soviet political leadership were considered by the Jews anti-Semitic schemes planned in advance.

The fact is, that during an entire year of Soviet rule, **n o t h i n g** was said (in the press or by the authorities) about what had happened to the Polish Jews who lived in the area occupied by the Germans, nothing about what was expected to happen to the Soviet Jews if the hand of the Germans would catch them. Great speakers who came to Akkerman indeed spoke about the danger of war against the Germans, but not one word was said about the great danger for the Jews in particular. No wonder that many still believed that it would be possible to make arrangements with the Romanians through various "payments," as was the custom to do. This was why it happened, that in contrast to the flight to the interior of the Soviet Union, which many have chosen, the Akkerman Jews preferred to remain in place rather than take the risks of evacuation. This was the reason they perished. Even those who reached Odessa did not reach a safe heaven. The Romanians caught them and they perished as well. Some of them (like the mother and sister of Dr. Shaul Palikov and the parents of Riva Axelrod) did arrive at far-away places, but the cruel hand of the Nazis reached them there as well. Only a small number of Jews, who reached, after great suffering, Asia, survived.

After the war, the Akkerman Jews who survived preferred not to return to their town, but chose other Russian cities (Cernowitz, Kishinev and Odessa) because from there it was easier to go to Romania and then to emigrate to USA or Israel or other countries. This was the reason that so few of the surviving Akkerman Jews returned to their town of origin.

The fateful day was, as it is known, the 28 of June 1940, when, following a Soviet ultimatum, the Romanians were forced to leave Bessarabia according to the agreement and enable all the Bessarabians to return from Romania to their homes. The Jews preferred to endanger their property and remain where they were and not join the returning Romanians.

[Page 218]

Those who did return to Bessarabia (Akkerman included) were not followers of the leftists-communists, as for example Eng. Trachtman, former director of JCA in the Balkans or Eng. Grushmsn, director of JCA in Romania and former chairman of "Maccabi" in Akkerman. They died (the first on the roads of Bessarabia, the other committed suicide by hanging after his wife, his daughter and his grandson fell in the snow while running and remained on the side of the road. Among those who did return, were Jewish doctors, who succeeded in Bucharest, but preferred to leave their wealth and their professional success and return to Akkerman (Dr. Karadonski, Yellin and others), taking with them only a few packages and suitcases. None was sorry about the property that was lost. They tried to get used to the new conditions, hoping that in time they will overcome the difficulties. Soviet citizens, who came to Akkerman, began to buy everything from the stores, and formed long lines, never seen in Akkerman before. It was possible to notice at first sight the lust for money of the Russian officials who had come to town. However, during the beginning of the Soviet occupation it seemed as a paradise on earth. Actors came from Odessa and performed theater pieces and reviews, fat lady singers sang Soviet songs, but unfortunately together with the artistic groups came people of the NKVD who made nightly raids and arrested "suspected elements": former merchants, Zionists, public activists, Hebrew teachers and the like. And so life went on: in the morning they were making jokes and at night every person feared for his own life and the lives of his family members – who knows who will be the prey of "the black crow" tonight?

Towards the New Year, the authorities gave us a "present" – paragraph 39 of the Soviet Law, which defined the place of residence of the citizens and forced many to relocate in 3 days to a village which was at least 30 km. from the former residence in the city center. This was a smart move, which enabled the new residents to get good apartments and working places.

As a son of a wealthy person, I too received the "present". I decided to check the justice of the Soviet law and I appealed to the general Attorney of the area. He listened, then asked me whether I know the Russian saying that "when one cuts wood, splinters are flying around".... This was the end of our discussion and I was ordered to leave my town, my home and my work and relocate to a village, without taking with me my things, when my wife was six months pregnant. Thus I had the opportunity to understand the meaning of the Soviet Communism...

It didn't take long, and the Nazi soldiers invaded almost all of Europe, from Greece in the south to Norway in the North. The Nazi "Barbarossa Plan" was activated and the great strategist, the "Sun of the Nations" did not listen to the warnings of an invasion of Russia by the Germans coming soon. Ten days before the invasion they "took measures"...On the night of 12 June Jewish old and sick people (among them my mother, who was sick and blind) were awakened from their sleep and, defined as "dangerous anti-Soviet elements" were taken to investigation or chased out of town. The German residents in town were not touched. Neither were the Ukrainians, who, as was well known, immediately began collaborating with the Germans. The evacuated people were not allowed to take their clothes and not even medicines. It is easy to imagine how the Soviet justice looked in their eyes. It is worth mentioning, that many communists and former underground fighters were deeply disappointed from the Soviet regime – they felt well this "justice" on their own bodies...

When war broke out, on 22 June 1941, the Romanian prime-minister Antonescu spoke to his Romanian citizens, saying: Romanians, cross the River Prut and liberate our Bessarabia, punish the Jewish population for its bad behavior and attitude toward the Romanian army and kill 10% of the Jewish population! On 29 June the authorities took "measures" and, among others they accused the Jews of the city of Yassy [Iaºi] that they signaled the Soviet airplanes and shot through their windows at German soldiers. They carried out a terrible pogrom in town and killed over 12,000 Jews. This was a general rehearsal before the Romanians invaded Bessarabia.

The Soviet propaganda hid from the public Antonescu's speech as well as the Yassy pogrom. It is possible, that if the Jews had known about those terrible acts, they would have understood what was awaiting them and would have reacted differently – they would not have believed in a possibility to "make an arrangement" with the Romanians and would have escaped in time.

All units of the Romanian army hurried to perform Antonescu's instructions concerning killing Jews, and as the soldiers entered the Bessarabia villages and towns their first acts were to rob the Jews and then kill them, men and women, young and old. In towns where the number of Jews was large, they gathered them in one place and murdered them without mercy.

The 35th infantry battalion, which had been stationed in Akkerman before the Russians came, returned to town. One of the captains, the son of a local peasant, born in Akkerman, Okishor by name, was responsible for

[Page 219]

killing the Akkerman Jews. During the first days of August 1941 they gathered all Jews in the Craftsmen's Synagogue after they had robbed their belongings. More than 1600 men, women and children were kept there several days without food, then they forced them to run through the main streets, in front the old man Feigin, naked, to the "Karnitchka," where in the past we used to hold the Lag Ba'Omer festivities. By the command of captain Okishor all were shot and buried in a pit that they had themselves dug before. Another officer should be infamously mentioned, Freulich, son of a former German resident, who conducted the murder of the Shaba Jews. On 9 August this Freulich came to Tatarbonar and, together with the local commander of the ghetto captain Bato Jonas robbed and killed 451 Jews in the ghetto. On pages 71-72 of the Black Book by M. Karp, former secretary of the Jewish community in Bucharest, is printed the document that describes this event.

I, my wife and our baby miraculously succeeded to escape, thanks to our acquaintance with some rare and charitable farmers. The engineer Ivan Ivanovitch Baloban endangered his own life and helped me in the winter of 1942 to get from Odessa to Bucharest with my baby. The Christian Greek Saropolo hid me and my wife in Odessa during two months of the winter of 1941-1942 and so saved us from being sent to the concentration camp. I want to mention, with good blessings, he engineer Gregory Andonianetz from Akerman, who was the head of the Goltianesk Region. With his help, I succeeded not only to help myself but also to establish a Jewish Committee after the war. Dr. Feldstein was the deputy head of the committee and I was given the possibility to act through it for the benefit of the Jews. With the help of Eng. Andonianetz I managed to send to Bucharest a memorandum describing our situation and connect with Dr. Corneliu Iancu, deputy head of the Zionist Federation in Romania. Thanks to this connection we received from Bucharest financial aid, which helped us to open medical clinics, an orphanage, a pharmacy and several workshops that employed Jewish people. I managed to save, feed and educate 90 children, many of whom are now in Israel with us, as the sisters Gerzberg from Sarata. One of them, who is called now Lily Bardev and lives in Ashdod, I took out from the death camp Achmatchatka in a sack of bread. About a year later I managed, with the help of the Red Cross, to take Lily to Eretz Israel. Her elder sister came later, through Cernowitz.

After we were liberated from the camp, I managed to stay in Bucharest and I worked at finding the Romanian murderers and bringing them to justice. Among others, I managed to find the above mentioned Okishor; he was arrested by the Romanians and I testified concerning all his terrible acts in 1941 in Akkerman.

On the mass grave in Karnitchka, where over 1600 Jews are buried, there is no memorial stone.

Among the Jews who fled to Odesa and survived all the horrors of the war and returned to Akkerman: Dr. Yeshayahu Feldstein and his wife, his son Dr. Musia Feldstein and his wife and daughter, Dr. Tesia Elberg, Huna Kapelnikov with his wife and two children, Brand Soya and several others. Dr. Tchobotaru from Tatarbonar and his wife and children are now living in Kishinev. Eng. Brodeski with his wife and children are now living in Bucharest. Every one of them has a long story to tell about the road of suffering that they had to take and how they survived.

[Page 220]

Jewish Survivors in the 1980s
by Yakov Zigloks
Translated by Sara Mages

The Jewish community of Akkerman was one of the first communities of Eastern Europe. Throughout the centuries of its existence it has known periods of ups and down, but reached its peak in the 1920s and 1930s of this century. Vibrant community life, extensive social activities, vibrant spiritual life, cultivation of Jewish tradition, schools and synagogues, kindergartens, "OZE" institution [Association for the Preservation of Jewish Health], lending and saving fund, libraries, sports associations, Zionist clubs, nursing home, a club for Yiddish culture, and much more. The marvelous infrastructure of Jewish culture has also given rise to important public activists who have become famous in and around the city: the rabbis Moshe Zukerman and Roller, the philanthropists Milstein, Alman and Kroschkin, the Zionist leaders Kestretz, Berger, Serper, the communal workers Kishpon, Kushner, Schildkrauth and many others. It was the golden age of the community of Akkerman.

The decline of this community came at once with the entry of Soviet Russia into Bessarabia in 1940, while the tragic end came in the days of the Nazis. Indeed, even today, about fifty years after the Holocaust, Jews still live in Akkerman, but they are in terms of the survivors left among the ruins, and they mourn the glorious past.

In the summer of 1945, I returned to Akkerman from the battlefront against the Nazis. At the same time additional Jews started to return from the front to the neglected and ruined city. There was hunger in the city. Bread, potatoes, milk and all the essential commodities for a person's existence were out of reach. People went to the market every day, but only a few, especially those that had items to exchange, could get the essentials there. On a street corner it was possible to find a barrel of wine, from the wines that my father, and many others, drowned their grief and poverty in the red drink. I remember that once, when I passed through the market among a lot of junk for sale, I discovered at a Russian woman, who sold all kinds of haberdashery in the market, a "*Mahzor*" that was published in Hungary in 1860 and was already partly charred. I took this "*Mahzor*" from her and kept it for a long time as a remnant of the sanctity of the past.

The market served as a meeting place for Jews who congregated in Akkerman, most of them are no longer alive, but let us mention the last of the Mohicans by their names.

Meir Kogen - a wise Jew, religious and advanced who bought all kinds of haberdashery at exorbitant prices from businessmen in Odessa and sold them in Akkerman. Avraham Greenshpon - a blacksmith with a healthy body who, at every meeting, lamented his fate and always repeated one saying that was common in his mouth: "see what they've done to us, what was left of us." Nachum Feldstein, whose pipe never left his mouth, was a sexually transmitted disease doctor. For a long time he was under investigation by the Soviet security organizations who tried to incriminate him, but he defended himself and told them: "my father, Isak Feldstein (also a doctor), and I always served the public in faith, why are you harassing me?" Boris Roitman, a watchmaker by profession, decent and orderly man who miraculously survived together with his family. Gedalia Sterltz, an entertainer and comedian, a lover of Jewish folk songs and cantorial music. He was always willing to give "*A shtikl Hazzanut*" to every passerby, especially his hit, "*Mizmor *leDavid*" [A Psalm to David]. Mendel Gelman, a slaughterer who was knowledgeable in the Bible and Mishnah, lived and even prayed alone. His impressive white beard also earned him respect by the Russian residents. Ajzik Blinder, one of Akkerman's veterans, was observant and jealous, small, gaunt, and wrinkled. He seemed a little strange in the eyes of the street children who called him Cheetah. Tulia Skliar, a carpenter, a former *Yiddishistl* who was a member of the "*Bund.*" He left his wife and lived with a Russian woman. Isak Tendenik, a beggar, sloppy in his clothing and appearance, passed among the rows of sellers of dairy products and innocently tasted from the cheeses and other food products, and in this way he satisfied a little his constant hunger. Yeshayahu Jaroslavsky, an old bachelor who loved to eat. He offered his friends delicacies that were rare in those days and found in the back pocket of his pants. He sold bread, flour, sugar, etc. Isak Stetzky, lame and asthmatic, but a man who loved life. He always hoped that he would be able to reach his son, Shmuel, who immigrated to Israel, but he took his hope with him to the grave.

[Page 221]

The Beginning of Recovery

By the spring of 1946, several hundred Jewish residents had already concentrated in the city. A considerable number came from towns and villages in the area. Among them were: Isak Wallier from Shabo, the Komarovsky brothers from Tuzla, Surka Telmzan from Dyviziya, David Rozanskie, Olishenty Slepoy from Volontrikova, the family of Hassid and Isak Katchalski from Sarata, Hersh Kleitman from Artsyz, the brothers Aspis and Alexenberg from Tatarbunar, Isak Greenberg from Kiliya, Yisrael Yagolnitzer from Bologard, and many others.

The first to try to reorganize the life of the Jewish community was David Berkowitz. With his meager strength he renovated the neglected Great Synagogue and the "*Kloyz.*" He obtained Torah scrolls, candlesticks, prayer books and other ritual articles, and in the fall of that year the Jews celebrated Rosh Hashanah and Yom Kippur in accordance with law and custom. At Simchat Torah, the children waved flags with apples and candles attached to them. The authority soon banned this religious activity. The disappointed old man obtained a permit from the chairman of the Supreme Council of Russia to leave the country and immigrate to Israel to reunite with his many family members.

City life slowly returned to normal. There were a lot of problems of job search, food and housing, but the situation of the Jewish residents continued to be serious and the locals treated them with overt or covert hostility. Once, as I passed a cafe on Moskovskaya Street, I saw drunk drivers harassing the brothers, Abraham and Solomon Shorr, who came to Akkerman from Kantemir. The brothers said something to them, a boxing match ensued, and I noticed that the drivers' faces were badly bruised and bleeding.

Another incident took place in the city center near the council building to Baruch Weini, a daring fighter who was severely wounded in a battle near Tashkent and even received a medal for his heroism. A Christian called out to the mustachioed Baruch "Zyd!" In response, Baruch lowered his pants and revealed to the crowd, who had gathered at the place, his buttocks with the deep scars - a result of the wounds he sustained in this part of his body when he was in the battlefront. In his act, Baruch wanted to emphasize his part in defending the Russian homeland, and the audience understood the "thin" hint...

Over time, the abuse of Jews took on more serious dimensions, Jewish public institutions and houses of worship became sports halls, dance halls and vocational schools for the youth. The magnificent Craftsmen Synagogue ("*Remesline Shul*") became a supply and clothing warehouse for the army. The Jewish Nursing Home - to students' dormitory, the building of "Tarbut" gymnasium - to a hospital for the disabled. There is no trace left of Jewish culture, tradition and Jewish life. It can be said: the last Jewish spark has faded. Tired of the hardships of the war and the great Holocaust, the Jews succumbed to the dictates of the new life and began to adapt to the new circumstances.

The new Jewish cemetery (the old was destroyed in the Holocaust) in Akkerman

[Page 222]

On the Ties with Israel and Judaism

In early 1948 fragmented news, which were published in the government press or other communication tools, began to reach Akkerman about the struggle of the Jewish settlement in Israel for political independence. There was nothing in these news items to give us an idea of what was really happening in Israel, about the struggles of the *Palmach*, *Etzel* or *Lehi*. The establishment of the State of Israel was described as a Soviet political victory to ensure the legitimate rights of the people of Israel. The news of Israel's declaration of independence was received, of course, with great joy, but also with a certain restraint, since it was clear to us that any manifestation of identification with the State of Israel could be interpreted by the authorities as an "anti-revolutionary" move.

In the fall of 1948, a funeral service was held for the remains of Jews who had been shot in Akkerman by the Nazis. They were discovered in the pits of the quarry south of the city, behind the meat factories. The funeral procession proceeded to the new mass grave that was excavated in the Armenian cemetery on Shabskaya Street. In the inscription above the mass grave it was not mention at all that the victims were Jews, even those who spoke at the ceremony did not say the word "Jew," but everyone knew that most of the murdered were Jews. We, the Jewish survivors who attended this funeral, knew very well who we were accompanying for eternal rest. We knew that we were accompanying the bones of entire Jewish families (Zimmerman, Folkman, Farberski, Kafelnikov, Brand, Erlich and more). We accompanied, but we kept our grief within us as we feared that any such expression might be harmful. I can bring up the names of the Jews who were present at this sad ceremony, and these are: Aharon Trachtenbroit, Yehciel Sztulman, Mendel Tabchnik, Yoel Nidriker, Yisrael Solomon, Boris Steinberg, Chaim Vorotnikov, Pinchas Milman, Zalman Glabonski, Dr. Shvarzman, Wilkomirski, Pipergal, Izia Chamilkis, the midwife-nurse Fidelman, the accountant Risenzon and many more.

At the time, this kind of power was Israel's victory in the Six Day War. Despite the unrestrained anti-Israel propaganda of all the Soviet media, which presented Israel as occupying territories not belonging to it, there was an awakening in the Jewish public, feelings of Jewish pride arose and Jewish identification erupted spontaneously. At the same time, there was also a rising wave of anti-Semitism. Discrimination against Jews in all aspects of life gained legal validity. For no reason they started ousting the Jews from government jobs. The thugs also raised their heads, painted swastikas on Jewish homes, desecrated tombstones, etc. The Jewish youth began to see the current situation, realized that their chances of taking root in the new reality were nil, and began to look for a way out. Like a thunderbolt on a clear day, the news spread about the failure of the escape attempt of Sylvia Zalmanson's group and Eduard Kuznetsov, and the hijacking of a plane at Leningrad airport. Not only did it not weaken the hands, but gave an emotional boost to the beginning of mass immigration to Israel. The youth began to learn Hebrew, the publications of "*Ikhud*" - the Zionist movement in the underground, appeared, the number of "*Refusenikim*" increased, and at the same time deportations and imprisonments began in the big cities of Russia. Many of Akkerman's natives made their way to Israel and were absorbed in many settlements in the country. The authorities tried to stop the wave of immigration to Israel that swept the Jewish population, but they could not. A typical case: The shoemaker, Isser Frank, informed the chairman of the city council that if they did not provide his family with a suitable apartment, he would immigrate to Israel - he was immediately provided with a suitable apartment. I remember how warmly the Jews of Akkerman accompanied me when I immigrated to Israel in the spring of 1974. My childhood friend, Chain Zunis, asked me to kiss the earth of our homeland in his name. Yosef Friedman, a Jew from Zhitomir, who now lives in Akkerman, asked me to make sure that those, who reluctantly remained in Soviet Russia, were not forgotten. Also a Christian neighbor gave me her blessing for the road and also added that she read in the Bible about the return of the children of Israel to their promised land.

When I looked, for the last time, at the city's clean streets and the residents who walked in them, I felt how the life that once forcibly flowed under the clear skies of Southern Bessarabia was disappearing…

It was not even possible to think of Zionist activity under the conditions of those days, although there were already quite a few Zionists in the city such as: Dora Goldman, Fania Druze, Lipa Wolozyn, Keila Weissberg, Anya Guchman, Chancza Frechter, Yasha Yusim, Chaim Zunis, Izia Shinkrovsky and others. We were separated from each other, there was an atmosphere of fear and suspicion and fear of betrayal and provocations. The Zionists, David Kogen, Efraim Abramowitch and Dvora Blanowitz, were imprisoned in Siberia at the time and their fate stood before our eyes. I also received a letter

[Page 223]

from David Kogen, through the Christian Butshai who sat together with him in jail in exile. In this letter there were clear hints of incessant investigations being conducted by the men of the KGV about the Jews who returned to Akkerman. Therefore, it was natural that we avoided the risk of Zionist activity in the underground.

Meanwhile, anti-Semitism has also increased and its marks were well visible everywhere. In the government shops, in which Jews were employed, they slowly began to dismiss all the Jews and replaced them with the young people of the "Komsomol." Having no choice, the Jews began working in various factories as technicians, locksmiths, carpenters, painters, etc. Only a few Jews were accepted to study at universities and higher education institutions. Jews were not given any senior position. Moreover, the entire country began to eliminate everything that was left of Jewish culture and the highlight was the murder of Jewish writers, the director Mikhoels, and the plot against the Jewish doctors headed by Professor Vofsi. There were plans to deport masses of Jews to Siberia and Birobidzhan, and only Stalin's death delayed their execution. The days of mourning, which were declared in the country after his death, were days of restrained joy for us. We breathed a sigh of relief.

Restoration of Public Property

Another wind blew around. Hopes arose for a new life, and we hoped too. A problem of competent representation from every ethnic community arose. It was solved to us by the agile and resourceful Jew, Kalman Frechter, who undertook the task of establishing a special group that would represent, and also preserve, Jewish public property in Akkerman. The group began raising funds to rehabilitate the destroyed Jewish cemetery. Its eastern side was smashed to the gate, most of the tombstones were broken and traces of vandalism were visible everywhere. Also the historical monuments for the victims of the 1905 pogroms in Akkerman, and the mass grave for the victims of the First World War, were also desecrated. This group, headed by Kalman Frechter, erected a fence around the cemetery, organized the guarding of the place, resumed the activity of "Chevra Kadisha," and organized a *minyan* for prayer on the Sabbath and holidays. I will mention these activists by name:

Kalman Frechter, agile and flexible, with a matter-of-fact approach to every issue, nurtured the relations with the authority even during the Romanians' reign. He released, in exchange for "hush money," young people from good families who had been arrested for communist activity by the secret police. Velvel Jacobson, was the treasurer of the group and had a good sense of humor. Reuven Glickman, an educated and progressive man in his views, well versed in Jewish affairs and also in classical literature. It was possible to obtain from him literature that was banned by the censorship such as "The Warsaw Ghetto Uprising" or Graetz's history books. He was an honest man and his words could be trusted. Shaike Rotenberg, a redhead who was always meticulously dressed and wore suspenders. He obtained several prayer books from the rabbinate in Moscow and printed them for the needs of the community. As an employee of the "Wine Vodka" store, which opened at dawn, he was the first to know the news, who was born and who died. Kalman Kleiner, a leather worker by profession, who previously belonged to the Zionist-religious party "*Mizrahi*," had the "right" to recite "*Kaddish*," "*Yizkor*" and other prayers. He immigrated to Israel and lived with his daughter in Jerusalem. Avraham Telzman, a carpenter by profession and cantor by his hobby, led the prayers on the Sabbath and holidays and trilled "*El Male Rachamim*" in funerals. A proud Jew dedicated to public needs. Moshe Edelstein was educated in "*Betar*" and remained faithful to the movement's ideology. As a government employee he was also active in the trade union but also took an interest in the activities of the Jewish community. In his entanglement in unnecessary arguments, and being of a weak character, he was exploited by the Russian police and sometimes even told more than he knew. A propaganda booklet, in which former wealthy Jews were accused of being bourgeois and exploitative, was published in Akkerman and his name appeared on it as the author. Naturally, the Jews did not have too much affection for him, they insulted and cursed him. His conscience tormented him and he contracted a fatal disease and died. David Zonis, was the *shamash* in the synagogue. The poor laborer spent day and night in the cemeteries. He cleaned the gravestones, wrote in a notebook the names of all the deceased in chronological order and in return received a donation or alms from the Jews.

This group of communal workers couldn't continue its activity for a long time. From the outside they were harassed by the authorities and from the inside they did not receive much encouragement, for, as stated above, many chose the path of adaptation, joined the Communist Party and hoped to build their careers in this way. Such were, among others, Monish Trachtman, director of the municipal printing house, Yosef Flikov, director of the culture section of the local executive committee, Yerachmiel Goldman, in "*Promkombinet*." Alexander Meglnik, director of the Tea House and others. There were those who did not refrain from passing convicting information, some out of fear, some just for flattery and some for the benefit. There was no shortage of Akkerman Jews who were addicted to drinking alcohol and playing cards, and there is no point in naming them here. But most Jews worked hard and led a modest and fair lifestyle, such as Burok Buca, Moshe Kushnir, Yasha Guzmann, Schwinn Niuma, Lushak Filia, Zelig Tabachnik, Chaim Midman, Yafim Sordlik, Katz, Zufrik and others.

It should be remembered, that apart from Akkerman's longtime residents many Soviet Jews, who came from all over Russia, lived and settled in the city. They were steeped in the new Russian culture, removed from a Jewish way of life and excelled in excessive affinity with the Soviet regime. There is no doubt that most of the Jews

[Page 224]

did not trust the new regime, and even if they identified with it outwardly, then, within themselves, in their homes, they maintained loyal to Israel and the Jewish people.

During my travels throughout Soviet Russia for my work, I also met many Jews from Akkerman who did not return there after the war for various reasons. In Kiev I met the lawyer David Milstein, in Moscow - Hersh Cheritonov and the tailor Raphael Tukhman, in Lvov - Mendel Arbeit and Chaim Greenspan, in Stanislav - the blacksmith Moshe Weinstein and Osip Streich, in Chernivtsi - Chaim Zeff, Yoel Malinsky and Zerach Gorfield, in Chi?inău - David Weisser, Reuven Kaplinsky, Pluski, Gordon, Sania Shrira and his grandmother - his wife aunt Manya the kindergarten teacher who educated in her kindergarten generations of students for the Hebrew Gymnasium.

Today, close to six hundred Jewish families live in Akkerman. The older generation - passed away, the next generation - grew old, while the third generation - our children and grandchildren - are almost completely cut off from their Jewish roots, and except for section 5 of their identity card, which mentions their Jewish national affiliation, there is no sign of their Judaism in their way of life, education, culture, etc. Mixed marriages are very common, assimilation is increasing and only a serious force from outside may help the members of this generation to discover their Judaism.

Memorial conference of former residents of the Akkerman District in Israel in memory of the victims of the Nazis

[Page 225]

Yisrael Schildkrauth speaks at the memorial conference for the Jews of Akkerman

Dr. Shaul Zerling speaks at the memorial conference for the Jews of Akkerman

[Page 229]

Personalities and Characters of blessed memory

Avraham Ravutski z"l
Translated by Sara Mages

Avraham Ravutski, who was the Minister of Jewish Affairs in the Ukrainian Government, co-founder of the Jewish National Autonomy and, at a later stage, one of the leaders of "Poalei Zion" movement, was not born in Akkerman but came to this city with his parents when he was ten years old, but, it is appropriate to mention this distinguished man in this book because his qualifications were discovered in Akkerman already in his youth.

* * *

He was born in Smila (a city in the Cherkasy Oblast near Kiev) on 8 February 1889 to his father Shmuel Ravutski. His parents immigrated to Israel in 1891 together with their two daughters and their youngest son - Avraham. They settled in the village of Rehovot but, before they were able to take root in their new place of residence, a great deal of trouble came upon them. All members of the family were stricken by a severe trachoma disease and were in danger of blindness. At the doctors' request they had to travel to Vienna for treatment. The doctors in Vienna warned them that if they returned to Israel they would again be infected with trachoma. The Ravutski family received the sentence with heartbreak. They returned to Russia and settled in Akkerman. The father, Samuel, purchased a vineyard that served him as a source of employment and livelihood.

Avraham was about ten years old when he left Eretz Yisrael to be absorbed in a new and foreign environment, but he already made a name for himself as an outstanding student when he attended the gymnasium in Akkerman, and a few years later he also became famous in the Zionist circles in Akkerman. It was in 1906 when Ber Borochov's lecture, which drew a huge audience, was held in Akkerman. On this occasion the young yeshiva student, Avraham Ravutski, was presented before the lecturer. Borochov quickly introduced him to the complicated problems in the theory of "Poalei Zion" and captured his heart. Ravutski joined Borochov's movement and, from then on, his path in life was set. A few years later he stood out among the key personalities of "Poalei Zion" movement.

Minister of Jewish Affairs

Even before the October Revolution, and the establishment of the Soviet Government in Central Russia, a government was formed in Ukraine which, according to its personal composition, was considered a left-wing national government. This government was subordinate to the Ukrainian National Council ("Rada"), in which the national Jewish parties (Zionists, Socialists and Poalei Zion) were represented. The Ukrainian Government strove for a full national independence with a federative relationship with Greater Russia. In the course of time, the Ukrainian parties left the federative idea and declared an independent Ukraine with complete separation from Russia. When a left-wing Ukrainian Government was re-established, only socialist parties were represented in it. This government, which in principle recognized the national autonomy of minorities, suggested that they add their representatives to it. At that time, the minister's office for Jewish affairs was offered to "Poalei Zion" and not to the "General Zionists" which was considered a bourgeois party, and not even to the "Bund" because of this party's fundamental opposition to Ukraine's separation from Russia. After a lot of deliberations, "Poalei Zion" central committee decided to accept the proposal of the Ukrainian Government with a vigorous demand for an immediate cessation of the war with Russia. The choice fell on Abraham Ravutski who received the tenure of Minister of Jewish Affairs. It soon became clear that the Ukrainian Government, which pretended to be a socialist government, was in fact based on a thin layer of nationalist intelligentsia circles in the cities and wealthy peasant circles in the villages. The main supporters of the government were the military men that in their ranks gathered adventurers, inciting nationalists and rioters.

[Page 230]

When it became clear that the Ukrainian Government did not show any desire, and initiative, to fight the anti-Semitism that spread in the military ranks, and also treated the pogroms against the Jews with apathy - Ravutski left the government and all the Jewish parties also severed their ties with it.

His Activities in the Party

In March 1919, Ravutski fled from the Ukrainian hell on his way to Europe, and in August of that year he participated in the World Alliance Council of "Poalei Zion" in Stockholm. The party's emissaries from Eretz Yisrael, as well as the main leaders of the movements in the Diaspora, participated in this council. Avraham Ravutski played a very important role in this council. The main topic of debate was, "the ways of building the country and the role of the party in the processes of its construction." The delegation from Eretz Israel unveiled a comprehensive economic plan which was guided by the main idea of the realization of a socialist society by expanding the kibbutz settlement in the village, and developing a broad cooperative movement in the industry, building and trade. The keynote speaker, and the supporter of this plan, was Nachman Syrkin who based the assumption that if they built the country in such a way they would not end up in a class war. The leaders of "Ahdut HaAvoda" supported this idea but, in contrast to this perception, the Zionist-Marxist concept which requires the hegemony of the Zionist-Socialist labor movement as a major trend in the construction of the economy of Eretz Yisrael was raised at the council in Stockholm. The main supporters of this trend were Avraham Ravutski and Nahum Nir. The heated debates around the two plans proved the magnitude of the ideological gap that separated the two different parts of the movement and, which one year later, led to its split.

Ravutski in Eretz Yisrael

With the split, Ravutski joined "Poalei Zion Left" and also announced his settlement in Eretz Yisrael. The World Alliance Office appointed him to rescue the Israeli party from the plague of the Zionist liquidation because, following the October Revolution and the significant changes in the international labor movement, a fierce struggle developed between the loyalists of Borochov's Labor-Zionists and the communist wing in the movement which, in effect, demanded that the movement's leadership integrate into the Comintern [Communists International], even at the cost of denial to the main principles of "Poalei Zion." Several branches of the party in Europe centered around the communist faction, as well as the Socialist Workers Party in Eretz Yisrael, which was founded by the consolidation of members of "Poalei Zion" who did not join "Ahdut HaAvoda" when it was founded, with anti-Zionist communists who immigrated to Israel with the first immigrates of the Third Aliyah. Ravutski appeared on the list of the Socialist Workers Party for the Histadrut's founding conference, and even participated in the general debate at the conference.

The riots, which broke out in Jerusalem in 1920 and the blood riots in Jaffa (1921), aroused a deep shock in the Jewish *Yishuv* [population]. Many of the leaders of the Zionist movement, and leaders of the "*Yishuv*," continued to believe that the British Mandatory Government had no part in organizing the bloody riots. At that time, Avraham Ravutski published a booklet named "From Balfour to Samuel" in which he argued that the riots were nothing but a "calculated political step by the ruling circles in England who opposed the Balfour Declaration and Jewish settlement in Eretz Yisrael." He also did not remove the responsibility of the Jewish factor and imposed a heavy blamed on the Zionist Commission which, at that time, was the executive branch of the Zionist Organization in Eretz Yisrael. And those are his words: "every Jew in the country will testify that if you want to bury an essential idea or an important initiative - bring them before the "Zionist Commission"... The inability of the Zionist Organization to act, and the hostility of the British administration - these two created the psychological atmosphere for the wild riots against the Jewish *Yishuv*."

For the sin of publishing this booklet, Ravutski's name was blacklisted by the Mandatory Government and, some time later, when Ravutski left the country for the party's Sixth World Conference in Danzig - he was banned from entering the country by the Mandatory Government.

At the World Conference of "Poalei Zion" in Danzig, which took place in 1922, and the split between the communist wing and Borochov's wing became an existing fact. At that time, Borochov's loyalists, led by Z. Abramowich, A. Ravutski and others, organized themselves as an independent global movement whose center was in Berlin. Ravutski was given the task of editing the new movement's theoretical magazine, "*Der Kampf.*" In 1924, unity returned to the world movement, Ravutski left Berlin and moved to the United States.

The Turning Point in the United States

Ravutski arrived in the United States satiated with bitter disappointment and was no longer active in his movement. There were various reasons to this, but the most notable thing was the turning point in his views on principles that until now have been sacred to him. He developed an extensive literary-journalistic activity and many of his research essays were highly appreciated. In the early 1930s, he officially joined "Poalei Zion Right" and published many articles in the journal "*Yiddisher kemfer*" ["Jewish Fighter"]. He was also liked by a large number the readers of scientific magazines in the United States and Canada, and the editorial staff of the daily newspaper "Der *Morgen Zshurnal*" [The Jewish Morning Journal] gave him the responsibility of editing the political section of the newspaper.

[Page 231]

His regular participation in the daily newspapers did not prevent him from devoting himself to writing research articles on various subjects in the fields of economics, sociology and history, and in all these he stood out as a man of in-depth analysis and broad coverage.

In the United States, Ravutski lived his spiritual and public life with special intensity. Among others he devoted himself to exploring the prospects of the economic development of Eretz Yisrael, its absorptive ability and its implications for future of economic development. Many of the economic guidelines he has put forth in his articles on these issues have long been proven to be well-founded and correct. He published a book on Eretz Yisrael and the Near East, which aroused many echoes in the public and received an enthusiastic review in the American press. This book, which was published in three editions and translated into several languages (including Hebrew and Yiddish), was used for a long time as a guide for researchers in the history of Eretz Yisrael and the Near East. It was also recommended for teaching in high schools in Israel and the Theological Seminary in New York. He was also the partner of Walter Clay Lowdermilk in the writing of his book "Palestine, Land of Promise." In 1933 he visited Eretz Yisrael and this visit served him as an additional push to support the idea of "*HaMilve HaLeumi*" [National Loan] which, for him, was initially sort of a project and after visiting Israel turned into a passionate desire and a thought that strives for purpose.

In 1946, Ravutski fell ill and was confined for a long time to a deathbed. But, even when he was confined to his bed, he continued to write his articles and sent them to the editorial boards of many newspapers. When his physical strength ran out and he could no longer hold a pen in his hand, he dictated his articles to his wife Chana. He passed away on 6 February 1946 in Yonkers, New York.

(A summary from a large biographical study written by L. Tronopoler and published in "Al HaMishmar" on 30 September 1970)

Our Ministers
Translated by Yocheved Klausner

(Introduction in Hebrew)

Our town Akkerman had the privilege to possess two ministers "of its own," both of them Jews. One was A. Ravotzki, who was minister in the Kranski government and the other, S. M. Gutnik, was minister of commerce in the government of the Hetman [military commander] Skoropedski. We saw fit to bring in this book some biographical details of both, as well as a chapter of Ravotzki's book (in Yiddish) "During Ukraine's Difficult Days" (Memories of a Jewish minister), which reveals the relationship between "our" two ministers, as well as an interesting and almost unknown affair from the days prior to the Bolshevik revolution. The chapter is given below in the original Yiddish.

On the same First of January, after the talk with Tchechovski, I went to my Bessarabia Landsman the esteemed M., where I was invited to New-Year's lunch. In town they already knew about my scheduled arrival. During lunch, M. introduced me to a blonde middle-aged lady and said:

- This is Sergei Michaelowitz's wife.

- Which Sergei Michaelowitz? – I asked quickly.

- Naturally, Gutnik, smiled M. to me. S.M. Gutnik – the Jewish financier, the minister of commerce in the Hetman's government, was almost a landsman of mine; he came from Akkerman, Bessarabia Gubernia, where his father had a small bank. I didn't know him well personally. During the war I saw him a few times in the offices of the Odessa newspaper, where I worked at that time. After the fall of the Hetman, Gutnik, who had been one of his most reactionary ministers, disappeared, and the new regime looked for him everywhere.

[Page 232]

So, as the French say, I put on a pleasant face for a nasty game, and I used one of the sentences that people use when they have company and have nothing to say, or when there is something that they do not want to talk about:

In the middle of the short discussion, I asked quickly:

- So, your man is, it seems, already on the other side of the border?

- Naturally.

My conscience calmed down.

Several months later, after I left my position, while walking on the street in Odessa, where the "Freiwillige" ruled at the time, I met the same good M. He was happy to see me and invited me to his home. Suddenly he said:

- Do you remember how in Kiev I introduced you to Mrs. Gutnik?

- Yes, I remember.

- And do you know that Gutnik was at the same time right in the next room?

I was really surprised and remained silent.

- Yes, Gutnik was hiding in my place, and for three weeks he did not leave the locked room. Later we razed his beard and entirely changed his appearance, so that even his own mother would not have recognized him, and I took him from Kiev to Odessa. We used to joke about the fact that a Hetman minister would hide in the same apartment where a minister of the government used to be a regular guest, who was looking for him as a great criminal...

The same day that I related to one of my Odessa friends this piquant episode, he asked me:

- Tell me, if you had known that Gutnik was in the next room, would you have informed the authorities?

Would I have done that in the case of a threat of the death punishment?

It was a difficult question...

Theoretically, I would have certainly done it, although I would have seen it as my duty to make every effort to avoid a death sentence. Practically, however, it would have been much more difficult. I am still too much of a "Freedom-Socialist" and the idea of "informing" – even for the benefit of a progressive power, even for the defense against reactionary persons – would have scared me very much. And besides that, by doing so I would have put my host M., who hid Gutnik, in a difficult situation. However, if I decided not to divulge the fact of my meeting, I would, in any case, present my resignation; or rather: I would simply give up my candidacy. It is, naturally, impossible that a minister, member of the cabinet, provide cover, even by keeping silent, to one of the most important criminals.

[Page 233]

Yakov Shmuel Halevi Trachtman z"l
Translated by Yocheved Klausner

He was born in 1831 in Ovrotch (Wolhyn District) and in his early youth he came to live in Akkerman. He was a scholar, was ordained as Rav, and a known writer at the time, known by his pseudonym "Ish Tam." He was familiar with the Russian literature and a devoted communal worker. He published many books in Hebrew: *Agada Achat* [One Legend] (Odessa 1870), *Or Tora* [The light of the Torah] (Warsaw 1881), *Sha'arei Gan Eden* [The Gates of Paradise] (Jerusalem 1909), *Sukat David Hanofelet* [David's fallen Sukka] (published in the journal "*Talpiyot*" Berdichev 1895) as well as books for young people as: *Haduda'im, Baruch Mibanim* and others. He published tens of articles and hundreds of reports in the Hebrew newspapers *Hamelitz, Hatzefira, Hachavatzelet* and other Hebrew periodicals. Apart from that, he published articles in the Russian press, and it became a sort of tradition that before every Jewish Holiday the local Russian newspaper published an article by Y. S. Trachtman, in which he explained the history and the importance of the Holiday. These "Holiday" articles were very popular and were read by the Christian readers of the newspaper as well.

He was a smart Jew, with a sharp eye and a sense of humor and a large education; no wonder that he was appreciated by the Jewish as well as by the Christian population. He served the public not only by his pen, but also by his speeches at every important public event. His 50th birthday was celebrated in Akkerman with much splendor. In the 147 issue of *Hatzefira* from 1913, M. Startz relates about the Jubilee party that was held in his honor: "These days our community celebrated the jubilee of the veteran Hebrew writer, the last of the pioneers and fighters of the Enlightenment, the wise Rav R'Shmuel Halevi Trachtman, on the day he was 82 years of age and 60 years of his public and literary work. The leaders of the town, the intelligentsia and many of the local residents gathered in the "Culture House." As R'Trachtman walked through the entrance he was presented with a bouquet of flowers and Mrs. Shoshana Litvin gave him a picture album and greeted him in Hebrew. The cantor Mr. Rabinowitz sang "Welcome" [*Baruch Haba*] and other songs. The teacher M. Startz congratulated him in the name of the Hebrew readers and described shortly his activities and his devotion to the education of the young generation. He spoke about R'Trachtman's literary work and mentioned his articles published in *Hatzefira* and his books. A young man, B. Keplauch, presented him with greetings written in Hebrew "in the name of the young people of Akkerman who read Hebrew."

Y. S. Trachtman lived a long and peaceful life, and experienced happiness with his children. One of them, Immanuel, occupied the important position of general manager of JCA in Bessarabia.

He died at the age of 99. Many of the Jewish and Christian Akkerman residents accompanied him at his funeral as he was taken to his eternal rest.

I. Schildkraut

Havatzelet, Jerusalem 1909, published Trachtman's piece "The Jewish handkerchief." We bring here a few passages:

"...The Jewish handkerchief, the "handkerchief of the people of Israel" is a sort of "hold-all" or "all-in-one," a tool for holy as well as for secular use. Besides its main function – keeping one's nose clean – it serves many other functions, in public and in private:

The Jew uses it to cover: his holy *challa* [special bread] on Shabat, his three special *matzot* reserved for the Pesach Seder, the dish in which he puts the presents that he sends on Purim to his friends and neighbors, his own face – against mosquitoes and flies on the Sabbath day while taking a nap after the *kugel* for the 'pleasure of the Sabbath," or, finally, as a head cover against rain and snow.

[Page 234]

Transforms it into a "sponge" and uses it to wash his body, his face, his hands and his feet with hot water in the bathhouse.

Uses it to wipe his eyes – on *Yom Kippur* and *Tish'a beAv*, so he would look as if he were shedding tears; to wipe dry his glass, his knife and fork, his mouth and his hands after washing them for the blessing after meal; also before the *Asher Yotzer* blessing; to clean the crumbs from his table and the dust from his clothes.

Wraps it: around his neck during weekdays against the cold, and around his leg on Shabat, in order not to trespass the commandment that prohibits to carry things on Shabat; around his face, eyes, cheeks or head – against a head ache or tooth ache; on a wound, burn or blow, God forbid; around his middle, during prayer, instead of a sash.

Gathers in it charity money from the townspeople.

Uses it at weddings while dancing in honor of the bride.

Carries in it: meat from the butcher, fish, onions from the market and other foods.

Ties knots in it, to remember things and be saved from forgetting, – and this is a true and well-tested method.

Spreads it on the edge of his table like a little table-cloth, when he eats alone and is in a hurry, in his home or his shop or in the market, or when he sits in the train and eats comfortably and leisurely, together with other Jews like him.

Wraps in it his Tallit, and his big prayer book.

And other uses, which I would not want to specify.

And our Rabbi, Gadi, did more than all that: he turned his handkerchief into an apron on his knees – an invention that we hadn't known up to this day.

Sergei Michailowitz (Israel) Gutnik

He was born in Akkerman to his father Michael Gutnik. He was a typically assimilated Jew and he kept away from Judaism and Jews. His father, Michael, was a manager of a commercial bank in Odessa and would come to spend the weekend in Akkerman with his family after a week of work in Odessa.

Israel studied Law in Odessa and opened an attorney's office there.

Since he was fully assimilated, he was of the opinion that being a Jew obstructs his progress in the Russian society. And one day in 1912 he informed his father that he intends to adopt the Christian religion. His father tried to prevent that, and a compromise was reached: his father will give him money to enter in business, and he will change his name from Israel to Sergei...

With the collapse of the Russian front in the Ukraine in 1917 The Germans and Austrians occupied the region, and they appointed a puppet-government headed by the Hetman Skoropedski of the "White Russians." Sergei Gutnik served as minister of commerce in Skoropedski's temporary government.

When the Revolution broke out, the German and Austrian armies retreated from Ukraine and the puppet-government dispersed. Gutnik escaped and fled to Bucharest.

In 1926, he ran for Parliament in the party of General Averescu and was elected. According to the testimony of Zvi Manueli (Miniali), Gutnik spoke at an election meeting in Akkerman and, among others, addressed the assembly with the following moving words: "I am Srul Gutnik, resident of your town, I know all of you in this town and all of you know me. Those of you who are older than I know how old I am, and those who are younger than I – I know how old they are…"

His political career was not long and he quickly disappeared from the political map – and it is not known where his fate has taken him.

Written by N. Amitay, from information supplied by Z. Manueli and Alexander Shapira

Sergei Michaelowitz (Yisrael) Gutnik

Written by N. Amitai from the words of Tzvi Manueli and Alexander Shapira

Translated by Sara Mages

Was born in Akkerman to his father, Michael Gutnik. He was a typical assimilator and distanced himself from Judaism and Jews. His father, Michael, was the manager of a commercial bank in Odessa and came to spend the Sabbath in Akkerman with his family after a week of work in Odessa.

Yisrael studied law in Odessa and opened a law office there.

Since, as stated, he was distinctly assimilated, he tended to think that his Judaism interferes with his progress in Russian society, and one day, in 1912, he informed his father of his intention to convert to Christianity. His father tried to dissuade him from this move and the compromise reached between them was, that his father would give him money to enter the industrial business, while he will change his name and instead of Yisrael he will be called Sergei…

With the collapse of the Russian front in Ukraine in 1917, the Germans and Austrians took control of this part of the country and appointed a puppet government headed by the Hetman Pavio Skoropadskyi of the White Russians, who accepted their authority and did as they wished. Sergei Gutnik served as a minister with an economic portfolio in the Provisional Government established by Skoropadskyi.

With the outbreak of the revolution in Germany and Austria, their armies withdrew from Ukraine and the puppet government fell and dispersed. Gutnik fled and reached Bucharest.

On the eve of the election to the Romanian Parliament in 1926, he appeared as a candidate on the list of General Averescu's party. Averescu won the election and Gutnik was elected as a Member of Parliament. According to the testimony of Tzvi Manueli (Miniely), Gutnik appeared at the Akkerman election rally on behalf of his party, and among others he addressed those gathered in these excited words: "I, Srul Gutnik, your townsman, know everyone in this city and everyone knows me. Whoever is older than me – knows how old I am, and whoever is younger than me – I know how old he is"…

His political career did not last long, he quickly disappeared from the political map and it is not known where he directed his steps.

[Page 235]

My Brother Yakov Berger z"l
Translated by Sara Mages

From the day I matured I have always been accompanied by the image of my brother Yakov, who in my eyes has always been portrayed as the character "*Ha–Matmid*" ["The Talmud Student"] of Bialik. Now, various memories of him come to mind and I will bring up some of them in this article.

First memory: my brother studies the Gemara with Rabbi Yossi, and one evening he puts me on his shoulders and brings me to a graduation party held to mark the end of the study of one tractate. Second memory: my brother walks outside on bright summer nights and memorizing his lesson in the moonlight. Throughout the year he studied in the Great Yeshiva in Odessa and in the summer he prepared for the external exams for the gymnasium. Due to the "restrictive norm," according to which Jews were not allowed to constitute more than ten percent of all high school students and graduates, he could not take the external exams because he had to present nine non–Jewish "external students" – and apparently no such students were found at the time. The book never came out of his hands, even when he helped our father in his store. In one hand he held a book and in the other – the "*mabok*" spoon…

Third memory: Yakov is preparing for his studies at the University of Bern in Switzerland. I see him practicing his English in front of the mirror and trying to adapt to the correct, and appropriate, accent of this language, which he did not have the time to study in the Russian Gymnasium.

He studied at the Great Yeshiva in Odessa for four years under the guidance of great teachers such as *"Rav Z'air"* (Tchernowitz), Professor Klausner, his favorite poet Hayim Nahman Bialik (in time, my brother called his son, Hayim Nahman, after the poet and others). These teachers, as well as the doctrine of Ahad Ha'am [Asher Tzvi Hirsch Ginsberg], determined his path in Zionism. He also tried to fulfill Ahad Ha'am's motto who called on the Zionists to conquer the communities.

He combined sacred studies with secular studies, and later – to the Faculty of Philosophy at the University of Bern for the study of Semitic languages. Our father had a hard time understanding this goal that my brother has chosen for himself, since most of his peers in those days chose to study medicine or engineering that supported their owners, but, was it possible to make a living from philosophy?... Father poured his heart our before me on this matter and suggested that I would write my brother and ask him to study a useful profession in addition to philosophy. I've done as he suggested, and I remember that I added a poetic phrase in my letter (I corresponded with him in Hebrew): "because two are better than one." He replied that he was very pleased that I was using proper phrases, but added that there is also another phrase in this regard: "and a three–stranded cord will not quickly be broken."

My brother spent a year at the University of Bern, and I remember that when he came home for a vacation he brought with him Hassidic and Israeli melodies. He then moved to the University of Berlin which stood at a much higher level in the study of Semitic languages. From the beginning, my brother aspired to be admitted to this university, but could not get there due to the lack of a matriculation certificate. There were well-known scholars in Berlin at the time (among them Zalman Ruvashov – in time the President of Israel) who worked on the preparation of Encyclopaedia Judaica. It was a great program and my brother also wanted to be among the scholars helping to make this program a reality. And indeed, he prepared some entries for this encyclopedia and the salary he received allowed him to continue his studies.

At the outbreak of the war, Yakov left Berlin on the last train and during the years of the war managed to be accepted to the Higher Institute for Language Studies in Petrograd, but, after the outbreak of the 1917 revolution, studies at this institute ceased. Yakov managed to participate in the All-Russian Conference of *"Tzeirei Zion"* in Petrograd and returned to his birth place – Akkerman and in his hand, so to speak,

[Page 236]

an unwritten certificate of "eternal student," like the one that was in the hands of many young Jews who did not have the time to finish their studies. Upon his return to Akkerman, our home became the center of the Zionist activity and was noisy just like a swarm of bees. The "flowers" of Akkerman's students (P. Berkov, the brothers Krasenyanski, David Kushnir, Danovich, Yisrael Rabinowitch) and young activists came, sometimes even several times a day, and planned all the many activities because the years of darkness and depression ended and a wide field of action was opened, new horizons were opened for all dreamers of good dreams immediately after the revolution. At that time all the parties wanted to attract followers with meetings, lectures and artistic performances. As long as Odessa was open, and transportation was regular, we brought lecturers from there. I personally remember two lecturers that impressed me in my youth, and they are: Granovskiy, who later became head of the Jewish National Fund, and Yosef Shechtman.

I especially remember the great assembly held in the glorious Craftsmen Synagogue on the occasion of the Balfour Declaration in 1917. All in the representatives of the parties and national minorities were invited to this solemn assembly. My brother, Yakov, was the chairman and appeared in a top-hat and tailcoat as was the custom of diplomats, and he was then only 25 years old.

In fact, it is worth noting, that my brother did not excel as an excited and enthusiastic speaker, but in his painstaking work, in gaining fans for the Zionist idea and recruiting "every good guy" who was willing to devote his time, or even as they said then – to join the effort. His first activity was the opening of a club and a library, which was managed by the dedicated guidance of Moshe Schildkrauth z"l, who came to our house every Saturday to consult with my brother regarding the club. Apart from Yosef Sarper also came, and later, Yakov Trachtenbroit, who joined the public activity and also served as deputy chairman of the Zionist Organization. It is especially worth noting that Leib Stambul joined the Zionist Organization as the craftsmen's representative. With this accession the anti-Zionist claim that the Zionist Organization is bourgeois and has no place for those who work a hard physical labor, was taken of the agenda. With the help of Leib Stambul the Craftsmen Synagogue became a meeting place for Zionist gatherings.

I remember that among the first to join "Tarbut" activities were Hersh-Tzvi Brudski, Meir Stretch, Aharon Cohen, Yehudit and Yitzchak Arbeit. These formed the nucleus that initiated the opening of the kindergarten and, later, the gymnasium. Fortunately, Menora Milman-Sharira, who completed a course for kindergarten teachers in Odessa, lived in our city at the time. She was added to the "Tarbut" committee and was the first kindergarten teacher in Akkerman. A year later, the kindergarten expanded and the kindergarten teacher, Shoshana Puzis, known by the name "Aunt Shoshana," who is with us in Israel, entered to work.

He devoted quite a bit of hard work and efforts to get the building, which previously served as a Yiddish school, for the gymnasium. He headed the delegation that conducted the negotiations in this matter with Milstein, the well-known philanthropist in Akkerman, who agreed to make his building available to the gymnasium.

The building had to be renovated, but since the days were days of emergency it was impossible to obtain glass for the windowpanes. A strange idea came to Yakov's mind: he bought old negatives from the photographers and all members of the household, and everyone who happened to be in our home, sat down and cleaned the negatives that were used as a replacement for the glass. It was a long and tedious job, but Yakov conducted the work, encouraged many to do so, and in this manner solved the problem of the glass...

The main problem was – how to ensure the continuation, and my brother solved this problem. When he was at a Zionist conference in Kishinev, my brother met the teacher, Fishel Stern (father of Mr. David Stern who, for many years, was the director of the Settlement Department of the Jewish Agency for Israel). He was a teacher in Eretz Yisrael and remained stuck in Bessarabia during the First World War. He invited him to teach the gymnasium's first grade. Later, it turned out that this was a real "find," because the teacher Stern succeeded in instilling the Israeli spirit in the gymnasium.

It is hard to describe the many difficulties and problems that stood in the way of operating the "Tarbut" institutions. The most essential equipment for maintaining a kindergarten and school was missing, and apart from that the harsh conditions caused by the Bolshevik Revolution and afterwards – the Romanians' entry into Bessarabia. My brother went to all the stationery stores in town, collected everything he could lay his hands on, pictures, maps and any object that appeared useful for the school. He worked days and nights and translated into Hebrew all the names, foreign terms and concepts. He decorated the walls of the kindergarten and the school to instill a pleasant atmosphere for the students and teachers alike. To my knowledge, he has done everything without getting paid. Only after the institutions expanded, and the teacher Stern returned to Eretz Yisrael, he succumbed the parents' pressure and in the years, 1919–1920, he began teaching at the gymnasium and serving as the pedagogical and administrative director of the institutions which had grown considerably.

I left Akkerman in 1920 and immigrated to Eretz Yisrael. For that reason I could not follow closely my brother's blessed activity. On the other hand, my sister, Sara Zarfin, continued to live in Akkerman until 1924. Therefore, I would give her "the right to speak," and from here on, what I have heard and recorded from her.

[Page 237]

How did Yakov turn the kindergarten into a gymnasium? – only with dedication and tireless work. All of a sudden the parents, who were invited to various celebrations and ceremonies, noticed that their children were singing Hebrew songs and dancing Israeli dances. They simply did not believe what they've heard and were full of joy when they realized that the Hebrew language was alive again in their children's mouths. Yakov – had a big part in this "miracle."

Yakov was a soft and humble man, but he also knew how to stand as a fortified wall in time of need. When the Romanian authorities began to harass the gymnasium, and raised the problem of a diploma from a Romanian university that Yakov lacked as a gymnasium principal, Yakov enrolled in the university's law school, worked hard to study the Romanian language and state laws – all in addition to his role in the gymnasium and the "Rabbinate." Sometimes I saw him fall asleep with the books in his hand and his glasses on his nose.

He had many opponents and it was not easy for him to stand in battle. He struggled with his rivals in the various meetings and before and after the elections. Sometimes he came home with his straw hat completely crushed and his glasses broken. It was the work of the opponents, especially the socialists who did not avoid physical injuries, but after a while they sent their children to the Hebrew Gymnasium.

He had more friends than enemies. I remember the delegations that came to our house to implore Yakov to place himself as candidate for the office of *"Rav Mitaam"* (Rabiner) [rabbi appointed by the government] in place of the old rabbi whose time had come to retire. His many pursuits prevented him from accepting the offer, but it was his loyalty to the slogan "conquest of the communities" that motivated him not to consider the difficulties piled up on his way. He also knew that the duty of "Rabiner" will allow him to develop the institution he nurtured – the Hebrew Gymnasium. By the way, as *"Rav Mitaam"* he had to struggle hard with the Romanian authorities regarding the absorption of refugees from Ukraine and Russia who came to our city over the years 1922–1923. I remember that Yakov took many of these refugees under his wing. They arrived at night, on the icy road of the frozen Liman, and when they were captured the government officials returned them the same way. Yakov managed to save them from the hands of the authorities and brought them to Akkerman.

As an employee in his office, I witnessed cases of intervention on my brother's part for the benefit of prostitutes who were about to be imprisoned in a Romanian prison. Yakov did not hesitate and exerted his influence even in such cases.

Yakov was able to fulfill many of his aspirations, but not his strongest aspiration – to immigrate to Eretz Yisrael and cultivate its land. He perished along with his wife and only son in a concentration camp. There is some comfort in the fact that many of his students were able to do so.

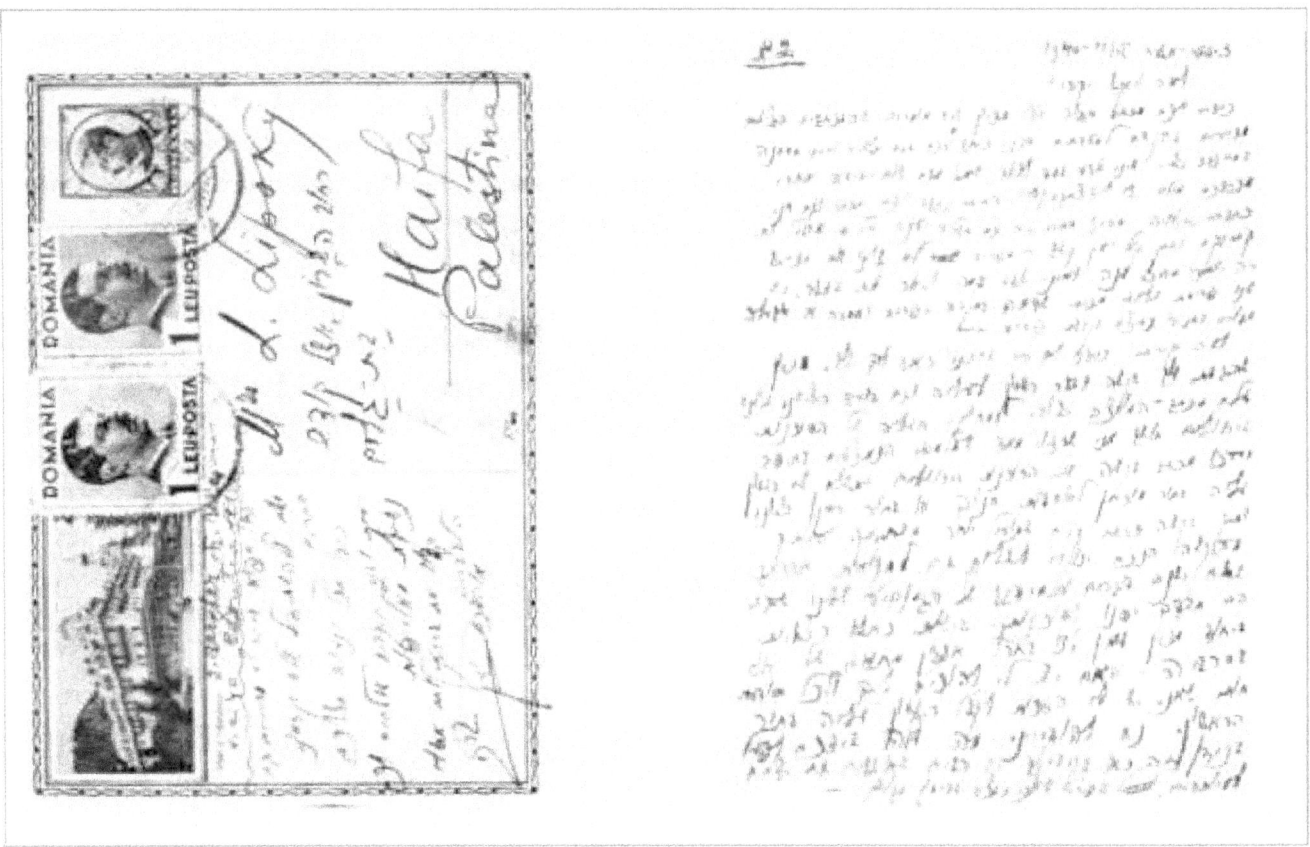

Postcard of the principal Y. Berger to his sister, 1940

[Page 238]

Dov Shrira z"l
Member of Kibbutz Kabri
Translated by Sara Mages

Was born on September 1897 in Akkerman. His father was wealthy, the owner of a saw mill. In his youth he was orphaned from his mother who was a descendant of a family of rabbis. He did not receive a traditional education at his parents' home and became an assimilated youth. He graduated from high school in Odessa and then from Rostov University with a law degree.

During the First World War he encountered the phenomenon of anti–Semitism, which did not harm him personally but served as a reminder of his Jewish origin. His friends were mostly left–wing Russian students, but he was not affected by their enthusiasm and thought of his way, and in a decisive decision became an ardent Zionist.

In 1920, when he was 23, he immigrated to Israel with the Crimean group, which was formed in Russia, and when they arrived at the Port of Jaffa they joined the founders of "*Gdud Ha'avoda*"

["The Work Battalion"]. Shrira first joined the company that paved the Tiberias–Tzemach Road and later the Migdal company. There, he first met Berger who influenced his way and his life.

During his stay near the Sea of Galilee he met his future wife, Chaya Yanovski, and when they were in the "Gdud's" company in Jerusalem their daughter, Raisa, was born.

From Migdal, through intermediate stops, the Shrira family arrived to the quarries near Jerusalem. In 1925, the family moved from the Jerusalem area to the vicinity of Kibbutz Kfar Giladi – Metula where the "*Gdud*" founded Givat HaHotzvim with the aim of establishing a marble industry in the area. In this place a son was born to the family. At that time, quarrels began in the "*Gdud*" between the right and the left, and most of the left wing left Israel and returned to Russia. Shrira was among the stubborn opponents of the left wing. He always believed in the correctness of the "*Gdud's*" path and its varied activities – agriculture, quarrying, the work in the British army camps and more, and loathed the blind fidelity, the worship of Russian communism. On the other hand he argued, for many years, with those who opposed the existence of the "*Gdud*" due to the deviations of some of its members.

He had a serious accident when a block of stone crushed one of his legs. After the recovery his leg shortened and caused him great physical suffering. However, he insisted and continued to work in quarrying in Jerusalem, this time in the area where the land was prepared and the construction of Beit HaKerem neighborhood has begun. After that, he worked on the construction of the power plant in Naharayim while the family lived in Kfar Yehezkel. From there he moved to the building of the Port of Haifa. Yitzchak Landoberg (in time, Sadeh) and Shrira built a shed for their families next to the Atlit quarries, from which large blocks of stone were transferred for the construction of the breakwater. Yitzhak Sadeh and Shrira took on themselves the management of the quarrying work. In original and innovative methods, they managed to produce very large amounts of stone with a small amount of explosive. The construction of the breakwater was completed in 1933, and the Shrira family moved again. Before him were a number of alternatives: building a house in Kiryat Haim or transition to agriculture in Gush Tel-Mond. However, he was not ready to abandon the quarrying work and decided to settle in Beit HaKerem and continue to work in his favorite profession.

Then, again, in early 1936, he entered large-scale quarry work in the Tzova quarry to provide stone slabs for "Hadassah," the university on Mount Scopus and other buildings. Tzova quarry has become the largest and most sophisticated in the country. Every day, 20-ton blocks were hewn there. They were hoisted by crane to the cutting machines that were used to make the stone slabs for construction. Shrira invested the best of his initiative and ability in this work. He improved the separation of stone blocks and their sawing, and increased the quarry's production.

The 1936 riots began. Workers' cars were attacked on the way to and from the quarry. A suggestion was made to stop quarrying until the rage passed. Shrira was unwilling to hear about it and the work continued with the typical picture – Shrira in the car on his way to the quarry, or in the quarry's area, with his pistol in his hand, to make sure that there wouldn't be an interruption during the work. He helped the families of the victims, took care of their needs and even donated much of his little money to them. All his life he gave charity in secret. Friends or neighbors in distress, including Arab co-workers, were helped by him with money and care, when everything was done modestly.

Shrira created a warm social atmosphere for everyone who came to his home, among them simple workers, Jews and Arabs. He dreamed that most of the construction, at least for residential and public buildings, would be stone construction that would dominate the solid landscape of the country, and that quarrying will become a major economic industry that will support thousands of families with dignity and even become an export industry.

With great sorrow Shrira left his quarry in 1940 (among others also for health reasons that have bothered him since his leg was crushed in Givat HaHotzvim) and moved to coordinate the Department of Industry in the Histadrut Executive Committee. He has always seen the combination of various productive works, agriculture and industry, as a necessary combination in the conditions of the country. He began his activity with momentum, not only provided funds for working capital but also provided professional advice, advanced training, sought financial sources for basic research on water desalination and development issues related to infrastructure industries, and for existing enterprises in accordance with their development dynamics. He encouraged the expansion of factories and helped with the establishment of new factories,

During the War of Independence Shrira joined the Corps of Engineers as a fortification officer. He was mainly involved in the fortification of the Jerusalem corridor outposts and in the breakthrough of Burma Road. His extensive experience in quarrying greatly contributed to meeting the schedule. After the war Shrira returned to work in the Department of Industry.

In his twenty years of work in industry he often returned to the subject of quarrying. He was consulted when new quarries were opened, when there were difficulties in digging tunnels for the National Water Carrier and in Timna Copper Mines, and when the granite quarry opened in Eilat. Shrira always responded to inquiries, encouraged the expansion of existing quarries and expressed his joy at any progress in the quarrying industry.

In 1961, Chaya and Dov Shrira moved to Kibbutz Kabri. His health, vision and hearing deteriorated and his strong heart weakened. They had to move to a nursing home in Ra'anana where Shrira passed away at the age of eighty and eight days.

Dov Shrira was a great role model to his sons, grandchildren, and many who lived in his company.

[Page 239]

Professor Yitzchak Starec z"l

Nisan Amitai

Translated by Sara Mages

Was born in Novocherkassk in 1894 to his father, Meir Starec, Was a dedicated Zionist and a Bible and Hebrew teacher at the "Tarbut" gymnasium in Akkerman. As a child he moved with his parents to Akkerman and attended school in Akkerman and Odessa. He acquired higher education in Leningrad (B.A. in mathematics) and at the age of 32 received a doctorate in mathematics, physics and astronomy. In 1922, he was the principal of a semi-governmental gymnasium in Tatarbunar.

During the First World War he was drafted as an officer in the Russian army. His stories from the days of the war, imagination and reality, were used interchangeably as the stories of Baron Munchausen. Like his father, he clung to Zionism and became one of Ze'ev Jabotinsky's ardent admirers. Against this background, a conflict broke out between him and his father, who was a General Zionist, and for a while the ties between them were severed.

In 1928, he was invited to lecture at the Technion in Haifa and instructed members of the "Haganah" in weapons training. The Mandatory government put him on the blacklist because of his excessive interest in buying weapons for the "Haganah," and when he left the country to attend a conference of scientists he was not allowed to return to Israel.

He attended many international scientific congresses and, in 1931, was appointed to the Academy of Sciences in Cadiz. During the Spanish Civil War he fought alongside the republicans and at the end of the Civil War fled Spain. In 1937, he immigrated to Israel with his wife Anna of the Carlos–Schorer family. He was a mathematics teacher in several high schools, in the last years of his life lectured at Bar–Ilan University and conducted many studies in the fields of astronomy, mathematics, and biomechanics. He lost his only son to a serious illness that infected him. He showed a special interest in the field of music and in the 1930s, with the encouragement of Dr. Biram the principal of the Reali School in Haifa, he initiated and founded an amateur symphony orchestra in Haifa and also conducted it.

In the last years of his life, he adopted a hobby in the field of carpentry and farming and conducted various agricultural experiments on his plot of land in Petah Tikva. He passed away in 1982, lonely and childless, and he was 88 years old.

[Page 240]

Moshe Hellman z"l
Told by Y. Schildkrauth and Nissan Amitai
Translated by Sara Mages

Moshe Hellman, chairman of the Jewish community of Akkerman, was one of the most prominent figures in our city. He was born to his father, Azriel, together with two more sons and a daughter (Sonia – wife of the lawyer Yosef Serper). Moshe married the daughter of the great oil agent and merchant, Warschawski. His father–in–law entrusted him with the management of the oil business in Odessa and he was very successful in his business. His daughter Miriam, and son Aba, were later among the activists of "*Tzeirei Zion*" in Akkerman. When the 1917 revolution broke out, Moshe fled penniless from Odessa to Akkerman. His father–in–law rehabilitated him and gave him the management of one of his oil businesses in Akkerman, and once again the business began to flourish. His interest in public affairs came by chance and unintentionally. At the cornerstone–laying ceremony for the hospital building, when everyone's contribution to the institution building was announced, a voice suddenly announced a donation that surpassed the contributions of the city's wealthy. The eyes of all those gathered turned towards the announcing voice – it was the voice of Moshe Hellman who, out of a sudden awakening or out of some other impulse, made a great contribution. Since then, he began to show excessive interest in public affairs and was soon elected chairman of the community.

He was an educated man, a Zionist (general), honest and dedicated to public affairs. Thanks to his sincere and humane approach to every person he was very popular with Jews and Christians alike. He had a great initiative and the fruits of this initiative were felt on various levels in the city and the district. He maintained honesty and sincerity in all matters of trade and merchandise and many had trade relations with him. It is said, that when he married his daughter the burden of the young couple's arrangement fell on him. He encountered difficulties and reached bankruptcy. He sat and wrote letters to all his creditors and informed them that he could not repay his debts and bills. It soon became clear that none of the creditors submitted his bills for repayment, everyone agreed to give him an unlimited extension which allowed him to recover financially and repay his debts.

He attended almost all the regional and national conventions in matters of the Jewish communities. He pursued peace by nature and in the days of the rabbis' conflict in Akkerman he has done a lot to make peace between the rival factions. He was active for all Zionist fundraisers and attended Zionist conventions held in Bessarabia.

When the Russians entered Akkerman in 1940, he was arrested because of his Zionism and exiled to Siberia together with his wife who passed away during the deportation period. After the war, he returned to Akkerman, the city for which he worked so hard for, broken and shattered in body and soul. He lived in Akkerman for two years in great distress, financially and mentally. He saw the destruction of his community until he passed away in the city he so loved.

May his memory be blessed.

[Page 241]

Pava Berkov z"l

by Yehoshua Harari z"l

Translated by Sara Mages

Pava was the son of an assimilated dentist. I remember his father who came to Beit HaMidrash on the High Holidays with a Russian-Hebrew "*Mahzor*" in his hand. His place in Beit HaMidrash was next to my father's place and I followed closely how he prayed in Russian. If Pava came to a national Zionist recognition, despite the assimilated atmosphere in his home, it was mainly thanks to the influence of Borya (Dov) Shrira who was his friend and also lived in his neighborhood. When he was expelled from the Russian gymnasium, Pava began learning Hebrew with the help of Y. Grozovsky's dictionary and reached full control of speaking Hebrew in a Spanish accent. He also translated poems from Hebrew to Russian and, to the best of my knowledge, also printed a booklet of Tchernichovsky's poems in Russian translation. He showed it to the poet himself in Odessa and Tchernichovsky approved the translation.

A group of Russian gymnasium students, who were also from assimilated homes, gathered around Pava and, thanks to Pava's influence, these young people later became an influential factor in the cultural life of the city. After the 1917 revolution, he successfully passed the final exams at the gymnasium and received a matriculation certificate. I remember that at a celebration held in our city on the occasion of the Balfour Declaration, Pava delivered an impressive speech while wearing a student uniform. After the cornerstone was laid for the university on Mount Scopus in Jerusalem, Pava decided that he should study at this university and immigrated to Eretz Yisrael together with Aharon Kaminker and Noah Zukerman. The university had not yet been built. Therefore, he went to Borya Shrira, who immigrated with the Krymchaks group, and worked with him on the Tiberias-Tzemach Road which, in those days, served a first place of work for many "*Halutzim*" (new immigrants). Borya quickly adapted to the work, the harsh conditions and the main food portion - bread with mustard. Not so Pava. Also the conditions in the "*Gdud*" and life of sharing and permissiveness were not to his liking. He returned to Haifa and when I arrived there after my immigration I found him in a very serious condition - hungry for bread. After a while he got a job at the train station at a low wage that every Arab worker got, and even that thanks to his knowledge of the English language. He did not last long. His fiancée, who remained in Akkerman, sent him money and he left the country and went to study at the University of Vienna. From there, he moved to Moscow and married his fiancée. He finished his studies and even reached the rank of professor at one of the Russian universities.

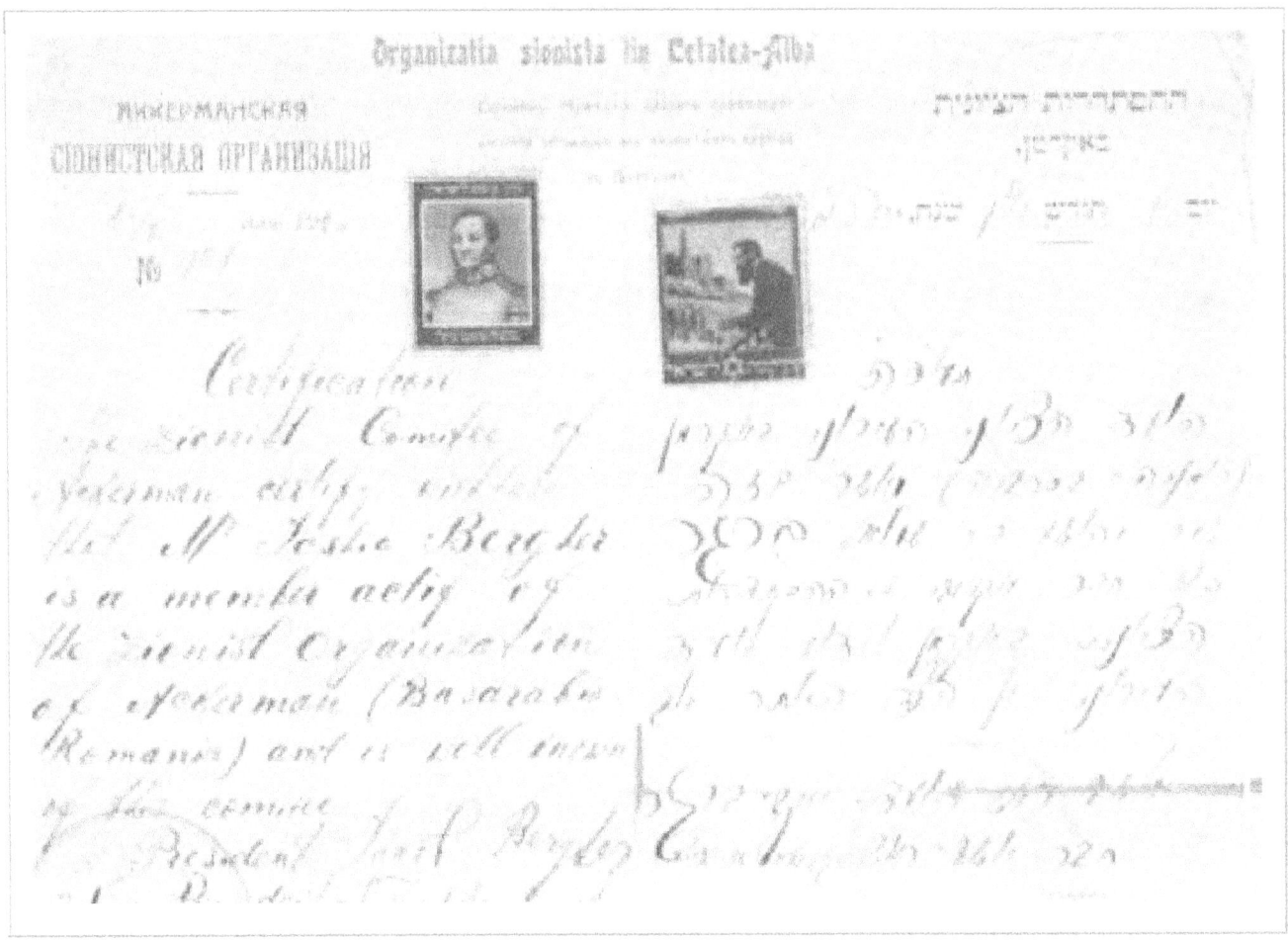

[Page 242]

Our Brother Moshe Zukerman z"l

by Shmuel, Leib & Noah Zukerman

Translated by Sara Mages

I always had kind of a feeling of respect for our eldest brother, Moshe, and this was not only because he was the eldest, but because he was always at the center of events in our home. He was a member of a Zionist association and received to his home the [Hebrew newspaper] "*Ha-Tsfira*" edited by Nahum Sokolow. He was alert and interested in everything that was happening in the Zionist movement. He defected from the Russian army and managed to reach Austria safely. There, he was caught by the First World War, and as a foreign national of an enemy state was placed in detention in a prisoner of war camp. He went through five years of hardship and suffering, hunger, danger of blindness, etc., but his spirit was not broken. Someone sent my father the tragic news that he had been shot to death while trying to escape from the prisoner of war camp and grief prevailed in our home. But my father did not stop believing that Moshe was still alive, and indeed he was.

I would never forget his great devotion to our father while he was sick. He completely neglected his job and his family and took care of father. Moshe immigrated to Eretz Yisrael about a year after my father passed away and here, too, he went through many hardships, especially the great tragedy of the death of his beloved son, Nahum (later he called himself Avi-Nahum). All his days Moshe bore in his heart the bitter pain and the bereavement. Nahum's fall in the battle over Malkia in the War of Independence filled the cup of grief from which he drank a lot, far too much.

By nature he was kind-hearted, pursued peace and loved people. He made sure that peace was maintained in our large family. I will never forget with how much love and devotion he received Bozia and me when we arrived in Israel. He "jumped" to us from time to time during the period when I was "green" in the country, to check how I was adapting and taking root, and guided me with good advice and instructed us on how to live modestly and frugally. When our brother, Zadok, arrived with his family in Israel, he again showed the same devotion and has done his best to advance Zadok in his work in Herzliya. This is how he treated all his brothers.

Shmuel

I remember that the Hebrew author, Hillel Zeitlin, wrote once in "*Hashiloach*" that the difference between an opponent and a Hasid is that the opponent is cold in his studies and prayer, while the Hasid is the opposite - hot in prayer and also in his studies, in the terms of "all my bones shall say." Moshe was a Hasid in the full meaning of the word. Even when we studied at the yeshiva he prayed enthusiastically. I remember that when the Pashkaner Rebbe z"l was about to come to us, Moshe told me in these words: take a good look at the Rebbe, Leib, when you will give him "*Shalom aleichem*" you will see that the Divine Presence rests upon his face. When we left the synagogue he asked me: "well, have you seen the Divine Presence?, and when I answered, no, that I did not notice anything special in the Rebbe's face, he scolded me and said: "you are not a Hasid and you do not understand anything."

At first he was very devoted to the Sadigura Rebbe, and all the descendants of the Rizhiner, and this devotion was later passed on to other family members. He really admired our grandfather, Zadok, and later, when he was caught up in Zionism, he was willing to sacrifice himself for Zionism. I remember my father telling me in 1917, that if he had known that by sacrificing his life he could save Israel - he would not hesitate for a moment and sacrifice his life. Moshe's grandson fulfilled it with his body. After all, sons of sons are like sons.

Leib

Moshe loved to read and was also interested in books of thought, philosophy and history. He planned to travel to Frankfurt after the war to attend a continuing education program, but all his plans failed. He encouraged me to immigrate to Eretz Yisrael and even helped me to pay for the journey. He himself emigrated five years after my immigration. His first work in Israel was in Zikhron Ya'akov, drying the Kabara swamps. It was a hard work and I remember his first day of work when he fainted in the middle of the work, but soon recovered and continued working. After the Palestine Jewish Colonization Association [PICA] fired the workers, he worked in Petah Tikva and Kefar Saba, and finally moved to Herzelya where he worked in a supermarket until retirement aged. He gave his full love to his only son, Nahum, was happy with him and cared for him. A day after the declaration of the State of Israel his son, his pride and joy, was killed, but Moshe did not break despite all the pain and deep sorrow. His words, in one of the memorials, resonate in my ears: "with all the pain and sorrow we are proud of such sons, and blessed is the nation that such are its sons."

After the tragedy, he bequeathed his home to the Workers' Council in Herzelya, to "*Hapoel*" Association to commemorate the memory of his son. He invested all his energy and time with activities for "*Ha'aguda Lema'an Hachayal*" [Association for the Soldier], and maybe this helped him to overcome his deep grief.

My uncle, Moshe, was loved by all his brothers and sisters, their sons and daughters. All of them will always remember him.

Noah

[Page 243]

Leib Stambul z"l
by Bruriah Ben-Zion
Translated by Sara Mages

Who in Akkerman did not know Leib Stambul? He was a unique figure that stood out against the background of public life in Akkerman. He had a tailoring workshop in the center of Akkerman, but it was also kind of a public center and a lot of threads (not sewing threads) led there, for there was hardly an institution, or a public enterprise, in which Leib Stambul was not involved in. He was the Chairman of the Trade Union, member of the Jewish Bank Council, founder of the Charitable Welfare Fund, member of all committees of the Zionist Funds, one of the founders of "Tarbut" gymnasium where his children were educated, and was involved in every enterprise or activity for Eretz Yisrael. In all these he acted voluntarily, adopting for himself an ancient rule: virtue is its own reward.

He was a handsome man, and his every public appearance left its mark and charm. He made a living from manual labor and was proud of it. Therefore, it is no wonder that the craftsmen in the city, and in the synagogue in which he also invested a lot of efforts, saw him as their most prominent and important representative.

His main ambition was to immigrate to Israel, and this was fulfilled after the emigration of his son Nissan. He immigrated with his wife and daughter and, again, opened a workshop near Merkaz Ba'alei Hamelacha Street, Tel Aviv. And again, the wheel turned, the wheel of the sewing machine, and again, he was at the center of public life and his home served as an address to every

Jew who came from Akkerman and needed some advice or help. By the way, he also initiated and founded the Society of Emigrants from Akkerman in Israel.

I remember well the day when the entire family gathered at the home of Atya (his daughter) and Gershon, to mark the day that Leib reached the age of eighty. It was the fifth day of Hanukkah. My uncle did not feel well at that time but overcame, wore a dark suit, a white shirt that accentuated his handsome appearance, blessed the candles and, as was his custom every year, handed out envelopes with Hanukkah-money to his great-granddaughters, grandchildren, relatives' children, and finally - to his son and daughter-in-law, his daughter, son-in-law (to the last he gave gifts). He then turned to the whole family and said: my beloved, I thank you from the bottom of my heart for coming to rejoice together with me. Please, go to the set table and treat yourself. Everything is at your disposal. In response to this brief greeting all present started to sing - "Today is grandfather's birthday." The joy did not overflow because it was mixed with sadness and tears flowed from the eyes of a few. There was a feeling that our beloved uncle's day was approaching. The next morning he was rushed to the hospital and passed away at night. It was a kind of death with a kiss that only the *tzadikim* receive according to Jewish tradition, and Leib Stambul was a *tzadik*. He always prayed that, God forbid, he wouldn't be a burden to others. His prayer was answered. Only outstanding people, like our uncle, get to say goodbye to the family in such an event, with a head held high and a clear mind.

His life dream came true. He had the time to see his children as he wanted to see them, rooted in the Jewish state, and rejoiced with the success of his many descendants. He walked proudly on the land of the country for whose redemption and freedom he worked daily and collected penny for penny.

In light of your deeds and way of life, our beloved uncle, we will continue to walk in the future, and your image will enchant us even after your death as you have enchanted us in your life.

[Page 244]

My Uncle Yehoshua Harari (Berger) z"l

by Yossi Shiloh, Ma'ale Shomron

Translated by Sara Mages

Yehoshua was a beloved and revered uncle, but I saw in him a second father, a symbol of an idea, of an era. He was carved from a unique material, a kind of compound of absolute honesty, undisputed belief in the path of Pioneering Zionism, love of others, devotion to family, diligence and manual work. Indeed, a very expensive and rare material.

I always liked to talk to him in private, and even to argue with him, and Yehoshua loved and knew how to converse. When he started talking about the past, and the different periods in his life, it seemed to me that they were living right before my eyes. I've often asked myself: how is it possible that despite the large age gap between us (fifty years) and despite the gap in our views on various issues, such closeness and understanding has developed between us? The answer is without a doubt - Yehoshua's values and virtues caused this. Even when we were divided on a certain subject, Yehoshua knew how to listen to his opponent, treat his views with respect and try to understand him.

Since he moved to Givat Haim I've often talked to him on the phone, and we usually sailed in our conversations to very important matters and did not limit them to matters relating to family and the environment, and the very fact that I've lived in Shomron for the past two years has added a local touch to our conversations.

In settling in the Shomron - the mountain overlooking Ein Iron - Yehoshua saw real pioneering, and even made me understand that he sees that my wife and I are continuing on his path, but he was not happy with the fact that I chose this place for permanent residence. He really wanted to visit our home in the Shomron, but was unable to do so. He shared with me the pain, sorrow and rage, on the evacuation of Hevel Yamit and Ofira, the displacement of settlements and settlers from the land of Eretz Yisrael, and prayed for a miracle that would eliminate the evil decree. His attitude of what was happening in the Israeli society, and in the country, in the last year of his life ranged from the pole of disappointment to the pole of faith, and so he used to say: "when I came to Israel sixty years ago, I found nothing there. Since then a real revolution has taken place. We have to believe, we must believe, and only if we believe - we will succeed."

I remember the last conversation with him when he said to me, and the tone of sorrow was well felt in his words, "I feel as if I've gone back sixty years"...

I understood his heart well and his words were like a sword's stab in my heart.

I will miss you very much, uncle Yehoshua.

[Page 245]

Dov Harari z"l
Translated by Sara Mages

As a native of the steppes of Bessarabia he absorbed within him their landscape: endless green fields, blue skies covered in autumn with heavy clouds, black clouds, which infuse gloom in a person's soul and arouse in him a strong desire to struggle, vegetable and fruit gardens on the quiet shores of the Dniester.

Was a student of the Hebrew gymnasium "Tarbut" in Akkerman and absorbed the old and renewed Jewish tradition. Upon his immigration to Israel he immediately entered a youth movement and public activity. Had a raging and creative soul, a student of Berl [Katzenelson] and a man of public and national morality. He believed in the dignity of man, always sought the good and the superior in him, and was always ready to encourage others. From this, one can understand why Dov has always been among people, always striving to help them. He reached the point of personal identification, with nationalism and socialism in the sublime sense of these concepts. In the educational movement he guided, instructed and educated, by the personal example he set for his students. He clung to the spiritual world of Berl Katzenelson. In his home, on the wall in his room, in quiet times and in the underground in the Diaspora, wherever he worked, he was accompanied by a picture of Berl, his spirit and his way. In adolescence he left his educational movement, and his home, and moved to Kibbutz Beit Oren in the Carmel Forest. He worked, and worked well, in full recognition of the destiny in the act. He thought about work and its purpose for the people who return to build their homeland while connecting with nature and work. And from the summit of Mount Carmel, when he looked out over the spectacular view, he became closer, in his body and soul, to the things he had strived for all his life: nature, perfection, and all that is good and just.

It did not last long, the World War broke out and the beautiful scenery "became ugly." From time to time, enemy bombers appear in the skies of Mount Carmel and Haifa, sowing death and destruction. From the summit of Mount Carmel Dov Harari sees smoke rising from burning factories. The whole enterprise of his life is in danger, society is in danger, the country is in danger and life is in danger. And for the sake of life, he decides to enlist in the army and fight the enemy, to encourage his people who are being destroyed by the Nazis and defend the homeland. He enlists in the artillery. He wants to harn the enemy that carries death and save lives. He is an artilleryman in Israel and abroad, he is also a driver and in constant motion. The constant struggles in Israel against the Mandatory authorities, against the White Paper, against the locking of the country's gates to immigration - accompany him in all his ways. He stirs up emotions and inspires struggle.

"We will fight against Hitler as if there was no Mandate, and we will fight against the Mandatory Empire as if there was no Hitler!" - Ben-Gurion's slogan accompanies and guides him day and night, and to its light he operates wherever he is. He carries out missions, performs assignments, fight for the opening the country's gates, the salvation of the people and the independence of Israel.

The situation in the Diaspora is getting worse. Information about the extermination arrives in Israel. The *Yishuv* [Jewish population] is agitated. The soldiers of the Brigade rebel: they want to reach the front, to Europe, to the Jews. And when the news of the possibility of parachuting into enemy lands arrived - he is among the first volunteers. In heated debates over the form of parachuting, he is among those demanding a blind jump, a direct jump, a shortcut. Among the trainees he is the first. A talented radio operator, a driver, speaks English, a man of good manners and the link between us and the British. I remember that at the end of June 1944, the plane in which we flew to Romania broke down and we were forced to return to the base. Our flight was postponed to the end of July. The two of us left on a trip to the area of liberated Italy. We traveled to Naples. How excited he was from the spectacular view of Naples. When we climbed Mount Vesuvius he was truly enchanted, and out of enthusiasm he muttered endlessly: "just like in our country, on the Carmel!" When we descended to Pompeii, he seemed to go down to the depth of the period in which the people of Pompeii lived, and it always seemed to me that this was his special feature: to concentrate on the matter and feel as if he was living the period unfolding before him. In the Colosseum in Rome, in the catacombs where first Christians concentrated, and in the Vatican where the most recent Christians concentrate, I saw him excited to the depths of his heart and happy from this human right, to see and feel human history.

[Page 246]

We parachuted together. Together . I remember how he lay on the airplane iron door and pondered. What was he thinking then? We could not talk, the airplane's noisy buzz interfered, and in the dim light I only saw his watchful good eyes wondering in wide open space.

Later, in Bucharest, in military uniform, he continued his activity. He worked in the British legation in the uniform of a British sergeant, and at the end of his work - he printed books and booklets at the "*Halutz*" printing house, at the meetings of the *Ha'apala* delegation and the *Bricha*, in the Zionist organization, in "*HeHalutz*," in the youth movements and the Jewish quarter, in one word - everywhere. He explained, urged and organized, and he was always with people. He stayed three years in Romania and was among the last paratroopers to leave the Diaspora and the Jews.

When he returned to Israel he was among founders of *Tsva ha-Hagana le-Yisra'el* [Israel Defense Forces], in the cultural service headquarters. He explained, coordinated the information, reached the rank of *Sgan Aluf* [Lieutenant Colonel] and managed the officers' school. In Jerusalem, which he loved so much, on the border, across from his school and his home, stood the former governor's house, which is now used as the home of the chairman of the UN delegation in Israel.

On the tenth anniversary of our parachuting we decided to meet in Kibbutz Ma'agan. We met. All those who parachuted in Romania came. We all sat together, also Arye Fichman z"l and Liuba Gukowski z"l, and may they live long - Mendel Moskowitz, Lupo, Mialo and Markesko. We all sat, but not all of us got up. We lost the best in us in the disaster in Kibbutz Ma'agan, the beloved and talented, the pioneers, the loyal to man and the homeland. Among them, the radiated, the noble and lovable figure of Dov Harari, the beloved and revered.

From the Letters of Dov Berger z"l

To Chana -

...it was my destiny to work for "*HeHalutz*" and the youth. Well, a job that is - more or less - really suitable for me. But, the tradition of the movements here is terrible: terrible separation. The movements are unable to work together and used to looking at each other as enemies. There is a happy phenomenon here in the country of a common front between the Social Democrats and the Communists. The professional associations are shared. While, in our country I need tremendous efforts to pass some joint action, stop the mutual slander and mutual accusations and harness all the people to some action instead of quarreling and chatting. But, I hope that we will succeed. There are already some fruits, but, in what difficulties they have been achieved! I also work in the movement "*Dror-Habonim*" - the practical union between "*Dror*" and "*Habonim.*" This is also something I have invested a lot of energy in, and I don't know how it is viewed in Israel. I'm imbued with the hope that separation is a crime, and the best of my efforts are invested in certain areas in accordance with this recognition of mine.

Bucharest 11.10.1944

... today, Victory Day, but there is no joy in my heart for many reasons: because I still don't know what this victory means for the remnants of our people, and because I see before my eyes Chana and Aba and Tzvi and Peretz and those who paid so dearly - so dearly - for this victory, and because I don't know for how long we will have "peace." Oh, little girl! Sometimes it bothers you so much, and just last night - on Victory Day - something heavy was bothering me...

Bucharest 5.5.1945

...I'm depressed to the ground. The day before yesterday news reached me that the bodies of Tzvi, Rafi and Haviva were found in one mass grave. If so, the balance of our victims so far is: Chana, Aba, Rafi, Haviva (the paratroopers). There is no knowledge about Chaim and Pertz. I'm afraid they are lost too. We are after the war - it has been over a month and a half - and if they were captives, they would have reported to an Allied army camp.

This is the balance. The hand cannot write what is happening in the heart. You will understand that. I daydream. I see horror scenes. I think that all these hallucinations are symptoms of madness. If I wouldn't go mad, it is a sign that I'm stronger than steel. Am I really like that?

... but I will not kill myself. It would be foolish to share their fate. This - no! But it is clear to me that all the days of my life I will seek for myself a way as their way, for the sake of dying in the way they died. Not only will I be prepared, over and over again, for such acts, but it seems to me that I will deliberately seek my death in this way in order to pay for the fact that I stayed alive.

... therefore, please think well of your way. Our relationship has not yet reached a point where it is impossible to sever them. Think of Haim's girlfriend with her three children, think of Tzvi's girlfriend - with a girl. Think about Rafi's girlfriend with a girl. I simply don't want your fate to be like their fate, and I know that if you cling to me, your fate would be like theirs.

Bucharest 25.6.1945

...in fact, I want to answer about one thing: what has changed in me over the past year and a quarter.

I've always been ... I don't know what to call it, let say: sensitive. When I was a child I burst into tears when I read a story about a dog that was killed or hurt. Even now, a good book, or a good movie, brings me to tears.

[Page 247]

Once, I ran over a dog with a car and killed it - and this sight has not been erased from my eyes. I don't know what to call this feature. I don't know if the word "sensitive" is correct.

And here are things that happened this year and penetrated deep into me, when nothing deepened into me before:

The ship Mefküre sank with 300 immigrants from Romania.

Berl died.

The death of Chana, Sereni, Aba, Peretz, Haviva, Rafi and Tzvi.

Eliyahu's death.

To all this must be added what my eyes see: refugees, refugees, orphans, diseases, poverty.

I've always felt the pain of others. I told you, I think, once: " I'm prepared for the entire constitution of future human society to be included in one sentence: "respect your fellow-man, don't do to him - what is not desirable to you." This is the whole theory in a nutshell, and this - in the national and social field, in relationship between him and her, in everything, in everything. And here, the pain of others has always touched my heart. And how much of it did I see here?

And so I would say: I was deepened. I live things more deeply, my feelings are warmer. And I must say: what I'm - became deeper. I'm closer to you, and you - closer to me. In this, I feel and I'm sure. The relationship between us can only benefit from this change that has taken place in me. Actually, I don't know if this is a change. It is more correct to say, that it is an overemphasis and deepening of one feature, which has existed in me for a long time.

There is also a change in me in the field of consciousness. I've lived a year or so with the Russians. I see their way of life, and I see the face of the Communist Party when it is next to the helm of power. And it is good for a person to keep his eyes open. I did not become anti-Soviet, but I will say: d e m o c r a c y. With that all is said.

And here, as you can see, also in this area I got closer to you. Therefore, the relationship between us can only benefit from this change that has taken place in me.

I also learned something in the movement's field. I'm in favor of the unification of all our movements and in favor of the unification of the Kibbutz Movement. I oppose, with all my might, the current situation in this area in Israel.

If so, I also got closer to you in this area.

As you can see - you have nothing to be afraid off. Only good has come out for us from the last year, and when we meet again - we will understand each other even better than before.

And there are other changes in me, which, of course, resulted from the changes listed above, and it is impossible to write about everything that is in my heart. We will meet and talk. Let's hope that it wouldn't be in the most distant future.

You write, at the end of your letter, that when many people return to Israel they will isolated themselves in their own corner. I'm not afraid of it. The greatest happiness of man is that he thinks that he is living a life of happiness and living according to his conscience. He is not arguing an empty quarrel, not insulting a friend, not harming a fellow-man, he seats and study until he is called again to duty, according to his spirit and integrity. I'm not afraid of it and I'm ready for it. Obviously, I will not join the party's turmoil in the country. And it will be good for us to sit in Beit Oren and live our lives. Why in the kibbutz? Because it is good for a person to know that he lives life that is the closest realization of his desire.

Bucharest 11.10.1945

Dov Harari (Berger)

(Biographical details)

Dov was born in 1917 in Byeramtcha, studied at the local school where he already stood out with his talents and quick perception. At the age of 10 he was sent to Akkerman to study at "Tarbut" gymnasium and with the establishment of "Gordonia" he joined the movement. In 1932, he immigrated to Eretz Yisrael with his mother and sister, started working in "Egged's" garage and also continued his studies. He was a member of "*HaNoar HaOved*" [Working Youth], in 1933 joined "*HaBacharut HaSocialistit*"[1] and was also active in the "*Haganah.*"

Dov was gifted with excellent writing and speaking ability and a unique personal charm that he radiated to all his friends. In the years 1939-40, he served as secretary of "*HaBacharut*" and rode his motorcycle to all the branches. He activated and encouraged, and his vigor and dynamism knew no bounds. He established the movement's labor camp and was among the founders of Kibbutz Beit Oren. In 1941, he enlisted in the British Army and then, as recounted below, parachuted into Romania and did everything he could to help the Romanian Jews who were then under Nazi rule. During this period he has done a lot for the renewal of the Zionist movement, "*Dror,*" "*Habonim,*" "*HeHalutz,*" etc. He translated into Romanian books and booklets, which were used by the instructors in the various movements, about Zionism, the Labor Movement and the political struggle in Israel. In 1946, Dov returned to his kibbutz and at the outbreak of the War of Independence enlisted in Israel Defense Forces. He headed the education department of the army's cultural service, was the commander of the Israeli Infantry Corps, and his last duty was - head of the Army Intelligence School.

Dov was killed in the disaster in Kibbutz Ma'agan in July 1954.

Translator's footnote

"*HaBacharut HaSocialistit*" was the young chapter of "*Mifleget Poalei Eretz Yisrael*" ("Workers' Party of the Land of Israel"). It was founded in 1926 in order to secure a political reserve amongst young people of 17 to 23 years of age.

[Page 248]

Yehoshua Drory (Shura Volovich) z"l
N. Amitai
Translated by Sara Mages

Was born in Akkerman in 1913, grew up in a traditional home where the influence of his grandfather, who was careful with a light commandment as with a grave one, was evident, but Yehoshua's parents were not as religious as their father. At the age of five he went to the first Hebrew kindergarten in Akkerman, continued in the elementary school and "Tarbut" gymnasium where he completed his studies. He was influenced by his eldest sister who attended a Russian high school and in his youth often read the books of Russian classics.

He was among the best students in the gymnasium and stood out mainly in his sense and talent for leadership. Was among the founders of the association "Speak Hebrew" and "Gordonia," and in 1931, upon his graduation from the gymnasium, was elected to the main leadership of "Gordonia." He immigrated to Israel in 1933 and settled with his family in Hadera.

In Israel he continued in public activity, was active in "*Mifleget Poalei Eretz Yisrael*" ["Workers' Party of the Land of Israel"], and for a long time served as secretary of the Hadera branch. He enlisted as a noter (guard) and was a member of the "Haganah." After the Second World War, at the beginning of the great immigration of the survivors of the camps, he worked in the Immigration and Absorption Department of the Jewish Agency for Israel, and did his best for the absorption of immigrants, and their guidance in the first years of their settlement in the country. He acquired many friends from among these immigrants, who were also invited to his home, because they came to know that he was not doing his job out of a normal routine but, saw it as a mission and has a great interest that they will adapt to life and work in Israel. When the immigration of Jews from North Africa began he was very devoted to this matter and his knowledge of the French language greatly facilitated his work. He went from *ma'abarah* [immigrant absorption camp] to *ma'abarah*, instructed and explained, to alleviate the suffering of these immigrants.

Upon completing his position in absorption he moved to work for the Histadrut's tax bureau in Hadera. He was given the role of liaison with the public because everyone knew how to appreciate his skills for contact with the public.

In 1964, he was elected secretary of the Workers Council in Hadera. When the layoff of many workers began in 1966, with the onset of the "recession," he was in great mental distress. It was difficult for him to withstand the pressure of unemployed workers who literally arrived to a slice of bread. Since he could not see them in their suffering, he proposed a plan to alleviate their distress and submitted it to the authorized institutions. But, when he realized that even the institutions were powerless, and he himself could not help, he decided to resign from his job. Many of the workers in Hadera regretted this move because they knew that he always supported and cared for them. He returned to work at the tax bureau, continued his activities in the city's institutions, the Histadrut and party institutions, until he contracted a fatal illness and died in 1975.

May his memory be blessed.

[Page 249]

Zev (Wobcha) Kamin z"l
Tzvi Menuali
(from words at the memorial in 15.3.68)
Translated by Sara Mages

    We gathered this evening to commemorate the memory of Zev that we all knew and respected. We have not yet come to terms with the thought that Wobchik, who was always cheerful and lively, full of vigor and joy of life, suddenly fell silent, fell silent forever.

    I knew Zev since his childhood, and although he was not my age friendly relations developed between us, especially in the Zionist activity in the city in which Wobchik actively participated. As a child he was a naughty prankster and a great joker, and it seems to me that he also remained like that. However, in his pranks and clowning there was a core of seriousness and idealism that characterized our youth in Akkerman. He grew and developed in his movement. He excelled in his organizational skills, speech and leadership talent, so much so, that over time he reached key positions and proved his great ability. When young Wobchik began to stand out in Gordonia's ranks I noticed his special demeanor, and I remember that once, when I met his father, R' Mattel Kaminker, I told him: "a typical Kaminker from Beit HaMidrash." Maybe I owe a certain explanation for this definition, well, Beit HaMidrash in Akkerman was not only a synagogue where people came to pray, but a kind of a center, or a social club of a certain public whose influence was well felt in the Jewish street. People used to say: "Beit HaMidrash decided," or "Beit HaMidrash will not," or "Beit HaMidrash is against." And there was a kind of verdict in that statement, if "Beit HaMidrash" opposes – what good is it talking in favor of? Before prayer, after prayer and in between prayers, the fates of institutions and individuals were decided in Beit HaMidrash. And I dare say that many came to Beit HaMidrash mainly for this purpose and not necessarily for the purpose of prayer. Among them were the Kaminkers – an entire tribe, sort of a dynasty: Haim Kaminker, Haim Chava–Lubes, Shike Kaminker, Mattel Kaminker, Aizik Kaminker, Arish Kaminker etc. All the Kaminkers were rebellious, spoke passionately and were lively and zealous, eternal oppositionists who waged wars and struggles, but, God forbid, not for self-interest, but disputes for Heaven's sake. Therefore, when I say here that Zev was a type from Beit HaMidrash – I meant the uniqueness of the Kaminkerim tribe. Admittedly, the struggles he waged were on different terms from those of his ancestors and forefathers, but this fervor of the Kaminker dynasty remained in him and he invested it in his struggles for the benefit of the movement, the country and all that was dear to him. He died while he was in the middle of the road, and surely he would have gone fare if he had not died at a young age.

[Page 250]

The Lawyer Yosef Serper z"l

Translated by Sara Mages

He was one of the respected public figures in our city. A native of Akkerman, involved in all its affairs, knowledgeable in legal matters, and therefore also served as the community's legal counsel during the tenure of Moshe Helmam as the community's chairman. For a time he was vice chairman of the community. He was also active in the cooperative institutions and served as deputy chairman of the board of "*Kupat Milve Vehisachon*" ("The Jewish Bank"). His Zionist activity (he belonged to General Zionists) was evident in many areas: *Keren Kayemet LeYisrael, Keren, Hayesod*, "Tarbut" gymnasium and others. He was a good and kind man and tried his best to help those who needed him. As a lawyer he did not take any payment for legal advice unless it was related to a trial. Instead of a fee, he asked those who needed his advice to put a donation in *Keren HaKayemet* box. For this reason the blue box in his office was often full and it was necessary to empty it once a week and not once a month as was customary. He kindly contributed to every fundraising campaign and to every public institution. He perished in the Holocaust in Odessa in 1942.

Doctor Shapira z"l
Alexander Shapira
Translated by Sara Mages

"Issac Osipovich" – this is how his colleagues in the profession used to address him. He was involved in extensive public activity and many of "his" patients were non-Jews.

He was born in Akkerman as the eldest son to Yosef son of Yeshayahu Shapira. Upon graduating from medical school he returned to his hometown and began to engage in private practice. Thanks to his devotion to his patients, his great patience and kindness, he soon became popular with the residents of the city and the surrounding area, Jews and non-Jews alike.

He devoted quite a bit of his time and energy to public activity, proved to be a gifted speaker, and greatly contributed to the establishment and management of institutions. Two examples prove the extent to which he was acceptable to the public.

A. In 1904, when the news arrived of the sudden death of Herzl, the Zionist circle in Akkerman decided to hold a memorial service in the synagogue and, although Doctor Shapira was not one of the members of the circle, they offered him to be the only speaker at this memorial service after the religious service.

B. When, with the help of the municipality and its sponsorship, a large public library was established in Akkerman (on Mikhailovsky Street), and he was elected chairman of the library even though most of the readers and subscribers were non-Jews.

He was the chief physician (without pay) of the Jewish Hospital in the city, and also served as chairman of the board of directors of the hospital. In this role he initiated the establishment of the new and modern hospital and persuaded the philanthropist, Max Krolik, a native of Akkerman and a resident of America, to donate the money to this cause. He was also one of the initiators of the establishment of the "Jewish Bank" and for years headed its management.

With the outbreak of the Russian Revolution, the Jewish population organized and established an umbrella organization to represent it, managed its affairs and be responsible for the existence of all its institutions. In the free elections, in which all Akkerman Jews participated, the first community committee was elected and Doctor Shapira was elected chairman of the community.

I've said only a little of the praise of the man who has been at the center of Jewish public life in Akkerman for a long time. When the storm began, with the entry of the Red Army into Bessarabia, he managed to reach Odessa, but due to his advanced age was unable to continue to migrate east and try to save his life. When he correctly evaluated what awaits him – he decided to inject himself with the injection that put an end to his life.

[Page 251]

Mendel Gellman z"l (Shohat)

Dr. Rachel Gellman-Neiger

Translated by Sara Mages

My father was a slaughterer by profession and for that reason everyone called him Mendel Shohat. This profession was passed to him by inheritance from his father, but he also "inherited" a mother and five children, who were left destitute after his father's death, and he had to support them. He was one of the most excellent ritual slaughterers and circumcisers in our city. I remember that in 1926 he performed a circumcision on an 11 year old boy who, due to various circumstances was not circumcised. The circumcision was performed at the local hospital in the presence of the doctors: Shapira, Schwartzman, Feldstein and the surgeon Zubowski. At the end of the circumcision ceremony, the surgeon, who was very pleased with my father's work, smiled and said: "our luck is that you aren't a surgeon"…

My father studied Hebrew, Mishnah, Talmud and other subjects, but his main skills were discovered in the field of mathematics. During the gymnasium exams many students asked him to help them solve complicated mathematical problems.

He married at the age of 19, children were born, and at a young age he already had a heavy burden of feeding ten people. The economic situation at home was dire and our mother, the granddaughter of HaRav Zadok Zuckerman, was not accustomed to the conditions prevailing at home. But, she did everything to overcome and help maintaining the house. Despite her poor health she did not refrain from any work. She prepared kosher lunches for the teachers of the Hebrew gymnasium, provided accommodation for students who came from the outside to study in Akkerman, and similar jobs. Thanks to her help all her children were able to get a high school education and three of them (in total she had six children) also had a higher education.

My father's special talents were also discovered in a field that had nothing to do with slaughtering – he drew up plans for buildings which were approved by certified engineers without any reservations. He also participated in the building of the Jewish hospital where I worked for many years. Apart from that he was active in various institutions of the Jewish community and his opinions and advice had great weight. One episode is worth noting: at one of the meetings of the hospital building committee, a proposal was brought by the contractors and the engineers on the amount of bricks to be bought for the needs of the building. My father, who knew that the hospital was built with donations from Jews from America, was convinced that savings should be taken and submitted a counter-proposal for the use of a smaller amount of bricks. After examination it was proved that he was right. The engineer in charge of the building said angrily: I am not ready to work with the "engineer" Mendel the slaughterer... The engineer's prestige was damaged, but my father continued to supervise the construction until the construction of the hospital was completed.

He was gifted with a calligraphic handwriting, was a scribe and repaired Torah scrolls, in which various letters were damaged or distorted, with great talent. His talent stood out after the Second World War when torn Torah scrolls were found in many cities in Russia. They were brought to my father who managed to rehabilitate them flawlessly. In his spare time he read the books of Tolstoy, Chekhov, Dostoevsky and the rest of the Russian classics.

After four years of uprooting we returned to our city, but, under the conditions of the Soviet regime he could not make a living from his profession – kosher slaughtering. Therefore, he started to grow grapes in his yard and after the grape harvest produced considerable quantities of wine. At the same time, he gathered around him the Jewish survivors who returned to Akkerman after the war, to protect the embers, the Jewish spark, so that it doesn't fade. Kalman Frechter made his house available to the public and it served as a synagogue. They bought a Torah scroll and my father was "*Baal Korei*" [reader]. The authorities allowed them to pray only on holidays and festivals. My father also prepared a calendar which was updated fifteen years forward and twenty years back. Of course, all the Jewish holidays were listed in this calendar, but due to his illness and old age he did not have the time to complete the calendar. The Soviet authorities did not allow him to visit Israel as a tourist. He passed away in 1973 at the age of 93. One of the city's residents expressed himself after his death: "The high priest of our city has passed away, and with his death our Judaism was lost."

[Page 252]

Characters
Shmuel Geber
Translated by Sara Mages

A wide and varied mosaic of Akkerman characters accompanies me even today. Among them are characters that arouse a smile or anger, remind me of forgotten sounds, sights that have faded over time, etc. Sometimes, when these characters come to mind I try to recreate events and acts from the past, but I don't always succeed. I will try to bring up only a few lines in memory of these characters, and I'm sure that the former residents of Akkerman will remember them while reading these lines, and maybe will bring up additional lines as well.

Musiri the Redhead

Engraved in my memory are the last words I heard from him on the day I immigrated to Israel. "You're the only one who can throw me across the sea" – so he said to me when we parted as tears glistened in his eyes. He was short and in his gaze was an expression of surrender. He was always ready for any work. He helped the person of duty to clean the clubhouse and every member who needed any help. Because of his short stature he always stood last in line and he came to terms with this fate, but, by no means, he was able to integrate in drilling exercises. It was beyond his ability.

Shura Volovitz

His performance in the movement was quiet and modest, but he was always among the men of action. It seems that his departure from life was also simple and modest. He was not praised and glorified even though he deserved it. I remember that day when Shura was elected to the duty of head of the branch of "Gordonia." He secluded himself for a few days with the books of A.D. Gordon, read them as if they were about to train him for the duty, and then began to get into things and managed the branch. He always had a serious expression on his face and seldom, in time of success, a smile appeared on his face. There was a great friendship between him and my sister, Chava z"l, who was one of "Gordonia's" activities.

Yakov Berger

Was a figure that radiated to anyone who happens to be on his way. In his elegant attire he seemed to be different from others and formed a buffer between himself and other teachers at the gymnasium, all the more so on the students. But, anyone who exchanged a few sentences with him immediately felt that there was no "distance," since the gymnasium principal knew how to listen well to the words of a fellow-man, whoever he was. A student who had to talk to him – if he got into a conversation with stress, he ended it completely free. It is amazing how he knew to evoke concentrated listening and complete silence in his lectures without making any effort in that direction. One of his traits was: in many cases he was chairman of various meetings and conventions, but he did not move from his seat before the oldest member left the presidency table.

Liss, the Medical Practitioner ("feldsher")

Like in the stories of grandma-Liss, he was the miracle-doctor who arrived to every home in which was a sick child and brought the magic medicine. He examined the children, dripped into their mouths syrup from the bottle that was always in his pocket and, when necessary, also fed them from the porridge that was also known to be a virtue for health... He performed all the duties even when the child was left alone at home, and when the mother returned from her shopping – she immediately felt that the "feldsher" had visited the house in the morning and the sick child – was no longer ill and the porridge was also gone... In addition to medicines, he also kept candies in his black bag, and these were used to capture the hearts of children who had not yet become accustomed to, or did not accept his medicines. I remember that Dr. Feldstein eulogized him after his death and, among others, said: all the doctors accompany him on his last journey because they learned from him how to treat sick children.

The Librarian – the Teacher Shternsaus

It seems as if he was destined by the Supreme Providence to be a librarian, and fulfilled this role with awe and reverence. He saw it as a real mission. He always knew which book to give and especially helped those who needed certain books for a certain purpose. When we were children, we, of course, asked for new books, but he knew how to get our attention to "an old container full of new wine," meaning, to books that were like an unturned stone but in his opinion there was a lot of treasure in them. He also knew how to convince those who exchanged books in his library what to read. His recommendation for certain books always came after he himself has read them. There was no book in the public library that Shternsaus did not take home to read. We would linger in the library more than necessary, simply because it was nice to be with him and see him in his "Holy Work."

[Page 253]

Shmelke

(I don't remember his last name) belonged to *Shlomi–Emuni* [Union of the Faithful] to Yiddish literature and in his private library it was also possible to find ancient books printed a hundred years ago and more. Anyone, who wanted to enjoy reading Shalom Aleichem in the original language (Yiddish), Y.L. Peretz or another author, was able to find whatever his soul desired in Shmelke's library. When the controversy between the "Bund" and "Poalei Zion" intensified, Shmelke knew how to find reference material that would provided us with argumentation in the inter–party debates. He was a short Jew, wore glasses with very strong lenses, squinted a little, his hairstyle was neatly made and the Russian Roveshka, which he wore frequently, befit him. The cigarette never came out of his mouth, even though it was not always lit, and I never saw him nervous. When something bothered him during a political debate, he used to bite his well–groomed black mustache, which was a sign of vigorous opposition to the opinions of his interlocutor. He didn't enter our clubhouse, but frequently came and left our house with an excuse in his mouth: he found new material that I've asked for. My mother always gave him a shot of vodka and herring.

Moshe Helman, the Community Leader

I remember that evening when he received a verified report that the residents of one of the Christian villages were preparing to commit robbery and riots against the Jews. Helman was revealed then with all his might and glory. He soon managed to recruit hundreds of young people ready for battle, among them many that did not belong to the Zionist youth in Akkerman, and also members of the "Bund." He knew how to impose his authority and influence. Nowadays, we can say that he was a kind of a "bulldozer" and, indeed, this was how he looked like from externally, but he was also able to act as a "bulldozer" when needed. On the evening I've mentioned, it was not necessary to use the forces that Helman had mobilized (and this is told in another article in this book), but if it was needed– everything was in place. Those, who stood out most in the preparation of the tools for defense, were: Magzinik, Ilusha Bundy, the Rosenthal brothers and Moshe (Mishka) Kvitko, but the person who activated them all was Moshe Helman.

Moshe Wieder

Lived in one room in our yard, lonely and isolated. He was not sane, but he was a quiet man and never hurt anyone. I could not find out when he came to Akkerman and what the source of his illness was. When asked how he was, he answered that all the people are crazy and he is the only one who tries to live with everyone in peace... He had a great voice, loved to sing, and sometimes sang opera passages. He responded to requests and sang cantorial chapters, but was always careful with three: he sang the prayer "*El Malei Rachamim*" only next to an open grave, the "*Kiddush*" only on Friday when a glass was in front of him, and "*Sheva Brachot*" when the bride and groom stood before him at the wedding ceremony... Outside, he was always seen with clean clothes, blue coat and a straw hat on his head. When he was asked to sing a song – he lingered until he felt that the applicant had slipped a coin into his pocket, and only then opened with a song. Any attempt to meet him in his secluded room failed. He never agreed to that.

I last time I saw him he stood on the wall of the "fortress" on the Liman shore, his gaze frozen and staring into space of the world. From a distance he looked like the statue of the "Troubadour" from Akkerman.

The Kvitko Family

In every city there is a home, or a family, that preserves the ancestral tradition, the assets of the past, a home in which it is possible to received certain assistance in time of distress to the body or the soul, quietly and modestly, a kind of "giving in secret." Many former residents of Akkerman will testify that such was the home of the Kvitko family, may they be remembered for the better and for blessing. A bitter fate befell the elders of this family in the snowy fields of Soviet Russia, but they bequeathed the spark to their son, or maybe their flame. He too, like his parents, knows how to be "Ahiezer and Achisamach" [one that helps and can be trusted]. He went through wanderings and adventures until he reached his homeland, but kept the spark. Even today, in the homeland, his home is open to anyone who needs him, and since he immigrated to Israel he was able to help, to a greater or lesser extent, anyone who asked for his help. Also guests from abroad, who visit his home, thank him for his fascinating conversations and for explaining what is happening in our country. With Kvitko you can sit for many hours and not get bored. Also his conversations and memories of the distant "Akkerman days" indicate that the spark has been preserved.

[Page 255]

The Society of Emigrants from Akkerman and the Diaspora

[Page 256]
[blank]
[Page 257]

Guests from the United States at a memorial gathering for the martyrs of the Akkerman district, M. Ginzburg and his wife

The Society of Emigrants from Akkerman in New-York
Translated by Sara Mages

It was only natural that the first immigrants from Akkerman to the United States will try, immediately upon arrival to the "Golden Land," to locate those who came earlier from their city to this country, to try, with their help, to pave a way for themselves in the new conditions that required a lot of effort: difficulties in acquiring a new language, difficulties in adapting to the new environment, to new professions, etc. So it was with former residents of other cities – and so it was with former residents of Akkerman.

The first gathering of former residents of Akkerman in the United States took place on 21 January 1905, at the home of Mr. Pesach Ginzburg on 219 Foresight Street, Manhattan in New York, and this is how the history of the Society of Emigrants from Akkerman in the United States began. Among the participants in this meeting were: Ben Berkov, H. Zepllin, Yosef Brenard, Chaya and Harry Krausman, Nathan Fildman, Willie Prachtenberg, Pesach Ginzburg, Charles Prachtenberg, David Goldstein, Morris Gobsevich, Harry Grazenstein, Kishiniovski, S. Krasner, Isaac Litvak, Akivah Margolin, Prelis, Issac Rosenblith, Lewis Shechtman, Philip Seibleband, H. Spitzirman, David Tabachnik, Harry Weinzweig. The chairman of the meeting was Ben Berkov, the secretary and the register of the protocol – Akivah Margolin.

This group laid the foundation for the Society of Emigrants from Akkerman in New-York and their names should be remembered for the sake of history. The first step was to call a special meeting for the election of committee members. And indeed, the elections took place on January 29, 1905, in Mr. Spitzirman's shop on 14 Canal Street in Manhattan. The first members of the Benevolent Association of former residents of Akkerman were: chairman – Kishiniovski, vice chairman – Bernard Krausman, treasurer – Grazenstein, secretary – Akivah Margolin, secretary registrar – Berkov. Trustees: Kipnis and Harry Krausman.

It has not been long since the organization was founded, and it proved its right to exist by responding to various requests for assistance that came from Akkerman, and among others – assistance to the victims of the pogrom following the 1905 revolution.

Nine years later, in the summer of 1914, the First World War broke out and left orphans, widows and great distress in Akkerman. The former residents of Akkerman in America saw it their duty to provide help. And so it was after the February 1917 revolution, which overthrew the Tsar and the House of Romanov dynasty, when pogroms befell Akkerman and the men of Denikin, Petilura and Semyonov vented their anger on the Jews and their property.

[Page 258]

As is well known, in November 1918 Bessarabia was annexed to Romania – and again the Jews in Akkerman were put to a bitter test. Many fled for their lives, some to Eretz Yisrael, some to the Soviet Union and some to the United States. Also, at this time, the Akkerman Benevolent Association, proved its solidarity with the Jews of Akkerman, whether by sending aid to the victims of the pogroms or by assisting the new immigrants who arrived from Akkerman.

The organization undertook a major task after Akivah Margolin and his wife visited Akkerman and realized that it was necessary to establish a new hospital in the city. The organization set up a special fund for this purpose, and from 1925 to 1932 managed to raise over fifty thousand dollars for this purpose and the money was transferred to the hospital building committee in Akkerman. In September 1934, we received an invitation to the inauguration ceremony of the new hospital building.

Also after that, we continued our humanitarian activities for various constructive projects in Akkerman, and one of our most important operations was the assistance to the Jewish Cooperative Bank in Akkerman by depositing some of our savings in it.

After the Second World War, and the great Holocaust that befell the Jews of the world, including Akkerman, we conducted a relief operation for the surviving members of our city. After locating the survivors' addresses, we sent packages to faraway Siberia and Turkestan, a place where our townspeople found temporary refuge. With the end of the war, and in cooperation with the War Refugee Council in Russia, we sent several hundred packages with food and clothing to the Jews in Akkerman whose name was changed to Bilhorod–Dnistrovs'ky. When we started to receive information about the survivors who returned to Akkerman, the survivors of the concentration camps and various refugees, we sent personal packages, food and clothing, according to the addresses we had, and we received confirmations and letters of thanks from those who received the packages.

M. Ginzburg and his wife at the memorial service in Israel

[Page 259]
The Society of Emigrants from Akkerman and the Vicinity in Israel
Translated by Sara Mages

In the first years of the founding of the State of Israel, various conversations took place among the former residents of Akkerman about the establishment of the organization. For some time there was a need to establish this organization to create a contact among the former residents of Akkerman, for mutual aid in the economic sector, for the preservation of the rights of the first members of the Zionist movement, etc., but this only came to fruition in 1950.

The talks on the establishment of the organization were conducted in the meetings between Yisrael Schildkrauth, Dr. Zerling (a Zionist activist who immigrated to Israel and worked here as a doctor), Leib Stambul (father of Nissan Amitai), Sheraga Cohen (of the senior workers at the Agricultural Center) Utca Cohen and others. After a preparatory operation, former residents of

Akkerman in Israel gathered at the Pioneer House in Tel–Aviv (1950), and in this meeting the foundation was laid for the Society of Emigrants from Akkerman and the vicinity. The chairman of the conference was Dr. Zerling, the secretary – Yisrael Schildkrauth, and apart from them sat in the presidency: Leib Stambul, Leah Krolik, Leah Rabinowitch, Dina Bass, Moshe Zukerman (Nachum's father), Yanchik Zukerman from Kibbutz Nir Am, Avraham Schechter (Tzvi Schechter's father) and Matya Lifshitz.

At this meeting the national committee was elected in this composition: chairman – Dr. Shaul Zerling, secretary – Yisrael Schildkrauth, Leib Stambul and Sheraga Cohen. Moshe Zukerman from Herzliya was elected honorary president of the organization. After the death of Dr. Zerling, Yisrael Schildkrauth was elected chairman of the organization and Tzvi (Hershel) Gronich as secretary. Leib Stambul and Sheraga Cohen were members of the committee.

In 1962 Schildkrauth resigned from his duty and the engineer, Yakov Trachtenbroit, was elected chairman in his place. Zev Kamin was elected chairman after him and he served in this position until his death. From 1967 to this day (1982), Baruch Kamin serves as chairman of the organization.

From among the activities of the organization we must note in particular: assistance in the absorption of immigrants from Akkerman and their guidance, financial help to the needy through the organization's Kupat Gemilut Hassidim, annual memorial services for Akkerman's martyrs, publication of the Yizkor Book – Akkerman and the Towns of its District, issuing certificates of approval to Akkerman immigrants for Zionist and public activities for the purpose of calculating the pension, etc.

The memorials are held every year and the number of participants varies from 200–300 people.

The largest operation, which required maximum efforts of the committee and all the activists, is – Akkerman and the vicinity book. From the beginning there were many concerns about the possibility of implementing this task, both due to lack of financial means and due to difficulties in gathering suitable material for the book, but the committee did not give up. In recent memorials the members were encouraged to write and submit appropriate photos, and after Nissan Amitai was chosen as coordinator of this operation, the matter was given serious impetus and the doubts and fears disappeared.

[Page 260]

At the last meeting a committee of the following composition was elected: Baruch Kamin, Herzlia (chairman); Nissan Amitai Hadera (coordinator of the book committee); Yisrael Schildkrauth, Tel–Aviv; Yakov Steinberg, Tel–Aviv; Chava Barnea, Tel–Aviv; Bruriah Har–Zion, Hadera; Binyamin Girshfeld, Neta'im; Reuvan Manos, Kfar Haim; Binyamin Giker (Tatarbunar), Haifa; Geber Shmuel, Rishon LeZion; Shmuel Gorfil, Moshav Nordia (Artsyz); Shmuel Brilliant, Tel–Aviv (Tarutino); Menachem Beider – Petach Tikva (Artsyz); Shoshana Ramba, Tel–Aviv (Byeramtcha); Tzvi Schechter, Ramat–Gan (Sarata).

To the audit committee were elected: Shmuel Naamani, Tel–Aviv; Asher Brodsky, Rehovot; Shmuel Miniali, Natanya. To *Kupat Gemilut Hasadim* committee: Baruch Kamin, Yakov Steinberg and Binyamin Girshfeld.

The Loan Fund, of former residents of Akkerman and the vicinity, was established in 1952 with the initiative of Y. Schildkrauth and L. Stambul. The sum of 500 Israeli pounds was collected in an internal fundraiser, and later the sum of 1000 Israeli pounds was received from the organization of former residents of Akkerman in the United States. The fund was named after Mendel Komarovsky, one of the major activists of former residents of Akkerman in America. After a while, the fund was changed to *"Keren Gemilut Hasadim* in memory of Marta," the late daughter of Mr. Ginzburg who donated 1000 dollars to the fund. The fund helped many former residents of Akkerman with minimum interest rate loans. Over time, inflation eroded the value of money and the value of the loans that only a few needed, and with the start of the publication of the Yizkor Book for Akkerman and the vicinity the committee decided to buy paper with the fund's money, and with that the fund ceased to exist. What was left of it is used for the existence of the organization and its ongoing operations.

A conference in honor of the first halutzim from Akkerman on the 40th anniversary of their immigration to Eretz Yisrael

[Page 261]

A conference of former residents of Akkerman: Leib Stambul speaking

Rabbi Ingerleib speaking

[Page 262]

[Caption inside the photo: Welcome teachers and students of the "Tarbut" Gymnasium]

[Page 255]

Sons Who Fell in the Israeli Wars

[Page 264]
[blank]
[Page 265]

Meir Zaltzhendler z"l
His parents: Efraim and Malka
Translated by Sara Mages

Was born in Kfar Hess on 19 Iyar 5711 (25.1.51) to his parents, Malka and Efraim Zaltzhendler. His mother arrived in Kfar Hess from Tarutino when she was a little girl together with her parents, and his father arrived in Israel as an illegal immigrant after his military service in the Second World War. Meirke demanded and received maximum attention from his parents, and when he was still young all the paths of the farm were clear to him and everyone predicted that he would be an exemplary farmer. He was cheerful, playful and welcoming to everyone, and at the same time sensitive to the suffering of others. He was ways busy and active. He traveled extensively in the country and got to know every corner and every town. He liked to hang out with his friends but, if his help was needed in the farm, he was willing to give up any pastime and help faithfully.

After graduating from public school in Tel-Mond, he began studying at the high-school of Emek Hefer region. Later, he moved to study at the Israeli Air Force Technological College. He devoted the little time he had left until his enlistment in the army to work on the family farm in Kfar Hess, and at the same time also worked as a youth counselor in Kfar Hess. He enlisted in the army in the last months of the War of Attrition and served in the Paratroopers Brigade. When he finished his basic training, and arrived to a parachuting course, it turned out that he was suffering from high blood pressure. Even though he was not allowed to parachute in this condition, it was decided to keep him in the unit in auxiliary positions, but Meir did not agree to this and was transferred to the Air Force. Meir reconciled with the transfer to the Air Force but not to its uniform. He continued to wear the paratrooper uniform he wore in his unit in Sinai, as well as the army boots of a combat paratrooper. Therefore, in his new unit in the Air Force he was called "Meir in the paratrooper's clothes." No one at home knew any details about his role in the military. We used to joke at the expense of his leave, and he himself joked while preparing the salad that he is in the special role of a cook in the camp...

His fervor for agricultural work cannot be described. As he passed the threshold of the house, in every leave he had, he immediately set out to work on the farm, ran to the orchard, to the greenhouses, planted ornamental plants that he like so much and found something to do in every branch of agriculture. Together with all the members of the household he planned to expand the farm in the course of time, when he would be discharged from the army and be able to devote all his time to activities on the family farm. He did not achieve that and neither did we.

He fell on duty on 15 Tamuz, 5731 (08.7.1971).

[Page 266]

Avraham Neiman z"l
Translated by Sara Mages

He was born in 1913, in the village of Rozvinitz on the border of Bessarabia and Bukovina to his parents, Yehezkel and Bluma. At the beginning of the First World War the Russian authorities ordered to expel the Jews from the settlements near the border. Therefore, his family moved to Khotyn and later settled in Akkerman. In his youth, Avraham studied at "Tarbut" gymnasium, but he was unable to complete his studies because he had to help his parents to support the family. He studied to be a watchmaker and his instructor in this art stated that he came from the biblical Bezalel family because, he too, was gifted with a creative talent and was proficient in fine mechanics and complex mechanism.

At the age of 16 he joined the "Gordonia" movement, left for *Hakhshara* and in 1934 immigrated to Israel. At first he worked in Hadera, later moved to Bitanya in the Jordan Valley and lived there for fifteen years. From Bitanya he moved to Moshavat Kinneret and during the riots of 1936 enlisted in the Notrim[1] and served until the day of his death.

As a corporal he was responsible for the Notrim station in Kinneret. For many years was a member of the "Haganah" and served in the duty of a gunsmith in the Jordan Valley. During the

War of Independence, when the heavy fighting began in the Jordan Valley, he was added to the elite division of the agricultural settlements in the area and after vigorous training his unit was sent to defend the power plant in Naharayim. From there, the unit moved to Zemach and withstood heavy fighting against the Syrians. He was given a twenty-four-hour leave, but was called back to his duty when the Syrians surrounded Zemach. Avraham was placed at the police station building where the weapons and ammunition were stored. In the midst of the heavy shelling, Avraham risked his life and climbed on the roof to take down the weapons that endangered the building and its defenders. Shortly after the weapons were taken down the retreat from the building began. During this retreat a shell hit his stomach, but he did not let go of the machine gun despite his fatal wounds.

He fell on 18.5.1948 and was brought to burial in the mass grave in Degania Alef. He left a wife, elderly parents and sisters.

Translator's footnote

Notrim (lit. guards) – Jewish Police Force set up by the British in the Mandatory Palestine in 1936 to help defend Jewish lives and property during the 1936–39 Arab revolt in Palestine.

[Page 267]

Avraham Feldman z"l
Translated by Sara Mages

Was born to his parents, Edit and Bezalel (Zuli) from Akkerman, on 13 Nisan 5711 (19.4.474) in Kibbutz Shamir. Fell on Mount Hermon on 23 Nisan 5734 (15.4.74).

Avraham was a graduate of the educational institution of "Hashomer Hatzair" in Amir. When he graduated he volunteered to work as a counselor at "Hashomer Hatzair" branch in Karkur. After a year of guidance – the thirteenth year – he volunteered for a combat duty. In the two and a half years of his service in the Israel Defense Forces, he participated in many daring operations against terrorists across the border. In the Yom Kippur war he fought in Mount Hermon. He was wounded in one of the battles, but after recovering from his wounds returned to his unit. He was Samal Rishon [Staff sergeant] in the Israel Defense Forces. His commanders appreciated his fearless spirit and readiness for any action.

His counselor at the educational institution wrote about him: "His loyalty and kindness were known to all. No one hesitated to ask for his help with the lessons, in groups' activity and on hikes. Avraham always gave an answer to someone's request, always helped, always took on every task – all in humility and modestly. He never put himself at the center and was also blessed with academic talents. Worked slowly and thoroughly and delved into problems. Did not like to stand out in group conversations, listened intently, but spoke little. He did not know how to insult a person and everyone loved him. Even though he was introspective you felt he was still looking for his way. Towards the end of the studies at the educational institution, the group was required to appoint representatives for the thirteenth year of the educational movement. I talked to Avraham about this and I was under the impression that he was ready to leave. He wanted to prove himself in the new reality and felt that there were forces within him that could not be expressed in the institution."

One of his commanders in the army wrote to Avraham's parents: "From the first moment I received the team into my hands Avraham stood out among his friends. He had great physical strength, endowed with kindness and was willing to fulfill any task assigned to him. He never resented anyone, and if something seemed wrong to him – he knew to come and tell me in good spirit and did not complain and scream as soldiers usually do. When I needed to select soldiers from the team for a special operation – I had no doubt about Avraham's participation in the mission. – – – the team members always knew that Avraham was the address for all sorts of problems."

[Page 268]

Yisrael (Srulik) Frank z"l
Translated by Sara Mages

Was born to his parents, Haim and Ester, on 21 Elul 5681 (1921) in Artsyz. He acquired his first education at the elementary school "Tarbut" in Artsyz. Upon graduation, he continued his studies at "Tarbut" gymnasium in Akkerman and in a high technical school in Kishinev where he studied building engineering.

With the entrance of the Soviets to Bessarabia he was exiled together with the members of his family to Central Russia, lived for some time in Tashkent, served in the Russian army and even participated in various battles. In 1946, he immigrated to Israel in the illegal ship "Haganah." The ship was discovered by the British and the illegal immigrants, Yisrael included, were locked up for three months in the Atlit detainee camp.

When he was released from the detainee camp he joined the ranks of the "Haganah." He immediately enlisted in the Israel Defense Forces and participated in military operations of behalf of the "Haganah" even before the outbreak of the War of Independence.

On 13 May 1948, on the eve of the declaration of state, when the soldiers of the Iraqi army approached the borders of Eretz Yisrael, Srulik set out to lay mines on the roads used by these soldiers, and since then his traces have been lost.

[Page 269]

Avinoam Schechter z"l
His father
Translated by Sara Mages

Was born to his parents, Rivka and Tzvi former residents of Sarata, on 22 Nisan 5713 (7.4.53) in Ramat-Gan. Fell in enemy containment the Yom Kippur War, 14 Tishrei 5734 (10.10.73), in the central sector of the Suez Canal.

He graduated from "Nitzanim" elementary school near his home, and completed his high school education at "Ohel Shem" and "Dvir" schools in Ramat-Gan. He had tendency for natural science subjects and his teachers praised him for his intelligence and quick perception. He demonstrated resourcefulness, showed initiative in everyday life and excelled in manual labor. He had many hobbies: fishing, chess, stamp collecting and more. He carved, in good taste, birds in flight to the heights and his carvings remained silent witnesses to what our beloved son loved. He was connected in heart and soul to the country's spectacular landscapes and loved to wander in its expanses. The basalt stones he collected during his travels were placed on the shelves of his bookcase, and the seashells from Eilat adorned his desk. Whenever he was at home – many friends gathered around him, as everyone felt the tenderness and love, simplicity and sincerity that his soul radiated, and for this reason he was respected and loved. He felt the distress of every needy person. In his last leave he talked about soldiers from poor families and the need to improve their situation.

He completed his two year military service in the Sinai Desert impeccably, or as his commander said – "with courage and love." He also wrote me "Avinoam was an excellent team member who worked to the satisfaction of his commanders." On the evening of Yom Kippur, his tank crew was instructed to move to the "Hizaion" stronghold to rescue all the casualties and to extend help in repelling the waves of enemy that stormed in masses. For many hours Avinoam and his friends fought in fierce and cruel armored battles, and in the battle that took place on 14 Tishrei, he was hit and fell.

In an article published in the Israel Defense Forces weekly magazine, "BaMahane," about the crew of the black tank that Avinoam was one of them, it was said among others: the gunner, Avinoam Schechter, who later fell in the war, hit hard targets while driving very fast, and anyone, who is a tank-crew man, knows that this is not a simple thing. It should be written about the team members, that Avinoam z"l was among them, that they had done wonderful job. They were great. It's important that it wouldn't be forgotten."

Page 272]

The Towns in the District
Tarutino
(Tarutyne, Ukraine)
46°11' 29°09'

Facts and Numbers About the Jews of Tarutino
by Eliyahu Feldman

See http://www.jewishgen.org/yizkor/pinkas_romania/rom2_00357.html

A street in the residential section of Tarutino, 1912

[Page 273]

Our Town Tarutino
by Shmuel Brilliant
Translated by Ala Gamulka

The following article, dedicated to the Jewish Community of Tarutino, requires an explanation.

At first, the former residents of Tarutino had intended to publish a special book about the village and its Jewish life. This way there would be a commemoration of all those who were murdered in the Holocaust. We quickly discovered that the task was too difficult for us. Some people tried to deter us since there was some indifference towards the topic. Also, much has been forgotten and whatever remained would not interest former residents of Tarutino. These allegations strengthened the hands of the group, but the first attempts came to naught. We were not discouraged since we felt the need to somehow honor the Jewish community of Tarutino and on we went. We continued to collect material and to encourage those who had difficulty writing. This is how we obtained what we did. It was not enough for a complete book about Tarutino so we were obliged to accept the invitation to include our articles in the Akkerman and Surroundings Yizkor Book. Tarutino was a neighbor of Akkerman. It was not only a geographic closeness, but also one of friendship and economics. The former residents of Tarutino who were consulted agreed to this proposal and this is how the following section was born.

It is probable that more could have been added to some topics, however, we were not successful in finding the appropriate material. We even tried to research the National Library and other places for books, but we could not find any. We saw the need for concentrating on those personalities that had contributed to Jewish life in Tarutino. We hope that our decision is acceptable. We especially thank the widow and the son of Dr. Yosef Lerner, z"l, Judge Efraim Laron, who were able to provide us with notes of their husband and father about Tarutino. We also thank all those who participated in this section. May they all be blessed!

[Page 274]

History of the Jewish Community in Tarutino

There is no trace of Jews in Tarutino and we do not see the need for research on the history of the village itself. We will add only a few lines about this topic. The village changed regimes and names in different times. It was originally known as Anchiokrak and then as Nagergrak and Agikrak – named after the river which went through it and cut it in two. Tarutino is situated about 198 kilometers from Odessa on the Akkerman–Bessarabskaya rail line. It is about 6 kilometers from the train station in Rezina. The name Tarutino came from another village in the Kaluga district near Moscow. It had served as a military base of the Russians during Napoleonic times. The Russians used to reuse names that were connected to military battles under Marshall Kutuzov. This is how the ancient name was given to Tarutino.

In 1812 the Russians captured the village from the Turks who had ruled it previously. German farmers came to inhabit this area. Jews were not allowed to settle in Tarutino because it was near the border. Eventually, the regulation was lifted and Jews came to Tarutino from Poland, Lithuania, Podolia and other places. In the 19th century the Russians brought German farmers to about 100 villages and settlements near Tarutino. This was not a novelty, but still it resulted in the growth of the Jewish population in Tarutino at a greater pace than other settlements in southern Bessarabia, except for Akkerman. The growth was probably due to the German residents who developed the village from an economic and commercial point of view and thus drew more people.

The German High School in Tarutino where there were some Jewish students

In 1870 it was officially permissible for Jews to settle in Tarutino and at the beginning of the 20th century Jews constituted one third of the entire population. It, in turn, was mostly German. Eventually, Tarutino became the second center in southern Bessarabia, after Akkerman. It helped in the growth of other villages in the vicinity. It is obvious that the Jews who arrived in Tarutino were influenced by the level of development of the Germans and they learned much from them. In time, there was a division of tasks: the Germans worked their farms and in industry and the Jews dealt in commerce. It is noteworthy that the only German language newspaper in Bessarabia was published in Tarutino.

In contrast to what happened later, the German residents did not show signs of anti-Semitism, in spite of the general hatred of Jews by the Russians. Relations between Germans and Jews were decent and even friendly. Nearly all the Germans in Tarutino knew some Yiddish and so the Jews were careful in conversations between them not to use words that could be understood by them. The expression "The uncircumcised understands everything" was quite common and served as a warning. When they spoke among themselves they used typically Jewish words such as "in loyalty", "For sure", etc. There is a story about two Germans from Tarutino who, on the way to Kishinev, stopped in a Jewish inn and ordered wine. As they were leaving the innkeeper asked for a specific price, but the Germans only offered half that amount. When the Jew asked what this meant, they replied: We heard how you gave our order to your wife and told her in Hebrew "half water". So since you only served us half of the wine, we are only paying half…

The ability of the Germans in Hebrew and Yiddish also was a result of the fact that there were German youth who attended Heder together with Jews. We remember some of them: Sasha Bross who became a lawyer, Robert Hirshkorn, Bugner and others. We even remember a German called Vanka who used to bring goods from the train station and he would write notes in Yiddish to his Jewish customers...

The German priest, Haze, used to come to synagogue on the High Holidays to listen to the chanting of the cantor. During Nazi times, when German youth tried to bring in Nazi propaganda into the church, the priest forbade it.

It did not take long for the priest to be dismissed from his job. He committed suicide.

The German students in the Heder learned everything the Jewish ones did, but they were exempt from two tasks: putting on Tfilin and reciting Kiddush. From this point of view, Tarutino was unique in Bessarabia and perhaps in the rest of the world.

The change in relations between the Jews and the Germans occurred as Hitler came to power in Germany. Instigators came from Transylvania and Germany and they trained the local Germans in Tarutino in how to behave with Jews and how to disconnect relations with them. In addition, young people from Tarutino who had gone to study in Germany, returned full of anti-Semitism. They did their best to cut any relations between the Germans and the Jews in Tarutino.

[Page 275]

The majority of the Jews in Tarutino rented apartments from German landlords. I know of many cases when the Jews could not pay the rent on time, the Germans waited without resorting to the law. All this changed when the war broke out in 1939. There were closer ties with German groups in Transylvania. German cooperatives and workshops were established so there would not be a need to work with Jews. There was also military training on Sundays and holidays. A new atmosphere prevailed and relations between Germans and Jews changed completely.

All the houses in Tarutino were built of stone, which was uncommon in villages. Some stores were built with wood and stood on top of the bridges. It was rare to find a house built of wood. This was quite common in villages in Poland and Ukraine. There were some houses with several stories. Tarutino was also different from other villages by the fact that it had beer parlors, bakeries, bars, a ball club, etc. I recall that there was in the village a small diner owned by a bearded, tall Jew called Zalman Vineberg. The ice cream he served was renowned. He did not sell to Jews before 6 in the evening to make sure that anyone who had eaten meat at lunch would not have waited the required 6 hours.

Zeirei Zion in Tarutino

Seated in first row from right to left: **Gurfel, unknown, unknown, Gedalya Imas**
Seated in second row from right to left: **teacher Braz, Yosef Gnessin, Sosia Rosenberg, teacher Kripitz. Ida Falik, Yerucham Klorfeld, unknown**
Standing in third row from right to left: **unknown, Israel Ronzberg, unknown, teacher Gersh Zilberman, six unknown, Gershon Shlovitz, Zelig Wexler, unknown**

Education and Culture

The first high school in Tarutino was founded by the Germans in 1912. Its language of instruction was Russian. Most of the students were Germans and a few were Jewish or other minorities. In 1919, when the regimes changed, the Romanians changed the language of instruction to German. One of the first Hebrew High Schools was founded in Tarutino, in the early 1900s by the beloved teacher Gersh Zilberman. In 1919 there was also an elementary Hebrew school– 4 classes as was customary in Romania. The first principal of the school was Levi Fanish who returned from Eretz Israel in 1915 after he finished his studies in Herzliah High School in Tel Aviv. The Hebrew High School was closed by the Romanians in 1925. It was reopened a year later when its new principal was the lawyer Sperling– a well-known jurist. This is discussed in another article. The principal that followed him was Gedalya Rosenthal who was exiled to Siberia for being a Zionist.

[Page 276]

Male and female students in the elementary Hebrew school in Tarutino in 1934

Seated, Row 1 from left to right: **Kenner, Zaltshendler, Chariton, Zeltser, Rozitchner, unknown, Sugitin, David Kisliansky, Aaron Melament**

Seated row 2 from left to right: **Ovadia Kopilovitz, Hershel Kreizel, Herzl Lainzon, teacher Teperman, Principal Levi Fanish, teacher Lily Bronstein, Moshe Shtilman, Yosef Stromberg, and Zvi Gildish**

The teaching of Hebrew to children was a primary concept and even those youngsters who did not attend Heder, before the establishment of the Hebrew Elementary school, were sent to special tutors. The writer of this article was taught Hebrew when he was six years old by the famous Zionist teacher Michael Kovlanov. May his memory be a blessing!

Tarutino was often visited by some of the best theater troupes from Bessarabia, Romania and Poland. Those I remember who performed between the two wars– Vilna Theater with Ida Kaminska, Sigmund Turkov, Stein, etc., the Fishezon group from Kishinev, Azazel from Bucharest, Sidi Tal and various casts from Bukovina. There were also local troupes that put on mainly plays by Shalom Aleichem. There is a description in one of the other articles. The schools also encouraged artistic activities and would occasionally put on plays. Those were usually about Biblical themes with the students performing and the teachers directing. Most notable are the celebrations at Hanukah and Purim organized by the Hebrew High School. An article in Unzer Tzeit (Our Time) describes as follows:

"On March 23 there was a costume ball for Purim organized by the Hebrew High School. Most notable were the costumes of Mrs. Brachot who depicted the importance of the local high school as an educational institution and of Mrs. Sh. Hellman. The latter portrayed the activities of the societal institutions in Tarutino. The ball was a financial success. The participants were Mesdames M. Hellman, R. Sirota, R. Shulman, Fisher and others. Messers I. Hellman, B. Sheinman, M. Katz, V. Leitman, Kh. Royzen, E. Schwartzman also contributed. In particular, Mr. N. Sirota was very helpful.

On Wednesday afternoon there was a celebration for the students with their parents subsidized by the public institutions. The Principal, Mr. G. Rosenthal, opened the festivities with a beautiful speech in which he emphasized the importance of the educational institution from a national point of view as well. On the program were songs sung by the choir, recitations, live pictures and sporting events"

Zionist activities in the village

It is essential to discuss the many Zionist activities in Tarutino. Unfortunately, there are no documents that survived. Although we have some testimonials it is difficult to describe clearly and succinctly these activities. It must be emphasized that the Jewish community always had a distinct trait– Zionism.

[Page 277]

In the diary of Dr. Yosef Lerner, z"l, we find more proof of the Zionist flavor of the Jewish Community. Even before 1899 (year of birth of Dr. Lerner) there was Zionist activity organized by many businessmen who spent their time developing Zionism in the village and among the youth. We remember in this context: Y.L. Baratz, Yekutiel Rosenberg, David Schwartzman, Nachum Sirota, I. L. Grinberg, Moshe Cooperman, Yeshayahu Itzkovich, Levi Fanish, Gersh Zilberman, M. Sperling, G. Rosenthal, Rabbi Bronstein, Israel Haham, Avraham Haham, Avraham Rotenberg, Mordehai Haklai (Kuris), and others. It is noteworthy to mention that the first group of Hovevei Zion in Bessarabia was founded in Tarutino on the eve of Yom Kippur 1884.

In the chapter about the Zionist movement in Bessarabia, Israel Kloisner writes about its beginnings in Tarutino:

"In the German Colony of Tarutino, where there were about 300 Jews, a group of Hovevei Zion was established at the end of 1885. On the eve of Yom Kippur the group placed bowls in the synagogue and collected 34 rubles. There was also income from membership dues and other sources: engagements and weddings, circumcisions, and pledges on Simchat Torah. The group decided to try to get revenue from the collection of cattle bones in town.

In a letter from the first day of Hol Hamoed Succot 1885 addressed to the head office of Hovevei Zion in Warsaw, Yehuda Leib Baratz proclaims in the name of his group: "Our income is growing from day to day and has reached 150 rubles. The committee is not sure where to send the funds, either to Petach Tikva, to Warsaw or to Petersburg." It is amazing that there is no sentiment towards it in Kishinev (Israel Kloisner).

The founders of Zeirei Zion in Tarutino, Elul 1919:

Seated from left to right: **Rachel Schwartzman–Gordon, Yocheved Bronstein, Der. Eli Epstein (brother–in–law of Jabotinsky), Avraham (Bazia) Haham, Mordehai Haklai (Kuris), Avraham Sofer**

Standing left to right: **Yeshayahu Friedman, Ozer Rotberg, Yosef Lerner (Laron), Mordehai Rosenblatt, Zev Friedman (Velvel)**

[Page 278]

Zionist leaders and the Keren Hayesod executive with visitors from Kishinev:
Seated from right to left: **Yekutiel Rosenberg, Y.L. Baratz, M. Segal, Dr. I. Sapir, Az. Dubinsky (3 emissaries from Kishinev), Mrs. Krassiuk, Dr. Krassiuk**
Standing: **Mordehai (Monia) Levitt, Avraham Rotberg, Yeshayahu Itzkovich, Yosef Leib Grinberg, Eliezer Berger, I. Kh, Reznik. 1925**

Prior to the Katowitz Hovevei Zion conference the group sent its recommendations to Warsaw. These were: "choose a wealthy man to be the executive director in the central committee, all business of the movement should be handled by this central committee and the smaller groups should only be involved with collecting money". It is important to note the following: representatives of Zionist movements in Tarutino took part in the first congress of the Zionists of Russia which occurred in Warsaw in 1898. In Av 1900 a representative of the Tarutino Zionists, Israel Haham, came to Bendery to a conference. Also, in Tishrei of the following year, I. Haham participated in another conference there. Activities for the benefit of Jewish National Fund began at the turn of the 20th century. At certain times, the funds collected in Tarutino for Jewish National Fund and Keren Hayesod were greater than those received in Akkerman.

In Tsarist Russia there was a prohibition against Zionist activities. Any such meetings only took place in synagogues. The only group active at the time in Tarutino was Hovevei Zion.

In 1919–1920 about 60 members of Hovevei Zion from Tarutino made Aliyah. Among them were: two Schwartzman brothers (sons of David Schwartzman), Yeshayahu Perper, Mordehai Kochuk, Haim Goldstein, Ben Zion Kreber, Avraham Sofer, Pivnik, Yosef Rotberg, Mordehai Haklai, Dubobis, Efraim Averbuch, Zev Stoliar, A. Malamud, Yaakov Zaltshendler, Efraim Poliakov, Toporov and others. Some of them participated actively in the establishment of settlements and the development of various institutions. There were some who came back. Until the end of 1900 there were about nine different Zionist groups in Bessarabia and one of them was in our Tarutino. On 25.11.1906 there was a gathering in Tarutino and the collection of funds for Jewish National Fund was started. Some of the attendees at this gathering were the tailors in the village. A week later there a meeting of the store owners and a discussion about a tax levy in favor of JNF.

The activities of Maccabi, founded in January 1918, are worthy of discussion. It was headed by Dr. Strechilevitch, followed by Mark Shalem. In the second decade of the century there were also sport groups, such as "Victory" and "Forward".

[Page 279]

In Tevet 1928, to commemorate the 10th anniversary of Maccabi, Zvi (Hersh) Altzofein donated 25 000 lei to Zionist institutions in the village (a report in "Our Time") . In the same newspaper, in the October 1923 edition, a list of JNF contributors was published. This was on the occasion of a Bris in the family of Yehoshua Leizerovitz: Israel Rosenberg (Yekutiel's son) and Michael Kovlanov (the teacher). In the Great Synagogue the following were the donors: Y.L. Baratz and David Schwartzman. In various editions of "Our Time" we found lists of donors to JNF at Bar Mitzvah celebrations and other occasions.

The Beitar activities are discussed in a special article by Eliezer Shulman.

Hashomer Hatzair in our village is described by Blumke Schwartzman-Glazer:

The founder of Hashomer Hatzair in Tarutino and its first counselor was, according to her, Zalman Yoeli (Sioma Shneirson). He now resides in Petach Tikva and was a member of the editorial board of Davar. He came to Tarutino in 1924 after he had established a Hashomer Hatzair group in nearby Romanovka. The leaders of the movement arrived from Kishinev. The members of the group used to meet in the evenings in the forest outside the village. They would sing songs from Eretz Israel, listen to lectures about pioneers and they dreamed of making Aliyah. The first to achieve this wish was Tema Gochberg-Nudelman. She was quite young at the time. She joined Hechalutz where she also met her beloved and together they made Aliyah. They live in Kibbutz Hephzibah. All the other members of the movement were jealous of her because she was able to achieve her dream. Other members of Hashomer Hatzair who first went to a preparatory kibbutz were Yehiel Averbuch and Yosef Kochuk. The preparatory kibbutz was in Kishinev, but there were others in Prauni and Bereni.

Blumke's older sister, Rachel, had studied in Odessa. She brought in a lively spirit when she came to Tarutino– the spirit of Eretz Israel being rebuilt. She recited poems by Bialik, sang songs from Eretz Israel and taught them to others. Blumke herself had attended a Hebrew Kindergarten (a rarity in those days) and she had continued in a Hebrew Day School. She was quite young when she was accepted at the Kishinev Teachers College. It was run by the well-known educator Alterman (father of poet Natan Alterman). The atmosphere at home was Zionist– as it was in many homes in the village. The emissaries from the various Zionist groups would lecture in the synagogues. After these enthusiastic speeches the listeners would donate money and women would hand over their jewelry.

There was also, in Tarutino, a Zionist Women's Organization. In one of the editions of "Our Time" there is an article about the Bazaar held by this group in the Maccabi Hall. We read in this article that at the opening of the bazaar, Mrs. M. Reznik emphasized the special importance of the participation of the women in the redemption of Eretz Israel. Others who spoke were B. Gurfel from JNF, Fanish on behalf of the school and I. Grogerman in the name of culture and the local high school.

Hashomer Hatzair group in 1923:

Seated in row 1 from left to right: **Bluma Schwartzman–Glazer, Pessia Reznik, Leah Averbuch, Ida Roichman, Yehiel Averbuch, Bina Poliakov, Aidel Reznik, Soibel Gochberg, Averbuch, Leah Harmoy, Ida Kogan, Ida Taraday, Shaindl Katz (Hemda Ben Israel), Gershon Lerner, Riva Arbeitman, Enta Lerner, Niusa Roichman, Beigeldrot, Tema Gochberg–Goldman, Hannah Otchkovskaya, unknown**

[Page 280]

In addition, the article continues, the secretary of the Women's Organization responded to the words of welcome and thanked the many guests who came to participate in this festive occasion. The honor of cutting the blue and white ribbon at the entrance to the hall was given to Mrs. Dina Grinberg for 800 lei. The total income from the bazaar was 10 000 lei. During this economic depression it was considered in Tarutino to be a large sum.

The Jewish Community and its Organization

Even before the Jewish community had organized itself there were some institutions in Tarutino that had been established independently: Mikvah, cemetery and synagogue. In 1910 there was also a hospital. When the community was organized (a separate article) a few more institutions were established: "Assistance to the Sick", "Fund for Poor brides", "Food for the Poor" and "Help for the Indigent". This fact shows solidarity of spirit and a mutual help atmosphere within the Jewish community of Tarutino.

There were four synagogues in Tarutino– the same as in Akkerman: the Polish, the Tailors', the Great and the Successful. There was also the same number of ritual slaughterers: Moshe Friedman, Yitzhak Rosenblatt, Falik Grinberg and Shlomo Malamud. Every synagogue had its own ritual slaughterer. Rabbi Bronstein prayed in the Great Synagogue.

After the 1917 Revolution when the Jewish Community was awarded certain rights by the Temporary Soviet Regime, there was great happiness. The Jewish Community was officially established. In 1917-1918 there was also a Jewish Self Defence group since in the upheaval after the revolution there was fear of attacks. At the same time a city council, with Russians Germans and Jews was founded.

When the Romanians came to the village in 1918 their first task was to disconnect everything from the previous Russian regime. There was even a prohibition against using Russian in the schools. The worst crime was Bolshevism.

Council of the Women of JNF in Tarutino

Seated in row 1 from left to right: **unknown, Clara Gochberg, unknown, Matya Reznik, Mania Kushnir, Ita Rosenblatt, Ita Brachot (Brochis)**
Standing in row 2: **Dorfman, Falik, Rosa Schwartzman(Retza), Frank, Goldstein, Krikun, Glickman, Yocheved Bronstein, Riva Shtilman, Freda Feisher, Batya Sternshus, Zilberman, Rotberg, Mussia Kushnir**

[Page 281]

When we scanned various editions of "Our Time" to find articles about Tarutino, we found, among others, that in May 1929 the Tarutino community donated 113 000 lei to the "Hunger Committee" while the Jews in nearby villages only gave 40 000 lei. In an edition from 1928 an article was published which speaks about the establishment of a Charitable Organization at the initiative of Yekutiel Rosenberg. The article, written by Haim Framan, discusses the attempt to found a new community along democratic lines.

The community institutions were helped tremendously by the women volunteers who often organized charity balls to benefit them. Quite often there was a selection of a beauty queen or a ball queen. These balls were held in a theater or movie house. Weddings were also held in these locations and lasted two days. This was especially true if one of the families was not local. On the evening following the official wedding there was a party called "After the Festivities".

It was customary for the bride to weep at the chuppa. If she could not do so on her own, others would make her cry at a ceremony called "Making the bride cry". Of course, the special entertainer took part in it. In Tarutino there was a special wedding orchestra. However, there was also another orchestra from out of town. It was directed by Haim the Blind One. He played the clarinet and was famous throughout southern Bessarabia for his expertise. Among the members of the local orchestra were Pinye Lainzon and Hisia Skolnik. The daughter of the donations collector in the village was married to the shoe polisher and the local women organized the wedding. It was a fancy wedding where the liquor was flowing and the orchestra was playing. There was no difference between this wedding and one of rich people.

A typical article about the Jewish community of Tarutino was published in the 18.5.29 edition of "Our Time":

"Recently there was a meeting in the Great Synagogue in order to elect two candidates for the Executive Committee of the community. The local rabbi spoke about the need to choose observant candidates who could defend the honor of the religion and the Torah. When he finished speaking he proposed two candidates. However, when he asked if someone objected to Mr. Shtilman (the wealthy man in the village) a riot broke out. Mr. Shtilman was present at the meeting and many people wanted the rabbi to do what is usually done. The rabbi was afraid that his candidates would not be chosen and he did not agree to elections where the candidate is not present. Some of his supporters understood the situation, but the rabbi stood his ground and found an original method of having his way. He asked those in favor of the candidates to stand on the one side of the hall, while those opposed would go to the other side. Is it any wonder that due to these tricks the rabbi's candidates were successful".

Kitchen for the Poor in Tarutino in 1923

Standing left to right: **Avraham Rotberg, Dr. Poliak, pharmacists Motniak and Kopilovitz, Mrs. Dorfman**

On the right: **Yonah Shafir, Markovsky, teacher Teperman, Hava Zaltshendler, Clara Gochberg, Manya Kushnir, Retza Schwartzman, Yonah Zukerman, Mrs. Kiner**

[Page 282]

Members of the Maccabi Orchestra in army uniforms on the occasion of Romanian Independence Day May 10, 1932

Economic activities

In Tarutino there were many factories and workshops. Among them should be mentioned the following: two metal casting plants, a paper factory, a beer distillery, two textile factories –one for dying and the other for finishing cloth, printing press, factories for the manufacture of oil and of soap. One street in the village was completely filled, on both sides, with stores selling cloth. The owners of these stores had worked in their youth at the large commercial establishment of Rosenberg, Breitburd, Reznik and others. This is where they learned their craft and opened their own businesses.

There was also a large business which exported feathers to Germany and its owners and workers were Jews. Also, there was a syndicate for the collection of wheat in the villages and its sale in the Danube ports. This syndicate was also handled by Jews only. The heads of the feather export business were Brachot (Bruches), Krikun, Shternsis, Schwartzman brothers, Leitman and Tcherkis. The wheat syndicate was run by Kiner, Shalem, Imas, Slimovitz, Berman and others.

In 1906 an office affiliated with the United Jewish Cooperative in Bessarabia was established. In 1925 a Loan Fund was founded with 285 members: 17 farmers, 57 craftsmen and 172 merchants. Except for a few farmers, everyone else was Jewish.

Commerce in the village was in the hands of Jews in the first decades of the 20th century. One store was owned by a Russian and another by a Hungarian. Every two weeks there was a fair and hundreds of farmers from the area would stream to it with their produce.

[Page 283]

Notes From A Legacy
by Dr. Yosef Laron z"l
Translated by Ala Gamulka

At the beginning of 1900 the general population of Tarutino was 6 000 residents. It seems one third was Jewish and two thirds German. The Jewish population had no civil rights and its members could not vote in local elections. They also were not permitted to own property. It was only after the 1917 revolution that the Jews obtained these rights. Until then there was no organized Jewish community, but there were some institutions that received some funds from the government. However, the government managed to take back these funds in the form of additional taxes levied on the Jewish population. After Akkerman, Tarutino was considered to be the most developed and progressive village in southern Bessarabia.

A river, called Hadgi Krak by the Turks, divided the village into two sections. There were 20 bridges across it. The bridges were mostly made of stone and a few made out of wood. Eventually, the residents of Tarutino renamed the river Tchikrak or Anchiokrak.

There were almost no observant Jews–with ear locks and traditional Hassidic garb– in the population. The Jews were concentrated in the center of the village. Their children played with German children and these, in turn, learned Yiddish. In the years 1910-1912 a change occurred and the religious position grew among the Jews. However, even the observant Jews were liberal and there was no religious jealousy in the village.

A big change came into the lives of the Jews, as mentioned above, after the 1917 revolution. The Zionist movement began to organize and many cultural institutions were established. There were a Hebrew elementary and High School where the language of instruction was Hebrew. Later it became Romanian. The Jewish Community grew at the same time.

Jews dealt in commerce and on Shabbat and Holidays the stores were closed. My grandfather was also a merchant. However, earlier he had been a sexton in a synagogue called "The Polish Shul". The name is a bit misleading since all the participants came mostly from Podolia, but they were nicknamed "Polish". I remember, when I was five the building burned down. A new Polish synagogue was built in its place. It had stained glass windows. The official opening of the new building was a big event in the village. The governor of Bessarabia arrived from Kishinev.

The majority of the Jews were members of the middle class, but there were some wealthier people. There were very few poor ones. Those who could afford to do so sent their children to study in Akkerman, Odessa and Kishinev. The German residents in the village also followed this practice.

Tarutino served as the cultural center for nearby small villages. In 1907 'Pirhei Zion' was founded. I was a Zionist at the age of 8. In my father's generation the following were active Zionists: Yekutiel Rosenberg, the owner of a grocery store and the treasurer of the Polish Shul; he was an educated man with an attractive appearance and an excellent speaker, as well as Rabbi Bronstein and Y.L. Baratz. My father was also active in Zionist circles and contributed much to the establishment of the cultural center and the library in the village.

[Page 284]

Zeirei Zion in Tarutino saying good-bye to Dr. Grebois (General Zionist)

Standing left to right: **Vinitsky, Pinhas Rosenberg, Nissan Imas, Avraham Sofer, Ozer Rotberg, and Mendel Gochberg**
Seated left to right: **Yeshayahu Friedman, Israel Rosenberg, Dr. Yitzhak Grebois, Mordehai Rosenblatt, Mordehai Haklai (Kuris)**

Our Zionist activities in the years 1900–1910 were mainly for the benefit of the Jewish National Fund and collecting of money for the Odessa Committee for the Establishment of settlements in Eretz Israel. I received my early Zionist upbringing in those gatherings organized by Yekutiel Rosenberg. When I grew up and completed my academic studies I, too, became one of the featured speakers in Zionist gatherings. After WWI I founded, in Tarutino, a branch of Zeirei Zion. It came as a result of my participation, as a delegate from Teleneshti, to the Zionist conference in Kishinev in 1919.

In 1911-1912 two important personalities arrived in Tarutino. These were Dr. Avraham Grabos and Dr. Eli Epstein. The former had studied law in Berne, Switzerland. During his studies there he established a Zionist organization called 'Friend'. He was an outstanding speaker and a talented organizer. He was also the first president of the Zionist Organization of Tarutino.

At the same time a bank was founded in Tarutino with the help of a wealthy Jew from Akkerman – Milstein. The bank was run by two Germans and the above mentioned Dr. Grabos. In 1919 Dr. Grabos went to Odessa intending to make Aliyah. However, he was stuck in Odessa where he ran the national bank. Later he became the head of a large national concern dealing in transportation.

Dr. Epstein was a medical doctor and ran the government hospital in Tarutino. He, too, was a Zionist and an excellent speaker. However, he did not have an extensive Jewish education. He was also the brother-in-law of Zeev Jabotinsky (married to his wife's sister).

In addition to the above it is important to mention several young and talented people who stood out in Tarutino: Nahum Sirota who was active in the Zionist Union and who eventually held an important position in it and Avraham (Bazia) Haham who was an active Revisionist and who later was part of the Hasmonaim movement in Bucharest. For a while we were both leaders of Zeirei Zion in our village.

Both of them made Aliyah and died in Israel.

[Page 285]

In 1905 there was a group of Jews who intended to immigrate to Argentina to join others who had established colonies of the Jewish Colonization Association of the Baron de Hirsch.

My father was one of the members of this group, but in the end the group dispersed and no one left the village.

The wealthiest Jew in the village was Shmuel Breitburd who owned a large textile business. He was observant and was well regarded by the members of the Jewish community. His family originated in Moldova, but he moved to Kishinev and from there he arrived in Tarutino. He was one of the few people who knew the Romanian language well. He led a life of a wealthy man and traveled in a cart with two horses. In his cellar there were old wines and he loved to entertain important people in his home. When the governor of Bessarabia came to the launching of the renovated synagogue he stayed at Breitburd's house. He also had an extensive collection of Jewish art. In 1910 my grandfather became a partner to Breitburd and they established a private bank. Breitburd's wife was observant and charitable. Under her influence and my father's, Breitburd decided, in his old age, to open an inn for Jews who came to Tarutino. One time, there was a Bris in our home and Breitburd donated an amount of 10 000 rubles. This was a large sum at the time. The money was intended for the founding of an elementary school and a high school. Next to the school building he built a Matzoth factory.

He died in 1917. A tent was erected over his grave and was decorated in marble and gold. This was a very special gravestone in the Tarutino cemetery.

Another donor who should be mentioned is Leib Shtilman. He was well educated and observant, but he wore European clothing. He had arrived in Tarutino from Kishinev, leased a flour mill and later bought it. Thanks to this mill there was always enough flour in the village during WWI. He also led the life of a wealthy man. He even had a car with a chauffeur.

Pioneers from Tarutino in Eretz Israel in 1921 with visiting Zionists from Tarutino

Standing left to right: **Israel Schwartzman, Yaakov Zaltshendler, Avraham Sofer, unknown, Mordehai Kochuk, Mordehai Haklai (Kuris), Schwartzman**

Seated in the middle row from left to right: **Yosef Rotberg with his young son Aaron (eventually Superintendent of Police, Aaron Sela), David Schwartzman, Yekutiel Rosenberg, unknown, Aaron Kuris**

Seated in first row from left to right: **Yosef Dubobis, Yitzhak Stromberg, Moshe Toporov, Zeev Stoliar, and Pivnik**

[Page 286]

After the 1917 revolution there was much social and Zionist activity in the Jewish community. Soon a few hundred Soviet soldiers were sent to Tarutino. They established a Council. Some Germans joined it as well as the author of this article. There was great fear among the Jews and no one knew what would happen next. The representatives of this Council also were part of the local municipal council and this caused more fear of the future. I organized a group of Jews called ESOB – Jewish Section for the Public Defence. It was a self–defence group that also trained with arms. We sent people to Bolgrod and they came back with 100 guns. However, in 1918, when the Romanians arrived, we gave up these guns. The task of the members of the unit was to guard the markets and entrances to the village so that the hooligans would not be allowed in. It must be mentioned that ESOB saved Tarutino from pogroms in the stormy days of winter 1917.

The Romanians behaved cruelly when they entered Tarutino. There were, in Tarutino, about 50 university students who studied in Russia. Among them was Fishman who was the secretary of the Zamir choir. He had a list of all participants in the choir. One night the Romanian police arrested Fishman and tortured him. They accused him of plotting against the new regime. Under duress Fishman admitted that the Zamir choir were a group of Bolsheviks. All members of the choir were arrested. Among them were: Avraham Lerner and Attorney Sperling– a socialist from Bendery who lived in our home and later became Principal of the Tarbut School. I, too, was arrested by the Romanians. They burned all my books.

When it comes to artistic activity in our village I can say that, as of 1910, there were drama groups. They presented 'MIrel Efros' and 'The Slaughter'. Residents of Tarutino also traveled to Odessa to see plays as well as to concerts by the singer Isa Kremer. There were amateur groups that put on literary trials and occasionally, Cantorial concerts (Kvartin, Blazer, etc.) In 1925 Maccabi was active in the village and it was headed by Dr. Strahilovich.

Jewish Education

Prior to 1917 there were, in Tarutino, a Heder and a Talmud Torah. The language of instruction in both was Yiddish. I remember two teachers from 1905. One had a white beard and was nicknamed Yankel Smetene (Sour cream). His family name was Rikenberg. The other was Kardman. He was better educated and his Heder operated like a school. I studied with him for half a year. There was also a teacher from Podolia who taught Tanach and also knew Russian.

[Page 287]

My father used to bring him daily to our house so he would teach the children Russian and Hebrew. In the years 1907–1909 there was a private school in Tarutino where Hebrew, Yiddish and Russian were taught. The school was founded by Zvi (Gersh) Zilberman. He also published novellas about Jewish life in Bessarabia. He was an active Zionist and an interesting personality. I remember two Hebrew teachers in this school. One was Krisman who was a Hebrew writer and had come to Tarutino in 1908. He had come from Eretz Israel where he had been an agricultural worker. He brought a Zionist spirit to our village. It is due to him that there was Zionist education in the village. I used to accompany him to Zionist gatherings. Another teacher was Alesker who had come to us from Galicia. He later immigrated to Argentina and eventually made Aliyah and settled in Jerusalem.

Other teachers in the school were: Lieberman, Kripitz and more.

In 1915 a Kindergarten was opened by the Silberstein sisters and a teacher by the name of Zilberleyev. My brother and sisters learned Hebrew in the Tarbut School. In 1919 I also taught in the school.

Pioneers leaving Tarutino for a preparatory Kibbutz

Standing from right to left: **a man from Bacau, Sonia Berman, Devorah Lainzon, Devorah Skolnik, Yehuda Bronfman, Leah Sverdlik, and Fira Melament**
Seated: **Hannah Ganegorsky, Leib Toporov, Golda Lainzon**

Members of Hashomer Hatzair in Tarutino in 1933–34

From left to right: **Bassya Finkelstein, Deutch, Treistman, and Leah Grinberg**

Row one: **Hannah Malamud, Sonia Friedman, Manya Berman, Haya Auerbach, Dolia Shulman, and Shura Frank**

Row two: **Riva Sirota, Rozalia Zuckerman, Vaskovnik, Vinitsky Rosenthal, Yocheved Bronstein, unknown, Baratz, Lota Sirota**

Row three: **Esther Leizerovitz, Rosa Zuckerman, Hinda Rostetcher, Hannah Arbeitman, Leah Lainzon, Perper, Tzirel Rotberg, Ethel Katz**

Standing from left to right: **Yaakov Schwartzman, Zuckerman, Yitzhak Rostetcher, Kalman Cooperman, Gersh Berger, Moshe Zaltshendler, Sioma Fisher, Boria Kochuk, Eli Hellman, Israel Leitman**

Last row: **Leib Schwartzman, Shuka Katz, Sioma Kogan, Iliusha Lerner, unknown, Velvel Dorfman, Haim Trachtman**

Students in Tarbut High School in Tarutino with teacher Lily Bronstein in 1933

Left to right: **Isia Brilliant, Nahman Shulman, Melech Shafir, Lily Bronstein. Fira Gnessin, Avraham Stoliar, Feiga Katz**

[Page 288]

From My Memories Of Tarutino
by Shmuel Rosenberg
Translated by Ala Gamulka

After the Napoleonic wars in Russia, as happened in many other settlements, the village of Anchiokrak renamed itself Tarutino. It was the name of a location where Napoleon had been defeated. The same custom occurred in Rezina, Borodino, Krasnaya, Kolm, Pereshemfunaz and others. Tarutino, located in the northwestern part of the Akkerman District, was surrounded on three sides by tall mountain ranges and on the east was the Kugilnik River.

In the last years before WWII the population consisted of 5500 Germans and about 2500 Jews. There were dozens of Russians who were mostly government employees. The majority of the Germans were farmers and some had large areas. The Jews were merchants and their ancestors had come from Poland, Lithuania and Old Russia. Until the advent of Hitler relations between Germans and Jews were cordial. It is important to note that the German residents in Tarutino had opposed the passage of the railroad through the village because they wanted to keep the rural atmosphere of the settlement. The railroad tracks were moved a distance of several kilometers from the village.

Tarutino was a commercial and industrial center for the entire area. There were plants for casting of metals, production of beer and paper, flour mills and textile dying. There were many businesses selling cloth, metal and small wares. There were banks, pharmacies, a hospital, mail and telephone service and two cinemas. In the educational field there were two high schools, one of them a Hebrew one–one of the first in the world. Prior to the establishment of the Hebrew High School there were two Heders. The Jewish community also founded a large public library. Four synagogues served the Jewish public– a third of the entire population. The Germans –the majority– had only one church.

One of the teachers in the Heder was Yankel Smetene (real name Rikenberg). One of his students was a German, Albert Bugner who eventually moved to Artsiz. His uncle, Rudolph Hirshkorn also studied in this Heder. Both continued their studies in the German High School together with Jewish youth. I was among them. During exams in Russian, Bugner would sit close to me. We had a special "code" so that he would know when to add "Yad". As was true for many of the German youth in Tarutino, he also knew Yiddish. When I was studying in Odessa he sent me a letter half in Russian and half in Yiddish. He wrote that his uncle, Rudolph had become a habitual drunk...

During WWII Rudolph served as a military doctor and arrived with Rommel to Africa. He was injured and was taken prisoner by the British. I was told that in the medical clinic a doctor from Eretz Israel came to look after him, but he pushed him away and said, in German:" I do not want to receive any help from a Jew..."

[Page 289]

During The Days Of The Holocaust
by Yehuda Bronfman
Translated by Ala Gamulka

June 28, 1940 was a bitter day for the Jews in our village and in all of Bessarabia. The Russians who came to "free" us managed in a few days to create upheaval in Tarutino. They closed the stores, confiscated possessions and turned most of the residents into unemployed and poor people. No one knew what to expect on the following day. People were exiled without any trial and for no reason. The first to go were Tzadok Gochberg, Israel Kochuk and Michael Katz. They were expelled by the Soviet Inquisition and no one knew what happened to them. There were several textile plants in Tarutino and workers came from Bucharest and other places. Their daily wage was 8 rubles. I met a family that lived near my house. The head of the family came to Tarutino from a small village and his wife was from the Gammer family in town. They had three children and needed to buy 2 kg of bread daily at a cost of five and a quarter rubles. The head of the family worked in a textile factory and I saw how he and his family suffered more and more each day. After three months of working in a factory under the Communist regime, the head of the family hanged himself at home. This is how terrible things were during the "redeeming and liberating" regime.

In June 1941, when the German–Soviet war broke out there was a general draft. I joined the army together with Israel Glickman. He was an outstanding accountant, but had a weak physique. We both served in various divisions of the Russian artillery. The regiment was camped on the border between Bessarabia and Romania on the banks of the Prut River–near the villages Liova-Kaul. Soon the order to retreat was given. We retreated at night and in the daytime we dug trenches. We also had to look after tall and fat horses. We had to put saddles on these tall horses which weighed 25 kg. It was not easy to do especially for Israel Glickman who was quite weak. Every time he tried to raise the saddle onto the horse he would fall. I ran to him many times to help him. In the end I was forbidden from doing so. Israel's sergeant was a cruel anti–Semite and he used to yell at Israel, in front of his superior: "Srulik, Kike Face. You are a s–t eater". In spite of the fact that we were in different divisions, I tried to visit him in the evenings. The last time I saw him he felt ill and complained that he had been badly beaten by the sergeant. On the next day I searched for him in various locations and I was unable to find him. When I asked the superior officer where Israel Glickman had disappeared, he replied curtly:"This is not the appropriate time to look for various Israels." All this happened even before the first shot was heard on our front and prior to our battle with the German army.

Nearly all the Jews of Tarutino escaped from the village before the Germans came. Only a few families were left and I only heard about their fate after I returned to Tarutino after the war.

Israel, son of Menahem, Melament–about 21 years old, a real hero– and Avraham, son of Eliezer, Leizerovitz were hung in the town square. Their bodies were only removed eight days later. The residents of the village and nearby areas were ordered to come to market to see how the Jews were punished.

Binyamin Sheinman and his family (wife and two sons) were slaughtered by shooting. In the family courtyard a similar fate awaited a couple of elders– Zalman and Elka Vineberg. They were neighbors of the Sheinman family who owned a diner in the village.

A most tragic end awaited the sisters Bricker, daughters of a businessman who sold newspapers. On the morning of the first day at 10 am the Germans brought the two miserable sisters to the town square. A large crowd was gathered. There were soldiers and a military band. The killers tore off their dresses and ordered the sisters to dance with their arms pointing upward. The commander had promised them that they would remain alive if they complied. They refused to obey. The sisters began to dance and the band played music. Those gathered laughed at them. They were elderly and they could not keep their arms up. The commander began to shout and the sisters understood what their fate would be. They stopped motionless and hugged each other. Helplessly they yelled "Shema Israel" and fell down–never to rise again.

[Page 90]

The ritual slaughterer Yitzhak Rosenblatt, his wife and their baby remained in Tarutino after the Russians left. (The oldest daughter was saved and lives in Israel today). The Nazi beasts came to their house and ordered them to go out into the yard. When they came out the SS officer forced the mother to give her baby to the soldiers. The mother refused to obey the order and held the baby closely. The commander ordered two soldiers the pull the baby from the mother's arms. The mother prostrated herself in front of the officer and begged him to kill her before they shoot the baby. The Nazi beast replied that they did intend to shoot the baby but to tear her in half and ordered the soldiers to do it. When the mother heard the command she fainted and was shot by the German soldiers. Yitzhak was watching these events and he screamed and fell on the ground. He was paralyzed and unable to move even though the soldiers tried to make him stand up. He fell again. The next command was for two soldiers to hold him up, put a rope around his neck and bring him to the slaughterhouse in the village. This is where animals were slaughtered. The fate of other Jewish families in our village was similar. Many died on the roads from hunger or other illnesses. Many young people were killed on the battlefield in the service of the Red Army.

When I arrived in Tarutino after the war I could not find the graves of my ancestors. I froze when I saw the condition of the cemetery. It had been completely destroyed. I was unable to find the graves, but I searched for the gravestones. I found some of them in the yards of some Christian residents. They were used to pave sidewalks and the letters were upside down. The new residents were not familiar to me. Most of them were Bulgarians who came from surrounding villages. I stopped in one of these yards and I said Kaddish in their memory. There was no sign of the four synagogues that had stood in Tarutino and the buildings were used for various purposes. It is difficult to believe that there is no sign of the lively Jewish life of the recent past.

I walked around the village imagining my wife and only son who were burned in the army fortress in Odessa. I was hearing my son's first words. We who remained alive are the only monument to our dear ones. Let us hope that we preserve the tradition left to us by our ancestors and the memory of our dear ones who perished.

It is important to note that some of the youth of Tarutino, born in the last generation, are now well-known scientists. Among them is Israel, son of Tzadok, Gochberg. He was a famous mathematician in the Soviet Union and now serves as a professor at Tel Aviv University. Another is Avraham, son of Aaron, Stoliar who is a Physics professor.

There are other scientists born in Tarutino who work at the Hebrew University and in the Soviet Union.

(Translated from Yiddish by Sh. Brilliant)

Another account of the terrible lot of the Jewish community in Tarutino is told by Dr. Eliahu Feldman in Pinkas Kehilot Romania:

"Several divisions of the Romanian army entered Tarutino. The majority of the Jewish population had not left with the retreating Soviet army. During the first days the Romanian soldiers and Christian residents went wild. They did not spare the lives and possessions of the Jews. After they stole their money and other valuables, the Romanian soldiers gathered the Jews in a large field. They were placed on benches brought in advance. They were told that they were being photographed for identity cards. However, instead of a camera there was machine gun covered with a black cloth – to pretend that it was a camera. This machine gun eliminated the Jews of Tarutino. The bodies were placed in a large trench near the road. Prior to that some men were selected to do forced labor- mainly to maintain the roads. There was a lot of rain at the time and the burial place of the Jews of Tarutino was uncovered and these men had to put earth all over the grave. These were their brethren. There are no other details about the fate of these people".

Shalom Kochuk speaks:

In September 1978 I visited Tarutino. There was nothing left of what was dear to us. The homes were gone and the businesses, workshops and factories had disappeared. Tarutino serves these days as the center for the Odessa District. Instead of the destroyed buildings new ones were erected by the cooperative. Near the Hebrew high school, still standing, there is a business called "Univermag". Shtilman's flour mill is also standing. As to the Polish synagogue, only the walls are still standing. Our High School building now serves as a district school and the German Sport Club is a cultural center. The power station built in 1938 is still standing.

[Page 291]

I went to the cemetery to search for my family, but you cannot even go in. On the road from Berezina one can see the broken stones as proof that it had been a Jewish cemetery. No Jews are left in the village. The local residents told me that the cemetery was razed by tractors. The entire village was destroyed by the Soviet army. They burned anything made of wood without paying attention to what it was. They tore out windows, doors, floors and roofs to use as firewood.

Ritual slaughterer Yitzhak Rosenblatt and his wife, z"l and their daughter Nusha who survived

[Page 292]

About Beitar In Tarutino
by Eliezer Shulman
Translated by Ala Gamulka

Tarutino stood out from other villages in southern Bessarabia by the fact that there were cordial relations between the Jewish and German residents. In my time there were only 320 Jewish families from among a population of 5 000 people. It must be said that on all levels the relations were friendly and mutually respectful between the Germans and the Jews. My best friends were German boys. I remember well that until 1939 even my father's good friends were German. There was much business between Germans and Jews based on a handshake without any written contracts. I was never afraid of the Germans and I wandered on my own in the fields without any fear. I was scared of "Grisha Rasputin" the Russian and perhaps a few other Russians in the village. It never occurred to me to fear the Germans.

It seems to me that we, the Jews, learned much from them–especially order and discipline. The Germans learned about human relations from the Jews. They themselves would say that their society did not achieve what the Jewish community was able to do. In my time the Jewish community was well organized and it was based on mutual assistance. An example: my father was a wealthy man and paid 10 000 lei annually for my tuition in High School while other students did not pay anything. They even received the official school uniform for free. This is only one example.

Another fact that differentiated Tarutino from other villages: there was not much poverty or unemployment. Everyone worked. All the crafts were handled by Jews: tailors, glass makers, tinsmiths, painters, electricians, hat makers, barbers, saddlers, etc. There were also Jewish taxi drivers and a shoe shiner.

In Kishinev I had the occasion to see Jewish poverty. I saw many Jews selling rags. We did not see this in Tarutino.

In my time there were no Heders in Tarutino–something typical of any Jewish shtetl. We had an elementary school (4 years) and a high school (continuation). However, the High School did not have government backing and anyone who wanted to matriculate had to be tested by a special committee. This committee consisted of teachers from Akkerman, Odessa or Kishinev. It was not an easy examination since those being tested were required to know more than the students in the government schools. There were some Jewish students in the German High School and, as far as I know, they did not suffer anti-Semitism. It was only in 1933 after Hitler was in power that Nazi theory arrived in Tarutino. Still, there were no physical attacks on Jews.

I became a member of Beitar in an "illegal" manner at the age of nine and a half. This is how it happened: My parents had a calendar on the wall published by "Our Time". Every page in the calendar was dedicated to a specific event in Jewish History or to a particular personality with biographical data and a picture added. I remember that when I was only five or six my father lifted me and showed me the picture of Yosef Trumpeldor in a Russian army uniform. He read to me the inscription: "Yosef Trumpeldor, born in Piatogorsk in 1880". These words are etched in my memory.

In the winter of 1933 I noticed that in Grisha Weismann's yard many young people would gather in the evenings in a rickety shack. My child's inquisitiveness was awakened and I came closer to the shack. I peeked through a hole and saw a picture on the wall which was well-known to me. It was the picture of Yosef Trumpeldor. I dared enter. When Grisha Weismann, one of the leaders of Beitar, asked me why I had entered I replied that I, too, wished to join these young people. Grisha asked how old I was and I replied: nine and a half. Grisha said– come in a half a year when you turn ten because that is the minimum age for membership. I was quite disappointed and I held on my life saver–Trumpeldor. I told Grisha: I know who the man in the picture is and I began to recite: "Yosef Trumpeldor, born in Piatogorsk in 1880"...

[Page 293]

Grisha was surprised with my knowledge and allowed me to join Beitar as an unofficial member. When I brought 10 lei to pay for my monthly membership they would not accept the money because I was not yet an official member in the movement.

Almost all the young people of Tarutino belonged to Beitar. Before that only Maccabi Union had existed. The latter dealt mainly in sports and even had a band which was the pride of Jewish Tarutino. Eventually the two groups merged and became one–Beitar. There had also been a Hashomer Hatzair branch, but when its members made Aliyah the group disintegrated.

The Beitar branch was well supported and by the Jewish residents. We can even say that it was not only the Jewish residents. I remember that on Lag Baomer 1933 there was a parade of all high school students to the hill out of town that we called "Mount Sinai". A Romanian officer with a troop of soldiers paraded through the gate of honor, decorated with a Hebrew banner. This was done to honor the organized Jewish youth. In Tarutino this was a real holiday and all Jewish stores were closed.

In the best times Beitar had 130 young people organized in different levels. There was a change in the attitude of the Jews towards Beitar after the murder of Arlozorov. I remember the day when my father was reading in "Our Time" an article about the murder. He immediately became angry and shouted at me: "You are not to step into their branch from now on. I forbid it!" Even mother said to Grisha Weismann at the time that her sons were no longer to attend Beitar. I was in shock, but my parents and others in Tarutino believed that if they read in "Our Time" that Revisionist hooligans killed Arlozorov, it must be so. This was the only Jewish newspaper in Bessarabia and everyone believed everything in it was true.

The movement suffered a temporary setback after this episode. In the elections to the Zionist Congress that year 158 from Tarutino voted for list No. 5– the Revisionist list. Only 56 people voted for the General Zionists. It seems the Jews soon saw that there was no truth to the accusation of murder.

I remember another episode from those days: I did some chores for my father and he paid me. I bought two shekels with that money and I gave them to my grandfather and grandmother to use to vote in the elections for Jewish Congress. My grandmother took the shekel and went to the election booth saying she wished to vote for list no.5. When she was asked "Number 5?" she replied "My grandson, Leyzer–Ber told me to do it". On the other hand, grandfather did not go to vote and when I asked him why, he replied: "Why? Did the Messiah arrive? One does not dance before the wedding". He meant that one should wait patiently for the Messiah as is written in our holy books.

The young people in Beitar were given a thorough upbringing. One could recognize a member of Beitar by his clothing and his gait. I was very careful with that. This Beitar education helped me in my years of exile in Kazakhstan and allowed me to overcome many difficulties. There were some Beitar members who forgot their upbringing when the Soviets entered. There were some cases of tattling. This breakdown happened to adults as well. "If the flame has fallen among the cedars–what will the wall moss say?"

I believe the Holocaust began not with the entrance of the Germans to Tarutino, but with the coming of the Bolsheviks. They immediately tried to destroy any signs of Judaism and Zionism. The Jews were afraid and we were cautioned not to have any Zionist activity as this could cause a pogrom. When the Soviet tanks entered, our leaders saw them as our saviors. Everyone ran to the Soviet soldiers, including the girls, and they threw flowers on them. There was a wealthy Jewish merchant who opened his store and invited the Soviet soldiers to take whatever they wanted without payment. My branch leader invited me to go greet the Soviet army. I could not accept the atmosphere in the village. I left and went to Bendery, about 80 kilometers from Tarutino. I then went to Kishinev, but I returned six weeks later.

I will never forget one episode. After my return a youngster from the village came to me and said:"Do you know? Our library is now in Weismann's barn". I went there and I broke out in tears when I saw it. It was probably the first time I cried because in Beitar I was taught to never cry. I remember the three books I saw among the others in the pile.

[Page 294]

These were: "The Heart" by De Amicis, Poems by Haim Nahman Bialik and "The Hunger" by Knute Hansen. I could not hold back my tears. This was a symbol and a warning for what awaited us in the future from the Soviet "Messiahs".

The saddest part of my life was the period of the Communist regime. I had no illusions about them. I wanted to run away with the Romanian army, but the chairman of the community, Dr. Pollack and the high school principal, Mr. Rosenthal, came to my house and convinced me to stay with my parents. We were to wait for an international committee which would make a list of all the residents who designated where they wished to go. Instead, a committee came to extract the Germans from Tarutino. The Jews had no saviors. In 1941 I was arrested and exiled. I did not even know what my punishment was exactly, but I knew what my "crime" had been. I was listed as a Fascist and there was no relief from that sin. Many others who had been arrested with me were freed, but I remained Kazakhstan for many years.

Eliezer Shulman offers his book "Stories in the Bible" to President Yitzhak Navon in 1941

[Page 295]

Personalities And Charcters In Tarutino
by Shmuel Brilliant
Translated by Ala Gamulka

Dr. Yosef Laron (Lerner) z"l

He was born in Tarutino in 1899. His father was Meir and his mother was Sarah, daughter of Avraham Acher. He studied in the local German high school and after graduation he continued his Hebrew and Judaic studies. His higher education was obtained in Odessa, Iasi and Bucharest. He completed his law degree in Bucharest and in 1924 he began an extensive public career as well as in journalism.

He was active in the Zionist movement from childhood and founded "Flowers of Zion" in Tarutino. In 1918 he was an active member of Zeirei Zion in Kishinev. He returned to Tarutino in 1920 and for a while taught in the Hebrew High School. He was one of the founders of the newspaper "Our Time" and had a regular column in it. For a certain period he was the secretary of the editorial board of the newspaper. He was an outstanding speaker and traveled on behalf of Keren Hayesod throughout Romania. In Iasi he established the Union of Zionist Students and was chosen as chairman of the first Students Conference in Bucharest in 1922. In 1923 he married Dr. Rosa Meirson from Beltz. That year he was also appointed secretary of the Jewish National Fund. He served in that capacity for seven years.

The ties of the family of Yosef Lerner to Tarutino begin in 1890. That year his two grandfathers arrived in Tarutino from Balta and Mariograd and settled there. They were both observant (his father's grandfather was a rabbi in Raigrod) and were well educated. Lerner's father was in textiles as well as the oil and wheat businesses. He was among the first Jews in Tarutino to develop industry in 1910. In 1941 he escaped to Russia with his wife. He was murdered together with her in Turkestan. His sister Hava, a teacher in Rostov, was also slaughtered together with her daughter.

Yosef Lerner was a leader in Zeirei Zion and united it with Poalei Zion. In the united movement he was on the executive committee. He was a candidate for Parliament in 1930 and 1934. He was also a candidate of the Zionist bloc to become vice president of the Jewish Community of Bucharest, vice-chairman of the central Eretz Israel office, a member of the Vaad Hapoel Hazioni (Zionist Workers Committee) and a delegate to many Zionist congresses.

He made Aliyah in 1938 and became a director of a group of insurance companies. When the State of Israel was declared he was appointed to be in charge of the Latin America department in the Economics section of the Jewish Agency. In 1951 he was on staff at the Israeli Consulate in Warsaw. In 1947-1950 he was a Zionist emissary in South America. Among his public assignments, those in the field of art must be especially noted: chairman of Friends of Betzalel and member of the Steering Committee of the Israel Museum. Y.L. published articles in various newspapers in Israel and outside it. He was also the correspondent of ITA in 1924-1931. He used to sign his articles with different names: Y. Lerner, Y. Lamdan, Y. Lamed, Y. Razin, Y. Schwartzman, and Y. Laron. He also wrote articles about insurance in American and British newspapers.

His main hobby was to collect paintings by Jewish artists. His collection was well known. There was an article by Yehuda Ha'ezrachi about it in the monthly Gazit. In his collection, among others, are paintings by Isserles (father and son, Chagall, Hirshenberg, Isidor, Kaufman, Kissling and others.

He died in Jerusalem in 1974 after a difficult illness.

[Page 296]

Mordehai Haklai (Kuris) z"l

He was born on Tu B'Shvat, 1900 in Tarutino and studied in Heder, high school and advanced courses in Economics in Odessa. He was the secretary of the Tarbut School and the Jewish Public Library. He was also active in Poalei Zion, chairman of Zeirei Zion in Tarutino, delegate to various Zionist councils in the area and also part of Keren Hayesod.

He left Tarutino in 1921 to make Aliyah, but he was detained for some time in Turkey. There he was the secretary of Former Residents of Russia in Turkey. He settled in Eretz Israel in 1921 and in 1923 he married Sarah Feldman. From the day he arrived in the country he saw himself- and was seen by others- as the patron of Former Tarutino residents in Eretz Israel. He helped many with his contacts when they searched for employment. He was one of the first residents of the Borochov community (now Givatayim) and was on the area council for 10 years. In 1928 he opened the first cooperative grocery store and took part in the founding committee of Hamashbir Latzarchan. For some time he served as the chairman of a section of bank employees in the Histadrut. M.H. filled many roles in the field of credit cooperatives and he also served as chairman of the National Institute of Accountants. His public positions were: member of the administrative committee of Kfar Haishuv in the Dan area, member of the committee collecting funds for volunteers, chairman of the national committee of Friends of the university in Givatayim, and chairman of the national council of the Fund for Soldiers. In the fifties he also was chairman of Former Resident of Bessarabia and was instrumental in establishing Kiryat Israel, the area for Bessarabian newcomers.

He died on 15 Tammuz 1958

Public Servants and Other Active Members of the Jewish Community
Translated by Ala Gamulka

The public servants and other active members of the Jewish community in Tarutino are worthy of an extensive discussion on their devoted work. They can serve as examples to public servants of our day. It is also essential that their descendants should know about them and their devotion. Unfortunately there is no one who followed their activities and could write about them. Following are just a few details about some of them who worked loyally for the common good and did their best for the Jewish community in Tarutino.

Yehuda Leib Baratz

It is supposed that his family arrived in Tarutino from Lithuania. He stood out in his public service as a central figure in the Jewish community and as a Zionist leader. For a while he ran a Heder and was himself a teacher and educator. He later had a notions store. He was one of the first members of Hovevei Zion in Tarutino. A postcard he sent to Hovevei Zion in Warsaw in the name of the local branch is copied in this book. In it he writes about the development of the organization in Tarutino. He was an educated man and an enthusiastic speaker with great influence on local youth. In a Tarbut conference in Kishinev in September 1922 he brought greetings from the local branch in Tarutino. He was also chosen as a member of the Executive. It can be said that his influence was evident in all aspects of public life in the village.

M. Sperling

He was the Principal of the Hebrew High School as of 1926, but after a few years he practiced law in Tarutino. He was well regarded by the community and among his colleagues, Jews and Germans alike. When he appeared in court his words were clear and well thought out and very few people would disagree with him. It is important to add that he never accepted a case that had any shady real estate dealings. He was honest and was appreciated by everyone.

Golda and Aaron Schwartzman

Aaron came from a traditional family and continued in the ways of his ancestors. He was a merchant and also served as the Gabbai of the Great Synagogue. He was killed on Yom Kippur by bombs from German aircraft. He was escaping from the Nazi murderers. His wife, Golda, was involved in public life. She was president of a Women's organization called "Women's Auxiliary". She was also active in Help for the Sick and Help for Poor Brides. Secretly, she helped those who were needy and families that had lost their possessions. She was a beautiful person who collected and wrote down lyrics to Jewish folk songs. She often hummed Goldfaden songs that were performed on stage. She died young.

[Page 297]

Yekutiel Rosenberg

He was an educated Jew, tall and bearded. He was an active Zionist, a community leader and a talented speaker. He served as a Gabbai of the Polish Shul and made sure the cantor would pronounce Hebrew words properly. He was a talented organizer and always invited speakers and lecturers to his synagogue. In 1922 he visited Eretz Israel with a group of Zionist delegates from Tarutino. He met the pioneers from his hometown. In the Beth David Museum in Tel Aviv there is an exhibit of an exchange of letters between him and the famous Zionist leader of the Jews of Bessarabia, Y. Bernstein-Cohen as well as Sh. Bendersky.

Rabbi Bronstein

He served as the rabbi of Tarutino in the years 1910-1940. In addition to his deep knowledge of rabbinic lore he also knew Russian and was an educated man. He was an enthusiastic Zionist and he organized observant Jews inside the Zionist movement. He was the first and main speaker at every gathering in the village. His daughter Yocheved was a science teacher in the high school. He influenced Tarutino Jews to not be swept into ultra-Orthodoxy, to wear European clothes and not the long coats.

Avraham Rotberg

He was an educated man and was one of the founders of the Hebrew High School. He was active in the Savings and Loan Fund and national funds. He was a member of the municipal committee and wrote all his letters in Hebrew. His brother, Yosef, was one of the founders of the Borochov District and one of the first pioneers from Tarutino to have made Aliyah in 1920. His two sons and their families live in the State. His youngest daughter died here.

The two sons of Yosef Rotberg were: Aaron Sela, z"l who was the General Commander of the Police and Colonel Haim Sela, z"l who died in the Peace to the Galil War together with Major Yekutiel Adam.

Levi Fanish

He arrived in Tarutino in 1919. He had graduated from Herzliah High School in Tel Aviv, Third graduating class. For various reasons he ended up in Tarutino where he married Paula, daughter of M. Goldenberg. He was the principal of the Hebrew High School. He was totally devoted to national Hebrew education and many Tarutino natives who are now in Israel still praise him.

The beginning of our national education came from him. He was a fanatic about the Hebrew language and only spoke Hebrew with his students. If a student forgot his knowledge of Hebrew, Fanish would refuse to speak any other language. We remember in particular our outings with him on Lag Baomer to "Mount Sinai" outside of the village as well as the discipline he instilled in the school. In the mornings, before classes began, all the students would gather at the entrance to pray "Modeh Ani". They then marched to class to the tune of "You are our homeland".

Nahum Sirota

He was active in all Zionist, community and cultural institutions in Tarutino. He was among the founders of the Hebrew High School and also its treasurer throughout its existence. He was born in Tarutino in 1886. His house was open to all Zionist emissaries who would stay with him. It must be noted that he organized an amateur band in Tarutino. They played, voluntarily, for charity events as well as at weddings of poor people. He was active in the Revisionist party. He made Aliyah in 1972 and he died.

[Page 298]

Eliezer Shulman,
The Bible Researcher From Siberia
Translated by Ala Gamulka

Eliezer Shulman, whose article is published above, was a special personality. He brought good publicity and honor to the Jewish community of Tarutino. He was liberated from Soviet exile in 1974 after dozens of years and arrived in Czernowitz with his wife. He was an expert in railroads and iron tracks and served the Soviets in this capacity in the Gulag. At the same time, all during his exile, he continued to do research on the Bible.

When the Shulmans applied to make Aliyah he was immediately fired from his job. His wife, a doctor, was sent to work as a porter. After Shulman sent a letter to Israel describing the attitude of the Soviets towards his wife, they were both given permission to leave.

When Shulman arrived in Israel he was welcomed enthusiastically by the President. He was interviewed by various newspapers and soon his research was published. He had dedicated much time and effort to the research while he was in exile.

In "Maariv" of 26.08.1981 there is an article by Yaakov Ha'elion titled "The Bible Researcher from Siberia". Here are some quotes from it:

Recently the Defence Ministry published his research thesis entitled "Order of the Chronicles in the Pentateuch". It is an outstanding book that was born in the Gulag where God is a disreputable name that does not exist. He was determined to personally teach the Bible to his daughters.

One of his daughters asked: did Noah, who was saved by being in the ark, abandon his father and grandfather? This is a moral question that requires a clear answer. This question pulled him to do his research on the Bible. His tools were a deep personal knowledge, a pocket calculator, Tanach volumes and commentaries he obtained in secret in the permanent snow fields. He eventually was able to tell his daughter that Noah did not abandon his elders, but that they had died before the flood. During his research he found more amazing facts such as that Abraham was able to see his grandsons Jacob and Esau since he lived an additional 15 years after their birth.

His work also includes an exact family tree of all figures in the Torah. An interesting fact is that although the State of Israel was declared in 1948, this was also the year BCE when God gave Abraham Canaan. There were many special details that he found, but he was most proud of the table called "Declaring the Covenant on the Land". In it he quotes specific times when God promised Avraham Isaac and Jacob the rights to Eretz Israel.

Naomi Shemer has always been aware of Shulman. She knows that in Siberia he "worked" on the song "Four Brothers" and made them to be four brothers in the Soviet Union. He showed her his research and she wrote: "This is a document with depth, clear thinking and strong diligence". Rabbis read his work and are amazed by it. The chief Rabbi of the Air Force is charmed by the "personal dedication and perseverance needed to complete this holy work". Issar Frenkel, chief Rabbi of Tel Aviv describes the research as "giant work". The President of Israel, Yitzhak Navon, encouraged him to publish his work and said it was "miraculous". Everyone saw this work as something that could open eyes and was easy to digest because he simplified details.

Eliezer Shulman– the immigrant who was quickly absorbed in the country two weeks after his arrival – feels like a complete Israeli citizen.

[Page 299]

No.197.The High School in Tarutino, Grades A and B, 1927

In the center, from right to left: teachers

Bronstein, Unknown, Principal Gedalya Rosenthal, Yeshayahu Vinitsky, Unknown

Female students of Tarbut High School in Tarutyno with their teacher Mikhael Kovlenov (1922)

Student Khemda Ben Israel (Sheindl Katz) describes teacher Kovlenov as "a nice man, but quick to get angry and considered mean. After four years with us it was difficult to say goodbye. Only then did we discover his goodness. He was tearful. We used to call him Kovlenchik or Mishika."

Standing: R. to L. **Feiga Shchiglova, Khaya Umansky, Riva Shtilman, Khedva Ben Israel(Sheindl Katz), Niusia Reikhman**
Seated: R.to L. **Lisa Kharmoy, unidentified, teacher Kovlenov, Feiga Grinberg, Bina Poliakov**
Front row: R. To L. **Ita Taraday, Bliuma Shvartzman, Tema Gokhberg**

[Page 300]

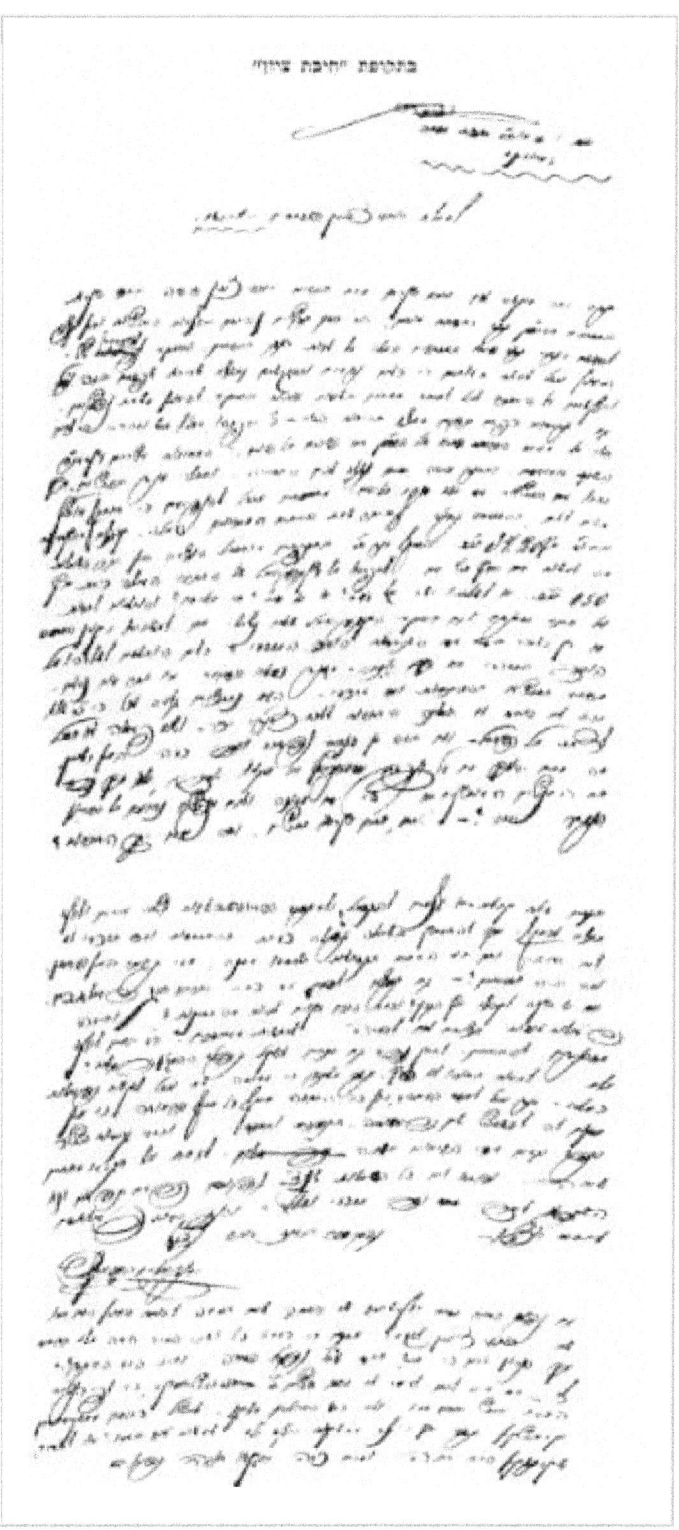

During the Hibat Zion Era:
A letter from Hovevei Zion of Tarutino to Hovevei Zion in Warsaw

[Page 301]

Delegates to Hashomer Hatzair conference in Kishinev in 1925

From right to left: **David Tabachnik, Bluma Schwartzman, Yosef Kochuk, Niusa Roichman, Hemda Ben Israel (Shaindl Katz)**

Delegates to Hashomer Hatzair conference in Kishinev in 1925

[Page 302]

Students in the Tarbut High School in Tarutino with their teachers and the principal Gedalya Rosenthal

Male and female students of the elementary Hebrew school in Tarutino with the teachers and Principal Levi Fanish in 1930

[Page 303]

First Grade of the Tarbut High School in Tarutino in 1926

Row 1 standing from left to right: **Shimon Levitt, Eli Elman, Moshe Schwartz, Israel Leitman, Yitzhak Rostetcher, Moshe Zaltshendler, and Yaakov Schwartzman**

Middle row from left to right: **Kalman Cooperman, Leibl Schwartzman, Sioma Kogan, Haim Trachtman, Ilusha Lerner, Leah Lainzon, Etel Katz, M. Baratz**

Seated bottom row from left to right: **Hannah Malamud, Rozalia Zuckerman, Leah Averbuch, Raizel Schwartz, teacher Voskovoinik, Sioma Feisher, Sonia Friedman, Dolia Shulman, Nehama Zaltshendler, Rosa Zuckerman, Deutch, Haya Averbuch**

Female and male students in Second Grade of the Tarbut High School in Tarutino in 1931

Seated from left to right in row 1: **Avraham Stoliar, Moshe Bronfman, Gedalya Schwartzman**

Row 2 seated from left to right: **Ida Brilliant, Fira Gnessin, teacher Volkovitz, Hannah Kanner, and Rosa Kanner**

Standing: **Nahman Shulman, Feiga Katz**

[Page 304]

Dedication of first homes in Kiryat Israel (1951/2)
L. to R. : **Mordekhai Khakla'i, Rabbi Maimon(Fishman) - Minister of Religious Affairs, author Shlomo Hillels and his wife**

[Page 307]

Artsyz

(Artsyz, Ukraine)
45°59' 29°25'
by Shmuel (Milya) Gurfil
Translated by Yocheved Klausner

Artsyz was half village half small town, its geographical location in the Akkerman district, southern Bessarabia, at a distance of 6–7 hours travel by train from the big and famous city – Kishinev. The traveler from Kishinev to Artsyz would change trains at the Bassarabyeska station and after two hours of travel would reach Artsyz. The beautiful train station was encircled by a wooden fence. Carriage owners would usually be stationed nearby, waiting for passengers, most of them Jews. Some 500–600 meters from the station was the main street of Artsyz, several kilometers long.

The Artsyz streets did not have names nor were the houses numbered. These were not needed: here everybody knew everybody.

The trip in a carriage through the streets of Artsyz was no great pleasure: the swinging and swaying of the carriage could cause pain through the entire body. In the summer a cloud of dust would follow the wheels of the carriage, in the winter black mud would be scattered by the wheels and the horses – not the type of "gallant" horses...

Whoever happened to come to Artsyz could gather, from the carriage owners, all the local news. They were an unlimited source of jokes and sayings as well. They knew, at first glance, where to drop every passenger. And if they spotted that you were not one of the local people, they would take you straight to one of the two inns in Artsyz, where there would always be room for a passing guest [the latter would, obviously, not expect to find there any modern luxury, as in our time today...].

Two widows were the owners of the two inns. One was Mrs. Schwarzman, whose apartment was situated in Zev Yankelewitz's courtyard, the other was Mrs. Sara Altstein, in the courtyard of Reuven Fischman.

Livelihood and Survival

The population of Artsyz was mainly German Christian Protestants. There were about 250 Jewish families in town, and the relations between the two minorities – Jews and Germans – were correct. The Jews erected in town a commercial center with houses built of stone as well as barracks, and one could obtain anything in the various shops – including agricultural machines, porcelain dishes etc. On Tuesdays, which was market day in Artsyz, the Jews would buy vegetables, fruits and fish for Shabat. Since refrigerators did not exist in Artsyz, they kept the food in the cellar situated in the courtyard of the house. In the cellar one could find barrels of pickled cucumbers, tomatoes and watermelons, as well as wine.

Artsyz was the home of many Jewish craftsmen of all kinds: cobblers, harness makers, tailors, furriers, hatters, soda-water bottlers, etc.

The town had two coffee-houses, which also served as domino and backgammon playing places, as well as meeting places of the grain traders, or plain idlers.

In the neighborhood of Artsyz there were villages of Germans, Russians, Ukrainians, Bulgarians and Moldavians. The Artsyz merchants would buy from them eggs, poultry and grains and sell them in the big cities. The greatest eggs-trader was Asher Reznik, a warm-hearted Jew, active in public affairs and a great Zionist (lives today in Netania). The length of the main street was lined by pubs and taverns, mostly owned by Jews, but the customers were local or neighborhood Christians. Many Jews also liked the taste of alcohol, especially the wagon and carriage owners. During cold and snowy winter days, they usually could not afford to buy a drink or food to wash down the drink, so they kept in their pocket a piece of herring and after each sip they would take it out and lick it, then put it back into the pocket, to keep for the next "round." No need to mention that the piece of herring was not wrapped hygienically. The Artsyz wagon owners did not pay much attention to hygienic stuff...

[Page 308]

In the morning, at sunrise, Artsyz resounded with the noise of the whiplashes of the cattle shepherd. This was the signal for the cattle owners, most of them Germans, that it was time for the morning–milking and for taking out the cattle to pasture. In the late afternoon the shepherd would return the cattle to the owners, raising a cloud of dust through the entire town.

In the center of Artsyz, opposite the commercial quarter, stood a German Protestant church built in 1880, with a huge bell in its tower. A cemetery was situated in the backyard of the church, mainly for the rich and privileged. Flowerbeds, cared for by a special gardener, decorated the front of the church. A sidewalk paved with concrete, near the church, served the Jewish youths as well as the others. A tall pole carried on top a lighting installation called "Petromax." It was filled with gas or petrol and lit, and it spread its light around. Here young couples took their "walks," ate sunflower and pumpkin seeds and talked over the politics of the day. At night it was pitch–dark, since electricity had not yet reached Artsyz in those days, and only the barking of the dogs could be heard in the stillness of the night.

On Education and Charity

Artsyz had a big and beautiful synagogue that fulfilled the religious needs of the 250 Jewish families. It had a beautiful Holy Ark of the Torah and, of course, a Women's Section. On weekdays and regular Sabbath Days, the cantor was usually the Artsyz Rabbi, R'Yeshayahu Mendel Geiser z"l or the Shochet [slaughterer] R'Leizer Kolomiski z"l, and during Holidays they invited a special cantor, mostly it was the local cantor R'Avigdor Polonski, who also owned a grocery shop. The *shamash* [attendant] of the synagogue was R'Idel z"l and after he died the position was "inherited" by his son–in–law R'Michael Kaganowitz z"l, who was a cobbler. At a distance of about 700–800 meters from the synagogue, was the slaughterhouse for cattle and near the synagogue a smaller place for slaughtering chicken and geese.

In our town we had an eight–grade *Tarbut* Hebrew school and a Hebrew kindergarten. All community institutions were centered near the river. A building that was in the past a flour mill and was almost destroyed by fire, was renovated and enlarged, and became the school. Mrs. Mosia Chananovna Bilostotzki z"l, the wife of the local doctor, served for years as the principal of the school. Most Jewish children went to the Tarbut school, and only a small number of parents, who did not come to an agreement with the community concerning tuition, sent their children to the government school, where most of the pupils were Germans. The Hebrew School was under the supervision of the Community council.

[Page 309]

In Artsyz we had institutions, or rather public charity committees, of help for the poor, visiting the sick, help for poor brides, burial society [*Hevra Kadisha*] and others. The Artsyz Jews excelled in their work and donations for the National Funds (JNF and *Keren Hayesod*). Many were those who performed the commandment of *Matan Baseter* [giving secretly], the most outstanding being R'Avraham Gurfil. He never argued about the sum of money he was required to give. He would ask only: how much?

In the area of cultural–artistic activity we should mention the association of members and supporters of the Theater, and the Wind–Instruments Orchestra under the direction of Shika Aharonowitz z"l, who became famous as a conductor not only in Artsyz, but as conductor of orchestras in the capital Bucharest. After Bessarabia became part of the Soviet Union, he directed the official Orchestra of the Moldavian Republic.

The Community organized special dinners for various charity enterprises, in particular during the holidays of Chanuka and Purim. The women would bring cakes and other delicacies that were sold at the party. It is worth mentioning that all local Jews responded gladly to these charity drives. The local orchestra helped, by playing for the pleasure of the guests. I remember that the director of the orchestra, Chaim Schwartzman z"l played the trumpet, Efraim Braverman z"l the violin, Moshe Kleitman the saxophone, Shmuel Gurfil the accordion, Shmuel Ben-Chaim Bodyeski the guitar, Freink Shmuel the mandolin, Syoma Korol the drums, Chaim Frank the violin, and there were others, whose names I could not remember.

The students of the Hebrew school Tarbut with the teachers and Parents Committee

There were three Jewish doctors in town: Dr. Bilostotzki, Dr. Gordon and Dr. Korol, and two pharmacies – one owned by Yasha Gamoshewitz and the other by Pasternak. There were also two dentists (Mrs. Notov and Mr. Averbuch), and we shall not forget our devoted midwife Mrs. Sochmalinova. She was Christian, of a noble family. When the Bolshevik revolution broke out she fled from Russia and settled in our town. She had Jewish friends and spoke well Yiddish. The postmaster of the town, a German by the name of Schmidtka, spoke fluent Yiddish as well. This was no wonder, since he came in constant contact with Jews.

R'Chaim Freink served as president of the community until World War Two, and his deputy was Asher Reznik. The chairman of JNF was R'Yosef Yankelewitz z"l, the chairman of "help for the poor" was R'Avraham Gurfil z"l. The religious institutions in town were represented, beside the rabbi and the shochet by R'Mordechai Beider z"l, Mordechai Braverman, Hillel Apelboim, Goldinger, Pevzner, Yitzhak Averbuch, Shimshon Zhabgoreski and others.

The First *Halutzim* [Pioneers]

One night in June or July 1941, at midnight, the authorities assembled all Jewish leaders in Artsyz and send them to concentration camps in Central Asia. Most of them died there of hunger and diseases.

Teachers and pupils of the Hebrew School

[Page 310]

The Zionist youth movements in Artsyz were: *Gordonia, Hashomer Hatza'ir* and *BEITAR*. There was also the "chaliastra" (a nickname given to communists and leftists). As a former "commander" of the local BEITAR branch, I can tell that we were helped by the BEITAR branch in Sarate, in particular by Zvi Schechter and Yechezkel Altman. We kept also close contact with the town Starbonar.

The first *Halutzim* from our town made Aliya in 1924–1925: Israel Beider, Mordechai Bodyeski and Zvi Tzirolnik – may their memories be blessed, and Chaim Lerner, may he long live. Some of them returned after a short time. The last to make (illegal) Aliya, on the ship "Astor" on Passover 1939, were: Menachem Mendel Kaganowitz (lives in Ashkelon) and Yosef Gurfil (now in Dimona). After WWII, some of the "chaliastra" members also managed to come to the country. It is worth mentioning that Professor Yehuda Pevzner z"l, an expert on heart surgery at the Belinson and Tel Hashomer hospitals, was a native of our town. One can find former residents of Artsyz on the Kibbutzim, in agricultural villages and other various localities in the country.

Artsyz was a small Jewish town, but it was dynamic, lively and very Zionist. The Russian occupation brought an end to the Jewish life and activity in Artsyz. It ended and continued no more. Only the memories of those days remained, and they are bringing light to our lives to this day. May these pages be a memorial–candle for the Jews of Artsyz and their life, for our parents and parents' parents, who have planted in us the prized values that have brought us to this point.

Grades 1 and 3 of the school, with the teacher I.A. Vinitzki

[Page 311]

Artsyz my Town

by Arie Kleitman

Translated by Yocheved Klausner

Our town was a small town. According to the census conducted by the Russian authorities in 1897, its population numbered 1728 residents, 337 of them Jews – 18.4%. In 1930, the Romanians, then the rulers of the region, held a general census and this time the number of residents was 2951, 842 of them Jews, which was 28.5% of the population. The Christian population was not homogeneous: the majority – 60 percent – were Germans, and the rest Bulgarians, Romanians etc.

Most of the Germans, who were brought by the Russians at the beginning of the 19th century, were farmers, and the Jews, as was the situation in other Bessarabia towns, were engaged mostly in commerce and craftsmanship. The local soil was rich, but its cultivation was quite primitive. Yet, in a good year the soil yielded some 200 pood [unit of weight] grains to the hectare. Vegetables and fruits were abundant. Once a week, on Tuesday, was "market day" and the peasants from the region came to Artsyz, sold their crops and bought all their necessities, from needle–and–thread to cattle. The Jews were a very important factor on these market days, as well as among the grain traders, who were called "Cerealists."

The town had two elementary schools, of 7 grades each. One was Romanian and was free of tuition; the other was a Hebrew school of the *Tarbut* chain, where tuition was paid. It can be said, that this school was the glory and pride of Artsyz. The mere fact that such a small Jewish community could maintain a Hebrew school was undoubtedly a great achievement, enabled by the devotion of the parents and the Zionists in town and thanks to the principal of the school, Mrs. Misia Chananovna Bilostotzkaia. D. Vinitzki, in his book "Jewish Bessarabia" provides numbers about the school in the 1930–1931 school year: the kindergarten employed one kindergarten teacher for 11 children and its yearly budget was 29.000 Lei, and the school employed 4 teachers in 6 grades, with 95 pupils. The yearly budget of the school was 328.000 Lei. In D. Vinitzki's words: "Two small towns served as an example for others, in their organization and readiness to carry the school budget and pay the teachers a good salary, in spite of the small number of students: Artsyz in the Akkerman district and Rany in the Ismail district. Artsyz, of 170 Jewish families, kept for many years a kindergarten and a seven–grade elementary school, only thanks to the few well-to-do parents (the Yankelewitz, Freink and other families), who were ready to pay a double and triple sum as tuition, compared to the other towns."

Lag Ba'omer festivities of the Hebrew School in Artsyz, grades 1 to 7, with the teachers and the principal Mrs. Belstotzki (in the center). The year 1935.

[Page 312]

The community imposed an obligatory tax for the support of the school; the tax applied, as well, to the parents who sent their children to the Romanian school. On the other hand, the principal of the school filled not only her own job: she was at the same time secretary, accountant, etc. of the school; all this, in addition to teaching (mathematics and geography) and doing the regular principal's work. In her devotion to the school and her diligence she was an example for all.

When the children finished the local school they usually continued their study at the Magen David School in Kishinev, or in other places. Some of them became famous; among them it is worth mentioning Professor Yehuda Pausner, a famous heart surgeon in the Beilinson and Tel Hashomer hospitals, who had been a pupil of the school in our little town. Also the composer and conductor Shika Aharonowitz, who is now in the USSR, was one of the pupils of the school. I would like to mention one of the excellent teachers at the school, Weissman, who lives now in Israel. He came to us from Kishinev and soon gained fame as an outstanding teacher and educator; he won the hearts of his students and paid great attention to each and every one of them. His lessons were fascinating, no wonder that none of his students failed at exams. He knew how to arouse interest in any subject that he taught.

The Jewish Community

The Jewish community in Artsyz was considered one of the best organized communities in Bessarabia – and rightly so. It left its impression in all areas of Jewish life. The only synagogue in town, which was supported by the community, was comfortable and large enough to accommodate all, except during the High Holidays, when it was necessary to organize prayers in some of the private houses. The prayers were led by the Rabbi R'Yeshayahu–Mendel Geiser or by the *shochet* [slaughterer] R'Leizer Kolomyeski, both well–versed in all matters of religious ceremony. For the Holidays the community hired the cantor Avigdor Polonski, who was blessed with a pleasant tenor voice, and he would lead the prayers. In the thirties, his young son joied him, and the congregation enjoyed them both. To this day, my ears resound with the beautiful prayers of the cantor and his son, every person in the room following every sound. Although the fee requested by this cantor was higher than usual, the Artsyz congregation preferred his services.

It should be stressed, that the community never forgot the needy in its midst, and the council organized "progressive taxes" – the rich being asked to pay a higher tax. Among those who helped the poor in many ways, especially by "giving secretly" [*matan baseter*] we shall mention in particular R'Avraham Gurfil z"l.

Whenever he heard about a family in need he hurried and sent his people to help them, on the explicit condition that they do not divulge the source of help. I can testify on that – since I served as R'Avraham Gurfil's "good messenger" [*Sheliach mitzvah*] to a family whose daughter was about to get married and they did not have the means to organize the wedding. I brought to this family 5,000 Lei, which was considered a large sum at the time, without revealing to the family who their saving angel was. R'Avraham did not make any distinction between Jew and Christian, and in many cases he helped Christians as well. During the Soviet occupation, when the NKVD arrested him and his family as "capitalists" many Christians went to the commander asking to release them. "He gave his money to the aid of the poor" – the Christians pleaded – but it did not help. He and his family were sent to Siberia, and his wife died in the Siberia steppes.

The Artsyz community participated in the general activity of the Bessarabian Jewish communities. In A. Feldman's book, mentioned above, we read that delegates from the Artsyz Jewish community participated in the Conference of Jewish Communities in Romania, held in Bucharest in 1930, in a regional conference of Southern Bessarabia communities held in Romanovka in 1935 (whose main topic on the agenda was finding the means to overcome the heavy hunger in the region following years of drought) and other conventions. In the first Bessarabia Economical Conference, held in Kishinev on 3 December 1935, the Artsyz delegates were I. Schusterman and I. Hellman. In the second convention of the communities, which took place in 1936, one of the Artsyz delegates, I. Schusterman, was elected to the Council.

The Zionist Activity

The first immigrants to Eretz Israel from Artsyz made Aliya in the early twenties, after the First World War. However, part of them returned since the difficult economic conditions in the Land have not enabled them to become part of the Eretz Israel settlement. Among the first to make Aliya were: Shlomo Abramowitz, Yosef Brener, Berl Portnoy and others. In the early thirties a new Zionist wave began, with the organization of the youth movements: *Hashomer Hatza'ir*, *Gordonia* and *Brit Trumpeldor*. Many of the youth movements' members went to a "training camp" on a farm in Ambrovka, 35 Km. from Artsyz, and when their training was completed they received "certificates" and made Aliya. Obviously, the youth movements have not grown on barren soil; they were the result of the Zionist atmosphere in town and the Zionist activity of the adults. In the Encyclopedia of the Bessarabia Jews we read that already in 1899 a delegate (or delegates) of the Artsyz Zionists participated in the Regional Zionist Convention in Kishinev, as well as in the regional Zionist Conventions in Bender and Akkerman. From the twenties of the 20th century we have more detailed knowledge about Zionist activity: we know, for example, about the sale of shares of *Bank Hapo'alim* by a messenger of the *Tze'irei Zion* Center, in 1922. David Ravelski, while fulfilling this mission, visited Artsyz as well. In general, Artsyz was active in the contribution to the various Zionist funds. For example, in 1928, a year of drought in Bessarabia, Artsyz donated to JNF 40,316 Lei and to *Keren Hayesod* 88,750 Lei. In 1939, when anti–Semitic activity in Romania increased, the Artsyz Jews contributed to the National Funds 178,028 Lei – a notable increase compared to other years.

[Page 313]

The Relations between the Jews and the Germans

Until the thirties, the relations between the two groups in Artsyz were friendly and the cooperation between them correct. However, as the Nazis came to power in Germany, pamphlets in German inciting against Jews began to arrive to Artsyz, and the local commercial relations and cooperation between Jews and Germans stopped gradually. The Germans opened more and more shops and the Jewish merchants and store owners were restricted. In the encyclopedia mentioned above, Theodore Lavie describes the relationship in the following words: "In Artsyz, a German woman visited the Jewish doctor Korol. Since she belonged to a pre–military unit, she was brought to a court of the Nazi party and was reprimanded and lowered in rank. In order to be restituted to her former rank she was forced to issue a complaint against the Jewish doctor, the pharmacist Caushanski and other Jews in Artsyz. In the complaint she stated that the Jews have given her money to conduct propaganda against the country. The Jews were arrested and kept several days in jail." The attorney B. Klepner, who was sent by the Jewish National Party to examine the situation of the Jews in Southern Bessarabia, found in Artsyz 225 Jews, who lived "in conditions of poverty and hunger." The signs of destruction had already begun to show, and no doubt caused many young people to seek Aliya to the Zionist and pioneering country.

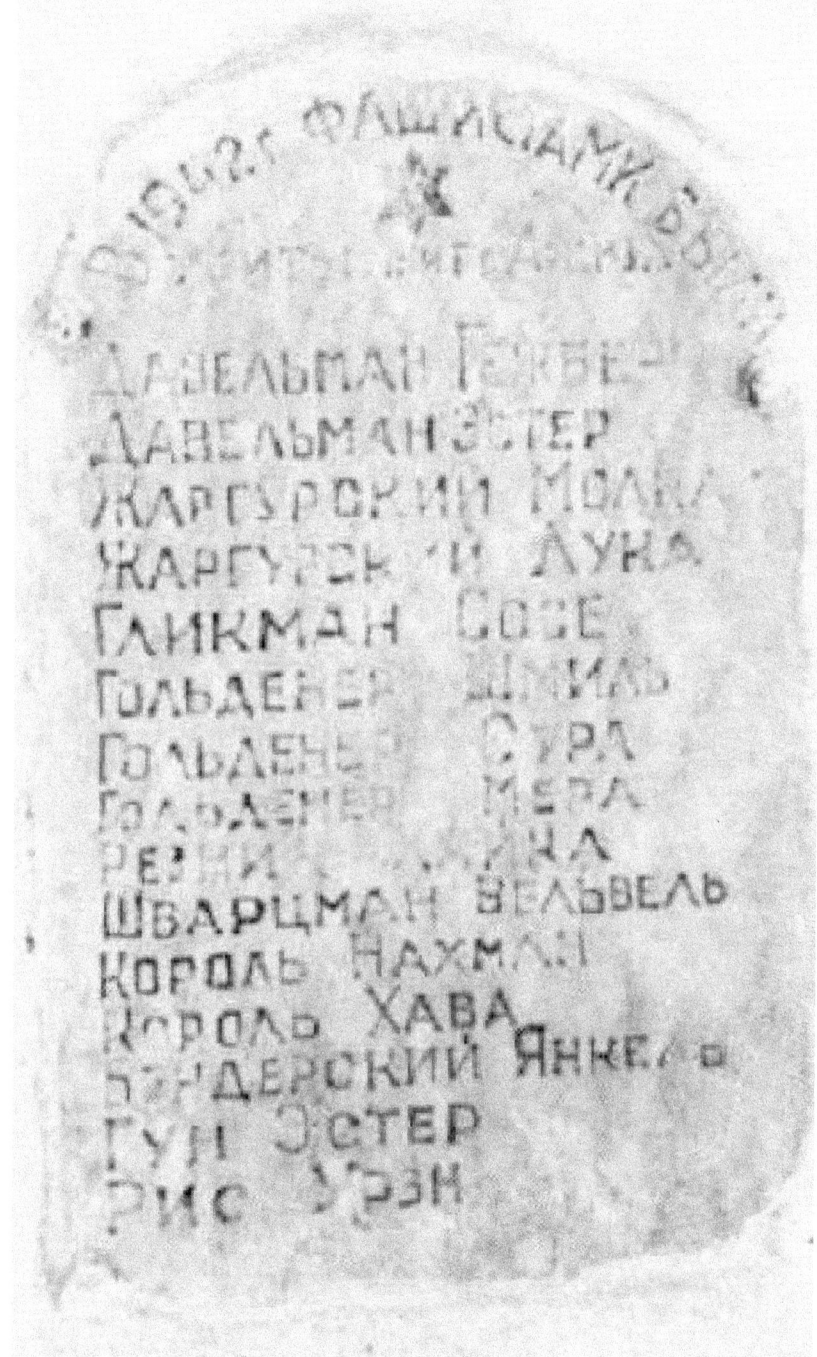

A memorial stone for part of the Artsyz Jews, murdered in 1942

The names of the people engraved on the stone: **Debelman Hersch-Ber, Debelman Esther, Zavgorski Malka, Zavgorsli Luca, Glickman Sosa, Goldner Shmuel, Goldner Sara, Goldner Moshe, Reznik Chaika, Schwarzman Velvel, Karol Nachman, Benderski Yankel, Gon Esther, Riess Aharon**

The teachers of the Hebrew School in Artsyz and the kindergarten–teacher (second from left)

[Page 314]

A group of Artsyz Jews. The photograph is from 1938

A cheap kitchen in Artsyz in 1936 (the kitchen was near the school)

Standing are the members of the committee, from right to left: **Avraham Pausner, Melech Margolies, the teacher Ritech, Helman**

The women in the committee (on the left side of the photo) from right to left: **Perlmutter, Litman Rachel, Abramowitz, G. Shivitz, Kos, Katz**

An assembly of public activists in a forest in Artsyz

Sitting from right to left: **Unidentified, Klozeski, Kiprosser, Kapelman, unidentified, Pausner**
The rest are unidentified. The second from left is **Chaia Ita Pausner**

[Page 315]

The Tarbut School in Artsyz

Sitting are the teachers, from right to left: **Chaia Ita Pausner, the principal Blostotzkaia, Marlin, Grishnog, Tzeitin–Zhemni**

The Hashomer Hatza'ir branch in Artsyz

[Page 316]

The Hebrew School in 1922

The kindergarten with the kindergarten–teacher in Artsyz

[Page 317]

Prof. Yehuda Pausner z"l

He was born in Russia in 1910 and after the 1917 Revolution his parents Aba–Moshe and Chana z"l relocated to Bessarabia and settled in Artsyz. He finished his secondary studies "cum laude" and in 1929 went to Belgium, studied medicine and was certified as a doctor there.

He made Aliya to Eretz Israel in 1938 and began his medical career as a doctor in the *Choma Umigdal* settlements in the *Bet She'an* Valley. Later he worked in the *Beilinson Hospital* in Petach-Tikva and was among the first founders and doctors in the *Tel Hashomer Hospital*, with his friend Prof. Chaim Shiva z"l. In Tel Hashomer he was the head of the department of chest and heart surgery until his retirement.

Prof. Pausner was also among the founders of the School of Medicine of Tel Aviv University and the head of its Department of Surgery. Many well-known doctors were his students. His many scientific publications added to his fame in the country and abroad, and he was often invited to important scientific conferences.

Until the sixties he served as a military doctor as well and was appointed as chairman of the Superior Medical Committee of the Ministry of Defense.

Returning in his car from a meeting of the medical staff in *Tel Hashomer*, Prof. Pausner suffered a heart attack and died on 17 November 1968, at the age of 68. He left his wife, Jenia, a son David and a daughter Chana, both doctors.

May his memory be blessed.

[Page 318]

[Page 321]

Tatarbunar

Tatarbunar
(Tatarbunary, Ukraine)
45°51' 29°37'

Translated by Yocheved Klausner

This town does not have a long history. It was founded in 1809, and in 1861 it was registered by the general statistical authority as a town in the Bessarabia region. As anti–Semitism grew in Russia, the Bessarabia District Management decided in 1882 that Tatarbunar was a village, not a town. The significance of this decision was that the temporary decrees that prohibited Jews to live within a certain distance (50 Verstas) from the border applied to Tatarbunar as well and the Jews living in this "village" should expect to be deported. All attempts to change the decree failed – and several Jewish families, who had lived tens of years in Tatarbunar, were deported. Only in 1890 did the Senate decide, after discussing the Jewish plea, to annul the decree of the District management and return to Tatarbunar the status of town.

From various articles that were published in the press in the 80's of the 19th century we learn about the life and activity of the Jews in town. In *Hatzefira*, issue 9 1882 we read about the *Hachnasat Orchim* Society [free accommodation for guests, lit. "Welcoming guests"] "that rented a beautiful house and furnished it with beds and tables, and appointed a devoted man to take care of the needs of the house." It seems that this activity was well suited within the framework of other activities of this kind, organized by the Jewish intelligentsia in town and aimed to establish modern charity institutions, free of the influence of "attendants" of various kinds.

In a report published in a local newspaper (issue 20, 1882) we read about organizing an Association for Aliya and Settlement in Eretz Israel, with 100 registered members, each paying 100 Rubles. However, issue #23 of the same newspaper published a slight "correction:" not 100 registered members, but 20, and they did not bring any income. The Association wanted to send delegates to Eretz Israel to buy land, and for this purpose it got in touch with the *Central Committee of the Associations for Settlement in Eretz Israel* that was active in Romania (the main offices were situated in GalaÈ›i), and received a report expressing "a good opinion" about Eretz Israel. The Association turned to Sir Olifant asking support and he replied, that the money of the London Committee for the support of Jewish refugees from Russia is designated for those who immigrate to America; the Turkish Sultan, for political reasons, prohibited the Jews to immigrate to Eretz Israel, and "until Olifant and other activists succeeded in changing the Sultan's mind, the Jews should be patient."

We know from another source about another association that was formed that year, to help and support needy Jews. The founders were 19 young men from the town, who collected a considerable sum to help poor families to make Aliya, but this association did not last long.

Some reports from 1898 said that the Zionist Association in Tatarbunar sold *shekalim* and passed the proceeds to the Zionist management.

That year, the association *Dorshey–Zion* held a grand Chanuka ball with the participation of more than 200 people.

A delegate from Tatarbunar participated in the Zionist meeting in Warsaw, which took place after the Second Zionist Congress, and another delegate from Tatarbunar participated in the Regional meeting held in Kishinev, as preparation for the Third Zionist Congress.

The *Nes–Ziona* Association in Tatarbunar sent a congratulations letter, in the form of a poem, to the Second Zionist Congress and to the most honored chairman Mr. Theodore Herzl, signed by 20 Tatarbunar Zionists.

The Central Zionist Archives keeps a letter from the *Zokhrei–Zion* Association in Tatarbunar to Dr. Herzl, announcing that he was elected by the Association as delegate to the 4th Zionist Congress; the Association grants him the authority to pass the mandate to whom he saw fit. The letter is dated 8 July 1900, and the Jewish date, mentioning the weekly Torah Portion, is added. The letter is signed by the chairman Chaim Glickman, his deputy Avraham Greenberg and the secretary Zvi Silberman.

In 1902, the Congress of the Russian Zionists took place in Minsk, and the Zionist Associations that had sold *Shekalim* had the right to send delegates. The Tatarbunar Zionists received that right and sent a delegate. After the congress, an intensive Zionist activity began in Bessarabia and many JNF [*Keren Kayemet*] stamps were sold. The Tatarbunar Zionists ordered stamps for 26 Rubles.

The threat to the Zionist Movement posed by the Uganda dispute caused distress to the Tatarbunar Zionists, and when they found out that at the meeting of the Great Executive Committee in Vienna (April 1904) an agreement was reached between the "Zionists of Zion" and Herzl – the *Zokhrei–Zion* Association in Tatarbunar sent a letter of appreciation and encouragement to Dr. Herzl.

(From the book on Bessarabia by A. Feldman)

[Page 322]

Tatarbunar and its Jews
by Binyamin Gieker
Translated by Yocheved Klausner

The general Population of Tatarbunar (the meaning of the name – a Tatar water source, hinting at the many sweet water springs in the region) was 15,000 souls, including 520 Jewish families. Most of the Jewish families lived in the center of town and their occupations were commerce and crafts. The institutions that served the Jewish population were The Jewish Community Committee and the Association for Helping the Needy, headed by Nushka Weissman. At the end of 1920, by the initiative of Dr. Wollman, a bank was founded, mainly for the purpose of giving loans to those of limited means. Two synagogues served the religious population in town, and they were enough, since the Jewish population in town was not particularly religious. There was, however, an intensive and lively cultural activity in town, especially theatrical activity, led by Ita Wilk, Zvi and Ita Albert and others. The local performances of the Jewish theater attracted a large public.

Several young people opened a library in a small room in the house of Pinya Feigin; in time it turned into a large and beautiful library in a new building, and became a cultural center of the town.

The youth in Tatarbunar

The young people of Tatarbunar have grown up in the shadow of WWII, the Russian revolution and the transition from Russian to Romanian rule. These events have undoubtedly left their marks on the development of the young people.

Leaders and public activists

Sitting on the floor, from right to left: **Rosa Tzvoter, Liuba Brodeski, Sofa Weissman, Riva Silberman, Yosef Silberman, Bluma Silberman**
Second row sitting, from right to left: **Nushka Weissman, in back of him Mrs. Weissman, Dr. Fischman, Sara Midovoy, Hirsch Silberman, Mrs. Teitelbaum, Tona Teitelbaum, Akiva Brodeski, Yosef Litvin, Zvi Albert**
Standing: **Dr. Wollman, Riva Wilk, Mrs. Tzobotar, Gardintchik, Mrs. Gardintchik, Dr. Komorovski, Isak Wilk, Mrs. Slotzki, Mrs. Litvin, Wilik, Mrs. Wilik.**

[Page 325]

The Tatarbunar *Gordonia* Branch
by Arie Shochat
Translated by Yocheved Klausner

The first steps to organize Zionist youth activity in our town were taken after the Balfour Declaration. Some 20 young people formed a small organization with the purpose of making Aliya to Eretz Israel. Indeed in 1920–1921 most of them went to Eretz Israel, but after that there was a period of about 7 years of low activity in this area. There was no initiative to organize young Zionists, the main Zionist activity in town being contributions to *Keren Kayemet* (JNF) and *Keren Hayesod*.

In 1929, after the riots in Eretz Israel, a group of friends, headed by Yitzhak Goldman, Arie Shochat (Leibl), Yosef Silberman, Yosef Specterman, Israel Gieker, Riva Silberman and Fania Gardentzik began organizing young local people aiming to establish a framework for their Zionist education and personal development. With the help of the Akkerman *Gordonia* they established a *Gordonia* branch in Tatarbunar. Most of the members came from the working youth who, due to the economic difficulties at home were forced to interrupt their studies and start working at a young age. For them, the *Gordonia* branch was a study place as well, and there they completed their education, expanded their knowledge in the history of the Jewish people, learned the Hebrew language etc. The Community provided *Gordonia* with a location for its activity, and the members worked at collecting money for the Zionist Funds.

A group of Zionists at Hakcshara [training camp] in Orchayov

A group in training (Orchayov), among them people from Tatarbunar

[Page 326]

Members of Gordonia, "graduated" in 1931

The "Boselia" branch in Tatarbunar

[Page 327]

Dr. Solomon Shalem
by Binyamin Gieker
Translated by Yocheved Klausner

He was a well-known doctor on Tatarbunar, but first of all he was a human being, in the full sense of the word. His pleasant ways and his fatherly attitude toward any patient instantly removed a large part of the aches and pains. He responded to any call, day or night, even when he was certain that he might not receive any recompense for his work. More than that: more than once has he paid for the medicines, when he realized that the patient was in need. Healing the sick he considered a holy humane mission. Everybody knew him, and as he walked in town with his wide hat in the summer and his fur cap in the winter, leaning on his heavy walking stick, every person saluted him with respect.

He was always working, since he was the doctor of the Jewish and Christian population; in particular on Sundays and Christian Holidays, when people celebrated and drank, and from the quarrels many came out hurt and wounded… Often he served as arbiter in disputes between Jews or between Jews and non-Jews, since all respected his reasoning, and his decisions were never contested. For these arbitrations he was also never paid.

His library was full of medicine books and art books, and he was busy reading every free hour. Many used his library, and in his will he bequeathed it to the local doctors and to the general library of the Community.

We should also mention his wife, a very intelligent lady who devoted much of her time to public and Zionist activity in the framework of various organizations. Their two sons, Leonia and Mark, both university graduates, served as teachers. His only daughter, who had been my friend and my school-mate in high-school, is still living now in the Soviet Union, alone and without a family.

The Ladies' Committee in Tatarbunar

The picture was taken on the occasion of the return of the Rabbanit [the Rabbi's wife] Posk from a visit in Eretz Israel

A group of Gordonia members

[Page 328]

My Home in Tatarbunar
by Riva Zukerman – Silberman
Translated by Yocheved Klausner

The Jewish community in Tatarbunar was a lively community, blessed with activity – and most of its members were Zionists. My father z"l, Zvi Silberman, was born in Akkerman and for some time he was teacher in Tarotino. From his early youth he was active in the Zionist movement and he represented the town at Zionist meetings in Kishinev. In 1902 he took part in the Congress of Russian Zionist in Minsk, with the participation of Dr. Herzl. At this important and historic congress he was one of the two delegates from Southern Bessarabia. After he married Feiga Glickman from Tatarbunar he moved to his wife's town and became active in all areas, until his Aliya in 1934.

My father was blessed with writing talent and published articles in the newspapers of those days. He witnessed the pogrom in the town Biremtcha at the beginning of this century and expressed in writing the horrible sights that he has seen. He published in the Russian newspaper that appeared in Bucharest, in *Unzer Zeit* in Kishinev and he also sent articles to a Jewish newspaper in distant Harbin, where a great number of Jews who fled from the 1917 revolution, had found shelter. His articles and stories were filled with love of Zion and of the Jewish people.

Our home was wide open to all and served as a meeting place for Zionist assemblies. Father would host delegates from the Kishinev Center, and since he was one of the founders of the local Hebrew School and kindergarten, meetings and discussions about Jewish education in town were often held in our home, with the participation of teachers and other people involved in education. Father wrote reviews and plays, for performances held in school for the students and in town for the general public. They were usually accompanied by songs and melodies written by Ladyzhenski. The teacher Titinschneider was the director of these performances, which educated many and prepared them for Aliya.

In 1922, as the San-Remo declaration – which affirms the British Mandate in Eretz Israel – was made public, father received a telegram from the Jewish Center in Kishinev (I still have the telegram) and he organized a festive parade in town in honor of this event. All Tatarbunar Jews marched, dressed festively and carrying blue-white flags, danced in the street and handed out flowers. Father gave a speech, and he didn't need a loud speaker to be heard. The German authorities were liberal at that time and permitted unlimited Zionist activity.

In 1932, the youth movement *Gordonia* was founded in Tatarbunar, and all young people in our family joined. Father helped as well, and he would speak about the history of Zionism. My brother, Yosef Silberman, followed in the steps of father, was very active in *Gordonia* and founded a new branch in Kiliya. An article by father about the *Gordonia* meeting in the summer of 1933 in the Akkerman District was published in the newspaper "Bessarabskaia Slovo" that appeared in Kishinev, and is included in this book.

Four years our father lived and was active in Eretz Israel, he helped the writer and poet Yakov Fichman and supported *Moznaiym*, the magazine of the Writers' Association, edited by Fichman.

A group of Gordonia members in Tatarbunar

Sitting from right to left: **Moshe Kogan, Zev Binenbaum (from Akkerman), Specterman Yosef**
Standing from right to left: **Schusterman, Peretz, Riva Silberman, Arie Shochat, Shoshana Silberman, Elik Liebman, Rozha**

[Page 329]

The *Gordonia* Congress
(From an article by Zvi Silberman in the Russiann newspaper "Bessarabskaia Slovo," 1937)
Translated by Yocheved Klausner

This week, the *Gordonia* Congress of Southern Bessarabia took place in the *Bet-Ha'am* [People's House] in Tatarbunar. 90 delegates participated, from the branches: Akkerman, Birmatcha Serta, Tatarbunar, Kilia, Ismail Bulagdard, Tchedar-Longa, Komart, Romanovka and Liova, as well as 140 *halutzim* [pioneers], former members of *Gordonia*. One of the delegates, Chaim Yankelewitz from Kilia, missed the truck that went to the Congress on foot – walked 50 km. to Tatarbunar, and reached it exactly at the time of opening.

The chairman of the Congress was Binyamin Gershfeld from Akkerman. The representatives of the public institutions and of the Zionist organization in Tatarbunar extended greetings: Dr. Wollman, Dr. Fishman, Weissman, Gardenychik, Rabbi Posk, Dr. Komarovski, Schwerin and Zvi Silberman…

Mr. Elkana Margalit, member of the General Management of *Gordonia* in Romania, lectured on the topic: "Between Coercion and Freedom." He exhibited much wisdom and talent as speaker.

The festive opening of the congress – which was open to the general public – ended with Zionist songs and folk-dancing. After that the discussions and lectures began, continuing three days, and decisions were taken; the main topic of the discussions was the organizational problems of the movement. The concluding lecture was given by A. Margalit, on the subject: "Birobidjean or Eretz Israel." The lecture left a strong impression on all listeners.

The participants in the Congress left full of enthusiasm and satisfaction, their hearts filled with feelings of hope and encouragement concerning the future of the Zionist and pioneer movement.

Students of the High–School in Tatarbunar

[Page 330]

On the eve of the Second Zionist Congress that took place in 1898 in Basel, 20 Zionists from Tatarbunar sent the following letter of greetings (in the form of a poem) to Dr. Herzl:

The Zionist in the town Tatarbunar, Bessarabia district, hereby present greetings and blessings to the elected members of the Congress in Basel and to our most respected Chairman Dr. Theodore Herzl:

> May our blessings cover his head
> May God be with him,
> He Who sits in Heaven
> Shall give him His blessings
> For the well–organized Congress.
> From this Congress
> Learning will emerge
> For all those who are expecting its light.
> We shall keep away from any jealousy,
> From any competition or hate,
> That are coming from Satan,
> And we shall witness miracles
> As in the time of the Exodus from Egypt.
> May God give you a long life on this Earth.

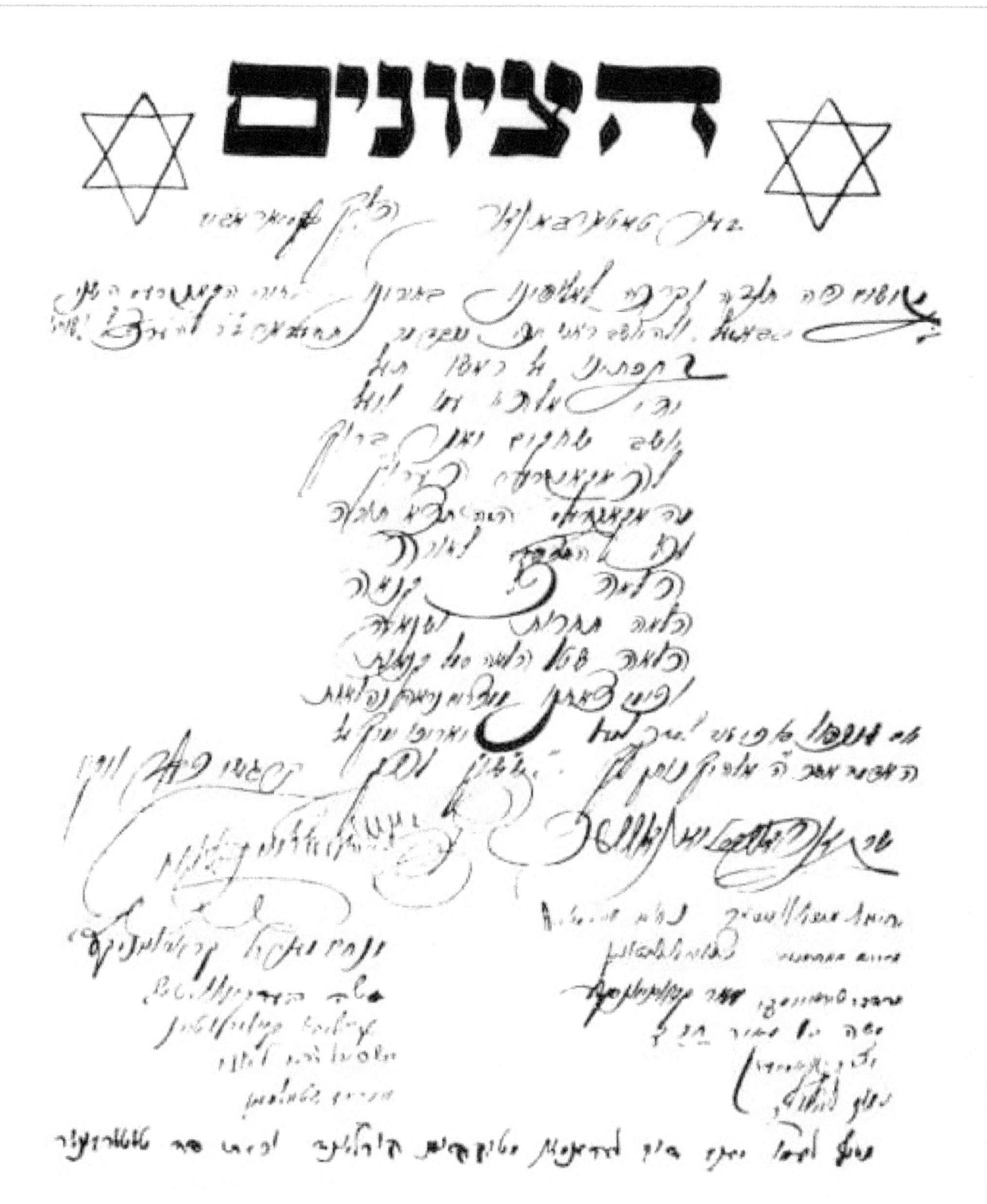

The letter of greetings in the form of a poem, from the Nes–Ziona Association in Bandar to Herzl

[Page 331]

The Keepers of the Flame
(In memory of those who keep the candle of the Tatarbunar community still burning)
by Berurya Har–Zion
Translated by Yocheved Klausner

In 1966, I went with my husband on a visit to Russia. When we arrived in Kishinev, uncle Avraham and aunt Batia came from Tatarbunar to meet us. My uncle was very ill, suffered from very high blood–pressure. The family begged him not to make the 12–hour trip from Tatarbunar to Kishinev, but he insisted and argued that one dies only once. Maybe it was this time for him, he said, but maybe he will have the good luck to see the children who had come from Israel – the trouble and the risk were worthwhile.

He was privileged and he met us. Since he had to be in bed, I would sit with him every day and answer his questions about relatives and acquaintances from Tatarbunar who had made Aliya to Eretz Israel. He was very happy to meet with us, thanked us for the presents we brought, and asked secretly, when we were alone: I hope you also brought what I asked you specially to bring. I felt a tremor over my entire body. Before we left, we received a letter from our uncle, asking us to bring him a prayer book [siddur]. I explained that many have warned us and advised not to take anything that would compromise us or our family. My uncle did not accept the explanation and said:

It is a pity, Manitchka, a pity. You know that I never was very religious. Only on the *Days of Awe* [*Rosh Hashana* and *Yom Kippur*] I went to the synagogue. But now times have changed. We have lived through the terrible Holocaust and we have grown old. We collected some money in town to build a synagogue. Twenty people gave each a promissory note. The authorities gave us a small room, which was to serve as a synagogue and also as a meeting place for the few Jews in town, to listen on the radio to news about Israel, to keep up the "Jewish spark," to tell each other our troubles and worries, to be together. There are still two Jews among us, who remember the silver–covered prayer book and the etrog [citrus fruit] that you sent me before the war. When I told them that I am traveling to Kishinev to meet relatives from Eretz Israel, they said to me: Avrum, we hope that your niece will bring us a prayer book. It is true that there is still one of us who knows all the prayers by heart and he also has an old and torn prayer book, but what will happen if that Jew, nicknamed Zalman the Red, will one day return his soul to his Maker? Then we will lose the last drop of Jewishness. Everything will end. Now you understand why I – and not only I – waited so impatiently for you and for the prayer book that you will bring me? And now you came and did not bring a *siddur* – – – – –

The Women's Committee in Tatarbunar

[Page 332]

Thus spoke my uncle, and his words were like stabs of swords in my heart. I saw in my uncle the last "keeper of the flame" – I was ashamed that I did not fulfill his request. I decided: be as it may – I have to fulfill his wish, which may be the last wish of the few remaining Jews in Tatarbunar.

After his sad words, I said to him: Don't despair, uncle, I will do everything to obtain a *siddur* for you. I will ask my friends, perhaps some of them has brought one and doesn't need it, maybe Shmuel will succeed to obtain one in Moscow and we will send it to you. Don't worry, the prayer book will be here.

Shmuel promised me that he will do all he can. The ambassador Katriel Katz was his friend, and he will certainly help. Indeed, when we came to Moscow we received a prayer–shawl, two pairs of *Tefillin* [phylacteries], two *mahzorim* [prayer-books for the High Holidays] and eight *mezuzot*. We were very excited, but we also feared: how will be able to hide all these things in our hotel? I said to the cleaning woman that she was working too hard and asked her not to clean our room, since we were only two people and we don't make a mess. I also gave her some nylon socks as a present. She didn't know how to thank me for that. I wrote immediately to my cousins asking them to be at the train station at a certain hour since I have to return something that I had taken by mistake. When we arrived at the Kishinev train station we were amazed to see hundreds of people, who had come to say "farewell" to the Israelis who were leaving and to hear the song *Hevenu Shalom Aleichem*. I embraced my cousin Nelly and gave her the parcel, wrapped in the "Pravda" newspaper. I felt relieved.

I waited a long time for some sign that the parcel had reached its destination; the sign arrived, albeit a little late. My aunt Batia wrote: "Good children do not forget their mother even if they live far away, Greetings to the good sons, who promise and do not forget their promise." We were glad that we had the good fortune to fulfill this small mission for the Tatarbunar Jews, the last to "keep the flame."

Meeting in Haifa of former residents of Akkerman

[Page 333]

The Double Miracle
by Berurya Har-Zion
Translated by Yocheved Klausner

During our visit in 1966 in Kishinev we heard several stories from our aunt Batia Wilk from Tatarbunar. Below is one of these stories, which, in my opinion, deserves to be published so that many people could read it

And this is what our aunt told:

It happened during the war. My husband Avraham was in the army, and I with my three children lived in the Kolkhoz Azbekikova Tzotkovski, in the Rostov District. Our life was not easy.

Almost the entire population was old men and women, who were not recruited to the army. Every morning we would go out in the field, to gather grass and roots, remnants from last year's crop, and I was ready to do any hard work if it would enable me to feed my children.

One day, several German soldiers appeared, with the command: All people in the Kolkhoz should assemble at the train station, to go on a trip. We had no doubts about the nature of this "trip," but we had no choice and we joined all the others. The girls were 16 and 18, but the boy Izia was young and sick with a high fever. We walked slowly until we reached a corn field. That year it was a good crop and the corn was taller than a man's height. As we walked, Izia fainted and collapsed, and we decided to stay with him, since we realized that we had nothing to lose. We were so tired that we all fell asleep. We were at a distance from the others. My mother came to me in my dream (I knew that she was dead a long time) and I burst in tears: Mother, save my children, we are taken to be murdered! Mother looked at me with a look that I shall never forget: "Go straight until you come near a very tall tree. From there turn and go left, never go to the right, only left" she said and disappeared, and I woke up crying so loudly that the children woke up as well.

We drank some water, ate some sweet corn and started to walk. Soon we reached a tall tree, and as my mother instructed me, we went to the left. According to the soldiers' command we should have gone to the right, but we preferred to listen to mother.

We kept on walking after darkness fell. The children said that we had lost our way, and I myself didn't know where we were and where we were going. When day came, we saw in front of us a small town. We went in the direction of that place and several hours later we reached the kolkhoz that we had left the day before. Some people seeing us crossed themselves in wonder "How have you escaped" – they asked – "all were killed." How could I explain?

We continued living in great fear among the few gentiles. Soon I received a message that I should come immediately to the post office. Somebody was looking for us. My first thought was: we have been discovered. They probably didn't find us among those who were killed and now they have come to take us.

I decided to go to the post office without the children. As I arrived, I was told to sign, since there was a parcel waiting for me. I was embarrassed and frightened: a parcel? Who knew where I was? It could be only from Eretz Israel. I opened the little parcel and my eyes lit up: needles, sewing thread, pins of various sizes, razor blades, shoe strings etc. I had an idea: I took one of the needles and showed to a neighbor. "This is a treasure nowadays – how did you get it?" And so we made a deal: In return of a few needles and some sewing yarn I received a little milk, some potatoes, beets and a piece of pumpkin. So we managed to stay alive, thanks to these deals, thanks to the treasure that had come from Eretz Israel.

So you see – my aunt ended her story – a double miracle happened to us: thanks to my mother's instructions in my dream and thanks to the parcel you sent from Eretz Israel, we are alive today.

[Page 337]

Sarata

Sarata
(Sarata, Ukraine)
46°01' 29°39'
by Zvi Schaechter
Translated by Yocheved Klausner

Sarata was surrounded by wide green fields of wheat and corn, stretching to the horizon. Fruit trees bloomed across the bridge – a meeting place for young people and young couples, who enjoyed the charming landscape of the little hill and the smell of hay and fresh fields. The town was located near the train station, and it included a Jewish settlement among German farmers. It was surrounded by Russian, Bulgarian and Romanian villages.

The Jewish settlement in Sarata started during the 1905 pogroms; the first Jews to settle there were refugees, who escaped from the pogrom raging in Akkerman and Farmacia, and in their flight reached Sarata.

The local German farmers refused to receive the Jews among them. The refugees from the pogrom addressed the Committee of the Kishinev Jews and following their appeal the authorities intervened and the German settlers received instructions to allow the Jews to settle in the village.

The German residents were well–to–do, with large agricultural assets. The houses, about 400 in number, were built in a beautiful rural style, surrounded by large courtyards. Each courtyard had a fountain and the water was drawn by a pump. In the yard there were a chicken coop, a cow shed, a stall for the horses and pens for the sheep, as well as large bales of hay.

The neighborhood villages would bring their agricultural produce to the local market, where the shops belonged mainly to Jews.

The main roads in the village were dirt roads. During the winter rains the heavy dirt turned into sticky mud and it often happened that a shoe or a galosh remained stuck deep in the mud. In some places, however, there were stone sidewalks.

The Sarata Jews were honest workers, healthy in body and soul and full of national feelings. The life in town, in the agricultural setting, increased their national longing. Eretz Israel was identified with hard agricultural work, which was seen by these Jews in their close neighborhood.

One hundred and fifty Jewish families lived in Sarata, in rented homes; only few of them owned their homes. The German residents avoided selling homes or plots to Jews; they did not like the fact that strangers lived among them and possessed property.

Beginning in 1923, the Jewish settlement increased. Many Jews from the neighborhood were accepted in the village, and remained there. They felt welcome by the warm and hearty Jewish atmosphere that prevailed among the Jewish families in Sarata.

Livelihoods

Most of the Sarata Jews earned their livelihood by commerce and work connected with agricultural produce. Beginning in 1935, the number of Jews in town increased day by day. Jewish families from the neighboring villages joined, and Jewish merchants from Kishinev and other cities came to buy agricultural produce, part of which was exported.

Sarata and its environs were a rich center of grains, milk products, meat, eggs, wool and leather. It was an administrative center as well; it had a Justice of the Peace, a Tax Department and other offices.

The market place was in the center of town, and around it the shops that provided the daily needs of the farmers: there were wood and iron warehouses, kosher butcher shops, bakeries, coffee houses, groceries, and shops that sold textiles, building material, household utensils, etc. Most of the shops were built of stone; some of them were just whitewashed sheds.

Once a week, there was "the fair" – the official market day. Many farmers from the neighborhood villages arrived, to sell their produce and buy what they needed. Special stands were kept in the market place for the Jewish merchants from the neighboring villages that came to sell their wares,

[Page 338]

mostly textiles and haberdashery. The fair was held in the market place and nearby streets. We had a friend, who sold notions; and for many years he would come a day before the fair to our house, take his ware out of the boxes, and our family members would help sort it out and arrange it carefully – treads, combs, needles etc. to have it ready for the fair. One of our relatives would come once every 10 days to sell tobacco, although tobacco was under government monopoly.

Many of them were trading in wheat – they were keeping the wheat in the warehouses until they had a sufficient amount for loading.

The center of marketing was the train station. Many earned a substantial livelihood around the train station. There was a constant movement of activity and effort. Jewish agents would lease the warehouses of the station and receive the wheat shipped by the merchants. They would also load the ware on the train cars and send it to its destination.

Many of the residents worked taking the grains to the station warehouses, on wagons pulled by horses. That was hard work, but profitable. There were also peddlers, who bought produce, leather and farm animals in the neighboring villages and sold the ware to the wholesale merchants. Some of the peddlers traded in textiles and notions, others sold sewing machines.

Special agents would travel on the train back and forth, taking care of the commercial relations with Kishinev and other cities. Their role was to relay urgent letters and urgent orders from the various shops, and to bring or exchange missing items. On their way to town, they carried with them local agricultural produce – butter, broiled geese and salami – to sell in town. They carried their ware in packages, and were therefore called "the package agents." While on the train, they were very careful, paying attention that a package wouldn't be stolen. Everybody recognized the package carriers, and many Jews joined them in the train car, turning the journey into a pleasant meeting of jokes and stories.

The Jewish Community

As the Jewish population increased, the community began to organize. Jews from the neighboring villages and towns came to Sarata, where it was easier to make a living. Beginning in 1923, they felt the need for religious and educational institutions. A rented apartment in the center of town served as a prayer house during weekdays. It was, however, too small for the Holiday prayers; for the "Days of Awe" and other Holidays they rented a large warehouse for that purpose.

They began to organize, intending to build a synagogue for the Holidays, which would serve during the rest of the year as a place for meetings and cultural activity. Among the activists were Nachman Altman, the *Gabay* of the synagogue, and Melekh Lublinski. They bought a plot of land in a Jewish neighborhood in the center of town, and building began. The plan was for a large building but the funds were sufficient only for the erection of the walls, and the structure remained several years without a roof. It was feared that the rain and winds would destroy it.

Several years later the "People's House" [*Bet Ha'am*] was completed and served as synagogue during the High Holidays. During the year, cultural and Zionist activity was taking place there, as well as community meetings, festivals, plays, elections to the Committee and the Zionist congresses, lectures of Zionist representatives and meetings of the youth movements. Theater groups playing in Yiddish performed their plays in this hall as well.

In the center of town they kept a rented apartment, which served as a synagogue during weekdays and a Hebrew School for the town children. The Community had a ritual slaughterer [*shochet*] who also served as cantor during the High Holidays. Our *shochet* was Chaim Baruch and after he became ill others filled his place.

Education

The Sarata Jews invested great efforts in the education of their children in the spirit of national Judaism. They hired teachers, who worked permanently in the rented apartment in the town's market place.

The teachers made great effort to teach the children basic elements of Jewish customs and Hebrew language, reading & writing and preparation for the *Bar-Mitzva*. There were times when the town also had a kindergarten, for the pre-school children. However, the support of the community was limited; some of the parents hired private teachers, on their own account. The teachers were full of national spirit and worked hard, despite their low salary, because they considered their work a national mission. Some of the parents had financial difficulties – yet they sent their children to the Hebrew high-schools *Tarbut* in Akkerman and Kishinev.

The Library

In many of the homes one could find private libraries in Russian, Yiddish and Hebrew. Whoever wanted to read a book – could find it. In 1933, by the request of the readers, the Community Committee of Culture founded a public library. It was first located in the home of Mrs. Chefetz, a wise and educated woman, who served as the librarian in her own home. Later, the library was transferred to *Bet Ha'am*. The librarians were volunteers, young girls from the youth movements *Beitar* and *Gordonia*. They were diligent and devoted workers.

[Page 339]

The Women's Committee

The *Damen Komitet* was the women's organization that included all women in town and helped all and every social and national activity in town: organizing festivities, visiting homes to collect donations for the JNF or charity, secret charity [*matan baseter*] etc. Their help was felt in the other community activities as well, in particular in the department of culture and education.

Among the active women were: Mrs. Bat Sheva Gertzberg, Mrs. Allensohn, Mrs. Krasnov, Mrs. Feldman.

The community was responsible for religious matters, kosher slaughtering, upkeep of the *Bet Ha'am*, support of the needy. Its income came from the "bowls" [*ke'arot*] placed on Yom Kippur in the synagogues, where every Jew would pay the sum imposed on him by the community, according to his means. The activists of the community were: Chaim Chefetz, G. Feldman, M. Hasid, Lublinski, A. Schaechter, N. Altman. N. Altman was elected as the *gabay* of the synagogue.

Entertainment

A Drama Group, which provided the artistic part of the community festivities, was active in town, with the help of the women's committee. The income of the performances was devoted to charity and cultural needs. Some of the festivities and parties donated their income to the JNF (*Keren Kayemet LeIsrael*). All Sarata Jews were going to see these performances. This was also the occasion to display the latest fashion in dresses. Usually there was also a raffle and the servings were plentiful and delicious – all prepared by the women's committee. The guests were delighted and the atmosphere was joyful; sometimes the spectators joined the performers in song and dance. There were also literary discussions and debates concerning the various plays.

Zionism

The Zionist ideas spread in Sarata with the first Jewish family that settled in town. As the settlement grew, so did the Zionist activities, expressed by collection of donations for the National Funds and various other activities of the Zionist organization: distribution of the *shekel*, election to the Zionist Congresses, etc.

Since 1928, the coordinator of the funds management and the local activities was my father z"l Avraham Yitzhak Schaechter, who recruited people to the Zionist cause. Our home was always open for the delegates.

Among the activists were: G Hasid, I. Rabinowitz. The Sarata Jews donated to all fund raising projects.

In 1929, the youth movements *Gordonia* (headed by Elkana Altman) and *Beitar* were established, and the Zionist activity increased. All the young people remained friends, however, in spite of the ideological differences.

A group of young people in Sarata

Sitting from right to left: **Ch. Foigel, S. Altman, Unknown, L. Schwarzman, Hershel Tzirolnik**
Standing from right to left: **A. Ostrovski, M. Korol, P. Schwarzman**

[Page 340]

One of our basic principles in educating our youth was love of the Jewish people. In 1940, the Soviet occupation put an end to the Jewish Zionist activity.

Anti-Semitism

Already at the beginning of the thirties, envy and hate of the Jews was felt in Sarata. The local Germans were very active, had close and constant contact with Berlin and spread the anti-Semitic poison. The town, where honest and rich Germans had lived, turned into a snake-pit of wild hate against Jews. The Sarata Germans adopted totally the Hitler theory.

Since 1933, the boycott, aiming to dispossess the Jews of their property and hurt their economical standing was working well. A constant propaganda was conducted, urging the German population and the other minorities not to buy in the Jewish shops. This propaganda was accompanied by the regular Nazi abuse and insults.

The Germans, with financial help, opened stores in all commerce branches. They incited the farmers in the surrounding villages and the hate increased day by day. One of the Nazi activists, who had studied dentistry in Germany, wore the Nazi uniform and went from store to store spreading evil Nazi propaganda and hate.

The German Youth also wore clothes similar to Nazi uniform. They were organized in an association by the name of "Good Friend" – but in their deeds they were far from the concept of "good." Once they caught a Jewish little boy and forced him to salute and pronounce in a loud voice the Nazi salute. Often they would throw stones to break the windows of the synagogue, in the market or in *Bet Ha'am*.

The farmers in the surrounding villages also conducted wild anti-Semitic propaganda and incitement and prevented non-Jews from entering Jewish shops. The Sarata Jews looked into the bitter reality with wide open eyes. The sharpened knives, ready for the final solution, were in front of them.

We shall mention here some of the Jews active in the public life:

Tzipora Altman – her home was the meeting place of the youth movements *Beitar* and *Gordonia*. Her sons, Zinia and Yechezkel, were active in *Beitar* and her son Elkana in *Gordonia*. She helped with the activity of the movements, hosted delegates, and her house was always full of young people. Her husband, R'Israel Altman, educated his children in a national spirit, to work and perform good deeds. He was an example for them.

Mrs. Cheifetz – a noble and educated woman. She promoted social and cultural life among the local Jews; was very active in the Community Cultural Committee and one of the initiators of the library, which was located in her home for some time and she was the librarian. Together with her husband Chaim, who was one of the leaders of the Sarata community, she raised their children in a national spirit; they went to school at the Hebrew High-school *Tarbut* in Akkerman.

N. Grinberg – a well-to-do pharmacist, helped every needy person, supported every Zionist activity and made large donations for the youth movements.

G. Hasid – one of the most active of the Jewish community, in particular in matters of Judaism and Zionism. As a teacher, he was obviously active in educational matters – library and cultural events, and was the local correspondent of the Russian newspaper.

Feldman – one of the owners of the flour mill; a handsome and honest man, he helped in the community activity and liked to help others. He was respected by all residents of the town.

Nachman Altman – Goodhearted, had a Jewish soul. He was one of the first to devote himself to the building of *Bet Ha'am* and invested many efforts to finish the building, which became an important property of the Sarata Jews. He was also the permanent *Gabay* of the synagogue.

Netzik Perlman – a warm and goodhearted Jew. Russian literature was an integral part of his education. He loved books, and had a large number of Russian books in his home. He was one of the writers of the "Petition" in Russian and fully identified with its content. He and his family were murdered in the German torture camps.

R'Israel Galperin – "the Jew from Eretz Israel." He was a religious man with a beard, dressed in Hasidic garb. His speech was mixed with Torah teachings. He was always busy working or reading a book, and set aside special times for Torah study. Even in his little store of flour and bran, where there was never a long line of customers waiting, he was reading a book. At home he worked hard and was devoted to the few farm animals he kept for the needs of his family – which earned him his nickname. His wife was a true "woman of valor" (Proverbs 31:10) – at dawn she was in the yard milking the goat and collecting the eggs. She was also learned in the sayings of our Sages. The family perished by the Nazis.

David'l Seltzer – had a warm and hearty look and was always in a good mood, "to the spite of all Jew–haters." He was working in the trade and transport of grains. His work never provided him with enough sustenance for his family, but he was always confident and joyful. He loved singing about freedom, and would say "life is short, and without singing and dancing it is also bitter" and was active in the drama group. At the signing of the "Petition" (to open the gates of Eretz Israel to Aliya) he was asked by the writer of these lines whether he will sign, and he replied "Of course, I want to make Aliya to Eretz Israel." He was not saved; he perished together with his devoted wife.

[Page 341]

Sarata
by I. Ben–Hur (Altman)
Translated by Yocheved Klausner

In my childhood I lived in the town Prival in the Kishinev County. Hundreds of Jewish families, their homes and their businesses, were concentrated on one very long street.

The two teachers in the Hebrew school, who were nicknamed, according to their hair color, "The Red" and "The Black," taught us the love of Zion. Every year on *Lag Ba'omer* they would take the town's children and sometimes the parents as well to an outing in the midst of Nature, to a large forest where we enjoyed ourselves with Hebrew songs and dances.

Once, the President of the Zionist organization, Nachum Sokolov, stopped in our town while traveling by train to Kishinev. The train stopped for a long time, to give all the townspeople the possibility to see the President. My uncle, Shmuel Tabakman, went with me to Sokolov's car and asked him how will the Jewish farmers go to Eretz Israel? This conversation became etched in my memory.

I followed the Schwarzbard trial by reading in the newspapers the reports about the trial. The hero of the trial obviously earned my total admiration.

After some time, a pioneer [*halutzim*] training camp was established in town; the pioneers lived a few kilometers from the town, in buildings that belonged to a rich Jew from Kishinev named Balaban, who possessed a large farm and vineyards. He provided for the *halutzim* their main sustenance and lodging. I would spend days in their camp, in particular Saturdays, and I learned about their organization and way of life.

The town was not really a Zionist town, but the youth was Zionist. Most of the young people in town felt like members of one big family.

Following the work of my father z"l, who was a supplier of food and grains for the army, a short time before my *Bar–Mitzvah* we relocated to the Southern part of Bessarabia and settled in the little town Sarata, in the Akkerman Province.

Most of the local Jews lived in German farmers' houses; the Germans were the majority of the population in town. After some time, the Jews concentrated in the North of the town and founded a Jewish neighborhood.

Here too, the Jews were the shop owners and merchants, and the Christians, especially the Germans, were the land owners. Bulgarians and other Christians in the neighborhood helped with the work in the fields. This work was done in a primitive way, with the help of farm animals; it was very hard work, in particular during the long rainy season.

While still living in Prival I was doing agricultural work. I would join my uncle Yakov Fikhman (cousin of the writer Yakov Fikhman) in his inspection tours of the village fields, and I loved the huge sunflower fields, the corn plantations and the wheat and barley fields.

Even after my *Bar–Mitzvah*, during the summer vacation months and during vacation days from school I would go with the farmers to their fields and join them in their work – easy or difficult – in the field: plowing, sowing, harvesting, primitive threshing in their own courtyards etc.

One of the tasks I remember in particular was cleaning the corn cobs that the farmers would bring to the big storehouses. Tens of German youths would work together removing the kernels from the cobs while singing, and I joined them often.

Considering the town from a Jewish and national standpoint, it can be said that it was a "sleepy" town, without Hebrew cultural activity. Apart from very few groups that met in private houses for chats or a little dancing, the connection between the young people in town was insignificant. A major change occurred in the beginning of 1929, when Zvi Schechter and his family came to live in Sarata. After a few discussions in his home, it was decided to open in town a branch of BEITAR "Brit Trumpeldor" and a lively activity began, in particular among the young people.

[Page 342]

Soon we enjoyed in Sarata a visit by the president of BEITAR in Eretz Israel. During his visit he had a difficult conversation with my brother Elkana (Nyona) and as a result several members left BEITAR and established a branch of the Gordonia movement and so we had two youth clubs in town. It should be noted that despite the ideological differences between BEITAR and Gordonia and the heated discussions, the close friendship between the individual members of the two groups was preserved.

With the establishment of the youth movements, other cultural institutions were established as well: a Hebrew library serving both parties, a drama club and others.

In time, I began making preparations for *hakhshara* [training for Aliya]. The first BEITAR member to make Aliya was Yitzhak Hershkowitz z"l; all townspeople escorted him to the train station, and after some time he came for a visit with his wife, native of Rechovot in Eretz Israel; the visit left a strong impression on all of us.

After our local branch was consolidated, I started visiting the neighboring towns, to try to establish BEITAR branches. I would walk from village to village, at first alone and later accompanied by a few members of the branch. We did our best to encourage the young people to join BEITAR.

We visited many times the town Artsyz, which was known as a center of activity of Jewish communists, and we managed to open there a BEITAR branch. I owe thanks to this town for the fact that my Aliya was reset for an earlier date – and this was how it happened: one evening, when I had come to lecture at the branch, I spent the night at the home of a friend. I woke up when the Security Police rounded up the young people of the town and began to sort out the communists. I was arrested together with the other BEITAR members. My explanations that there was no connection whatsoever between BEITAR and the communists were of no avail, neither was our formal authorization from the Ministry of the Interior to manage the branch legally. The officer was severe and what infuriated him against me was the fact that I was not a local member. Only after my father z"l came at noontime with instructions from the regional police was I released. After this event I was called to the *BEITAR* delegation in Bucharest and told that my Aliya was be soon.

In the beginning of 1933 I went to *hakhshara* (training) in Beltz. Here I had a cousin who had been previously at *hakhshara* in Prival, but he did not make Aliya. In another part of the town there was a Gordonia training camp and I would visit them to learn how to organize the camp.

Jabotinsky's visit at the BEITAR training camp in Zastavna
Sixth from left is R. Schoenfeld from Sarata.

[Page 343]

At the end of my training period – which was shortened because I was wounded in my leg – I tried to go on Aliya illegally. I went to Galatz and with the help of relatives of my father z"l I met some Yugoslavian sailors, and was supposed to join them as a sailor and begin my journey to Eretz Israel. They put me on a boat on the way to their ship, but as I boarded the little boat they robbed my money and put me down far from the port of Galatz. Depressed and tired I arrived at noon to my relatives in Galatz, who called my parents and my sister was sent with some money for me. I went home, and this was the end of my illegal Aliya.

BEITAR at the elections to the Zionist Congress

First row standing from right to left: **S. Kaprishanski, Zvi Schachter, I. Grinblatt**
Second row standing: **Milia Ohrbuch, D. Gratzberg**

As a compensation for this adventure, my mother HY"D sent me to her brother's family in Kilya. Maybe she intended to prevent another attempt of illegal Aliya. When I returned home I found another invitation to come to the *BEITAR* offices in Bucharest in order to arrange my Aliya. I was certain that I was going just to make the technical arrangements, but as I arrived in Bucharest the *BEITAR* representative Schieber informed me that I shall board the first ship to Eretz Israel, and even did not let me go back to say farewell to my parents and friends. I never saw them again.

Between Rosh Hashana and Yom Kippur 1935 I made Aliya to Eretz Israel with the Bulgarian ship Borges and my first stop was the Absorption Center in Bat Galim, near Haifa.

BEITAR Sarata 1932

Sitting first row (from right): **G. Glazer, A. Seltzer, W. Kaprishanski, S. Schachter. B. Krasnov**
Sitting second row: **A. Korol, S. Altstein, Z. Schachter, L. Schwarzman, S. Hasid**
Standing third row: **R. Gerstein, B. Altstein, Ch. Kapeishanski, R. Seltzer**
Standing fourth row: **Ch. Foigel, A. Wasserman, A. Ostrovski, A. Finkelstein, L. Galperin, S. Soybel, A. Goldenberg, M. Altman**

[Page 344]

The *BEITAR* Branch in Sarata

by Zvi Schachter

Translated by Yocheved Klausner

In 1929 the *BEITAR* branch in Sarata was founded by the writer of these lines. Soon the "branch" found its way to the hearts of the young people in town and many of the Sarata Jews. A great number of young and adult Jews showed interest in the activity of the branch and joined the meetings. The parents of the *BEITAR* members, Jews healthy in body and soul, totally identified with their children, and Zionism was their aspiration and longing.

The Sarata Jews felt strangers among the local German population. They read correctly the menacing signs of what was about to come. They did not oppose Zionism and the number of parents who desired a national education for their children and sent them to the Zionist youth movements increased constantly.

Our educational aims were: educating a true pioneer–fighter; training toward building our country and defending it; acquiring extended knowledge in the geography and history of the country, the nation and Zionism; doing physical exercises and learning songs about the homeland and its landscapes.

During one of the festivities we performed a play that included songs about the Kineret [the Sea of Galilee] and Mount Hermon – "*My Kineret*" and "*My Hermon.*" Indeed, in Sarata Kineret and Hermon were ours, we grew up with them. Our young people, who were raised in a rural region, absorbed the smell of the field, the love of work and the aspiration to live a healthy life in our homeland.

Beginning in 1935, our activity met with difficulties, because of the attitude of the German residents, who refused to rent us a place for our activity. They would attack us with obscene words and with shouts "Jude!" and often, while we were working in the field, German boys would assemble nearby and with sticks in their hands would make the Hitler symbol, the swastika. Once, in 1937, as we were training in the yard of the Galperin family, the "Hitler–Jugend" [Hitler Youth] called the gendarmes with the pretext that we were "disturbing the peace" and bothering the residents. The *BEITAR* members were arrested and fined. The German population and the local authorities did everything to interfere with the activity of *BEITAR* and *Gordonia*, but the movements continued their national and educational activity with double energy.

The Activity in the "Branch" [of the Movement]

We would assemble in rented apartments for our regular activity; the rent was paid by the savings of the members. Some time before the meeting, the "attendants" (members of the movement) would come to clean and make a fire to heat the place. I remember that once there was a leak of CO from the burning stove, and all members became sick with headaches and vomiting.

Since 6 January 1930, we celebrated every year the "Day of the Inauguration of the Flag." We always had a rich program, which expressed the achievements of our branch and also enabled us to collect donations. Members of all age–groups would perform national songs in Hebrew. All Jews in town were invited, and came willingly to take part in the festivities.

Announcements and newspapers that arrived from the central offices, as well as organized assemblies helped to spread the ideology of *BEITAR* in town.

The *BEITAR* members participated in general public activity, such as working in the community library. Many members, in particular young girls, participated in the Drama Club; the income of the performances was devoted to charity. *BEITAR* took part in the collection campaigns for the National Funds and helped the Zionist delegates who visited Sarata. These delegates arose much interest and all were eager to hear their speeches. One of the most loved delegates was Shmuel Gaber, who came several times to help us; many residents fought among them for the honor to be his host.

The *BEITAR* activity was not limited to Sarata. Relationships were established with other branches in the neighborhood, as Tatarbonar and Artzyz and visits and common festivities took place. In 1937, the Tatarbonar *BEITAR* branch hosted their Sarata friends in a camp that they erected on the road between the two settlements. The close relationship with the neighboring *BEITAR* branches increased the activity and brought a feeling of friendship like one big family. Jabotinski, during his visit in 1938 in Akkerman, expressed this feeling: "I have come to bring you greetings and wishes of success from the *BEITAR* branches around the world, including those that I have not visited. I am sure that every *BEITAR* member feels as you do: we are indeed one big family." The Sarata branch helped preparing the visit and a large delegation participated in the welcoming party.

[Page 345]

A BEITAR training group in Radautz with a pioneer woman from Sarata, R. Schoenfeld

The Zev Jabotinski BEITAR farm.
First at right R. Schoenfeld, first at left S. Frank.

[Page 346]

Our first and main worry was Aliya to Eretz Israel. Our members were trained at several training camps (Zastavna, Radautz, Gura Humorului etc.) aiming to develop the ability to adapt to the conditions in the country and prepare to the expected struggle. In 1930, Sarata *BEITAR* members began going to the training camps. The locked gates of the country prevented many from fulfilling their aim of Aliya; the number of "certificates" was limited, sometimes null, and the chances to obtain one were low.

The former *BEITAR* members and the revisionist circle helped us in our work. On their initiative and with their support, we organized a memorial assembly, in memory of Shlomo Ben Yosef on the day he was executed by hanging; we participated in the preparations for the elections to the Zionist congresses, we signed the "Petition" that requested from Britain to open the gates of the country etc. Among the activists were: Netzik Perlman, Milya Ohrbach and David Rabinowitz.

A few words about two *BEITAR* members who are not with us any more:

Leibl Galperin

He came from a religious-national home, joined the *BEITAR* activity with great devotion and was ready for any assignment that was given to him. He was responsible for the administrative part of the activity: he rented a locale and took care of its maintenance. He was full of life and loved jokes, but in his work at the *BEITAR* branch he was serious and always ready to meet any call and to extend help to his friends whenever needed. He lost his life tragically near Tashkent.

David Gerzberg

He went to the Hebrew High-School, was devoted to the national idea and was active in the movement branch with much energy and talent. He was an artist and for over a year his illustrations decorated the *BEITAR* educational publications. He could not make Aliya, and fell in battle against the Nazi enemy.

* * *

The *BEITAR* Members in our Country

A strong will and national devotion produced the building and fighting youth. With a pioneer enthusiasm, the Sarata *BEITAR* members filed their mission of building and liberating the country. Wherever they were sent, they fulfilled their tasks with courage and talent. We shall mention some of them:

Yehezkel Ben-Hur (Altman)

In 1935 he arrived in Eretz Israel, by an illegal and dangerous way. He was part of the *BEITAR* "Road Company" [*plugat hakvish*] stationed on the Kastel Hill near Jerusalem. In December 1937, as Arabs were murdering Jews, Yehezkel reacted by shooting at a bus full of Arab passengers and was sentenced to death. The sentence was then changed to life imprisonment. In 1944 he was released from prison, and after he took part in capturing the city of Jaffa he joined the Jerusalem *ETZEL* brigade and was among the group that founded the settlement *Ramat Razi'el* in the "Jerusalem Corridor" and the youth village in the name of Johanna Jabotinski.

Yitzhak Gershkowitz

He was the first Sarata *BEITAR* member to make Aliya in 1931. He joined the recruiting companies in Rosh-Pina. For his active opposition to the "population census" he was sentenced to 30 days in the Akko prison. After that he relocated to Rechovot and continued, with the others, the struggle for the State. But he was arrested again and was sent for 11 months to the Mizra prison and then to Latrun. He died in 1976 in Netania.

Rivka Schoenfeld

She was in the Zastavna training camp and made Aliya in 1935. She reported for service at the *Hakotel* [the (wailing) wall] Regiment in Zikhron-Yakov and completed her service in 1937 in the *plugat hakvish* ["the Road Company"] near Jerusalem. She was a member of *ETZEL*, carried "instruments" (weapons) to the Old City in Jerusalem and participated in the transport to Jerusalem of the shofar that was blown on Yom Kippur at the Wall.

Israel Lublinski

Was at training camps in Zastavna and Radautz and made Aliya in 1939. As he arrived in the country he reported to the recruiting unit in Rishon LeZion and later in Mishmar HaYarden. While he served in Yesud Hama'ala he became ill with malaria. By the order of the Movement he joined the Jewish Brigade and fought on the Italy, Belgium and Holland fronts. In 1946 he was discharged from the army.

[Page 347]

About "*Gordonia*" in Sarata
by Elkana Altman
Translated by Yocheved Klausner

I grew up in the town Sarata, situated about 60 Km. from the county capital Akkerman. Most of the residents were German, but about 150 Jewish families lived among them. This fact left an imprint on the life in town. Like in other towns, the Jews were mostly merchants and provided the needs of the farmers in the neighborhood. A certain percent of the Jews were craftsmen; it should be mentioned that the relations between the Jews and Christians were good.

It is interesting that from the point of view of the political landscape there was almost no difference between the little town Sarata and the large cities – all the parties and movements present in Akkerman or Kishinev were active in Sarata as well: General Zionists, Revisionists, *Tze'irei Zion* [The Young People of Zion], *Po'alei Zion* etc. Naturally, since the population was small, the number of members could sometimes be counted on the fingers of two hands... The *Gordonia* movement was different, however – most of the youths in town were members. I myself joined the movement at the age of 13, and at 16 I already was the secretary of the local branch. When I was 18 I became the manager of the Sarata branch and I represented it in the main offices of the movement in Akkerman. The leaders of the Akkerman branch were: Baruch and Zev Kamin, Hirschfeld, Sheftel Zuckerman and others.

Our activity was well felt in town, whether by the various Zionist donation campaigns, or by the *Hehalutz* activity and other areas of activity, where the young people took a significant part. A special mention deserves the activity for Aliya to Eretz Israel, in particular the illegal Aliya. We invested great efforts to send on Aliya as many people as possible, and no wonder that so many young people (at that time they were young, that is...) from Sarata live in Israel.

The Theatre Club in Sarata

[Page 348]

The Holocaust

by Zvi Schächter

Translated by Yocheved Klausner

In June 1941 the Nazi invasion began. With the thunder of the cannons, the Jews of Sarata heard the bells of alarm – a warning, that it was time again to pick up their wandering sticks, the sticks that had been kept in a dark corner since 1905, when they fled to Sarata to escape from the riots in the Akkerman region.

The Jewish youth was recruited to the army in the war against the Nazis and the entire community was worried. The Sarata Jews were not bothered by illusions – they knew the Nazis and what they meant. They also knew the neighborhood and some of the villagers; they knew that those would be the first to rob and murder, in particular when it was clear that the Jew and his property were "free-for-all." The Jews felt what was coming: hate was palpable in the air, and bad news was coming from the front, indicating the approaching storm.

The Sarata Jews began evacuating; thus began the great wandering on the road from Sarata to Akkerman and to the Dniester passes, on the way to Odessa and other regions in Russia. First they evacuated the women and children and the men remained. Long convoys moved day and night, wagons loaded with house objects, on top of which the women and children were sitting, their eyes expressing sadness and worry. The Soviet authorities used some of the wagons to transport materials and machines as well.

When darkness fell, I recognized on one of the wagons two women, their faces smeared with soot so that they would not be recognized. I tried to speak to them but they replied in Ukrainian. They were Hinka and Niora Gurewitz, well known in Sarata and Akkerman.

By mid-July the rest of the Jews, except for a very few, had left Sarata. Already in the morning of the evacuation day, the Jewish shops were broken into, robbed and destroyed.

The Siege of Odessa

When the approach of Hitler's soldiers became known, it was impossible to continue the journey eastward. Odessa was under siege and all roads were blocked. Not all the refugees succeeded in their flight toward the depth of Russia. The Nazis surrounded Odessa and blocked all roads. Very few managed to escape by way of boats. Yet Odessa became a temporary shelter for most of the Jewish residents of Southern Bessarabia.

Day and night the Nazis bombed the city. Many houses were destroyed. All night the skies of Odessa were lit by fire-bombs and burning buildings. Frightened Jews ran from place to place looking for shelter. The bombings of the Jewish neighborhoods continued sometimes for days on end – without having any military purpose, but just to kill Jews. Some of the Odessa Russians were influenced by the Nazi propaganda and were waiting impatiently for the day of riots and plunder. One day in August, a Russian announced that the Germans were killing Jews and robbing their property and the rumor spread through the entire city.

One night, while fleeing from the bombings, we passed near a Russian's house and noticed a shelter in the courtyard. We asked to enter and find some shelter, and were refused: "Impossible! Where there are Jews, many bombs are falling!"

Yet, most of the region's Jews stayed in Odessa, including the Sarata Jews, most of them outside, under the sky, in the public park or on the promenade at the sea. They would sit and sleep on bundles, sacs and suitcases – a deplorable sight of wanderers lacking a roof over their heads. Day and night the Nazi oppressor murderously bombed them from cannons and planes. Buildings collapsed, culture houses and synagogues were destroyed. Odessa was besieged by the Nazi army and there was fighting in the outskirts of town. The Odessa Jews joined in the battle against the enemy and helped with great devotion in the effort to push them back.

The Nazis in Odessa

In October 1941, the Nazi army entered Odessa, and the spilling of Jewish blood began.

[Page 349]

An order was issued, that all Odessa Jews must appear for registration and they will be given proper documents. When they did, they were immediately sent to the Delnik death camp. A month later, a similar order was issued, this time with the purpose to annihilate the Odessa Jewry. The heavy hand of the Nazi animal would not rest. The number of the Sarata Jews was reduced daily.

Several weeks later, mass-deportation began, to regions around Odessa: Atzikov, Berezovska, Bogdanovka. On their way, the deported people met groups of Jews taken to be murdered. Near the villages they saw Jews digging large pits – it was well-known for what purpose: the Nazis did not try to hide their crimes. From Berezovka they took 34,000 Jews and sent them to work in the Kolkhozes. Many of them did not reach their destination, dying on their way as a result of torture.

The murderous machine worked day and night – during the winter storms, in the snow, in clear summer days, in the eyes of the entire world. Jews were forced to dig their own graves and the Germans murdered them. The Nazis subjected them to torturing labor, and when they were at the end of their strength they killed them.

We do not know the details of the murder of many of the Sarata Jews, nor of their burial places. With awe we bow our heads over their unknown graves. May these lines serve as an eternal memory to all of them; they excelled in their national pride, devotion to their families and courage, in life and death.

Memorial service for the Akkerman martyrs
Second from right: A Schachter from Sarata

[Page 350]

Yosef Kaprushanski and his wife could not stand the suffering of the Odessa Jews. He took his wagon and horses and they returned to Sarata. They were murdered near the Bulgarian village Kamtchik.
Israel and **Devora Galperin** and their son **David** - religious people – were killed near Odessa.
Tzipora (Feiga) **Altman**, **Mania Altman** and her baby-girl perished near Odessa.
Betty Tzirolnik, **Zonia Galia** and the daughter **Anna** perished near Odessa.
Nachman amd **Polia Altman** perished near Odessa.
The **Hefetz** family, the **mother**, **Bosia** and **Mika**. Bosia was a doctor. When he worked in the deportee camp, he saw a German soldier beating a Jewish boy and hitting him with his boots. This murderous act, the humiliation and subjugation enraged him. He approached the murderer and with a stroke of his fist threw him to the ground. As a punishment, the Nazis murdered his entire family in sight of all the deportees in camp.
Grisha Gertzberg and his wife, a rich merchant arrived to Odessa and was deported to Bogdanovka and from there to a deserted Kolkhoz, Achmatzotka. They were put in a pigsty and perished of hunger. Their two daughters survived.
Netzik and **Chana Perlman** and their two daughters were murdered in one of the camps near Odessa, after hard work, humiliation and hunger.

Yakov Kolpetzki and his family were murdered near Odessa.
Neshil Kolpetzki and his family were murdered near Odessa.
Yosef Kolpetzki was murdered near Odessa.
Yakov Glazer, his wife and his son **David** perished near Odessa.
Chana Kaproshanski and her family – the evil hand reached them in the Caucasus, where they were murdered.
Yosef Kornblit perished near Odessa.
Beril Streicher, his wife and the daughter **Tzila Gerstein** and her two daughters perished near Odessa.
Shimon Gershkowitz and his wife perished near Odessa.
Munia Gershkowitz and his wife perished near Odessa.
Avraham Peltz, his wife and his daughter were murdered.
David Rabinowitz, his wife and his daughter were murdered near Odessa.

On the Way to Eretz Israel

In July the Nazis occupied Sarata. The villagers in the neighborhood raided the town and began robbing the Jewish houses, but not only the content of the houses. They took windows and doors and stones from the walls. The Altstein's house was entirely destroyed, not one stone remained in place – they destroyed even the foundation of the house. They also smashed the tombstones and used them for building purposes.

Moshe Leib Lublinski, a 70 years old Jew, could not stand the hardships of the road. Most of his life he worked among the German residents of Sarata and he did not imagine that his life was in danger. After the Nazis murdered him in the yard of his house, for several days they did not allow the neighbors to bury his remains.

Shmuel Lublinski, about 30 years old, son of **Moshe Leib** was cruelly murdered in one of the neighborhood villages. He was a pleasant young man, with a permanent smile on his face.

Tzila, a young woman who could not leave the place, was murdered in Sarata.

Zvi Halperin, a student at the *Yeshiva*, wearing his traditional clothing, was tortured and abused physically until he returned his soul in purity. He was murdered by his neighbor, a young Ukrainian.

Welwel Schwartz, an old man, perished in Sarata.

Fanny Steinberg, her daughter **Miya Wakertchevski** perished in Shaba, in a cruel, horrendous death.

Several families, learning after the war what had happened to their families, came to Sarata, but soon left the place on their way to Eretz Israel.

Many of the Sarata Jews perished – by suffering and torture they paid for being Jews. But their spirit was inherited by their descendants, who lived to realize their aspiration in life and their last wish: they established the State of Israel.

The Fighters

From Odessa to Stalingrad, and from there to the occupation of Berlin, the Sarata young Jews fought the Nazis courageously and heroically until their surrender. Some of them, including invalids, returned from battle with medals, others fell in battle.

Eternal Glory for These Heroes:

Lublinski Aizik; Lublinski Gedalyahu; Rieder Danny; Y. Tomashpolski; D. Gerzberg; M. Altman; D. Roizman; Motil Ostrovski; Yitzhak Streicher; Shlomo Bronfman; Avraham Finkelstein.

[Page 351]

Iziya's Story
by Zvi Schächter
Translated by Yocheved Klausner

In the month of July 1941, on the road stretching through yellow cornfields, a wagon pulled by horses was moving among a long line of wagons. The wagon had left Sarata early in the morning, on the journey to the bridge on the River Dniester. The sound of tractors pulling damaged cannons and other heavy weapons blended with the sound of the wheels of the loaded wagons. The weapons were taken from the approaching front and the human voyagers were escaping from the Bessarabia villages. Everywhere one could see and feel defeat. Even the tired horses pulled the wagons heavily. The convoy was progressing slowly. There were rumors that a day earlier the Germans had bombed the convoy and sent paratroopers for the purpose of sabotage.

On the wagon that came from Sarata, four people, pale and worried, were sitting. One of them, holding the reins, was David Seltzer; but it was not the usual joyful and happy David'l. His face was sad, and he was deep in thought. David'l was traveling to his family, his wife Zenia and his twins, Iziya and Dora. They were waiting for him in Odessa.

Two Russian soldiers standing on the road stopped the wagon, announcing: "No entry to Odessa." They ordered him to turn around and take the road to Ukraine. David explained to the soldiers that he must go to Odessa where his wife and young children were waiting for him – to no avail. He decided to take another road and go to Odessa by way of Ovidiopol.

His son Iziya, one of the few who survived the murder pit in the camp, told us what had happened – a shocking testimony, drenched in the blood of tortured Jews, who even on the threshold of death preserved their dignity. -

In October 1941 the German army entered Odessa. An order was issued, that all Jews should register in a place called Fontenia and receive identity cards. Some 60,000 Jews came, including old people and children. They were taken to Delnik, a deserted army barracks, with some buildings and huts. On the way, the Gestapo soldiers beat them with sticks and rifle butts. Babies on their mothers' hands were crying bitterly. The Germans urged the helpless walking people and shot into the crowd without reason. Finally they reached Delnik and the Gestapo pushed the crowd – thousands of them, one on top of the other – into the mined buildings. Horrible cries were heard, there was no air to breathe. The murderers activated the mines in the huts and blew up the Jews inside. The air became filled with sounds of terrible explosions and foul smell of smoke and blood, alongside with the victims' cries of despair.

We – my father, my mother and my sister – approached the place; we were a step from certain death. But, for some reason the Nazis postponed the annihilation acts and we managed to return to the empty apartment and remained there.

In November 1941, the Gestapo issued an order that all remaining Jews in Odessa appear in the prison yard for work. My father heard that whoever went there was immediately murdered.

My father did not go. My parents spoke to a Ukrainian peasant, gave him a fur coat and my mother's golden jewels, and he promised to hide us. He led us to a hidden corner in the attic of his house. From there we could follow the movements of the Gestapo. We saw them go from house to house and cruelly pull out the Jews. Again an order was issued, for the Jews to appear at the Slobodka, and from there they were deported to the Atzikov, Berezovska and Bogdanovka Regions. Three weeks later, the peasant who had taken our jewels brought the Gestapo to our hiding place.

The Nazis sent us, together with many other Jews, to a deportee camp in Berezovka, 28 Km. from Odessa. The remaining Odessa Jews were crowded there, having been forced to walk during the cold winter days in the snow storms. They walked through snow and mud, crying and listening to their children's heartbreaking cries. They had no strength to continue, due to the hunger

[Page 352]

that they had suffered in Odesa, where many members of their loved ones had perished. Many were wounded, their clothes torn and blood-stained from the beatings. Many fell and couldn't get up and the Nazis kept on shooting and killing the weakened walkers.

From Berezovka they deported the Jews to the villages Gulievka, Sofievka and Zlatosteva, to the Kolkhozes – a short "rest." But the Nazi Satan planed meticulously his destruction work and the murder-machine kept accurately the time-table.

We were sent to the Sofievka Kolkhoz, for agricultural work. My father brought to Sofievka some Sarata people who were in the neighborhood, Fishel and Tzirna Rieder and their daughter-in-law with her baby, as well as Yehoshua Hersh Apteker, his wife and their son Sioma. We worked on a Kolkhoz in Sofievka. Our family lived in the house of a Ukrainian peasant, a Baptist family, who despised the Nazis. The villagers told us about the horrors of the Nazis, the murders that they had seen with their own eyes, and the constant shooting of Jews. We knew that the fate of the Jews was decided and the murder was executed systematically. The region was populated by Germans, who collaborated with the Nazis, as did some of the Ukrainians. We were living in the Kolkhoz, alert to any noise, to the barking of a dog, to the sound of steps in the long winter nights. It was great suffering on our poor shoulders.

In the spring of 1942, in the dawn of a day in the month of May the Gestapo surrounded Sofievka. The "Aktzia" was approaching – they will soon begin searching the houses and taking the Jews. We the children and Mother hid in the haystack in the yard and our father remained in the house. The Nazis turned the house upside down looking for us, also shot to the haystack but did not hurt us. My father and others were taken outside the Kolkhoz; the pits were ready; but before the shooting they picked from among the Jews several craftsmen – and my father, Fishel, Rieder and Apteker said that they were craftsmen, harness makers. They were among the few who remained alive after this Aktzia; the others, several thousand, were killed.

When my father returned home, he heard constant sounds of shots. As night fell, we became afraid. Any noise worried and frightened us – any moment they could come. Long were our nights in Sofievka. The Nazis turned our day into night.

On a hot summer day, in August 1942, the Nazis again surrounded Sofievka. 3000 Jews had remained in the place. We were staying with the Baptist Ukrainian family. The woman told us that the Aktzia had begun. She asked us to leave with them my twin sister Dora, since the Nazis, they said, would not recognize her as Jewish. She dressed Dora in a typical Ukrainian dress. She was afraid to take me, since the Nazis checked the boys, by taking off their pants.

The Germans surrounded us. Early in the morning they took us all out of the house and beat us cruelly. They checked every corner of the house. They were experts in "Jew-hunting." Some Jews who tried to escape were immediately shot. Iziya's fate had been the death march and other suffering; now he is with me and is well physically, but the wound in his heart is still bleeding for the loss of his loved ones in the Valley of Death.

Early in the morning we were taken outside the village, to a fenced place: myself, father and mother, Fishel and Tzirna Rieder, Riva Rieder and her baby, Yehoshua Hersh Apteker with his wife and their son Sioma. Near the place there were long ditches. Before that they had brought Jews who had been ordered to deepen the ditches. The Nazis ordered all of us to undress, either just for humiliation or with the added purpose to "kill and inherit" our clothes. Naked, humiliated and depressed we stood there, not understanding why they tortured us and shot at us. The sun sent its rays and lit the sad picture. The crying of the mothers was heard over the distance. I was standing and saw with my own eyes the massacre, I saw the Nazis and their evil faces full of satisfaction and pleasure, caused by their murderous acts.

As Riva came close to the pit, she asked for mercy for the baby in her hands. A Gestapo woman, in Nazi uniform, hit the head of the baby with the iron stick in her hand. A horrible cry came from the mouth of the mother, but she was immediately silenced with a bullet. Silence came over the place, but it was very soon broken: shots were heard again and the murder machine continued working. Yehosua Hersh Apteker, his wife and their son Sioma approached. On the edge of the pit Apteker embraced his wife and kissed her – love in front of murder. On the threshold of death they preserved their dignity. The bullets ended their lives. The 14-year-old son Sioma was shot and thrown into the pit while still alive.

It was near sunset and the sun sent its last rays. The murder continued. The number of Jews, naked, weak and suffering, which was about 3,000, decreased from minute to minute. They knew what to expect, every minute – many of them accepted reality; the majority was waiting in silence.

From the pit, desperate cries were heard, from mothers asking mercy for their children – what was their sin? But none of these cries could move the heart of the Nazi animals. I was standing some 5 meters from the edge of the pit and I saw Satan at the peak of evil. My father and mother were approaching. My mother was holding my hand and asking for mercy.

[Page 353]

Standing in front of a Gestapo platoon that was shooting with sadistic pleasure, she fought with the last of her strength, not to let me out of her hand. A shot silenced her awful cry, as she was protecting me with her body and pulling me with her toward the pit. I fell with her, heard another shot and lost my conscience. That was how my mother saved me from death.

Iziya's face was red and a tremor went through his body -.

When I woke up, I found myself on a pile of murdered people. Heartbreaking sighs were heard. Some of them were still dying and buried alive. I was covered with blood and hurting in my entire body. I was hit by a bullet in my leg, while I was thrown into the pit. With my last strength, after a great effort, I managed to climb out.

It was dawn. The first rays of the sun could be seen through the morning fog. I saw Sioma Apteker, wounded in his entire body; he could not climb out of the pit and together with Avrasha I helped him. Avrasha was a 14 year old boy from Odessa, who was also saved from the bullets fired at him in the pit. We managed to lift the wounded Sioma out of the pit.

As we came out, the German soldiers charged with keeping guard at the pit, fired at us. Sioma was hit again, fell and did not get up. Avrasha and I ran to the nearby grove of trees while the Nazis shot at us and bullets were flying all over. But we reached the grove and hid there. In the morning we saw through the trees how the Germans poured gasoline into the pit and burned the corpses.

For some 12 days Avrasha and I remained in the forest. We were afraid to go out; German peasants were living in the neighborhood and we were certain that they would report us to the Nazis. We were hungry and thirsty. The days were hot and we were dehydrated. We ate what we found on the ground – rotten potatoes, beets.

The Ukrainian peasant in whose house we had lived came out to the field and brought us a bottle of milk and some bread. He told us to be careful, since the region was full of Nazis and their helpers. He also told us that Jews deported from Romania were living in the Mostovia camp, and the Nazis were not shooting at them.

We were still hiding among the trees of the little grove of trees. The neighborhood was hostile, shots were heard often. We saw, from the distance, people digging pits. The region was full of mass-graves. Was our road again leading us toward the Nazis? Weak, covered with rags, tired and hungry we would walk during the nights and during daylight hide in the cornfield. How will we reach Mostovia?

Suddenly we saw a wagon loaded with green animal feed, making its way on the road to Mostovia. Without the wagon driver knowing, we climbed onto the wagon. But a passing German peasant observed what we had done, climbed the wagon as well and held us. Suddenly a motorcycle passed making great noise; the horses became frightened and began galloping. The wagon swung from side to side, we managed to free ourselves from the hold of the German and jumped from the wagon. With our last strength we ran toward the corn field and hid among the tall corn plants. Will we succeed? The German arrived to the closest village and alerted other villagers, who began searching the corn field. We held our breaths, several times they passed on their horses close to us, but they did not discover our hiding corner. So we were saved again from certain death.

We lived in constant fear. Death loomed over us. But salvation was still far away; we were pursued from every side and the hope that we would escape decreased; every road led to the hangman. Every day Jews were digging new graves; shots were heard in the area all the time. However, even young boys aged 12 years and swollen from hunger – the strong will of life pushed them forward looking for salvation. It was rumored that in the camp of the Romanian Jews they don't kill the prisoners, only kept them hungry.

Two more days passed, two hot days of hunger, thirst and exhaustion. At night we passed near a small village – just a few houses. We heard the dogs barking. Going out of the forest was dangerous, but we had no choice. We entered the cellar of one of the houses; there we found cheese and sour milk, we ate and drank. But our systems were not strong enough to process the food, and as we left we were hit by diarrhea. Who knows whether we will have enough strength to overcome our many troubles? Still, we continued walking toward Mostovia – at night on the road and during the day through side roads and groves.

About half a kilometer before Mostovia we saw again Germans shooting Jews; later we learned that gypsies were also among those shot. We saw the bloodthirsty Nazis in their uniforms and heard the horrible cries of the victims – I remembered my beloved and my blood was boiling in my veins.

When we approached Mostovia, we met a Russian peasant who told us to be careful since our lives were in danger.

Iziya continued his story. He was breathing heavily as if he was carrying a heavy load on his shoulders -.

[Page 354]

While we were talking with the Russian peasant, a Romanian Gendarme appeared and asked in Romanian: "Who are you?" I replied in Romanian. Avrasha did not know Romanian. The Gendarme took us on his wagon to his commander in Mostovia, who was guarding the Jewish deportees' camp. The Commander asked us where we came from. I told him that my parents were murdered and we escaped from the death pit, and added: "We are in your hands, do with us as you see fit." The Commander asked "What will happen if I shoot you?" and added: "Don't be afraid, here you will receive clothes and food and you will not be harmed."

The Gendarme took us into the kitchen and gave us food and clothes and army boots. He told us that they have an order to shoot Jews who came from Russia and Bessarabia, but they will not harm us. In the evening, the head of the Romanian Jews' Committee in the camp came and told us that we have been saved. We were included in the camp of the Romanian Jews – about 600 Jews – and sent to work in the kitchen. We stayed there about seven months.

In 1943, an order came from the Romanian Red Cross to set us free. With the help of the Red Cross and under its protection we went to Sofievka to take our sister who was still living with the Ukrainian peasant family. When the Baptist peasant woman saw me – knowing what had happened at the Aktzia – she was frightened, thinking that I had risen from my grave. I took Dora and returned to Mostovia and the Red Cross transferred us, together with many other children, to Tiraspol. There, 1200 children were put in quarantine, to avoid spreading of diseases. They cut our hair, gave us new clothes and by the end of 1943 we were sent to the city Iasi (Yassy).

The Yassy Jews welcomed us warmly. When the front came close we were transferred to other towns in Romania. Everywhere, the local Jews took care of us and we lived with Jewish families. Later we were taken to Bucharest and waited for the Russian occupation. The Russians took the Russian children and sent them to Donbass, where there was a coal mine. I worked in a brick factory, but I didn't find rest in Donbass; I wanted to find a relative or an acquaintance and relate what my eyes had seen, about the bitter end of my parents and the thousands of Jews whose graves were scattered throughout the fields of Transnistria. I left Donbass and went for a few days to Sarata. I found there a few Jewish families who were about to leave the destroyed town.

I went to Odessa, which was again in the hands of the Soviets. I informed the authorities about the Ukrainian who had informed the Nazis about us. He was sentenced to 25 years in prison.

When Iziya mentioned the Ukrainian, his eyed sparkled and his breathing became heavy – his whole personality said "revenge!" -

I continued my journey and came to Kishinev.

Iziya drank some water and stopped talking for a short minute. The horrors rose again before his eyes, sweat covered his face. How great the will of life, the courage and the power of struggle for existence of a young Jewish boy. At the table Iziya's son was sitting, looking like his grandmother who had remained there. This will not happen to him; he is living now in his own country.

[Page 357]

Byeramtcha

(Mykolayivka–Novorosiyska, Ukraine)

46°08' 29°54'

My Shtetl Byeramtcha

by Moshe Shochet (Nahariya)

Translated by Yocheved Klausner

The official name of the town in the time of Czarist Russia was Nikolayevka Novorusiskaya, but the Romanians changed its name to Byeramtcha, and this was actually its name at the time of the Turks. Byeram means Holiday. In 1945, when the town went under Russian rule, they changed its name to what it was before, and now it is again Nikolayevka Novorusiskaya.

The town is situated about 35 km. from Akkerman and 10 km. from the train station in Colvatcha. When Czarist Russia began to populate the fertile lands of the "Budzhak" they brought to Byeramtcha Cossacks, as they did in other villages. In time, other people began to buy the Cossacks's lands and settle there, since the Cossacks were not too willing to till the land. The new settlers (Russians, Ukrainians, Moldovans, Jews) were considered in Czarist Russia as foreigners, and at the various assemblies only the Cossacks had the right to vote. I remember on Sundays, when the Christians went to Church, the Cossacks walked through the streets in their official uniforms. One of them was guarding the Jewish cemetery, his name was grandfather Gordey; on Yom Kippur he was going to the Jewish synagogues and taking care that the candles would not be extinguished. Before Pesach, the *Hametz* was sold to grandfather Gordey; he would appear to the selling ceremony dressed in his official Cossack uniform, on his chest all the medals he had received during his service in the Czar's Army.

Another event from the distant past is etched in my memory: in 1913, when they celebrated 300 years of the Romanov Dynasty, they distributed wine to everybody at the entrance to the house of the Municipal Council. And there, too, the Cossacks appeared in full uniform.

The 1905 Pogrom

There were some 1200 courtyards in Byeramtcha and the Jewish population numbered 280 families. The 1905 pogrom severely hit the Jewish population. The members of the "Black Hundreds" gangs robbed the Jewish houses and set fire to houses and shops. I heard about this pogrom from David Schor, who was a resident of Akkerman, but lived with his family in Byeramtcha. When he returned to his home after the pogrom, he did not find even a pillow to put his head on; everything had been robbed. Gabriel Wolman and Israel Boganov fought heroically with the rioters, but they were killed and left widows and orphans. Gabriel Wolman was buried in Akkerman together with the other victims and a gravestone (*matzeva*) was erected on his grave. The desecrated Torah Scrolls were buried in the same place.

In the Encyclopedia of the Jewish Diaspora, Berman and David Vinitzki write: "A local policeman took part in the preparations for the pogrom, and so did the priest, who used to read in the church the "hate pamphlets." On 22 October, four days before the pogrom began, the Jews were invited to the opening and dedication of a new church, and they donated 25 Rubles to cover the cost of the festivities. But this was also used against the Jews. A shot in the air was the signal. The sound of the church bells meant an invitation for the peasants to enter the town. The police senior officer, who a day earlier advised the Jews to organize self-defense, disappeared from the place. At first several rioters were brought by the defense to the police, but they were soon released and even given new weapons. The director of the seminary for young priests tried to stop the rioters but without success. The Jewish newspaper *Hatzefira* of 7.11.1905 wrote among others: "On the day of 26 October, a frightening pogrom began in our town, and continued the next day. Most of the rioters are residents of our town. With axes, hammers, wooden logs and other 'instruments' they destroyed the shops and robbed the contents.

[Page 358]

After emptying the shops, they poured kerosene and burned them. Then, divided into groups, they marched through town, spared every Christian house and burned every Jewish one, after breaking all the furniture. – – – Many of the Jews escaped to the nearby German colonies, but many of these also closed their gates, some saying that they were afraid as well, some openly endorsing what was being done to the Jews. Tens of families, with suckling babies, wandered from village to village, sleeping at night under the sky, wet from the rain, trembling from fear and from the cold of the night. – – – –

The material damage reached 300,000 Rubles. The rich became poor, and 570 souls remained naked, hungry and without a place to rest their body. They needed urgent help. The rumor said that the initiators of the pogrom informed the peasants from the neighboring villages asking them to come with their wagons to collect the spoils. They waited for hours at the entrance of the town, until some of the bandits rang the church bells signaling that the head of the police had left the place and they could come in – – – – First aid was received from the charitable society in the name of Rabbi M. Rabelenski, Byeramtcha, Bessarabia."

Signed this report: The glazier.

Before WWI, Czarist Russia built a railroad connecting Akkerman with the town. According to the plan, the railroad should pass through Byeramtcha, but the assembly of the Cossacks and the residents of the town decided to oppose the plan whereby the railroad passed through their fields, fearing that their cattle would be hurt while in pasture. Later they understood that the decision was a mistake, but it could not be changed, and the station was built about 10 kilometers from town. This, however, did not stop Byeramtcha from becoming the center of the villages of the region and a connecting point between the Kolvatcha station and the Black Sea. All the farmers in the neighborhood brought their grains to Byeramtcha, and from there to Kolvatcha.

The Jews were mostly merchants, buying and selling agricultural products. Among them were also craftsmen and shop owners, in particular of textile and haberdashery. There was no industry in town. The Jewish population was, in general, not rich, and there were many needy families among them. Many were peddlers, and they would spend the entire week walking through the neighboring town and trying to sell their merchandise, and only on Friday they would come to join their families.

The football (soccer) team in Byeramtcha, Jews and Christians

[Page 359]

The town was a center of raw leather trade. Jewish merchants would travel to the neighboring villages, reaching even Volontirovka, and buy from the peasants the leather. Others would buy cattle, poultry and eggs and transport them to Galatz. Some had connections with banks in Akkerman and could obtain loans, in order to be able to conduct the trade in wool and grains.

Jewish Institutions

As early as 1915 a "Loan–and–Savings Fund" was established in town; its manager was B. Brodetzki and after him B. Droz Makerman. When he left he was replaced by Leib Hellman, who officiated until 1940. This Fund was a great help, and its loans reached 30,000 Lei and more.

The town had two synagogues, on opposite sides of the same street – the Jewish street: The Old Synagogue and the New Synagogue. Both were beautiful stone buildings. In 1910 our family arrived in town, and there was already a Hebrew school. Among the teachers were real scholars, for example Danilka, Rosenberg, Schochen, Glaznik, Magazinik and others. The rabbi of the town, Ravelski z"l, has done a great deal for the school. He was a member of the Mizrahi Party, participated in the activity for *Keren Hayesod* and made speeches at assemblies and conferences in Kishinev and other cities. After he left Byeramtcha, he was replaced by Rabbi Bunimowitz from Lithuania, a great scholar who, among others was fluent in the English language. He had a very rich library. When he left town, he planned to entrust his library in the hands of M. Pik, but he could not reach him and in those troubled times the traces of the library were lost. Before the October Revolution, the Rabbi was invited by the Odessa Community to serve there, and rumor said that after that he went to America.

After Rabbi Ravelsi left, the local school lost much of its reputation and most of the good teachers left it. My father z"l took upon himself to take care of the school, went to Toltchin and invited two teachers, Lipman and Farfel, who worked there until 1918, when Bessarabia was annexed to Romania. Later the teachers returned to Toltchin and the school became a government school; the government appointed Chichelinski as principal, but after serving a few years he left, to direct the *Talmud Tora* in Akkerman. After him, Mr, Furman was appointed principal, but not for long, since the school closed.

Until 1923, a good Russian school was also active in town, but when the Romanians began to act against the schools that taught in a language other than Romanian, this institution suffered as well. The Romanian secret police accused the school of harboring a communist cell and arrested five students on the charge that they belonged to this cell. They were taken to Akkerman for investigation, but on the way they were shot and killed, on the pretense that they tried to escape. Among those killed were Abramovici and Kacerga. When the Russians occupied Byeramtcha, they arrested all those involved in this affair.

The government hospital in town was managed by Dr. Yakov Bilostotzki, a devoted Zionist and a member of *Po'alei Zion*. His wife was the principal of the Hebrew School in Arciz. Among the young people who returned from Odessa after the October revolution were many who considered the new regime as salvation, but many of the students were true Zionists – like Alexander Kiefer, Komarovski and others – and they began to spread the Zionist ideas among the youth. Kiefer went to Eretz Israel and died in Tel Aviv. The Zionists established a Zionist Organization, published a local magazine and assembled around them the local young people, among them: Chana Korol, Z. Rabinowitz (Gesser) who lives now in France, Liza Geller (Chaimovici) who in 1925 made Aliya with her husband and lives now in Rechovot, A. Greenman, Roza Schor and Yakov Feldman. They spread among the Jews the *Keren Kayemet* (JNF) "blue boxes" and reached the Jews in the neighboring villages as well. The JNF Committee was headed by S. Perski, who organized festivities and lotteries and used to participate in every joyful occasion, collected donations from the guests and registered names in the "Golden Book" [*Sefer Hazahav*].

It is worth mentioning that the Jews made donations willingly, each according to his means.

Members of the Jewish Orchestra in Byeramtcha

[Page 360]

The Orchestra and Public Library

In 1925 we began to organize a Maccabi branch and our first aim was to assemble an orchestra of wind instruments. We collected money among the residents and when we had a suitable sum I went with A. Hellman to Kishinev and we bought instruments. A. Hellman, who was a musician, was the conductor of the orchestra and its manager until 1940. The players were totally devoted to the orchestra and Hellman was an example in his devotion to the matter. On the Purim holiday the same year, the orchestra played, for the enjoyment of the residents, at a ball held for the benefit of the National Funds. In time, the orchestra gained fame in the neighborhood and they began receiving invitations to festivities, Jewish and Christian – and the income was devoted to Zionist matters. With the Russian occupation in 1940, the orchestra operated under the management of the authorities, and Christian players joined it as well.

Our other undertaking was to establish a Public Library. Until that time, lending books was the task of Yankel Goldstein. He was by profession a carver of tombstone letters, but he had a collection of all kinds of books which he would lend against a small payment. For the library we arranged a collection among the Jewish residents and when we had a considerable sum we went (Avraham Greenman, Roza Schor and the writer of these lines) to Kishinev and bought a number of books in Yiddish, Russian and Romanian. In time, the library grew, as did the number of registered persons. Members of the Romanian Secret Police were permanent "visitors" in the Library, checking the accounting registers as well as the books. In 1930, we transferred the Library to the ownership and management of the Jewish Loan-and-Savings Fund. It should be mentioned that among the registered members were Christians as well.

Members of the Maccabi Sport Organization in Byeramtcha

[Page 361]
The Zionist Activity

Among the Zionist organizations, the first that should be mentioned was the Association of the General Zionists, headed by B. Brodetzki, A. Goldstein and Z. Otzertinski, in whose house all the meetings were held. All three of them helped any emissary who arrived from the big cities to arrange collections for the Zionist Funds.

Mrs. Feiga Berger, a dentist by profession, managed the activity among the youth. Helped by Chana Corol, she established the *Gordonia* branch in town. Every year on 20 Tammuz (the day Herzl died) they held in the synagogue a memorial service and planted trees in the Herzl Forest. In the 1930s Feiga and her two children made Aliya. Her brother came in 1920 and later fell by a rioter's bullet. I remember that in Byeramtcha they spoke about him as "a hero the son of a hero" since his father was killed during the 1905 pogrom, as we wrote earlier. Feiga's son, Dov, fell by rioters and his wife Shoshana lives in Tel Aviv. At the beginning of the 1930s, A. Gershkowitz made Aliya, as well as Rachel, daughter of A. Goldstein; she lives in Rechovot.

I was working, spreading the Zionist idea among the young people and I participated in several congresses held in Bessarabia: the Congress in Kishinev, with the participation of M. M. Ussishkin z"l, another congress with the participation of Nachum Sokolov z"l and a third one in Kishinev with the participation of the President of the Zionist Organization Chaim Weizman z"l. When I returned from these congresses I would give a detailed report to the Organization about the discussions and the decisions taken (from 1927 to 1932 I lived in Bendery, joined the Revisionist Party and was elected the head of the local branch).

The Jewish Community

Due to the difficult economic situation, many of the local Jews were forced to "pick up the wanderer's stick" and immigrate to other countries, like Brazil, the United States, Mexico etc., looking for means to make a livelihood. Entire families were uprooted from their birth place: the families of Chaim Chaimovici, Hersh and P. Perski, Kalman Chaimovici, Motl Getzuletzki, D. Dobrish, Shalom Kooper, Moshe Geller, P. Komarovski, Khorol Daniel and Noah and others. The Jewish emigration from Byeramtcha didn't stop, until the Russians occupied the place.

In 1934, the local Jewish Community, approved by the Authorities was organized. The Community Council was elected by regular elections. I was elected Head of the Community, the secretary was the dentist Kaplanski, the treasurer was Shkolnik and the accountant was Aharon Goldman. The Gabays [attendants] of the synagogues I. Kalnitzki and S. Balinowitz were also members of the Community Council. The " *Appointed [by the authorities] Rabbi*" M. Kolker was in charge of registering the local Jewish population and of the Archives; the income from the registration and the various documents issued was given to the Community. The Community Council included 15 councilmen, representatives of the various parties, and every Jewish resident paid a membership fee. The community was responsible for baking *Matzot* for the Passover [*Pesah*] holiday, for the residents of the town and the Jews from the neighboring villages. It was a serious source of income for our community. Orphans, sick people and needy people were supported by the community, and Dr. Goldenberg, who received a regular salary from the community, gave the needy sick people regular medical care.

Entertainment, Cantors and the Like

In 1918, an amateur Drama Club was organized, managed by Chaim Otzertinski and S. Perski. The Club performed various plays, of which I remember the play "The Massacre." The first members of the club were older, and after they left the scene, younger people took their place. The drama club existed until 1940; the Byeramtcha Jews liked theater, and many well-known actors visited us, among them the famous Russian actor Vronski, who fled from the Bolshevik regime. Usually the actors lived in private houses during their stay in town, since we did not have suitable hotels. When the Vilna Drama Group [*Di Vilner Trouppe*] visited us and performed "The Dibbuk" by Anski and "Midnight in the Old Market Place" by Y. L. Peretz, I had the honor to be for two weeks the host of the actors Alexey Stein and his wife.

The most famous cantors in Bessarabia visited us, and crowds would go to the synagogues to join the prayers. I remember the cantor Leibele Glantz. Often we would hold literary discussions, of which I particularly remember the discussions about "Bontzie Shweig," Motke Ganev," "With Lowered Eyes." The discussions were well organized and a large public attended.

The Political Activity in Town

Our little town played a role in the general political life as well. Some of the members of Parliament received our full support, as, for example, Att. Peter Vorvitzki from the Romanian Liberal Party and Att. Popovici, the representative of the Romanian National Farmers Party. When the Jews decided to send a representative of their own to the elections to the Parliament – it was Mr. M. Landau – we gave him our full support. I was one of the members on the Akkerman list. When the Russians entered Bessarabia, I had great trouble on the account of my name being on that list. The "Culture–League" people and the Communists acted against the Jewish list. Esteemed in particular was the Parliament member from the Liberal Party, Attorney Peter Verbitzki, who managed to establish and keep a situation of friendship between the Jewish and the Christian youth. The treasurer of the community, Z. Kaplanski helped him in this task. They organized a soccer team of Jews and Christians together, playing against groups from Tatarbonar, Kilia, Bolgrad, Ismail and others. It was not easy to create an atmosphere of friendship between Jews and Christians, at a time when Hitler was already active. Many Jews were saved thanks to this friendship.

[Page 362]

A class in the elementary school in Byeramtcha

In 1938, when the anti-Semitic party of Cuza-Goga came to power, the town Divizia held the regular market-day, on a Tuesday. Jewish merchants used to start at night the journey to the market, so that they would arrive early. On Monday, a day before the market-day, I was informed secretly that the ironsmith in Divizia prepared for the villagers chains, irons and other weapons, for a pogrom on the market day. Immediately I called the Council and we decided to tell the merchants not to go to the market the next day. However, some of them were already on their way and we could not reach them, and there were the Divizia Jews as well. I got in touch with the merchants' Stock Exchange in Akkerman, talked to S. Barg and K. Goldman and told them about the expected events. An hour later, I received a telephone call from Moshe Hellman, the head of the community in Akkerman, telling me that he had spoken to the Governor of the Province, who promised him that he will take the necessary measures to prevent the riots. The same night, soldiers from the 35 Infantry Regiment in Akkerman were sent to Divizia and prevented the villagers from entering the town. The market was cancelled and the Jews were saved from tragedy. A short time later the Goga-Cuza government fell; it happened on the night of Purim and for the Jews it was "another Purim miracle."

In 1933 there was a famine in Bessarabia, which did not miss our town as well. The community established a Committee to fight the famine and we received help from the JOINT, through the Central Committee for the fight against the famine in Kishinev. The Red Cross helped with food for the "soup kitchens" and we opened kosher soup kitchens for the Jews – hundreds of Jews came to these kitchens and received food for low prices. Some were ashamed to come, and we helped them by giving them money, until their situation improved.

After the Bolshevik Revolution there were no rabbis in Byeramtcha, and their tasks were performed by two *shohatim* [ritual slaughterers]. By the Romanian law, they were recognized as spiritual leaders of the Jews and were exempt from military duty.

[Page 363]

In 1940, with the Russian occupation, an outspoken anti-Semite was appointed head of the Farmers Council. He severely abused the shochet B. Gurewitz, who was accused that he did not hold special prayers for the well-being of the country on the Romanian national holidays. When the war against Hitler started, all those born in 1904 were recruited. Many of the town residents fell in battle; among them I remember: Chaim Braverman, Israel Rabinowitz, Moshe Leizerowitz, Yitzhak Rabinowitz, Chaim (Fima) Schor, Yankel Lowitz, Zelig Rabinowitz, Bilostotzki, Goldenberg. The evacuation of the population to Akkerman had begun, but many remained in Odessa and perished by the Nazis. Only a few families, who had suffered from Russian persecution and did not want to leave, remained in Byeramtcha. It was said, that when the German and Romanian soldiers entered the village Jews waited together with the Christians and welcomed them with bread and salt, as was the custom. But on the first day of the occupation, the Germans arrested all Jews, separated between the men and the women and took the men outside the village; there they forced them to dig a pit and shot them. During the night, the *shochet* Gurewitz, who was only wounded, crawled out from the pile of corpses, returned to the village and went to the house of the carpenter Gortchenko, who told later that he bandaged Gurewitz's wounds and fed him. Then he went to Velitchko, father of Nina who was a servant in his house, and he accompanied Gurewitz to his house. There, Velitchko received from Gurewitz a large amount of valuables, which had been in his possession for generations, but that was not enough for Velitchko and he informed the murderers. The Christians said later, that many Christians, among them the priest of the place made an effort to keep Gurewitz alive, but without success. To this day we don't know what had happened to him. The Jewish women were taken to the house of K. Gurlatchev, were abused and then taken to Akkerman. Among the murdered was my mother, two sisters and their children. I was told later that a Romanian lieutenant-general took two of the three children and transferred them to Romania, but all my efforts to find them were in vain. After the war, the Russian residents in Byeramtcha related to the authorities about the deeds of Velitchko.

He was called for an investigation, then he went home and committed suicide by hanging.

There is no trace of the Jewish settlement in Byeramtcha, and even the cemetery was entirely destroyed and the land turned over by plowing. May God avenge the blood of all who perished.

Meir Berger z"l

Meir Berger, father of Dov Harari, born to his father Dov Berger, was a central figure in the Jewish community of Byeramtcha. He died at a young age, and the following eulogy was published in the local Russian-German newspaper:

On 4 May, the known high-school teacher Meir Borisowitz Berger left us at the young age of 33, after a severe illness. He was active in all public institutions in Byeramtcha, traveled through the entire Akkerman Province as a guide, in the framework of the Central Committee of the Zionist Organization in Bessarabia and participated in the election campaign to the All-Russian Jewish Congress.

The late Mr. Berger was the initiator and the central figure of the local Jewish newspaper and served as the secretary of the Jewish Community Council to his last day. He was a member of the Court of Justice of the Parliament, but his greatest efforts, during his short life, were devoted to the Zionist Movement. He was one of the leaders of the Zionists in the region.

On the day of his funeral, all the institutions and stores were closed and many accompanied him to his eternal place of rest – high school teachers and students, simple folk and public leaders, young and old – the entire town.

The eulogies stressed the exceptional personality of the deceased and his devotion to public affairs. The Jewish community of Byeramtcha remained orphaned. We will all miss the good and loyal Meir.

Signed by Tchozoy

[Page 367]

Shabo

(Shabo, Ukraine)
46°08' 30°23'

My Shtetl Shabo
by Aharon Kaminker
Translated by Yocheved Klausner

Shabo was quite a famous shtetl, but it is doubtful whether someone tried to investigate its history and the events that took place there. It is probable that it was founded about 200 years ago. The entire region was not populated, the scenery was wild and desert was all around. The first steps to cultivate the area were made by the government of Czarist Russia, by inviting Germans to settle there, allotting plots of land and supporting them, so that they could develop the backward province. This explains the fact that many Germans lived in the area, at times reaching the number of 750,000 people.

Shabo consisted of three regions: the Northern Region, not far from Akkerman, was named Kolonia. The population included French, German and Swiss citizens, perhaps other nationalities as well. Some of them were wealthy and property owners, and most of them – diligent working people. In time, the residents of this region erected large farms, wine-cellars, beautiful houses with large courtyards, cowsheds, stables etc.

The farmers of Kolonia employed Russian peasants in their farms, paying quite low salaries; the regular workday began at dawn and ended at sunset.

The Kolonia region was nicely developed and was admired by every visitor. The beautiful houses, covered by red tiles, were surrounded by gardens, the streets were wide, bordered by trees and the vineyards could be seen in the distance. I remember that as a child I dreamt that in Eretz Israel we will build our villages by the example of Kolonia.

The residents of the area felt proud and haughty. They were very careful not to let other – lower – nationalities mingle with them…. in particular not Jews. Yet, during the summer crowds of Jews visited the area. Since the climate was pleasant and healthy, the Jews "adopted" the place as a summer resort. The residents would rent them accommodation in their own homes and provide produce from their farms, like fresh milk, grapes etc. The prices were not low, but since Kolonia became famous for its good climate, many preferred to spend their vacations there and paid willingly.

In contrast to the beautiful Kolonia, the residents of the Southern region in the direction of the Black Sea, owned small and undeveloped farms. Most of them were Ukrainians; among them were also a few Jewish families. The entire area was – and looked – poor. The houses were low, built of clay and covered by straw. The farms did not bring enough income for the sustenance of the family; therefore the members of the family needed additional work, outside the farm. The difference between the Northern and Southern regions was very great.

There was a third area, between the two regions, where Ukrainians, Germans and Jews lived in peace. The area was called "Psada-Shabo." Here were the institutions of the local authorities, the public services, shops, workshops, the market place, the slaughterhouses, etc.

At the length of the three regions, the waters of the Liman (a brook of the Dniester) flowed 10 kilometers to the Black Sea. The waters of the Liman were clear and flowing softly, generating an atmosphere of tranquility in the entire area.

The Dniester itself, on the other hand, was a strong river of an independent nature and a unique tempo and flow. In my young eyes the relationship between the Dniester and the Liman was similar to that between our own Jordan and the Sea of Galilee [the *Kinneret*]...

[Page 368]

During our youth, we were attracted to the shores of the river and we used to spend many hours there, admiring the beauty of the scenery and its ancient splendor.

It is worth mentioning, that the Liman contained many good fish that served as food for the population in the area, and were also exported to Odessa.

Thanks to the good climate, the quiet Liman waters and the rich fields and vineyards, Shabo became famous in Russia. It seemed that it was a natural resort place, and so it was nicknamed: "the healing place." The season opened in the spring, right after the Passover Holiday and it lasted five-six months, until autumn, by the end of the grapes harvest. The visitors were mostly (and perhaps only) Jews, coming mostly from Odessa. Many were wealthy, but there were also simple folk among them, who came to Kolonia to "gather strength" and find relief from the heat of the big city, in the clean air of the cool forests.

Many suffered from all kinds of aches and pains, and went to Shabo by the advice of their doctors. I remember that among them were famous people: Bialik, Tchernichovski, Ravnitzki, Tchernowitz (a young rabbi), Frug, Tchodanovski and others. Apart from the economic benefit, these guests brought to the place a cultural atmosphere and an interesting experience, and left pleasant memories.

The Jewish Community in Shabo

When did the Jews first come to Shabo? I cannot answer this question. It is probable that the first Jewish settlers came to the colony at the very beginning of the settlement. They came from all parts of Big Russia – Lithuania, Poland, The Ukraine, Caucasus etc. Understandably, they brought to the place new customs and ways-of-life, new styles of prayer etc., but through the years all these merged and a new blend, common to the entire Jewish community, was formed.

[Page 369]

At the time of my youth, about sixty families were part of the Jewish community in Shabo. Few of them owned property; most of them fought hard to maintain their modest sustenance. Many were merchants, but there were also craftsmen, workers in various services, waggoneers, butchers – as was the custom of the Jews in the Diaspora shtetls from time immemorial. The wine industry and commerce, which was particularly developed in Shabo, employed many Jews in its various sectors.

Members of the Zionist Organization Council in Shabo, in 1922, on the occasion of the Aliya of the first pioneers (halutzim): Slomo and Tzila Lerner and Penina Sitner (Berechyahu)

Sitting from right to left: **David Sitner, Penina Sitner (Berechyahu), Yoel Meirson, Shlomo Lerner, Berl Kishinovski, Tzila Lerner, Nechama Vidit, S. Lerner, Kaminker, Yitzhak Meirson**
Standing from right to left: **David Meirson, Pesia Nifomanishtchen, Elka Sternberg, Mania Steinberg, Yachna Steinberg, Sasha Meirson**

As in the other shtetlach, there were in Shabo many religious Jews, who observed all *mitzvoth* [commandments] strictly, and conducted their lives according to the Torah and tradition, but there were also secular families, who could be recognized by their way of dressing and their general lifestyle. However, even the secular families had respect for the Jewish tradition and the things that have been holy for many generations. It can be said, that a Jewish-national atmosphere was felt in every home in our town. On the eve of Shabbat and Holiday, a festive air spread over the Jewish community in town. Shabbat candles were seen in every home, the tables were set in a festive way with special food, and almost all Jews went to the synagogue. When Shabbat or a holiday came, the simple "everyday Jews" turned into "holiday Jews." That is how it was in all Bessarabia towns – and so it was in ours.

During vacation time, when all the visitors came, the synagogues were too small for all the people, and we would rent halls and large rooms in private homes to hold prayers.

I remember well the "Old Synagogue" on the central street. This was the spiritual center – sort of a Temple – of the little community. A wall separated the women's area from the main hall. The Holy Ark was built into the Eastern wall; in it were kept the Torah Scrolls and various religious objects. The Ark was covered by the special curtain embroidered with golden letters and the place for the cantor was nearby. In the center there was a large square table for the Torah Scroll during reciting the weekly Torah Portion. At the two sides of the table, the two elected and respected *Gabbays* [attendants, managers] would stand: R'Berl Steinberg and R'Yoel Meirson z"l, who would announce the names of those "called to the Torah." The Torah Reader, R'Binyamin Kaminker z"l, would stand there, ready. He was also the ritual slaughterer of Shabo.

The synagogue served also as the place where we performed weddings, Bar-Mitzvah ceremonies, Memorial days and so on. It was an institution that united the local Jewish public. Assemblies, lectures, social meetings etc. were also held there, and the entire Jewish population used it constantly. To this day I keep in my heart special ties to our synagogue, and I think that all former residents of Shabo remember this small spiritual center with love and respect.

For many years, the community leaders planned to build a new, big synagogue and collected money for that purpose, but the plan was never realized, unfortunately.

In the Shadow of Persecutions and Riots

If I described above he quiet waters of the Liman – the reader must not deduce that our lives flowed quietly like the Liman waters. The contrary is true. From my early childhood days in Shabo, memories of riots, pogroms and other predicaments are haunting me. It was the same as in other Jewish communities, bigger and older than Shabo. I almost don't remember days of calm, but I do remember times of horror and fear. The echoes of the Kishinev pogrom, which was the background of the great poem *Be'ir Haharega* by our national poet Bialik are always sounding in my ears, although I was still a small child at the time of this pogrom, which has become part of the Jewish history.

Regimes rose and fell, and the changes left an imprint on the life of the small Jewish community. Every change in government brought worry in the hearts of the Jews, because they never knew what to expect from the new regime and what suffering it may bring. I remember in particular the moments of dread and horror in the days of the 1905 pogroms. I can see clearly our hiding place in the attic – father z"l, my brother Moshe, I and a Jewish refugee who escaped from the pogrom in the town Ovidiopol, near Odessa. He told us that 38 Jews were murdered in one day; writing these lines, his terror story is fresh in my memory as if it happened yesterday.

I remember a dark autumn night, when our family escaped from bloodthirsty Russians, our hearts full of fear. We managed to arrive to the shore of the Liman and miraculously our lived were saved from certain death.

[Page 370]

The hatred of Jews never stopped. Sometimes it was overt and drastically expressed, sometimes it was hidden, but it was always there. Every political event, whether in the country or outside it, aroused anti-Semitism not only in the big cities but in the towns and small settlements as well, Shabo included.

I can still hear the echoes of the Russian defeat in the war with Japan. Many tried to put the blame on the Jews... and there were always those who "made them pay" by riots. In 1909, when a Jewish student made an attempt to murder the minister Stolipin, the entire country was terrified, but most of all the Jews, who were sure that the whole community will be accused and attacked – and so it was.

The Beilis trial, following the well-known blood-libel in 1911, lit again a big fire. Together with all Russian Jews, the Jews of Shabo trembled like a leaf in the wind. We never knew what tomorrow will bring; we were all horrified – waiting for a new wave of cruel pogroms.

Not much later, with the outbreak of WWI, which caused death and destruction over all of Europe, the Jews were again the first victims. I remember the talks and discussions, at the time, in every Jewish home. It seemed that, unconsciously, the Zionist idea materialized in the hearts of the Jews of our community. It became clear that there is no life for us in the Diaspora, where we could expect only destruction and death without mercy. But only few acted upon that tragic conclusion; as has happened so many times – the Jews believed in false Messiahs, but the illusions proved false very soon.

Kindergarten in Shabo

[Page 371]

One of these illusions was the Kerenski revolution in February 1917. His short rule (February-October 1917) was considered by many a good omen, a prediction of change. In the Jewish communities, there were many who felt relief and were led to believe that a new period of peace and calm was coming . . . until the new revolution (the October Revolution) broke out and brought with it chaos, confusion, collapse of all elements of existence etc. Again was the Jew the scapegoat, seen by the new regime – the regime of "equality and justice" – as the enemy number one, who should be fought to the bitter end.

When the Balfour Declaration was issued in November 1917, with the hope of a national home for the Jews, hope and new beliefs arose again. The Zionist Movement, which was totally inactive during WWI, awoke to a new life and a wave of Zionism spread through the Jewish Diaspora. This wave reached Romania and Bessarabia as well: branches were reopened, assemblies and regional congresses were called and hot discussions were renewed, new Zionist institutions were established – salvation was near!

However, it must be mentioned that at the same time, opposition rose as well. There were those who believed that the universal revolution will bring salvation to the Jewish people, without the need for a Jewish national home. They increased their activity and propaganda in the "Jewish Street," causing new turbulence and storm. We, the young people, were forced, through fiery discussions and arguments, to stand against this movement, which considered any Zionist activity as "contra-revolutionist" and dangerous: the Jews were distracting the population and preventing it from dealing with the main issue: the great revolution...

When I remember now these arguments and discussions held in our little town, I am smiling to myself. How much innocence did they contain?! How much enthusiasm?! How many illusions?! How much courage?! And how much timidity and fear?! True, those were days....

The Zionist Organization in Shabo

As I said before, the tumultuous times did not spare our little town. But here the Zionists had the upper hand. We, the young people, and many of the adults, were inspired by the national ideas. The hearts were open to listen to the Zionist information – in particular Aliya to our homeland. I remember the activity to sell shares of the Zionist Colonial Bank. We respected these shares very much – in our eyes they were the real expression of Zionism, a symbol of honor for their owners.

We elected R'Yoel Meirson, a veteran Zionist, valued and respected in our community, to be chairman of the Zionist Organization in Shabo. Kishinovski followed him in this position, and in time Aizik Kaminker was elected chairman.

As I am reviewing now those old days, I come to the conclusion that the Zionist activists did a great deal to strengthen the national feeling and Zionist consciousness among the Shabo Jews. They worked day and night, without expecting compensation, fully believed in their ideas and their work and thus were able to instill in others the same fire, the same belief. We organized many lectures, about the situation of the Jews after the World War, trying to convince the listeners that Zionism is the true solution of the Jewish problem, and all the solutions suggested by the Leftists and the believers in the October Revolution are false solutions. Lecturers would come from the nearby towns, in particular from Akkerman, but from our own Shabo as well. We had hot and enthusiastic discussions, coming from deep belief and faith. The participation of the public was lively. It was the best time for the Zionist movement in our shtetl Shabo.

The Zionist Branch in Shabo strengthened the connection with the Zionist institutions in Akkerman as well as with the central institutions in Odessa; often they sent to Shabo a lecturer, who spoke about general Zionist topics, but also about the Zionist literature of those times. The managing committee of the branch, in collaboration with the youth movement, organized evening courses of Hebrew, created a Drama Club and opened a kindergarten, which introduced a new spirit in town and increased the Zionist feelings. About these I shall relate below.

The activity for the benefit of the various National Funds deserves special mention. The young generation was particularly active in this area: they went from house to house, not only collecting money but also "explaining the cause" – and so the Zionist ideas took roots and gave fruit.

The Young Guard

At that time, when the revolutionary ideas, preaching for changes in the world and using attractive slogans charmed the youth and brought many young Jewish people to the revolutionary flag, the Shabo youth stood strong and were not dragged by the general current; they did not give up their Jewish national values and the Zionist consciousness in exchange for

[Page 372]

the benefits of the great revolution. I don't know how we had the strength to stand against the general current which was ruling the young circles. It was a fact, that the majority of the young people in town knew indeed how to "separate the chaff" from the grains and joined the national Zionist movement. Only very few were captured by the revolutionary slogans and followed them. We did not use the empty revolutionary talk that was an integral part of the discussions of the young people in the big cities, but instinctively, unconsciously perhaps, we followed the right way. The despair of the Diaspora, the deceptiveness of the non-Zionist solutions and illusions had an effect, and the national ideas grew in our midst.

The life and activity of the young people was full of interest and content. We still keep in our memory many impressive experiences from those days. We demanded from ourselves real action, not empty phrases. We demanded from ourselves more than we demanded from others – and this was our power, this was our secret weapon. All the Jews in town knew that if required we will be ready for deed and for sacrifice. As early as 1921, the first group made Aliya, and was soon followed by other groups. The many former Shabo residents living in Israel are proof of our activity and of our right way.

The young people of Shabo were the main initiators and of the social and Zionist activity in town, and they realized the ideas as well. I remember the devotion and enthusiasm with which we founded the library and the reading room, organized "cultural evenings" and managed to establish a cultural center. We went from house to house to collect money and books for the library. We considered it a national mission and the residents of the town responded accordingly.

We must mention Yechiel Steinberg, the son of R'Berl Steinberg, who donated to the library all his books in Russian. He served as an example to others. With the money we collected we bought many Hebrew, Yiddish and Russian books, in particular books that would strengthen the national consciousness among the youth. We brought newspapers and magazines in the three languages to the reading room. I remember the festive opening ceremony of the library and the feelings of satisfaction that filled our hearts. We performed with devotion the various tasks – changing books, supervising the reading room, lighting the petrol lamps and cleaning. I remember that we were a little disappointed by the small number of visitors to the reading room, but on the other hand, the number of people using the library grew. It was a pleasure to see the people waiting in line to change books. We had the good feeling, that we introduced knowledge and culture in our little town. The reading room was given to us by R'Binyamin Kaminker, and was later transferred to the house of the Farna family.

The above was only part of our activity. I do not remember all we did, but I do know that a spirit of volunteering and devotion was felt among us, a great and good spirit.

The Drama Club

The Drama Club in Shabo was active many years. It has introduced a feeling of liveliness in town; the population was proud of it and many participated in its activity. The rehearsals, the assemblies, the preparation of the stage, selecting the actors for the various characters – all this was done on a grand scale. It was the activity of young people mainly, but many of the adults showed interest in the performance of the Club.

In time, more and more members joined the Drama Club. Jews crowded the Shlomo Meirson Hall and after the performance hot discussions were held, reviewing and criticizing: who was good and who was less so, who showed talent and who was about to become a great star, and so on ... the entire public enjoyed what we did.

In a big city, full of possibilities, such activity is not rare. However, we should not forget the size of our town, the limited number of Jewish residents and our very limited material means. In those days, keeping a drama club was a real challenge for us, and I think we met it with honor. True, we did not provide many "stars" for the Jewish stage, and those who did remain successful actors did not realize all our hopes, but it is doubtful whether a town of this size, with a Jewish population of several hundred people could have maintained a drama club for so many years.

[Page 373]

The Drama Club in Shabo

[Page 374]

Crochmaz
(Crocmaz, Moldova)
46°27' 29°59'

The Village Crochmaz
by Yosef Koren
Translated by Yocheved Klausner

The village Crochmaz was situated at a distance of 35 km. from Akkerman, on the shore of the Dniester, which at that point was 150 meters wide.

Most of the village residents were Jews and Moldavians; they kept good neighborly relations and lived peacefully with each other. The Jews made their livelihood from commerce, crafts and farming. They owned plots of hundreds of Dunams and grew wheat, barley and other grains, and had also fruit orchards and vineyards. Every Jewish family in the village had riding horses and a wagon which they used to connect between the neighboring villages and the town Akkerman. Almost all Jews in the village kept the Jewish tradition and the synagogue served as the religious center, but only on Shabat and Holidays public prayers were held. All tried to preserve "the Jewish spark" as much as possible, and hired special teachers from the city to teach their children Hebrew and Yiddish; only when the children grew up they were sent to study in a real school in Akkerman.

About 7 Km. from Crochmaz the village Olineşti was situated. Once a week a fair was held in the village, and merchants and farmers flocked into the place from the vicinity. The Crochmaz people had good commercial relations with Olineşti and at the day of the fair they brought fruits, vegetables and cattle for sale, and bought for themselves the necessary groceries, textiles etc. The connection between the villagers and the Akkerman Jews were strong; Akkerman served them as a commercial as well as a spiritual–cultural center.

In 1910, my parents relocated from the village to Akkerman, but they continued working on their farm and vineyard in the village, selling the produce in Akkerman. The relocation to the town enabled them to give the children a Hebrew education in the "Tarbut" school.

My father worked with one of the export companies, which was connected with the Moldova Bank that had branches in Akkerman and Galatz. He managed the export sector. During summers we would move back to Crochmaz and stay there until the end of the harvest.

At the outbreak of WWII, my parents fled from Russia and wandered all the way to Almahata in Kazakhstan. With their own hands they built clay shacks near one of the mountains and lived there until the end of the war. When they returned to Crochmaz at the end of the war, they found that their land was given to the Kolkhoz.

[Page 375]

Former Residents of Akkerman and Region in Israel

by The Editorial Board

Translated by Yocheved Klausner

As is told in one of the chapters of this book, hundreds of years ago there were already roads from Akkerman to Eretz Israel, but these roads were taken only by very few and by groups of Crusaders. The road to Eretz Israel with the purpose of living there and building one's future there opened in 1920, when the first pioneers from Akkerman and surroundings made Aliya - their story is told in this book. Many roads led to Eretz Israel since then: through the home, the Hebrew High–School, the youth movement, the pioneer [Halutz] movement, all the Zionist Organizations. All these pointed the way.

Even when the Aliya gates were locked with seven locks, the young Zionists found ways to come to Eretz Israel. These were "illegal" ways, but in the eyes of the youth there was nothing more legal than the "illegal Aliya." According to a careful estimate, hundreds of people from Akkerman and the region made Aliya starting from 1920. The Second World War put an end to the hopes of many of our townspeople to reach the shore of the homeland; but it remained the only aim for so many of the Holocaust survivors who, even during their most terrible hours continued to aspire, to dream and to think of the homeland. Many of them did succeed to reach that safe shore.

In many settlements in Eretz Israel one can meet former residents of Akkerman and surrounding towns. Many of them were elderly when they arrived, but all joined the task of building our homeland, each in his profession and according to his means. We intended to bring here a full list of the former residents of Akkerman and the region in Israel, and we hope we will be forgiven by those whose names were not included.

Lists translated by Judy Petersen

[Pages 377-378]

Akkerman émigrés in Israel

Surname	Given name	Residence in Israel	Page
ABRAHAMSON	Yosef	Moshav Kinneret	377
ABRAMOVITZ	Nesya	Tel Aviv	377
ADELIS	Avner	Zichron Yakov	377
ADELIS	Orna	Tel Aviv	377
EIDELMAN	Manya	Netanya	377
ICHT	Luba	Carmiel	377
ICHT	Malka	Jerusalem	377
ITZKOVITZ	Klara	Holon	377
AMITAI	Nisan	Gesher Haziv	377

(STAMBOUL)			
ASPIS	Yosef	Holon	377
ASPIS	Lyuba	Bat Yam	377
ARBIT	Dov	Kiryat Tivon	377
ARBIT	Walodia	Haifa	377
ARBIT	Yitzchak	Carmiel	377
ARBIT	Shlomo	Haifa	377
BADNI	Eliahu	Netanya	377
BOTOSHANSKY	Esther	Tel Aviv	377
BOTOSHANSKY	Sura	Netanya	377
BOYOKANSKY	Dr.	Haifa	377
BOROCH	Eliezer	Rehovot	377
BILER	Gita	Kibbutz Shamir	377
BINENBAUM	Abba	Pardes Hanna	377
BINENBAUM	Bluma	Natzrat Ilit	377
BINENBAUM	Grisha	Dimona	377
BLUM	Miriam	Zichron Yakov	377
BANDERSKY	Eliahu	Holon	377
BASSAT	Zerach	Talmei Eliezer	377
BRONSTEIN (INGERLEIB)	Sarah	Tel Aviv	377
BRAIER (LAPIDA)	Esther	Holon	377
BRAND	Aharon	Talmei Eliezer	377
BARNEA	Chava	Tel Aviv	377
BERKOVITZ	Yakov	Kiryat Ata	377
GABER	Shmuel	Rishon Letzion	377
GAVRI	Yakov	Kibbutz Nir Am	377
GUZMAN	Tzvi	Tel Aviv	377
GUZMAN	Shlomo	Haifa	377
GOICHMAN	Yitzchak	Beersheva	377
GOLDENBERG	Tzipora	Even Yeuda	377
GUNZMACHER (GORDON)	Sonya	Nahariya Hanita	377
GUR ARYEH (INGERLEIB)	Eliezer	Tel Aviv	377
GUR ARYEH (INGERLEIB)	Yosef	Tel Aviv	377
GUR ARYEH (INGERLEIB)	Yisrael	Jerusalem	377

GUR ARYEH (INGERLEIB)	Moshe	Tel Aviv	377
GURFIELD	Moshe	Tel Aviv	377
GIA (BERKOVITZ)	Etya	Yafo	377
GILBOA	Syuba	Haifa	377
GLONSKY	Vitya	Kiryat Binyamin	377
GILADI	Tzvi	Kibbutz Masrik	377
GARBITZ (INGERLEIB)	Shoshana	Tel Aviv	377
GERTNER	Ada	Hadera	377
GRINFELD	Pira	Nahariya	377
GERSHFELD	Binyamin	Netaim	377
GERSHFELD	Baruch	Rishon Letzion	377
DEVORIN	Aharon	Ashkelon	377
DEVORIN	Chaim	Sderot	377
DOLEV	Etya	Givataim	377
DORFMAN	Efraim	Tel Aviv	377
DORFMAN	Amalia	Tel Aviv	377
HADAR (KAHALSKY)	Nechama	Kibbutz Masada	377
HOROVITZ	Aryeh	Kiryat Chaim	377
HOROVITZ (ELISHKEVITZ)	Shifra	Kiryat Chaim	377
HALPERIN (BRAND)	Devorah	Haifa	377
HARTZION	Bruria	Hadera	377
WLOSHIN	Shlomo	Tel Aviv	377
WEITZMAN	Golda	Rehovot	377
WEITZMAN	Roza	Hanita	377
WEININGER	Mora	Even Yeuda	377
WEINSTEIN	Moshe	Haifa	377
WEISMAN (COHEN)	Teshura	Kibbutz Nir Am	377
WEISMAN	George	Binyamina	377
WEISMAN	Tzvi	Binyamina	377
WELITZKO (KLEINMAN)	Ruta	Holon	377
WASSERMAN	Philip (Attorney)	Bat Yam	377
WAKSMAN (SHTERMBRAND)	Devorah	Netanya	377
WERSHAVSKY (WEINSTEIN)	Ita	Yavne	377

SIEGELWAKS	Yehuda	Haifa	377
SIEGELWAKS	Yakov	Kiryat Ata	377
ZELTZER	Eliahu	Azor	377
ZELTZER (MANOS)	Channah	Kfar Vitkin	377
ZESELEVSKAYA (KOGAN)	Zina	Rishon Letzion	377
ZEF	Shevach Dr.	Nahariya	377
HODES	Asya	Kibbutz Shamir	377
TOYERMAN	Yitzchak	Petach Tikva	377
TROP (ELISHKAVITZ)	Miriam	Hadera	377
YESHA (RABINOVITZ)	Raya	Tel Aviv	377
YISRAELI (KORN)	Leah	Kfar Ata	377
COHEN (NEUMAN)	Leah	Kibbutz Masada	377
COHEN (BOYOKANSKY)	Shoshana	Kibbutz Masada	377
COHEN	Shraga	Netanya	377
KAFRI (DORFMAN)	Avraham	Kfar Hess	377
KARMI (FRENKEL)	Yehudit	Tel Aviv	377
LEV	Eliahu	Haifa	377
LEV	Yakov	Haifa	378
LEV	Nachman	Haifa	378
LEBOVSKY	Mendel	Kiryat Tivon	378
LEBOVSKY	Sarah	Kiryat Tivon	378
LAHAV (BRAND)	Zev	Kibbutz Nir Am	378
LEVIT	Shlomo	Netanya	378
LITMAN (GECHT)	Tzviya	Tel Aviv	378
LIPSKY (BERGER)	Leah	Rishon Letzion	378
LANDAU	Yosef	Petach Tikva	378
MOLDAVSKY	Avraham	Tel Aviv	378
MALINSKY	Aharon	Givat Shmuel	378
MANUELI (MINIELI)	Tzvi	Holon	378
MANUELI (MINIELI)	Shmuel	Netanya	378
MALAL (BERKOVITZ)	Leah	Tel Aviv	378

MANOS	Reuven	Kfar Chaim	378
MANOS	Yisrael	Tel Aviv	378
MASTERMAN	Nesya	Petach Tikva	378
MARGALIT	Avraham	Zichron Yakov	378
MARKUS (KOCHOK)	Frima	Petach Tikva	378
NOVOBROTZKY (MUTCHENIK)	Rakhel	Givataim	378
NOTOV	Moshe	Rehovot	378
NEUMAN (WASSERMAN)	Leah	Ramat Gan	378
NEUGER (GELMAN)	Rakhel Dr.	Haifa	378
NAAMANI (TZUKERMAN)	Baruch	Kibbutz Masada	378
NAAMANI (TZUKERMAN)	Shmuel	Tel Aviv	378
SEGAL	Simcha	Zichron Yakov	378
SUDEK (GELMAN)	Sarah	Kiryat Chaim	378
SOCHER (AVIRBUCH)	Esther	Ramat Gan	378
SOFER	Devorah	Rishon Letzion	378
STRULOVITZ (TOYERMAN)	Malka	Pardes Hanna	378
SPEKTOR	Yosef	Hadera	378
SPEKTOR	Rakhel	Hadera	378
EINIS	Fruma	Netanya	378
FUCHS	Zelig	Tel Aviv	378
FEIGENBLATT	Chaviva	Jerusalem	378
FINKEL	Yisrael	Petach Tikva	378
FISCHMAN	Lev Dr.	Haifa	378
FELDMAN	Amnon	Hadera	378
FELDMAN	Betzalel	Kibbutz Shamir	378
FELDMAUS	Sarah	Netanya	378
FLEISCHER (GOCHBERG)	Manya	Kfar Saba	378
PAT LACH	Gita	Holon	378
PERLMUTTER (KAMINKER)	Shoshana	Tel Aviv	378
TZUKERMAN	Chaim Avraham	Haifa	378
TZUKERMAN	Noach	Kfar Hess	378

TZUKERMAN	Tzadok	Hertzliya	378
TZUKERMAN	Sheftel	Kibbutz Hulda	378
TZUR	Nisan	Kibbutz Nir Am	378
TZITRON	Mordechai	Netanya	378
TZAMIR	Chaya	Holon	378
TZAMIR (CHEMERINSKY)	Chaim	Holon	378
TZAMIR (CHEMERINSKY)	Miriam	Holon	378
CHAPLIN	Eliezer	Haifa	378
CHAPLIN	Yosef	Kibbutz Masada	378
CHERNILOV	Yitzchak	Moshava Kinneret	378
CHERNILOV (NEUMAN)	Malka	Moshava Kinneret	378
KEVES	Aharon	Rishon Letzion	378
KAVITKO	Michael	Tel Aviv-Yafo	378
KORNBLIT	Avraham	Rehovot	378
KORN	Yosef	Kiryat Chaim	378
KUSHNIR	Viktor	Bat Yam	378
KUSHNIR	Rakhel	Bat Yam	378
KOMOROV	Fanya	Pardes Hanna	378
KLEIMAN	Miron	Bat Yam	378
KLEIMAN	Roza	Jerusalem	378
KAMIN	Baruch	Hertzliya	378
KAPLAN	Aharon	Kibbutz Ruchama	378
KAPLANIKOV / KAPELNIKOV?	Menashe	Kibbutz Ruchama	378
KAPLANIKOV / KAPELNIKOV?	Arnold	Jerusalem	378
RADEK	Raya	Rishon Letzion	378
RABINOVITZ	Esther		378
RABINOVITZ (ELISHKEVITZ)	Carmela	Kiryat Motzkin	378
RABINOVITZ (SPERBER)	Stella	Kibbutz Hanita	378
RABINOVITZ	Pesya	Kiryat Motzkin	378
RABINOVITZ	Rakhel	Givataim	378
ROZENBERG		Holon	378

(KAPLAUCH)			
ROZENTHAL (LICHT)	Klara	Kibbutz Masada	378
ROIZMAN	Katriel	Kibbutz Hanita	378
RESNIK	Asher	Tel Aviv	378
RIESENSON	David	Tel Aviv	378
RANEN (RIBELNIK)	Emanuel	Tel Aviv	378
SCHVARTZMAN	Leonid	Jerusalem	378
SHOSHOK	Yochanan	Natzrat Ilit	378
SHEHORI (SCHVARTZMAN)	Yehuda	Netanya	378
STEINBECK (TZUKERMAN)	Leah	Kibbutz Ruchama	378
SCHEIN (TZUKERMAN)	Nesya	Kibbutz Masada	378
SCHILDKRAUT	Dov	Beersheva	378
SCHILDKRAUT	Yisrael	Tel Aviv	378
SCHILDKRAUT	Channah	Tel Aviv	378
SCHACHTER (ELISHKEVITZ)	Tova	Petach Tikva	378
SCHLEIZER (KOGAN)	Tova	Pardes Hanna	378
SHMUELVITZ	Bat-Zion	Beersheva	378
SHMUELI (INGERLEIB)	Rivka	Tel Aviv	378
SHAPIRA	Alexander	Tel Aviv	378
SHAPIRA (BRAND)	Sarah	Jerusalem	378
SHKOLNIK	Siuma	Kibbutz Hanita	378

[Pages 379-380]

Tarutino émigrés in Israel

Surname	Given name	Residence in Israel	Page
EIMES (GECKER)	Nechama Dr.	Haifa	379
AVIRBRUCH	Yechiel	Netanya	379
AVIRBRUCH	Channah	Ashkelon	379
ANTALSON	Yosef	Ramat Gan	379
BRILLANT	Shmuel	Tel Aviv	379
BELNEK	Yakov	Natzrat Ilit	379
BRONFMAN	Yehuda	Haifa	379
BEN YISRAEL	Chemda	Rehovot	379
BUBIS	Channah	Rehovot	379

BELCHER	Yisrael	Jerusalem	379
BERMAN	Zev	Tel Aviv	379
BACHMAN	Avraham	Tel Aviv	379
BLUMENFELD	Sima	Tel Aviv	379
BARASCH	Polya	Jerusalem	379
GURFIL	Yosef	Rehovot	379
GURFIL	Binyamin	Rehovot	379
GORBITZ? / GUREWITZ?	Chaim	Kiryat Ata	379
GORFBERG	Klara	Ra'anana	379
GOLDBERG	Yosef	Hadera	379
GOCHBERG	Fani Dr.	Ashdod	379
GOCHBERG	Channah	Tel Aviv	379
GLAZER	Bluma	Netanya	379
GALPERIN (ROSENBERG)		Tel Aviv	379
DOBRISHMAN	Binyamin	Rishon Letzion	379
DRORI (FRIDMAN)	Channah	Ramat Gan	379
HADAR (REZNIK)	Zhenya	Netanya	379
HOCHBERG (MELMANT)	Esther	Haifa	379
HERENSTRAUS (BRURMAN)		Hadera	379
ZAHAVI (ROSENBERG)	Chaya	Netanya	379
SINGER (STRENSHUS)	Manya	Bat Yam	379
ZELTZER	Isser	Pardes Katz	379
ZALTZHANDLER	Efraim	Kfar Hess	379
ZALTZHANDLER	Dora		379
ZALTZHANDLER	Michael	Pardes Katz	379
HAKLAI (KORIS)	Sarah	Givataim	379
TOBBIN	Yosef	Bat Yam	379
YANKO	Leah	Holon	379
YAVETZ (SIROTA)	Zlata	Haifa	379
KOGAN (ROSENBLATT)	Nusha	Holon	379
KOGAN	Shmuel	Or Yehuda	379
LEVIT	Gersh	Petach Tikva	379
LEVIT (SCHVARTZMAN)	Yehudit	Tel Aviv	379

LOTZKER	Reuven & Leah	Kiryat Yam	379
LIEBMAN (SOFER)	Channah	Givat Shmuel	379
LIFSHIN	Zissel	Pardes Katz	379
LICHTJEGER	Chava	Netanya	379
LANGBER	Milya	Ashkelon	379
LANDAU	Lipa	Petach Tikva	379
LEHRER (KRIKON)	Ida	Holon	379
MOTNIAK	Munya	Yafo	379
MILMAN (DORFMAN)	Mintza	Beersheva	379
MELAMNET	Yosef	Netanya	379
MELAMNET	Yakov	Rishon Letzion	379
MASTERMAN	Moshe	Ramat Gan	379
MENDEL (STERNSCHUS)	Ziva	Hadera	379
MARGALIT	Aharon	Ein Vered	379
MARGALIT	Elchanan	Tel Aviv	379
MERLIN	Roza	Rehovot	379
NUDELMAN (GOCHBERG)	Tema	Heftziba	379
NISENMAN	Bella	Rishon Letzion	379
SOLOMONOVITZ (SCHVARTZ)	Roza	Bnei Brak	379
SOFER	Savya	Tel Aviv	379
SORKIS	Lyuba	Ashdod	379
SIGALIT	Roza	Haifa	379
SAPIRSTEIN STERNSCHUS	Miriam	Hertzliya	379
PAZI (ROTBERG)	Mosya	Tel Aviv	379
PASTERNAK (MOTNIAK)	Fruma	Tel Aviv	379
PERLSON (ROSENBERG)	Pira	Holon	379
PARPAR	Efraim	Hod Hasharon	379
PARPAR	Dr.	Tel Aviv	379
TZIPRIN (ZAIETZ)	Shifra	Tel Aviv	379
KABKOV	Etya	Tel Aviv	379

KUPERMAN	Frida		379
KUPERMAN	Kalman	Or Yehuda	379
KOTCHUK	Yosef	Rehovot	379
KOTCHUK	Polya	Hadera	379
KOTCHUK	Shalom	Rehovot	379
KISLIANSKY	David	Tel Aviv	379
KUSCHNIR	Yitzchak	Bat Yam	379
KLEIMAN RISIS	Golda	Ramat Gan	379
KESSLER	Aryeh	Arad	379
RABINOVITZ KUSCHNIR	Zina	Ramat Gan	379
RABINOVITZ ROSENBERG	Tusya	Haifa	379
ROSEN	Levi	Beersheva	380
ROZITCHNER	Avraham	Netanya	380
ROSENBERG	David	Tel Aviv	380
ROYSTCHER	Yitzchak	Tel Aviv	380
ROYSTCHER	Boris	Petach Tikva	380
RUSIS	Tzvi	Yavne	380
ROSENBERG	Shmuel	Yad Eliahu	380
ROSENBERG	Sonya	Jerusalem	380
ROSENBERG	Shulamit	Jerusalem	380
ROTBERG	Ozer	Givataim	380
ROTBERG	Moshe	Ef'al	380
SHULMAN	Eliezer	Bat Yam	380
SHULMAN	Devorah	Kfar Ata	380
SHULMAN	Nachman	Jerusalem	380
SCHVARTZ	Yitzchak	Tel Aviv	380
SCHVARTZ	Moshe	Tzfat	380
SCHVARTZMAN	Berna	Givataim	380
SCHVARTZMAN (GERSH)	Tzvi	Yavne	380
STEIN FINKELSTEIN	Batya	Ramle	380
STROMBERG	Yosef	Kiryat Yam	380
STROMBERG	Yosef	Beersheva	380
STROMBERG	Yisrael	Netanya	380
STERNSCHUS	Batya	Bnei Brak	380
STERNSCHUS	Yakov	Haifa	380
SCHLIMOVITZ	Yosef	Kiryat Ata	380
SKOLNIK	Devorah	Kibbutz Dalia	380

[Pages 380-381]

Artsyz émigrés in Israel

Surname	Given name	Residence in Israel	Page
AVERBUCH (STEINMETZ)	Chaike	Tel Aviv	380
ABRAMOVITZ (BRAZ)	Lyuba	Tel Aviv	380
ABRAMOVITZ (BEN-YOSEF)		Hadera	380
ABRAMOWITZ	Miriam	Bat Yam	380
BODAISKY	Shmuel	Netanya	380
BRODETZKY	Aharon	Bat Yam	380
BRODETZKY	Ulya	Bat Yam	380
BRODETZKY	Mara	Bat Yam	380
BEIDER	Menachem	Petach Tikva	380
BEIDER	Sonya	Petach Tikva	380
BRAZ	Yakov	Tel Aviv	380
BRENER	Tzipora	Haifa	380
BRENER	Rivka	Haifa	380
BRENER	Rozika	Haifa	380
BRENER	Yosef	Netanya	380
BRENER	Moshe	Hadera	380
GETZOLSKY	Shmuel	Beersheva	380
GOLDINER (GOLAN)	Mendel	Kiryat Tivon	380
GEMESHIVITZ	Anya	Gedera	380
GURFIL	Aryeh	Hadera	380
GURFIL	Yosef	Dimona	380
GORFINKEL	Yakov	Ramat Gan	380
GURFIL	Shmuel	Moshav Nordia	380
GEIZER	Yocheved	Petach Tikva	380
GEIZER	Yente	Petach Tikva	380
GLEIZER	Manya	Haifa	380
GLEIZER	Shmuel	Hadera	380
GEMESHIVITZ	Manya	Gedera	380
GERSHBERG (GLICKMAN)	Tzipora	Dimona	380
DORFMAN	Shlomo	Dimona	380
WALMAN	Fanya	Kibbutz	380

		Magen	
ZHEBGORSKY	Burya	Bat Yam	380
ZHEBGORSKY	Lyusya	Bat Yam	380
ZEITZEV	Marina	Bat Yam	380
ZISLIS	Frida	Krayot	380
TOKER	Sarah	Netanya	380
YANKILEWITZ (GETZOLSKY)	Bluma	Beersheva	380
YANKILEWITZ	Zalman	Givataim	380
YANKILEWITZ (BRONSTEIN)	Zhenya	Tel Aviv	380
YANKILEWITZ	Yehuda	Tel Aviv	380
YANKILEWITZ	Munya	Tel Aviv	380
YANKILEWITZ	Misha	Ramat Gan	380
YANKILEWITZ	Fraidel	Kibbutz Yakum	380
KAHANOWITZ	Menachem Mendel	Ashkelon	380
LISOVSKY (ROITMAN)	Leah	Beersheva	380
LERNER (GILADI)	Esther	Kibbutz Masrik	380
LERNER	Hinda	Kibbutz Evron	380
LERNER (LAMDAN)	Chaim	Akko	380
MOSKOVITZ	Ettel	Petach Tikva	380
MOSKOVITZ	Riba	Hod Hasharon	380
MILSHTER		Rehovot	380
MENDELOVITZ	Fraidel	Holon	380
MASTERMAN (BENKOVITZ)	Chaya	Ramat Gan	380
STKOLSHCHIK (FISHMAN)	Batya	Jerusalem	381
STKOLSHCHIK	Munya	Jerusalem	381
PAUZNER	Genya	Holon	381
PAUZNER	Matus	Petach Tikva	381
PAUZNER	Relya	Holon	381
PAUZNER	Rafael	Holon	381
POLINOVSKY (TUKRO)	Ettel	Ashdod	381
POLONSKY	Rochla	Petach Tikva	381

POLLAK	Lyuba	Beersheva	381
FILVITZ (DORFMAN)	Pira	Ashkelon	381
FILVIT	Shaike	Ashkelon	381
FISHMAN (BRAVERMAN)	Susel	Lod	381
FISHMAN	Reuven	Lod	381
PEKKER (JURMAN)	Esya	Bat Yam	381
PEKKER	Khasya	Bat Yam	381
PEKKER	Nechama	Bat Yam	381
FRIEDMAN (KISHINYOVSKY)	Ettel	Ashdod	381
FRIEDMAN	Lyonya		381
FRANK	Esther	Ramat Gan	381
FRANK (EDELSTEIN)	Chaya	Ramat Gan	381
FRANK	Channah	Kibbutz Revadim	381
FRANK	Yosef	Ramat Gan	381
FRANK	Yakov	Hadera	381
FRANK (SCHVARTZMAN)	Kreina	Yahod	381
FRANK	Shmuel	Hadera	381
TZUR (TZROLNIK)	Chaim	Givataim	381
TZROLNIK	Chava	Givataim	381
TZROLNIK	Tzipora	Bat Yam	381
KOLOMAISKY (BEN DOV)	Riva	Ramat Gan	381
KOLOMAISKY (ELAZAR SHAI)	Shaike	Tiberias	381
KUSHNIR (YUDKOVITZ)	Rakhel	Bat Yam	381
KIPERWASSER	Akiva	Nahariya	381
KISHINOVSKY	Moshe	Haifa	381
KOLOZHENSKY		Beersheva	381
KLEITMAN	Aryeh	Beersheva	381
KLEITMAN	Malka	Bat Yam	371
KLEITMAN	Moshe	Haifa	381
KLEITMAN	Charna	Bat Yam	381
KOPELMAN (LISOVSKY)	Rivka	Beersheva	381
RUSHKOVAN	Bozya	Rishon Letzion	381

REZNIK	Esther	Givataim	381
REZNIK	Asher	Netanya	381
REZNIK	Hershel	Kiryat Ata	381
REZNIK (ZISLIS)	Chaya	Kiryat Ata	381
REZNIK	Musya	Netanya	381
REZNIK	Akiva	Natzrat	381
REZNIK	Riva	Netanya	381
SHUSTERMAN	Buma	Bat Yam	381
SCHVARTZMAN	Kreina	Or Yehuda	381
SHTEIDMAN	Yitzchak	Tel Aviv	381

[Pages 381-382]

Tatarbunar émigrés in Israel

Surname	Given name	Residence in Israel	Page
OHTSHITEL (BLECHMAN)	Esther	Haifa	381
OHTSHITEL (SEIDMAN)	Channah	Haifa	381
ALBERT	Ita	Afel	381
ALBERT	Burya	Kiryat Motzkin	381
ALBERT	Milya	Tel Aviv	381
BEIDNER (STREICHER)	Esther	Haifa	381
BEIDNER (KOSOVSKY)	Roza	Haifa	381
BECKER (MATZBECKER)	Gita	Petach Tikva	381
BRAGOTIN (WEINER)	Tanya	Haifa	381
BRODSKY	Yuzya	Pardes Hanna	381
BERKOVITZ	Ida	Kiryat Yam	381
BERKOVITZ	Zlata	Tel Aviv	381
BERKOVITZ	Channah	Natzrat	381
BERKOVITZ (GLICKMAN)	Sonya	Rehovot	381
GOLDMAN	Isser	Nahalal	381
GOLDMAN	Yitzchak	Kiryat Ata	381
GICKER	Binyamin	Haifa	381
GELBINSKY (GITELMAN)	Tova	Tel Aviv	381
GLICKMAN	Ronit	Haifa	381
GALPERIN (CHACHAM)	Manya	Haifa	381

GALPERIN (BOVIAT)	Golda	Tel Aviv	381
GRADANCHIK (RABIN)	Fanya	Petach Tikva	381
WEINER	Avraham	Hadera	381
WEINER	Leibel (Aryeh)	Tel Aviv	381
SILBERMAN	Bluma	Netanya	381
SILBERMAN	Yosef	Haifa	381
SILBERMAN (TZUKERMAN)	Riba	Hulda	382
ZEF	Sarah	Kiryat Chaim	382
CHACHAM	Bela	Holon	382
CHAMUDIS	Manya	Givataim	382
LITWIN	Izya	Haifa	382
LASKIN	Esther	Haifa	382
LASKIN	Genya	Haifa	382
MARISIS	Nachum	Nes Tziona	382
STRILITZ		Kiryat Chaim	382
SLUTZKY	Ben-tzion	Ramat Gan	382
SPECKTERMAN	Yosef	Rehovot	382
POSAK	Zelig	Tel Aviv	382
KLEIMAN	Shifka	Tel Aviv	382
KREMER	Moshe	Netanya	382
ROIZMAN (MICHILIBOTZ)	Esther	Jerusalem	382
ROITMAN (GOLDFARB)	Roza	Ashdod	382
ROITMAN	Sarah	Tel Aviv	382
ROICHMAN	Yechezkel	Ramat Gan	382
SHOCHET	Elik	Kfar Saba	382
SHOCHET	Aryeh	Rishon Letzion	382
SHIRIN	Yosef	Tel Aviv	382

[Page 382]

Sarata émigrés in Israel

Surname	Given name	Residence in Israel	Page
AVERBUCH	Fanya	Rishon Letzion	382

ITZKOVITZ	Raya	Kfar Saba	382
ALTMAN	Elkana	Holon	382
ALTSTEIN	Zlota	Rishon Letzion	382
ALTSTEIN	Scheindel	Moshav Shoeva	382
ALENSON	Leib	Beersheva	382
BABENSKY	Gita	Holon	382
BEN HUR (ALTMAN)	Yechezkel	Moshav Shoeva	382
BERDOV	Lilli	Ashdod	382
GRINBERG ZEF	Lyusya	Nahariya	382
GRETZBERG	Bat Sheva	Bat Yam	382
GRETZBERG	Avraham	Bat Yam	382
GRETZBERG	Yakov		382
GERSTEIN (MONDIOK)	Riba	Beersheva	382
GERSHKOVITZ	Esther	Netanya	382
GERSHKOVITZ	Marianna	Bat Yam	382
DEUTSCH	Zev		382
WADWEZ	Rivka	Pardes Hanna	382
WEISBEIN	Zunya	Beersheva	382
WANKERT (SCHEINFELD)	Riba	Jerusalem	382
ZELTZER	Izya	Bat Yam	382
LUBLINSKY	Yisrael	Rishon Letzion	382
LUBLINSKY	Leah	Holon	382
LITWIN	Eizik	Beersheva	382
LIFSHIN	Motel	Haifa	382

LUBLINSKY	Rita		382
MINTZ	Yisrael		382
FISHELVITZ	Rita	Tel Aviv	382
FOIGEL	Chuna	Petach Tikva	382
KOROL	Anika		382
KOROL	Moshe	Carmiel	382
KOROL	Sarah		382
KAWASH	Batya	Ramat Eliahu	382
KOROL	Leibel	Netanya	382
KLEITMAN	Tsarna	Bat Yam	382
ROITMAN	Malka		382
SCHVARTZMAN	Rakhel		382
SCHACHTER	Tzvi	Ramat Gan	382
SCHACHTER	Moshe	Rishon Letzion	382
SCHACHTER	Shmuel	Tel Aviv	382
SHTILWASSER	Paulina	Azor	382
SHMULEVITZ	Bunya	Sderot	382
SHMUELI	Tzila	Beit Shearim	382
SHIMONOVITZ	Frida	Holon	382

[Page 383]

Bairamcea émigrés in Israel

Surname	Given name	Residence in Israel	Page
ALLINSON (GERSHKOVITZ)	Leah	Beersheva	383
GESSER (RABINOVITZ)	Tzviya	Afula	383
GETZOLSKY	Kalman	Akko	383
GERSHKOVITZ	Fishel	Bat Yam	383

CHAIMOVITZ	Leah	Rehovot	383
NAHARI (GOLDSTEIN)	Rakhel	Rehovot	383
TZUKERMAN (OTCHERTINSKY)	Chaya	Hertzliya	383
KIPPER	Miriam	Tel Aviv	383
KIRSHNER (GETZOLSKY)	Rivka		383
KLEIMAN	Daniel	Jerusalem	383
KAPLANSKY (PICK)	Etya	Tiberias	383
RABINOVITZ	Natan	Beersheva	383
ROSENSTOCK		Carmiel	383
REMBA (BERGER)	Shoshana	Tel Aviv	383
SHOCHET	Wolf	Nahariya	383
SHOCHET	Tova	Nahariya	383
SHOCHET	Zahava	Nahariya	383
SHOCHET	Moshe	Nahariya	383

Shabo émigrés in Israel

Surname	Given name	Residence in Israel	Page
NUR	Malka	Haifa	383
KAMINKER	Aharon	Haifa	383
STEINBERG	Yakov	Tel Aviv	383

[Pages 390- 507]

Necrology - Bilhorod-Dnistrovs'kyy (Akkerman), Ukraine

Last Name	Maiden Name	First Name	Date of Birth	Gender	Father's First Name	Mother's First Name	Spouse's First Name	Date of Death	Page no.
ALTMAN		Tzipora	1886	Female	Isser		Yisrael	01/01/1942	493
ARBEIT		Yehudit	1888	Female			Yitzkhak	01/01/1942	392
ARBEIT		Yitzkhak	1888	Male			Yehudit	01/01/1942	392
AVRAHAM			14/11/1885	Male	Shlomo	Klara	Josefina	13/08/1942	447
BARGUTIN		Gedalia	1890	Male			Zinia	01/01/1942	485
BARGUTIN		Grisha	1917	Male	Gedalia	-		01/01/1941	485
BARGUTIN		Zinia	1895	Female			Gedalia	01/01/1942	485
BARSKI		Masha		Female			Yehuda		401
BARSKI		Yehuda		Male			Masha		401
BATUSHANSKI		Khaia Klara	1884	Female			Shlomo	01/01/1942	393
BATUSHANSKI		Shlomo -	1886	Male			Khaia	01/01/1942	393
BATUSHANSKI		Shmuel		Male	Shlomo	Khaia		01/01/1942	393
BEIDER		Mordekhai	1876	Male	Moshe Shlomo				478
BERG		Eliahu		Male					397
BERG		Gitel		Female					397
BERG		Mordekhai		Male					397
BERG		Yisrael	1916	Male				01/01/1941	397
BERG		Yura		Male				01/01/1942	397
BERGER		Barukh	1901	Male	Shmuel			01/01/1942	398
BERGER		Khaim		Male	Yaakov	Paula		01/01/1942	399
BERGER		Polia		Male			Yaakov	01/01/1942	399
BERGER		Yaakov	1892	Male	Shmuel	Khaia Roza	Paula	01/01/1942	399
BIDNER		Bila	1876	Female			Eliahu	01/01/1941	486
BIDNER		Eliahu	1871	Male			Bila	01/01/1941	486
BLINDER	EDLIS	Charna		Female	Avraham	Sima	Moshe	01/01/1942	390
BLINDER		Dusia		Female	Moshe	Charna			391
BLINDER		Khsanie		Female	Moshe	Charna			391
BLINDER		Moshe		Male			Charna	01/01/1942	390
BRENER		David		Male			Khaia		391
BRENER		Ester		Female	Khaia		David		391
BRENER		Khaia		Female			David		391
BRENER		Khaim		Male	Khaia		David		391
BRENER		Malka		Female	Khaia		David		391
BRENER		Tzipora		Female	Khaia		David		391

Surname	Maiden	First Name	Birth	Gender	Father	Mother	Spouse	Death	Page
BRENER		Yisrael		Male	Khaia		David		391
BRILIANT	GRINBERG	Ida	1920	Female	Moshe	Khava		01/01/1941	460
BRILIANT	GRINBERG	Khava	1892	Female	Efraim		Moshe	01/01/1941	460
BRUDSKI		Brakha	1942	Female			Leib	01/01/1942	395
BRUDSKI		Etel	1884	Female			Tzvi	01/01/1942	395
BRUDSKI		Leib	1873	Male			Brakha	01/01/1942	395
BRUDSKI		Tzvi	1881	Male			Ester	01/01/1942	395
CHAPLIN		Beniamin	1886	Male			Paula	01/01/1942	450
CHAPLIN		Polia	1887	Female			Beniamin	01/01/1942	450
CHERNILOV		Khana	1889	Female			Zalman	01/01/1942	441
CHERNILOV		Zalman	1890	Male			Khana	01/01/1942	441
DORFMAN		David	1928	Male	Pesakh	Fruma		01/01/1942	412
DORFMAN	SHMULEVITZ	Fruma		Female			Pesakh	01/01/1942	412
DORFMAN		Pesakh	1896	Male			Fruma	01/01/1942	412
DORFMAN		Rakhel	1934	Female	Pesakh	Fruma		01/01/1942	412
DVORIN		Avraham	1891	Male			Bentzion	01/01/1942	409
DVORIN		Etie	1895	Female			Aharon	01/01/1942	409
EDLIS	PREIS	Erna		Female					391
EDLIS		Mania		Female			David		391
EDLIS		Yaakov		Male	Avraham	Sima	Ilana	01/01/1945	390
EDLIS		Yehoshua		Male	Avraham	Sima			391
EDLIS		Yosef		Male	Avraham	Sima			391
ELFER	BERGER	Ita	1897	Female	Shmuel	Khaia Roza		01/01/1942	398
ELFER		Mira	1925	Female			Ita	01/01/1942	398
ELFER		Sara	1931	Female			Ita	01/01/1942	398
ERLIKH	HIRSHHORN	Josefina -	30/9/1891	Female	Filip	Berta	Avraham	13/08/1942	447
FALIKOV		Bunie		Female					393
FALIKOV		Dolie		Female					393
FALIKOV		Liza		Female					393
FALIKOV		Mania		Female					393
FALIKOV		Moshe		Male					393
FALIKOV		Rivka		Female					393
FALIKOV		Roza		Female					393
FALIKOV		Shlomo		Male					393
FALIKOV		Shulim		Male					393
FELDMAN		Avraham	1907	Male	Zusia	Miriam			437
FINKEL		Aharon	1885	Male	Meir		Khana	09/09/1941	436
FINKEL		Bela	1931	Female	Aharon	Khana		09/09/1941	436
FINKEL		Faia	1929	Female	Aharon	Khana		09/09/1941	436
FINKEL		Khana	1886	Female			Aharon	09/09/1941	436

Surname	Maiden/Other	Given	Birth	Sex	Father	Mother	Spouse	Death Date	Page
FRANK	SERPER	Roza		Female	Shlomo	Khava		01/01/1942	435
FRIDMAN		David		Male					393
FRIDMAN		Eliezer		Male					393
FRIDMAN		Khana		Female					393
FRIDMAN		Nina		Female					393
FRIDMAN		Soie		Female					393
FRIDMAN		Yeshayahu		Male					393
GEBER	RAPOPORT	Sara	1887	Female			David Tzvi	01/01/1942	402
GEKHT		Rakhel	1889	Female				01/01/1942	404
GELFER		Malka	1866	Female			Zavel	01/01/1942	486
GELFER		Zanvil	1866	Male			Malka	01/01/1942	486
GERSHFELD		Batsheva		Female				01/01/1942	407
GERSHFELD		Khava	1905	Female				01/01/1941	408
GERSHFELD		Malkh	1931	Female	Khava		Barukh	01/01/1941	408
GERSHFELD		Mordekhai	1916	Male	Yaakov			01/01/1942	407
GERSHFELD		Yaakov	1869	Male				01/01/1941	407
GERSHKOVICH		Monie		Male				01/01/1942	
GERSHKOVICH		Unknown		Male			Menukha	01/01/1942	
GERSIIMAN		Aba -		Male				01/01/1942	431
GERSHMAN		Yenta		Female	Shmuel	Gitel		01/01/1942	431
GERTZBERG		David	1911	Male	Yitzkhak	Fani		01/01/1942	498
GERTZBERG		Ester -	1/5/1902	Female			Hertz	01/10/1942	493
GERTZBERG		Hertz -	1900	Male			Ester	01/08/1942	493
GERZON		Avraham		Male					393
GERZON		Neli Sara		Female					393
GERZON		Soiba		Female					393
GIKER		Avraham	1872	Male	Moshe		Reiza	01/01/1942	485
GIKER		Raiza	1876	Female	Reuven		Avraham	01/01/1942	485
GIKER		Tauba	1904	Female				01/01/1942	485
GIRSHFELD	GIRSCHFELD	Khava	1904	Female	Kalman	Malka	Barukh	01/01/1941	501
GIRSHFELD		Khava	1931	Female	Barukh	Khava		01/01/1941	501
GNESIN		Fania		Female					393
GNESIN		Moshe		Male					393
GNESIN		Pola		Female					393
GNESIN		Yisrael		Male					393
GNESIN		Yosef		Male					393
GRINBERG	BERG	Rakhel		Female					397
GRODENCHIK		Berta	1886	Female			Shmuel	26/10/1941	487
GRODENCHIK		Iasha	1920	Male	Shmuel	Berta		01/01/1941	487
GRODENCHIK		Shmuel	1886	Male			Berta	26/10/1941	487
HELMAN		Sara		Female				01/01/1942	494

Surname	Maiden	First Name	Birth	Gender	Father	Mother	Spouse	Death	Page
HELMAN		Zoia		Female		Sara			494
HORIO		Tzipora		Female				01/01/1942	494
KAHALSKI		Khaia	1868	Male			Yehuda	01/01/1942	451
KAMINKER		Asnat		Female			Moshe		505
KAMINKER		Beniamin		Male	Zeev	Khaia	Batsheva	01/01/1941	505
KAMINKER	BLANK	Brana	1892	Female	Aizik		Mordekhai	01/01/1942	445
KAMINKER		Feiga		Female	Moshe	Asnat		01/01/1942	505
KAMINKER		Khaim		Male	Zeev		Tzipora	01/01/1942	444
KAMINKER		Mordekhai	1888	Male	Beniamin		Brana	01/01/1942	445
KAMINKER		Moshe	1894	Male	Beniamin	Batsheva	Asnat	01/01/1942	505
KAMINKER		Peretz	1900	Male	Beniamin	Batsheva		01/01/1941	506
KAMINKER		Zeev		Male	Moshe	Asnat		01/01/1942	505
KAPLAN		Eliahu	13/10/1904	Male			Khana	10/06/1942	451
KAPLAN	ROIZMAN	Khana	25/10/1905	Female			Eliahu	10/06/1942	451
KLEIMAN		Pesakh		Male			Miriam	01/01/1942	431
KLEINER		Brana	1900	Female			Kalman	01/01/1942	441
KOCHEK		Etie	1914	Female				01/01/1944	397
KORNBLIT	MATZEBAKER	Sima		Female			Yosef	01/01/1941	489
KORNBLIT		Unknown	1932	Male	Yosef	Sima		01/01/1941	489
KORNBLIT		Yosef	1905	Male			Sima	01/01/1941	489
KOTZIUK		Aliza	10/9/1939	Female	Meir	Ester		01/01/1944	443
KOTZIUK	BERG	Etie	25/1/1914	Female				01/01/1944	443
KOTZIUK		Klara		Female	Moshe		Tzvi	01/01/1942	443
KOTZIUK		Moshe	30/11/1930	Male	Tzvi	Klara		01/01/1942	443
KOTZIUK		Tzvi	1908	Male	Elimelekh	Ester	Klara	01/01/1942	443
KRIKUN		Sheindl	1890	Female			Shmuel	13/08/1943	466
KRIKUN		Shmuel	1885	Male			Sheindl	20/07/1942	466
KUPERMAN	DOKTOROVITZ	Khaia	1888	Female	Yisrael		Yehuda	01/01/1942	474
LEKER		Feiga		Female	Moshe				426
LEKER		Moshe		Male			Tzipora	01/01/1942	426
LEKER		Rakhel		Female	Moshe			01/01/1942	426
LEKER		Tzipa		Female			Moshe	01/01/1942	426
LEKH		Musia		Female	Abrasha	-			393
LEKH		Musia		Female	Abrasha	-			391
LERNER		Aharon		Male	Feibush	Sobel			506
LERNER		Feibush		Male			Sobel		506
LERNER		Sobel		Female	Beniamin	Batsheva	Feibush		506
LERNER		Zeev		Male	Feibush	Sobel			506
LEV		Abrasha		Male				01/01/1942	391
LEV		Mera		Female	Abrasha	Yulia			391
LEV		Yulia		Female				01/01/1942	391

Surname	Maiden	First	Born	Sex	Father	Mother	Spouse	Died	Page
LINDENBAUM	BRUTZKI	Sara	1/5/1910	Female				01/01/1944	395
LINDENBAUM		Yisrael	1932	Male				01/01/1944	395
MATZEBAKER		Datze	1913	Female	Barukh	Rivka		01/01/1941	489
MATZEBAKER		Rivka	1885	Female			Barukh	01/01/1941	489
MATZEBAKER		Sakhah	1911	Male	Barukh	Rivka		01/01/1942	489
MATZEBAKER		Siome	1915	Male	Barukh	Rivka			489
MATZEBAKER		Unknown	1938	Male		Yente Riszi		01/01/1941	489
MATZEBAKER		Yenta -	1913	Female	Barukh	Rivka		01/01/1941	489
MISIONEZHNIK	RASHKOVETZKI	Malka	1883	Female			Moshe	01/01/1942	441
MONASTIRSKI		Shlomo	1870	Male	Melekh		Khava	01/01/1942	465
MOSHKOVITZ	EDLIS	Sima		Female					391
ORBUKH		Mordekhai Yitzkhak	1877	Male	Moshe Tzvi	Frida Lipsha	Batia	01/01/1942	477
ORBUKH		Shmuel	8/8/1906	Male	Mordekhai Yitzkhak	Batia		25/05/1942	477
OTZARTINSKI		Gitel	1933	Female	Yosef			01/01/1942	501
OTZARTINSKI		Kalman Zaidel	1880	Male			Malka	01/01/1941	501
OTZARTINSKI		Rivka		Female	Kalman	Malka		01/01/1941	501
PAUZNER		Avraham	1893	Male	Moshe	Khana			480
REZNIK		Dvora		Female			Yehoshua	01/01/1942	466
REZNIK		Nate	1880	Male				01/01/1944	466
REZNIK		Sonia		Female				01/01/1942	469
REZNIK		Yehoshua		Male			Dvora	01/01/1942	466
REZNIK		Yitzkhak		Male				01/01/1942	469
RIDER		Dani	1909	Male	Fishel	-	Rivka	01/01/1941	
RIDER		Rivka	1919	Female	Yitzkhak		Dani	01/01/1942	
ROIZMAN		Abrasha	6/8/1912	Male				15/07/1942	451
ROZENBERG		Shalom		Male	Simkha	Zinaida			467
ROZENBERG		Simkha		Male			Zinaida		467
ROZENBERG		Zina		Female			Simkha	01/01/1941	467
SERPER		Barukh		Male	Shlomo	Khava		01/01/1942	435
SERPER		Moshe		Male	Shlomo	Khava		01/01/1942	435
SERPER		Yosef		Male	Shlomo	Khava		01/01/1942	434
SHAPIRA		Ester		Female			Hirsh	01/01/1942	432
SHAPIRA		Mania	1887	Female			Yeshayahu		433
SHAPIRA		Mira	1912	Female					433
SHAPIRA		Misha	1905	Male					433
SHAPIRA		Rakhel -	1916	Female	Yaakov	Rivka		01/01/1941	433
SHAPIRA		Shaia Yeshayahu	1886	Male			Mania		433

Surname	Maiden	Given	Year	Gender	Father	Mother	Spouse2	Spouse	Date	Page
SHAPIRA		Yaakov	1897	Male				Rivka	01/01/1941	433
SHAPIRA		Yitzkhak Reuven	1866	Male	Yosef				01/01/1942	432
SHAPIRA		Zinia	1917	Female	Yeshayahu	Mania				433
SHAPIRA		Zinia		Female	Yeshayahu	Mania				433
SHKOLNIK		Arie Leib	1885	Male				Slava	01/01/1942	456
SHKOLNIK		Slova	1890	Female				Arie	01/01/1942	456
SHRIRA	SHARIRA	Lea		Female				Shaul		452
SHRIRA		Shaul		Male				Lea		452
SHRIRA		Yitzkhak		Male	Shaul	Lea				452
SHTEINBERG		Rakhel	1939	Female	Elisha	Sara			01/01/1942	507
SHTEINBERG		Sara	1886	Female				Elisha		507
SHVARTZMAN		Yosef -	1913	Male	Shimon	Sheina			22/08/1941	452
SPERBER	SHAPIRA	Mania	1885	Female				Efraim	01/01/1942	432
SPERBER		Tzvi	1928	Male	Efraim	Mania			01/01/1942	432
TOIERMAN		Frida	1873	Female					01/01/1941	402
TOIERMAN		Mania	1941	Female	Avraham	Frida			01/01/1941	402
TOIERMAN		Riva	1909	Female	Avraham	Frida			01/01/1941	402
TUKHMAN		Mordekhai	1923	Male	Rafael	Charna			01/01/1942	430
TZUKERMAN		Eliezer	1890	Male	Efraim			Zinaida	01/01/1942	440
TZUKERMAN		Yisrael -	1906	Male	Moshe	Brakha			01/01/1941	438
TZUKERMAN	GOTLIB	Zina		Female				Eliezer	01/01/1942	440
VASERMAN		Dvora Dora	1890	Female				Tzvi	01/01/1943	424
VASILEVSKI		Bentzion		Male						393
VASILEVSKI		Roza		Female						393
VOLVITZ		Dvora		Female	Khaim	Miriam			01/01/1942	420
VOLVITZ		Khaim		Male				Miriam	01/01/1942	420
ZALTZHENDLER	LERNER	Khava	1904	Female	Meir	Sara			01/01/1942	462
ZALTZHENDLER		Mira		Female				Khava		462
ZELTZER		David	1905	Male				Zinia	01/01/1942	498
ZELTZER		Zinia	1907	Female				David	01/01/1942	498
ZIGELVAKS		Asher	1921	Male	Yitzkhak	Khaia			01/01/1942	421
ZIGELVAKS		Dan	1914	Male	Yitzkhak	Khaia			01/01/1942	421
ZIGELVAKS		Khaia	1884	Female	Asher			Yitzkhak	01/01/1942	421
ZIGELVAKS		Khana		Female	Yitzkhak	Khaia			01/01/1942	421
ZIGELVAKS		Slova	1921	Female	Yitzkhak	Khaia			01/01/1942	421
ZIGELVAKS		Yitzkhak Moshe	1882	Male	Faivel				01/01/1941	421
ZONIS	SHILDKRAUT	Busi		Female	Moshe	Khana			01/01/1942	454
ZONIS	SHILDKRAUT	Khana		Female	Bentzion	-		Moshe	01/01/1942	454
ZONIS		Moshe		Male				Khana		454

NAME INDEX

A

Aarale, 32
Abelis, 276
Abrahamson, 484
Abramovich, 24, 95, 96
Abramovitsh, 214
Abramovitz, 484, 494
Abramowich, 269, 270, 300
Abramowitch, 61, 72, 73, 104, 108, 126, 128, 191, 204, 206, 269, 293
Abramowitz, 230, 408, 412
Abramowitz, 494
Adam, 24, 389
Adelis, 484
Adlis, 61, 62, 72
Adlizki, 237
Adumah, 217
Afendopolo Ben Eliyahu, 19
Agol, 62
Aharon, 6, 19, 22, 46, 49, 75, 76, 77, 78, 93, 96, 120, 121, 122, 136, 138, 150, 155, 159, 160, 161, 162, 163, 164, 168, 211, 212, 216, 225, 228, 237, 246, 271, 292, 308, 315, 410, 471, 475, 484, 490, 494, 501, 503
Aharonovich, 63
Aharonowitz, 402, 407
Akkerzsher, 212
Aksler, 174
Akslrod, 178
Alberg, 160
Albert, 377, 421, 422
Albert, 497
Aleichem, 192, 204, 227, 235, 335, 359, 435
Alenson, 498
Alexander I, 12, 24
Alexandru, 12
Alexenberg, 290
Aliechm, 157
Allensohn, 441
Allinson, 500
Alman, 289
Alperson, 42
Alterman, 214, 363
Altman, 404, 440, 441, 442, 443, 444, 448, 452, 453, 457, 459
Altman, 498, 502
Altstein, 401, 448, 458
Altstein, 498
Amitai, 6, 7, 98, 117, 118, 181, 185, 238, 261, 268, 305, 312, 313, 327, 340, 341
Amitai, 484
Amitay, 227, 305
Anatre, 211
Ancel, 77
Andonianetz, 288
Andrew, 17
Andreyev, 238
Anski, 471
Antalson, 490
Antonescu, 105, 287
Apelboim, 403
Appelbaum, 260
Apteker, 460, 461
Arbeit, 219, 294, 308
Arbeit, 502
Arbeitman, 364, 375
Arbit, 61, 70, 72, 73, 136, 137, 138, 153, 230

Arbit, 484

Arlozorov, 228, 272, 382

Asbsorov, 169

Asfis, 258

Asodorov, 85, 90

Aspis, 290

Aspis, 484

Auerbach, 158, 375

Averbuch, 214, 257, 363, 364, 398, 403

Averbuch, 494, 498

Avirbruch, 490

Avirbuch, 484

Avoka, 78

Avraham, 200

Avraham, 502

Avraham Ben Yehudah, 19

Avromtzes, 218

Axelord, 174

Axelrod, 230, 286

B

Babel, 11

Babensky, 498

Bach, 9, 193

Bachman, 490

Badni, 484

Bailis, 215

Bakhmetyev, 12

Balaban, 28, 444

Balebottish, 214

Balfour, 75, 76, 163, 299, 307, 315, 423, 480

Balinowitz, 471

Baloban, 288

Baltaksa, 106

Bandersky, 46

Bandersky, 484

Barany, 104, 105

Barasch, 490

Baratz, 360, 362, 363, 370, 375, 388, 398

Bardev, 288

Barg, 473

Bargutin, 502

Barkan, 248

Bar-Kochba, 281, 282

Barkov, 93

Barnea, 6, 127, 189, 341

Barnea, 484

Baron De Hirsch, 371

Baron Hirsch, 40, 41, 42

Barski, 137

Barski, 502

Bartov, 235

Barulke, 212

Bar-Yochai, 281

Bass, 212, 216, 341

Bast, 77

Batushanski, 502

Batya, 134, 223, 365, 490, 494, 498

Bayokansky, 45

Becker, 497

Bedgi, 77, 78

Beg, 18

Beider, 6, 216, 341, 403, 404

Beider, 494, 502

Beidner, 497

Beigeldrot, 364

Belcher, 490

Belkin, 235, 237

Belnek, 490

Belstotzki, 406

Belzer, 172

Ben Dov, 494

Ben Hur, 498

Ben Israel, 364, 392, 394

Ben Yisrael, 490

Ben Yosef, 451

Ben–Daniel, 81

Benderski, 409

Bendersky, 215, 389

Ben-Gurion, 260, 323

Benkovitz, 494

Ben-Yehudah, 171

Ben–Yehudah, 225

Ben-Yosef, 494

Ben-Zion, 157, 167, 174, 319

Ben-Zvi, 277

Berdov, 498

Berechyahu, 477

Berenstein, 47

Berfel, 96

Berg, 16, 55, 70, 73, 120, 230

Berg, 502, 503

Berger, 22, 47, 54, 55, 58, 63, 65, 70, 73, 75, 76, 77, 78, 79, 81, 82, 91, 93, 94, 96, 97, 104, 108, 120, 121, 123, 162, 163, 164, 168, 171, 189, 191, 204, 205, 214, 218, 219, 223, 224, 226, 230, 232, 289, 306, 310, 311, 320, 324, 326, 334, 362, 375, 470, 474

Berger, 484, 500, 502, 503

Berkov, 74, 75, 97, 160, 163, 307, 314, 338

Berkovic, 165, 255

Berkovitz, 216

Berkovitz, 484, 497

Berkowich, 226

Berkowitch, 153, 256

Berkowitz, 22, 41, 78, 230, 290

Berman, 81, 212, 223, 230, 256, 368, 374, 375, 465

Berman, 490

Bernstein, 159, 389

Bezprozvanne, 212

Bialik, 84, 175, 227, 306, 307, 363, 383, 476, 478

Biazet Ii, 9

Bidner, 502

Bignbaum, 120, 121, 124

Biler, 484

Bilhorod–Dnistrovskyi, 7, 11, 83

Bilinowitch, 128

Bilostotzkaia, 406

Bilostotzki, 402, 403, 468, 473

Bimbolov, 102

Binenbaum, 430

Binenbaum, 484

Biranbaum, 78

Birmatcha, 431

Bistritzky, 130

Bitelman, 191, 230

Blank, 503

Blanowitz, 293

Blazer, 373

Blecher, 217

Blechman, 497

Blinder, 65, 70, 73, 149, 181, 182, 213, 215, 256, 290

Blinder, 502

Blinovitch, 271

Bloch, 130

Blostotzkaia, 414

Blum, 484

Blumenfeld, 490

Bodaisky, 494

Bodyeski, 403, 404

Boganov, 465

Bolgar, 215

Borisowitz, 474

Boroch, 484

Borochov, 47, 84, 298, 299, 300, 387, 389

Botoshanski, 230, 248, 249

Botoshansky, 75, 78, 93, 103, 104, 159, 162, 164

Botoshansky, 484

Boviat, 497

Boyokansky, 484

Brachot, 336, 360, 365, 368

Bragotin, 497

Braier, 484

Brand, 55, 65, 70, 75, 93, 124, 149, 159, 162, 164, 168, 172, 230, 256, 257, 288, 292

Brand, 484

Braner, 70

Braski, 136, 138

Bratini, 271

Braverman, 213, 403, 473

Braverman, 494

Bravmann, 120

Braz, 358

Braz, 494

Breitburd, 368, 371

Brenard, 338

Brend, 32, 73, 78, 93, 151, 256, 269

Brener, 155, 408

Brener, 494, 502, 503

Brenson, 61, 69

Briliant, 503

Brillant, 490

Brilliant, 6, 341, 355, 376, 379, 385, 399

Britava, 230

Britva, 67, 174

Brochis, 365

Brodeski, 230, 288, 422

Brodeskki, 230

Brodesky, 96

Brodetsky, 22, 176

Brodetzki, 467, 470

Brodetzky, 494

Brodsky, 6, 87, 88, 89, 96, 341

Brodsky, 497

Brodtzky, 215

Brofman, 234, 237

Bronfman, 374, 377, 399, 459

Bronfman, 490

Bronshtein, 211

Bronstein, 49, 70, 73, 230, 359, 360, 361, 365, 370, 375, 376, 389, 391

Bronstein, 484, 494

Bross, 357

Brotzky, 37

Brudski, 54, 62, 219, 224, 226, 308

Brudski, 503

Brudsky, 49, 57, 58, 60, 61, 67, 69, 70, 72, 73, 153, 234

Brukhaus, 13, 14, 82

Brun, 137

Brurman, 490

Brutzki, 503

Bubis, 490

Bublitshnik, 211

Buca, 294

Buchner, 218

Buganov, 50, 90

Bugner, 357, 377

Bulagdard, 431

Buloshin, 78

Bun, 9

Bundy, 335

Bunimowitz, 467
Burotzin, 93
Butshai, 293
Bvolovitz, 78

C

Caesar, 8, 11
Camblack, 17
Caushanski, 408
Celler, 276
Chabad, 148
Chacham, 218
Chacham, 497
Chaimovici, 468, 471
Chaimovitz, 500
Chalomot, 215
Chamilkis, 292
Chamudis, 497
Chanoch, 228
<u>Chaplin</u>, 78, 240, 241
Chaplin, 484, 503
Chariton, 359
Charol, 223
Chava–Leibes, 149, 150
Chava–Libes, 32
Chava–Lubes, 330
Chavis, 235
Chazan, 212
Chechelnitsky, 38
Chefetz, 230, 440, 441
Cheifetz, 443
Cheikis, 218
Chemerinsky, 46, 127
Chemerinsky, 484
Cheritonov, 294

Chernilov, 484, 503
Chichelinski, 468
Chlapik, 126
Citron, 105
Clapouch, 139
Cohen, 22, 47, 69, 70, 73, 77, 78, 89, 137, 159, 168, 169, 190, 223, 224, 248, 269, 276, 308, 340, 341, 389
Cohen, 484
Constantiner, 147, 284
Cooperman, 360, 375, 398
Cornbleet, 77

D

Dainow, 27
Dailsh, 215
Dan, 273, 387, 503
Danilka, 467
Danilovich, 147
Danovich, 75, 93, 307
Danowitch, 75
Danziger, 246
David, 41
Davidovna, 36
Davidson, 117, 223
Davidzon, 17, 18, 19, 20, 22, 82
Debelman, 409
Deutch, 375, 398
Deutsch, 498
Devorin, 484
Disconti, 247
Dissentchik, 136
Djokovic, 88, 89
Dobrish, 471
Dobrishman, 490

Doktorovitz, 503

Dolev, 484

Dorfman, 75, 77, 78, 96, 120, 123, 127, 150, 213, 230, 365, 367, 375

Dorfman, 484, 490, 494, 503

Dorpman, 6, 189

Dostoyevsky, 224

Dostrovsky, 160

Doyben, 237

Drori, 98, 100, 114, 116, 118, 122, 157

Drori, 490

Drory, 327

Druze, 88, 293

Dubinsky, 362

Dubobis, 363, 372

Dudelzak, 96

Dudlzek, 97

Durfman, 93, 159, 162, 164

Durpman, 77, 78

Dvorin, 120, 121

Dvorin, 503

E

Echselrod, 237

Edelstein, 294

Edelstein, 494

Edlis, 55, 65, 77

Edlis, 502, 503

Edliss, 211

Efrat, 50

Egul, 55

Eibinderr, 256

Eidelman, 484

Eigenheim, 216

Eimes, 490

Einbinder, 37, 38, 53, 55, 62, 69, 73

Einis, 484

Eisenberg, 235

Eisman, 230

Elazar Shai, 494

Elberg, 212, 288

Elfer, 503

Elishkavitz, 484

Elishkevitsh, 218

Elishkevitz, 484

Elman, 398

Epstein, 27, 171, 219, 223, 225, 361, 371

Erlich, 257, 292

Erlikh, 503

Esvodorov, 87

Eybeschutz, 29

F

Fagin, 212

Failand, 78

Falik, 358, 365

Falikov, 72, 104, 108

Falikov, 503

Fanish, 358, 359, 360, 364, 389, 397

Farberski, 292

Farfel, 468

Feidel, 105

Feigenblatt, 484

Feigin, 38, 67, 74, 75, 168, 288, 422

Feiland, 234

Feinbelt, 171

Feinblatt, 223, 225

Feinland, 174

Feisher, 365, 398

Fejland, 237

Feld, 218
Feldman, 12, 17, 20, 24, 26, 82, 96, 120, 213, 217, 225, 237, 247, 257, 270, 350, 354, 379, 386, 408, 421, 441, 443, 468
Feldman, 484, 503
Feldmaus, 484
Feldstein, 54, 55, 58, 62, 65, 67, 73, 74, 273, 288, 289, 332, 334
Felik, 55, 69, 70, 73, 238
Feyman, 234
Fichman, 324, 429
Fiddelman, 214
Fidelman, 70, 237, 292
Fikhman, 445
Filand, 104
Fildman, 67, 338
Filia, 294
Filot, 96
Filvit, 494
Filvitz, 494
Finchlet, 81
Finegersh, 217
Finkel, 201
Finkel, 484, 503
Finkelshtein, 216
Finkelstein, 375, 448, 459
Finkelstein, 490
Finsburg, 230
Fischman, 401, 422
Fischman, 484
Fishelvitz, 498
Fisher, 223, 360, 375
Fishman, 50, 90, 91, 213, 373, 400, 431
Fishman, 494
Fishzun, 235

Flikov, 294
Florence, 62
Foigel, 442, 448
Foigel, 498
Fokkelman, 38
Folkman, 292
Fraldnski, 94
Frank, 95, 137, 191, 231, 292, 351, 365, 375, 403, 451
Frank, 494, 503
Frechter, 179, 235, 293, 333
Freida, 77
Freink, 403, 406
Freldansky, 93
Freldensky, 72
Frenkel, 137, 231, 390
Frenkel, 484
Fridman, 235
Fridman, 490, 503
Friedman, 223, 292, 361, 365, 370, 375, 398
Friedman, 494
Frug, 136, 476
Frumer, 191
Frumin, 230
Fuchs, 484
Furman, 468
Fyvelles, 212

G

Gaber, 135, 143, 144, 230, 449
Gaber, 484
Gacht, 61, 65
Gadi, 304
Gafni, 122, 126
Galperin, 443, 448, 449, 452, 457
Galperin, 490, 497

Gamoshewitz, 403

Gamshievitsh, 216

Gamshiyevitsh, 212, 213

Gamulka, 355, 369, 376, 377, 381, 385, 388, 390

Ganegorsky, 374

Ganpolsky, 105, 134

Gapon, 83

Garbitz, 484

Gardentzik, 423

Gardenychik, 431

Gardintchik, 422

Garin, 46, 49

Gavri, 484

Gavshevits, 49

Gazettshik, 215

Geber, 6, 79, 118, 120, 333, 341

Geber, 503

Gecht, 72, 73, 77, 230

Gecht, 484

Gecker, 490

Geiser, 402, 407

Geisman, 237

Geizer, 494

Gekht, 503

Gelbinsky, 497

Gelbord, 256

Gelfand, 36, 37, 70, 93

Gelfer, 503

Geller, 468, 471

Gellman, 332

Gelly, 212

Gelman, 47, 55, 65, 73, 78, 165, 212, 215, 216, 230, 255, 290

Gelman, 484

Gemeshivitz, 494

Gerber, 78

Geret, 63

Gernik, 256

Gersh, 490

Gershberg, 494

Gershfeld, 6, 116, 118, 120, 121, 123, 124, 125, 230, 245, 431

Gershfeld, 484, 503

Gershkovich, 503

Gershkovitsh, 216

Gershkovitz, 498, 500

Gershkowitz, 136, 452, 458, 471

Gershman, 503

Gershon, 90, 228, 320, 358, 364

Gerstein, 448, 458

Gerstein, 498

Gertner, 484

Gertzberg, 441, 457

Gertzberg, 503

Gerzberg, 288, 452, 459

Gerzenshtein, 96

Gerzon, 503

Gesser, 468

Gesser, 500

Getz, 212

Getzis, 150, 216

Getzolsky, 494, 500

Getzuletzki, 471

Getzy, 212, 216

Gevet, 156

Gewirtzman, 176

Gezetshik, 211

Gia, 484

Gicker, 497

Gieker, 6, 421, 423, 426

Giker, 341
Giker, 503
Giladi, 129, 131, 311
Giladi, 484, 494
Gilady, 234
Gilboa, 484
Gilbord, 46, 230
Gilburd, 49
Gildish, 359
Gilman, 70
Ginsberg, 307
Ginzburg, 213, 337, 338, 339, 342
Girschfeld, 503
Girshfeld, 137, 165, 166, 191, 230, 341
Girshfeld, 503
Giser, 114
Gitelman, 497
Givony, 130
Glabonski, 292
Gladstein, 46, 49, 63, 70, 73
Glantz, 472
Glassman, 124
Glazer, 363, 364, 448, 458
Glazer, 490
Glazman, 120, 218
Glaznik, 467
Glefend, 69
Gleichman, 223
Gleizer, 494
Glickman, 120, 293, 365, 377, 409, 421, 428
Glickman, 494, 497
Glikman, 78
Glinberg, 223
Glonsky, 484
Gnesin, 503

Gnessin, 358, 376, 399
Gobsevich, 338
Gochberg, 363, 364, 365, 367, 370, 377, 379
Gochberg, 484, 490
Gohberg, 97
Goichman, 484
Gokhberg, 392
Golan, 494
Golani, 193
Goldberg, 78, 123, 146
Goldberg, 490
Goldenberg, 389, 448, 471, 473
Goldenberg, 484
Goldenshtein, 211, 216
Goldenstein, 235
Goldfaben, 238
Goldfaden, 234, 235, 388
Goldfarb, 174
Goldfarb, 497
Goldfled, 234
Goldiner, 494
Goldinger, 403
Goldman, 55, 58, 65, 95, 96, 105, 137, 139, 191, 217, 223, 230, 235, 293, 294, 364, 423, 471, 473
Goldman, 497
Goldnberg, 104
Goldner, 409
Goldshtein, 216
Goldstein, 37, 38, 53, 54, 55, 61, 69, 70, 73, 108, 338, 363, 365, 470, 471
Goldstein, 500
Golobow, 179
Gon, 409
Gonopolsky, 235
Gorbitz, 490

Gordey, 465

Gordion, 78, 150

Gordon, 63, 77, 78, 96, 118, 121, 124, 126, 128, 134, 168, 228, 230, 235, 245, 268, 270, 273, 294, 334, 361, 403

Gorfberg, 490

Gorfield, 294

Gorfil, 341

Gorfinkel, 494

Gorin, 90

Gortchenko, 473

Gotlib, 74

Gotlib, 503

Gottlieb, 200, 244, 245, 246

Gottloib, 215

Goy, 215

Grabos, 371

Gradanchik, 497

Granick, 168

Granovski, 102

Granovskiy, 307

Gratzberg, 447

Grazenstein, 338

Grebois, 370

Greenberg, 290, 421

Greenman, 468, 470

Greenshpon, 96, 106, 289

Greenspan, 294

Greenstein, 39, 106, 174, 234, 246

Gresfeld, 99

Gretzberg, 498

Gribaldi, 136

Grinberg, 360, 362, 364, 365, 375, 392, 443

Grinberg, 498, 503

Grinblatt, 447

Grinfeld, 484

Grinshpun, 212, 215, 216

Grinstein, 39, 50

Grishfeld, 168

Grishnog, 414

Gritshevsky, 217

Grodenchik, 503

Grogerman, 364

Grohovcky, 235

Groshman, 104

Grossman, 118

Grossmann, 106

Grozman, 204, 223

Grozovsky, 315

Grushmsn, 286

Grynszpan, 173

Guberman, 105

Guchman, 293

Gukowski, 324

Gunmacher, 271, 272

Gunzmacher, 484

Gur Aryeh, 484

Gur-Arye, 153

Gur–Aryeh, 6

Gurevich, 260

Gurevitsh, 214

Gurewitz, 230, 455, 473

Gurewitz, 490

Gurfel, 358, 364

Gurfield, 484

Gurfil, 6, 55, 400, 402, 403, 404, 407

Gurfil, 490, 494

Gurin, 147

Gurlatchev, 474

Gutnick, 88

Gutnik, 301, 302, 304, 305

Guzik, 260

Guzman, 234, 235, 236

Guzman, 484

Guzmann, 294

Guzmanzogger, 213

Gvirtzman, 37, 54, 55, 60, 61, 65, 69, 70, 73, 152

H

Hacham, 32, 74, 75, 93, 178, 235

Hadar, 484, 490

Ha'ezrachi, 386

Hagaon, 199, 200

Haham, 360, 361, 362, 371

Haimovich, 160, 271

Hak, 211

Hakham, 41

Haklai, 360, 361, 363, 370, 372, 386

Haklai, 490

Halevi, 7, 226, 302, 303

Halevi, 194, 199, 200

Halperin, 458

Halperin, 484

Hamavet, 216

Hansen, 383

Harari, 47, 83, 91, 94, 158, 159, 162, 164, 169, 272, 314, 320, 322, 323, 324, 326, 474

Hararit, 6

Harav R' Eliezer, 19

Harav R' Yom Tov Dayan, 19

Harav R' Yosef Dayan, 19

Harkavy, 22

Harmatz, 37

Harmoy, 364

Harol, 74, 75

Hartzion, 484

Har–Zion, 281, 284

Har–Zion, 6, 127

Har–Zion, 341

Har–Zion, 434

Har–Zion, 436

Hasid, 317, 441, 443, 448

Haskin, 49

Havdolah, 215

Hefetz, 457

Helfend, 46

Hellman, 106, 256, 313, 360, 375, 408, 467, 469, 473

Helmam, 330

Helman, 46, 54, 55, 57, 58, 62, 63, 65, 73, 74, 81, 95, 96, 97, 104, 217, 223, 237, 335, 412

Helman, 503

Herenstraus, 490

Herman, 177

Herodotus, 7

Hershkowitz, 137, 445

Herzl, 186, 260, 278, 331, 359, 421, 428, 432, 433, 470

Hikkevotte, 212

Hillels, 400

Hirschbein, 238

Hirschfeld, 32, 96, 165, 453

Hirschfield, 77

Hirshenberg, 386

Hirshhorn, 503

Hirshkorn, 357, 377

Hirsh–Wolf, 35

Hitron, 61

Hochberg, 490

Hodes, 484

Hohberg, 96

Hon, 213

Honigman, 7
Horio, 503
Horovitz, 193
Horovitz, 484
Horowitz, 226
Hurtzele, 212
Hyde, 7

I

Iancu, 288
Icht, 46, 47, 147
Icht, 484
Ilyinsky, 26
Imas, 358, 368, 370
Imias, 38
Ingerleib, 155, 230, 344
Ingerleib, 484
Iorga, 7, 12, 17
Isidor, 386
Itseles, 149, 150
Itsikson, 273
Itzelles, 216
Itzkovich, 360, 362
Itzkovitsh, 216, 218
Itzkovitz, 67
Itzkovitz, 484, 498
Itzkowitz, 90, 124, 245
Izbelinsky, 218

J

Jabotinski, 449, 451, 452
Jabotinsky, 84, 96, 139, 158, 159, 185, 260, 312, 361, 371, 446
Jacobson, 293
Janowitz, 76
Jaroslavsky, 290
Jonas, 288
Josipovich, 89
Jurman, 494

K

Kabkov, 490
Kafelnikov, 292
Kafri, 484
Kagalsky, 78
Kagan, 211
Kaganowitz, 402, 404
Kahalski, 120, 230
Kahalski, 503
Kahalsky, 484
Kahanowitz, 494
Kalechnik, 247
Kalkin, 256
Kalnitzki, 471
Kaloshnik, 215
Kamin, 6, 123, 206, 271, 272, 275, 277, 329, 341, 453
Kamin, 484
Kaminker, 6, 22, 32, 70, 75, 76, 77, 93, 120, 122, 123, 124, 128, 149, 160, 161, 162, 163, 164, 214, 223, 230, 256, 275, 315, 329, 475, 477, 478, 480, 482
Kaminker, 484, 501, 503
Kaminska, 359
Kaninker, 96, 126
Kanner, 399
Kanterovitch, 47
Kapeishanski, 448
Kapelman, 413
Kapelnikov, 288
Kapelnikov, 484
Kapelush, 213

Kaplan, 484, 503

Kaplanikov, 484

Kaplanski, 471, 472

Kaplansky, 63

Kaplansky, 500

Kaplauch, 484

Kaplinsky, 191, 235, 294

Kaprishanski, 447, 448

Kaprushanski, 457

Karadonski, 286

Karalik, 57, 67, 70

Karaninsky, 74, 75

Karasik, 26

Kardman, 373

Kardonsky, 213

Karmi, 484

Karnaliyevikker, 218

Karol, 409

Karolik, 54, 55

Karp, 288

Karpovitz, 211

Katchalski, 290

Katz, 258, 294, 360, 364, 375, 376, 377, 392, 394, 398, 399, 412, 435, 490

Katznelson, 322

Kauchansky, 126

Kaufman, 31, 36, 37, 386

Kaufmann, 37

Kavitko, 484

Kawash, 498

Keiselman, 247

Kelbel, 216

Kelzon, 215

Keminer, 127

Keminker, 155

Kenig, 235

Kenner, 359

Kentor, 169

Keplauch, 303

Kernkurs, 247

Kesselman, 230

Kessler, 490

Kestretz, 289

Keves, 484

Khakla'i, 400

Khalifa, 18

Kharmoy, 392

Khorol, 471

Kiefer, 468

Kilia, 431, 472

Kilimenik, 247

Kilometer, 147, 148

Kiner, 367, 368

Kiperwasser, 494

Kipnis, 338

Kipper, 500

Kiprosser, 413

Kirshner, 500

Kiselewski, 87

Kishiniovski, 338

Kishinovski, 477, 480

Kishinovsky, 494

Kishinyovsky, 494

Kishpon, 289

Kisliansky, 359

Kisliansky, 490

Kissling, 386

Kitzis, 186, 187

Kizlman, 175

Kizzelman, 217

Klaiman, 237

Klarfeld, 89

Klausner, 45, 47, 82, 226, 231, 240, 244, 278, 281, 283, 284, 285, 301, 302, 307, 400, 405, 420, 421, 423, 426, 428, 431, 434, 436, 438, 444, 448, 453, 455, 459, 465, 475, 483, 484

Kleiman, 130, 234

Kleiman, 484, 490, 497, 500, 503

Kleinberg, 235

Kleinbord, 245

Kleiner, 294

Kleiner, 503

Kleinman, 90, 245

Kleinman, 484

Kleitman, 290, 403, 405

Kleitman, 494, 498

Klepner, 408

Kliger, 148

Kloisner, 360

Klorefeld, 256

Klorfeld, 181, 358

Klozeski, 413

Klurfeld, 214

Klyuchnik, 11, 14

Kminker, 168

Kochanski, 235

Kochek, 503

Kochok, 484

Kochuk, 363, 372, 375, 377, 379, 394

Kogan, 88, 118, 128, 191, 212, 215, 230, 245, 246, 279, 364, 375, 398, 430

Kogan, 484, 490

Kogen, 38, 54, 61, 62, 67, 70, 73, 74, 79, 81, 93, 99, 174, 177, 223, 289, 293

Kolker, 471

Kolomaisky, 494

Kolomiski, 402

Kolomyeski, 407

Kolozhensky, 494

Kolyesky, 212

Komarovski, 431, 468, 471

Komarovsky, 290, 342

Komorov, 484

Komorovski, 422

Komorovsky, 96, 97

Kooper, 471

Kopelman, 494

Kopilovitz, 359, 367

Korean, 69

Koren, 191, 483

Korin, 230

Koris, 490

Korn, 484

Kornblit, 120, 124, 458

Kornblit, 484, 503

Korol, 403, 408, 442, 448, 468

Korol, 498

Korotkin, 45

Kos, 412

Koskov, 62

Kosovsky, 497

Kosoy, 258

Kostirin, 91

Kotchuk, 230

Kotchuk, 490

Kotter, 213

Kotziuk, 120, 127

Kotziuk, 503

Kovlanov, 359, 363

Kovlenov, 392

Kozak, 218

Krankurs, 169

Krasenyanski, 307

Krasik, 237

Krasner, 49, 338

Krasniansky, 212, 214

Krasninski, 256

Krasnov, 441, 448

Krassiltshik, 215

Krassiuk, 362

Krausman, 49, 338

Kreber, 363

Kreizel, 359

Kremer, 373

Kremer, 497

Krichevsky, 90

Krikon, 490

Krikun, 365, 368

Krikun, 503

Kriper, 49

Kripitz, 358, 373

Krolick, 237

Krolik, 65, 332, 341

Kroschkin, 289

Kroshkin, 95

Kroyt, 273

Krushkin, 37, 70, 72, 73

Kruskin, 55, 60, 61, 62, 65, 67, 69

Krylov, 148

Kumarovsky, 37, 38, 39, 41, 46, 47, 49, 53, 83

Kumorowski, 83, 84

Kunicher, 77

Kuperman, 490, 503

Kurin, 78

Kuris, 360, 361, 370, 372, 386

Kuschnir, 490

Kushner, 289

Kushnir, 38, 65, 73, 93, 94, 120, 217, 230, 235, 294, 307, 365, 367

Kushnir, 484, 494

Kutchuk, 245

Kutshiuk, 216

Kutuzov, 355

Kuznetsov, 88, 292

Kuzniyetz, 212

Kvartin, 373

Kvitko, 62, 65, 256, 273, 335, 336

L

Ladizshensky, 217

Lahav, 484

Lainzon, 359, 366, 374, 375, 398

Laker, 230

Lamdan, 386

Lamed, 386

Landau, 472

Landau, 484, 490

Landoberg, 311

Langber, 490

Lapida, 77, 137

Lapida, 484

Laron, 355, 361, 369, 385, 386

Laskin, 497

Lavie, 408

Lazar, 104, 106, 212

Lebovsky, 484

Lechte, 120, 123

Lederman, 78

Lehrer, 490

Leibele, 32, 255, 472

Leibeles, 215

Leibeshis, 217

Leitman, 360, 368, 375, 398

Leizerovitz, 363, 375, 378

Leizerowitz, 473

Leker, 32, 256

Leker, 503

Lekh, 503

Lender, 117

Lenin, 261, 275

Lerner, 58, 355, 360, 361, 364, 373, 375, 385, 386, 398, 404, 477

Lerner, 494, 503

Lestschinsky, 56

Lev, 78, 120, 126, 191, 484

Lev, 484, 503

Levin, 32, 96, 97, 215, 226, 230, 256

Levinton, 186, 187

Levit, 85, 104, 105, 110

Levit, 484, 490

Levitt, 362, 398

Levitzki, 247

Lezer, 126

Liber, 77

Licht, 78, 104

Licht, 484

Lichtjeger, 490

Liebman, 430

Liebman, 490

Lifchitz, 105

Lifshin, 490, 498

Lifshitz, 88, 260, 341

Lindenbaum, 503

Linder, 216

Liova, 378, 431

Lipman, 468

Lipsky, 484

Lis, 47, 230

Lisovsky, 494

Litman, 412

Litman, 484

Litvak, 216, 338

Litvin, 303, 422

Litwin, 497, 498

Loker, 276

Lotzker, 490

Lowdermilk, 300

Lowitz, 473

Lublinski, 440, 441, 453, 458, 459

Lublinsky, 258

Lublinsky, 498

Ludizenski, 235

Ludvipol, 50

Lupo, 324

Lushak, 235, 294

Lushek, 191

M

Magalnik, 214, 216

Magazinik, 245, 467

Mages, 4, 7, 83, 91, 93, 98, 102, 113, 117, 127, 129, 135, 146, 153, 158, 159, 161, 165, 169, 170, 173, 176, 179, 181, 185, 189, 193, 197, 201, 204, 206, 219, 234, 237, 255, 258, 266, 268, 272, 289, 297, 305, 306, 310, 312, 313, 314, 316, 319, 320, 322, 327, 329, 330, 331, 332, 333, 337, 340, 346, 348, 350, 351, 352

Maglnik, 235

Magzinik, 275, 335

Makerman, 467

Malal, 484

Malamud, 223, 363, 365, 375, 398

Malchin, 77, 78

Malinsky, 294

Malinsky, 484

Malkin, 78, 131, 133, 134, 216, 230, 243, 247

Malkkin, 243

Malmud, 165, 230

Mamenyu, 158, 216

Maniali, 103

Manne, 172

Manoles, 91, 92

Manos, 77, 78, 93, 121, 123, 134, 341

Manos, 484

Manueli, 22, 73, 74, 102, 103, 104, 255, 305

Manueli, 484

Manus, 230

Marcellinus, 8

Marcus, 127

Margalit, 75, 77, 78, 93, 159, 161, 162, 164, 230, 431

Margalit, 484, 490

Margolies, 412

Margolin, 46, 49, 69, 70, 338

Marinyansky, 49

Marisis, 497

Markesko, 324

Markotin, 217

Markovsky, 367

Markowitz, 104

Markus, 89, 216

Markus, 484

Marlin, 414

Marx, 275

Masliansky, 29, 31

Massliansky, 45

Masterman, 484, 490, 494

Matusis, 85, 87

Matzbecker, 497

Matzebaker, 503

Meglnik, 294

Meir, 260

Meirson, 386, 477, 478, 480, 482

Meisel, 84

Melament, 359, 374, 378

Melamnet, 490

Melchin, 96

Meller, 125, 126

Melmant, 490

Melnik, 212

Mendel, 490

Mendelovitz, 494

Menuali, 93, 95, 96, 97, 273, 275, 329

Merlin, 490

Meshi, 114, 121

Meyrson, 176

Mialo, 324

Michael, 285

Michaelowitz, 301, 305

Michilibotz, 497

Mickiewicz, 24

Mickiewiczs, 146

Midman, 294

Midovoy, 422

Mikhoels, 293

Miletus, 8

Milman, 70, 175, 214, 215, 218, 230, 292, 308

Milman, 490

Milshter, 494

Milstein, 37, 54, 55, 62, 63, 65, 73, 103, 104, 149, 177, 224, 289, 294, 308, 371

Miniali, 127, 131, 133, 134, 278, 305, 341

Minieli, 230

Minieli, 484

Miniely, 108, 305

Minkovski, 244, 247

Mintz, 498

Mishal Hadalponi, 36

Misionezhink, 234

Misionezhnik, 129, 131, 133, 134

Misionezhnik, 503

Misionzink, 236

Misonzik, 78

Missonzshnik, 213

Modistke, 212

Moldavsky, 484

Moldovon, 213

Molodowsky, 75, 78

Monastirski, 503

Mondiok, 498

Mordechai'le, 46

Moshe–Wolf, 35

Moshkovitz, 503

Moskovitz, 494

Moskowitz, 70, 96, 97, 324

Motniak, 367

Motniak, 490

Motzkin, 50, 484, 497

Mukumel, 214

Multiner, 96

Munishes, 216

Mushinski, 228

Mutchenik, 484

Mutchnick, 104

Mutshnik, 218

N

Naamani, 223, 341

Na'amani, 226

Naamani, 484

Nachmans, 215

Nahari, 500

Navon, 384, 390

Navrotzki, 213

Neami, 81

Neiman, 77, 120, 123, 124, 204, 223, 245, 348

Neizl, 218

Nestor, 9, 17

Neuger, 484

Neuman, 484

Nicomedia, 19

Nidriker, 148, 292

Nifomanishtchen, 477

Nikolaevna, 86, 91

Nir, 58, 232, 299, 341, 484

Nisenman, 490

Niuma, 78, 294

Nodelman, 235

Notov, 403

Notov, 484

Novak, 70, 223, 237

Novobrotzky, 484

Nowakowsky, 46

Nudelman, 213, 363

Nudelman, 490

Nur, 501

Nusatte, 215

Nutov, 223

O

Obet, 70

Ohrbach, 451
Ohrbuch, 447
Ohtshitel, 497
Okishor, 288
Okishur, 256
Olifant, 420
Oliphant, 45
Orbukh, 503
Osipovich, 331
Osipowitch, 283
Ostropoler, 148
Ostrovski, 442, 448, 459
Otchertinsky, 500
Otchkovskaya, 364
Otzartinski, 503
Otzertinski, 470, 471
Oved, 122, 123

P

Pakkenarreger, 213
Palikov, 61, 230, 279, 286
Parkansky, 212
Parladansky, 212
Parpar, 490
Pasternak, 403
Pasternak, 490
Pat Lach, 484
Pausner, 407, 412, 413, 414, 418
Pauzner, 494, 503
Pazi, 490
Pegger, 216
Pegorski, 96
Peker, 90
Pekker, 494
Pelikof, 189, 190, 191

Peltz, 458
Perelmuter, 238
Peretz, 235, 245, 324, 325, 335, 430, 471, 503
Perldansky, 61
Perlin, 211
Perlis, 70, 72, 73, 215
Perliss, 216
Perlman, 443, 451, 457
Perlmutter, 412
Perlmutter, 484
Perlson, 490
Perper, 363, 375
Perski, 468, 471
Pertz, 208, 324
Pettifer, 237
Pevzner, 403, 404
Pick, 500
Pieterman, 237
Pik, 467
Pimilidia, 15
Pineles, 159
Pinsker, 49
Pipergal, 292
Pippergal, 216
Pippik, 216
Pivnik, 363, 372
Plehve, 186
Plock, 106
Pluski, 294
Poliak, 367
Poliakov, 363, 364, 392
Polinovsky, 494
Pollak, 494
Polonskaya, 235
Polonski, 402, 407

Polonsky, 494

Pomoshtsh, 217

Popov, 85, 88

Popovici, 472

Porlodonski, 97

Portnoy, 270, 408

Posak, 497

Posk, 427, 431

Potash, 238

Prachtenberg, 338

Prechter, 212

Prectman, 32

Preis, 503

Preladenski, 69

Preldenski, 96

Prelis, 46, 62, 65, 338

Puchslman, 234

Pushkin, 24, 148, 159, 224

Puterman, 234

Puziniok, 214

Puzis, 93, 223, 308

R

R' Binyamin Aharon, 18

R' Binyamin Meir, 18

R' Caleb Aba, 19

R' Dov, 200

R' Efraim, 199

R' Eliyahu Of Bashyazi, 19

R' Gedalia, 18

R' Heschel, 199

R' Idel, 167

R' Keleb Ben Eliyahu Tarno, 19

R' Leizer, 167, 181, 182

R' Mendel, 70, 165, 179, 180

R' Yakov, 19, 41, 201

Rabelenski, 466

Rabelski, 53

Rabin, 497

Rabinovitch, 223

Rabinovitsh, 215, 218

Rabinovitz, 212, 214, 223

Rabinovitz, 484, 490, 500

Rabinowitch, 22, 28, 61, 73, 74, 75, 76, 93, 94, 96, 97, 120, 137, 159, 162, 164, 191, 270, 271, 307, 341

Rabinowitz, 136, 230, 303, 441, 451, 458, 468, 473

Radek, 484

Radzivitzke, 218

Rafaleks, 58

Ramati, 20

Ramba, 6, 341

Ranen, 484

Rapoport, 503

Rashi, 161, 162

Rashkovetzki, 503

Ratner, 213

Ravelski, 408, 467

Ravnitzki, 476

Ravotzki, 301

Ravutski, 58, 69, 160, 297, 298, 299, 300

Razin, 386

Razomani, 244, 247

Rebelski, 38

Reginowitz, 230

Reifman, 90

Reikhman, 392

Remba, 500

Resnik, 484

Reuven, 49, 78, 216, 230, 235, 293, 294, 401, 484, 490, 494, 503

Reznik, 214, 362, 364, 365, 368, 401, 403, 409

Reznik, 490, 494, 503

Ribak, 96

Ribelnik, 484

Rider, 503

Riebak, 212, 218

Rieder, 459, 460, 461

Riesenson, 484

Riess, 409

Rikenberg, 373, 377

Risenzan, 55

Risenzon, 78, 292

Risis, 490

Risnzon, 61, 72

Ritech, 412

Ritenberg, 257

Rivelnik, 96

Rivkin, 46, 47, 63, 70, 93, 147, 158, 211

Roichman, 364, 394

Roichman, 497

Roitman, 67, 174, 230, 244, 249, 289

Roitman, 494, 497, 498

Roizman, 96, 97, 128, 230, 257, 459

Roizman, 484, 497, 503

Roler, 168

Roll, 99, 118

Roller, 289

Romanovka, 116, 120, 126, 363, 408, 431

Ronitch, 237

Ronzberg, 358

Rosen, 490

Rosenbaum, 96, 230

Rosenberg, 358, 360, 362, 363, 366, 368, 370, 372, 376, 388, 467

Rosenberg, 490

Rosenblatt, 361, 365, 370, 378, 380

Rosenblatt, 490

Rosenblith, 338

Rosenstock, 500

Rosental, 191, 230

Rosenthal, 104, 105, 106, 285, 335, 358, 360, 375, 383, 391, 396

Rostetcher, 375, 398

Rotberg, 361, 362, 363, 365, 367, 370, 372, 375, 389

Rotberg, 490

Rotenberg, 105, 293, 360

Rotenshtern, 269

Rotenstein, 201, 202

Rottenshtein, 218

Roystcher, 490

Royter, 149

Royzen, 360

Rozanskie, 290

Rozenbaum, 95, 120

Rozenberg, 484, 503

Rozenthal, 484

Rozitchner, 359

Rozitchner, 490

Rozman, 116

Rozumani, 249

Rubinstain, 257

Rubtzinsky, 212

Rushkovan, 494

Rusis, 490

Rutshka, 216

Ruvashov, 307

Rybak, 169

S

Sacerdati, 249

Sadeh, 311

Saint Peter, 17

Sapir, 362

Sapirstein, 490

Sapoznikov, 213

Saropolo, 288

Sarper, 308

Schachter, 447, 448, 457

Schachter, 484, 498

Schächter, 455, 459

Schaechter, 438, 441

Schbartz, 96

Schechter, 6, 136, 341, 352, 353, 404, 445

Schectman, 95, 96

Schein, 484

Scheinfeld, 96

Scheinfeld, 498

Scher, 178

Schieber, 447

Schildcroit, 226

Schildkraut, 93, 94, 95, 96, 97, 127, 247, 303

Schildkraut, 484

Schildkrauth, 6, 14, 15, 16, 21, 22, 32, 35, 37, 45, 54, 56, 57, 61, 66, 67, 70, 73, 74, 75, 79, 83, 146, 176, 179, 273, 274, 289, 296, 308, 313, 340, 341

Schinkovsk, 96

Schleizer, 484

Schlimovitz, 490

Schneider, 235, 237

Schochen, 467

Schoenfeld, 446, 450, 451, 452

Schor, 465, 468, 470, 473

Schuman, 235

Schusterman, 408, 430

Schvartz, 490

Schvartzman, 218

Schvartzman, 484, 490, 494, 498

Schwartz, 223, 225, 398, 458

Schwartzman, 6, 55, 62, 65, 77, 120, 123, 127, 139, 332, 360, 361, 363, 364, 365, 367, 368, 372, 375, 386, 388, 394, 398, 399, 403

Schwarzbard, 444

Schwarzman, 401, 409, 442, 448

Schwerin, 431

Schwien, 90

Schwinn, 176, 294

Segal, 102, 103, 104, 106, 199, 213, 214, 217, 362

Segal, 484

Segel, 63, 96, 176, 235

Seibleband, 338

Seidman, 497

Sela, 372, 389

Selinger, 49

Selnik, 18

Seltzer, 444, 448, 459

Semmen, 212

Serfer, 93, 96, 97, 159, 162, 177, 223

Serper, 46, 49, 55, 57, 58, 60, 61, 62, 63, 65, 67, 72, 73, 75, 90, 93, 257, 289, 314, 330

Serper, 503

Serta, 431

Sforim, 24

Shabolatter, 212

Shadmi, 130

Shafir, 367, 376

Shafrir, 114, 120, 122

Shagansky, 32

Shaibes, 213

Shainer, 78, 213

Shakhnazarov, 235

Shalem, 363, 368, 426

Shankarovsky, 124, 126

Shapira, 32, 37, 39, 54, 55, 58, 67, 69, 73, 77, 88, 89, 95, 96, 97, 168, 219, 223, 231, 256, 305, 331, 332

Shapira, 484, 503

Shapiro, 268

Shar, 49

Sharett, 276, 277

Sharira, 45, 55, 61, 123, 204, 308

Sharira, 503

Shaul, 73, 74, 104, 150, 151, 223, 286, 297, 341, 503

Shchiglova, 392

She'ar, 86, 87, 88

Shechter, 98, 99, 100

Shechtman, 158, 159, 216, 307, 338

Shehori, 484

Sheinberg, 41

Sheinkin, 46, 47

Sheinman, 360, 378

Shemer, 390

Sherira, 89, 230, 282

Sheyner, 148, 149

Shifra, 78, 133, 134, 484, 490

Shikkeles, 216

Shildkraut, 103

Shildkraut, 503

Shildkroit, 212

Shimonovich, 97

Shimonovitz, 96

Shimonovitz, 498

Shinkarovsky, 216

Shinkrovsky, 293

Shirin, 497

Shivitz, 412

Shkolnik, 471

Shkolnik, 484, 503

Shlein, 279

Shlovitz, 358

Shmoish, 121, 125, 134, 230, 256

Shmuel, 6, 19, 20, 41, 46, 49, 65, 69, 70, 73, 74, 77, 78, 79, 96, 97, 104, 105, 106, 131, 133, 134, 135, 150, 157, 168, 185, 194, 196, 200, 204, 214, 218, 223, 228, 230, 256, 275, 278, 290, 297, 302, 303, 316, 317, 333, 341, 355, 371, 376, 385, 400, 403, 409, 435, 444, 449, 458, 484, 490, 494, 498, 502, 503

Shmuel Ha-Ramati, 19

Shmueli, 484, 498

Shmuelvitz, 484

Shmukler, 257

Shmulevitz, 498, 503

Shmunis, 77

Shneirson, 363

Shneur, 153

Shochat, 255, 423, 430

Shochet, 402, 465

Shochet, 497, 500

Shohat, 22, 58, 332

Shohet, 106

Shorr, 18, 290

Shoshok, 245

Shoshok, 484

Shpiegelman, 217

Shrira, 125, 126, 147, 223, 294, 310, 311, 312, 314, 315

Shrira, 503

Shteidman, 494

Shteinberg, 85, 120, 217

Shteinberg, 503

Shterenshis, 194

Shtermbrand, 484

Shternberg, 88, 89, 91

Shternsis, 368

Shteydakot, 191

Shtilman, 359, 365, 366, 371, 379, 392

Shtilwasser, 498

Shtink, 214

Shtukes, 218

Shtulman, 49

Shulman, 360, 363, 375, 376, 381, 384, 390, 391, 398, 399

Shulman, 490

Shusterman, 494

Shutina, 94

Shvartzman, 392

Shvartzman, 503

Shvarzman, 292

Shwartzman, 283

Sidikman, 69

Siegelwachs, 245

Siegelwaks, 484

Sigalit, 490

Silberfarb, 230

Silberman, 421, 422, 423, 428, 429, 430, 431

Silberman, 497

Singer, 490

Sinilnikov, 230

Sirkis, 9, 18, 193

Sirota, 58, 360, 371, 375, 389

Sirota, 490

Sirotin, 57, 62, 65

Sitner, 477

Siyoma, 191

Skliar, 290

Skliarov, 237

Sklyarov, 235

Skolnik, 366, 374

Skolnik, 490

Skoriski, 63

Skoropadskyi, 305

Skoropedski, 301, 304

Slabay, 218

Slepoy, 290

Slimovitz, 368

Slon, 212

Slotzki, 422

Slutzky, 497

Smetene, 373, 377

Smulbard, 55

Socher, 484

Sochmalinova, 403

Sofer, 81, 361, 363, 370, 372

Sofer, 484, 490

Sokoloski, 230

Sokolow, 316

Solomon, 234, 235, 290, 292, 426

Solomonovitz, 490

Soloveitchik, 198, 200

Sordlik, 294

Sorkis, 490

Soya, 230, 288

Soybel, 448

Speckterman, 497

Specterman, 423, 430

Speevak, 279

Spektor, 484

Sperber, 484, 503

Sperling, 358, 360, 373, 388

Spinnern, 104

Spir, 63

Spitzirman, 338

Spivak, 213

Sposov, 215

Sprinzak, 276

Stalin, 275, 293

Stambol, 123, 125

Stamboul, 484

Stambul, 6, 7, 47, 61, 62, 63, 65, 67, 73, 77, 118, 120, 123, 124, 126, 173, 174, 181, 227, 229, 230, 308, 319, 320, 340, 341, 343

Starec, 22, 38, 46, 47, 49, 53, 63, 70, 73, 75, 76, 81, 136, 312

Starozumne, 215

Startz, 230, 303

Stefan, 9

Stein, 359, 471

Stein, 490

Steinbeck, 484

Steinberg, 6, 45, 50, 57, 87, 91, 156, 179, 249, 292, 341, 458, 477, 478, 481

Steinberg, 501

Steinmetz, 494

Stembul, 98, 238

Stephen The Great, 18

Sterenhuss, 118

Sterltz, 289

Stern, 223, 225, 230, 308, 309

Sternberg, 50, 235, 477

Sternsaus, 63, 73, 74, 79, 81, 223, 225

Sternschus, 490

Sternshis, 135, 171, 230

Sternshus, 365

Stetsky, 78, 105

Stetzky, 290

Stkolshchik, 494

Stolberg, 58

Stolbrod, 61, 62, 65, 67, 72, 73

Stoliar, 363, 372, 376, 379, 399

Stolipin, 479

Stompotolo, 256

Strechilevitch, 363

Streich, 294

Streicher, 458, 459

Streicher, 497

Strenshus, 490

Stretch, 223, 308

Stretz, 106, 159, 171

Strilitz, 497

Stroganov, 26

Stromberg, 359, 372

Stromberg, 490

Strulovitz, 484

Stulbrod, 230

Sudek, 484

Sudkowitc, 257

Sugitin, 359

Sussy, 215

Sverdlik, 212, 235, 374

Sviadush, 49

Swet, 247

Syrkin, 299

Sztulman, 292

T

Tabachnik, 74, 75, 79, 93, 235, 294, 338, 394

Tabakman, 444

Tabatshnik, 217

Tabchnik, 292

Tal, 235, 359

Talmazan, 235, 258

Taraday, 364, 392

Tatarbunar, 4, 26, 116, 290, 312, 341, 420, 421, 422, 423, 424, 426, 427, 428, 429, 430, 431, 432, 434, 435, 436, 497

Tchechovski, 301

Tchedar–Longa, 431

Tcherkis, 368

Tcherniavskki, 281

Tcherniavsky, 96, 97, 223, 225

Tchernichovski, 227, 476

Tchernichovsky, 136, 315

Tchernilov, 179

Tchernowitz, 307, 476

Tchichelnitzky, 171, 234

Tchobotaru, 288

Tchodanovski, 476

Teitelbaum, 422

Telenofer, 149

Telmzan, 290

Telzman, 294

Tendenik, 290

Teodorescu, 256

Teperman, 359, 367

Teplizki, 256

Tepner, 235

Ternopol, 133

Ternopolski, 256

Teshmerinski, 174

Teuerman, 230

Tinkelman, 215

Tishby, 19

Tishler, 235

Tobbin, 490

Toierman, 503

Toker, 249

Toker, 494

Tolstoy, 224, 333

Tomashpolski, 459

Toporov, 178, 363, 372, 374

Toyerman, 78

Toyerman, 484

Toyrman, 191

Trachtenberg, 273

Trachtenbroit, 58, 292, 308, 341

Trachtman, 105, 128, 185, 286, 294, 302, 303, 375, 398

Trackman, 70

Trahtman, 41, 42, 45, 57, 73, 91, 96, 97

Tronopoler, 301

Trop, 484

Truker, 246

Trumpeldor, 118, 135, 381, 382, 408, 445

Tukhman, 294

Tukhman, 503

Tukro, 494

Tulchinsky, 96, 97, 255

Tultshinsky, 214

Turgenev, 158, 224

Tur-Kokhba, 274

Turkov, 359

Turlakker, 217

Tzamir, 484

Tzdik, 20

Tzeitin–Zhemni, 414

Tzibulevsky, 213

Tziprin, 490

Tzirlson, 249

Tzirolnik, 404, 442, 457

Tzitron, 484

Tzobotar, 422

Tzrolnik, 494

Tzsli Ben Eliya, 20

Tzukerman, 127, 128, 230

Tzukerman, 484, 497, 500, 503

Tzur, 484, 494

Tzvoter, 422

U

Umansky, 392

Ussishkin, 74, 471

V

Varrenik, 216

Vaserman, 503

Vasilevski, 503

Vaskovnik, 375

Vassilevsky, 212

Vattenmacher, 214

Vayser, 148

Vebtchik, 128

Veggele–Shtuper, 216

Veler, 207

Velitchko, 473

Verbitzki, 472

Vidit, 477

Vilderman, 97, 256

Vilkomirski, 87, 88

Vilkomirsky, 87

Vineberg, 215, 357, 378

Vineshtein, 216

Vinitsky, 370, 375, 391

Vinitzki, 405, 406, 465

Vinitzky, 75, 80, 82

Vinizky, 57

Vishenivsky, 120

Vishnevsky, 96

Vishnivetzki, 97

Vishnovitzki, 95

Vladimirsky, 215

Vodovoz, 213

Vofsi, 293

Volkovitz, 399

Volovich, 327

Volovitz, 98, 99, 114, 116, 118, 120, 121, 123, 334

Volvitz, 503

Voronovskaya, 235

Vorotnikov, 292

Vorvitzki, 472

Voskovoinik, 398

Vronski, 471

Vytzblit, 216

W

Wadwez, 498

Waiser, 104

Wakertchevski, 458

Waksman, 484

Wallier, 290

Wallman, 90

Walman, 494

Wankert, 498

Warschawski, 314

Warszawskaya, 237

Wasiniwesky, 174

Wasserman, 448

Wasserman, 484

Weiner, 497

Weini, 290

Weininger, 484

Weinstein, 41, 105, 138, 230, 294

Weinstein, 484

Weinzweig, 338
Weisbein, 498
Weisberg, 216, 217
Weiser, 89
Weisman, 257
Weisman, 484
Weismann, 382, 383
Weiss, 215
Weissberg, 230, 293
Weisser, 72, 294
Weissman, 407, 421, 422, 431
Weitzman, 260, 268, 270, 271
Weitzman, 484
Weizmann, 225, 273, 274
Welitzko, 484
Wellman, 58
Wershavsky, 484
Wertheim, 32, 153, 154
West, 228
Wexler, 358
Wieder, 336
Wienstein, 191
Wilderman, 235
Wilk, 421, 422, 436
Wilkomirski, 67, 104, 106, 108, 112, 292
Wisniewski, 191
Wisser, 61
Wizblat, 158
Wloshin, 484
Wollman, 421, 422, 431
Wolman, 37, 50, 465
Wolowitz, 227
Wolozyn, 293

Y

Yacobson, 78
Yagolnitzer, 290
Yakobsohn, 245, 246, 248
Yakobzan, 41
Yankel, 35, 38, 172, 186, 214, 215, 218, 245, 246, 373, 377, 409, 470, 473
Yankelewitz, 401, 403, 406, 431
Yankilewitz, 494
Yanko, 490
Yarnowski, 131, 133, 134
Yaroslavsky, 57, 61, 67, 72, 73, 218
Yashar, 160
Yashpan, 174
Yashpon, 61, 70
Yashpun, 279
Yavetz, 490
Yehenson, 139
Yehudah Ben Tanach, 22
Yelin, 95, 96, 228, 258
Yellin, 286
Yeroslavski, 255, 256
Yesha, 484
Yevazrav, 45
Yishpon, 69
Yisrael, 173
Yisraeli, 484
Yitsá, 78
Yizi, 35
Yoeli, 363
Yona, 35, 93, 246
Yoske, 191
Yossi, 35, 306, 320
Youngerleev, 137, 139
Yuchentzes, 212

Yudkovitz, 494
Yusim, 293

Z

Z.M – Y.S., 211
Zacharov, 249
Zadok, 161, 162, 193, 194, 196, 198, 199, 200, 201, 276, 317, 332
Zahavi, 490
Zaietz, 490
Zait, 271
Zalkind, 269
Zalmanson, 292
Zaltshendler, 359, 363, 367, 372, 375, 398
Zaltzhandler, 490
Zaltzhendler, 346
Zaltzhendler, 503
Zaltzman, 216
Zamir, 127, 266, 373
Zandberg, 228
Zarchi, 169
Zarchy, 216
Zarfin, 309
Zashtzuk, 26
Zaslavsky, 214
Zausmer, 37
Zavgorski, 409
Zavgorsli, 409
Zbarsky, 217
Zebler, 19
Zef, 61, 62, 72, 73
Zef, 484, 497, 498
Zeff, 294
Zehavi, 117
Zeider, 77, 78, 235

Zeitzev, 494
Zektzer, 212
Zeltser, 359
Zeltzer, 484, 490, 498, 503
Zenkler, 53
Zeplin, 191, 230, 235
Zepllin, 338
Zerling, 55, 62, 63, 67, 73, 74, 223, 297, 340, 341
Zeselevskaya, 484
Zhabgoreski, 403
Zhebgorsky, 494
Zieglwax, 275
Zigelvaks, 126
Zigelvaks, 503
Ziggelvaks, 214
Ziglevaks, 234
Zigloks, 289
Ziglwaxs, 269
Zilberberg, 97, 215
Zilberleyev, 373
Zilberlib, 96
Zilberman, 96, 218, 358, 360, 365, 373
Zimmerman, 292
Zislis, 494
Zlering, 104, 108, 150, 151, 152
Zohar, 130
Zonis, 126, 294
Zonis, 503
Zonnis, 213, 217
Zsheliyenzshik, 216
Zshida, 217
Zubowski, 332
Zuckerman, 32, 55, 223, 224, 245, 276, 332, 375, 398, 453
Zufrik, 294

Zukerman, 58, 75, 76, 77, 78, 81, 93, 96, 99, 113, 116, 120, 122, 127, 160, 161, 162, 164, 165, 170, 191, 193, 194, 195, 196, 197, 199, 200, 201, 223, 230, 273, 289, 315, 316, 341, 367, 428

Zuli, 350

Zunis, 96, 245, 292, 293

Zusman, 45, 185

Zwilling, 185

Zwillinger, 178

www.ingramcontent.com/pod-product-compliance
Lightning Source LLC
Chambersburg PA
CBHW082007150426
42814CB00005BA/255